THE WHICH? GUIDE TO

TOURIST
ATTRACTIONS

THE WHICH? GUIDE TO
TOURIST ATTRACTIONS

Edited by Kim Winter

CONSUMERS' ASSOCIATION

The Which? Guide to Tourist Attractions was researched by *Holiday Which?*, part of
Consumers' Association, and published by
Which? Books, 2 Marylebone Road, London NW1 4DF
Email address: *books@which.net*

Distributed by The Penguin Group:
Penguin Books Ltd, 27 Wrights Lane, London W8 5TZ

The publishers would like to thank the following for their help in the preparation of this
book: Diccon Bewes, Sophie Butler, Sophie Carr, Niamh Fitzgerald, Max Fuller, Sue Harvey,
Paula Hodgson, Lindsay Hunt, Roger Lakin, Julie Lennard, Andrew Leslie, Shereen Makarem,
Jonathan Mitcham, Steven Murray, Mike Pedley, Michael Proudlove, Gill Rowley, Lucy
Smith, Philip Taylor, Bob Tolliday, Peter Woolrich and Patricia Yates

Readers' competition – closing date **1 August 2000**.
For details see page 15.

First edition April 2000

British Library Cataloguing in Publication Data
A catalogue record for this book is available from the British Library

ISBN 0 85202 805 9

For a full list of Which? books, please write to Which? Books,
Castlemead, Gascoyne Way, Hertford X, SG14 1LH
or access our web site at *www.which.net*

Cover design by Sarah Watson
Text design by Julie Martin

Cover photographs: Grecian rotunda, Stourhead House © James Davis Travel Photography;
Legoland © Peter Kingsford/Eye Ubiquitous; Brighton Palace Pier © David Cumming/Eye
Ubiquitous

Photographs at back of map section: garden © Lost Gardens of Heligan/David Hastilow;
floodlit Royal Pavilion © The Royal Pavilion, Libraries & Museums, Brighton; elephant calf
© Chester Zoo; child with screen © National Museum of Photography, Film and
Television/Bob Cox/Paul Thompson

Typeset by Saxon Graphics Ltd, Derby
Printed and bound Clays Ltd, St Ives plc

Contents

Maps   centre of book

Introduction   7

Award-winning attractions   16

How to use this guide   19

Main entries

London   21

England   111

Scotland   395

Wales   451

Directory of other attractions

London   485

England   489

Scotland   516

Wales   523

List of attractions by category   527

Introduction

Visiting tourist attractions is big business in the UK – each household spent an average of nearly £120 on visiting attractions in 1998, a figure that is forecast to grow by over 30 per cent by 2003. The new millennium opened to a fanfare of publicity about new tourist attractions being launched, many of them using National Lottery funding, and all of them competing for our leisure spending.

Yet the press has not been short of stories about sights that are failing to bring in the numbers of visitors envisaged, among them the National Centre for Popular Music in Sheffield, the Earth Centre in Doncaster (both recipients of Lottery funding) and the Royal Armouries in Leeds. Various reasons for the low attendance have been suggested, including geographical location (these three northern cities, for example, cannot claim to be top-ranking tourist hotspots) and the fact that the bidding process for funds encourages organisations to be wildly over-optimistic in their visitor number projections. But perhaps the key question that should be asked is: are these places any good?

At the moment, trying to find a rewarding and fun day out often means wading through a heap of leaflets, some of which may promise more than they deliver. Some leaflets do not even give basic information such as admission prices or opening times. With admission for a family of four costing about £60 for somewhere like the major theme parks or the Dome, a disappointing visit can be a costly experience in terms of money as well as time.

In 1999, after inspecting 21 well-known attractions in England for *Holiday Which?* magazine, we concluded that some of Britain's best-known attractions leave much to be desired and called for the English Tourist Board, now the English Tourism Council (ETC), to introduce a grading scheme that would give consumers a better indication of the merits or otherwise of the country's attractions (the Scottish Tourist Board already runs such a scheme, and roughly three-quarters of the attractions in Scotland now receive regular inspections). Such a scheme would also help to improve standards within the industry, as sights strive to better their ratings. As we went to press, the ETC announced funding for one of the regional tourist boards in the East of England, to develop an inspection and assessment scheme for visitor attractions. Two other regions, Heart of England and the West Country, also have inspection schemes for attractions in their areas.

It has to be said that much of the industry is against such a grading scheme. The view seems to be that if visitors are disappointed this will not put them off going to attractions in general because they will just think they made a bad choice. And in the end poor attractions will fail anyway because nobody will go. What complacent humbug! Such a view assumes that we consumers can afford to spend any amount of time and money on finding out for ourselves. And how are we supposed to decide what to visit in the first place? From advertising, of course – and when was the last time you saw a publicity leaflet proclaiming 'We have so little to amuse you that you will be in and out in 20 minutes'?

Until there is a nationwide grading scheme, consumers will be stuck for objective information on popular sights. Hence this book. We sent our inspectors out anonymously to over 300 popular British tourist attractions, including theme parks, stately homes, dockyards, caves, prisons, mines, wildlife parks, heritage centres, gardens, nuclear power stations and museums, all selected on the basis of visitor numbers, and assessed each of them on:

- **quality of attraction** (welcome, what there is to see and do, interpretation, guides, range of appeal)
- **standard of facilities** (restaurant, shops, toilets, parking, maintenance) and
- **value for money**

all on a scale of 1 (poor) to 5 (excellent). (For more details, see 'How to use this guide', page 19.)

Not surprisingly, we found wide variations in standards, even at some of Britain's best-known sights. Here are some of our pet likes and dislikes.

Pricing

With the adult entry fee at some attractions now as high as £20, a family day out can be a costly enterprise. Even at a time of low inflation, prices seem to be spiralling ever upwards, so value for money is very important. From what we have seen, sights vary considerably in their pricing policies.

We like:

Free entry for all Excellent sights that remain free to everyone include the National Museum of Photography, Film and Television in Bradford, the Wallace Collection, the National Gallery, and the National Army Museum in London, and, politically incorrect though it may be to say so, Sellafield in Cumbria. Also a pat on the back for Glasgow, where the local authority has made a determined and laudable effort to keep all its museums and galleries free – no mean feat in this age of budget cuts and efficiency savings.

Free entry for children All national museums now offer free entry to children, and the intention is to extend this to pensioners from 1 April 2000, although there is now doubt about the government's commitment to let everyone in free the following year. The National Trust for Scotland is allowing children in free at all its sights during the year 2000.

Family tickets Many places now offer a discounted family ticket, usually covering two adults and up to three children, though more progressive sights, like the Royal Pavilion at Brighton, also have deals for, say, one adult and up to four children.

We hate:

Stingy discounts Most sights offer discounts for children – except Flamingoland in Kirby Misperton, where children aged over 4 pay the same as an adult (despite many of the rides having height restrictions), and Chatsworth Adventure Playground, which charges a flat rate for everyone.

Those who run these attractions might argue that they are aimed primarily at children, so why should youngsters not pay full price? In that case, why not let adults pay less (we didn't see any grandparents tackling the rope bridges or swings at Chatsworth)? In fact, pensioners do pay a lower price at many sights – though not at those that clearly appeal to older age groups, like the RHS Gardens at Wisley, or Wallington House at Cambo.

Discounts for disabled visitors and their carers also vary – and are not always advertised: incredible as it may seem, staff at Eureka!, the children's museum in Halifax, told our inspector that they do not offer discounts for disabled visitors because if they did 'everyone would claim a disability'.

Being short-changed Many sights charge the same admission price throughout the season, despite the fact that there is often much more going on at some times of the year than at others. For example, zoos such as Edinburgh have regular free talks or sessions where you can 'meet the animals' – but only from April to August. Holyrood Palace in Edinburgh runs good guided tours (included in the price) only from November to March – the rest of the time visitors have to rely on an expensive guidebook to get any idea of what they are looking at. Similarly, guided tours of HMS *Victory* at Flagship Portsmouth run only when the site is not busy.

Lots of extras First you pay to park; then you stump up the entrance fee; then you have to fork out for a guidebook because no labelling or interpretation has been provided; then you find that you have to pay a further fee to gain admission to, say, a particular part of the house or a special exhibition. And that is even before you have visited the restaurant or the shop. Canterbury Cathedral fell particularly foul of our inspector on this. 'I came away with the impression that they were a grasping lot,' she said. 'You have to pay to enter the *precinct*, let alone the church, and they even charged for the toilets – and then you exit through a large gift shop.' This set-up compares unfavourably with York Minster, where there is no compulsory charge for entry and the guided tour is free.

But for theme parks, our inspectors' views on the pros and cons of all-inclusive prices are more variable. Some prefer to pay an entrance fee up-front, as at Alton Towers: 'My kids tend to want to go on rides more than once, and it's good to know that I don't have to pay out each time,' commented one inspector. Others think that free entry to the park and payment for wrist-bands (which allow a set number of rides) or individual rides is far better: 'Then Granny, who doesn't want to go on any of the rides, can go in free and just watch the children having fun.' Some places, including Dreamland in Margate, offer both systems.

No information on prices Why do some publicity brochures not state admission prices? We have noticed such omissions even when the leaflet is clearly marked with the year, so the excuse of saving money on printing will not wash. We would like to see full details of prices, as well as information on the length of guided tours, opening times and suggested length of visit, supplied in all publicity leaflets.

And prices should also be clearly advertised *outside* the attraction so that potential visitors can see them before they walk through the door. Cathedrals and churches seem to be particularly at fault here, perhaps because of the sensitivity about charging. Many state that a 'voluntary donation' will be requested, but it is not until you're inside that the size of this suggested donation – which can be as much as £4–£5 – becomes clear.

Interpretation

The best attractions manage to inform and entertain at the same time. Those who sneer that this is simply 'dumbing down' should go and see the best of our national museums – particularly the revamped National Maritime Museum and its mind-expanding exhibition on time. On a smaller scale, well done to Down House in Kent, which avoids taking the easy way out – instead of simply confining itself to an account of Darwin's home life, it also explains the theory of evolution and its impact on the world.

'Worthy but dull' is no longer good enough for some of our most famous tourist sights – take note, Buckingham Palace and Apsley House in London. This is not just a matter of spending more money: a good story and a dash of imagination are much more important (as some of the zones in the Dome could have demonstrated).

We like:

Information included, not as an extra At some attractions so little information is available that you have to buy a guidebook or an audio tour simply to have some idea of what you are seeing – so it essentially becomes an additional entry cost. English Heritage is particularly good at providing free audio tours at its sites – for example, Battle Abbey (Sussex) and Eltham Palace (London). Audio points at Anglesey Sea Zoo in Brynsiencyn offer commentaries by David Bellamy on the different animals. Well-designed soundtracks, panels and pictures help bring the experience alive at the People's Palace in Glasgow.

Audio tours that exploit the medium A dull recitation of the fittings and furnishings in each room hardly makes interesting listening (Windsor Castle is guilty of this). What is the point of an audio tour that simply regurgitates information printed in a guidebook? Through the use of music, sound effects and actors a good audio tour can help to re-create the atmosphere and bring a place alive, giving a sense of place and the people connected with it – as at the Cabinet War Rooms in London. The audio tour at Hidcote Manor in Gloucestershire includes a conversation between Stephan Bucazski (the gardening author and broadcaster) and the head gardener; the one at Battle Abbey tells the story of the battle from the point of view of the Normans, the English, and King Harold's mistress; at Howletts Wild Animal Park in Kent you can hear the keepers talking about the animals they care for.

An audio tour is ideal for allowing people to explore particular areas of interest further. At several places, including Eltham Palace and Down House, you could get further information on specific subjects by keying in the appropriate numbers. The audio tour of the National Gallery in London allows you to pick and choose which paintings you want to hear about. By contrast, the one provided at the Banqueting House in London seemed to drone on endlessly.

We hate:

Poor control and sound insulation If you have several commentaries, audio or touch-screen information points, don't put them too close together or you will end up with the Tower of Babel (as at the Clink Prison Museum in London; and poor insulation was particularly noticeable at the National Centre for Popular Music in Sheffield). At Vinopolis in London we had problems with the automatic 'triggers' that were supposed to start the commentaries in each room.

Out-of-date and/or illegible labels Some museums present their exhibits as if we were still in the nineteenth century, not the twenty-first. The Ashmolean Museum in Oxford springs to mind, along with the Fitzwilliam Museum in Cambridge, while the Theatre Museum (London) should present all of its visitors with a magnifying glass, as the print on the labels is so small. By contrast there were good information plaques at Conwy and Caernarfon Castles.

Staff

However outstanding a sight may be, if the staff are unhelpful they can mar your day.

We like:

A warm welcome As in hotels, it is important to get the welcome right, as it sets the tone for the whole visit. This is one of the things that the Dome seems to have got right, with very visible greeters and staff who seem to like people. By contrast, at Vikingar! in Largs and Tullie House in Carlisle our inspector was unimpressed: 'About the same level of friendliness as your local bus station' was the comment.

Proactive, knowledgeable guides The guides at Castle Howard in Malton really make the visit – chatty, unpatronising, and happy to approach visitors and engage their attention. The volunteer guides at cathedrals we came across were generally superb, enthusiastic and keen, and clearly doing the job for love rather than money. Room guides at National Trust properties have often been criticised for being more interested in making sure visitors do not touch anything than for being helpful – something our inspector at Stourhead in Wiltshire felt still applied. On the other hand, we have nothing but praise for the guide in Churchill's study at Chartwell, who was full of stories about the great man that really humanised him; and the volunteer at Fountains Abbey who quite happily took our inspector on the garden tour even though she was the only visitor to turn up for it (and, what is more, offered to extend the tour to cover the abbey).

We hate:

Bored, negative staff who would rather be elsewhere, like the whinger at Osborne House on the Isle of Wight, who ruined the ride in the horse-drawn carriage by giving a lecture on the silly questions she was asked (like 'What is the horse's name?') and how fed up she was with answering them – she certainly silenced our inspector's two children. Staff at Marwell Zoo called another inspector stupid for stopping to ask where the parking for disabled visitors was. The cavern guides at the Heights of Abraham in the Peak District were clearly bored when we inspected, reeling off set speeches and making no effort to involve the children.

Child appeal

Far too many historical attractions advertise themselves as the perfect family day out, yet make little effort to interest youngsters in the history, apparently taking the view that the place for kids is the adventure playground (as at Leeds Castle and Blenheim Palace). Such facilities may help to enliven the visit, but the best places find ways to encourage children to find things out and learn a little too. At Flagship Portsmouth the galleries on Nelson have display cases arranged around a children's activity centre so that young visitors can play there while grown-ups have time to browse and then explain those parts of the exhibition that will appeal to their offspring.

The need to explain will change over time as well. At Chartwell, for instance, there was no introduction to or explanation about the context of Churchill's life – presumably not needed by the predominantly elderly visitors who had lived through World War II, but likely to be increasingly necessary for younger visitors. Nor was the advertised children's worksheet available on either of the two occasions when we visited.

We like:

Children's activities that show some imagination The best children's guides or discovery booklets and trails encourage youngsters to observe more closely and find out more for themselves – some even suggest activities that can be done after returning home (the children's guide to Blickling Hall in Norfolk contains ideas for making marbled paper and Jacobean gingerbread as well as providing stickers of portraits throughout the Hall). Some, however, are too worthy, less imaginative, or downright boring – the children's guide to Chatsworth seems to rely as much on general knowledge ('What is alabaster?') as on observation – and no crib sheet is provided to help frustrated adults.

Historical pageants and re-enactments These make history accessible, and children are entranced by the action and the stories. Top marks to Hampton Court and Warwick Castle for making efforts to entertain as well as educate. And the Millennium Show at the Dome is really stunning.

We hate:

Being overrun by school outings School groups can be a menace for those who want to concentrate on exhibits or just soak up the atmosphere of a place. It would be helpful if sights that are very much on the school trip circuit could put school term dates and schools' preferred times of day for visits on their publicity leaflets – as Eden Camp in Malton does – so that other visitors can choose quieter times.

Food

Our inspectors found plenty to grumble about on the subject of food.

We like:

A variety of reasonably priced, tasty food – for everyone Too many places rely solely on second-rate fast food (there are exceptions – we had some good fish and chips at Pleasure Island in Cleethorpes). Even if other options are available, they are not necessarily more appetising – the rock-hard pizza and congealed pasta at Flagship Portsmouth will linger in the memory for all the wrong reasons. Vegetarian inspectors consistently bemoaned their lack of choice. And why is not it possible to offer children half-portions of the adult dishes, rather than the inevitable nuggets and chips?

On the other hand, the home-made soups and cakes/biscuits offered have usually been very good. Some attractions try to reflect local traditions or carry their theme through to the restaurant – for example, Eden Camp has a wartime theme in its canteen, while the menu at Blickling Hall offers dishes based on local Norfolk recipes, and Erddig Hall in Wrexham includes Georgian dishes drawn from the archives of the Yorke family. Not surprisingly, the Centre for Alternative Technology in Machynlleth majors on organic wholefood.

At more upmarket places it is clearly thought that visitors should be willing to pay extra for the privilege of elegant surroundings – for example, £6.75 for three small finger sandwiches, a scone with jam and cream and a pot of tea in the Indian Room at Blenheim Palace.

Pleasant picnic areas If you prefer to bring your own food and drink, there should be somewhere attractive to sit, with plenty of litter bins so that you do not have to cart your rubbish around with you. Anglesey Sea Zoo is just one place that offers good picnic facilities.

We hate:

Long waits How many restaurant managers have stood in lunchtime queues at their self-service cafés at the height of summer wondering whether they would manage to get something to eat before the sight closed? Not many, we would guess, judging by the waiting times we have endured. Having just one person serving up hot food or working on the till inevitably leads to log jams and moans from customers (are you listening, Dover Castle?).

Lingering smells and slow clear-up At the other end, if tables are not cleared fast enough, you end up dining surrounded by other people's left-overs – hardly an appetising environment (at Bristol Zoo the slops trollies were left lying around). And the stale-food-mingled-with-ancient-mop smell

(Inverewe Gardens and Culloden in Scotland) is likely to put off all but the hungriest visitors.

Toilets

One of the most basic facilities is still difficult to get right. Cleanliness is the main bugbear: it is not good enough just to clean the lavatories once a day if hundreds of visitors are traipsing through. Overflowing bins by midday at the Dome are not a pretty sight, and a blocked toilet, no soap, and cigarette butts in the urinals at Blackpool Tower were the pits. Comfort (the loos were icy cold at Culloden and draughty at Lincoln Cathedral) needs some thought, too, as does the state of the décor (Stonehenge's facilities linger in the memory). And one of the toilets at Bamburgh Castle had been out of order for so long that a cobweb festooned the door handle. Also, why should functioning lavatories be closed before the site does?

Gold stars to Althorp, which not only has decent loos but has staff looking after them throughout the day, and to Glenturret Distillery, where amazingly smart, warm and comfortable toilets were described by our inspector as 'worthy of a five-star hotel'.

Baby-changing facilities seem to be on the increase; nowadays, the National Trust even provides them in the men's loos as well as the women's.

And finally . . .

We hope you find this guide useful in helping to plan your days out. But things change – prices go up, facilities are improved (or may deteriorate), special rides or exhibitions are added or closed down, new galleries open up. And of course expectations move with the times – unlike the attitudes of some tourist attraction operators. Do let us know, at the Which? Books address opposite the Contents page, of any good or bad experiences you may have. You can also email us – see page 485.

The good news is that there are some excellent sights out there – see pages 16–17 for our awards for the best (and worst) we came across. And if you want to tell us about your own experience, act quickly – you could win £150 to spend on a day out with the family (see competition details, opposite).

Readers' competition

Enter our competition and you could win free entry for you and your family to any UK tourist attraction of your choice.

All you have to do is to nominate your favourite attraction, visited within the last two years, and tell us, in not more than 30 words, why you enjoyed going there.

The winning entry will be the one which, in the opinion of the judges, best describes why the tourist attraction appealed so much.

Send your entry to Tourist Attractions Competition, Which? Books, 2 Marylebone Road, London NW1 4DF. Alternatively, fax it to 020-7830 7660 or email it to *books@which.net* (please include your name and address). Closing date 1 August 2000.

1st prize
Tickets to the UK tourist attraction of your choice, plus spending money, to the total value of £150, *plus* a year's subscription to *Holiday Which?* magazine.

10 runner-up prizes
Tickets to the UK tourist attraction of your choice, plus spending money, to the total value of £50, *plus* a year's subscription to *Holiday Which?* magazine.

All winners will be notified personally and their names announced in *Holiday Which?* magazine.

Award-winning attractions

Here are the bouquets – and brickbats – we have awarded to the best and worst sights we inspected in the following categories.

Animal attractions

Best ☺
Chester Zoo
Longleat, Warminster
Slimbridge Wildfowl and
    Wetlands Trust

Worst ☹
Blair Drummond Safari and
    Leisure Park
Dudley Zoo and Castle
Knowsley Safari Park
Sea Life Centre, Brighton

Thrills and spills

Best ☺
Alton Towers
Blackpool Pleasure Beach

Worst ☹
Butlins Family Entertainment
    Resort, Skegness

Heritage and history

Best ☺
Royal Pavilion, Brighton
Castle Howard, Malton
Hampton Court, London
Hartlepool Historic Quay
Lanhydrock House and Gardens,
    Bodmin
Warwick Castle
Wilton House

Worst ☹
Apsley House, London
Buckingham Palace, London
Stonehenge, Amesbury

Outdoor attractions

Best ☺
Beamish North of England Open
    Air Museum
Black Country Living Museum,
    Dudley
Fountains Abbey and Studley Royal
    Water Gardens, Ripon

Worst ☹
Paradise Family Leisure Park,
    Newhaven
Southend Pier
Waterperry Gardens

Ironbridge Gorge Museums
Lost Gardens of Heligan, St Austell
Royal Botanic Garden, Edinburgh
Westonbirt Arboretum, Tetbury

Churches and castles

Best ☺
Dover Castle
Glamis Castle
Lincoln Cathedral
St Paul's Cathedral, London

Worst ☹
Bamburgh Castle
Ludlow Castle
Canterbury Cathedral

Museums and galleries

Best ☺
Imperial War Museum, Duxford
National Maritime Museum, London
National Museum and Gallery,
    Cardiff
Natural History Museum, London
Science Museum, London
Tate Gallery, St Ives
Victoria & Albert Museum, London
National Railway Museum, York

Worst ☹
Dinosaur Museum, Dorchester
Theatre Museum, London

Themed experiences

Best ☺
Beatles Story, Liverpool
Big Pit Mining Museum, Blaenafon
National Museum of Photography,
    Film and Television, Bradford
Dynamic Earth Centre, Edinburgh
Eden Camp, Malton
Eureka!, Halifax
Galleries of Justice, Nottingham
Royal Yacht *Britannia*, Edinburgh
Sellafield Visitor Centre, Seascale

Worst ☹
Louis Tussaud's Waxworks, Blackpool
Clink Prison Museum, London
Earth Centre, Doncaster
Oxford Story

How to use this guide

The *Guide* is divided into two main sections: main entries and the directory of other attractions, both of which are sub-divided into four sections (London, England, Scotland and Wales). Within each regional sub-division the attractions are arranged alphabetically.

The attractions in the **main entry section**, all of which **have been inspected** by the *Guide* team, are described in detail. Practical information such as opening times, prices and directions are provided, and they are plotted on the maps in the centre of the book. The tourist attractions in the **directory of other attractions** at the end of the book **have not been inspected** by the Guide team and are not plotted on the maps, but, like those in the main entries, are some of the more popular destinations for tourists. Directory entries are listed by region, then alphabetically by name of attraction.

Finding an attraction

If you are looking for an attraction in a particular area: first go to the maps at the centre of the book. The main entry attractions are marked on the maps by name. Once you have chosen an attraction, go to the relevant section of the book to find the entry for it.

If you are looking for an attraction by name: turn to the section of the book depending on whether it is in London, England, Scotland or Wales, and find the attraction listed alphabetically. If it is not a main entry, it may be listed in the directory.

If you are looking for an attraction by type: turn to the list at the back of the book which features attractions by category (for example, animal attractions, museums and galleries), then find it in the main entries.

How to read a main entry

At the top of each entry you will find the name of the attraction, its address, telephone and fax numbers, and web site and email addresses if it has them.

The ratings for **quality of attraction** (★), **standard of facilities** (🍴) and **value for money** (£) follow. Each of them is on a scale of 1 to 5 (where 1 is worst and 5 is best). The main part of the entry covers: **What's there** (which describes the attraction); **Information/tours/guides** (which gives details of organised tours, audio tours and videos, guidebooks, etc.); **When to visit** (which advises on best times of year to visit and also when special events are held); **Age appeal** (which tells you which age groups each sight is best suited for); **Food and drink** (which lists options for eating); **Shops** (which tells you what merchandise is available at the sight); and, if relevant, **Other facilities** (which gives information on toilets, baby-changing facilities, etc. if appropriate). Bear in mind that prices mentioned in the text may change.

The **rubric** at the bottom gives practical information about the attraction, starting with details of **how to get there** by **car** (🚗) and by **public transport** (⊖). **Opening times** (🕐) are given and **admission fees** (💷) listed for adults, children, concessions, families; all prices in this section are for 2000 unless otherwise specified. **Access for disabled visitors** (♿) notes any special facilities and access problems. Details are correct at the time of going to press, but may change: telephone ahead if you have any special requirements or are travelling some distance to get there.

National organisations

The names of national organisations that help to preserve historic houses and gardens are often abbreviated: NT (National Trust), NTS (National Trust for Scotland), EH (English Heritage), Historic Scotland (HS), and Cadw (which manages historic monuments in Wales). Some of these organisations grant free admission to members. The full names and addresses are as follows.

National Trust 36 Queen Anne's Gate, London SW1H 9AS
☎ 020-7222 9251   📠 020-7222 5097
🖳 *www.nationaltrust.org.uk*

National Trust for Scotland 28 Charlotte Square, Edinburgh EH2 4ET
☎ 0131-243 9300   📠 0131-243 9301
🖳 *www.nts.org.uk*

English Heritage 23 Savile Row, London W1X 1AB
☎ 020-7973 3000   📠 020-7973 3001
🖳 *www.english-heritage.org.uk*

Historic Scotland Longmore House, Salisbury Place, Edinburgh EH9 1SH
☎ 0131-668 8800   📠 0131-668 8888
🖳 *www.historic-scotland.gov.uk*

Cadw National Assembly for Wales, Crown Building, Cathays Park, Cardiff CF10 3NQ
☎ 029-2050 0200   📠 029-2082 6375
🖳 *www.cadw.wales.gov.uk*

LONDON

Apsley House

149, Piccadilly, Hyde Park Corner, London W1V 9FA   ☎ 020-7499 5676
📠 020-7495 8525

Quality ★★	Facilities 🎫 🎫	Value for money ££

Highlights Monumental silver collection; some fine paintings; good audio tour
Drawbacks Dull presentation; poor access for disabled visitors

What's there Apsley House, once known as 'Number 1, London' was bought by the first Duke of Wellington in 1817 from his elder brother for £42,000. The Robert Adam house was to be the British hero's London home, and it is here that the Waterloo banquets, celebrating his famous victory over Napoleon, were held every 18 June. Although there are some fine paintings and spectacular silver here the presentation is old-fashioned and dull, and you will have to work hard to learn more about the Duke from your visit than you knew when you went in.

The highlights are the **plate and china room**, which houses the spectacular gifts from the grateful royal families of Europe. It includes the set of **Egyptian Sèvres porcelain** given by Louis XVIII – apparently originally offered as a divorce present by Napoleon to Empress Josephine, but rejected by her. On the wall is the magnificent **silver gilt Wellington shield**, depicting mounted soldiers with winged Victory above. The **candelabra** was presented by the City of London, while a display case alongside holds the very **sword Wellington carried to Waterloo** – its worn leather case indicates that it might have seen a bit of action. Surprisingly, perhaps, there are plenty of images of Napoleon – the most startling being the massive statue by **Canova** that dominates the hall.

Upstairs, the rooms are full of the pictures collected by Wellington – some bought at Paris auctions after Waterloo, others 'liberated' from the French after being looted from the Spanish royal family, including his favourite, **Correggio**'s *Agony in the Garden*. The most important works are housed in the Waterloo Gallery, a room added to the house for the Duke's banquets. It is furnished in white and gold 'Louis XIV style' – the windows are fitted with sliding mirrors to reflect the candlelight at night. Here you can see **Velázquez**'s *The Waterseller of Seville*, an enormous equestrian portrait of Charles I, and **Goya**'s portrait of a tired-looking Wellington also on horseback (his head hurriedly superimposed on an unfinished portrait) after the liberation of Spain. The painting was so disliked by Wellington that it was not displayed until the 1950s.

Pass through the striped drawing room, with Lawrence's portrait of the Duke in his red jacket, to the dining room, where an 8m-long silver centrepiece is laid out, topped with a winged Victory, one foot resting on the Iberian peninsula – a gift from the King of Portugal. Around the walls are portraits of other grateful monarchs, including George IV wearing tartan. Don't overlook the small basement gallery, where you can see some of Wellington's personal effects – a travelling canteen, campaign plate and a telescope – and many medals.

Information/tours/guides A good audio tour is included in the entrance price.

When to visit To miss the crowds, come mid-week when coach parties have gone (after 2pm).

Age appeal Apsley House is of limited appeal to children. The dull format is designed to attract enthusiasts only.

Food and drink No food or drink is available on site.

Shops A small selection of gifts from the V&A museum is available in the reception area.

Other facilities Toilets in the basement. No staffed cloakroom.

🚗 Not recommended. Nearest car park in Park Lane, about 10 minutes' walk. ⊖ nearest Underground station Hyde Park Corner (Piccadilly line). Buses 2,8,9,10,14,16,19,22,36,38,52,73,82, and 137 stop nearby. ◷ Tues to Sun, 11am to 5pm (last admissions 4.30pm). Closed Mondays (except bank hols), Good Friday, May Day Holiday, 24–26 Dec, 1 Jan. 💷 Adult £4.50; child (under 18 yrs old) free, student, senior citizen, unemployed, disabled visitor £3.00. Free admission on Waterloo Day (18 June). ♿ Very limited access. Steps up to entrance and down to lift.

Banqueting House

Whitehall Palace, Whitehall, London SW1 2ER ☎ 020-7930 4179

Quality ★ ★ ★   **Facilities 💷 💷 💷**   **Value for money ££**

Highlights Beautiful Rubens ceiling and Inigo Jones architecture
Drawbacks Only one room to see; overlong introductory video

What's there This is the only remaining part of the original king's **palace at Whitehall**. Its place in English history is secured by the fact that it was the building from which Charles I departed to be beheaded on the scaffold erected outside the building in January 1649. Cardinal Wolsey owned the site's original building, which was confiscated by Henry VIII, who renamed it Whitehall. After a fire, King James I commissioned **Inigo Jones** to design the Palace of Whitehall. Completed in 1622, it was used for royal banquets, entertaining foreign ambassadors and, perhaps most importantly, the stylised masques that emphasised kingship. Charles I paid **Rubens** £3,000 – a fabulous sum in those days – to paint the **ceiling panels**, which can still be seen in the Banqueting House. Their wonderful rich colours illustrate the principles of good governance, the amalgamation of the Scots and English crowns under James and the Divine Right of Kings – the principle that caused Charles to lose his head. The last great national ceremony to be held here was the offering of the crown to William of Orange. Today, the Banqueting House is again used for grand entertaining.

Unfortunately, there is only one room left to see of the original Palace of Whitehall. As such, a visit shouldn't take more than an hour.

Information/tours/guides A 20-minute introductory video downstairs and an audio tour to accompany your visit upstairs are both included in the entrance fee. They're both overlong and dry, and should you prefer to go at your own pace you can use the excellent guidebook (£3.50) instead.

When to visit It's quieter during the winter months and on Saturdays should you wish to avoid the crowds.

Age appeal There's little for younger children, and the video and audio tours are definitely not for little ones.

Food and drink No refreshments are available.

Shops A few souvenirs have been squeezed in round the receptionist's desk.

🚗 Not recommended as parking around Whitehall difficult. ⊖ Nearest Underground stations Charing Cross (mainline rail station, Northern and Bakerloo lines), Westminster (Circle, District and Jubilee lines) and Embankment (Northern and Bakerloo lines). ⊕ Mon to Sat, 10am to 5pm. Closed Sun, 24 to 26 Dec, 1 Jan, Good Friday and other bank hols and at short notice for functions. 💷 (1999 prices) Adult £3.60; child £2.30; student/senior citizen/unemployed/disabled people £2.80. ♿ Stairs to Banqueting Hall; no lift. Disabled toilets (but 3 steps to get there).

BBC Experience

Broadcasting House, Portland Place, Oxford Circus, London W1A 1AA
☎ *(0870) 6030304* 🖰 *www.bbc.co.uk/experience*

Quality ★★★★	Facilities 🏛🏛🏛	Value for money ££

Highlights Some very entertaining interactive exhibits for children
Drawbacks Not enough explanation of how television programmes are produced

---

What's there The BBC Experience strives to strike a balance between presenting an informative history of BBC broadcasting and providing a series of interactive activities designed to demonstrate aspects of broadcasting technology. The result is a generally entertaining melting-pot of games and audio-visuals aimed principally at children, with a strong emphasis on radio. It could do more to explore some of the themes that visitors might have anticipated – for instance, how television programmes are commissioned and produced. For those wanting to explore the world of television in greater depth, tours of Television Centre can be booked (over 16s only) by ringing (0870) 6030304.

The first part of the tour is guided and begins in the Marconi Room, where you can read about the very first wireless transmissions and see some of the earliest broadcasting equipment. From there, you are shepherded seamlessly through a series of rooms, beginning with an introductory video montage of BBC snippets. The highlight of the tour, at least for children, is likely to be the **recording studio**, where visitors can take part in the production of a short radio play, including acting and adding sound effects. When we visited, the play was *Gunfight in Cactus Gulch* – it went down a treat with the children involved, but the size of the tour group prevented everyone from participating. Following the recording studio, the next two rooms present an atmospheric and highly emotionally charged account of BBC broadcasting through a series of sound bites and film excerpts. It rapidly juxtaposes the coronation of Elizabeth II with Beatles interviews, the assassination of President Kennedy, and reports of the famine in Ethiopia – this whirlwind history of our century *à la* BBC could leave visitors feeling slightly dazed.

With the tour over, visitors are free to wander through the final, and arguably most enjoyable, sequence of rooms, which are devoted entirely to

interactive exhibits. There you will have a chance to present the weather, become a sports commentator, and even select your own desert island disc. The well-publicised opportunity to edit a scene from *EastEnders* suffers from an absence of playback – you are far too busy selecting cameras during the editing to really get any idea of what you have produced. A children's TV room allows you to animate characters like Badger and Mousie.

Information/tours/guides The Marconi Room is well labelled and all of the interactive exhibits are clearly explained. On the guided part of the tour, staff lead visitors from room to room rather than offering explanations or answering questions. A slim and glossy guidebook (95p) provides a little background information about the BBC.

When to visit Any time is a good time to visit. Some of the atmosphere may be lacking during very quiet times, but there will be less opportunity to participate when tour groups are packed out.

Age appeal The BBC Experience strikes a tentative balance between catering for adults and children. Although both will find elements that appeal to them, some aspects are likely to be trying.

Food and drink A stylish, minimalist restaurant serves a typical range of slightly pricey dishes, including Covent Garden soups (£2.25), pizzas (£4.45) and bangers and mash (£5.65).

Shops As you might expect, the largest BBC shop stocks just about the whole range of BBC merchandise, including videos, book tie-ins, T-shirts, posters and toys. Presentation is chic and service is efficient.

🚌 Traffic in this area is often extremely congested, so allow plenty of time if travelling by road. Expensive metered street parking available. ⊖ Nearest Underground stations are: Oxford Circus (Victoria, Bakerloo, and Central lines) with 5-minute walk up Upper Regent Street; and Great Portland Street (Circle, Hammersmith & City, and Metropolitan lines) with 10-minute walk. Several buses stop near Oxford Circus (3, 6, 7, 8, 10, 12, 13, 15, 23, 25, 53, 55, 73, 88, 94, 98, 113, 135, 137,139, 159, 176 and 189). ⏰ Mon, 11.00am to 4.30pm (last tour begins 4.30pm), Tues to Fri, 10.00am to 4.30pm (last tour begins 4.30pm), Sat and Sun, 9.30am to 4.30pm (last tour begins 3.30 pm). Times subject to seasonal variations. Tours start promptly, so allow plenty of time to arrive. Pre-bookings are recommended. 💷 Adult £6.95, child £4.95, child (under 5 yrs old) free, family ticket (2 adults + 2 children) £19.95, concession £5.95, student £4.95. ♿ Only three wheelchairs are allowed into the exhibition at any one time. Call in advance to ensure admission.

Bethnal Green Museum of Childhood

Cambridge Heath Road, London E2 9PA ☎ *020-8980 2415*

Quality ★★★★ **Facilities 🏛🏛🏛🏛** **Value for money ££££**
Highlights Fantastic dolls' houses and toys that take you back in time
Drawbacks Traditional presentation of toys with few interactive opportunities to help interest children; few of the children's books on display

What's there The Museum of Childhood is a branch of the Victoria & Albert Museum and since 1974 has concentrated on developing its own distinctive collections of things to do with childhood. There are toys, dolls, dolls' houses, games, children's clothes and items of childhood history. The latter range from a seventeenth-century Iberian nappy to teething rings and early feeding paraphernalia. You can even see a plastic Little Tikes 'push and ride coupe' car cordoned off on a display stand.

On the ground floor the central aisles are taken up with 30 fascinating dolls' houses, which were originally made for young girls to help them learn about domestic affairs. The earliest dolls' house on display is the **Nuremberg house** dating back to 1673, the kitchen full of pewter tankards and carved wooden furnishings. **Queen Mary's dolls' house** from the 1920s is altogether a plusher affair, while the **1930s Whiteladies house** is modernist in style and like an architectural model – though you have to wonder about its furnishings as you can't see the interior.

The rest of the ground floor features case after case of pristine dolls in all sorts of silks and laces, toy soldiers, board games, toy theatres and wind-up mechanical toys, including a clockwork Charlie Chaplin and a battery-operated table tennis game from China. **Toy trains** have been around since real steam trains were developed in the 1830s. You can see a broad range here, from pull-along-wooden models to **electric Hornby trains** that whizz around their tracks if you put 20p in the slot. There is also a section of traditional German wooden toys from the seventeenth century, when production began around Nuremberg and continued expanding well into the nineteenth century.

The displays on the social history of childhood are on the top floor. They include baby walkers (which can be traced back to the Middle Ages) and clothing from the early years, from miniature 'adult' outfits for children to teenage garb. You can learn about pioneers in child education, such as Maria Montessori, and there's a range of educational toys, from children's stoves and tea sets to brightly coloured beads on wire (a few can be played with too).

Information/tours/guides Leaflets giving details of workshops and soft play sessions are available by the entrance. The guidebook (£3.95) gives lots of detail on the items on display.

When to visit Visit any time. At weekends there are free activities, such as art and dressing-up workshops, and soft play sessions on Sundays.

Age appeal The museum is probably better for adults, though the few interactive features are popular with children.

Food and drink The café serves sandwiches, such as beef and ham salad, light snacks, carrot cake, scones, muffins, coffee and biscuits.

Shops You'll find souvenirs and dolls' house furniture, books and some old-fashioned toys.

Other facilities Disabled toilet and baby-changing facilities beside the entrance.

🚌 On A107 Cambridge Heath Road. Metered parking in nearby streets. ⊖ Nearest Underground station is Bethnal Green (Central line). Also buses 106, 253, 309, D6 on Cambridge Heath Road, 8 (Roman Rd), 26, 48,55 (Hackney Rd) stop nearby. 🕐 Sat to Thur 10am to 5.50pm. Closed Fridays (including Good Friday), 25 Dec, 1 Jan. 💷 Free. ♿ Ramps are available on ground floor and a lift gives access to all galleries. Parking at the rear of the building can be arranged for wheelchair users; call 020-8983 5204.

British Library

96 Euston Road, London NW1 2DB ☎ *020-7412 7332*
🖱 *www.bl.uk* 🖱 *boxoffice@bl.uk*

Quality ★ ★ ★ ★ ★   **Facilities** 👝 👝 👝 👝 👝   **Value for money** £££££
Highlights Numerous treasures of the John Ritblat Gallery and a tour of the building
Drawbacks No access to the actual books unless registered as a reader

What's there Some 34 years after the first proposal to rebuild the British Library, the new building finally opened in 1998. A cool £511 million had been spent, 10 million red bricks used, and Travertine marble, white oak, brass, leather and Purbeck stone combined to create an impressive interior. As a visitor you can go on daily tours of the building and access a small part of the collection in the John Ritblat Gallery, and visit the Workshop Gallery and the exhibition gallery.

The **John Ritblat Gallery** contains some of the treasures of the library, from **sacred texts** and **illuminated manuscripts** to **handwritten manuscripts** of George Eliot. '**Turning the Pages**' is a computer-based interactive system that allows you to simulate the experience of turning the pages of six notable works, including the Diamond Sutra, a Buddhist scroll from the ninth century and Leonardo da Vinci's notebook. You can also listen to extracts from the National Sound Archive, such as the account of the sinking of the *Titanic* by one of the officers on the ship or James Joyce reading an extract from *Ulysses*. The 'Sounds and Images' gallery traces the story of the earliest manuscripts, from the development of printing to the most modern digital technology.

Guided tours concentrate on the main concourse area and describe the development and workings of the library. Books are stored in four basement floors under the Piazza on 180 miles of shelving, and are categorised by size rather than author (it saves space!). Eight thousand new books arrive each day to take up three miles of shelving; and there are more books in German than in the German National Library. The only books you see outside the reading rooms are the 65,000 leather-bound volumes of the King's Collection donated by George III in 1863 and displayed in a 17-metre-high glass tower that can be inspected from various levels of the building. Beside it is the 80,000-item philatelic exhibition that you can browse through at will.

The mechanical book room is where books requested by readers will arrive after an hour's journey from the basement storage areas. They travel by way of some four miles of conveyor belt that circumnavigates the building. At the reader's desk in the reading room a light will illuminate to indicate the book has arrived.

Information/tours/guides There are two different guided tours. The shorter one takes place on Mondays, Wednesdays and Fridays at 3pm and on Saturdays at 10.30am and 3pm. The longer one includes a visit to a reading room and takes place outside reading-room hours on Tuesdays at 6.30pm and on Sundays at 11.30am and 3pm. It lasts about an hour and a quarter and is worth attending if you have the time (booking is advisable).

Free leaflets (with a floorplan) are available for each of the galleries, and a souvenir guide of the British Library can be bought in the shop (£4.95).

Various lectures take place throughout the year (extra charge) and in the Workshop Gallery there are free craft demonstrations. 'Meet the Author' talks are also arranged in the bookshop.

When to visit As an indoor attraction, it's good for wet weather.

Age appeal The Library is mainly of interest to adults and older children.

Food and drink A restaurant serves full meals and two cafés sell drinks, sandwiches, pastries and cakes.

Shops The well-stocked bookshop includes books on calligraphy, illuminated manuscripts, book binding and book craft, libraries, cartography and literature. A good selection of literature-inspired gifts include Jane Austen paperweights and T-shirts sporting literary quotes. But plain old souvenir mugs of the Library are also on sale.

Other facilities Toilets on all floors.

On the Euston Road close to Kings Cross and St Pancras mainline stations. Metered car parking on Midland Road and Ossulton Street and car park at St Pancras station. Nearest underground stations are Kings Cross (mainline station and Metropolitan, Circle, Hammersmith and City, Victoria, Piccadilly and Northern lines), and Euston (mainline station and Northern and Victoria lines). Buses along Euston Road 10, 30, 73, 91 SL1 and SL2. Mon to Fri, 9.30am to 6pm (8pm on Tues), Sat 9.30am to 5pm, Sun and Bank Holidays 11am to 5pm. Free. Guided tours (including a visit to a reading room) £4 (Tues and Sun £5), under-18/senior citizen/student/unwaged £3 (Tues and Sun £4) (booking advisable). All areas wheelchair accessible.

British Museum

Great Russell Street, London WC1B 3DG ☎ *020-7636 1555*
🖳 *www.british-museum.ac.uk*

Quality ★ ★ ★	Facilities 🏛 🏛	Value for money ££££

Highlights World-class exhibits including the Elgin Marbles, Egyptian mummies and Rosetta Stone
Drawbacks Confusing layout; dry and formal approach; pricey food; poor toilets

What's there Britain's premier museum is primarily a stunning collection of trophies and mementoes acquired from all four corners of the earth. It's rather like your granddad's attic after a lifetime of service and holidays abroad, though on a much grander scale. It has such a vast collection of artefacts and displays that you would need weeks if not months to see everything. All the more so because you are more than likely to get dazed and confused by the bewildering layout and lack of information. The situation isn't helped by the building work going on around the Great Court, which is due to open in autumn 2000. But grapple with the shortcomings and you'll be rewarded with a glimpse of some truly outstanding exhibits.

The best way to start, especially if you are pushed for time, is to pay for a highlights tour – probably the best £7 you'll spend that day. At least this way you don't run the risk of waltzing past the incomparable Portland Vase without realising it, and you will get oodles of background information on what you see. After that you can negotiate your own way – a feat made harder by the numbering (rather than naming) of rooms, which makes it easy to wander from Ancient Egypt into Assyria without noticing, and consequently get confused. Some individual galleries also have worthwhile free tours (see below).

Although the exhibits are clearly labelled, much of the museum assumes a certain level of knowledge, leaving the layperson to struggle. It has an air of being a place set up by archaeologists for archaeologists. Some rooms (the mummies and Roman Britain, for example) are more accessible, while only the Parthenon sculptures have their own CD tour (a very dull one at that for the suggested £3). The guidebook will help you some of the way, but even then you are still left a bit in the dark.

Give yourself plenty of time to explore hidden corners, but any visit must include the main highlights: the **Rosetta Stone**, a tri-lingual tablet that helped us decipher hieroglyphs; the oft-repaired **Portland Vase**, which inspired Wedgwood to porcelain perfection; the extensive and controversial **Parthenon sculptures** (aka Elgin Marbles); the amazing **Egyptian mummies** (expect huge crowds as this is the most popular room); catching up with our past with the **Sutton Hoo treasures** and the **Roman Britain gallery**; the perfectly preserved **Lindow Man**; and the horologists' heaven in the clocks and watches room.

Information/tours/guides The 90-minute guided tour (Mon-Sat 10.30am and 1.00pm, Sun 12.30pm, 1.30pm, 2.30pm, 4.00pm), which costs £7 (£4 for children), is an excellent introduction to the main highlights, though it can feel a little rushed at times. Our guide was full of anecdotes and witty asides, and whetted the appetite for independent exploration. Alternatively, there are worthwhile, free 60-minute tours of each of the seven main galleries (such as 'Roman Britain' or the 'World of Asia'), with a rotating programme every day (Mon-Sat 3.15pm, Sun 4.30pm). The guidebook is good value at £5 and fills in a bit of background but isn't comprehensive enough. The map (£1) has suggested tours, and some galleries have superb 50p-leaflets that pull out the highlights and provide detailed explanations.

When to visit Any time is a good time to come, although weekends, especially in the summer, are very busy.

Age appeal Despite the separate children's bookshop (but no separate guidebook), and the very child-friendly mummies, kids may find it a bit dry and lifeless. The labelling and interpretation are rather too adult. It's more like a school-trip than an outing of choice.

Food and drink The restaurant (run by Milburns) has a pleasant enough atmosphere but overall could be better. The food is fine, but expensive – the Museum of London has the same food by the same firm but at cheaper prices. Soup and a sandwich is £5.45, salmon salad £7.95, pot of tea £1.25. Our teatime visit was marred by dirty tables, uncleared clutter from lunch, and surly staff.

Shops The main shop has an imaginative array of gifts, though most are on the pricey side – Egyptian casket salt and pepper pots at £19.95 or a Rosetta Stone mousemat at £11.99. In comparison, the bookshop is cramped, crowded and untidy.

Other facilities Free cloakroom/bag check. The toilets were universally awful, with an unattractive assortment of dirty floors, a blocked loo, rusty mirror and dated fittings.

🚗 Central London. Metered car parking nearby. ⊖ Nearest Underground stations are Holborn (Central and Piccadilly lines), Russell Square (Piccadilly) or Tottenham Court Road (Central and Northern). ⊙ (in 1999) Open all year, Mon to Sat 10am to 5pm, Sun midday to 6pm. Closed Good Friday, 24 to 26 Dec, 1 Jan. £ Free (but donation of £2 strongly suggested). ♿ All areas accessible either by ramps or lifts. Wheelchairs provided if requested. Guide dogs welcome. For more information telephone 020–7637 7384.

Buckingham Palace

London SW1A 1AA ☎ *020-7839 1377 (general enquiries); 020-7321 2233 (credit-card bookings); 020-7799 2331 (24-hour recorded information)* �🖥 *www.royal.gov.uk*

Quality ★ **Facilities** 🏛🏛🏛 **Value for money ££**
Highlights Impressive art collection and sumptuous rooms
Drawbacks Sterile atmosphere; little information on the life of the Royal Family; guidebook expensive and dry

What's there If you're expecting an insight into the life and times of the Royal Family, you're likely to be severely disappointed. Although Buckingham Palace is the official London residence of the Queen, the State Apartments are used for court ceremonials and official entertaining and are thus somewhat lacking in human warmth. The only real flicker of human interest comes in the **Throne Room**, where the 1953 coronation thrones of the Queen and Prince Philip perch side by side on the dais: the Queen's is embroidered with the familiar ER II, while her consort's features a simple P.

The best way to approach the series of undeniably impressive State Apartments is to regard them as a sumptuous setting for the artworks in the Royal Collection. For art-lovers the highlight has to be the **Picture Gallery**, which displays **Van Dyck portraits** of Charles I and family as well as works by **Rembrandt, Rubens, Poussin, Vermeer** and **Canaletto**. The Marble Hall also contains a couple of sculptures by **Canova**. Elsewhere, **John Nash**'s splendid gilded plaster ceilings and coving soar above glittering chandeliers, faux onyx columns, ornate chimney pieces and Gobelin tapestries, not to mention the antique furniture and porcelain. Among all this luxuriance one of the most appealing rooms is the **Music Room**, which has a semi-circular bow window overlooking the garden and a plasterwork dome moulded with roses, thistles and shamrocks, representing England, Scotland and Ireland (respectively). The parquet floor includes a dazzling mix of satinwood, rosewood, mahogany and holly.

Information/tours/guides There are no guided tours or audio tours; the only information available is a guidebook, which costs an extra £4 and concentrates largely on the architecture and details of the fixtures and fittings. Small plans of each room with coloured keys to distinguish pictures, furniture, porcelain, etc. are not entirely successful, especially in the Picture Gallery. Here, pictures may be hung two or three deep, and visitors constantly have to look up and down to check that they are looking at the right painting. There's very little information on the significance of the rooms in the life of the Royal Family – other than the interesting snippet that the Queen's three eldest children were baptised in the Music Room in water from the River Jordan.

The publicity leaflet gives opening times and booking details, but no admission prices.

When to visit The State Apartments are open for only two months a year. Everything is under cover (the toilets and shop are in temporary tents in the gardens), so it's good for wet days. The queues and number of people in the Palace are smaller while the Changing of the Guard is going on, so if you can bear to miss the military spectacle this would be an ideal time to visit.

Age appeal Other than the excitement of seeing where the Queen lives, there is very little to keep children interested, with no special guidebooks or leaflets.

Food and drink With no refreshment facilities available in the Palace, the nearest options are at Victoria. Alternatively, there are kiosks in St James's Park and Green Park, near the ticket office.

Shops In a marquee in the gardens, the shop is clearly divided into sections, such as fine china, children's gifts, books and videos. Merchandise includes hand puppets depicting policemen, soldiers or princesses (£15 each), bone china patterned with a design based on the White Drawing Room (tea cup and saucer £30), silk scarves (£39 to £49) and ties, and a limited-edition carriage clock (£495). Souvenirs of the wedding of Prince Edward to Sophie Rhys-Jones include oven gloves (£10) and tea cosies (£10).

Other facilities You can leave belongings in the cloakroom and pick them up at the end. Toilets are available only at the end of the tour, in a specially erected tent in the gardens. They are nevertheless sturdy and clean, with baby-changing facilities and a nursing room. If you need to use a toilet beforehand you'll have to use the public toilets in St James's Park or Green Park.

🚗 Not recommended as no local parking (nearest car parks Victoria or Trafalgar Square). ⊖ Nearest Underground stations are Green Park (Victoria, Jubilee and Piccadilly lines) and St James's Park (Circle and District lines). ⊙ 6 Aug to 1 Oct. Entry is by timed ticket only and can be booked in advance by credit card (020–7321 2233). There is also a temporary ticket office in Green Park, where you can buy tickets in advance or on the day (no shelter if there are queues on hot or rainy days). 💷 Adult £10.50, child (under 17 yrs old) £5, senior citizen (over-60 yrs old) £8. ♿ Special route for visitors in wheelchairs, avoiding the stairs and using lift (book well in advance). Wheelchairs on loan (book in advance).

Cabinet War Rooms

Clive Steps, King Charles Street, London SW1A 2AQ   ☎ *020-7930 6961*
🖶 *020-7839 5897*   📱 *www.iwm.org.uk*

Quality ★ ★ ★ ★   **Facilities** 💰 💰 💰 💰   **Value for money** £££££
Highlights Evocative explanation of government during the Blitz; good audio tour
Drawbacks Narrow corridors toward the end can cause some crowding

What's there These basement rooms were the centre of government when the bombing of London was at its worst in 1940. The building was chosen because it was the only building in the area with a steel frame. The rooms are shown being prepared for a meeting (the clocks are stopped at two minutes to five on 15 October 1940), and have been kept exactly as they were when their wartime function ceased on 16 August 1945.

The first room very much sets the scene, with Chamberlain's wartime broadcast on the outbreak of war and Churchill's stirring 'We shall fight them on the beaches' speech. On display is the actual map used by Churchill at Yalta to decide the fate of post-war Europe. Churchill's wartime cabinet room shows the chairs squeezed in for the chiefs-of-staff, and just down the corridor is the trap door leading to the sub-basement, where all but the most senior staff would sleep.

Down the long corridors you can hear more sounds redolent of the times, including further wartime broadcasts by Churchill. You can even see the microphone and seat he used to make them. Don't miss the hot-line to the American President on the left – a lock showing 'engaged' was put on the door, to convince people working here that this was the only flushing toilet in the building and reserved for Churchill (in fact there wasn't one at all – you can see his potty at the foot of his bed further on). You can hear one of Churchill's wartime broadcasts down in this basement and see the microphones where he would have sat.

Perhaps the focal point is the **map room**, full of charts plotting the Allied progress. A line of telephones, known as the beauty chorus, which would be manned round the clock, divides the central desks. Every day a progress report, compiled from the intelligence fed into here, was on the desks of Churchill and the chief of staff by 8am. Past here you can see the individual cells where the most senior staff and Churchill slept – he merited rather nicer furniture and a fitted carpet.

The tour ends with an exhibition on Churchill during the war years using original documents from the archives that are changed every six months – they make fascinating reading.

Information/tours/guides An audio tour is included with the entrance fee; good guidebook (£2.70).

When to visit Outside summer months, early or late to avoid crowds.

Age appeal The good audio tour will appeal to older children.

Food and drink None.

Shops Small shop at exit selling lots of books, postcards and evocative wartime items such as ration books (£1.50).

🚗 Hard to park in central London. ⊖ Nearest underground stations are St James's Park (District and Circle lines) and Westminster (District, Circle and Jubilee lines). It's about a 15–20 minute walk from Charing Cross (mainline station, Northern and Bakerloo lines). ⊕ 9.30am-6pm Apr-Sept, 10am-6pm Oct-Mar. Closed 24-26 December. 💷 Children free, adult £4.80, senior citizen/student £3.50, unwaged £2.20. Reductions for groups. ♿ Lift to get down to basement, then pathway flat. Disabled toilet. Half price admission.

Chiswick House

Burlington Lane, Chiswick, London W4 2RP
☎ *020-8995 0508; 020-8995 5390 (information centre)*

Quality ★ ★ ★ ★   **Facilities** 🏛 🏛 🏛 🏛   **Value for money ££££**
Highlights The saloon, gallery and restored blue velvet room; beautiful grounds
Drawbacks Some of the unrestored principal rooms look tired and worn by
comparison with the blue velvet room

What's there A neoclassical gem in beautiful landscaped grounds, Chiswick House was the brainchild of the 3rd Earl of Burlington (1694–1753), whose travels on a European Grand Tour inspired him to build a haven away from the pressures of city and court in the style of ancient Rome. Like nearby Marble Hill House, this rural retreat was visited by the great figures of the day, including the writers Pope, Swift and Gay, the composer Handel, and William Kent, the artist and pioneer of landscape gardening. In the nineteenth century visitors to Chiswick House included Victoria and Albert, a king of Prussia and a Russian tsar.

Chiswick is a fine example of the **English Palladian villa**. Lord Burlington had studied Palladio's villas, adapted from Roman originals, in Vicenza. One known as La Rotunda was the direct inspiration for his design. Lord Burlington wanted somewhere for entertainment and a showcase for his collection of sculpture, paintings and antiquities. While he continued to live in the family's old house (demolished long ago) next door, here in this villa art and enlightenment reigned supreme.

The ground floor once housed the library, butler's pantry, linen room and bedchambers. No sign of these functions remains. Today these rooms, including the low-ceilinged **central pillared hall**, are given over to an exhibition about the origins and development of the house and garden. One previous occupant was Georgiana, Duchess of Devonshire (daughter of the 1st Earl Spencer and wife of the 5th Duke), who lived at Chiswick from 1744. As a pre-eminent supporter of the Whigs, she entertained lavishly to boost party morale. A bust of Napoleon (after Chaudet, 1763–1810), whom Georgiana and the Whig leader Charles James Fox greatly admired, can be seen in the former library. (Fox died in this house in 1806.)

An eighteenth-century lead sphinx, previously a garden feature, can also be seen in this part of the house, together with classical statues.

A corridor leads off the main house to the **summer parlour**, which in the eighteenth century was a garden room. Previously it was Lady Burlington's dressing room, decorated in magnificent style by the Burlingtons' close friend William Kent. The room now contains an exhibition about the restoration and re-creation of the estate, which fell into disrepair, came into public ownership in 1929 and was restored in the 1950s. The wings, housing the kitchen and other practical facilities, were demolished.

Upstairs, via a narrow spiral staircase, are the rooms where the social gatherings took place. Guests would have entered via the grand external staircase directly into the central octagonal **saloon** or 'tribune', immediately above the pillared hall on the ground floor. Under the saloon's lofty carved-plaster dome hang large-scale paintings, seven of which were in this room in Lord Burlington's day. The subjects include Anne of Austria and Louis XIII (with dog). Light comes from the drum of the dome, into which are set windows echoing those of the Roman baths of Diocletian. Twelve antique busts overlook the room.

Around the periphery of the saloon are a gallery, occupying the entire north-western side (back) of the house, three fine rooms identified by the colour of their wall coverings, two small closets either side of the passage from the entrance portico into the saloon, and a bedchamber. The **gallery** contains two massive porphyry vases brought back by Lord Burlington from his first Grand Tour, and two recently re-acquired marble-topped tables on gilded Baltic fir bases. The richly gilded ceiling features an oval painting depicting the defence of Scutari against the Turks in 1474, which Lord Burlington thought was by Veronese.

The **red velvet room** also has a notable ceiling: in the central painting, probably by William Kent, Mercury presides over figures representing the visual arts – painting, sculpture and architecture. More deities are depicted in the paintings by Ricci hanging at either side of the window, and on the wall opposite are paintings of classical ruins by Codazzi. Matching this room on the other side of the house is the **green velvet room**, with more paintings by Ricci, Albani's *Mars and Venus*, various views of the gardens, and a triple portrait by Michael Dahl that includes Lord Burlington's father.

While the décor of the red room and its counterpart, the green room, is somewhat worn and tired, the **blue velvet room**, now restored, shows how vibrant these rooms must have been in former times. It is like a jewel box – rich, gorgeous and glittering. Some 26 paintings were once displayed here, though it is not a large room, so it may have been a 'cabinet', to which connoisseurs were invited. It retains its ceiling painting by William Kent (1729), in which Architecture, crowned with a Corinthian capital, is flanked by boys holding drawing instruments. Above one of the doors is a painting of Inigo Jones by William Dobson.

Leave time to explore the gardens, especially the **avenue of stone sphinxes and urns** that leads to the exedra, a semicircular recess lined with statues; the orange tree garden, in the shape of an amphitheatre, where a classical temple overlooks a circular pool with an obelisk in its centre; and the recently restored **cascade** dating from 1738–46, at the southern end of the lake or 'canal'. The **Italian garden**, an intricate arrangement of paths and flowerbeds, features a pair of fine Coade stone vases – replicas stand in the garden, near the entrance to the 1813 conservatory, originals within it.

Information/tours/guides Although there is a good 10-minute introductory video and many display boards on the ground floor, floor plans, a suggested route and a little more on-the-spot explanation would be useful in the first-floor rooms. The guidebook (£2.50) is written for students of architecture, not the general visiting public. The guides are knowledgeable and happy to talk about the house.

When to visit Any time, but the gardens are particularly pleasant in summer.

Age appeal Mainly adult, though families can and do derive much pleasure from the gardens.

Food and drink The Burlington Café, despite its accommodation in a shabby glazed outhouse with lino floor, is rightly popular for its range of reasonably priced food, from the Burlington breakfast (£5) and main courses (e.g. lamb shank at £6) to filled ciabatta (£2.50), filled croissants (£2.95) and smoked salmon/scrambled egg on toast (£5). Tea is 85p, coffee £1. Tables outside and in.

Shops The shop occupies (with the ticket counter) a tiny space between the visitors' entrance and ground-floor rooms. It stocks books, including a history trail (40p) and a teachers' handbook (£1.95) about the house, teas, jams, soaps and foam bath, calendars, mugs (£2.99), clocks (£14.99), teddy bears, pencils, cards and traditional wooden toys.

Other facilities Toilets are in the house. Picnics are allowed in the grounds.

🚗 On the Great West Road, A4, follow car park sign, House a few 100 yards away. ⊖ Nearest Underground station Turnham Green (District line), then ¾-mile walk or bus E3 or 190 from Richmond station to grounds. Alternatively, train to Chiswick station then ½-mile walk. ◷ Apr to Sept, Mon to Sun, 10am to 6pm; Oct, Mon to Sun, 10am to 5pm (or dusk if earlier); Nov to Mar, Wed to Sun, 10am to 4pm. Closed 24–26 Dec, 1–18 Jan. 💷 Adult £3.30, child (under 16 yrs old) £1.70 (under-5s free); concessions £2.50. ♿ Wheelchair access difficult owing to spiral staircase. Ring for more information. Disabled toilet. Access in grounds.

The Clink

Clink Prison, 1 Clink Street, London SE1 9DG ☎ *020-7378 1558*
📠 *020-7403 5813* 🖥 *www.clink.co.uk*

Quality ★ **Facilities 📷** **Value for money ££**
Highlights Reasonably atmospheric; informative text on wall displays
Drawbacks Not a great deal to see; a struggle to read small print of some notices in the gloom; cacophony of competing taped voices

What's there The Clink Prison Museum endeavours to give visitors a taste of what it was like to fall foul of the law in a less enlightened age. The prison was named 'The Clink' because it stands in an 80-acre area known as 'The Liberty of the Clink', which was the London manor of the Bishops of Winchester. The prison served this area for nearly 300 years, from the fifteenth century until 1780, and what you see are a few underground rooms of it – windowless, painted black throughout and strewn with sawdust, with dim lighting and **wax models of** unsavoury-looking **prisoners** and their **gaolers**.

The customs of the day guaranteed a miserable time for all inmates, whether they were heretics, whores, thieves or debtors. The museum's first diorama shows the **fetters being fitted**. Prisoners were charged for this service, and for the eventual removal, as well as for their keep. They were also relieved of their clothes, money and valuables on arrival. An audiotape dramatises this scene.

The Clink was the first prison in which women prisoners were regularly confined, with their offspring if they had any. In the next room, an audio tape (unfortunately competing with the one in the first room) tells the tale of a woman pleading for mercy after being trapped into working as a prostitute. Text descriptions on the wall reveal that women were not spared the tortures, including branding and mutilation, handed out to the men.

The next diorama depicts a **priest in his cell**. Imprisonment for dissent was common after Henry VIII, breaking away from the Church of Rome, declared himself head of the Church in England. Dissent became a crime not only against the Church but also a crime against the monarch – and hence, treason.

After passing a rack and a torture chair, visitors enter a large room dealing with the many brothels, or 'stews' as they were known, once found in the Clink area. The brothel trade was regulated, as shown by the rules governing the activities of both the whores (once known hereabouts as 'Winchester geese', owing to their flapping white aprons) and their customers. Tyrannical bailiffs were in charge of both prison and brothel. Exhibits in this room include a pillory, stocks, which were once a common sight on the village greens of Merrie England, a block and axe for executions, and various kinds of prison door, including the Victorian model with peephole and food hatch which is still in common use today.

The final scene shows a **starving debtor**, who has just been lucky enough to catch a rat for his supper. His account of his sojourn can be heard on another audio tape. Visitors pass from here to the shop, where there are also some exhibits relating to hanging.

Information/tours/guides The background information for each diorama is on mis-spelt notices on the walls, which in some cases have been helpfully corrected by visitors. The four audio recordings by actors supplement the written word. Guided tours for groups can be arranged.

When to visit Any time at all: these subterranean rooms are inhospitable whatever the weather.

Age appeal The Clink is mainly for adults interested in the history of the penal system. Older children with a taste for horror and prurience will probably find it all hugely amusing.

Food and drink Despite the mention of 'light refreshments' on the board outside there was no sign of them when we visited. However, this riverside area has many tourist attractions and it is not difficult to find refreshment nearby. For example, Southwark Cathedral, which houses some of the tombs of the above-mentioned bishops of Winchester, has a café. There is also Vinopolis Cantina.

Shops The shop counter in the room from which visitors exit was unstaffed when we visited. It contained, under glass, a small range of souvenirs including T-shirts (£7.99), mugs (£4.99), pens, erasers, pencils, Clink rings (£1 silver, £1.50 gilt), Clink bracelets (£1 and £1.50) and postcards (50p). A booklet on the Clink's history and another by a priest describing his time at the Clink each cost £1 (£1.75 for both).

Other facilities No facilities whatever (including toilets) are provided.

🚗 Not recommended during the week, but on-street parking south of the river between London Bridge and Southwark Bridge. ⊖ Nearest Underground and mainline station London Bridge (Northern and Jubilee lines). ⏰ Mon to Sun, 10am to 6pm. 💷 Adult £4; student, senior citizen, unemployed, disabled £3; child (5-16 yrs old) £3; family ticket (2 adults + 2 children) £9. ♿ Not suitable for wheelchairs owing to stairs at entrance and exit.

Courtauld Gallery

Courtauld Institute of Art, Somerset House, Strand, London WC2R 0RN
☎ *020-7848 2526*   📠 *www.courtauld.ac.uk*

Quality ★★★   **Facilities 🏛🏛🏛🏛**   **Value for money £££**
Highlights   Small, intimate collection with a broad range of European paintings
Drawbacks   Absence of audio tours or guides that could provide enlightening background information

What's there   This small but impressive collection includes world-famous **Impressionist** and **Post-Impressionist paintings**, and a few sculptures. Its smallness provides an intimacy that larger collections lack, and the attractive setting of Somerset House gives it a pleasant ambience.

The Courtauld Institute of Art was set up by Samuel Courtauld, chairman of the famous textile company from 1921 to 1945, and his personal collection forms the heart of the Impressionist and Post-Impressionist section on the second floor. Included are **Cézanne**'s *Card Players* and **Degas**' ballerinas, as well as poor old **Vincent Van Gogh** minus his ear. Other famous images are **Manet**'s *Bar at the Folies-Bergère*, **Toulouse-Lautrec**'s *Jane Avril* of the Moulin Rouge, and **Gauguin**'s *The Dream* from his Tahitian period. Also on show are the Pointilism ('dot') paintings by **Seurat**, and work by **Pissarro**, **Renoir**, **Brueghel** and **Rubens**, among many others. There is also a small collection of early Italian and Flemish paintings on the ground floor from the Princes Gate collection donated by Count Antoine Seilern.

As we went to press the rest of Somerset House was being renovated, and a new museum for the Gilbert Collection of decorative art was due to open in May 2000, while works from the Hermitage in St Petersburg were to go on display in the autumn of 2000. There were also plans for a new bar and restaurant.

Information/tours/guides   There are no guided tours. A guidebook (£8.95) is available from the bookshop. Visitors are given a free gallery plan with their ticket. The marker panels for each painting are interesting and informative.

When to visit   This is a quiet, relatively little-known gallery, and is not frequented by hordes of schoolchildren or tourists, so visit any time.

Age appeal   The gallery runs 'Saturday drop-ins' and workshops for kids during school holidays, with activities like puppet-making and hat-making. Free thematic 'gallery trails' for 5- to 12-year-olds are available from the reception desk.

Food and drink   A café in the basement, run by friendly Italian staff, serves sandwiches (£2.50) and quiche, salads and pasta (all at £5.00) until 5.30pm.

Shops Located opposite the gallery entrance, a shop sells prints (£2.50) and books (£15).

🚗 On A4. Parking available at Drury Lane and the South Bank Centre. ⊖ Nearest Underground stations are Covent Garden (Piccadilly line), Holborn (Piccadilly and Central lines) and Temple (District and Circle lines). ◷ Mon to Sat 10am to 6pm; Sun and bank hols 12pm to 6pm. Last admission 5.15pm. Free admission 10am to 2pm every Mon except bank hols. Closed 24–26, 31 Dec, 1 Jan. 💷 Adult £4; child (under 18 yrs old) free; student, unemployed free; concession £3. Annual ticket £7.50. ♿ A separate entrance provides access for wheelchairs; lift to all floors.

Cutty Sark

King William Walk, Greenwich, London SE10 9HT ☎ *020-8858 3445*
📧 *www.cuttysark.org.uk*

Quality ★ ★ ★ ★   **Facilities 🚢 🚢**   **Value for money ££££**
Highlights Wealth of information and anecdotes from guides
Drawbacks Lack of facilities

What's there Now resigned to a sedentary life in dry dock, the *Cutty Sark* is perhaps the most famous of the tea clippers which raced from China to Britain laden with cargo in the nineteenth century. The ship has been restored to its current splendour by the Maritime Trust, and the rigging and brasswork certainly give the ship a majestic, graceful appearance, although she was actually one of the smaller vessels of the period.

The ship can be visited only on a **guided tour**, which begins on the middle of the three decks, starting with the origins of the ship's name and an account of its design and construction, the original shipyard now being the site of the Cutty Sark Whisky distillery. From there your guide moves on to recount the **story of the tea trade**, including the high price that tea once fetched, thanks to the social cachet of using the freshest leaves. This is useful as it places everything you learn in context and allows you to fully appreciate the ship's significance. The tour is packed with facts, anecdotes and other snippets of information about every aspect of the ship and the tea trade – for instance in 1866 three of the five clippers that entered the largest 'China Race' reached British ports within 20 minutes of each other, after a 99-day voyage!

On the upper deck, you can see the galley, inside which the cook some how rustled up food for 30 men, as well as the somewhat confined sleeping quarters. These and the food on display bring home the **hardships of life at sea** – sailors had to survive on a diet of salt beef or pork and the notorious hard biscuits, which were made to keep 'fresh' over a long period (one guide claims that he ate one which was 40 years old). The deck also holds chicken coops and a pigsty with sound effects (the pig kept on board, incidentally, was always called Dennis, and was always a black pig, so as to avoid problems with sunburn). From the stern you descend to the relative splendour of the **Captain's Saloon**, complete with fireplace and dining table, where the Captain tried to maintain a slightly more refined existence while planning the navigation.

The tour ends on the lower deck, which features an **exhibition of figureheads** from ships' bows, including the oldest in the world, dating from 1660.

Contrary to popular myth, these are not an array of bare-breasted women, but mostly classical characters and politicians of the day. The lower deck also has a video including footage of clippers in the 1920s, again stressing the rigours of life at sea (unfortunately, on our inspection the video had technical problems and at one point stopped for a short while).

Very close to the ship you can also see the *Gipsy Moth IV*, the yacht in which Sir Francis Chichester made his famous single-handed voyage in 1966–7.

Information/tours/guides The full-colour Pitkin guidebook (£2.50) is well written and packed with information about the origins and history of the ship. The knowledge of our tour guide, an ex-sailor born in Foochow in China, where the tea used to be loaded, made the subject matter come alive. The guides do tend to be fairly mature – ours was a sprightly 73-year-old.

When to visit The upper deck is exposed to the elements, so it's best avoided in bad weather, especially by older visitors. To avoid large parties of schoolchildren visit in the afternoon.

Age appeal The tour would appeal to all ages, although perhaps more to older visitors and those with an interest in history. Children and teenagers may find the historical facts a bit dry. A 'Seaman-for-a-Day' promotion allows groups of 20 to 30 children to spend a day aboard, learning how the ship was sailed and the cargo was handled. They are presented with a certificate at the end of the day. This promotion costs £2 per child as well as £25 for the party regardless of size.

Food and drink The site itself has no café or bar, but there are plenty of good pubs and restaurants in nearby Greenwich, many with seafood on the menu.

Shops The lower deck has a small shop – The Bosun's Locker – selling a variety of nautical souvenirs, including sweatshirts (£20) and jigsaws (£20).

🚌 Centre of Greenwich village (car parking), then 10-minute walk. ⊖ Train to Greenwich station (from Charing Cross or London Bridge stations), then short walk to riverside. Also Docklands Light Railway to Cutty Sark station. ⏱ Open all year, Mon to Sun, 10am to 5pm. Closed 24–26 Dec. 💷 Adult £3.50, child (5 to 16 yrs old) £2.50, senior citizen, student, unemployed £2.50, family ticket (2 adults + 3 children) £8.50. Discount of 20% for groups of 10 or more if one pays full price. An adult 'Passport Ticket' allows entry to the *Cutty Sark*, National Maritime Museum (which is free for children) and Royal Observatory for £12.00, concessions £9.60. ♿ No wheelchair access to the upper or lower decks (plus no prams or pushchairs can be taken on board).

Design Museum

28 Shad Thames, London SE1 2YD   ☎ *020-7378 6055*

Quality ★★   **Facilities 🏛🏛🏛🏛**   **Value for money ££**

Highlights   Good café and shop; pleasant location overlooking the Thames
Drawbacks   Level of interest depends as much on temporary exhibitions as on permanent displays; little to interest children; orientation could be better

---

What's there Located in a much-revamped area of the South Bank next to a clutch of Conran restaurants, this former warehouse by the Thames concentrates on **twentieth-century design**. The second floor houses the permanent Collection and Review Galleries, while **temporary exhibitions** (about five or six a year) take up the first floor.

The permanent Collection Gallery looks at the study of **design for mass production**, choosing particular objects, such as the telephone, and following them as they evolve over time with new materials, technology and social changes. Thus the kettle changes from the traditional hob variety through electric and cordless models to a design where form may take precedence over function, as in **Philippe Starck's Hot Bertaa kettle**, where the packaging reads 'Do not use when hot'! The range of wacky TVs from the 1960s is also interesting, including the **Videosphere**, a combined TV/radio/clock in fetching orange, designed to be suspended from a chain (the inspiration apparently came from *Sputnik I*). Chairs (which you can actually sit on), plastic packaging, tableware, and white goods such as washing machines are also covered.

The Review Gallery features a changing selection of new and innovative design concepts in areas such as furniture, transport and electrical equipment. Thus a radical toothbrush might crop up next to a backpack vacuum cleaner or hingeless spectacles.

The permanent collections are not very large, and the length of your visit and value for money will largely depend on whatever temporary exhibition is on at the time. Sadly, it's all very theoretical: while the galleries may be full of sketching students, there are few interactive activities for ordinary visitors.

Information/tours/guides The publicity leaflet gives details of the temporary exhibitions and their dates. There is no guidebook, and the layout of the permanent Collection and Review Gallery is a little confusing, as it's not always clear where one exhibition stops and another starts.

There are good explanatory labels within the exhibition cases, but these are sometimes difficult to match up with the items on display. Silent videos play on loops, but the lack of sound means they lose much of their appeal – nobody was watching them when we inspected. Audio guides are available for selected exhibitions.

When to visit The museum is all under cover, so it's a good wet-weather attraction, although fine weather is best for river views.

Age appeal There's very little to appeal to children. Some of the older designs may provide trips down memory lane for adult visitors.

Food and drink The café makes up part of the open-plan lobby on the ground floor, where the river can be viewed through full-length glass windows (and there's some seating outside for fine days). Tea, cappuccino (£1.30), home-made soup, sandwiches (salami and egg £2.80), and various cakes and pastries are available as well as more robust snacks in the form of Italian vegetable pie.

For full meals the pricier Blue Print Café (separate entrance), on the first-floor glassed-over balcony, offers Mediterranean-influenced dishes such as rabbit fricassee with peppers, olives and basil, or polenta with ceps, roast onions, mascarpone, rocket and Parmesan (main courses £12 to £20).

Shops The shop next to the café stocks plenty of books on various aspects of twentieth-century design. Specific Design Museum souvenirs include T-shirts (£12.99), notebooks (£1.50 to £2.50), and keyrings. But there is also a range of suitable gift ideas, from kitchenware (egg cups, kettles, jar openers) and watches, calculators and pens to models of the chairs in the exhibition (£81 to £175).

Other facilities Toilets are not as 'designed' as you might expect for a design museum, but are clean and functional. There's a separate disabled toilet with baby-changing facilities.

🚗 Multi-storey car park on Gainsford Street, SE1 and a coach and car park on Tooley Street SE1 (tel 020-7378 1147). ⊖ Nearest underground stations are Tower Hill (Circle and District Lines, Docklands Light Railway) and London Bridge (Northern Line and mainline rail) – both 10–15 minutes' walk from the museum. ⏲ Mon to Sun 11.30am to 6pm (last entry 5.30pm). 🎫 Adult £5.50, students £4.50, child (under 18 yrs old) and concessions (senior citizen, disabled visitors, unemployed) £4, family ticket (2 adults + 2 children) £12. ♿ Mostly wheelchair accessible; lift; disabled toilets.

The Dome

Greenwich, London SE10 0BB   ☎ *(0870) 241 0541*
Ticket line (0870) 606 2000 📠 *www.dome2000.co.uk*

Quality ★★★	Facilities 🏛🏛🏛🏛	Value for money ££

Highlights Outside view of Dome; Millennium Show; Play and Journey Zones; excellent staff; branded food outlets

Drawbacks High entrance price; queues; heavy branding by sponsors; variable quality of zones – Learning, Money, Faith and Work Zones are missable

---

What's there This vast site is rather a curate's egg – choose the right zones and you could have a great day, but some are frankly disappointing – and it is a shame that the sponsorship is so 'in your face' given that visitors are paying a high entrance fee to see the attraction.

Allow a full day to get your money's worth. On arrival you will be given a timed ticket to see a specially-commissioned episode of *Blackadder* (40 minutes) and the Millennium Show. If you arrive early you will probably be given the 11am screening, but if you prefer to be more active while you are fresh, ask for a later time. Note that the film is *not* shown in the main part of the Dome. The zone descriptions that follow are in descending order of preference.

The **Millennium Show** is a spectacular 40-minute acrobatic performance in the central arena. The best seats are probably the higher ones allowing a view over the stage, but children may like to sit on the floor near the round stage so that they feel more part of the action. Be warned that if you go first to the **Play Zone** with children you will have trouble getting them to see anything else. This big dark hall is full of brilliant virtual-reality games – and whatever your age you will want to join in, whether on the music machine where you can play a piano and make a light show by moving a rollerball, the virtual-reality tug-of-war, or the 100-a-side dog and cat team game. Allow at least an hour for this.

The **Journey Zone** is one of the few that conveys any sense of history and human progress (allow an hour for it). It starts with a time trail on the development of locomotion (Egyptians could swim the crawl, Roman chariots could move at about 17mph, *Apollo 10* travelled at 24,791mph), then progresses to transport problems of the future and possible solutions (with lots of high-tech models, including a simulation of the cockpit of a yacht in the Indian Ocean as a storm approaches) – and then, via a twinkling model of the Dome and Canary Wharf, looks at the journeys of tomorrow. Outside, a virtual rallying game attracts long queues.

Timekeepers of the Millennium is a Heath Robinson-like soft-play and climbing activity centre, appealing mainly to under-10s, that could be visited to break up the day. **Self-portrait** (allow 30 minutes) is an intimate zone for grown-ups – a photographic account of the British in the last millennium, with humorous and affectionate images of British life such as a jug of custard, a socks-and-sandals wearer ('how others see us'), beach huts and Radio 4. In the centre of the exhibition are sculptures by Gerald Scarfe giving a more fashionably negative view – the thug, the racist, the slob and the Establishment.

Home Planet, the only ride (10 minutes) in the Dome, allows you to travel with aliens as they explore the Earth. Experience iceberg chill and volcanic heat on this quest for human life. Queues are likely.

The most eye-catching element of the Dome is the walk through two huge human models of the **Body Zone** (allow an hour or more to queue – try to go when the Millennium Show is on – and 15 minutes for inside). This is unashamed entertainment rather than an attempt to educate. You start in the pubic hair area; next, embarrassment-proof volunteers can have their heads thermally imaged to see if they contain any bugs; then escalators take you up to the noisy heart area (rather scary for very young children), which leads into the womb, where sperm race to catch the egg to the noise of enthusiastic chanting. The brain room has Tommy Cooper's brain telling jokes to an audience of other brains, while in the eye room you watch a film designed to move you to tears. The rest of this zone is surprisingly dull and more like a science fair with individual exhibits showing the work of drugs companies.

Shared Ground (allow 30 minutes) is one for the grown-ups, where they can record their views on the minutiae of domestic life (what do you think about when ironing?) for inclusion in a time capsule. It is well designed and people's answers are often hilarious. The **Mind Zone** offers some interesting ideas about machines and human intelligence, throwaway-style. Note the starfish that reacts to the heat of your hand – demonstrating the principle of neural nets – and, if you are a football fan, the film of Manchester United (judge whether the Red Devils play so well because they have 'a collective mind'). Long queues form for the morphing machines where you can change your age or sex or graft yourself on to a famous person's (well, Carol Vorderman's) image. The **Talk Zone** (30 minutes), an extended commercial for BT's Internet service, reminds you that 'it's good to talk' while long queues wait to have their images manipulated with ET.

Living Island (allow 20 minutes plus time for games) is enough to kill off the British seaside resort. Your trip starts with a display of toilets blocked by items such as hypodermic syringes and razor blades and depressing warnings about pollution. The displays of some of the rubbish collected from Britain's beaches and statistics on the number of people poisoned by eating processed foods like hamburgers are bound to shock you. Arcade-type games – many not functioning when we visited – continue the pollution message and will keep children happy. The large white concrete interior of the **Rest Zone** soothes you with mood music, while the **Work Zone** (allow 20 minutes) whisks you through a battery of slogans on all the old 'new ways of working' to tables that test out some of the skills in demand (try beating the clock at mental arithmetic, taking a phone call to test listening skills or playing a huge table-football game to gauge your team skills).

The **Faith Zone** (20 minutes if it appeals at all) is a dull attempt to explore how Christianity has shaped us – lots of talking heads on screens that are impossible to follow against the level of background noise – and key facts about other religions. Activities in the tacky and incoherent **Money Zone** (30 minutes, and missable) include spending a million, for no apparent reason, walking through a tunnel that shows the horrors of what would happen if money were not managed (hyperinflation, and so on), and choosing an investment. Downstairs, look at the beautiful Millennium Diamond. Despite its good looks, the **Learning Zone** (allow up to 20 minutes) is a letdown. After watching another mawkish film in a mocked-up school room you move into a glittering grove full of terminals on which you can play around to very little effect.

Information/tours/guides Free map provided on arrival is not easy to understand. Audio tour (£2.50) is a complete waste of money unless you have difficulty with English.

When to visit Any time until end of 2000. A good rainy-day sight – but wear warm clothes in cold weather, as there is no heating.

Age appeal Children will probably be most enthusiastic; adults are more conscious of the drawbacks – and cost.

Food and drink Plenty of branded outlets, from McDonald's to Yo! Sushi and seafood and wine bar. High-street prices.

Shops Large gift shop with plenty of branded products and gifts, from pin badges (£1) to diamond pendants (£2,000).

🚗 In no-car zone with parking restrictions for 2 miles around. For Dome park-and-ride car parks around London phone (0870) 241 0541 to book, pay for a space and receive directions. ⊖ *Trains* Nearest Underground is North Greenwich (Jubilee line). One-day Millennium LT card allows unlimited travel on Underground, buses and DLR on the day of visit (adult £3.50; child £1). Ring (0870) 606 2000 or show your admission ticket at any Underground station. The M1 Millennium transit bus meets trains from Victoria and North Kent at Charlton railway station. *Buses* M1, M2 from Greenwich Station or 108, 161, 188, 422, 472 (call 020–7222 1234 for information). *Boats* City Cruises run boats from Waterloo and Blackfriars Piers direct to the Dome every 30 minutes. Ring 020–7740 0400 or visit *www.citycruises.com* ⏰ 10am to 6pm (gates open 9am); evening sessions 6pm to 11pm. 💷 Adult £20; child (5 to 15 years old) £16.50; family ticket (5 people) £57; student £16.50; senior citizen £18; unemployed £12. Tickets from ticket line (0870) 606 2000) and National Lottery outlets: do not rely on buying at gate. ♿ Highly accessible; motorised and manual wheelchairs available on free loan. Book orange badge parking in advance (tel (0870) 241 0540). Land train from Main Square to Meridian Point.

Eltham Palace

Court Yard, Eltham, London SE9 5QE ☎ *020-8294 2548* 📠 *020-8294 2621*

Quality ★ ★ ★ ★ ★   **Facilities** 🎫 🎫 🎫 🎫   **Value for money** £££££
Highlights   Impressive renovation of art deco mansion; moat and medieval wing; excellent free audio tour
Drawbacks   Very little to occupy children

What's there   Recently opened after a painstaking renovation by English Heritage, Eltham Palace is a gem of an attraction. The main house was built in the early 1930s for Stephen and Virginia Courtauld, of textile-family fame and – quite obviously – fortune. They chose a site where a **medieval palace**, bigger than Hampton Court, once stood, and which is now a remarkably tranquil setting on the edge of an unremarkable London suburb. The Courtaulds left Eltham in 1944, and the site was then occupied by the Army until 1992, but English Heritage has skilfully used period photographs to reproduce many of the lavish interiors.

Only the **Great Hall**, built for Edward IV in 1470, survives from the early palace. With the enormous timbers that form its lofty, hammer-beamed ceiling and the beautiful stained glass, it is one of the architectural highlights, and forms a major contrast to the rest of the house. The Courtaulds not only restored the Great Hall but added on a house that represented the **height of 1930s design and technology**, including a centralised vacuum cleaner, internal telephones in the bedrooms and a loudspeaker system that could broadcast records throughout the ground floor.

Each of the main rooms has a distinct design scheme. This ranges from a rustic Italian-style salon through to a classically inspired mosaic and marble bathroom. There are striking examples of **period decoration**, such as an **aluminium leaf ceiling** in the dining room and **elaborate inlaid marquetry** in Virginia's oval-shaped bedroom. Examples of the architectural fashions of the day include sweeping curves and modernist symmetry, inspired by the design of ocean liners. The entrance hall, in particular, is an art deco master-piece. Standing under the domed ceiling is like being in a giant salt cellar, as light streams in through the tiny glass portholes.

Even the Courtaulds' pets lived well. Mah-Jongg, a ring-tailed lemur, was bought as a pet by the family from Harrods, and his sleeping quarters were centrally heated and painted with forest scenes to make him feel at home. A bamboo ladder allowed him access to a small room off the entrance hall.

Despite the opulence, you still get a feel for the house as the Courtaulds' home. Bath taps still work and nothing is roped off or hidden behind glass. This makes the pleasure and interest of the visit as much about the people as the place they lived in.

Information/tours/guides   A clear and engaging audio tour, plus accompanying map of grounds, are included in the admission price. Making good use of the technology, the tour combines factual information – the dates, the original designers and the renovation – with an account of events in the house described by actors playing the Courtaulds and their guests. A keypad on the handset allows you to select more detailed information, on, for example, individual fittings and historical events. There's also an informative and well-illustrated guidebook (£3.95), which provides additional details on the Courtaulds and the restoration work by English Heritage.

When to visit The main interest of the house is the interior, so poor weather shouldn't deter a visit. In better weather the spacious, varied gardens make a good picnic site.

Age appeal Neither the guidebook, audio tour nor the explanatory panels offer much for children. There's plenty of space for a run around outside, but younger children in particular might be bored.

Food and drink A limited range of freshly prepared and good-value food is available in the small restaurant in the converted kitchens, and from a counter in the garden. The 1930s theme is carried through, with the staff in black and white lace uniforms, deco-inspired china, and the original cream and green colour scheme. Cream tea (£2.95), sandwiches (from £2), and quiche and salad (£3.80) are served.

Shops Given the potential of the art deco period, the small boutique is slightly disappointing; far more books, souvenirs and gifts relate to the medieval era (where English Heritage is presumably stronger) than the later period.

🚗 1 mile north of A20, then A208, off Court Yard (follow the brown signs). Free car park. ⊖ Train to Eltham mainline station, then 10-minute walk (follow signposts). ⊙ Wed to Fri, Sun, Apr to Oct, 10am to 6pm (5pm in Oct), Nov to Mar, 10am to 4pm. Open Bank Holidays. Closed 24–26 Dec, 1 Jan. 💷 Adult £5.90, child (under 16 yrs old) £3.00, senior citizen £4.40, English Heritage members free. ♿ Special route of house and gardens for disabled visitors outlined on map. Disabled toilet; disabled parking.

FA Premier League Hall of Fame

County Hall, Riverside Building, Westminster Bridge Road, London SE1 7PB
☎ *020-7928 1800*   ✎ *www.hall-of-fame.co.uk*

Quality ★★★★   **Facilities** 👜👜👜👜   **Value for money ££**
Highlights Evocative use of soundtracks and period settings
Drawbacks Ubiquitous adverts for museum's sponsors

What's there While the 'Hall of Fame' currently contains just a measly dozen players – the Premier League having been in existence since only 1992 – this museum actually rejoices in hundreds of years of football history. Pass through the scene-setting rotating '**time tunnel**' and you are taken back to the beautiful game's grubby medieval origins and on to a stroll through a century of British socio-political history with a soccer slant. A Victorian parlour gives way to **First World War trenches**, an austere post-war living room, a section of Wembley terracing with England perpetually winning the 1966 World Cup Final, and a corridor of **fashion disasters** from the 1970s. Songs, speeches and some choice artefacts put **iconic soccer moments** – like the Christmas Day kick-about between the trenches in World War I, the White Horse Final of 1923 and the Munich air crash – into the appropriate period settings. Touch screens and storyboards provide skimmable snippets or sufficient detail for the obsessive.

The **Hall of Fame** holds life-sized models of the chosen 12 (Adams, Bergkamp, Cantona, Ferdinand, Gullit, Hughes, Rush, Schmeichel, Seaman, Shearer, Wright, Zola) which resemble giant Subbuteo players, each equipped with touch screens so visitors can call up their career statistics and footage of them in action.

A small cinema shows a ten-minute playground-to-Premier League schoolboy fantasy film, and **computer-generated soccer skills** can be put to the test at the controls of the many Sony Playstation units available in the Virtual Stadium area.

Information/tours/guides The glossy souvenir programme (£2.50/ 2 for £4) is basically a take-home copy of the Hall of Fame players' statistics, with a smidgen of behind-the-scenes-at-the-museum details thrown in, several pages of adverts, and the same practical information as can be gleaned from the free promotional leaflets.

When to visit Any time, though Saturdays are busiest.

Age appeal Football fans of all ages should find enough to hold their attention for up to two hours among the whizz-bang graphics, animatronics, touch screens, video clips and computer games.

Food and drink Limited to just tea, coffee, fizzy drinks and chocolate bars.

Shop A spacious and stylish operation cashes in on the demand for replica kits. Supplements include mugs, baseball caps, caricature figures and assorted small knick-knacks emblazoned with club logos.

🚗 Nearest car parks located by the Royal Festival Hall, the National Film Theatre and Waterloo station (about £3 for 2 hours). ⊖ Nearest Underground stations are Waterloo (Bakerloo, Northern and Jubilee lines) and Westminster (Circle, District and Jubilee lines), 5–10 minutes' walk away. Buses 12, 53, 76, 77, 159, 211, 507, D1 and P11 pass close to County Hall. ☉ Mon to Sun 10am to 6pm (last admission 5pm). Closed 25 Dec. 💷 Adult £9.95; child (4 to 15 yrs old) £6.50; senior citizen, student £7.50; disabled £5. ♿ People with disabilities can use the entrance on Belvedere Road. The museum is on two floors, with lifts. Disabled toilets.

Geffrye Museum

Kingsland Road, London E2 8EA ☎ *020-7739 9893/8543*
📠 *020-7729 5647* 🖥 *www.geffrye-museum.org.uk*
🖥 *info@geffrye-museum.org.uk*

Quality ★★★★★   **Facilities 🍴🍴🍴🍴🍴**   **Value for money ££££**
Highlights Attractive room displays and creative workshops for all age groups
Drawbacks Narrow passages through room displays can mean congestion –
especially with a pushchair or wheelchair

What's there This enjoyable museum, which presents the changing styles of **English domestic interiors**, is located in some charming eighteenth-century former almshouses set in pleasant gardens with mature trees. The museum was opened in 1914 as a reference collection of furniture and woodwork to educate and inspire the local workforce involved in the furniture industry. In the 1930s the collections were reorganised into a series of period rooms to provide a unique resource for schools to learn about domestic life.

Now visitors can walk along a narrow passage through a series of room displays that takes you through time, from the oak panelling and furnishings of the seventeenth century to the **loft living** of the 1990s – visitors can enjoy trying to spot at least one item of furnishing they may have (or have had) in their own homes. A panel describes how each room was used and gives information on the trends and furnishings. In the late Georgian room the ritual of having tea is described: chairs and tables were moved into the room for the occasion, the urn of hot water has its own table, and there is a locked satinwood tea caddy. The style of the **Aesthetic Room** (1875–1890) was influenced by Japanese art and design.

In 1998 a major new extension was built to house four new period rooms, some temporary galleries and a design centre, and to provide more space for educational activities and workshops as well as a new shop and restaurant. Not apparent from the front of the almshouses, this has created a light and modern space to house the twentieth-century displays and resulted in an attractive restaurant overlooking the period gardens at the rear. Only developed in the last few years, these are now becoming more established and include a herb garden, Edwardian garden and Victorian garden.

Information/tours/guides Each room has a display board describing the room and listing the furnishings, and there are wardens in some of the areas, but the guidebook (£5) is the main source of information. A range of talks and teaching sessions for schools, colleges and adult groups is available through the education department.

When to visit There is a lively series of exhibitions and workshops throughout the year. Around Christmas there are special activities such as a candlelight concert and Twelfth Night event as well as an annual exhibition of 400 years of Christmas traditions in English homes, with rooms decorated in the festive style of each era.

Age appeal Free workshops during school holidays and half term will appeal to all, with many geared to children of specific age groups, for example, 'Look at me' for 3–5 year olds explores self portraiture, or a fabric workshop for 13–15 year olds.

Food and drink The modern restaurant serves full meals as well as snacks: for example, grilled trout with vegetables, salmon fishcakes on a bed of creamed spinach, or bangers and mash (£5). Afternoon tea (£4.75) and home-made cake (£1.85) are available. During holidays a selection of children's meals is provided.

Shops The attractive shop sells ceramics and gifts and a wide selection of postcards and books on furniture, design and garden history.

Other facilities Highchairs are provided in the restaurant. There is a reference library and interactive database of designers in the design centre.

🚗 Limited metered parking in neighbouring streets. ⊖ Nearest Underground
Liverpool Street (Central, Metropolitan, Hammersmith and City lines) then bus 242 or
149, or Old Street Underground (Northern line) then bus 243. ⊙ Tue to Sat 10am to
5pm, Sun and bank hols 12pm to 5pm. Closed Mon, 24-26 Dec, 1 Jan 💷 Free. ♿ Full
access for wheelchairs.

Ham House

Ham, Nr Richmond, Surrey TW10 7RS ☎ *020-8940 1950*
📠 *020-8332 6903*

Quality ★ ★ ★ ★	Facilities 📔 📔 📔	Value for money ££££

Highlights Carvings on staircase; portraits by seventeenth-century masters; opulent
state rooms and lovely formal gardens

Drawbacks Not a great deal to interest children

What's there When it was owned by the Duke and Duchess of
Lauderdale, this fine Stuart house (now National Trust) was one of the most
fashionable in the country. Built in 1610 for one of James I's officials, it was
later leased to William Murray, who had been 'whipping boy' to the future
Charles I. Murray remodelled much of the interior, commissioning the
magnificent staircase and the first-floor state rooms. The king made him Earl
of Dysart as a reward for his loyalty during the Civil War. The title and
property both passed to his 'beautiful, ambitious and greedy' daughter
Elizabeth, who married first Sir Lyonel Tollemache and later, in 1672, John
Maitland, 2nd Earl (later Duke) of Lauderdale. After he was appointed Lord
High Commissioner for Scotland the couple held court there and revamped
Ham House, their London base, for entertaining the highest in the land.

The ambience created by the Lauderdales is conjured up today by the decoration, furniture, pictures and tapestries on view.

The entrance to the house is via the courtyard of the north front, where
marble busts are set into the curving sweep of its boundary wall and a statue of
the Thames river god, lounging on a plinth, greets you. Inside, the **great hall**,
hung with family portraits, is open to the carved Inigo Jones ceiling of the
floor above. Just off the hall is the chapel. An imposing **staircase**, with its
carvings of armour and weaponry, leads to the floor above and a museum
room where upholstered chairs and bed hangings are on view. The white satin
cover with couched embroidery in the central case is especially fine.

As you enter the gallery overlooking the hall, note the painting of the 6th
earl as a boy, with battledore and shuttlecock, and the **Lely portrait** of the
Duke and Duchess of Lauderdale on the end wall. As this area was once, before
most of the floor was removed, the great dining-room, a drawing room
adjoins it. The 1660 ivory cabinet here, though impressive, looks strangely out
of place against the **Mortlake tapestries** that line the walls and the chairs with
their carved-dolphin armrests.

The **long gallery** contains portraits of the patrons of William Murray and
the Duke of Lauderdale, including Charles I and Charles II, and some notable

pieces of furniture. Off it, a cabinet room known as the **green closet** is a treasury of miniatures and other small-scale pictures. Don't miss the beautiful **painted ceiling**.

The first of a suite of rooms extravagantly decorated in the 1670s in honour of Charles II's consort, Queen Catherine of Braganza, is an antechamber lined with wood painted to look like olive wood, and also blue and gold hangings. The **Queen's bedchamber**, adjoining, was used for court business as well as sleep, but no longer contains the state bed and since the 1730s has functioned as a drawing room, which is how it is presented today. The Queen's closet, beyond, to which few visitors would have been admitted, retains most of its original decoration and contents, including an adjustable 'sleeping chair' and scagliola fireplace. It also has a lovely **ceiling painting** by Verrio.

Downstairs, the windows of the garish birdcage room are no longer flanked by birdcages. The adjoining white closet (with summer hangings) and Duchess's **private closet** (winter hangings) offer a better insight into aristocratic life, for it was here that her ladyship entertained private guests and wrote letters at her walnut scriptor.

The floor of the 'marble' dining room, which gave it its name, has been replaced by parquetry. Its leather wall hangings, from the 1750s, were chosen in preference to fabric because leather does not harbour cooking smells. French taste is evident in the dramatic red hangings (reproductions) in the **Duchess's bedchamber**, where the bed stands on a recessed platform, to signify its importance. In this room, note the **Peter Lely portrait** of the Duchess as a young girl, in stark contrast to the blowsy matron portrayed with her husband (also by Lely) in the hall gallery.

A door leads from this room down narrow stairs to the Duchess's **bathroom** – a very early (1675) example and great luxury for this time. The basement also contains the kitchen and other rooms now used for educational purposes: early fire-fighting equipment stands alongside an explanatory panel; other display boards explain how the house was heated, and a rather good 10-minute **video** brings the house's social history to life.

Outside, on the south side of the house, the 'platts' (lawns) and 'wilderness' beyond are being restored to their seventeenth-century appearance: 'parterres, flower gardens, orangeries, groves, avenues, statues, perspectives, fountains and aviaries', as the diarist John Evelyn recorded. In the **cherry garden**, once the Duchess's private domain, hornbeam arbours surround formal beds of lavender and santolina outlined by clipped box – once the fragrant backdrop to many a stately promenade.

The **rose garden** (early 1900s) is overlooked by what is probably England's oldest orangery, built for over-wintering the Duchess's citrus trees and other tender shrubs. It was later used as a laundry and now serves as a tea-room.

Information/tours/guides The house leaflet (70p), which includes a map, is very useful. The guides are also very happy to talk about the house, its contents and former occupants. The illustrated souvenir guide costs £4.50. Guided walks/tours available.

When to visit Mid-summer is the best time to see the rose garden in bloom. Weekends can get busy.

Age appeal The main appeal is to adults. Children will get more from their visit if they have one of the children's guides (40p), written from the point of view of one of the Duchess's housemaids of the 1670s. Occasional special events for families are arranged.

Food and drink The orangery tea room (open Saturday to Wednesday, 11am to 5pm) serves coffee (£1.05) and tea (£1.05 per pot) and lunches (soup £2.70, main course £5.75 to £5.95) based on seventeenth-century recipes. Wine, cakes, scones and afternoon teas are also available.

Shops Books and the usual range of National Trust shop items are on offer. Opening hours as for tea-room.

Other facilities Licensed for weddings.

On south bank of Thames, west of A307, at Petersham. Car parking. ⊖ Nearest Underground station is Richmond, then 1½-mile walk along Thames path (signposted); or train to Twickenham station, walk via Church Street and Riverside to foot ferry that crosses to house. ⏱ 1 Apr to 29 Oct, Sat to Wed, 1pm to 5pm (last entry 4.30pm). *Garden*: open all year 10.30am to 6pm (or dusk if earlier). Closed Thursdays, Fridays, 25, 26 Dec, 1 Jan. 💷 Adult £5, child (5 to 17 yrs old) £2.50, family ticket £12.50. Garden only £1.50. ♿ House not accessible for wheelchairs. Braille guide available.

Hampton Court

East Molesley, Surrey KT8 9AU ☎ *020-8781 9500*
www.hrp.org.uk/hcp/indexhcp.htm

Quality ★★★★★	Facilities 👜👜👜	Value for money £££££

Highlights Excellent organised daily programme; variety of presentation methods, including audio tours, guided tours, and videos; lots of activities for children

Drawbacks No admission prices on publicity leaflet; Privy Kitchen Coffee Shop too small to cope with crowds

---

What's there Although Hampton Court is usually associated with Henry VIII and his various marital relationships, much of the eastern part of the building actually dates from the seventeenth century, when Sir Christopher Wren was commissioned by William and Mary to rebuild the palace. However, he ran out of time and money before he could demolish the whole building, so what remains today is a mixture of Tudor and baroque.

The **six tours** of the different parts of the palace allow you to get an idea of how it developed over the years under different monarchs, from Henry VIII to George II, who was the last member of the Royal Family to use it as a court.

Henry VIII's state apartments begin with the Great Hall. Used as a communal dining room, it features a magnificent hammer-beam roof and tapestries of gold and silver thread. The Chapel Royal also has a splendid vaulted pendant ceiling added by Henry, as well as a carved altar screen by Grinling Gibbons, installed by Sir Christopher Wren when he refitted the chapel for Queen Anne in the eighteenth century.

To cater for the 1,200 members of the court, the Tudor Kitchens took up 50 rooms and 36,000 square feet. They are one of the most atmospheric parts of the palace, where real (dead) wild boar and rabbits await dismemberment on the butcher's block. Finally you pass through the Great Wine Cellar, where some of the 300 barrels of ale were stored.

Cardinal Wolsey was the original owner of Hampton Court (before he gave it to Henry). The main attraction in his former rooms is the collection of Italian and Northern European paintings, including works by **Holbein**, **Raphael**, **Titian**, **Bellini**, and **Cranach the Elder**. In **Bruegel's** *Massacre of the Innocents* you can see where the bodies of children were overpainted by animals.

Jump 150 or so years when you enter the King's Apartments in the 'new wing' built by Sir Christopher Wren. The king in question was William III, and the grandiosity of his ceremonial state apartments upstairs (painted staircase by Verrio, fantastically detailed carvings by Grinling Gibbons, ostrich feathers festooning thrones and beds) contrasts markedly with his private apartments downstairs (lower ceilings, cosy panelling, portraits of the Hampton Court Beauties in his dining room).

There's a similar contrast in the Queen's State Apartments. Although these were originally intended for Mary II, William III's wife, they were not completed before her death in 1694, so what you see today dates largely from the time of Queen Caroline, wife of George II (reigned from 1727 to 1760). In the Guard Chamber, grinning carvings of Yeomen of the Guard support the mantelpiece, while in her private apartments you can see locks on the doors that could be operated from the bed to guard her privacy.

The **gardens** deserve a couple of hours in themselves. Most visitors head for the **Maze**, but the beautifully restored formality of the Privy Garden to the south and the avenues of the East Front Gardens are worth a wander. The Maze, almost an acre of yew-lined paths, was planted in 1690 for William III. Other wonders in the garden are the 1,000-year-old oak tree, and the oldest and longest vine in the world, planted in 1768. Also, don't miss **Mantegna's** outstanding series of paintings of the Triumphs of Caesar, tucked away in the Lower Orangery.

Information/tours/guides The daily programme that comes with your ticket is extremely helpful in helping to plan your day. All tours and times are listed, together with the length of time, and those that need to be booked in advance. Tour guides, who are usually costumed for the occasion, tell you not just about the history of the palace, but about everyday life of the period; they are also happy to answer questions. Although numbers are restricted, some of the groups can still be quite large – the earlier tours tend to have fewer people.

The free audio tour, which covers the Tudor Kitchens, the King's Apartments, and the Georgian Rooms, gives you the basic information, but also goes into more detail about, for example, particular paintings or Queen Caroline's bathing habits. There are also introductory videos or models for Henry VIII's State Apartments, the Tudor Kitchens, and the King's Apartments.

The beautifully illustrated official guidebook (£3.95) is well written and yet another source of information. It also makes a nice souvenir. There are also separate guidebooks to the Tudor Kitchens (£3.95) and the King's Apartments (£2.50).

Given how useful all the information provided on site is, it's a shame that the publicity leaflet fails to give admission prices – just a phone number to call for further information.

When to visit The palace is open year round, and there's enough under cover to keep you occupied even on rainy days. However, it would be a shame to miss out on the gardens, which are superb. Special events throughout the year include a flower show, music festival, Tudor Christmas and New Year activities, story telling and workshops at half-term, and lantern-lit tours in the winter. For information telephone 020-8781 9540.

Age appeal Great appeal for all ages. The free Family Trails leaflets, aimed specifically at children, offer quizzes and activities pitched at different age ranges. There are also special guided tours for children, and activities like making helmets or trying out seventeenth-century games.

Food and drink Don't be confused by the names: the Tiltyard Tea Room, in the gardens south of the Maze, actually has the widest range of hot and cold food, and plenty of seating inside and out. A choice of hot dishes is served at lunchtime, including a vegetarian option, for £5.50–5.95. Wine and beer are also available, along with salads, cakes and sandwiches (Brie and pesto ciabatta as well as bacon, lettuce and tomato sandwich).

The Privy Kitchen inside the palace is more of a coffee shop, its hot dishes limited to soup and a roll. Straightforward sandwiches (cheese and tomato, ham salad, beef and horseradish) and delicious cakes (carrot cake, chocolate fudge cake, cheesecake, scones and clotted cream) make it better as a snack stop than for substantial meals. Benches and tables surrounded by whitewashed walls and two enormous fireplaces provide an authentic Tudor atmosphere, but because it is relatively small the lunchtime queues can be horrendous.

There's an ice-cream kiosk in the North Gardens, and picnics are allowed in the Wilderness and on the grass around the Tiltyard Tea Room.

Shops There are four shops, all of which sell fairly high-quality goods with an historic theme (although not necessarily relevant to the sight). The Tudor Kitchens Shop sells pewter tankards and birch wine, porcelain dolls of Henry VIII and his six wives (£160–175), Tudor teapots (£19.99), Tudor activity packs for children (£1.99). Christmas also comes early – when we inspected during the October half-term, Christmas carols were already being piped over the speakers, and there were special displays of Christmas decorations on sale.

🚗 From the M25 take exit 10; from A307, exit 12; and A308 exit 15 and A312 and follow brown signs. Parking (in grounds £3) or free parking at Hampton Court Green. ⊖ Nearest rail station is Hampton Court (30 mins from Waterloo). Alternatively, a number of buses from Richmond and Kingston, and Green Line Coach number 718 from Victoria. ◷ Mid-Mar to mid-Oct, Mon 10.15am to 6pm, Tues to Sun 9.30am to 6pm. Mid-Oct to mid-Mar, Mon 10.15am to 4.30pm, Tues to Sun 9.30am to 4.30pm. Last admission 45 minutes before closing. Gardens open all year round till 9pm (or dusk if earlier). Closed 24–26 Dec, 1 Jan. 💷 Adult £10.50, child (5–15 yrs old) £7, child (under 5 yrs old) free, senior citizen, student £8.00, family ticket (2 adults + 3 children) £31.40. Season ticket valid for one year £68.00. ♿ Visitors in wheelchairs or with limited mobility should ask a warder for help. Battery-powered cars available free of charge for use in the gardens. Disabled toilets in Fountain Court, Base Court and in the North Gardens. Helpers of disabled visitors admitted free. Wheelchairs available.

HMS Belfast

Morgans Lane, Tooley Street, London SE1 2JH   ☎   *020-7940 6300*

Quality ★★★   **Facilities** 🚶 🚶   **Value for money** ££££
Highlights   An insight into naval life; fascinating for those with an interest in military history
Drawbacks   Lack of tour guides to bring the attraction to life

What's there   This floating museum is a formidable, 11,000-ton reminder of Britain's former maritime power in the last days of Empire. She is now moored close to London Bridge following a lengthy naval career. During World War II, she helped protect the Arctic convoy and was involved in the Battle of North Cape, where she played a major part in the sinking of the German battle cruiser *Scharnhorst* in 1943. Following that encounter, she served during the Normandy Landings, in the Far East, and also in the Korean War.

From the quarterdeck you clamber up inside the **6-inch gun turret**, and then round to the 4-inch guns and **Boatdeck**. An accompanying and informative video shows footage of that area of the ship during the war, when a Walrus seaplane was launched. The tour then moves on to the stern and the outside of the 6-inch gun turret, whose guns are trained on the Scratchwood motorway services, some 20 km away – a sobering thought next time you travel along the M1. From there you head for the Compass Room and Operations Room – the nerve centre of the ship, with a dramatic reconstruction of the engagement with the *Scharnhorst*, based on eyewitness accounts. The tour then leads to the four **Bofor anti-aircraft guns**, which can be elevated and aimed manually – children love these. Care should be taken when moving around on these high decks, as the wire-rails which surround them are only waist high.

Back inside is the '**HMS *Belfast* in War and Peace**' exhibition, with touchscreens and an audio commentary detailing the history of the ship. From there you enter the cramped forward **mess decks**, recreated to show a sailor's existence during the Arctic tour of 1943, when temperatures frequently dropped to minus 30 degrees. The tour next takes you down into the bowels of the ship to the heavily protected shell rooms and magazines where, if fire were to break out, the Captain could order it to be flooded in seconds, leaving its occupants little chance of escape. Further down still you find the boiler rooms with accompanying explanation. The last element of the tour covers the day-to-day workings of the ship, including the galley, NAAFI, dental surgery, and – most important – the barrel from which rum was issued daily.

Information/tours/guides   There are no guided tours. Your ticket unfolds into a basic map with minimal information on layout and facilities, but it's better to use the free guidebook you receive with your ticket, as its map is better and it contains much more information. Well-positioned videos help to move you in the right direction as you go round the ship.

Navigation can be difficult. If you miss a stairwell you can end up going in circles, and the video and audio commentary can be unhelpful in using nautical terminology. A stern naval voice tells you to 'proceed aft to the starboard side', which doesn't mean much to non-sailors, although it does add to the atmosphere.

When to visit It's not ideal in bad weather, as some of the tour is on exposed decks. School parties can be avoided by going in the afternoon.

Age appeal This should be of interest to everyone, as the ship's interior is highly atmospheric, but it may hold more interest for boys or older visitors.

Food and drink The Walrus Café close to the Boatdeck is perhaps a bit too authentic; you're better off heading for one of the many restaurants or pubs on Tooley Street.

Shops A shop situated ashore sells a wide-range of T-shirts (£7.95) and posters (£3.25) with a military theme.

🚌 Europark car park 400 metres to the east along Tooley Street. ⊖ Nearest Underground and mainline station is London Bridge (Northern and Jubilee lines). Also, Monument (Circle and District lines), then walk across London Bridge. ⊕ Mon to Sun, Mar to Oct and Easter 10am to 6pm; Nov to Feb 10am to 5pm. Closed 24–26 Dec. 💷 Adult £4.70, child (under 16 yrs old) free, senior citizen, student, unemployed £2.90. Groups of 10 or more: adult £3.70. ♿ A wheelchair lift provides access to the ship, with entry to the upper deck via ramps, and a disabled toilet, but much of it is inaccessible.

The House of Detention

Clerkenwell Close, London EC1R 0AS   ☎ 020-7253 9494   📠 020-7251 1897

Quality ★★   **Facilities** 🍴   **Value for money ££**
Highlights Gives a good impression of prison conditions in earlier days, especially the Victorian era
Drawbacks Quite a few of the information panels have been rendered illegible by water seepage; visitors also get dripped on

---

What's there This underground prison museum gives visitors an insight into what it was like to have been incarcerated a century or more ago. Its dank atmosphere, dark passages, wet stone floors and dripping walls and ceilings convey the nature of the experience as vividly as the waxen models of wretched former inmates, rusty bars and instruments of torture.

The tour takes you first through a brick-lined **ventilation tunnel** constructed partly from the exterior walls of an earlier prison on this site: the first, the Clerkenwell Bridewell, a house of correction, was established in 1616 and swiftly joined by the New Prison, a house of detention built alongside it in 1618, burnt down during the Gordon Riots of 1780 and rebuilt in 1775. In 1847 the prison primarily known as the House of Detention, comprising three levels of cells above ground plus a basement, was constructed, incorporating some of the building you see today. This 'model' prison, with 286 cells, was designed on similar lines to Pentonville. It closed in 1877 and was largely demolished in 1890 to make way for a school.

The **cells, passageways and underground chambers** through which the tour takes you contain information (some of it washed away) and displays featuring wax models on various themes of crime and punishment. In one of the first cells the long history of penal institutions in this area is recounted, starting with the Bridewell, a royal palace given by Edward VI in 1550 to the City of London for the relief of the poor. In this workhouse prison the 'workshy' were reformed by means of enforced labour and physical punishments. Vagrants were whipped on arrival 'until his or her body is bloody' and by 1600 the regular floggings of half-naked inmates had become popular public spectacles. The audience watched the proceedings from a purpose-built viewing gallery.

When the first prison, or House of Correction, was built in 1615, to relieve overcrowding, it accommodated petty criminals. This place, which was constructed mainly of wood and had little security, was closed in 1794, but meanwhile in 1618 another gaol, the New Prison, had been built as a house of detention – a remand prison for people awaiting trial.

The house-breaker and highwayman Jack Sheppard, who had trained as a locksmith, famously escaped from here with his girlfriend, 'Edgworth Bess', in 1724 (John Gay's *Beggar's Opera* is based on his exploits). However, he went to the gallows, following further escapes from Newgate, later the same year, aged 22.

The prison system in the eighteenth century was highly corrupt: some inmates could pay fees to escape the hardships, while others were stripped of all they possessed and were left to die. The overcrowding was appalling – for example, 60–70 women were confined in two wards 7.5 square feet in area – and 'scenes of the greatest licentiousness' were a nightly occurrence.

A common punishment was transportation, introduced in preference to executions, which had become unofficial public holidays, caused social unrest and made heroes out of criminals. On the grossly overcrowded transport ships ('hulks') death by starvation or disease, if not by shipwreck, was a common fate. Survivors faced being sold into slavery on arrival. The practice of transportation continued until 1868, by which time 162,000 people (one of them was 'Edgworth Bess') had been deported; the initial destination was America, and later Australia.

The prison reforms of the Victorian era gave rise to improved conditions and a concern for health, hygiene and moral discipline. However, it also introduced the 'silent system', employed at the House of Detention, which sought to prevent association between prisoners: hence the single cells, in which the occupants spent 23 hours a day, the enforced wearing of masks and thick veils, and insistence on silence. Prisoners who chose not to work (in silence) could pray or do nothing. It was eventually realised that this silent régime had a devastating effect on prisoners' sanity.

In the **fumigation room** clothes taken from new arrivals were hung in a large oven and subjected to high temperatures and sulphur fumes to purge them of disease-carrying agents, including body lice. The **laundry** facilities demonstrate how exhausting this work – carried out by prisoners – must have been, and why laundry workers were allowed a pint of beer a day.

The rest subsisted on 2,000 calories a day – 'enough for nourishment and health, nothing more'. Food was prepared in the **kitchen**, an insalubrious cavern that retains its original ovens and dumbwaiter.

Via a **wardens' room** you then pass through a **second ventilation tunnel** to the **women's cell block**, where the displays in the various cells provide further accounts of different aspects of the lives of Victorian criminals. One cell contains instruments of torture while the one next door features surgeons' implements; others describe the treatment of what would now be called young offenders, one is a replica bathroom, another focuses on prostitution, another on the activities of cat burglars, and yet another describes the futile tasks prisoners were given to do, such as turning a treadmill that drove a large fan on the roof, to no purpose whatever. Two cells are now the ladies' and gents' toilets.

Information/tours/guides A 'tour guide programme' is provided on arrival but is ill-written, begs as many questions as it answers, and is in such tiny type that it is hardly possible to read it in the subterranean gloom, so the information on the display panels, of which there is a great deal, is the visitor's best bet, unless the wet conditions have washed away the text. No tours or guides were advertised when we visited.

When to visit Any time of the year. Whatever the weather is doing, you will be glad to emerge into fresh air.

Age appeal Mainly for adults and older children. Not for the claustrophobic.

Food and drink None was available. Nearest refreshments are probably at Clerkenwell Green.

Shops Although there is no shop, a few books and booklets are displayed in a glass case outside next to the entrance. *Crime and Punishment* and *Clerkenwell and Finsbury Past* were two of the titles visible.

Other facilities Inside toilets (with modern plumbing) in the women's cell block. Outside toilets (closed when we visited) near entrance.

🚗 Difficult parking. Possible on-street parking around Clerkenwell Green. ⊖ Nearest Underground station is Farringdon (Hammersmith and City, Circle and Metropolitan lines), then 8-minute walk to museum. Buses 19, 38, 55, 171a also pass nearby. ○ Open all year, Mon to Sun 10am to 5.15pm (last admission). Closed 25 Dec, 1 Jan. £ Adult £4; child (under 12 yrs old) £2.50; child (under 5 yrs old) free; student, senior citizen £3. Family ticket (2 adults + 2 children) £10. ♿ Not suitable for wheelchairs: stairs at entrance and exit, and some passages have raised brickwork at floor level to negotiate.

Imperial War Museum

Lambeth Road, London SE1 6HZ
☎ *0900 1600140 (information); 020-7416 5320* 🖥 *www.iwm.org.uk*

Quality ★★★★★   **Facilities 🎫 🎫 🎫 🎫**   **Value for money £££££**
Highlights Sheer breadth of exhibits, from soldiers' letters to planes; excellent use of different media to interest all the family; free for children
Drawbacks Layout can be confusing; indifferent welcome from front-of-house staff

What's there This national museum tells the story of war in the twentieth century with spirit and sensitivity. The collection is stunning by itself, but there is also a refreshing endeavour to make it accessible to all, with excellent use of interactive displays and contemporary archive footage to bring events alive. Add to that a lively programme of temporary exhibitions and events, and the result is a museum with enormous vitality that is a pleasure to visit.

The **display of fighting hardware** is so good that you could easily spend a couple of hours here. You can't miss the V2 and V1 rockets and the film telling their history, the enormous World War I Mark V tank, and the Sopwith Camel and Spitfire overhead. Easy to overlook, yet probably more destructive than all of them combined, is Little Boy, an atomic bomb of the type dropped on Hiroshima.

If you want to put all this in its historical perspective head downstairs to the displays that tell the story of the two World Wars. The World War I route leads you through an explanation of why it happened to a model of the front line with films of the battles and the sound of fighting songs. Somehow the most moving testaments are the journals and letters from the men at the front. One display tells of the famous 1914 Christmas truce, not to be repeated, when the troops fraternised and put up Christmas trees. There's also a message carved on an army biscuit (easier to write on than eat, they said). Older children will enjoy the **Trench Experience** – a walk through a trench with life continuing while the noise of battle rages around.

You enter the World War II section to the sound of Chamberlain's broadcast on the outbreak of war. Different galleries tell of specific aspects of the war, such as the Battle of Britain and the ferocious fighting on the Eastern Front. The **Blitz Experience** will give you a feel for what it was like to be caught in an air raid in London – it's all too realistic, so no under-5s or unaccompanied children are allowed. If you are short on time, go here first, as there tends to be a queue and you could wait 20 minutes or so. Children are also not allowed in the narrow room that tells of the horrors of Belsen, though they are likely to find the pictures of men liberated from the Japanese just as shocking. Just to the left as you leave is a gallery dedicated to all the conflicts since 1945 – it's a depressingly long list.

Up on the first floor is more big hardware: the children's favourite is the **walk-through cockpit of the Halifax.** More reflective is the gallery of Victoria and George Cross medals, which tells the stirring stories of courageous acts carried out by their recipients. A recent addition is the Secret War gallery, looking at the undercover world: apparently MI5 managed to arrest or turn every German spy sent to Britain during World War II – 16 were executed and 47 turned. The film when we inspected showed how the Special Operations Executive trained its agents, and is followed by two presentations – on a three-man team's raids on a German airfield in North Africa in 1942, and the SAS involvement in the ending of the Iranian Embassy siege in 1980.

Up on the second floor is the museum's extensive art gallery, showing works with a wartime theme.

Information/tours/guides The guidebook costs £2.70 and makes a good souvenir but is not really needed on your visit.

When to visit Avoid school holidays and weekends as the museum gets busy then.

Age appeal All ages will find a great deal to interest them.

Food and drink The attractive modern – and unfortunately popular – café serves lunches and snacks throughout the day: pot of tea costs £1.05, a hot dish and salad £5.50. A picnic room is available at weekends and outside school holidays.

Shops The large shop stocks a wide range of wartime themed goods and a variety of pocket-money items, such as Battle of Britain mint humbugs (£2.95) and top secret multi-writers (99p).

On A3203. Car parking (with charge) on Westminster Bridge Road. ⊖ Nearest Underground stations are Lambeth North (Bakerloo line), Waterloo (Northern and Bakerloo lines, also mainline station), and Elephant & Castle (Northern and Bakerloo lines). Buses 1, 3, 12, 45, 53, 63, 68,159,168,171,172,176,188, 344 and C10 stop nearby. ⏲ Mon to Sun, 10am to 6pm. Closed 24–26 Dec. ⊞ Adult £5.20, child (up to 16 yrs old) free, student, senior citizen, unemployed £4.20, disabled visitor and helper £2.60. Free after 4.30pm. ♿ All galleries wheelchair accessible; lifts. Disabled toilets on each floor.

Kensington Palace

Kensington Gardens, London W8 4PX ☎ 020-7376 2452

Quality ★★ **Facilities** ♨ ♨ ♨ ♨ **Value for money £**
Highlights Lovely setting; King's gallery and wind-dial; stylish café
Drawbacks Complex route; over-long audio tour

What's there Most modern-day royal watchers will connect Kensington Palace with Diana, Princess of Wales, but you will see nothing here to commemorate her (although there was a temporary exhibition of her dresses). What you will see is a collection of court dress and the state apartments used by the Royal Family in William and Mary's day, and later rooms used by the young Queen Victoria.

The tour starts with dimly lit tableaux of two young debs getting ready to be presented at court in the 1920s. The fashions of the day sat rather oddly with the court requirements for trains on the dresses and white ostrich-feather headdresses. A ceremonial tailor gives an idea of the dress appropriate to different male ranks – the most eye-catching being the primary-coloured tunic of a royal herald. The workroom of a fashionable ladies' dressmaker shows the exquisite embroidery worked on the dresses while the audio tour reminds you of the hard life endured by the seamstresses. A collection of the present Queen's dresses, in this **'Dressing for Royalty' display**, is surprising for the thinness of the waist, but the stars of the show are the Coronation robes of George V and Queen Mary.

As you head upstairs to the state apartments, pay attention to the **audio tour**, as it is easy to get lost at this stage. The first few rooms are shown as used by the young Queen Victoria, who was awoken in her bed here to be told that her uncle was dead and that she was now queen. Then it's on to grander things, starting with the **King's Staircase**, built by **Christopher Wren** after the house was bought for the Royal Family in 1689. George I had the walls filled with portraits of his courtiers leaning over a marble balustrade to catch sight of the approaching visitors. In the first of the **King's Rooms** look up at the ceiling, painted in the very fashionable antique Roman style, a theme echoed in the heavily gilded Roman gods of the Cupola Room. On the ceiling here, though, is the Garter star – for George I was very conscious of his foreign origins. The centrepiece clock shows the four greatest monarchies of antiquity on its faces.

The **King's Gallery** is perhaps the most stunning room, with its red walls and white and gold decoration. Above the mantelpiece is a map of Europe with a hand, connected to a weather vane on the roof, showing the prevailing wind direction. You can also see a large copy of Van Dyck's portrait of Charles I.

The Queen's Apartments are more intimate in scale and decoration and show Queen Mary's affection for the style of her Dutch homeland. The finest is probably the **wood-panelled Gallery**, where the ladies of court would amuse themselves. It was in these rooms that the queen died from smallpox in 1694.

Outside, do have a wander round the lovely **sunken garden**, built in the early twentieth century to recreate the garden as it had been before the landscaping of the eighteenth century.

The tour takes about one and a half hours.

Information/tours/guides The audio tour comes free with entry. Alternatively, there's a good guidebook (£3.95) if you prefer to go at your own pace.

When to visit Come mid-week on a fine day.

Age appeal There's little to interest children here – and a warning to this effect at the entrance.

Food and drink The elegant Orangerie, with light flooding in through the windows and views over the lawns, provides stylish surroundings for pricey tea (£1.60) and cake (coffee and walnut £3.15). Light lunches are also on offer (Stilton and leek tart with red leaf salad £6.75).

Shops The Palace's shop is good, selling a wide range of knick-knacks.

🚍 Not recommended. ⊖ Nearest underground station is High Street Kensington (District and Circle lines). Also, buses 12, 94, 9, 10, 33, 49, 52, 52A, C1 stop nearby. ⊘ Mid-Mar to mid Oct, Mon to Sun 10am to 5pm (last entry 4pm); mid-Oct to mid-Mar, Wed to Sun 10am to 4pm. 🎫 Adult £9.50, child (5 to 15 yrs old) £7.10, senior citizen, student, unemployed, disabled visitor £7.70, family ticket (2 adults + 2 children) £29.10. ⅙ Steps up to state apartments, no lift. Ramp to Orangerie. Disabled toilets.

Kenwood House

Hampstead Lane, London NW3 7JR   ☎ *020-8348 1286*
🌐 *www.english-heritage.org.uk*

Quality ★★   **Facilities** 🛏🛏🛏🛏   **Value for money** £££
Highlights   Notable art collection; free admission; friendly staff; good café
Drawbacks   Presentation a little dry; unimaginative merchandise in shop

What's there Kenwood House, remodelled by **Robert Adam** from 1764 to 1779, sits on the crest of a ridge on the edge of **Hampstead Heath**, blessed with a view over lakes, heathland and the skyline of London. It's home to the Iveagh

Bequest, a collection of **seventeenth-century Dutch and Flemish art** and late **eighteenth-century British art** bequeathed to the nation in 1927 by Edward Cecil Guinness, 1st Earl of Iveagh.

Unfortunately, most of the furnishings designed by Adam as part of his decorative schemes were sold off at auction in 1922, though some 'lost' pieces have been traced, and other furniture from the contemporary period is also present. Nevertheless, the house should be viewed more as an art gallery than as a model example of an eighteenth-century home.

The most spectacular of Adam's rooms, the Library, was, together with its Ante Chamber, the only part of the house built on by the architect. A major example of eighteenth-century neoclassical style, it was not entirely rapturously received in its day: the ceiling was decorated with 'cheesecakes and raspberry tarts', according to one critic. Mirrored recesses reflect back the images of painted ceiling panels, allegorical roundels, sugar-almond colours, and gilded filigree stuccowork, while windows along the southern wall look out over the grounds.

By contrast, the Upper Hall contains an extraordinary chinoiserie chimney piece, also by Adam, incorporating painted marble tiles, carved mermen and cherubs. Sadly, the rest of the furnishings for the room have been lost.

Elsewhere, the gems of the art collection include *The Guitar Player* by **Vermeer**, a self-portrait by **Rembrandt**, and other portraits by **Van Dyck**, **Hals**, **Reynolds** and **Gainsborough**.

In addition to the picturesque views over the lake and bridge, the grounds also feature **sculptures** by **Barbara Hepworth** and **Henry Moore**.

Information/tours/guides Although the handbook and publicity leaflet mentioned an audio tour, none was available when we inspected. We were told that because the paintings were constantly being rearranged during temporary exhibitions, it had been impossible to produce an up-to-date audio tour.

Visitors thus have the choice of an explanatory leaflet for £1.25 or a souvenir colour guidebook for a rather hefty £5. Both contain maps. The guidebook has plenty of colour photos and lots of additional details on former residents and visitors as well as the house and artworks, though it can be rather dry. Laminated lists of paintings in each room, describing the artists and giving background details, provide further information, as do the guides in each room, all of whom were approachable and happy to chat about the exhibits.

When to visit The house and grounds are open all year round: call for details of temporary exhibitions. In the summer, concerts and firework displays are held by the lake (admission charge).

Age appeal Children can run around the grounds but are likely to find most of the house very boring.

Food and drink The Brewhouse and Garden Café (open 9am to 6pm) offers cooked breakfasts (£4.75 to £4.95) as well as hot and cold lunches (organic carrot and coriander soup, £2.95; braised chicken breast with saffron and mushroom sauce, £6.95) and afternoon teas. You can eat in the former coach house, with stone floor, or, in fine weather, there's a pleasant outdoor area with canvas parasols and trellises twined with plants.

Shops There are two shops – one as you exit the house and another near the café. Both stock a similar range of goods. There is some porcelain with patterns based on the Adam ceiling designs, but most merchandise is generic English Heritage stuff, from medieval and Celtic jewellery to cherry preserve and tapestry cushions.

🚗 No parking on site except for disabled visitors. On-street parking at West Lodge on Hampstead Lane, NW3. ⊖ Nearest underground stations Archway and Golders Green (Northern line), then 210 bus. ⏰ Daily 10am to 6pm, Apr to Sept; 10am to 5pm, Oct; 10am to 4pm, Nov to Mar (closed 24, 25 Dec and 1 Jan). 💷 House and grounds free; charge for temporary exhibitions. ♿ No access to the upper floor for visitors in wheelchairs. Toilets for disabled people.

Kew Gardens

Richmond, Surrey TW9 3AB   ☎ *020-8332 5622*   🖰 *www.kew.org*

Quality ★★★★   **Facilities 🏛 🏛 🏛 🏛**   **Value for money ££££**
Highlights Glasshouses and the Princess of Wales conservatory; the museum and the
                gardens with their ever-changing landscapes
Drawbacks   Amount of time (and energy) needed to do justice to Kew – and best in
                fine weather, even though there is a lot to see indoors

What's there The Royal Botanic Gardens at Kew, to give Kew its full title, cover 300 acres. The largest and most diverse collection of living plants in the world, with one in eight of all flowering species, it is also a repository of preserved plant specimens, plant-based products and botanical art and literature.

One way to tackle Kew is to board the Kew Explorer (extra charge), which makes a 40-minute circuit of the gardens. You can get off whenever you wish, and the ticket is valid for a whole day. Whether you do this or walk (from the Main Gate to the pagoda is about a mile), be sure to see the glasshouses – which close earlier than the gardens – and the museum, as well as the areas of particular seasonal interest (consult the map leaflet).

The famous **Palm House** is the oldest glasshouse at Kew, designed by Decimus Burton and built 1844–8 by the engineer Richard Turner. Heraldic beasts carved from Portland stone stand on guard in front of this curvaceous glazed structure overlooking a formal lake. The Palm House's interior is divided into three geographical zones – the Americas, Africa and Australia – each closely packed with plants typical of the region. The humid rainforest atmosphere supports hundreds of species, including bananas and oil palms; the 'traveller's tree' of Madagascar, which traps water at the base of its leaves; the world's oldest pot plant (*Encephalartos altensteinii*); the panama hat plant; the sealing wax palm; the coconut and the tamarind; the peach palm and the giant bamboo; and coco-de-mer (the double coconut, with the largest seed in the world).

The **Temperate House** is another Decimus Burton design, built 1860–99. Among the tender woody plants jostling for attention, and again arranged geographically, are many with medicinal uses, including quinine, tea

(*Camellia sinensis*), China root (*Smilax china*) and the dragon tree from the Canary Islands. Others are food plants (clementine, olive and grapefruit) or have exotic flowers. The world's tallest glasshouse plant, *Jubaea chilensis*, is here, too: raised from a seed collected in Chile and planted in 1846, it is now nearly 18 metres high.

Other glasshouses to visit include the **Waterlily House**, near the Palm House, the **Evolution House**, near the Temperate House, the **Filmy Fern House** (for plants that like humid shade) next to the Orangery, the **Alpine House** and the magnificent **Princess of Wales Conservatory**. Built in 1986, the latter is the largest area under glass at Kew (4,490 square metres). It has no side walls but comprises a series of interlocking aluminium, steel and glass triangles, making maximum use of sunlight for heating and containing ten different zones, from desert to cloud forest. Each environment is centrally monitored and controlled by computer to maintain ideal growing conditions. Wander from a landscape of sand and cactus to a mangrove swamp, through temperate and tropical ferns, via outcrops of begonias and tropical orchids, festoons of dangling epiphytes and sinister carnivorous plants.

Three of Kew's glasshouses are numbered among the 39 listed buildings on the site. These include Kew Palace (built in 1631 and due to re-open to the public in 2001); the ten-storey pagoda (to which there is no admittance); the **Japanese gateway** (a replica of a Kyoto temple); Queen Charlotte's cottage, used for picnics by George III's wife; a ruined arch and classical temples. There are two art galleries and a small **museum**, which has an excellent permanent exhibition, 'Plants and People', demonstrating the myriad uses to which we humans put these organisms. The innovative presentation includes touch screens, sounds to listen to and smells to sniff.

Leave time to explore some of the grounds for their own sake, too – woodland glades and dells, innumerable species of trees, and **gardens** devoted to everything from roses, rhododendrons and azaleas to heathers, grasses, bamboos, bees and lilacs.

Information/tours/guides The map leaflet provided at the ticket office is useful. Informative plant labels often include photos showing different aspects of the plant or its uses. The booklet about Kew Gardens and Wakehurst Place, *A Resource for the World* (£1.50), is an educational souvenir rather than a guide. The video presentation in the audio-visual theatre (Princess of Wales conservatory) is worth seeing, but not essential. One-hour guided tours leave from Victoria Gate at 11am and 2pm in March to October, at 11am in November to February (with extra tours at 12 noon at weekends during this winter season). Travellers on the Kew Explorer (£2.50) also hear a commentary.

When to visit Although there is much to see indoors, fine weather will help you to enjoy exploring the rest.

Age appeal Everyone can enjoy Kew, though children might need the motivation of a trail (certain plants are marked 'Kids' Kew'). Ask about trails at the Friends desk at the Victoria Gate visitor centre. The Princess of Wales conservatory is a glorious environment for children to explore in its own right.

Food and drink Of the four cafés, the Orangery and the Victoria Gate coffee shop are open all year round, the Al Fresco and the Pavilion summer only. A reasonable range of refreshments and lunch dishes is available, such as tea (90p), mug of coffee (£1.20), cakes (from £1), soup (e.g. carrot and orange for £2.75), chilli con carne (£2.75) and a meat dish (£5.95).

Shops The Victoria Gate and Orangery shops are open until 4.30pm and 3.30pm respectively. The former is larger and stocks a greater range, including up-market gift items (such as framed prints of plant paintings ranging from £165 to £200 and a wooden Noah's Ark costing £85). Also available are mugs (£6.50), jams, ceramic vases, large umbrellas, walking sticks, small garden tools, stationery, postcards and a video about Kew (£14.99), and an impressive range of books on horticulture. Children's books are also sold here. The Orangery shop has seeds, bulbs and more items for small children.

Other facilities In so large an area, toilets are important, and Kew fortunately has several: at Victoria Gate, Brentford Gate, the Orangery, near the Museum, at the Pavilion restaurant, and so on, with baby-changing facilities at three of them.

🚗 Just south of Kew Bridge. Car parking near Brentford Gate (round the green in front of the Main Gate), and on Kew Road after 10am. ⊖ Nearest Underground (and rail) station is Kew Gardens (District line), then short walk away. Alternatively, take train to Kew Bridge station, then half a mile walk. ⊙ Mon to Sun, 9.30am to 4.30pm (last admission 4pm). Conservatories close at 4pm. Closed 25 Dec, 1 Jan. 💷 Adult £5, child (5 to 16 yrs old) £2.50, child (under 5 yrs old) free, senior citizen, student £3.50. Late entry (3.15pm or later) £3.50. ♿ Generally good wheelchair access, although some stairs in the Princess of Wales conservatory. The Kew Explorer can accommodate one wheelchair but the user would need to negotiate one low step to access. Disabled toilets.

Leighton House

12 Holland Park Road, London W14 8LZ   ☎ *020-7602 3316*
📠 *020-7371 2467*

Quality ★★★   **Facilities 🏛 🏛 🏛**   **Value for money ££££**
Highlights   Dazzling Arab Hall; Victorian paintings
Drawbacks   Need to buy the guidebook to learn about what you are seeing

What's here This unconventional house was built as the home of the notable Victorian, Frederick, Lord Leighton (1830–96), who was a painter and President of the Royal Academy. It was designed to be a private palace devoted to art, so don't be fooled by the rather ordinary red-brick exterior. Step inside, and the tinkle of water will draw you to the exotic splendour of the **Arab Hall** with its domed ceiling and wonderful blue Iznik tiling collected by Lord Leighton on his travels in the Middle East. Walk back towards the hall, and on the right-hand side is the library with the only Old Master owned by Leighton remaining in the house – a sixteenth-century religious scene from the school of **Tintoretto**. If your taste runs more towards the **Pre-Raphaelites**, cross the corridor into the drawing room to see **Burne-Jones'** *Wheel of Fortune* and Lord Leighton's own sentimental

Widow's Prayer, with the light falling on the young child sitting on the stairs while her mother prays. Though both this room and the dining room are rather short on furniture, you can see the lovely garden through the large picture windows.

Upstairs reflects the priorities of the owner, with a very modest single bedroom (the only one in the whole house), while most of the floor was given over to his studio. Originally, this room would have been filled with artist's clutter and props – you can see photos of the studio as it was – whereas now the only clutter are the pictures on the wall. However, the tradition of using it for musical evenings continues. After the Arab Hall was built downstairs, the space upstairs was extended to create a top-lit picture gallery, where Leighton could display the pictures given to him by his contemporaries – such as the wonderfully tranquil women shelling peas by **John Millais**.

An hour will give you plenty of time for a leisurely visit.

Information/tours/guides Guided tours, which last 45 minutes, are given on Wednesdays and Thursdays at midday (£2 charge). If you are going round on your own do splash out on a guidebook for £3 as much of what you see will make little sense otherwise.

When to visit It's a good rainy-day choice.

Age appeal Leighton House is ideal for art enthusiast adults.

Food and drink No refreshments are available on site, although there is a spot for picnics.

Shops Nothing to be bought at the actual House.

Other facilities Toilets on site.

🚗 Off A315 (Kensington High Street). On-street parking in Melbury Road (metered). ⊖ Nearest Underground station is High Street Kensington (District and Circle lines). Buses 9, 9a, 10, 27, 28, 31, 33, 49 pass nearby. ⊘ Mon to Sun 11am to 5.30pm. Closed Tues, 25 Dec, 1 Jan. 🎟 Free (donations welcomed). ♿ No wheelchair access (stairs to studio).

London Aquarium

County Hall, Riverside Building, Westminster Bridge Road, London SE1 7PB
☎ *020-7967 8000* 🖥 *www.londonaquarium.co.uk*

Quality ★★★   **Facilities** 🏛 🏛   **Value for money ££££**
Highlights Giant Atlantic and Pacific tanks
Drawbacks No place to pause for refreshments inside

What's there In this subterranean aquatic world on the banks of the Thames, an essentially broad, split-level circuit of darkened corridors carries you through a series of habitats, from British rivers to Amazonian rainforest, accompanied by a swooshing and gurgling soundtrack.

The visit begins with an explanation of the ecology of the river flowing just a few metres away, using storyboards and interactive video clips. Exotic lionfish and the like from the Indian Ocean follow, then you're back to more familiar mackerel, bass and cod cruising around a vast two-storey tank, accompanied by other Atlantic chip-shop favourites. The encircling walkways provide 360-degree views. Every day (usually at midday, but check at reception) divers enter to feed the huge conger eels lurking around the granite rocks.

There's a chance to play 'feel the flatfish' and 'stroke the starfish' at the **touch pool**, before crowding around the main attraction: **6-foot sharks** circling around submerged Easter Island statues in the **Pacific tank**. Titbits on invertebrates and coral follow, then triangular angler fish among a mocked-up mangrove swamp. Finally, large **catfish** and charismatic **piranhas** inhabit rainforest settings, before you spill back out into the London air after no more than a couple of hours underwater.

Information/tours/guides Ten-minute talks about sharks and rainforest fish are given at intervals throughout the day (check the noticeboard in the entrance foyer for times). Digestible snippets of information about the specimens are attached to most tanks, and numerous touch screens provide short educational packages on the aquatic environments. At 30p, the exhibition guide is cheap, but adds nothing to what can be gleaned from the plans and information panels around the exhibits.

When to visit A visit to the Aquarium is good at any time as it's pretty weather-resistant. However, school holidays are particularly busy.

Age appeal This attraction's appeal is across the board, with quiz leaflets (30p) to keep younger children interested.

Food and drink No food or drink is available within the Aquarium, but there is a McDonald's in the same building, opposite the exit from the shop. The adjoining Marriott Hotel provides more upmarket options.

Shops Not surprisingly, the Aquarium's shop stocks a mix of fish-related souvenirs (such as squid-shaped bottle openers or shark staplers), educational books and videos about fish, and shelves of unrelated toys and games.

🚌 On the River Thames, by Westminster Bridge. Car parking at Royal Festival Hall, the National Film Theatre and Waterloo station (£3 for two hours). ⊖ Nearest Underground stations are Waterloo (Northern, Bakerloo and Jubilee lines) and Westminster (District, Circle and Jubilee lines), then 5–10-minute walk away. Buses 12, 53, 77, 109 and 211 pass close by. ⊙ Mon to Sun, 10am to 6pm. Last admission 5pm. Closed 25 Dec. 💷 Adult £8, child (3 to 14 yrs old) £5, child (under 3 yrs old) free, senior citizen, unemployed, student £6.50, family ticket (2 adults + 2 children) £22, wheelchair users free. ♿ Wheelchair access to entrance via County Hall on Belvedere Road. The two floors are wheelchair accessible. Lift. Disabled toilets. Two wheelchairs available for loan.

London Dungeon

Tooley Street, London SE1 2SZ ☎ *020-7403 7221*

Quality ★★★ **Facilities** 🎫 🎫 **Value for money** £££
Highlights Good family entertainment in realistic grimy settings
Drawbacks Dingy café; toilets are too authentic

What's there The overhead rumble of trains leaving London Bridge has helped to give visitors to the dank London Dungeon a perfect taste of subterranean squalor ever since it opened in 1975. Promoted as a museum of the macabre, the 'Dungeon' is not for the squeamish. It leads you chronologically through the multitude of tortured ways in which people have been killed since medieval times, exhibiting a sadist's **treasure trove of torture antiques**, such as a mantrap 'in working order' and the Halifax Gibbet, a precursor to the guillotine.

At first, customers can enjoy the exhibits at their own pace as dioramas show medieval folk vomiting from the Black Death or being disembowelled and then historical figures, such as Thomas Becket and Anne Boleyn, being persecuted in the well-designed **ecclesiastical section**. On reaching the market outside a **reconstruction of Newgate Gaol** (not as good as at Madame Tussaud's Chamber of Horrors), children will want to buy the eyeballs and other 'real' body parts on sale. From here, you and your fellow visitors become a group of criminals awaiting judgement and are literally prisoners, unable to choose what you see next. Being a passive onlooker is not permitted; in the entrance queue, everyone must put their head in the pillory for the obligatory photo – later expect to be goaded by the judge or gaoler. Finally, you are sent on a **boat ride** (don't expect a white-knuckle ride) through Traitors Gate to execution, followed by a tour of the authentic fog-filled Victorian streets where Jack the Ripper attacked (dealt with in extensive, graphic detail). The final guillotine section is also better done at Madame Tussaud's.

Allow up to one and a half hours to walk around the one-way route. Once you are part of a group, you may be herded too quickly between rooms to take in the scenery and information boards in each.

Information/tours/guides A glossy colour guidebook (£2.50) provides historical information, souvenir pictures and a layout map. No information about what to expect is given on arrival – you are there to be surprised. Most exhibits are accompanied by minimal written information, some of which can be hard to decipher in the dim light. The guides are roaming ghouls – actors who are there primarily to entertain, asking visitors whether they are in league with the devil. Shrinking violets beware; their witty banter could easily be the highlight or the ruin of your visit.

When to visit As with most attractions in London, it can get very, very crowded between July and September. Opt for a rainy, foggy, late autumn day to set the perfect scene. How about Hallowe'en?

Age appeal Notices are posted at the entrance warning parents that children may find the experience frightening, and unaccompanied minors are not permitted entry. However, the ghoulish atmosphere can affect any person of a squeamish or nervous disposition, regardless of age (particularly when the horrific actors suddenly appear at your side). The attraction is best suited to families with older children. Adults without children or a sense of humour could find the actors annoying.

Food and drink You must walk through the café to reach the exit. The décor of the 'Blood and Guts Tavern' continues the grimy theme, set in a 1600s street of London. The sackcloth hanging from washing lines, along with the old lanterns, Frankenstein prints and rum and port barrels adorning the walls rather jars with the bright blue 1990s litter bin and fast food being served. Bland burgers, potato wedges and ice creams are on offer, but prices are reasonable. The £10-family deal includes one large pizza, four portions of chips, soft drinks and coleslaw. Despite the *Addams Family* film playing while you eat, the deafening noise of the video games next door encourages you to eat quickly and leave.

Shops There is little here to enhance the visit educationally, apart from a small bookshelf selling *Goosebumps* books for children and *The Book of Execution* (£8.99) for grown-ups. Instead the shop resembles a horror fancy dress and joke shop – great for children to spend pocket money on glow-in-the-dark masks and 'terror toffees' (£2.25).

Other facilities There's only one block of toilets, near the entrance/exit, with few facilities. Enjoy the toilet humour – fake blood on the toilet floor, green slime on the walls and goldfish swimming around skulls in their tank. The grubby nature of the loos, however, can be a little too authentic, with a hand drier out of action and grafitti when we inspected.

On the south bank of the Thames. From the south, the A3, A2, A23 and A24 lead to Tooley St. From north of the river, drive over Tower Bridge. NCP car parking on junction of Tooley St and Tower Bridge Road. ⊖ Nearest Underground station is London Bridge (Northern line and mainline station). Dungeon a 100-metre walk away. ⏱ Mon to Sun, 10am to 5.30pm. Closed 25 Dec. 🎫 Adult £9.50, child (up to 14 yrs old), senior citizen, disabled visitor and helper £6.50, student £8.50. Group rates (20 people minimum and 1 free ticket for every 10 visitors): adult £6.95, student £5.95, child, senior citizen £5.25. ♿ The majority of the rooms are on the same floor and accessible. Access to the boat ride could be a problem for some.

London Transport Museum

Covent Garden Piazza, London WC2E 7BB ☎ *020-7836 8557*
🖥 *www.ltmuseum.co.uk*

Quality ★★★★★ **Facilities 🎫🎫🎫🎫** **Value for money £££££**
Highlights Attractive and imaginative presentation; interactive gadgets for children
Drawbacks Can get congested in busy periods

What's there This museum takes a potentially dry subject and makes it in turn fascinating, fun and thought provoking. The subject is public transport in London and the story starts in the nineteenth century. In chronological order you are shown the emergence of the bus service, from horse trams to motor buses, before moving on to the story of the Underground. Other issues tackled are the expansion of London, a look at the transport workforce and the **architecture and design heritage** of the public transport system. There is even a section describing how the **Underground map** became a design classic, thanks to draughtsman Harry Beck. All this means that the museum is as much about the social history of London as about the technical details of buses, trams and tubes.

As well as the immaculately polished collection of original engines, ticket offices and even escalators, there are videos, a chance to **drive a tube train** using the dead man's handle and **actors playing characters**, such as a 1916 bus cleaner and a 1930s tram driver. For children there are plenty of **interactive gadgets** that let them design their own bus or work out bus fares in different decades.

Information/tours/guides Free guided tours are arranged at weekends. A helpful guidebook (£1.99) tackles the exhibition section by section and includes copy for children. Occasional events, such as talks and film shows, are provided, but some need to be pre-booked.

When to visit It's an all-year round attraction, but will get busy in the peak tourist season.

Age appeal Plenty of emphasis is put on keeping children amused, with friendly actors dressed as conductors or tram drivers. There's a 'fun bus' for those under 5 and a ticket that children can have stamped as they visit each section. There is also a large, good-value (99p) children's fun book.

Food and drink A fairly ordinary café serves ordinary snacks – for example ham-salad baguette (£2.69) and custard cake (95p) – but no hot meals, and it can get crowded.

Shops The very smart shop sells a huge range of items. There are books, videos, postcards and posters, and Paddington and Thomas the Tank Engine sections. Tube boxer shorts cost £6.99, mugs £3.50, and collectors' model trains go for £12.99.

🚗 Off B401 Bow Street. NCP car parking on Wardour Street. ⊖ Nearest Underground stations are Covent Garden (Piccadilly line), Leicester Square (Piccadilly and Northern lines) and Holborn (Piccadilly and Central lines). Alternatively, buses to the Strand or Aldwych (buses 1, 4, 6, 9, 11, 13, 15, 23, 26, 68, 76, 77A, 91, 168, 171, 171A, 176, 188, 501, 505, 521). ⊙ Mon to Sun 10am (11am on Fri) to 6pm. Closed 24–25 Dec.
💷 Adult £5.50; child (5 to15 yrs old) £2.95; child (under 5 yrs old) free; student, senior citizen, unemployed, disabled visitor £2.95. ♿ Full access throughout the museum.

London Zoo

Regent's Park, London NW1 4RY ☎ *020-7722 3333*
🌐 *www.zsl.org www.weboflife.co.uk*

Quality ★★★★	Facilities 🏛🏛🏛	Value for money ££££

Highlights Web of Life exhibition; children's zoo; animal talks
Drawbacks Not enough information on the species in the aquarium or small-mammal house

---

What's there London Zoo has all the large animals you would expect to find, such as lions, elephants and rhinos, but is on quite a small site, so the crowds can easily build up at the various enclosures. Popular enclosures around the zoo include **Bear Mountain**, where bears, monkeys and waterfowl mix together, and the attractively laid-out **children's zoo**.

The new **'Web of Life'** exhibition building is a bold and original attempt to look at animals in the context of the wider issues of ecology, including some fascinating displays, such as the cross-section of an active beehive. When we visited the exhibition there was also an excellent talk on insects and spiders.

With its outstanding selection of **animal talks and demonstrations**, clear signposting and a suggested route around the zoo, this is a very easy attraction to get to grips with. Indeed it's possible to spend all your time moving from talk to talk throughout the day. The **'Animals in Action' demonstration** is a very slick and entertaining presentation on the abilities of various animals, including a **puzzle-solving kookabura** and a leaping lemur. Meanwhile, the predatory birds show lets you see several birds in flight.

Although there is plenty to hold your attention, there are still some areas where little or no information on the animals is displayed, such as in the aquarium and the gloomy small-mammal house.

Information/tours/guides A handy leaflet at the entrance has a timetable of animal talks, feeding times, and animal rides. The guidebook (£2.50) provides lots of information about animals and conservation. The 'Web of Life' guide (50p) is a little light on content.

When to visit A visit during fine weather would be best, as a large part of the visit will be outdoors, even though there are some indoor enclosures.

Age appeal The keeper talks will appeal to children as will the children's zoo where they have a chance to touch the animals. Other activities include face painting and craft activities in the activity den.

Food and drink There's a good choice between the Fountain Café, a fish and chip shop, a pizza outlet and a sandwich bar. The Fountain Café is attractive, with tasty food, good presentation and enthusiastic staff. The menu included chicken pie with vegetables (£5.85), regular salad (£4.75), sandwiches (from £2.45 to £2.85) and coffee (£1.15).

Shops The main outlet is the Fountain Gift Shop, and there's another smaller one at the children's zoo. The Fountain is excellent, with lots of stock, including toys and cuddly animals, but also a selection of serious animal books and videos, games and puzzles. Animal puzzles cost £10, T-shirts are from £5 to £12, cuddly toy animals cost £4.99 and plastic animals go for £1.

Other facilities The new toilets at the 'Web of Life' exhibition have set a standard not reached by any other conveniences on site.

🚗 Within Regent's Park. Zoo car park plus pay-and-display on the Outer Circle.
⊖ Nearest Underground station is Camden Town (Northern line). Buses 274 or C2 stop nearby. ⊕ Mon to Sun, 10am to 4pm (last admission 3pm) March to Oct 10am to 5.30pm (last admission 4pm). Closed 25 Dec. 💷 Adult £9; child (3 to 15 yrs old) £7; student, senior citizen, registered disabled plus carer £8. ♿ Zoo not fully accessible. Some manual and automatic wheelchairs available (book at least four days in advance).

Lord's Cricket Ground and MCC Museum

St John's Wood Road, London NW8 8QN ☎ *020-7432 1033*
🖥 *www.lords.org*

Quality ★★★	**Facilities** 🏛🏛🏛🏛	**Value for money** £££

Highlights Opportunity to see inside ultramodern press box and the traditional old pavilion

Drawbacks Limited time allowed in the museum

What's there This prime piece of central London real estate was first established as a cricket ground in 1787 by the eponymous Thomas Lord. Through centuries of development, it has mellowed into a wonderfully harmonious combination of ancient and modern design – at least in the eyes of sports architecture aficionados. Lord's is the headquarters of the Marylebone Cricket Club, the guardians of the game, so for adherents, a tour of the ground may be something of a pilgrimage, and the only way to see inside hallowed sanctums like the pavilion, otherwise the preserve of the exclusive MCC membership.

The visit is by guided tour only, which covers the pavilion, museum, Mound Stand, Media Centre, the real tennis court and the indoor school (though not all may be accessible on every tour).

After a few welcoming words from your guide, you will be led first into the **Long Room**, the appropriately named central hall of the Victorian Pavilion, for an outlook across the greensward and a clear appreciation of the slope (the left side is eight-and-a-half feet higher than the right) so often referred to by commentators. Players pass by the portraits of past cricketing greats and through the central doors on the way to and from the wicket.

Upstairs in one or other of the scuffed and spartan dressing rooms, the guide will regale you with anecdotes about cricketers past and present, while pointing out the favoured pegs of famous players and drawing your attention to the roll of honour pinned on the wall.

The small museum is a repository of portraits, historic scorecards, trophies and curiosities – most notably **the original Ashes**, an urn no bigger than an egg cup containing the figurative 'remains' of English cricket, which died on 29 August 1882 (and seemingly on a thousand other occasions since). The stuffed sparrow despatched by a killer delivery from Jehanger Khan in 1936 is also on display.

A brisk stroll the length of the ground, weaving through the seating, gives you a chance to admire the new grandstand and the distinctive tented Mound Stand, before climbing into the ultramodern spaceship-shaped **Media Centre**, which will leave you envious of the fine view of the wicket afforded to the world's journalists.

Cricket enthusiasts should find the one-and-three-quarter hour tour fascinating; those with a less than a passing interest in the game are likely to find it dull and the commentary overly reverential.

Information/tours/guides The guides, all immersed in the game, are very knowledgeable and full of entertaining anecdotes.

When to visit Most aspects of the attraction are indoors, or under cover of the stands, so the weather should not be a deterrent. Demand is usually much reduced out of the cricket season (during the season it is advisable to book ahead to ensure places are available). For a full day out, make a booking for the 10am tour on a day when Middlesex Cricket Club is playing at home, and stay for the day's play afterwards.

Age appeal Provided you are cricket mad, you'll love it whatever your age.

Food and drink No food or drink is available inside the ground, though you can get a 10 per cent discount on food at the Lord's Tavern (a neighbouring pub), which serves bar meals such as salmon fish cakes with salad (£6.95), or lamb sausages with mash and mint gravy (£6.50).

Shops The Lord's shop has a wide selection of souvenirs for the enthusiast (Panama hats from £19.95 or baseball caps fitted with ear piece radio at £15.99), a broad range of cricket books and biographies, and equipment for the serious sportsperson.

🚗 Off the A41, about 1 km north of Marylebone Road. On-street parking with meters (Mon to Fri, £1 per hour, maximum stay 4 hours). ⊖ Nearest Underground stations are St John's Wood (Bakerloo line) and Baker Street (Bakerloo, Circle, Hammersmith and City, Jubilee and Metroplitan lines), then 10-minute walk or 15-minute walk respectively. Nearest mainline station is Marylebone, then 15-minute walk. Buses 13, 46, 82, 113, 139, 189 and 274 pass by the ground. ⏱ Apr to Sept, Mon to Sun, tours at 10am, midday and 2pm; Oct to Mar, tours at midday and 2pm. No tours 24–26, 31 Dec, 1 Jan (also ring to check availability on Good Friday, Easter Sunday), and the preceding day and the days of major matches. On other match days, only the 10am tour is allowed into the pavilion. The museum (open 10am to 5pm) can be visited separately on match days. 💷 Adult £6, child £4.40; student, senior citizen, disabled person, unemployed £4.40; family ticket (2 adults + 2 children) £18. MCC members free. Museum-only ticket £2 (available only on match days). ♿ Some of the ground is inaccessible; an abbreviated version of the tour covers the pavilion, some of the stands, and usually the Media Centre. Disabled parking possible if arranged in advance.

Madame Tussaud's

Marylebone Road, London NW1 5LR   ☎ *020-7935 6861*

Quality ★ ★ ★ ★　　　**Facilities 🏛 🏛**　　　**Value for money £££**

Highlights　Excellent range of unbelievably life-like historical and contemporary figures

Drawbacks　Lack of biographical information beside models; crowded rooms

What's there One of the UK's oldest and biggest tourist money-spinners, Madame Tussaud's exhibition of waxworks has been in London since 1835. Madame Tussaud came to prominence during the French Revolution, making a death mask for the guillotined Marie Antoinette and a live sculpture of Napoleon Bonaparte in 1801. Echoes of the Napoleonic era appear throughout the exhibition; Napoleon is shown lying in state with Wellington looking over him, Josephine's ivory satin coronation robe is on display, and an interesting French Revolution/guillotine section forms part of the 'Chamber of Horrors'.

Madame Tussaud's has continued to move with the times, however, and the majority of the waxwork models featured are the rich and famous from the second half of the twentieth century. The most current 'stars' appear in the first themed room, the 'Garden Party', where the very authentic looking **Chris Evans** and **Joanna Lumley** rub shoulders with **Brad Pitt** and **Sean Connery**. Taking a camera with you is *de rigueur,* but the swarming crowds of snappers can be frustrating. There are no guided tours, so you are free to wander through the exhibition's one-way system at your own pace.

The various themed sections are well-designed, particularly the 'Garden Party' terrace with fountain, vines and Dudley Moore tickling the ivories, and the ghoulish 'Chamber of Horrors', featuring the actual Newgate Prison execution toll bell, used from 1775. The **'Superstars and Legends'** pose on a film set and the glitzy staircase of a realistic TV chat show set. The **'Sporting Greats'** room is tiny, while the enormous 'Grand Hall' houses the current **Royal Family** (at Edward and Sophie's wedding), virtually every religious and political leader you can think of, and an inconspicuous Bob Geldof. Ruminating on the inclusion – and the absence – of particular stars is part of the fun.

'Chamber of Horrors' is perhaps the highlight of the visit, providing enough grisly scenes to rival the London Dungeon. The final, and most recent, attraction is the **'Spirit of London'** ride, where you board a London black cab and are taken on a tour through 400 years of the capital's history. The idea is excellent, and the animatronic figures, special effects and models of Shakespeare, Dickens and Nelson are portrayed well. Unfortunately, the ride is so fast that it is almost impossible to fully appreciate what you're seeing or to learn anything.

Allow 2 to 3 hours if you have an interest in history, politics, sports and the entertainment industry. Others may be content to scoot around in an hour. For the time spent here, it is rather overpriced.

Information/tours/guides No map of the site is given, which would be useful. All models are labelled with at least their names but most would benefit from further biographical information. The modelling dates are given for some of the kings and presidents but not their periods in power. The room of '200 years' is more descriptive, explaining how models are sculpted and put together. Even at £4, the colourful, glossy guidebook is good value, giving interesting historical information and trivia about the characters in factboxes. It's just a shame that the same information isn't provided next to the actual models.

When to visit Madame Tussaud's is one of London's most visited attractions so expect to queue for entry any time of the year. The summer months see an influx of families and foreign visitors, but it can be equally busy with school groups during term-time. Queues are often at their worst around opening time. It is advisable to book tickets in advance to save queuing time at the entrance.

Age appeal With exhibits from all periods of history as well as the present, there should be something for everyone. Children will enjoy having their photo taken next to the stars but may find the 'Chamber of Horrors' scary and the 'Spirit of London' bewildering.

Food and drink The service-station restaurant, through which you have to go to get to the 'Spirit of London' ride, serves up typical fast-food fare; bland, pricey veggieburgers and roast beef sandwiches are on offer, as is the better value 'Combo deal' (pizza slice, fries and coke for £3.50), although the pizza was suitably waxy. The staff are efficient and the room is clean, if unimaginatively designed. Surprisingly, there isn't a gent's toilet – the nearest one is by the exit, after the 'Spirit of London' ride.

Shops Most items for sale in the spacious shop are London tourist souvenirs, unrelated to Madame Tussaud's. Few of the products could enhance the visit educationally. The small hardback book *Kings and Queens of England* (£5) is of interest, while children may enjoy the *Assemble your own guillotine* (£5.60).

Other facilities The small toilets – one at the entrance and one at the exit – are clean and fairly well-maintained, but badly sign-posted. Baby-changing facilities available.

🚗 Not advisable as parking difficult. ⊖ Nearest tube station is Baker Street (Jubilee, Metropolitan, Circle, Bakerloo, Hammersmith and City lines). Buses 13, 18, 27, 30, 74, 82, 113, 139, 159, 274. ⏱ (in 1999): Mon to Fri 10am-5.30pm, Sat and Sun 9.30am-5.30 (opening earlier in the summer months). 🎟 Adult £10.50, child (under 16 years old) £7, child (under 5 years) free, senior citizens (over 60) £8. *Group Rates (minimum 10 people)* adult £7.95, child (5–16 years old) £5.25, senior citizen £5.95 (1 free ticket when group of 20 people pay). ♿ Wheelchair users are advised to phone ahead to make arrangements. All exhibitions accessible except 'Superstars' and 'Spirit of London' theme ride (difficult for those with limited mobility). Free entry to wheelchair users and their helper. Disabled toilets are available.

Marble Hill House

Richmond Road, Twickenham TW1 2NL ☎ 020-8892 5115

Quality ★★★	**Facilities** 🏛 🏛 🏛	**Value for money £££**

Highlights The Great Room and the second-floor gallery
Drawbacks Lack of period furniture; ground floor seems rather institutional and less well presented than the rest

What's there This magnificent Palladian villa was built in 1724–9 as the Thames-side retreat of Henrietta Howard (later Countess of Suffolk), mistress of the Prince of Wales, who became George II. Midway along the river between St James's Palace and Hampton Court, it was in an ideal location for royal visitors and courtiers seeking respite from the cares of court life.

An intelligent and cultivated woman, the Countess became the patron, correspondent and friend of some of the most important literary figures of the day, including Alexander Pope, Jonathan Swift and John (*Beggar's Opera*) Gay, who all visited the house.

The building was designed by Colen Campbell and constructed under the supervision of Lord Henry Herbert (the future 9th Earl of Pembroke) to proportions inspired by the Italian architect Palladio (1508–80), whose taste was strongly influenced by the architecture of ancient Rome. The villa of Lady Suffolk's time survived virtually unchanged until 1902 when the state acquired it from the Cunard family and rescued it from the threat of destruction. The original furnishings had by then been dispersed and the building was used as a public tea room. It was reopened in 1966 as a **historic house museum** containing some fine early Georgian paintings, chinoiserie and furniture (including a few pieces previously belonging to the house). Since 1986 it has been in the care of English Heritage.

The **entrance hall** is at the 'back' of the house facing the river, from which most guests would have approached. Low-ceilinged and quite plain, this tetrastyle hall (so-called because its ceiling, under the Great Room, is supported by four columns) echoes Palladio's idea of the central court of a Roman house. It also establishes the villa's essential structure, based on an internal cube. On the walls are marble reliefs of Jupiter, Juno, Ceres and Bacchus, installed about 1720.

Off the hall are a dining room, used for a while as a tea room, and a breakfast parlour now containing information boards and prints of people associated with the house. Lady Suffolk would have used the breakfast parlour for informal entertaining.

A fine mahogany staircase leads upstairs from a passage adjoining the entrance hall to the **Great Room**, which after the restrained décor of the ground floor comes as a splendid surprise – truly a setting fit for a king. This massive cube, its symmetry preserved by the inclusion of blind doors in three corners, is embellished by gilded mouldings, four original Panini paintings of buildings in a Roman landscape, and a magnificent marble chimneypiece and overmantel surmounted by a classical pediment, graced by gilded cherubs. One of Lady Suffolk's elaborately carved tables (rediscovered in Australia in 1987) stands here, while portraits of Charles I, Queen Henrietta Maria (both after Van Dyck) and Elizabeth, Countess of Northampton (by Vanderbank) hang in panels on the wall.

Other rooms on this floor include the red damask bedchamber, with a mahogany four-poster bed and Chinese lacquered cabinet; the bedchamber of Miss Henrietta Hotham (a later occupant of the house); which has an attractive Reynolds portrait above the fireplace, and Lady Suffolk's pillared **bedchamber**, in which she died in 1767. This room, now once again lined with green silk damask, contains another mahogany four-poster, more architectural in style than Miss Hotham's. The same green damask is used for its cover and for the festoon curtains at the windows.

The second floor, reached by a functional internal staircase, contains a fine **gallery** echoing Jacobean rather than Palladian style. It offers fine views south towards the river and to Richmond Hill. Here the Duchess and her guests would have strolled in wet weather. The portrait (attributed to Amigoni) of an unknown lady wearing a fur-trimmed cape and holding a parrot is particularly striking.

Three further rooms, the Plaid Room, now decorated in yellow, the Wrought Room (probably named after the 'wrought' or worked hangings on the bed) and the Green Room, which retains more of its original features, would have been used by guests. These rooms contain items from the Lazenby bequest, including English *basso relievo* bird paintings, Italian glass paintings and chinoiserie.

Although the servants' wing of the house was demolished, the original eighteenth-century ice house can be seen in the grounds if, on turning left out of the exit, you walk towards the creeper-covered stable block which is now the Clock House tearoom.

Information/tours/guides Free audio tour and video (not in operation when we inspected) are included in the admission price. Interpretative display boards are on the ground floor, and guides on hand to answer questions. The souvenir book (£2.50) of the house is an informative complement to a visit. Guided tours are by appointment.

When to visit Any time.

Age appeal Mainly for adults, though a free activity sheet is available for children.

Food and drink The tea room in the stable block offers teas, snacks, lunches and children's meals. There are tables outside.

Shops The shop in the entrance hall, though small, has guides and other books plus a range of gift items.

Other facilities You can picnic in the grounds, which are a public park, used for walking dogs and playing ball games. Toilets on site.

🚗 Richmond Road, Twickenham (off A316). Free car park. ⊖ Nearest Underground station is Richmond (District line), then bus (33, 90, 290, H22, R68, R70). ⏲ Apr to Sept, Mon to Sun, 10am to 6pm (10am to 5pm Oct); Nov to Mar, Wed to Sun, 10am to 4pm. Closed 24–26 Dec, 1Jan. Last admission 30 minutes before closing time. 💷 Adult £3.30; student, unemployed, disabled person, senior citizen £2.50; child (under 16 yrs old) £1.70; child (under 5 yrs old) free. EH members free. ♿ Not accessible.

Museum of London

London Wall, London EC2Y 5HN ☎ 020-7600 3699
📱 *www.museumoflondon.org.uk* 📱 *info@museumoflondon.org.uk*

Quality ★★★★ **Facilities 👜👜👜👜👜** **Value for money £££££**
Highlights Brilliant overview of London's history; free for kids; great café; good shop
Drawbacks Not enough for children; little on modern London; down-at-heel toilets

What's there This must be one of the most logical museums and one of the easiest to follow. Starting with prehistoric times (lots of flint and bones) you progress chronologically through London's history to the present day. It's like starting at the bottom of a very deep archaeological dig and slowly working your way up to the surface. All the exhibits are clearly displayed, labelled and presented, and come complete with many a fascinating fact.

The excellent **Roman section** has reconstructions of streets and houses, as well as the still-vivid wall paintings from the Winchester Palace site, artefacts from the huge Temple of Mithras, and the most recent discovery, a skeleton from beneath Spitalfields. Equally good are the **medieval and Tudor rooms**, where a huge carved oak door frame from the fifteenth century and a model of London Bridge set the scene. The Great Fire Experience, however, where Pepys' diary is read out loud against a background display of London burning, could be so much more exciting than it is.

The museum comes into its own with the later nineteenth-century sections, charting London's population explosion when it became the world's largest metropolis. The exhibits encompass every aspect of the capital, though tend to concentrate on life among the richer parts of society. You'll see the cells from **Wellclose Square prison**, complete with the prisoners' inscriptions carved into the wood; **Charles Dickens' chair** in which he wrote *The Tale of Two Cities*; a window from the first Lyons Corner House (1909); a selection of Victorian Valentine cards; and an amazing – and still-working – **regulator clock made for the Great Exhibition**.

The first half of the twentieth century is covered in more detail than more recent times, with the 1928 lifts from Selfridges and really interesting sections on the **two world wars**, especially the second. Modern London could do with some more exhibits and space, though what's there is imaginatively displayed, not least the famous black-and-white painted placard of the Oxford Street protein man, who from 1968 to 1993 walked down Oxford Street holding aloft his placard, which stated 'less passion from less protein'. And you can see the Lord Mayor's coach in all its splendour, standing over a thin film of water to maintain the right humidity to stop the wood drying out.

All the way through, the larger exhibits are complemented by plenty of clothes, jewellery, household goods and personal effects giving each era great depth and a more personalised feel. The only drawback is that there are not enough interactive possibilities, making it more of a look-and-learn museum rather than a touchy-feely one. Children might find this especially disappointing.

Special exhibitions come and go, making a repeat visit some months later a worthwhile trip. You might get the story of Alfred the Great, a display on political fashion, or a gallery about topical issues, such as lesbian and gay life in today's London.

Information/tours/guides The guidebook is expensive (£7.95) and isn't necessary while you're there. It makes a better souvenir. The free plan is fine, but again you don't really need it, as the museum layout is self-explanatory.

When to visit Any time of year is a good time to come, although the summer months are busiest. Tickets are valid for a whole year from the date of issue, so you can go back whenever you fancy.

Age appeal Everyone will find something to interest them, but children might feel excluded and get bored. A lot of the labelling and information is a bit too adult in tone, and there aren't nearly enough opportunities for interaction and involvement.

Food and drink The café (run by Milburns) is a delight. It's actually in a separate building opposite the museum's entrance, and so gets a fair amount of non-museum customers, all making the most of the light, modern interior or the sunny terrace. The fare ranges from sandwiches (£2.50) or poached salmon with a choice of salad (£5.95), then cheesecake or crème brûlée (both £2.50). Hot dishes (from £4.95) and cream teas (£3.35) are also available.

Shops The only drawback to the spacious, tidy shop is its lack of fancy (and more expensive) gifts (unlike most museums). The merchandise here is aimed more at kids and tourists. So you can choose from a good range of London-themed stuff – maybe old Ordnance Survey maps of London (£1.75), Museum of London pencils (40p) or London chocolates (£2.75). There's also an interesting selection of children's books.

Other facilities Even though they are dated, the toilet fittings would be fine if their upkeep was better. As it is, we saw stained radiators, cracked tiles, rusty bins and dirty lino. The café toilets were the best of the bunch. There is also a free cloakroom/bag check.

🚫 Not advisable. ⊖ Nearest Underground stations are St Paul's (Central Line), Barbican (Circle, Hammersmith & City and Metropolitan lines) or Moorgate (Northern line). Buses 8, 11, 15, 23 or 25 pass nearby. ① (in 1999): open all year, Mon to Sat 10am to 5.50pm, Sun 12 to 5.50pm. Last admission 5.30pm. Closed 24-26 Dec, 1 Jan. 💷 Adult £5; child (under 16 yrs old) free; senior citizen, student, unemployed £3. Disabled person free. Free entry for all after 4.30pm. All tickets valid for 1 year. Adult groups of 10 or more get 20% discount, pre-booked school and college groups get free admission. Groups must book in advance (020-7814 5777). ♿ All areas are accessible either by ramps or lifts. Wheelchairs are provided if requested. For more information tel: 020-7814 5502.

National Army Museum

Royal Hospital Road, Chelsea, London SW3 4HT ☎ *020-7730 0717 ext 2210*
📠 *020-7823 6573* 🖥 *www.national-army-museum.ac.uk*

Quality ★★★★ | **Facilities** 🍴 | **Value for money** ££££
Highlights Early galleries, particularly Redcoats and 'The Road to Waterloo'
Drawbacks Gallery on the modern army; poor café with no prices; ugly institutional modern building

What's there This free museum tells the **story of Britain's soldiers** from the fifteenth century until the present day. The early galleries are well thought out and use a variety of media that make the displays appeal to children as well as enthusiasts. But the museum seems to run out of steam as it approaches the modern day – perhaps as the complete focus on the army and exclusion of other forces becomes more artificial.

Start on the ground floor with the **Redcoats gallery**, which tells the tale of the creation of the new Model Army by Parliament at the end of the Civil War, the beginning of a standing army after the restoration of Charles II in 1660, and its involvement in British adventures overseas. The use of **time lines** will help those with a hazy grasp of the history of this period to sort events into the right order.

On the first floor, start with '**The Road to Waterloo**'. Don't rush through the entrance section, as a sound-and-light presentation here tells you of the fight against Napoleon. There are some fascinating display cases of mementoes, including the **saw used to amputate the Earl of Uxbridge's leg** at the Battle of Waterloo. The **skeleton of Morengo**, Napoleon's favourite horse, is also on show, though it's not quite complete because two hooves were used to make snuff boxes. The exhibit culminates in a large **model of the battlefield** at Waterloo that was constructed from the accounts of British officers involved in the battle. You can choose from a selection of sound-and-light shows to tell you about various aspects of the battle.

The **Victorian gallery** reflects Britain's development of an Empire, with excursions in India and South Africa. Across the corridor '**The Nation in Arms**' recreates the years of World Wars I and II. Younger visitors can walk through a **mocked-up trench**, and there are **dioramas of wartime scenes**. In a case you can see a pair of **sniper's sunglasses** – the right-hand eyepiece is dotted with small holes to control the amount of light. Grainy archive film of the British Expeditionary Forces setting off brings the early days of World War I alive. The World War II section includes a good display on the conflict in south-east Asia, a theatre that can often get overlooked with a focus on the war in Europe. If you finish here you will have seen the best of the museum.

Upstairs is a small **art gallery** and a rather disappointing section on the **modern army**, which doesn't seem to have been put together with the same intelligence as the downstairs galleries. There is a dry display of the **history of women in the army**, lots of **recruiting posters** and a small display case on the Gulf and Falklands conflicts near the exit, which is a rather forlorn resting place for the **medals** awarded to Colonel H Jones after the battle of Goose Green.

A special exhibition gallery by the café on the ground floor is used to focus on specific themes and conflicts.

Information/tours/guides There is a regular programme of talks and temporary exhibitions. Visitors are given a plan showing the layout of the galleries as they enter, but there is no additional guidebook (the labelling and information is good enough for one not to be needed).

When to visit One to save for wet weather.

Age appeal Boys of all ages will probably enjoy it.

Food and drink The basic café will serve you a cup of tea and a cake – but no prices are displayed.

Shop The shop has plenty of books for the enthusiast, and model kits starting from £2.95.

🚗 Parking in King's Road and Battersea Park ⊖ Underground to Sloane Square, then 10-minue walk. Buses 11,19, 22, 211 and 137 stop nearby; 239 (not Sundays) stops outside the museum. ⊙ Mon to Sun 10am to 5.30pm. Closed 24-26 Dec, 1 Jan, Good Fri, early May bank hol. 💷 Free. ♿ All galleries accessible to people in wheelchairs, lift available. For more details call 020-7730 0717 ext 2210. 2 disabled parking spaces for Orange Badge holders.

The National Gallery

Trafalgar Square, London WC2N 5DN 📞 *020-7747 2885*
🖱 *www.nationalgallery.org.uk*

Quality ★★★★ | Facilities 🏛🏛🏛🏛 | Value for money £££££
Highlights Superb, wide-ranging collection; lavish interior of the building itself
Drawbacks Little to capture a child's attention

What's there This venerable national institution, firmly located in 'tourist country' on the north side of Trafalgar Square, houses a magnificent collection of Western European painting from medieval times to the beginning of the twentieth century. The gallery is divided chronologically into the Sainsbury Wing, West Wing, North Wing and the East Wing, and seeing them in this order is a good idea as it gives a better sense of continuity and evolution of artistic trends. The free floor-plan, available in the foyer, will help you plan your route.

The Sainsbury Wing houses early Renaissance paintings, including works by **Piero della Francesca**, **Bellini** and **Botticelli**, as well as **Leonardo**, **Mantegna** and **Raphael**. The northern Renaissance is represented too, most notably by **Van**

Eyck's Arnolfini couple. On the lower floor, temporary exhibitions are normally held (admission fee charged). Crossing over into the main building, the West Wing covers the fifteenth century, and includes paintings by **El Greco**, **Michelangelo**, **Caravaggio** and **Rubens**. Heroic, sculptural figures with a mythological or allegorical origin are popular, such as Rubens' *Samson and Delilah*, cleverly painted so as to incorporate natural light falling from outside. Works by **Holbein** include the famous *Ambassadors*, incorporating the distorted skull on the floor. The North Wing features a large collection of Dutch artists, such as the sombre, austere portraits by **Frans Hals**, and **Ruysdael**'s wintry landscapes. An interesting feature here is the Hoogstraten *Peepshow*, an ingenious three-dimensional visual trick designed to show the interior of a Dutch house.

The East Wing houses the artists of the eighteenth and nineteenth centuries, including **Constable**'s idealised view of country life in *The Haywain* and **Gainsborough** portraits. **Turner**'s formless, blustery depictions of early industrialisation feature quite strongly, including *The Fighting Temerare* and *Rain, Steam and Speed*. The gallery has even been faithful to the artist's will, which stated that his paintings be hung alongside those of his hero, Claude. Joseph Wright of Derby's striking comment on science, *An Experiment on a Bird in the Air Pump*, sits just along from the remaining fragments of **Manet**'s *Execution of Maximillian*, which was mysteriously hacked up, and was thought for many years to be so shocking that it was banned.

The early work of **Monet** and **Renoir** are contrasted, both featuring the transient effects of nature which they would later develop into impressionism. The same dappled examination of light can be seen in **Seurat**'s superb *Bathers at Asnières*, the audio commentary here explaining subtle references to class divisions in the painting. Javanese and Greek influences are visible in **Gauguin**'s dream-like Tahitian paintings, which, along with works such as **Van Gogh**'s *Sunflowers*, form the Post-impressionist section. Finally, with the dawning of the twentieth century, early Cubist influences can be seen in **Cézanne**'s angular, distorted landscapes.

Information/tours/guides There are helpful information desks in the main foyer and in the Sainsbury Wing. It is also worth checking the large computer screen for details of the day's events. On the first floor of the Sainsbury Wing a micro-gallery has 12 workstations, which even ardent technophobes can use easily to learn more about any artist and see their work on screen. You can get a printout of a suggested route round the gallery including all your favourite works. The Central Hall has similar catalogues specific to temporary exhibitions at the time.

The most comprehensive guidebook is the *National Gallery Companion Guide*, a full-colour, highly illustrated book for £9.95. A cheaper alternative is the leaflet '20 Great Paintings' (£2.50).

Two audio tours are available on one disc. One covers 'the highlights', features 30 paintings and lasts about two hours. The other covers almost every painting on the main floor as well as providing an introduction to each room – you simply key in the number of the painting you are interested in. It is available from the foyer, free of charge, although visitors are asked to make a voluntary contribution.

There are also tours led by professional, entertaining guides, who animate and enliven groups of visitors, and provide an explanation of the historical and social context behind each painting. They are free and last about one hour, and are on Monday to Sunday at 11.30am and 2.30pm and Wednesday at 6.30pm. Lunchtime lectures from Tuesday to Saturday start at 1pm, with films and special lectures on Monday at 1pm. A free copy of the monthly *National Gallery News*, which lists all current lectures, talks, events, films and exhibitions, is available from the information desks.

When to visit During term-time it will prove impossible to avoid the swathes of children being marshalled around, but this should not be unduly distracting. Overlooking Trafalgar Square, the gallery is also a mecca for tourists in summer time. On Wednesday evenings from 6 to 7.30pm the gallery is open late, and students from the Royal College of Music play in the Central Hall.

Age appeal The two trails aimed at children encourage them to look more closely at some of the pictures. 'Children's Way In' is a booklet with illustrations by Quentin Blake, while 'The Great Escape' has stickers that they peel off and place in the correct position. Donations of 50p per trail are requested.

Food and drink A branch of Pret à Manger sits in the basement, providing its normal mix of sandwiches, fruit, coffees and cakes. A brasserie in the Sainsbury Wing also offers sandwiches and snacks as well as more formal meals, with such main courses as roast salmon with potato and celeriac pancake and horseradish cream, or aubergine roulade with red pepper and goats' cheese. A set-price menu (£15) of two courses plus a glass of wine (also available on Wednesday evenings) is also on offer. Teas and cakes are served in the afternoons in the Sainsbury Wing brasserie.

Shops The main shop on the ground floor of the Sainsbury Wing has an array of art-related books, sweatshirts (£20) and posters (£8). There's another smaller shop in the main building selling postcards among other things.

Not advisable. Public car park in Whitcomb Street (at the back of the Gallery). Nearest Underground stations are Charing Cross (Northern and Bakerloo lines and mainline station), Leicester Square (Piccadilly and Northern lines), and Piccadilly Circus (Piccadilly and Bakerloo lines). Mon to Sun 10am to 6pm (9pm on Wed). Closed Good Friday, 24–26, 1 Jan. Free admission (except for special exhibitions). Access for wheelchairs through the Sainsbury Wing entrance, with lifts to all floors. Wheelchairs loaned on request. Disabled toilets. Large-print labels are available in main-floor galleries and for most temporary exhibitions. 'A Sense of Art' audio tour is for visually impaired visitors, available free from the information desk in the Sainsbury Wing.

National Maritime Museum

Romney Road, Greenwich, London SE10 9NF ☎ *020-8858 4422;*
020-8312 6565 (information line) 📠 *020-8312 6632* 💻 *www.nmm.ac.uk*

Quality ★★★★★   **Facilities ⚑ ⚑ ⚑ ⚑ ⚑**   **Value for money £££££**
Highlights 'Trade and Empire' and 'Nelson' galleries; hands-on experiences for children; mind-expanding 'Story of Time' exhibition
Drawbacks Layout of Main Galleries can be confusing

What's there With its collection imaginatively displayed in wonderfully light and airy new galleries, this is truly a museum to be seen in the millennium. The museum is made up of three buildings – the Main Galleries, the Queens House (showing a special exhibition on the story of time until 24 September 2000), and the Royal Observatory, home of the Prime Meridian Line, a short walk away up a steep hill in Greenwich Park.

Make sure you pick up a floor plan when you enter the Main Galleries – you'll need it to navigate your way around the rather confusing layout. The galleries are all clearly themed and labelled, so if time is short you can just pick out the ones you like the sound of – we'd suggest 'Explorers', 'Trade and Empire', 'Nelson' and, if you have children, the interactive 'All Hands' galleries.

Start by going downstairs to level 1, where you can see the *Suhaili*, Robin Knox Johnson's boat in which he sailed non-stop and single-handed round the world in 1968–9. One of the **'Explorers'** galleries (3) is designed so that you feel as if you are on board a boat as it tells of how nations explored new lands for trade. In the other (8) you can see Scott's sledging flag, with its motto 'Ready Aye Ready', that he flew at the South Pole on his fatal expedition; next to it is one of the special-recipe Huntley & Palmers biscuits included in their rations. The 'Cargoes' exhibition dismantles a car to show where all the component parts have been shipped in. The 'Passengers' exhibition reveals how the British class system reigned supreme even on the water – on the pre-World-War-One transatlantic liner *Mauritania*, the money was made from selling up to 1,300 passengers third-class one-way tickets for £6 rather than from the toffs' tickets.

Going up a level (2) you can have a sit-down at the start of the **'Trade and Empire'** exhibition and watch a selection of old films of happy smiling natives cut with a very modern ironic commentary. The gallery shows how Britain's maritime business was at the heart of its Empire. Don't skip the 'Seapower' gallery if you have small children – they'll get a chance to work in the ops room of a Type 22 Frigate while parents can read about Britain at war on the sea during this century. Out on the central balcony area you can learn about problems such as global warming and over-fishing, while the Global garden shows how the early explorers changed British gardens with the range of plants they brought home. The 'Art and the Sea' gallery displays images as diverse as seventeenth-century Dutch art to the stirring final speech in the classic British war film *In Which We Serve*.

The star of the third floor is the **'Nelson'** gallery, which does a fine job of putting the naval hero in historical context and has a computer simulation of the Battle of Trafalgar, which will leave you understanding Nelson's tactics. If you've an eye for the macabre, you can search out the tourniquet believed to have been used in the amputation of his arm (1797, Tenerife) and his blood-stained clothes worn when he was hit by the fatal French musket ball at Trafalgar. You can even see the hole where the ball passed through his jacket, just under the left epaulette. In the **'All Hands'** gallery children get a chance to learn by having a go – they can send messages by Morse code, load a ship or, most fun of all, fire a cannon in a computer simulation game. 'On the Bridge' continues in similar vein, with the chance to steer a Viking longboat and a paddle steamer up the Thames.

You could easily spend a whole day here with the family – even a reasonably paced dash round everything will take a good three hours.

Outside again you can puff your way up to the **Royal Observatory**, designed by Sir Christopher Wren under orders from Charles II to help solve the problem of British losses at sea by giving sailors more accurate charts of the moon and stars. The camera obscura needs bright light, so go here first if you are visiting on a dull day. You can see the beauty of Wren's design in the Octagon Room, with its tall windows designed to accommodate the long telescopes used in the seventeenth century. In a fascinating exhibition downstairs the **story of the search for longitude** is told. Sailors could easily tell latitude from the sun and stars but needed a second co-ordinate. So in 1714 the Board of Longitude, established by Parliament, offered a reward of £20,000 to the first person who could accurately measure longitude. The prize was eventually won by a clockmaker, John Harrison, who used the connection between time difference and degrees of longitude. His controversial story is told here. In 1884 it was agreed that the meridian passing though the Observatory would be the initial meridian from which all longitude and time would be calculated – so Greenwich is claiming for itself the privilege of being 'where the millennium really started'. You can see the line in the Courtyard – and play the tourist game of straddling it and being in both the east and west hemisphere. You can also continue your tour through some of the Observatories where the astronomers lived and worked. Allow an hour for your visit.

The third part of the museum is really one for adults rather than children. It is a stunningly displayed mind-stretching exhibition, **'The Story of Time'**, that juggles with ideas of time through different religions and cultures. Pick up the audio tour that gives you short descriptions of some of the best pieces, starting with the creation stories told throughout the world, and including the story of the development of the Gregorian calendar. Allow a couple of hours at least for this.

Information/tours/guides The guidebooks to Main Galleries and Royal Observatory cost £3 each. There's also an enormous catalogue to the 'Time' exhibition for £19.95. The audio tour of the 'Time' exhibition costs £2.50 and is highly recommended. A planetarium show (£2, £1.50 for children) is usually shown daily at about 2.15pm, but ring before you go to check it is on.

When to visit It's quieter during term time; and it's a good choice for a wet day.

Age appeal Both the Main Galleries and Royal Observatory are good for all ages. The 'Time' exhibition may be hard work for children.

Food and drink A café on level 2 sells cold snacks and drinks. The main restaurant off the 'Seapower' gallery serves hot lunches too, for example steak and kidney pie and vegetables (£5.95), chocolate fudge cake (£1.95) and tea at 95p a cup.

Shops The best gift shop is on level 1, with a range of educational toys and books for children and a wide range of branded gifts, mini telescopes (£1.50), ships in bottles (£10), Meridian Gin, vodka or scotch (£15), and champagne (£25).

🚗 A2 or A206 to central Greenwich. Free parking in Greenwich Park (often busy at weekends) and limited parking in museum car park (in Park Row) on Sat and Sun. Alternatively, pay and display public parking. ⊖ Train to either Greenwich or Maze Hill stations (from Charing Cross and Waterloo East), then short walk. Docklands Light Railway to Cutty Sark station. Alternatively, boat cruise from Westminster (tel: 020-7987 1185). Buses 53 (from central London), 54, 202, 380 stop at Greenwich Park.
⊙ Mon to Sun, 10am to 5pm. Closed 24–26 Dec. 🎫 *National Maritime Museum (Royal Observatory)* adult £7.50 (£6); child (5 to 16 yrs old) free; student, senior citizen, unemployed, disabled visitor and helper £6 (£4.80). *Combined ticket* adult £10.50, concessions £8.40. After 3.30pm adult £4, concessions £3.20. *'Time' exhibition* adult £7.50, child £3.75, concessions £6, family ticket (2 adults + 3 children) £20. ♿ For full details of facilities tel: 020-8312 6608. Main Galleries have lift. Queens House wheelchair accessible. The courtyard at the Royal Observatory accessible to see the meridian line, but steps to gain entrance to building.

National Portrait Gallery

2 St Martin's Place, London WC2H 0HE   ☎ 020-7306 0055

Quality ★★   **Facilities 👜👜👜**   **Value for money ££££**
Highlights Excellent overview of great figures in British history, right up to the present day
Drawbacks Rather overshadowed by the National Gallery next door; little in the way of explanations

---

What's there   Tucked away at the foot of Charing Cross Road, the National Portrait Gallery lives in the shadow of its larger cousin – the National Gallery (*qv*). Starting with Tudor times, visitors can glean a great deal about the major figures and events in British history from the portraits, sculptures and caricatures on display here. When we inspected, some renovation and building work was going on, so the arrangements described here are likely to change.

For observers of contemporary culture, the ground floor is probably the most interesting, as most of the subjects are well-known actors, sports people and politicians. Amongst the many familiar faces are portraits of **Bobby Charlton**, **Harold Macmillan**, **Stephen Hawking**, two of **Mrs Thatcher**, and many more. A spangly **bust of Zandra Rhodes** by Andrew Logan as well as two pieces by **Andy Warhol** stand out on this floor. The Wolfson Gallery houses temporary exhibitions, for which there may be an admission charge.

In temporary accommodation on the lower ground floor (during renovations) is the Tudor collection, including **Holbein**'s cartoon for his paintings of Henry VII and Henry VIII, as well as three of the latter's wives. Don't miss the exquisite **Hilliard miniatures** (protected under wraps in a display case) of **Elizabeth I** and her courtiers Francis Drake, Robert Dudley and Walter Raleigh.

The first floor concentrates largely on the nineteenth and early twentieth centuries, opening with an unusual sculpture of Victoria and Albert in Anglo-Saxon dress, looking rather like Arthur and Guinevere. Among the stiff, formal Victorian busts, look out for a **portrait of Chamberlain and Balfour** lounging on the front benches by Sydney Prior Hall, and **Max Beerbohm caricatures** of

David Lloyd George. Darwin, too, was the subject of satirists (a caricature compares him to an ape). You can also see a cast of an effigy of Lawrence of Arabia, in full Arab robes.

The top floor is devoted to the centuries in between, covering the Stuart and Hanoverian periods. Two vast canvases by George Hayter depict the divorce trial of Queen Caroline (wife of George IV) and the reformed House of Commons in 1833 (probably the most accurate architectural record of the building before it was destroyed by fire a year later).

An extension with new Tudor and twentieth-century galleries is due to open in May 2000, the intention being to display the collection in better chronological order. The new building will also have a restaurant and an IT Gallery with touch-screen catalogues.

Information/tours/guides There are no guided tours, but the audio tours, for which you pay a voluntary sum, cover the highlights. A guide (60p) gives basic information about the portraits as well as a floor plan. You can also buy booklets on the Tudor and Victorian collections (£2.50 each) in the shop.

When to visit It's a weather-proof attraction and rarely filled with tourists and children, so visiting at any time is fine. The most popular part of the gallery is the twentieth-century section on the ground floor.

Age appeal The gallery holds little interest for most children, as few of the subjects will be familiar to them, and the significance will be lost.

Food and drink A café in the basement provides teas and coffees, but is expensive (£1.50 for a cup of tea, £2.75 for a piece of fruit cake) and has a limited range. However, there is a wide variety of bars and restaurants in the area, including the café in the National Gallery around the corner. A new restaurant is due to open in May 2000.

Shops A shop on the ground floor has a similar range of goods to the National Gallery, including books (£20) and posters (£5).

🚗 Not advisable. Public car park in Whitcomb Street (at the back of the gallery). ⊖ Nearest Underground stations are Embankment (District and Circle lines), Charing Cross (Northern and Bakerloo lines and mainline station), Leicester Square (Piccadilly and Northern lines), and Piccadilly Circus (Piccadilly and Bakerloo lines). ☉ Mon to Sat 10.00am to 6.00pm, Sun 12.00 to 6.00pm. 💷 Free (possible charge for temporary exhibitions in the Wolfson Gallery). ♿ Wheelchairs can access the building via the Orange Street entrance, lifts to all floors.

Natural History Museum

Cromwell Road, London SW7 5BD ☎ *020-7942 5000* 🖥 *www.nhm.ac.uk*

Quality ★★★★★	Facilities 🗖🗖🗖🗖🗖	Value for money £££££

Highlights Galleries are clearly numbered; guides and information staff knowledgeable and pleasant; excellent bookshop

Drawbacks Layout of main self-service restaurant could be improved; baby-changing facilities and toilets (Life Galleries) were extremely untidy when we inspected

What's there Even the exterior of the Natural History Museum is impressive, in German-Romanesque style faced with terracotta interspersed with blue brick. In the main hall creatures and plants are carved into pillars and crevices. But the space is dominated by a **diplodocus** measuring 26 metres from tip to tail. The surrounding walls are split into 12 bays holding oddities such as a 225-million-year-old petrified tree trunk and a mammoth's skull that was found in Ilford.

Galleries are clearly identified (by numbers), easy to find, and divided into two distinct sections – Life and Earth. The highlights of the Life Galleries are the **Dinosaur** and **Mammal exhibitions**. A raised walkway that takes visitors past suspended skeletal models, including a Baryonyx found in Dorking, dominates the dimly lit dinosaur hall. Each model is labelled well and their complicated names are spelt out phonetically in a child-friendly way. A **robotic display of three dinosaurs** feeding on a fellow dinosaur (just killed) is located at the end of the walkway. On the ground, a well-organised display looks at the habits and eventual demise of these huge creatures. More life-size models of dinosaurs and nests, complete with newly hatched babies, are also shown.

The **Mammal Gallery** is split into two separate sections – one concentrating on land mammals, the other on those of the sea. The land mammals range in size from a tiny pygmy shrew to an elephant. A fierce-looking grizzly bear, a giraffe, tigers, lions and a polar bear are just some examples of the stuffed animals on display. A **life-size model of the blue whale** is the first thing you notice when you walk into the sea-life gallery. Skeletal remains of whales and models of dolphins hang from the ceiling. On the mezzanine level, interactive displays allow visitors to learn about their habits.

The 'Creepy Crawly' section is one to avoid if you don't like these creatures! At the back of the gallery, in No. 1 Crawly House, you can see just how many bugs you could be sharing your home with. Other exhibitions in the Life Galleries include an excellent and accessible section on **human biology**, a **marine invertebrates exhibition** with an 11-metre model of a giant squid, an **exhibition on the evolution of man**, a display on ecology, and a mineral and meteorite gallery.

Six galleries (and an earth lab) spread over three floors make up the **Earth Galleries**. The best way to see them is to start at the top and work down. The most dramatic way to reach the second floor is via 'Visions of Earth'. An avenue of bronze sculptures (including a Cyclops and Medusa) leads to an escalator that passes through a giant model of planet Earth. On either side, slate walls etched with constellations of the night sky and planets of the solar system hold specimens such as topaz, amethyst and a piece of moon rock collected by astronauts of the 1972 *Apollo 16* mission.

The 'Power Within' (the first gallery you come to on the second floor) focuses on the Earth's internal forces. Videos showing footage of famous volcanic eruptions give way to interactive displays on earthquakes, including a **simulation of the Kobe earthquake** (1995) in a reconstructed Japanese grocery shop. **'From the Beginning'**, **'Earth Today and Tomorrow'** and **'Earth's Treasury'** are the most interesting of the remaining Earth galleries. An engraved steel time-rail traces the development of planet Earth and the evolution of life forms, including humans, in 'From the Beginning'. Displays feature skeletal and stuffed animals and rock specimens. 'Earth Today and Tomorrow' throws up some surprising statistics – for example, a family of four eats 208 loaves and drinks the equivalent of 624 cans of soft drink per year. This gallery also focuses on the dangers our planet is facing, such as pollution and climate change. 'Earth's Treasury' is a showcase for a variety of gemstones, rocks and minerals. Coloured gems, gold, unusual mineral and rock formations are displayed in the peaceful, dimly lit gallery.

Information/tours/guides A full-colour, illustrated souvenir guidebook (£3.50) gives a good taste of what to expect from the various galleries. It also suggests a tour for visitors who do not have the time to see the entire museum and lists the galleries most popular with children. A free leaflet, which includes a map, is available at ticket and information desks. Children's activity sheets (30p) can be bought at the shops and information desks. Free tours (maximum of 10 persons per tour, lasting about 45 minutes) are available on the hour between 11am and 4pm and should be booked at the Life Galleries information desk. Guides are knowledgeable, enthusiastic and happy to answer questions.

When to visit This is a great place to go to when the weather is horrid, and because there is so much to see you can easily spend the whole day here. A changing programme of special events, including talks and demonstrations and temporary exhibitions, is held throughout the year for children and adults alike (additional charges may apply). Avoid school holidays, as the museum gets extremely crowded.

Age appeal This museum will appeal to all ages.

Shops There are four separate shops: the Gallery Shop (T-shirts, posters, games, toys and confectionery), Bookshop (a comprehensive range of books on subjects such as botany, wildlife photography and gardening) and the Dinostore (plastic dinosaurs, a small range of children's books, confectionery) are located in the Life Galleries section, while the Earth Store in the Earth Galleries section sells mineral specimens, jewellery, T-shirts and postcards.

Food and drink With three separate café bars and a self-service restaurant, there is no shortage of places to eat. Hot and cold meals are available in the Gallery Restaurant from 11.30am to 2.30pm. However, when we inspected there were long queues for no apparent reason, and the main hot dish (roast chicken, £5.25) was not available. Portions were on the small side and our inspection meal of pasta with shredded basil and tomato sauce (£5.25) was almost cold! Children's portions and lunchboxes (£3 for rolls, dinosaur cookie and juice) are available. A standard range of sandwiches (cheese ploughman's, egg mayonnaise, smoked salmon) and a selection of cakes, teas and coffees are also sold.

🚗 Off A4, Cromwell Road. Parking (charged) nearby. ⊖ Nearest Underground station is South Kensington (Piccadilly, Circle and District lines). Buses 14, 74 run nearby. ⏱ Mon to Sat 10am to 5.50pm, Sun 11am to 5.50pm. Last admission 5.30pm. Closed 23–26 Dec, 1 Jan. *Life Galleries Restaurant & Waterhouse Coffee Bar* (both licensed): 10am to 5pm; *the Globe Café:* 10.30am to 4.30pm; *the Snack Bar:* 11am to 4.30pm (5pm weekends). 💷 Adult £6.50; child (under 16 yrs old) free; student, senior citizen, unemployed, disabled visitor £3.50. Groups of 10 or more 50p reduction on admission price. Admission free for all after 4.30pm Mon to Fri and 5pm Sat, Sun and Bank Hols. A season ticket or membership is available. ♿ Wheelchair accessible. Wheelchairs are available free of charge. Tactile guides and guided tours for the blind arranged on request.

Rock Circus

The London Pavilion, 1 Piccadilly Circus, London W1V 9LA ☎ *020-7734 7203*

Quality ★★★	Facilities ♫ ♫	Value for money ££

Highlights Good animatronics in the multimedia show; life-like models in well-designed thematic layout

Drawbacks Limited appeal; minimal facilities; no interactive involvement

What's there Rock Circus is the musical offshoot of Madame Tussaud's waxworks (*qv*), and its success is principally due to its prime location on the site of the old London Pavilion in the heart of the touristy West End. What you might expect to see is pretty well what you get – dozens of very realistic wax models of the most famous stars of the pop world since the 1950s. There is nothing to entice people to come if they have no interest in rock legends.

The layout is a straightforward, well-designed one-way system. The stairs are cleverly turned into steps on the Beatles' **'Magical Mystery Tour'** double-decker with accompanying song and psychedelic Sixties video footage. The models appear thematically rather than chronologically (Buddy Holly is next to Eric Clapton), but are usually well positioned for the obligatory 'I'm next to a celebrity' photos. There is good use of various audio-visual media to add to the experience, such as a collection of TV screens playing Madonna's pop videos around her dummy and the unnerving video of Michael Hutchence as he posed for his wax double at Rock Circus just days before he died.

The first room is dedicated entirely to Michael Jackson – hardly a thriller – after which you meet a menagerie of stars in the VIP lounge as you wait for the exhibition's highlight, the **'Music Revolution Show'**. It is designed, quite successfully, to replicate the experience of going to see a show at the London Pavilion (once a music hall and then a cinema). This multimedia show rotates (literally) every 15 minutes and is a 10-minute (hit-and-miss) synopsis of recent pop history. You become part of the audience at an early Beatles concert, watch footage on cinematic screens and get dazzled by strobes and colourful lights. Animatronic models of Bob Dylan and Bruce Springsteen perform on stage. Springsteen's movements are brilliantly life-like; unfortunately Dylan's performance brings the show to an anti-climax (unless you're a big fan) with one of his songs awkwardly droning on too long.

After the show, continue through the themed rooms, such as the clever but eerie **Rock Cemetery** (where the gravestones look genuine and the effect is so gloomy that you can barely read the inscriptions), and the mock Soho street, where Jimi Hendrix plays outside Ronnie Scott's Jazz Club and George Michael is to be found busking opposite the Sex fashion store.

The promotional brochure indicates you'll have the chance to be 'hands on' in the recording studio, but don't expect anything of the sort. The opportunity to select a CD track is the only interaction you'll get here.

Allow up to 1½ hours for a visit. Most people will find an hour sufficient and the entrance prices excessive.

Information/tours/guides Come here to be entertained, not educated. There are no guided tours or maps but you will be shepherded by staff between themed areas. The glossy guidebook is fairly good value at £3, featuring colourful souvenir pictures of the best models, and plenty of information both about the stars' careers and about how a model is made. Unfortunately, too little of this information is next to the models themselves, and the Wall of Fame, displaying celebrity handprints, could have more explanation.

When to visit It's typically overcrowded in the July to September peak tourist months, when you can feel very herded. Try weekdays during term time if possible. It is a good place to escape the rain for a couple of hours if you're in the West End.

Age appeal Older visitors and young children could find the loud music and multicoloured flashing lights disturbing – but then the attraction is not really aimed at them: it's a totally passive experience likely to appeal only to teenagers and music fans.

Food and drink Hardly worth mentioning, the 'After Show Party' bar is more like a tuck shop, offering extortionately priced soft drinks (£1.20 for a can of Dr Pepper) and confectionery but no cooked food. Bar proppers Lenny Kravitz and Bono would certainly expect more.

Shops The small, rather cluttered shop has a grungy décor with industrial pipes running along the low ceiling. Merchandise includes framed photos of pop stars (£2.99) and kitsch inflatable guitars, while more serious musicians could buy the *101 Songs For Easy Guitar* book (£16.95). Plenty of photo-dominated, lightweight biographies are on the shelves but virtually no books on the history of rock. The service was efficient.

Other facilities The toilets are at the exit, badly signed and with very basic facilities; clean but hardly spick and span.

🚗 Not recommended. ⊖ Nearest Underground stations are Piccadilly Circus (Piccadilly and Bakerloo lines) and Leicester Square (Northern and Piccadilly lines). Numerous buses go to Piccadilly Circus. ⏰ Mon to Sun, 10am to 5.30pm. Easter and summer 10am-8pm, 11am-8pm (Tues). Closed 25 Dec. 💷 Adult £8.25; child (under 16 yrs old) £6.25; senior citizen, student £7.25. Disabled visitors and helpers free entry. Group rates (minimum of 10 people – one free ticket in every 16): adult £7; child £5.30; senior citizen, student £6.15. ♿ Wheelchair users (phone in advance) can take the lift and will miss only the 'Michael Jackson Tribute' room at the start. Disabled toilets.

Science Museum

Exhibition Road, London SW7 2DD   ☎ *020-7942 4455*

Quality ★★★★★   **Facilities 🏛️🏛️🏛️🏛️🏛️**   **Value for money £££££**
Highlights Hands-on games and experiments, presentations and shows; friendly staff
Drawbacks Medical exhibition on the top floor slightly confusing

---

What's there The UK's flagship science museum houses more than 10,000 exhibits from collections all over the country, and aims to illustrate the advances in science, technology and medicine that have helped shape the world in which we live today. The sheer size and range of the exhibits can be overwhelming, but the handy guidebook suggests some roughly timed routes for you to follow, and points out the best exhibits for children.

You can find fascinating displays on **chemistry**, **technology**, medicine, **flight**, **fossil fuels**, computing, transport, **outer space**, navigation, **optics**, the home and nuclear power among many, many others. Nearly all the exhibits are imaginatively displayed, with clever designs, innovative lighting and **hands-on experiments** or **interactive computer displays** to help explain what you are looking at. The emphasis is on participation and interaction with the exhibits, rather than simply reading about them.

Exhibits include the *Apollo 10* command module, still scorched from re-entry in 1969, some shrunken human heads, Babbage's very first calculating engine – the grandfather of all computers – and a real full-size landing gear from an Airbus A340 in the lobby. The scope of the exhibitions means that there will certainly be something of interest for everyone on a day out here.

Allow at least four hours for your visit, though it is easily possible to spend the entire day in the museum.

Information/tours/guides A guide is available on entry for £2.50. There's a packed programme of presentations and talks on an enormous range of topics. All activities are announced over the intercom before they happen, and the free 'What's on' guide, which gives details of the daily programme, can be picked up when you arrive.

Many other publications on individual exhibitions are available in the museum bookshop.

When to visit Visit any time of the year, although school holidays will be predictably busy.

Age appeal Children are especially well catered for, with a specific area called 'The Garden' set aside for 3- to 6-year-olds. But everyone will find something here to intrigue and inspire.

Food and drink There is a large buffet-style cafeteria on the ground floor of the museum, with a fair choice of food on sale, such as smoked salmon and cream cheese bagels (£2.85), smoked ham with lettuce and tomato sandwich (£2.65), hot meals of the day (£4.95), fizzy sodas, squash (50p), wine (£1.95 a glass), beer (bottles £2.45) and a range of pastries, biscuits and cakes. Good-value children's meals in pre-packaged boxes contain sandwiches, squash and crisps. Two other smaller cafés serve snacks and hot drinks only.

Shops The spacious, well-laid-out shop is split into literature in one area, and toys, games and souvenirs on the other. An excellent range of titles, from astrology to medicine, is sold in the bookshop, with a section for children's pocket-money buys. Prices range from around £2 to £15. The other section offers goods such as junior microscopes (£24.99) and binoculars (£10), as well as posters (£9.99), lava lamps (£49.99) and globes (£57).

🚗 Not advisable (street parking limited and expensive). ⊖ Nearest Underground station is South Kensington (Circle and District lines). Also buses 9, 10, 14, 345, 49, 52,

74, C1 stop nearby. ⏰ Mon to Sun, 10am to 6pm. Closed 24–26 Dec. 💳 Adult £6.95; child (under 16 yrs old) free; student, senior citizen £3.50; disabled visitor (and carer), unemployed free. Free entry after 4.30pm for all. 10% discount for groups of 15 or more. Season tickets available. ♿ Full wheelchair access. Wheelchairs are also available at the front desk.

Sir John Soane's Museum

13 Lincoln's Inn Fields, London WC2A 3BP ☎ *020-7430 0175*
📠 *020-7831 3957*

Quality ★★	Facilities 🦽	Value for money ££££

Highlights Series of Hogarth's paintings; work by Canaletto
Drawbacks Little attempt to explain the context of exhibits

What's there Sir John Soane was an architect in the late eighteenth/early nineteenth century who ran his house partly as a museum in his own lifetime, collecting classical pieces at the London sales to educate students of architecture. In 1833 he obtained a private Act of Parliament to ensure that the museum continued after his death. In the early 1990s the house was restored to look just as it did at Soane's death.

The museum is worth seeking out just for its setting, in Lincoln's Inn Fields. Inside, the house is a good example of a family home but shows Soane's passion for collecting. The corridors are narrow and the rooms are not grand, but you can see how Soane used some of his architectural themes in a domestic setting, with curved ceilings painted like an arbour in the breakfast room, and the use of skylights and an inner courtyard to create an illusion of space and light. Over the fireplace in the dining room is a portrait of Soane, said to be a good likeness, opposite **Reynolds**' *Love and Beauty*. Passing through his study and dressing room you start to get a feel for the wealth of marble he collected – notably in the central Colonnade filled with **classical busts and urns** and **fragments of sculpture**. The picture gallery to the right has two series of pictures by **Hogarth**: the *Rake's Progress* – telling the sorry tale of Tom Rakewell who squandered two fortunes to die in Bedlam – and *The Election* – a political satire of the electoral malpractice in Oxfordshire (which apparently was notorious for it). The pictures are double hung; ask the attendants to open the huge screens so you can see a number of Soane's designs for the Bank of England, a small **Turner** painting of Kirkstall Abbey and drawings by Piranesi of the Doric temples at Paestum in Southern Italy.

Downstairs lies the monk's parlour – a suite of rooms supposedly for the monk Padre Giovanni, whose tomb may be seen in the yard. In fact the tomb contains the remains of Fanny, Mrs Soane's lap dog, and is just Soane's little joke. There is also the real treasure of the **sarcophagus of Pharaoh Seti I** (died 1279 BC), which Soane bought after the British Museum turned down the purchase price of £2,000. Upstairs, again in the new picture room, are three **Canaletto paintings**, the largest and finest showing a view of Venice looking towards Santa Maria della Salute. On the top floor are the house's principal rooms for entertaining, painted in the then very fashionable lemon sherbet known as 'Turner's Patent Yellow'. There's also a painting of Soane's two sons, who were a sad disappointment to him (neither became an architect, and one became a dissolute writer who criticised his father). In the smaller dining room is Turner's painting of Admiral van Tromp's barge. Allow about an hour for a full tour of the house.

Information/tours/guides A good short guide costs £1 – do buy it as there is little labelling in the house. Guided tours are conducted on Saturdays at 2.30pm. Tickets cost £3 (free for students and unemployed people) and can be bought after 2pm on the day.

When to visit The busiest days are Tuesdays and Saturdays, so avoid them if you can.

Age appeal As it is a worthy site for enthusiasts, it offers little attraction for children.

Food and drink There is no café in the museum. However, there are plenty of refreshments available nearby on Kingsway and in Covent Garden.

Shops A small display of cards and books is on sale in the new picture room. Postcards cost 30p and 50p, a writing block £6.95.

🚗 Parking not easy – you may get space around Lincoln's Inn Fields. ⊖ Nearest Underground station is Holborn (Piccadilly and Central lines). ⏰ Tues to Sat 10am to 5pm (also open 6pm to 9pm on first Tuesday of the month). Closed Easter, 24–26 Dec, 1 Jan and Bank Hols. 💷 Free. Occasional charge for special exhibitions (free for students and unemployed people). ♿ Steps to gain entrance and more narrow steps inside. Once inside, the ground floor can be accessed using narrow wheelchairs provided.

St Paul's Cathedral

St Paul's Churchyard, London EC4M 8AD
☎ *020-7246 8348*   ✎ *http://stpauls.london.anglican.org*

Quality ★★★★★   **Facilities 🏛🏛🏛🏛🏛**   **Value for money £££**
Highlights Views from Whispering Gallery; tombs in crypt; service with choir
Drawbacks High entrance charge; expensive restaurant; crowds and queues

What's there More than 'just' a cathedral, St Paul's has been at the centre of national life since its distinctive dome was built (in 1710) by **Sir Christopher Wren** after the Great Fire of London. It almost wasn't built: Wren's designs for a dome were consistently turned down by the churchmen, who wanted a traditional Gothic cathedral, but he cannily managed to slip it in by persuading Charles II to authorise his final 'Warrant Design'. This allowed Wren to make such design changes as might become necessary in the building of the cathedral. You can see the compromises he went through to reach the Warrant Design in an exhibition in the crypt. The cathedral took just 35 years to build and was completed in Wren's lifetime, though his critics had Wren put on half-pay in 1697 to try to speed things up.

Once you are inside the building, stand by the Great West Door from where you can look down the full length of the nave. In the mosaic floor, a few paces in front of the doors, is a memorial plaque to the men and women of Saint Paul's Watch, who saved the cathedral from being destroyed by fire during the Second World War (it was hit by about 60 firebombs, and the altar was destroyed when one bomb detonated). Walk up the nave and you'll see the enormous monument to the Duke of Wellington – his tomb is in the crypt. Wren became disgruntled towards the end of the cathedral's construction, when he felt his views were being ignored, and he left the interior completely bare of colour and statuary. But look up at the dome and you will see monochrome scenes of the life of St Peter put in just after the cathedral's completion, and the start of **glittering mosaics** that continue up above the choir stalls showing scenes from the Creation. When Queen Victoria visited she thought the building needed brightening up and commissioned these mosaics – as well as having the altar screen moved to the side of the choir stalls to give the unimpeded view of the altar down the central nave.

The **choir stalls** themselves show some of the fine **carving of Grinling Gibbons:** the Lord Mayor's seat is distinguished by his sword and mace. In the North transept is **Holman Hunt**'s painting *The Light of the World*. Behind the modern altar is a memorial chapel to the American servicemen who lost their lives while stationed here during the Second World War. On the south side, a small exhibition shows St Paul's during the Blitz and a **monument to Nelson** with lions – a symbol that he died in battle.

If you have the puff do climb the steps to the **Whispering Gallery**; the views are beautiful and you can sit and survey the splendour. Keep climbing and you will come to two outside galleries that still give good views of the changing London skyline.

Downstairs in the **large crypt** are the **tombs of famous men**. Originally it was planned that Wren would be buried under the main dome – but pride of place was given to Nelson. Wren is buried to one side under the first foundation stone, and his famous memorial reads '*Lecter, si monumentum requiris, circumspice*' ('Reader, if you seek his monument, look about you'). Other tombs include those of artist **Joshua Reynolds**, and fighting men, such as Wellington. Memorials to those who died in the Falklands and the Gulf Wars can also be seen here. At the east end of the crypt is a small chapel housing the Royal Standards dedicated to the Order of the British Empire. If you have time visit the treasury containing the Cathedral's silverware.

Allow three hours to visit the cathedral, especially if you are doing a tour.

Information/tours/guides Guided tours by Friends of the Cathedral are at 11am, 11.30am, 1.30pm and 2pm. They last 1½ hours, and cost £2.50 for an adult, £2 for a student or senior citizen, and £1 for a child. They are recommended especially because they take you into some of the places that you can't otherwise access. Audio tours are also available between 8.45am and 3.30pm, and last 45 minutes. They cost £3 for an adult, £2 for a student or senior citizen, and £7 for a family ticket. The map of the site is free, the guidebook costs £3 and the activity book for children £1.99.

When to visit Mid-winter is a good time to visit. Big groups tend to go early in the day. Try to time your visit to coincide with a service. Weekday services are at 7.30am, 8am, 12.30pm and 5pm. On Sundays they are at 8am, 10.15am, 11.30am, 3.15pm and 6pm. The choir sings on Sundays at 10.15am, 11.30am and 3.15pm, and most weekdays at 5pm.

Age appeal The cathedral's history will interest young and old alike.

Food and drink A reasonably priced self-service café and an expensive table-service restaurant are in the crypt. A baguette and soup in the café cost £4.85, while in the restaurant the chocolate truffle torte and cream will set you back £3.50, and a pot of tea for one £1.25.

Shops The wide range of items on sale in the shop in the crypt include souvenirs, gifts, books and CDs.

🚌 From Blackfriars Bridge, up New Bridge Street and Ludgate Hill. NCP car park in Paternoster Square (£2.40 for 1 hour). ⊖ Nearest Underground station is St Paul's (Central line), then 5-minute walk. Nearest railway station is City Thameslink. Alternatively, buses 4, 8, 11, 15, 17, 23, 25, 26, 56, 76, 172, 242, 501 and 521 stop nearby. ◷ Mon to Sat, 8.30am to 4pm. *Café and shop* 9am to 5.30pm Mon to Sat, 10.30am to 5pm Sun. In Dec, tel in advance for additional closure times. 🖃 *Cathedral and crypt:* adult £4; child (6 to 16 yrs old) £2; student/disabled person/ senior citizen/unemployed person £3.50. *Cathedral, crypt and galleries:* adult £5; child £2.50; concession £4. Group rates available. ♿ Access to ground floor and crypt from the south side of the cathedral.

Syon House and Park

Syon Park, London Road, Brentford, Middlesex TW8 8JF ☎ 020-8560 0881

Quality ★★★★ **Facilities 🏛 🏛 🏛 🏛** **Value for money £££**

Highlights Entrance hall illustrating Robert Adam style and the wonderful Great Conservatory; lots for families to see and do within the grounds

Drawbacks A bit pricey

What's there The first building on this site was a Bridgettine abbey, established in 1431, which fell victim to Henry VIII's Dissolution of the Monasteries. In 1547 Edward VI gave the estate to his 'Protector', the Duke of Somerset, who pulled down the abbey and built a grand Tudor house. By 1761 the property had passed to Sir Hugh Smithson (later Duke of Northumberland), who asked Robert Adam to remodel the house. Adam's interiors, in vivid contrast to the building's uninviting exterior, are a delight – magnificent without being overpowering.

The public is admitted to the grand ground-floor rooms surrounding the central courtyard of the house, which is still the home of the Duke of Northumberland (the Percy family). The **entrance hall**, unrecognisable as the former timbered hall of the Tudor mansion, is a double cube of Italianate splendour. The shapes of the coffered ceiling are echoed in the mosaic of the floor below, and statues line the walls. At either end is a domed recess, one framing a statue of Apollo, the other Valadier's *Dying Gaul*, a moving study in bronze.

If the entrance hall has Roman connotations, so too does the **anteroom** beyond. Approximately cubic, with gilded columns and gilded statues of gods and goddesses, its architecture suggests that of a Roman villa, though perhaps no Roman interior was quite as flamboyant as this one. The striking design of the scagliola **floor** (a very rare material for so large an expanse and probably the only surviving example left today) is alluded to in other parts of the house.

The **dining room** was intended for entertaining on a lavish scale, though it is not an especially large room. Again, the décor is aglow with gilding – on the ceiling and columns, as well as in the tables and lamps – and more marble statues of deities survey the scene. At the far end of the room a musical clock, surmounted by a globe, stands in a corner on a scagliola stand, and nearby are busts of the 4th Duke and Duchess of Northumberland, who no doubt hosted some great occasions in this room.

The **red drawing room** contains yet another magnificent **ceiling**, this one incorporating 236 medallions by Cipriani. Its walls are lined with rich red silk – purportedly the first instance of silk being used as a wallcovering. **Portraits** by **Van Dyck** and Gerard von Honthorst (his study of Elisabeth of Bohemia indicating the family's link to the House of Hanover) hang in this room.

The **long gallery**, where exercise could be taken in bad weather, looks out on to the garden and the water meadows separated from it by a ha-ha. Formerly panelled in dark wood and rather tunnel-like, the impression now is of a light and airy space for relaxation. It is not a picture gallery, but contains books, furniture and many personal items belonging to the family. At each end is a small, exquisite boudoir.

The **print room** is used to display portraits of many of the house's former occupants, including the doomed Lady Jane Grey, and some of their possessions, such as the 1st Duke's coronet, worn at George III's coronation.

The **west corridor**, a nineteenth-century addition, runs along the side of the house to the main staircase. In this passage hang many more paintings – among them Van Dyck, Lely and Holbein portraits, especially of royalty. Majolica plates, a glass painting of Belshazzar's feast, a large framed map of 'Istelworth' (featuring annotations for tourists), equestrian bronzes and various curios can also be seen here.

The windows of the west corridor look out into the inner courtyard, with its formal beds and pool containing a fountain. Opposite on the roof stands the figure of a proud lion, tail outstretched – the symbol of the Northumberland family.

'Capability' Brown created the **garden** at the time of the 1st Duke. Its 35 acres include a man-made lake, fringed with willows and giant gunnera, a rose garden, some 3,000 trees (200 different species), wooded walks, a statue of the Roman goddess Flora, and the **Great Conservatory**, built by Charles Fowler. Extensively restored in 1987 by the 10th Duke of Northumberland, this *tour de force* was a strong influence on Joseph Paxton's design for the Crystal Palace.

Information/tours/guides An audio tour is included in the entrance fee, as is a plan of the garden. Allow 2 to 3 hours for a trip around the house and gardens, longer if visiting other Syon Park attractions.

When to visit To see the house, come between April and October. If you come out of season, you will find a lot to enjoy in the gardens, and the 'other facilities' will be open too.

Age appeal Mainly appealing to adults, Syon Park does, however, have much to interest children besides the house, including (at weekends and on bank holidays) the miniature steam railway in the garden. Syon Park also has a butterfly house, aquatic centre and an indoor adventure playground.

Food and drink The cafeteria next to the shop/ticket desk for the house serves tea and coffee (both £1), Danish pastries (£1.25), scones (£1.15), soups

(£2.50) and main dishes (e.g. chilli or peppered steak, deep-fried haddock, roasted stuffed peppers), all £6.50.

Shops The National Trust runs both the ticket counter and the shop, which has a typical range of National Trust merchandise.

Other facilities Syon Park's garden centre must be at least as famous as the house and garden. Also in the grounds are a farm shop, banqueting centre, needlecraft shop, art centre and trout fishery, as well as the attractions mentioned above.

🚗 Just south of the A4, on A315 between Hounslow and Brentford; enter by Park Road. Car parking. ⊖ Nearest Underground station is Gunnersbury (District line). Buses 237 and 267 stop at pedestrian entrance (Brent Lea). ⏱ *Syon House* Mar to Oct, Wed, Thur and Sun, 11am to 5pm. *Gardens* open all year, Mon to Sun, 10am to 5.30pm (closed 25, 26 Dec). *Steam railway* (extra charge) open Apr to Oct, weekends and Bank Hols. 💷 *House and garden* adult £6; student, senior citizen, disabled person, unemployed person, child (5 to 16 yrs old) £4.50; family ticket (2 adults + 2 children) £15. *Gardens only* adult £3; student, senior citizen and child £2.50; family ticket £7. ♿ Generally good. Woodland paths in garden can get muddy. Disabled toilets.

Tate Gallery

Millbank, London SW1P 4RG ☎ *020-7887 8000* 🖥 *www.tate.org.uk*

Quality ★★★★★   **Facilities 🏛🏛🏛🏛**   **Value for money ££££**
Highlights Extensive collection of stimulating painting and sculpture
Drawbacks Collection about to be split when we inspected, so lots of building work going on

---

What's there The Tate holds two vast collections of paintings and sculptures: British art since 1500, and international modern and contemporary art. In May 2000 the latter is to be moved to new premises in Bankside Power Station on the South Bank, and named Tate Modern. The building at Millbank will be renamed Tate Britain and retain the British collection. During our inspection, drilling and construction work was taking place as part of a programme of improvements known as the Centenary Development, with the aim of creating a new entrance, full disabled access and improved visitor facilities. These are due to be completed by spring 2001. Descriptions of exhibitions and facilities here are therefore subject to change.

Amongst the British paintings are bawdy scenes of London life depicted by **Hogarth**, portraits by **Gainsborough**, the semi-religious work of **William Blake**, and work by a number of the **Pre-Raphaelites**, including John William Waterhouse's *The Lady of Shallot*. The Clore Gallery houses the magnificent **Turner Bequest**, while **Francis Bacon**'s twisted images represent one of the giants of twentieth-century art. The annual controversy over the Turner Prize, with which the Tate is linked, usually brings in visitors to admire or tut over the shortlisted exhibitors.

On the international side, **Picasso**'s famous *Weeping Woman* and *Three Dancers*, the frenetic work of **Jackson Pollock**, and **Andy Warhol**'s multiple homage to Marilyn Monroe rub shoulders with works by **Matisse**, **Duchamp**, **Giacometti** and **Rothko**.

Information/tours/guides A guided tour of highlights takes place at 3.30pm (3pm on Saturdays). The guides themselves are not only well-informed, but also thought-provoking, animating the groups into interesting discussion. Other events are on offer with a more specialised theme – 'The Turner Collection' or 'Masters of Modern Sculpture', for instance – but these change monthly. In addition, each month a different painting is selected as the subject of a 15-minute talk, which is held in front of the painting on Mondays at 1.15pm and Saturdays at 2.30pm. Details of talks and events are listed in the 'Tate Events' brochure, available from the foyer.

Audio tours are available for £4 (£3 OAP/student/unemployed/disabled); these focus on key pieces and give fascinating details about the artist and place them in a historical framework. They last about two hours, and are highly recommended. A pocket guide (£2.95) and a companion guide (£14.95) are available from the bookshop but these will be replaced when the new gallery opens on the South Bank.

When to visit The gallery is visited by large parties of schoolchildren and tourists, who can usually be avoided by going late in the afternoon.

Age appeal Every Sunday from 2pm to 5pm the 'Art Trolley' – a series of kids' activities, games and gallery trails – makes the gallery appealing to children. Free children's trail leaflets are also available at the reception.

Food and drink The basement houses a café for refreshments and food, and an espresso bar, although these are somewhat pricey (tea £2.10, cappuccino £2.30). There is also a fairly swanky restaurant for a more formal meal (such as seared fillet of salmon £14, aubergine Parmigiana £13.50).

Shops The shop has a wide range of good-quality, relevant books (£15), postcards (£1.25) and prints (£2.50).

🚗 Parking available off John Islip street, behind the Tate and in Tate car park (pre-book). An NCP car park is on the other side of Vauxhall Bridge. ⊖ Nearest Underground station is Pimlico (Victoria line). Vauxhall station is the nearest railway station. Buses 88, 77a, C10 stop nearby. ⊙ Open all year, Mon to Sun 10am to 5.50pm. Closed 24–26 Dec. ⊞ Free. ♿ Access for wheelchairs through the Clore Gallery to the left of the main entrance, with lift access to all parts of the building.

Theatre Museum

Russell Street, Covent Garden, London WC2E 7PA ☎ *020-7836 7891*

Quality ★ ★	Facilities 🏛 🏛 🏛	Value for money ££

Highlights Enthusiastic guides and workshop staff; wide-ranging collection of video performances

Drawbacks Confusing layout; very dry information, some of which is of little interest to non-theatre buffs; lack of 'live' exhibits

---

What's there Housed in what was the Flower Market building of the old Covent Garden Market, the Theatre Museum is largely a historical collection of **theatrical memorabilia**. A ramp takes you down to the main gallery, past handprints from famous thespians, to the Paintings Gallery. Re-created to look like a foyer of an Edwardian theatre, the Gallery contains paintings, from the Somerset Maugham Collection, of famous British actors by such artists as **Reynolds** and **Zoffany**.

After a small section on the renovation of the Savoy Theatre to its original art-deco glory, you pass through the revolving doors into the Main Gallery. In the historical section a series of rather dry displays traces the development of theatre from Shakespeare onwards, including model stage sets, costumes, handbills and prints. You can compare a **model of the Globe Theatre**, which was open to the elements and had no scenery, with one from the Restoration, designed by Sir Christopher Wren, fully enclosed and with a raked stage and perspective scenery. The work of famous personalities, including actor-manager David Garrick, dancer Marie Taglioni (the first to dance on pointes), opera singer Jenny Lind, actor Henry Irving and the clown Grimaldi, is also covered, as is the career of Lilian Baylis, whose opera, ballet and theatre companies grew into the English National Opera, the Royal Ballet and the Royal National Theatre.

'The Wind in the Willows' makes an effort to explain how a theatrical production is put together, describing the roles of designers, casting directors, props and lighting technicians; there's also a video of the cast in rehearsal, learning to mimic the movements of stoats and weasels.

The video on how the two-hour make-up for the *Phantom of the Opera* is created is informative and interesting. If you're searching for a particular performance, whether it be theatre, opera or ballet, try the National Video Archive of Stage Performance.

Overall, the displays are disappointingly static and dull, capturing little of the excitement or magic of a live theatrical performance. The quality of the historical collection is not in doubt, but most of the presentation and interpretation is likely to appeal to true theatre buffs only.

Information/tours/guides There's no guidebook, just a leaflet (in several languages) listing the highlights of the Main Gallery and showing a map of the layout. Even with the map, orientation is a bit confusing, as it's not always clear where one exhibition in the Main Gallery stops and another starts.

Most visitors would do best to go on a guided tour, which lasts about half an hour and runs daily at 11am, 2pm and 4pm. The guide enthusiastically runs through a brief history of theatre in England, from Shakespearean romps at the Globe to the twentieth century, mixing anecdotes with fact to make it more interesting and accessible.

The workshops and demonstrations are also very good. Make-up demonstrations last 30 minutes and are at 11.15am, 12pm, 1pm, 2.30pm, 3.30pm and 4.15pm, using volunteers from the audience to show how special effects are achieved. Costume workshops (at 12.30pm and 3pm, and lasting 30 minutes) give you the chance to parade around for a few minutes as an extra in an opera, or play Macbeth wrapped in ermine, while you learn about how outfits are put together.

When to visit Everything is under cover and in the basement, without natural light, which adds to the theatrical feel and means that it doesn't matter if it's raining or dark outside. Try to time your visit to coincide with a guided tour or workshop to get the most out of your visit. There's a changing programme of temporary exhibitions.

Age appeal Some of the temporary exhibitions may appeal to children, but the main displays have little to hold their interest, apart from the videos of making up for *Phantom of the Opera* or the rehearsals for *Wind in the Willows*. The workshops are a much better bet – the staff actively encourage little ones to handle puppets and try on costumes.

Food and drink There are no refreshment facilities in the museum itself, but plenty in the immediate area, including Café Valerie next door (good coffee and cakes as well as light meals). Your ticket allows you to be re-admitted on the same day.

Shops The small shop next to the ticket desk has a limited range of stock, including Shakespeare T-shirts (£10), magnetic poetry kits (£14.99), books on various aspects of theatre, greetings cards, mugs, posters and (mainly cinema) postcards.

Other facilities There is an unattended cloakroom off the Paintings Gallery, where you can secure coats, but nowhere safe to leave bags.

No private parking; meter parking nearby. ⊖ Nearest Underground station Covent Garden (Piccadilly line). ◷ Tues to Sun 10am to 6pm (last admission 5.30pm). Adult £4.50, child (16 years and under) free, students, senior citizens, unemployed, Westminster residents, members of Equity, Bectu and Musicians' Union, and registered disabled visitors £2.50. ♿ Wheelchair access good (no steps, only ramps). The small print on exhibition labels may be difficult for partially sighted visitors.

Tower Bridge Experience

Tower Bridge, London SE1 2UP ☎ *020-7378 1928/020-7403 3761*
✆ *enquiries@towerbridge.org.uk*

Quality ★★★   **Facilities ✔ ✔**   **Value for money ££**

Highlights Good photographic displays of construction; heavy machinery in the engine rooms

Drawbacks Poor presentation of information through talking dummies; tiny windows at the top to look through; expensive

What's there Tower Bridge – one of London's most distinctive landmarks, built between 1886 and 1894 – was one of Europe's most innovative feats of engineering in its time. The Tower Bridge Experience tells the story of why it was necessary to build the bridge, explains how it works and displays a series of pictures taken throughout the construction process. The tour through the bridge – up the north tower and down the south – is punctuated by a series of presentations given either by film or by electronic dummies talking in Cockney accents (foreign visitors are provided with handsets to translate).

Entrance is a through a conservatory-type structure tacked on to the north tower. Visitors are taken up in a lift to the first presentation: a large wall clock on a screen that goes backwards, with famous pictures and quotes from the various years it stops at. After about seven minutes, during which time it imparts no relevant information about the bridge, it arrives at the requisite year. The second presentation is up one level and is given by an electronic dummy bridge-employee, Harry Stoner, who talks about the bridge's history, and why the bridge was necessary. The third presentation is at the walkway level and covers the debate between city officials for and against the bridge's construction. Horace Jones, the bridge's designer, features in this as a holographic image.

The glassed-in walkways between the towers offer limited views through tiny postcard-sized openings, thanks to the latticework in the construction of the walkway. **Displays of photos** taken during construction and of contemporary artwork are shown here.

The south tower has a film presentation on how the bridge hydraulics work, after which visitors descend in a lift and walk down to the south side of the bridge, where entrance can also be gained to the **engine rooms**. You'll find a series of **hands-on displays,** which are popular with children, and some seriously **heavy machinery** that was used to lift the bridge – 655 times in its first month of operation alone. A short film is shown at the end of your visit.

A visit to the Tower Bridge Experience will take about 1½ hours.

Information/tours/guides The full-colour guidebook (£2.50) covers everything from the Roman occupation of London to the reinvention of the bridge as a tourist attraction. The staff seemed more interested in herding the maximum number of tourists through the various presentations rather than being concerned that people were enjoying the experience.

When to visit Avoid the tourist season if you want to miss the crowds. If you do go during the summer season, aim to arrive early in the day or quite late.

Age appeal Older children and adults will get more from the historical and mechanical explanations on the how and why of the bridge, and younger children will enjoy the hands-on kids' area in the engine rooms and the views up and down the river.

Food and drink Vending machines are the only source of food and drink on site.

Shops Built into the south tower just opposite the engine rooms, the shop is quite small and sells a rather uninspired selection of models of the bridge (£7.50), mugs (£2.50), key rings and pens (£1 to £2), jigsaws (£20) and assorted confectionery. It is, however, well laid out and has an excellent big window looking out on to the river.

🚌 By Tower Bridge. Car parking (with charge). ⊖ Nearest Underground station is Tower Hill (Circle and District lines). Nearest railway stations are London Bridge and Fenchurch Street and Tower Gateway (on Docklands Light Railway). Alternatively, buses 15, 42, 47, 78, 100, D1, P11 stop nearby, and the riverboat stops at Tower Pier. ⏱ Apr to Oct, 10am to 6.30pm, Nov to Mar 9.30am to 6pm. Last entry 75 minutes before closing. Closed 24, 25 Dec. 💷 Adult £6.25; child (5 to 15 yrs old) £4.25; student, senior citizen £4.25. Family tickets £14.25 to £24.25 (1 adult + 2 children to 2 adults + 4 children). Ring for more information. Group discounts for 10 or more. ♿ Fully accessible.

Tower of London

Tower Hill, London EC3N 4AB ☎ *020-7709 0765*
🖰 *www.tower-of-london.com/*

Quality ★★★★   **Facilities** 🏛 🏛 🏛   **Value for money** ££
Highlights   Guided tours by the Beefeaters
Drawbacks   Royal Fusiliers Museum; lack of catering facilities

What's there Her Majesty's Palace and Fortress, the Tower of London, dates from the reign of William the Conqueror (1066–87). The main attractions of the fortress are the White Tower, which is the oldest part of the complex, the Medieval Palace rooms, several wall walks with views of the Thames and, of course, the Crown Jewels exhibition.

The historically informative and entertaining **Beefeater tours** are the best way to learn about the tower – the tours are a must, as they bring the place to life far more successfully than any of the static displays on offer. The tours leave from the main gate and stop off at various points, such as **Traitor's Gate**, before concluding in the Chapel Royal of St Peter ad Vincula. The **White Tower** houses a series of excellent **exhibitions on armoury and weapons**, including an execution block from 1747 complete with a sixteenth-century beheading axe. The **Crown Jewels** display in the Waterloo Barracks is both impressive and well laid out, not least because it keeps everybody moving. The massive safe doors are almost as impressive as the gold and diamonds on show, and visitors stand on a moving walkway so there are no bottlenecks.

The Medieval Palace Rooms are interesting to stroll through – the presentation of information using story boards makes them rather hard work, though staff dressed in period costume help make the exhibit more appealing. The **wall walks** offer excellent views of the Thames and Tower Bridge but can get a bit crowded. The Royal Fusiliers Museum costs an extra 50 pence, is poorly laid out, cramped and only mildly fascinating unless the military is of specific interest to you. One military display that really is worth making the most of is the **Changing of the Guard**, so check at the information kiosk for times.

Allow at least three hours for your visit.

Information/tours/guides The Beefeater tours leave from the main entrance every half hour, and last about an hour. Three other tours are conducted at certain times, but arrive early, as numbers are limited. Check tour times on arrival. Tickets for these are free from the kiosk at the Lanthorn Tower.

The official Tower of London guidebook is available on entry for £3.50. Each of the attractions inside the fortress has its own explanatory leaflet, many of which are free.

When to visit Any time of year is a good time to visit, but in summer the crowds can be prohibitive. Queues can get very long and the wall walks irritatingly crowded.

Age appeal The appeal of the tower is broad and for all ages – the best of the attractions are the tours, the armouries, the Changing of the Guard and the Crown Jewels.

Food and drink An inadequate coffee cart by the south wall sells a tiny range of snacks, coffees, biscuits and canned drinks. You have to exit the tower if you want anything more substantial from the larger café outside, so don't forget to ask for a re-admission ticket if you would like to get back in later the same day.

Shops Several shops in various parts of the tower sell a range of uninspiring souvenirs and expensive trinkets. Coronation videos sell for £16.99, key rings £4.99, tapestry cushions £29.95, collectors' teaspoons £12.99 and preserves £2.99. A range of engraved glassware is also on offer.

🚗 By Tower Bridge. Car parking on Lower Thames Street (with charge). ⊖ Nearest Underground station is Tower Hill (Circle and District lines). Nearest railway stations are London Bridge and Fenchurch Street and Tower Gateway (on Docklands Light Railway). Alternatively, buses 15, 42, 47, 78, 100, D1, P11 stop nearby, and the riverboat stops at Tower Pier. ① Mar to Oct, Mon to Sat 9am (10am on Sun) to 5pm; Nov to Feb, Tues to Sat 9am to 4pm, 10am to 4pm Sun and Mon. Closed 24–26 Dec, 1 Jan. 💷 Adult £11; child (5 to15 yrs old) £7.30; child (under 5 yrs old) free; student, senior citizen, unemployed person, disabled person (carer free) £8.30; family ticket (2 adults + 3 children) £33. ♿ Very limited access for disabled visitors – only the Jewel House in Waterloo Barracks is on one level.

Victoria & Albert Museum

South Kensington, London SW7 2RL ☎ *020-7938 8500* 📍 *www.vam.ac.uk*

Quality ★★★★★ **Facilities** 🏛🏛🏛🏛🏛 **Value for money ££££**
Highlights Sheer quantity and quality of collection has something for everyone, but Cast Courts and the dress collection stand out
Drawbacks Expensive (it was previously free) as large collection is best seen in several visits rather than one marathon visit

---

What's there This great treasure-house of art and artefacts has been described as a three-dimensional archive of the fine and applied arts. In addition it is a contemporary showcase and an educational institution providing instruction and reference for students and researchers. Its contents cross every geographical and cultural boundary. One moment you could be gazing at a Yuan dynasty (1271–1368) carved wooden figure of a *luohan* (holy man), the next at a massive fig-leaf made to adorn the museum's plaster copy of Michelangelo's *David* when Queen Victoria was visiting, and a minute later you could be picturing yourself in a vertiginous pair of **Vivienne Westwood platform shoes**, *circa* 1993.

The sheer range and quantity of exhibits is mind-numbing: the works of art, craft and design come from Europe, America, the Far East, Southern Asia and the Middle East and span 15 centuries. There are two main types of gallery: art and design, in which objects are arranged by place or date to show their visual relationships and cultural influences; and materials and tech-niques (such as silver, glass, textiles, jewellery, metalwork, or sculpture and carving). Other halls reflect the work of individual artists, such as **William Morris**, **John Constable** and **Frank Lloyd Wright**, while temporary exhibi-tions might highlight that of Beatrix Potter or the Pre-Raphaelites, or a theme such as seventeenth-century embroidery or iconography in the time of Mao.

Among the galleries and exhibits are the medieval gallery and the **Becket** casket (1180, gilded enamel), which once held the relics of St Thomas Becket, whose murder is depicted on the side; Tippoo's tiger, a fantastic mechanical toy (1790), in the India gallery (with audio-visual explanation); the **Raphael cartoons** (in the eponymous gallery), which were designs for Sistine Chapel tapestries; and the plaster replicas in the **Cast Courts** of, for example, the portal of the cathedral of Santiago de Compostela, Trajan's column in Rome and Ghiberti's bronze doors for the Baptistry in Florence. The vast Ardabil carpet (sixteenth-century) is found on the wall of the Islamic gallery. You'll also find **Canova**'s *Three Graces* (1814–17) and, by way of contrast, Agostino Carlino's bluff *Joshua Ward* (a quack doctor and philanthropist, who lived 1686–1761) in the sculpture gallery (the *Graces* will move to the British galleries in 2001). Within the dress collection, the preposterous, spectacular **court dresses** of the George II period sport side hoops wide enough to clear a swathe through any gathering.

Information/tours/guides Most exhibits carry informative labelling, though some (as in the dress collection) are poorly lit and difficult to read. A map of the museum is provided at the entrance, where there is also a list of gallery tours. Free introductory tours are held four or five times a day, take an hour and are very rewarding. Focusing on just a few objects chosen by the lecturer, they provide insights into distant times and cultures. More specialised introductory talks (for example, on the art and design of different cultures) are given twice a day. Gallery talks (for example, on 1960s photographs, or silver for the eighteenth-century dining table), lasting 45 minutes, are given once a day. All are free. In addition there are themed 'trails' highlighting specific exhibits (leaflet at entrance), and an ongoing programme of drop-in events (see leaflet). Other talks, lectures, demonstrations and workshops are offered on a regular basis.

When to visit Any time.

Age appeal The museum takes great care to be accessible to all, holding regular family activities/discovery trails and multi-cultural performances and demonstrations. Small folding chairs are provided for older visitors feeling foot-sore.

Food and drink The V&A's restaurant is justly popular, offering high-quality food all day. Coffee and tea are available outside the lunch period (11.30am to 3pm). The menu includes soups, salads, sandwiches, main courses (£5.95 to £6.95) and wine.

Shops There are two shops, the one at the entrance being a lofty, dazzling hall, flanked with architectural exhibits (an Adam façade, a French sixteenth-century staircase) and filled with displays of merchandise. As well as books on all aspects of art and design (*100 Highlights of the V&A*, £4.95, is a popular souvenir), the shop carries pictures, tapestries, jigsaws, postcards and greetings cards, calendars, tapestry cushions, Victoria and Albert paperweights (£5.95), sweatshirts and ties, modern ceramics, specially commissioned jewellery, tiles, chocolate mints – and a grand reproduction wine cooler at £195.

On A4, Cromwell Road, but not advisable (street parking limited and expensive).
Nearest Undergound station is South Kensington (District and Circle lines). Buses C1,

14 and 74 go to Cromwell Road entrance. ⏰ Mon to Sun 10am to 5.45pm (6.30pm to 9.30pm Wed late seasonal viewing). Closed 24–26 Dec. 💷 Adult £5; senior citizen £3; late viewing ticket £3. Free entry for all Mon to Sun 4.30pm to 5.45pm. Annual season ticket £15 (senior citizens £9). Admission free to under-18s, students, pre-booked educational groups, disabled visitors plus 1–2 carers, ES40 holders. ♿ Good wheelchair facilities. Enter via Exhibition Road.

Vinopolis

1 Bank End, London SE1 9BU ☎ *020-7940 8300* 🌐 *www.vinopolis.co.uk*

Quality ★★★ **Facilities 🍷🍷🍷🍷** **Value for money £££**

Highlights Imaginative presentations and use of video; chance to sample wines as you go round; good but pricey food and shop

Drawbacks No admission prices displayed; difficult to take a break in the middle of the Wine Odyssey

What's there Vinopolis bills itself as a City of Wine – perhaps that should be more like a World of Wine, because most of the 21 rooms making up the centrepiece of the Wine Odyssey are dedicated to various wine regions round the globe, which you explore with the help of an audio guide (available in six different languages). Apart from one room on the origins of winemaking, there are no traditional display cases of exhibits – all the information is relayed through your headset. Some imagination has gone into the presentation – in Italy, for example, you can **sit on a Vespa** and watch the countryside of Piedmont or Tuscany flash before you on the screen, while in Australia you take a seat in a jet plane for a flight across the continent.

Of course one of the main attractions of this travelogue is the chance to taste some of the representative wines as you go around. When Vinopolis first opened the 200 wines available were kept all together in the Grand Tasting Halls at the end, but now they are spread throughout the exhibition. With your entry ticket you receive **five tasting tickets** that you exchange for samples of your choice; you also have the chance to buy another five tickets for £2.50 if the first five are not enough. The range of samples, as you might expect, is largely determined by the sponsors – for example, bottles from Gallo and Mondavi dominate the Californian wines.

Commentaries on the **audio guide** are by respected and well-known figures such as Jancis Robinson, Hugh Johnson and Oz Clarke. Some of the commentaries are triggered automatically – for example when you enter a new room or stand in front of a video screen. Most of the time, however, you key in a number of the recording you want to hear. The tape holds four hours' worth of information, but most of it is in chunks of less than a minute.

We experienced a few technical problems: sometimes the sound cut out unless we stood in exactly the right place; occasionally the automatic commentary kept repeating; and if we passed too close to the entrance to the next room the introductory recording was automatically triggered. The automatic triggering also makes it rather difficult to nip off to the loo halfway round – so make sure you go before you start drinking!

It is sometimes difficult to judge what level of knowledge is assumed. For example, grape varieties are given jokey names like Omar Shiraz or Maxine Merlot, but the display case of bottles of Tokaj, covered in an impressive layer of black mould, fails to explain what Tokaj actually is. And there is very little information or advice on the best way to taste wine (apart from the chance to identify the odours associated with corking, excess sulphur and mould) – surely an opportunity missed.

Brief tasting details on cards are provided for all wines, with space for you to make your own notes. Serving staff are uniformly good-natured and helpful, and are generally knowledgeable enthusiasts, happy to pass on their own views and opinions.

The Hess Collection of contemporary art had not opened at the time of our inspection.

Information/tours/guides Visitors are given a Vinopolis Passport when they enter, containing a map showing the layout of the rooms and brief descriptions of their contents, plus the location of the toilets and other facilities. Just as well, because there are no internal signposts.

When to visit Summer weekends are very busy; the rest of the time it is much quieter.

Age appeal Vinopolis is very much an adult attraction; visitors under 18 must be accompanied by an adult. Accompanied children aged 16 and over are allowed to taste the wines.

Food and drink Cantina Vinopolis offers a cheaper Refectory menu and a pricier Brasserie menu. Both show a heavy Italian influence: typical Refectory main courses might be artichoke, olive, Serrano ham and mozzarella pizza (£8.50) – extremely thin and crispy – or home-made spaghetti with oven-roasted tomatoes and basil pesto (£6.95). Brasserie main courses are meatier and cost £10 to 14. Service is efficient and charming (service charge of 12.5 per cent added to bills).

The wine bar Root & Branch had not opened at the time of our inspection.

Shops As you might expect, Vinopolis Vaults is a classy outfit that stocks everything discerning oenophiles could wish for – glasses by Riedel and Schott Zwiesel, corkscrews and coolers of every description, an interactive CD (£12.99), and Le Nez du Vin, little bottles containing aromas of great wines, from new-mown hay to chocolate and cinnamon (£290 for the full set). You can also buy other comestibles like cheese, olive oil, chocolate or coffee – and of course there's the Majestic Wine Warehouse. This is the only branch in the UK where you can buy wine by the bottle rather than the case. The wines featured in the tasting halls are displayed separately.

Other facilities The toilets are immaculate. Vinopolis Academy offers a series of wine-tasting courses for all levels from beginners to sommeliers and retailers.

🚗 Off A300 Southwark Bridge Road, but not recommended as limited parking (NCP car park on St Thomas Street). ⊖ Nearest Underground (and mainline) station is London Bridge (Northern line), then short walk. Buses 17, 21, 35, 40, 43, 45, 47, 48, 63, 133, 149, 344, 501, P3, P11 stop nearby. ① Open all year. Mon to Sun 10am to 5.30pm (last admission 4.30pm). Closed 25, 31 Dec, 1 Jan. 💷 1999 prices: Tickets are cheaper if you book in advance through Ticketmaster on 0870 4444 777 (pick them up at the desk). *In advance (on the door)* adult £10.50 (£11.50); child (15 yrs or under) £4.50 (£5); senior citizen £9.50 (£10.50). For £30 a year you can become a member of Club Vinopolis, which entitles you to free admission for a year, free admission for a guest up to five times during the same year, and various other offers and discounts (tel: 020-7940 8320 for information). ♿ Fully accessible with ramps and lifts; disabled toilets.

The Wallace Collection

Hertford House, Manchester Square, London W1M 6BN　☎ *020-7935 0627*
(020-7563 9551 for events)　🖳 *www.the-wallace-collection.org.uk*

Quality ★★★★　　　　**Facilities 🏛🏛**　　　　**Value for money £££££**
Highlights　Famous paintings in a beautiful setting in the heart of London; free
admission; good shop
Drawbacks　A minimal level of disruption while building work for Centenary Project
continues

What's there　This sumptuous gallery, just behind Selfridges, was owned by the Hertford family and was once the French embassy. Bequeathed to the nation (at her late husband's request) by Lady Wallace in 1897, the collection comprises fine mainly **seventeenth- and eighteenth-century paintings**, together with furniture, bronzes, porcelain, majolica, arms and armour. For non-experts, its attraction lies in the accessibility of the paintings, mostly by French, Dutch, British and Italian masters, and the opportunity to see some extremely famous works. Themed exhibitions are mounted from time to time to explore different facets of the collection, including *objets d'art*.

The museum occupies two floors and 25 rooms, so it is possible to see everything in one visit (half a day is ample), but if you want to concentrate on the best-known works you should head straight up the magnificent staircase, hung with large pastoral fantasies by Boucher, and make for room 22, the largest gallery, to see **Frans Hals'** *Laughing Cavalier*, Poussin's *Dance to the Music of Time*, **Titian's** *Perseus and Andromeda*, *The Adoration of the Shepherds* by **Murillo**, **Rubens'** *Rainbow Landscape*, **Rembrandt's** portrait of his son Titus, and large portraits by **Gainsborough**, **Reynolds** and **Lawrence**. Among the **Van Dyck** portraits are a pair representing Philippe Le Roy and his child-bride Marie de Raet, each accessorised by a dog that seems to reflect its owner's character.

Nearby in room 23, among scenes of military campaigns and portraits of soldiers, Scheffer's sensual *Francesca da Rimini* (a painting that mesmerised George Eliot) draws the eye. In room 24 **Fragonard's** *The Swing* may be too chocolate-box for today's tastes, but its exuberance is undeniable. The Venice of Canaletto and Guardi can be found in room 17. Dutch landscapes hang in this room and also in room 20. Displays of miniatures adorn rooms 23, 24 and 25.

Fine furniture and ornate French clocks can be seen throughout the museum, while four rooms on the ground floor contain arms and armour, including knights on horseback and elaborately decorated weaponry from both Europe and the Orient.

Information/tours/guides A free floor-plan leaflet is provided and paintings are clearly labelled; laminated information sheets are available in some rooms. *The Wallace Collection Guide*, £3.50, has concise descriptions and photographs. General guided tours are available on most days and talks on special subjects are given frequently. External specialists give many of the lectures, the programme for which is posted near the entrance. You can also phone ahead for details of the lecture schedule.

When to visit Any time of year. Air-conditioning will be up and working by early 2000.

Age appeal Mainly adult appeal, although child-friendly features include discovery-trail quizzes; family events (for example the chance to try armour and brandish weapons); a 'see-and-scratch' engraving workshop; eighteenth-century dancing; and how to make your own costume in the style of a Van Dyck portrait. Book ahead for the events, which cost £1.

Food and drink From June 2000 the Collection will have its own restaurant and sculpture garden, beneath a glass roof constructed over the courtyard. Refreshments can also be obtained at cafés in nearby Marylebone High Street.

Shops A small shop sells books and high-quality goods relevant to the collection, including tiny handbag mirrors (99p), jigsaw puzzles (£5.50), 'Sèvres' picnic plates (£3.99), silk ties (£18.99), miniature enamel teapots (£19.99) and decorative alarm clocks (£32).

Other facilities Toilets were in temporary accommodation when we visited, but were clean and well maintained.

🚗 Not advisable (limited parking). ⊖ Nearest Underground stations are Bond Street (Central and Jubilee lines), Baker Street (Metropolitan, Bakerloo, Jubilee, Hammersmith & City or Circle lines) or Marble Arch (Central line). Alternatively, a bus to Selfridges, a few minutes' walk away. ⏱ Mon to Sat 10am to 5pm, Sun 2pm to 5pm. Closed 24–26, 31 Dec; 1–3 Jan; Good Friday and May Day bank holiday. 💷 Free. ♿ Ramp to front entrance; lift to first floor; wheelchair available on request.

Westminster Abbey

Parliament Square, London SW1P 3PA ☎ *020-7222 5152*
🖰 *www.westminster-abbey.org*

Quality ★★★★   **Facilities** 🏛 🏛 🏛   **Value for money** £££
Highlights   Henry VII chapel; Poets' Corner; the quire and sanctuary
Drawbacks   Inadequate refreshment facilities; scruffy gift shop selling tacky tourist
         souvenirs

What's there The fascination of Westminster Abbey lies in its **collection of tombs, memorials and monuments** – not just of the English monarchy but of great figures of state, politics and the arts.

Most of the Abbey as it's seen today was built on the orders of Henry III between 1240 and 1269 (although the Bishop of London established a monastic community on the site around AD 960). The association of the abbey with the monarchy is a long one, with the coronation of every monarch since William I in 1066 having been held on this site. The Coronation Chair, made in 1301, is on display (minus the Stone of Scone, which was returned to Scotland in 1996) and is surprisingly covered in graffiti – an effect of being left unprotected from the general public for many years!

Highlights include the **Chapel of Henry VII** (the Lady Chapel) with Henry VII's elaborate tomb, and breathtakingly **intricate fan vaulting on the roof**, embellished with Tudor badges and pendants. In **Poets' Corner**, many of Britain's finest poets and writers, such as Chaucer, Spenser, Dickens and Shakespeare, are buried or commemorated. For conservation reasons there is no access to the Chapel of St Edward the Confessor except on a guided tour – otherwise you can only peer at it between other tombs.

Some tombs, such as that of Elizabeth I and her sister, Mary, can suffer from queues of people filing past in a narrow space. The **quire**, with its splendid stalls, and the **sanctuary** are where royal weddings and funerals take place. In front of the high altar is a Cosmati marble mosaic floor dating from 1268 – unfortunately, because you cannot walk up the carpeted steps towards the altar, it is rather difficult to see.

Information/tours/guides A free colour leaflet and plan shows the suggested route and picks out the highlights. Rather confusingly, however, the numbers on the map do not correspond with the numbers on the audio tour (£2), which lasts about an hour and provides an adequate amount of detail in a lively manner. The colour guidebook (£3) picks out highlights and gives a limited amount of information: for more detail and a full listing of all the monuments you will need to buy the densely packed official guide (£8). Guided tours (£3) run regularly and last about 1½ hours. The maximum number in a group is 25 and the minimum is six. Efforts to beat the crowds by arriving early can backfire – on the day we visited the 10am tour was cancelled as there were not enough people.

When to visit Any time is a good time to visit, although you may want to avoid peak summer season – at the busiest times Westminster Abbey can have 16,000 visitors a day.

Age appeal The abbey is one for older children and adults only.

Food and drink The refreshments area in the north cloister is very much an afterthought rather than an integral part of a visit. The location in the cloisters is not ideal, as it is in a narrow, busy throughway with very limited seating, mostly on cushions on stone cloister benches. Although atmospheric and pleasant on a warm sunny day, it would be miserable if cold and wet. A small selection of sandwiches (£1.75 to £2.35), Danish pastries, muffins, coffee (£1) and tea (95p) are on offer, but no hot food.

Shops Unappealing and unimaginatively laid out, the shop shows signs of wear and tear and is rather tatty. It sells a large selection of standard tourist souvenirs and trinkets: T-shirts (£9), baseball caps (£4), mugs (£3 to £7) and fudge (£3). In addition it offers a good choice of books to buy.

Other facilities No toilet facilities are on site, but there are public toilets across the road from the Abbey.

🚗 Not advised as very limited parking in the area. ⊖ Nearest Underground stations are Westminster (Circle and District and Jubilee lines) and St James Park (Circle and District lines), then short walk. Buses 11, 24, 211, 88, 3, 77a, 159, 12, 13 stop outside the abbey or nearby. ⏲ Mon to Fri 9am to 4.45pm (last admission 3.45pm). Sat 9am to 2.45pm (last admission 1.45pm). Visitors advised to ring abbey to confirm times as it can occasionally close to visitors owing to special services and events. 💷 Adult £5; student, senior citizen £3; unemployed person £2.50; child (11 to 16 yrs old) £2; family ticket (2 adults + 2 children) £10. Guided tours additional £3; sound guide £2 (includes free entry to the Chapter House, the Pyx Chamber and the Abbey Museum). Abbey ticket holders pay a further £1 for entry to the three museums. Prices for admission to museums otherwise: adult £2.50; student, senior citizen £1.90; child (5 to 15 yrs old) £1.30; child (under 5 yrs old) free. English Heritage members free. Disabled visitors free. ♿ Steps and uneven surfaces can make it difficult for visitors with problems with mobility. There are some ramps provided, but not all steps have ramps. Severely restricted access to the Lady Chapel and no access for the Chapter House and Pyx Chamber. The abbey produces a leaflet detailing disabled access (tel: 020-7222 7110 for details).

ENGLAND

Abbotsbury Swannery

New Barn Road, Abbotsbury, Dorset DT3 4JG ☎ *(01305) 871858*
✆ *estates@abbotsbury.co.uk*

Quality ★★★   **Facilities** 🛥 🛥 🛥   **Value for money** £££
Highlights Seeing swans at close quarters
Drawbacks Little interaction or imagination used in presentation of information

What's there For at least the last six centuries (as far as records go back), but perhaps even longer, a huge colony of mute swans has flocked to the saline lagoon sheltering behind Chesil Bank. They make it their home for about eight months of every year.

The swans begin to arrive at the site in March, after wintering in a spot further east down the Fleet, and by the end of April all the prime nesting spots are occupied. Cygnets are born throughout May and June. For the next few months you can then watch them taking their first faltering steps and by September possibly a few crash landings. Come October they've finished their apprenticeships and gained their wings. With plentiful food further east, they begin to disperse.

Back in the days when the land was owned by the Benedictine Monastery, life wasn't quite so rosy: there was a high possibility that they would end up stuffed, seasoned and devoured on a feast night. Nowadays, they are left in peace (eating swans is illegal), and are seemingly unperturbed by visitors walking through their nesting grounds. They still have some less life-threatening uses. In the moulting season (July and August), the feathers are collected and supplied to Lloyds of London, who still use them as quill pens for logging shipping and other losses. The shorter feathers are used on the helmets of the Queen's bodyguards.

There is little to do at the Swannery other than to admire these graceful creatures, and a couple of hours is plenty for a visit.

Information/tours/guides There is a short, basic audio-visual show every half hour and an informative but dry education hut. A new edition of the guidebook (£2) should be available in summer 2000. Children are encouraged to help with the twice-daily feeding sessions. Two walking trails offer lots of information for lovers of the countryside and of birds in particular.

When to visit It's best from June to September. Swan feeding is daily at 12pm and 4pm.

Age appeal There is a very basic 'Ugly Duckling Trail' for children to follow (50p) – completed pamphlets can be posted on site for a chance to win a small prize.

Food and drink Seating in the small café is limited, though some tables and chairs are placed outside in fine weather. The café serves plenty of good home-cooked food, including hotpots, pies and ready-made sandwiches. Cakes, from Dorset Apple to Farmhouse Fruit, are especially tempting.

Shops The Abbotsbury shop stocks plenty of books, including *Abbotsbury and the Swannery* (£4.95), classics from Thomas Hardy, and volumes on wildlife and walks. Lots of country produce, from preserves to fudge and biscuits, are also on sale.

🚌 On the B3157 coastal road between Weymouth and Bridport. ⊖ Train to Weymouth, then bus (daily in July and Aug) to Abbotsbury. ◷ 18 Mar to 29 Oct, 10am to 6pm. Last admission 5pm. 💷 Adult £5, child (5 to 15 yrs old) £3, senior citizen, student, disabled visitor (helpers free) £4.70, family ticket (2 adults + 2 children) £15. ♿ Flat site allows for easy access. Wheelchairs available for loan. Disabled parking and toilets.

Althorp House

Althorp, Northampton NN7 4HQ   ☎ *(01604) 770107*
booking line (0870) 167 9000   📠 *(01604) 770042*   🖱 *www.althorp.com*

Quality ★★★★   **Facilities** 👜👜👜👜👜   **Value for money £££**

Highlights   Touching tribute to Diana, Princess of Wales; helpful young staff; pre-booking system sets some limit on numbers

Drawbacks   Queues at the Diana exhibition; narrow route through the house

What's there The fine country home of the Spencer family is increasing in popularity, primarily because of a loving exhibition to Diana, Princess of Wales, and her grave. Start your visit in the house itself to appreciate Diana's aristocratic pedigree, although many of its treasures are overlooked as people crowd round the contemporary photographs. Entrance is into a striking Georgian hall with chequerboard floor, paintings of country pursuits and a high ceiling decorated with a frieze of fox heads and hounds. On the walls of the Painters Passage you can spot a self-portrait by Sir Joshua Reynolds, who painted various Spencer family members through three decades – including the young Lady Georgiana Spencer, later Duchess of Devonshire, whose picture is seen in the south drawing room. The books in the warm library are the remnants of the collection amassed by the 2nd Earl; at the time it was reckoned to be the finest private library in the world. The 3rd Earl, whose portrait as a young boy by Reynolds hangs over the fireplace, founded the Royal Agricultural Society, and pictures of his favourite cattle can be seen in the Sunderland Room. The saloon was formed by the roofing over of the courtyard of the original Elizabethan house, and it is here that you will see a near life-size portrait of Diana, high on the walls, and modern photographs in silver frames on the bookcases.

The stables have been converted by the current earl, Diana's brother, into a touching **exhibition of Diana's life**. The first room covers her childhood: if the crowds are too great to see the collection stop a while and watch the film taken by her father. In the display is a letter to him from Diana aged 8, with the poignant plea 'Will you write back?'. The wedding room is dominated by the Emanuel dress, worn with the Spencer tiara, and two bridesmaids' dresses – look out, too, for the Christmas card sent in 1980 'from your tap-dancing partner Charles'. Another room covers her charity work. As you walk into the next room, room 5, you are hit by the smell of roses: a huge pile of petals is heaped beneath a screen showing a short film that ends with the car bearing her coffin turning into the gates of Althorp. You can see the copy of the speech the Earl gave at her funeral and the original draft too. You emerge past a glass wall of condolence books and then into a display of frocks, which somehow seem to lose their glamour without her inside them.

Once outside you can walk through the grounds, including around the lake that surrounds her **island grave**. Many visitors just sit and gaze, while others take flowers to the memorial temple and read the inscriptions – including a quote from Diana herself as well as her brother. Allow about three hours for the visit.

Information/tours/guides You are strongly recommended to pre-book tickets for a specific morning or afternoon session (telephone (0870) 167 9000). The colour guidebook costs £3.50 and provides details on items in the house.

When to visit Althorp House is open only in July and August each year. If you book a morning ticket you can wander round the site all day and may be able to pop back into the house and exhibition if queues aren't too bad.

Age appeal It's one for the grown-ups, particularly fans of Diana. There's nothing for children.

Food and drink A well laid-out café (with ice-cream kiosk) serves snacks, including sandwiches, scones and hot and cold drinks.

Shops Upmarket gifts are displayed in cases. Items are well organised but it's not ideal if you like to touch before you buy.

Discouraged, but the park is five miles west of Northampton on the A428. Large car park. ⊖ Train to Northampton station, then Silverlink coach meets train (full details are sent with your tickets). ⊙ Mon to Sun, July and Aug, 9am to 5pm. Last admission at 4pm. ⊡ Pre-booked admission charges: adult £10; child (5 to 17 yrs old) £5; senior citizen £7.50. The upstairs is open some weekday mornings; pay £2 on the day to see the rooms. ⅊ Most areas accessible by wheelchair. Orange badge parking; shuttle bus from parking area to stable block.

Alton Towers

Alton, Staffordshire ST10 4DB ☎ *(08705) 204060*
www.alton-towers.co.uk

Quality ★★★★★ **Facilities** 🏠 🏠 **Value for money ££££**
Highlights Premier Division theme park with a wide variety of entertainment and high thrill factor
Drawbacks Prepare to queue for nearly everything in peak season

---

What's there Set in 500 acres of rolling Staffordshire countryside, Alton Towers was once a stately home. But Pugin's 'Towers' (the neo-Gothic house at the park's centre) and the fine terraced gardens are not what pull in the 2.3 million punters a year. What Alton Towers is rightly famous for is its collection of high-adrenaline rides. If plummeting and rocketing, hurtling and inverting are your thing, and if you are stirred by being shaken, this is the closest you'll get in the UK to fairground nirvana.

A tour of the white-knuckle rides starts with the venerable **Corkscrew**, still capable of impressing the kids of the kids who rode the first-ever double roll-over rollercoaster. Then it's back to the future with space-age **Oblivion** and its gut-wrenching 110km-per-hour vertical drop of some 60 metres. **Ripsaw,** although inspired by the old-fashioned swing-boat, has clever hydraulics and water jets that make for a good-humoured, topsy-turvy ride you might want to go on twice. But even the most blasé of thrill-seekers can expect their come-uppance on hi-tech **Nemesis.** Unlike most rides, based on cars that run on tracks, the seats here are suspended, leaving your legs and feet to dangle beneath you. The ride is a terrifying high-speed flight beneath an overhead circuit of tangled track, of whooshing down and up, turning over and over . . . .

The size and layout of the park make it an effective crowd-swallower. Parking is well organised, and a cable-car cuts down on the walking. There are around 10 separate areas of the park, each with its own distinctive theme – for example, the Forbidden Zone, with its crimson-coloured stream and rusting metal props, could almost be a set for a post-apocalypse science-fiction movie.

There is more to Alton Towers than the big-name rides, thanks to a wide range of more gentle attractions. Younger children (who may not meet the minimum height requirements on some of the main rides) will appreciate **Adventure Land** for its bouncy castles and ballrooms, along with sedate sit-on rides such as Old MacDonald's Tractor. There's an interactive eye-spy water ride in Storybook Land, and prehistoric Ug Land features regular live shows from a family of singing and dancing cave people.

The down side? The theme park is not in the first bloom of youth and, in parts, it's a bit scruffy. Bored queuers have left their mark in the form of graffiti and discarded chewing gum, some of the buildings are shabby, and one or two of the rides are overdue a makeover – Haunted House and Toyland won't impress even the younger element of this video-gaming generation. It's quite a pricey family day out, and the abundance of fairground stalls and amusement arcades, strategically placed at ride exits, dispels any idea that the fun is on an all-inclusive basis.

Information/tours/guides   When you buy your ticket you are given a map showing the layout of the park, with location of toilets, restaurants, picnic areas, and so on. It also gives the minimum height requirements of the different rides.

When to visit   In peak season expect to queue for an hour or more for the big rides (Oblivion, Nemesis, Corkscrew, Ripsaw) and for at least half that time for the lesser ones. And, come rain or shine, with no protection while you wait, prepare to get wet or hot. The system is otherwise well managed – queues meander around the landscaped park and are continuously on the move.

A new system of 'virtual queuing' for Oblivion and Nemesis kicks in when the queuing time reaches an hour. This allows you to pick up a timed ticket at the entrance of the ride that tells you when to come back for a place towards the front of the queue.

The volume of traffic could mean you queue to get into the park and to leave it. Check the brochure for the busy dates.

Age appeal   Adults and older children will love the state-of-the-art rides, while younger kids have Adventure Land and Storybook Land. Senior citizens get a hefty discount on admission, and the house and gardens provide them with more sedate amusement.

Food and drink The shortest queues of all might be for one of the uninspiring, but numerous, fast-food outlets – mostly take-away burgers, fried chicken or pizza from the high-street chains.

Shops These are everywhere. A wide range of souvenir hats, clothing (such as Oblivion sweatshirts) and soft toys is on offer from these outlets. Action photos of riders, frozen in rapture or terror, are available as passengers disembark from many of the rides.

Other facilities Pushchairs and lockers can be hired from Guest Services at the top of Tower Street.

🚐 Follow signposts from M1 junction 23a and M6 junction 15 (if travelling north); or M1 junction 28 and M6 junction 16 (if travelling south). ⊖ During peak season Midland Mainline, Virgin Trains and National Express coaches offer packages, including travel and entrance fee. For further details call Midland Mainline on (0345) 125678, Virgin Trains on (0345) 484950, or National Express on (0870) 5010104. ⊙ Mon to Sun, 1 Apr to 29 Oct 9.30am until an hour before the last ride closes. This varies throughout the year – check at the entrance or ring before you go. Staying at the Alton Towers Hotel allows you early access to the park before it opens to the public. 'Exclusive Ride Time' (XRT) also allows a limited number of pre-booked full-price ticket holders into the park 30 minutes before it opens to the public (tel (0990) 664466 for details). 💷 *Peak days:* adult £19.99; child £15.95; senior citizen/disabled visitor £11; family ticket (2 adults + 2 children) £59. *Off-peak days:* adult £14.95; child £11.95; senior citizen/disabled visitor £11; family ticket £49. Ring for details of peak and off-peak days. *Return following day:* £9.50. *Season ticket* (to all Tussauds Group attractions) £70. ♿ Well organised with wide, level walkways and special provision for access to many of the rides.

American Adventure World

Ilkeston, Derbyshire DE7 5SX   ☎ *(01773) 531521*
🖳 *www.adventureworld.co.uk*

Quality ★★ **Facilities 🎫 🎫 🎫** **Value for money ££££**
Highlights A good handful of thrilling rides; moderate queuing
Drawbacks Unconvincing American theme

What's there As you approach the park, built on a former colliery site, you will notice the striking contrast between the black silhouette of the abandoned winding gear and the giant silver arches of the SkyCoaster ride. The contrast between this park and its more celebrated neighbour, Alton Towers, is equally great. American Adventure is smaller, with no pretty gardens, and far fewer rides and attractions. But it is also significantly cheaper, and there is much less queuing.

The park is arranged around a large lake. Some very respectable thrills are on offer from the brace of rollercoasters – particularly the **Missile**, which sends you forwards through the loops, then backwards. There is an exciting, if tatty, log flume, and a sure-fire drenching on the Rocky Mountain Rapids. The prime attraction for thrill-seekers, however, is probably the **SkyCoaster**. This involves a military-style performance where you are fitted snugly into a parachute harness and suspended by cables attached to arches. With two companions, you are hauled 200 feet into the air, to be left hanging and helpless. But by this time it's too late to turn back. A pull on your ripcord plunges you into near-vertical free-fall before you revert into a giant flying arc 30 feet from the ground, like an oversized swing. Unlike a rollercoaster with its combination of hi-G force twists and turns, this is a one-hit wonder of a ride – but it's a big hit! (Unless you are in a group of three, expect to pay a supplement to fly the SkyCoaster – £7.50 to go in a duo, £15 single.)

The American theme works well in **Silver Street**, very similar to a Wild West film set, which includes at regular intervals throughout the day a fast-paced show of cowboys (and girls) on horseback. But elsewhere, even if the rides themselves are satisfying enough, the American theme wears thin. The Aztec Kingdom, hiding behind a Mount Rushmore-esque façade, is a disappointing indoor games area – mostly a slot-driven amusement arcade. And although Twin Loper is a perfectly respectable rollercoaster that wouldn't be out of place at an Atlantic City fairground, it feels as if it's simply been plonked down on a south Derbyshire field – as indeed it has.

Free daily shows included in the entry price cover Lazy Lil's Saloon Show, Horses of the Wild Frontier, and a musical revue featuring 'glow-in-the-dark' characters.

Information/tours/guides Height restrictions on some of the rides are clearly shown on the map you are given on entry. You're also given a leaflet about the show times.

When to visit A nice summer's day would be best as most of the time you are outdoors. But queues are probably shorter mid-week and in poor weather. Various special events throughout the year include Hallowe'en fireworks (telephone (01773) 531521 for details).

Age appeal The train ride, boat trip across the lake and high-rise viewing platform are more gentle diversions for younger children, and there is a much reduced price for senior citizens. The daily shows are also family-oriented and suitable for all ages.

Food and drink Appropriately enough there is fast food, but not of the quality Americans would typically expect. The sit-down Fisherman's Wharf, however, offers quite acceptable British café food. The Frisco Wharf and Blue Fin offer take-away menus, including fish and chips for £4.25 and a 'family' meal based on breaded fried chicken for £13.95.

Shops Several outlets sell souvenirs, although very little branded to the park or its American theme. There is also a shop making and selling fudge confectionery, and an array of coconut-shy-style stalls.

🚌 Between Derby and Nottingham, signposted from M1 junction 26. ⊖ Bus from Ilkeston (Ilkeston-Heanor route), then 5-minute walk. ① 15 Apr to 10 Sept, Mon to Sun, 10am to 5pm; 11 Sept to 8 Oct, Thur to Sun 10am to 5pm; 12 to 29 Oct, Mon to Sun 10am to 5pm. 💷 Adult (12 yrs old and above) £13.50; child (up to age 11 or over 0.9m tall) £10.50; child (under 0.9m tall) free; senior citizen £2.99; family tickets (2 adults + 2 children) £39.99. ♿ Flat, smooth pathways; access to most rides possible for wheelchair users.

Anne Hathaway's Cottage

Shottery, Nr Stratford-upon-Avon, Warwickshire CV37 9HH
☎ *(01789) 292100*
📱 *www.shakespeare.org.uk* 📱 *info@shakespeare.org.uk*

Quality ★ ★ ★ ★   **Facilities** 🏠 🏠 🏠 🏠   **Value for money ££££**
Highlights   Wonderfully pretty, well-kept English cottage and garden; good guides
Drawbacks   Can get crowded, and the 'batch' system of visiting the house means you have to move through quickly

What's there   Anne Hathaway's family home, where she was courted by William Shakespeare before they married in 1582, is a **picturesque farmhouse**. A well-maintained **garden** filled with herbs and flowers of the nineteenth century, as well as several species popular around the sixteenth century, surround the beamed and thatched house. Inside, visitors follow a set route through the hall, the buttery and cold room, the upstairs rooms, the kitchen, and a small exhibition of linen and garments from recent centuries. The furniture and cooking utensils in the house date from the sixteenth to the nineteenth centuries, and friendly and knowledgeable guides tell anecdotal stories about the various pieces. You can even sit on the settle where Shakespeare is supposed to have parked his literary bottom. Guides explain the origins of expressions such as 'rule of thumb' and why beds had half testers – to stop rats falling from the roof above (ceilings had not yet been invented) on to the bed!

Outside, an orchard provides views over the fields that were once worked by the Hathaway family. In the newly planted Tree Garden, those trees mentioned in Shakespeare's plays, including aspens, elms, crab-apple trees and hawthorns, have quotations from his plays at the base of their trunks.

Allow 20 minutes to view the house, and an hour for the gardens, orchard and Tree Garden.

Information/tours/guides   A batch system operates in the house, whereby a guide waits until a group has accumulated before introducing the house and its contents in the hall. You then walk through the house and are met at the end, in the kitchen, for questions. A glossy guidebook (£2.50), which covers all the Shakespeare houses including Shakespeare's Birthplace (*qv*), gives information on Anne Hathaway's house. Alternatively, there's a short guide to the house and gardens for only 25p.

When to visit   To make the most of the visit and to appreciate the pretty garden, it is best to come in good weather, although the cottage is picturesque all year round.

Age appeal   The cottage will appeal mainly to adults. Those who find stairs difficult will not be able to see the upstairs of the house.

Food and drink   The Thatch Restaurant, across the road from the house, is an attractive conservatory-style cafeteria set in another lovely garden by a brook. It serves up cheap and cheerful Cotswold fare: cottage pie, soup, steak and kidney pie (£2.50 to £4.50), as well as the usual sandwiches and cakes. It is licensed to sell wine and beer.

Shops   The shop – selling books on Shakespeare, scripts, aprons, jams, lilac bath salts, and models of the Globe Theatre – leads on to a garden centre, with herbs and garden and pot plants, as well as some interesting old gardening tools displayed on the walls.

🚌 In Shottery, 1 mile from Stratford-upon-Avon. Signposted from Alcester Rd (A422), Evesham Place and Evesham Road. Car park (30p). ⊖ Train to Stratford-upon-Avon, then 'Guide Friday' bus from Bridge Street. Alternatively, walk (over 1 mile) from the station if you have adequate directions/map. ⊙ 20 Mar to 19 Oct, daily 9am (9.30am Sun) to 5pm; 20 Oct to 19 Mar, daily 9.30am (10am Sun) to 4pm. 💷 Adult £4.20, child £1.70, senior citizen/student/unemployed visitor £3.70, family ticket (2 adults + 3 children) £10. *Inclusive ticket for all five Shakespeare houses:* adult £12, child £6, senior citizen/student/unemployed visitor £11, family ticket £29. ⑁ House inaccessible and garden only partly accessible.

Aquarium of the Lakes

Lakeside, Newby Bridge, Cumbria LA12 8AS   ☎ *(015395) 30153*

Quality ★ ★ ★   **Facilities** 🏛 🏛 🏛   **Value for money £££**
Highlights   Well-presented collection of freshwater fish
Drawbacks   More variety needed

What's there   This smallish aquarium on the shores of **Lake Windermere** has one of the largest collections of **freshwater fish** in the UK. It's unusual to have an aquarium dedicated to freshwater fish, and there's probably a very good reason for that – they're not that interesting.

What makes this one a bit more engaging is that it features other species too. The **otter enclosure** at the beginning of the tour has running water and a holt, which makes an attractive and realistic environment for the animals, despite the use of fake rocks. At the end of the visit there is also a seashore and saltwater exhibition, providing a bit more variety.

The aquarium does try to be inventive in its exploration of freshwater life: although the 'Riverbank at Night' has lots of not very interesting fish, it is in a darkened room lit by neon stars. The 'River Runs On' appears more like a series of fish tanks initially, but when it moves into the 'Lake Windermere' section, a bridge leads over an open pool with glass walls, allowing you to see the fish and ducks from above. Downstairs from here is the most interesting sight of all – seeing the **ducks diving down** to the bottom from the surface above.

'Aquaquest' is a more educational element where visitors can look close-up, quite literally, under microscopes, at lakeland life. You'll find some common British animals, such as grass snakes and mice, in tanks, as well as some basic **interactive experiments,** which, for example, allow you to create your own whirlpool.

For a touch of drama, go to the saltwater pool, which features local **sharks and rays** along with lobsters, crabs and other species; there are points at which you can touch some of them. Allow 1½ hours for a visit.

Information/tours/guides   There are no guides or tours, but a beautifully illustrated field sketch book (£2.99) tells you all about rivers and their wildlife.

When to visit It is all enclosed and under cover so, unless you want to go for a walk next to the lake afterwards, it's an ideal rainy-day venue if you're in the area.

Age appeal The educational and interactive element is good for children and may appeal to adults, especially those with an interest in fish.

Food and drink The self-service café, in a separate purpose-built block next to the aquarium, has wonderful views of the lake, although the food is poorly presented – mostly unappealing pre-packed sandwiches, baked potatoes, scones and cakes.

Shops The brightly lit shop has, not surprisingly, a strong fishy theme, with everything from whale and shark T-shirts to ornaments, cuddly toys, games and a few books.

From M6 junction 36, take the A590 to Newby Bridge. Follow the signs from there. Train to Ulverston, then X35 bus to Newby Bridge and a 10-minute walk. Mon to Sun 9am to 5pm (closed 25 Dec). Adult £5.20, child (3 to 16 yrs old) £3.95, senior citizen/student £4.75, family ticket (2 adults + 3 children) £16.95. Full access, with lift and disabled toilets.

Ashmolean Museum

Beaumont Street, Oxford OX1 2PH   ☎ *(01865) 278000*
🖰 *www.ashmol.ox.ac.uk*

Quality ★ ★   **Facilities** 🏛 🏛 🏛 🏛   **Value for money** £££££
Highlights Wealth of material spanning the fields of art and archaeology; free admission
Drawbacks Extremely dated labelling; poor service in the restaurant

---

What's there From its controversial opening in 1638, when it was received with mixed acclaim, the Ashmolean has gone on to become one of the foremost collections of art and archaeology in United Kingdom. Now there is little left of Elias Ashmole's original bequest apart from Tradescant's Room (John Tradescant, head gardener to Charles I, built up the collection that passed to Ashmole). This is a fascinating cabinet of curiosities from the days of exploration, where visitors can still see Powhatan's Mantle – a decorated deerskin once thought to have been worn by the 'King of Virginia'.

It was around the turn of the nineteenth century that the museum really found its current feet under the directorship of Arthur Evans – the discoverer of Knossos. The natural history and anthropology collections were dumped in favour of archaeological material and classical bronzes, which all soon found their way into their present grand home on Beaumont Street, where they were to join forces with the university's art collections.

Today, the museum contains three main departments – **Antiquities**, **Western Art** and **Eastern Art** – and nearly 60 rooms: enough to keep you occupied for at least a week. Within the Department of Antiquities are artefacts from the Stone Age onwards, including a huge gallery of **classical sculpture** and, within the Egyptian rooms, an entire carved-stone shrine from the temple of Taharqa with its wonderfully evocative depiction of the Kushite king making offerings to the ram-headed Amon-Re. In the Department of Eastern Art, works range geographically from Asia Minor to Japan and chronologically from the Indus civilisation of ancient Pakistan to the Mughal lords of India. In the Department of Western Art, paintings and sketches from the Middle Ages onwards include works from such famous artists as **Giotto**, **Michelangelo**, **Rembrandt**, **Constable**, **Turner**, **Van Gogh** and **Picasso**, to name but a few. A collection of musical instruments even includes Stradivari's 'Messiah' violin of 1716.

Unfortunately, the quality of the presentation has not kept pace with the splendour of the collection, and many of the handwritten labels are virtually museum pieces themselves. This makes much of the Ashmolean, especially the archaeology, hard work for non-experts, who would be unable to establish a framework in which to make sense of what they are seeing. For instance, constant references to dynasties, rather than absolute dates, ensure that the Egyptian galleries remain the preserve of academics. Worse still, labelling from the 1920s can hardly incorporate more recent advances in knowledge, including the carbon-dating revolution of the 1950s. However, it is well worth visiting for the beauty and fascination of many of the items on display alone.

Information/tours/guides A map of the museum (50p) helps visitors to find their way around, but contains little more information than brief descriptions of some of the 'treasures'. An attractively presented but expensive souvenir guide (£6.95), *Treasures of the Ashmolean*, also contains very little general information. The rather infrequent gallery talks, which take place every Tuesday and Friday at 1.15pm (£1.50), are probably a better way to get to grips with parts of the collection. Monthly programmes are available from the Museum Information Desk and booking is recommended (telephone (01865) 278015). There are also Highlight Tours, which take place every Saturday morning at 11am (£1.50), and special tours for adults and children can be arranged through the Education Service (telephone (01865) 278015).

When to visit The museum is weather proof so any time is a good time.

Age appeal The sheer extent of the collection ensures that the Ashmolean has a very wide age appeal. In addition, children are specifically catered for by Gallery Trails.

Food and drink The attractive basement restaurant has a light, airy feel with its pillars and vaulting, and serves a tempting, if pricey, range of dishes made with good-quality ingredients, such as smoked-chicken salad with sundried tomatoes (£6.95) and fettucine with mozzarella, tomato and parmesan (£6.25). Unfortunately, although the museum was not particularly busy when we inspected, the service was extremely slow, inefficient and distinctly unfriendly on occasions.

Shops The well laid-out museum shop stocks a wide range of books on art and archaeology, postcards, greetings cards, calendars, diaries, jewellery, posters and some attractive replicas of artefacts.

🚌 Oxford city centre; car parks at nearby St Giles Street and Beaumont Street. ⊖ Train to Oxford station, then 10-minute walk. ⊙ Tue to Sat, 10am to 5pm; Sun and Bank

Holidays, 2pm to 5pm. Closed Mondays, Good Friday to Easter Sunday, 6 to 8 Sept (St Giles Fair), 25, 26 Dec. ⊞ Free. ⅰ Lift to all floors; four steps down to the first floor of Antiquities Galleries. Wheelchairs available for loan.

Audley End House

Audley End, Saffron Walden, Essex CB11 4JF   ☎ *(01799) 522842*
📠 *(01799) 521276*

Quality ★★★★   **Facilities** 🏛 🏛 🏛 🏛   **Value for money ££££**
Highlights Fantastic Jacobean ceilings; fine furnishings; newly restored organic
                walled gardens
Drawbacks Limited appeal for children

What's there Now in the care of English Heritage, Audley End was built for the 1st Earl of Suffolk, Thomas Howard, in the early seventeenth century. The Earl was Lord Treasurer for James I and hoped that he would stay in favour with the monarch long enough for James to come and visit him there – unfortunately for him, that did not happen. The house has been altered over the years, with two notable periods of expansion and enhancement: under Sir John Griffin Griffin a suite of reception rooms was added by architect **Robert Adam** in the late eighteenth century, and in the 1820s the owner Lord Braybrooke created several opulent reception rooms.

The set route through the house starts in the Great Hall, with its richly ornamented Jacobean oak screen at one end dating from 1605. The Jacobean theme was recreated by Lord Braybrooke, whose lavish schemes made great inroads into the family fortunes and whose descendants made no major changes to the house. The saloon has a fantastic **Jacobean plaster ceiling** with fish dolphins and sea monsters in bold relief. Upstairs, the picture gallery has a large collection of stuffed animals and birds whilst the chapel is a rare surviving example of the late eighteenth-century Gothick style with all the furniture intact. In the South Wing are the Robert Adam rooms, re-created in the 1960s and furnished with whatever original furniture survives. Throughout the house the picture collection includes some **Dutch Old Masters** and a **Canaletto**.

The River Cam runs through the extensive grounds. The landscaped park, devised by '**Capability Brown**', remains much as it was in the eighteenth century. The parterre garden stretches to the ha-ha at the rear of the house, the Elysian gardens include a bridge by Robert Adam and a cascade, and the walled kitchen gardens nearby have been re-established. Organic produce can be bought in the kitchen garden shop.

Information/tours/guides Short introductory talks (10–15 minutes) take place on the front lawn or in the Great Hall. Wardens are in most rooms and are informative and enthusiastic. The house guide (£3.95) and garden guide (£1.50) are glossy and detailed and provide enough information to explore both.

When to visit The gardens are best visited in dry weather. Various events take place in the grounds throughout the season.

Age appeal Not a lot in the house will interest children, though a leaflet for them has a short quiz.

Food and drink A waitress-service restaurant serves full meals such as spaghetti bolognese and chicken with potato wedges or jacket potatoes (£5.50), as well as sandwiches and cream teas (£3.50). A small coffee shop sells hot drinks and packaged cakes, and in summer, drinks and ice creams are available from the garden kiosk.

Shops The gift shop at the house entrance sells Audley End souvenirs including mugs, umbrellas, thimbles, Victorian and Georgian gardening books, toiletries and fudge.

Other facilities Disabled toilets and baby-changing facilities are available. Picnic tables are set out in grounds.

🚗 From M11, take junction 8 (junction 9 from Cambridge) and join B1383. Audley End is 12 miles from Stansted Airport. 🚇 Train to Audley End, 1½ miles from house. Taxis available at station. 🕐 1 Apr to 29 Oct, Wed to Sun and bank hol Mons 11am to 5pm. 💷 *House and gardens* adult £6.50; student/senior citizen £4.90; children (5 to 15 yrs old) £3.30; family ticket (2 adults + 3 children) £16.30. *Grounds only* adult £4.50; child £2.30; student/senior citizen £3.40; family ticket £11.30. ♿ All of grounds accessible. 3 electric buggies available for loan.

Babbacombe Model Village

Hampton Avenue, Torquay, Devon TQ1 3LA ☎ *(01803) 315315*
📧 *mvg@babbacombemodelvillage.co.uk* *www.babbacombemodelvillage.co.uk*

Quality ★ ★ ★   **Facilities 🏛 🏛 🏛**   **Value for money ££**
Highlights Well-cared-for miniature displays and gardens
Drawbacks Limited selection of food; souvenirs aimed mainly at children

---

What's there This model village has been on display to the public for over 30 years. The 4-acre site has **over 400 models** and figures that are one-twelfth their usual scale throughout. Mockington – based on the local thatched village of Cockington – is the epitome of an **English village**, with its thatched houses and narrow streets. There are examples of **Georgian and Tudor houses** too. Scarlet-coated huntsmen sit astride horses in the fields of Merrivale Farm, and further along the path is the 'House on Fire' complete with a blazing roof, firemen and a fire engine. The village is also **illuminated at night**.

The original idea – to portray the English countryside – has been broadened out to include minor industrial buildings, a model city and displays on the environment. There is even a tiny **scale model of Stonehenge**, a **miniature railway** and a waterfall that spills into the suitably scaled-down lake in the centre of the village.

Weather and earth satellite stations and world landmark sites are more recent additions. An indoor exhibition area of push-button display boxes tells the story of dinosaurs, the Stone Age, Vikings and Victorian England.

The site is splendidly landscaped and has an impressive collection of shrubs and dwarf conifers and carefully tended lawns. A complete duplicate set of all the models and figures allows the models to be changed and thoroughly renovated each spring. A visit will take at least two hours.

Information/tours/guides A full-colour guidebook (£1.50) covers the background and development of the village and some of the more popular displays and the gardens. A puzzle leaflet (free) for children includes a treasure trail to find the cartoon character Wally, who is hidden among the figures of one of the displays.

When to visit It's best to visit in good weather. The village is illuminated at night, with special 'Santaland Illuminations' over the Christmas period.

Age appeal The model village will appeal to all age groups, but small children may need help with the steep steps leading down from the arrival area into the village.

Food and drink The self-service tea room serves a limited choice of sandwiches and cakes. Cream teas, ice-cream and hot and cold drinks are also sold, but no hot food. Surroundings are modern and fresh with views over the village.

Shops The shop's small range of goods is aimed predominantly at children. Colouring books sat alongside a greenish concoction called Alien Slime when we inspected. Paperweights, bookmarks, fridge magnets and a souvenir video are also available.

🚗 Follow brown signs from Torquay town centre (1 mile away from centre). ⊖ Train to Torquay station, then bus (tel (01803) 613226 for details). Alternatively, free bus (11am to 5pm, Apr to Sept) from Torquay harbour (visitors must buy their tickets to the Village on the bus). ⏱ Easter to June, Mon to Sun 9.30am to 10pm; July to Aug, Mon to Sun 9am to 10pm; Sept 9.30am to 10pm; Oct 9.30am to 9pm; Nov to Easter, Mon to Sun 10am to dusk. Santaland Illuminations 9, 10, 16 to 23 Dec; *general illuminations* Easter to Oct. Closed 25 Dec. 💷 Adult £4.60; child (3 to 14 yrs old) £3; family ticket (2 adults + 2 children) £13.50; disabled visitors £3.40; wheelchair users free. Return visit: adult £2.50; child £1.50; family ticket £5.50. ♿ Wide, shallow steps from entrance to village and steep hill up to tea shop. A few wheelchairs are available for loan (free) but must be pre-booked.

Bamburgh Castle

Bamburgh, Northumberland NE69 7DF ☎ *(01668) 214515*

Quality ★   **Facilities** 🏠 🏠   **Value for money £££**
Highlights Magnificent setting and wonderful views; some interesting display items
Drawbacks Very old-fashioned presentation; a generally unloved atmosphere

---

What's there How are the mighty fallen! This once-great frontier fortress, built by the Normans as one of the strongest places in England, and a constant bastion against subsequent invasion, is now reduced to the kind of dismal tourist sight that leaves the visitor more depressed on exit than on entry.

Doomed as a fortress by the invention of artillery, Bamburgh suffered: first, neglect and ruination; second, a bizarre existence as a charitable institution for orphans; and finally life as a military hospital during the First World War and as military headquarters during the Second World War. 'Restored' and reconstructed according to the tastes and purses of its owners – most notably in the late nineteenth century by the 1st Lord Armstrong, engineer and armaments manufacturer *extraordinaire* – it appears now with the remnants of its Norman fortifications converted and extended into a High Gothic fantasy of medievalism.

There is a great deal that should be fascinating in this history, for the castle abounds in stories. But alas, what the visitor finds is just objects, not stories, and is left the poorer for it. For example, a page of neat copperplate handwriting from the days when the castle took in orphan girls and trained them to domestic service arouses questions that the visitor longs to have answered. What manner of life did these girls lead, here, in the middle of nowhere, under Dr John Sharpe, trustee of the charitable institution? What became of them? Why did the Russian ambassador of the time give the 1st Lord Armstrong the **collection of Asiatic armour**? Why should anyone want to re-create a medieval hall, complete with hammerbeam ceiling, in his new home? We are not told. Hand-written labels attached to display cases and a dry-as-dust description in the guidebook is as much enlightenment as is provided. Here is a place that cries out for someone to expend money and imagination to bring it to life. So far, it appears to have received neither.

It is not all disappointment, however. Bamburgh's setting is magnificent. The **Norman curtain walls** and **the keep** are perched high on a plug of basalt, and the **views** out over the sea to Lindisfarne and Holy Island are unparalleled. Approaching the castle, you can still feel overawed by it, and can imagine what a potent force it represented in medieval power politics.

Tucked away among the jumble of buildings, the **Armstrong museum**, for anyone faintly interested in engineering, is one of the better parts of the attraction, for there are pieces of aeroplane, models of hydraulic pumps and cogent explanations of the items on display.

Information/tours/guides Room guides may or may not be on hand. The guidebook (£1.50) is useful for the history of the castle and for a catalogue of the objects on display (some very interesting). Arrows point you from room to room, but it is sometimes hard to work out where you are. A fingerpost in the main courtyard indicates the various facilities.

When to visit Choose a windless day with good light for the sake of the views, which are worth lingering over.

Age appeal There's nothing special for children. The dungeon just might provide a chilling moment.

Food and drink The clocktower tea room is a respite from the wind, and a genial place. There's a mish-mash of décor: stags' heads, huge iron plates on the walls, and bunches of dried flowers. A fair range of snacks is on sale, including toasted sandwiches (£1.75 to £1.90), soup and roll (£1.85), toasted teacake (£1.45) and coffee (90p). A sandwich of locally caught crab (£2.55) is about as ambitious as it gets.

Shops The penultimate room on the tour is crammed full of merchandise, and the big notice about paying for breakages may well be needed. It's a classic souvenir shop with a wide range of small items, many of them branded.

Bamburgh Castle jam retails for a respectable £1.85, the mug is £3.30, and bookmark 50p. The many small items include horse brasses (£3.30) and magnetic writing pads (99p). There is a good selection of books on Northumberland and the area surrounding Bamburgh. All in all it is not wildly inspiring, but worth a quick rummage.

🚗 North of Alnwick, A1 then B1341. Small car park (70p) by entrance gate. ⊖ A bus runs to Bamburgh from Berwick or Alnwick approximately every 2 hours during the summer months. ⊙ 25 May to 31 Oct, Mon to Sun, 11am to 5pm (last admission 4.30pm). ▣ Adult £4, child £1.50, senior citizen £3. Free entry for wheelchair users. ♿ Access to the castle courtyard. Possible access to some ground-floor rooms (telephone for details).

Banham Zoo

The Grove, Banham, Norfolk NR16 2HE ☎ *(01953) 887771*
⌴ *www.banham-zoo.co.uk*

Quality ★ ★ ★ ★   **Facilities 🐾 🐾 🐾 🐾**   **Value for money ££££**

Highlights   Shady, well-maintained zoo with imaginatively designed enclosures, appealing to all ages

Drawbacks   Shop sells too many gimmicky souvenirs and not enough educational, animal-related books or activity packs

What's there   Over 1,000 animals and birds housed in 30 acres of parkland range from big cats to birds of prey – including **endangered species**, such as **Sri Lankan leopards**. There is also an **Activity and Education Centre**, Parrot Pavilion Food Hall, Jungle Clearing adventure playground, the Children's Farm Barn and a small art gallery housing animal-related temporary exhibitions.

Being a relatively small zoo, there is particular emphasis on **interaction with the animals**, and encounter sessions are organised between children and the more domesticated creatures.

Animals are housed in well-landscaped enclosures with effective use of woodland and water to create appealingly shady and varied environments. Cages are imaginatively designed to give animals space to move and conditions appropriate to their natural habitats. A good example is the **Tiger Territory**, which was recently built at a cost of over £100,000 and is a 2-acre setting of grassland and rock pools. Other attractions include a monkey house, reptile house, penguin pool, falconry centre and lemur island, as well as zebras, camels and wolves.

A tour of the zoo takes half a day, but allow a day to take in feeding times, talks and displays that are arranged at regular intervals between 11.30am and 3.45pm.

Information/tours/guides   A useful, if not entirely accurate, map (25p), including feeding and talk times, is available from the ticket office. The guidebook was being updated when we inspected. Zoo staff are friendly and knowledgeable about the animals. A free safari Roadtrain tours the park at regular intervals, taking ten minutes (sporadic service on weekdays in winter). Child-friendly information boards are clearly displayed by each enclosure, and there are interactive quizzes in some areas with touch-sensitive screens.

When to visit The park is large enough to absorb its visitors successfully but inevitably times outside school holidays are quieter. As the exhibits are outside, it is not a place to visit in very wet weather. Special events include Easter Eggstravaganza, Christmas Magic and evening barbecues.

Age appeal Face painting, hands-on animal encounters and soft play areas are designed to appeal to small children, while older children can run around the adventure playground and have a go at the interactive quizzes. Falconry displays, the heavy horse heritage, and the art gallery appeal to adults.

Food and drink The Parrot Pavilion Food Hall is an airy, barn-like area with a self-service restaurant and well-maintained seating section. It serves hot food at lunchtime for around £4.50 including lasagne, burgers, chips and beans. Sandwiches (around £1.75), baguettes and children's lunchboxes are also available. Tea (70p) is disappointing – a teabag dunked in a polystyrene cup – but the home-made shortbread (50p) is good. There is a spacious, outdoor picnic area with tables and benches provided.

Shops A small outlet in the ticket office sells a fairly good range of animal-related merchandise from zoo badges (45p), stickers (99p), and plastic animals (from 99p) to more expensive cuddly toys, notebooks, posters and games. However, there is little in the way of educational books or activity packs.

🚌 Between Attleborough and Diss on the B1113. Follow brown signs. ⊖ Train to Diss or Attleborough (approximately 7 miles away), then taxi. Bus from Norwich to Banham (tel (0845) 6020121). ⏱ Mon to Sun, Mar to June 10am to 5pm, July to Sept 10am to 5.30pm, Oct to Mar 10am to 4pm (closed 25, 26 Dec). 💷 Adult £6.95; child (3 to 14 yrs old) £4.95; senior citizen £5.95. Season ticket: adult £28, child £20, senior citizen £24, family (2 adults + 2 children) £80. Reduced rates for groups of 12 or more paying visitors. ♿ All but the woodland walks are wheelchair accessible; disabled parking; two wheelchairs available for loan.

Battle Abbey and Battlefield

High Street, Battle, East Sussex TN33 0AD   ☎ *(01424) 773792*

Quality ★ ★ ★ ★	Facilities 🏛 🏛 🏛 🏛	Value for money £££££

Highlights Good audio tour; story of events leading up to the battle well told
Drawbacks Little historical information on the implications of the defeat

What's there This is the site of the **Battle of Hastings** in 1066, the last successful invasion of Britain, when the forces of the Norman William the Conqueror beat the English supporters of King Harold, and hence claimed the English throne. In the course of the battle Harold was shot in the eye with an arrow and was killed. The battle was so bloody that William built a Benedictine abbey on the site of Harold's death to try to atone for the terrible loss of life.

A small museum up some rickety stairs by the gatehouse entrance tells the story of the Benedictine abbey and how the Normans introduced feudalism (by 1086, 20 laymen and 12 churchmen, none of them of English descent, held 40 per cent of English land between them). From the gatehouse, follow the path round to the **'Prelude to Battle'** exhibition, which narrates the events leading up to the battle from Norman and Saxon perspectives. It is probably also worth watching the video that tells the story of the battle before walking round the actual site of the battle. The path to follow is off to the right and easy to miss, but once you find it large display boards describe the battle's progress – the Saxons held the high ground, but were tricked into leaving their positions when the Normans pretended to flee. You can follow the stories of Harold's mistress, a Norman knight and a Saxon thane on the **audio tour**. The gentle slopes now lead down to a lake and are grazed by sheep, but with your audio tour, you'll be able to visualise the carnage of that day and hear how the Saxon women were refused permission to bury Harold's body (it is believed to have been buried on the beach in nearby Pevensey).

After looping round the battlefield you can wander around the **ruins of the abbey**, though little remains from Norman times. A plaque marks the spot where the high altar is believed to have been built on the site of Harold's death. It will probably take two hours to visit both the battlefield and abbey.

Information/tours/guides An excellent audio tour that will appeal to adults and children alike is included in the entrance price.

When to visit A crisp, bright day in autumn is an ideal time to visit. There are lots of special events, like battle re-enactments, but the audio tour is not available on these days.

Age appeal It's good for all ages. Older children will love the audio tour; younger ones can have a run round and enjoy the adventure playground.

Food and drink There's nothing on the site itself, so bring a picnic. For home-made cakes and light lunches try Milestones, just outside the entrance.

Shops The selection of English Heritage gifts is wide, with pocket-money trinkets, such as bookmarks (£1.25).

🚗 7 miles from Hastings; follow signposts from A259 (car park with charge). ⊖ Train to Battle station, then 355 bus (runs twice daily). Tel (01273) 474747 for more details. ◷ Mon to Sun, Apr to Oct 10am to 6pm (or dusk in Oct if earlier); Nov to Mar 10am to 4pm. Closed 24 to 26 Dec. 💷 Adult £4; child £2; student, senior citizen £3; family ticket £10. Free to EH members. ♿ Lots of steps on battlefield tour, but short walk and special audio tour for visitors in wheelchairs. Audio tour for the visually impaired and those with learning difficulties.

Beamish North of England Open Air Museum ☺

Beamish, County Durham DH9 0RG ☎ *(01207) 231811*
🖰 *www.beamish.org.uk*

Quality ★★★★★	**Facilities** 👜👜👜	**Value for money** ££££

Highlights Enjoyable re-creations; living history staff bringing the past alive

Drawbacks No family ticket; much less to see in winter (but admission price reduced accordingly)

What's there Beamish North of England Open Air Museum re-creates life in the north-east of England at two distinct points in history – 1825 and 1913.

Some of its sites, such as the drift mine, Home Farm and Pockerley Manor, are indigenous to the Beamish Valley and have been restored for exhibition, but most of the buildings have been transported from other areas of the north-east and reconstructed here. A **tram** trundles around the 300-acre site, allowing visitors to stop off at the places they wish to visit.

Be sure not to miss the **colliery village**, complete with pit cottages, village school and Methodist chapel. You can explore a real **drift mine** on a guided tour (lasting about 20 minutes), during which you can experience the horrific conditions for yourself – claustrophobic 4-foot-high tunnels and only candle-light to work by, which did the miners' eyesight no favours.

The **town** is dominated by a row of Georgian town houses. A co-operative store, the **Motor Cycle Works**, supplies everything from the latest car to gramophones, while the sweetshop stocks traditional confectionery including boiled sweets, nougat and fudge.

Pockerley Manor dates from the 1820s and conveys the lifestyle of that period well: you learn, for example, that the average family then bathed four times a year, while servants simply had an annual dip in the river.

Information/tours/guides As the museum aims to reconstruct the past, in some detail, information boards would be out of place. Instead, it offers living history, with real people impersonating men and women from the past. All are very knowledgeable and happy to answer questions as they conduct their daily chores. The full-colour guide book (£3) contains much useful additional information and makes a good souvenir.

When to visit Go when the weather is fine, and in summer, if you can, as so much of the site is outdoors and winter visits are confined to the town and tramway (admission charges are reduced accordingly in winter). A summer visit would take 4–5 hours; 2 hours would suffice in winter. Queues to go underground at the drift mine are shorter in the mornings, and Pockerley Manor is less crowded than other parts of the site, so try to visit these first.

Age appeal Visitors of all ages will enjoy the sight, though the bumpy tram and vintage car to the town (with a deep entrance step) could prove taxing for some visitors. There is plenty to entertain children.

Food and drink The Dainty Dinah Tea Room in the town, well situated on the high street, is a self-service, canteen-style cafeteria serving hot and cold food at lunchtime (sandwiches £2.10) and drinks and cakes throughout the rest of the day. A second, very small, cafeteria is located in the children's shop by the museum entrance. There is a picnic site near the railway station.

Shops Two gift shops in the entrance building cater for children and adults respectively. The former, also housing a cafeteria, is smaller. Merchandise is mainly stationery, books and soft toys – for example, old-fashioned teddy bears (£2.99), plastic spiders and books on the Victorians. The gift shop for adults sells hand-made biscuits (90p-£2.99), cards (£1.50), framed prints (£16.99) and Victoriana such as lace napkins (£1.99).

Other facilities Toilets can be found at each of the main sites, and baby-changing facilities in the entrance building and Pockerley Manor.

🚗 Follow the signs from the A1/M1 junction 63 (Chester-le-Street), 4 miles along the A693 towards Stanley. From the north-west take the A68 south to Castleside, near Consett, and follow the signs along the A692 and A693 via Stanley. ⊖ Rail: Durham City and Newcastle Central Stations are convenient for service buses to Beamish – both are on the main east coast line (Great North Eastern Railway). Bus/coach: service buses run from Durham City (Milburngate), colleges (summer only), Newcastle (Eldon Square) and Sunderland (Park Lane Interchange) to museum entrance. Call Go North East (0845) 6060260 for further information. ⊘ 8 Apr to 29 Oct 10am to 5pm, last admission 3pm. Closed Mon & Fri and 11 Dec to 1 Jan; 30 Oct to 6 Apr 10am to 4pm, last admission 3pm. Period exhibits close 15 mins before advertised closing time of museum and last tram leaves the town and Pockerley Manor 15 mins before closing time. Last guided tour of the drift mine is 30 mins before advertised closing time of museum.
£ *Summer* adult £10; child (5–16) £6; senior citizen £7. *Winter* all visitors £3 (town and tramway only). ♿ Good, with ramps, parking and toilets for disabled, but companion advisable for wheelchair users owing to size of site and occasional steep slopes. Guide dogs permitted in buildings. Free leaflet for visitors with disabilities available at main entrance.

The Beatles Story

Britannia Vaults, Albert Dock, Liverpool L3 4AA   ☎ *0151-709 1963*

Quality ★ ★ ★ ★ ★   **Facilities 🎫 🎫**   **Value for money ££££**
Highlights Imaginative and informative exhibition on a musical phenomenon
Drawbacks No toilets

What's there Set in the town where they were born, this is the definitive history of the Beatles, from their early failures to their ultimate triumph. The musical journey takes you from the back streets of Liverpool, to the Cavern Club, Germany and finally America. The museum also details their solo careers and ends with the deaths of both John Lennon and Linda McCartney.

In the basement of the historic and wonderfully restored Albert Dock, the Beatles Story is appropriately set amongst stone arches resembling the **Cavern Club**, of which there is an almost exact replica, complete with the cobbled street leading up to the club, black-and-white drum kit on the stage and a snack bar at the back. It's incredibly atmospheric, especially when the lights are dimmed and a recording of the band and their introduction by the original MC is played.

The story starts with a brief pre-war history of Liverpool and the importance of the docks, before moving on to the introduction of rock and roll from America, which sparked a flurry of copy bands in the UK. **Videos, display boards, life-sized models, photographs**, and a staggering array of **authentic memorabilia** are used to re-create the mood and energy of the times.

As you progress from room to room, a staggered video kicks in to describe the next stage in the Beatles Story – it's like an **automated guide**, and includes **interviews** as well as **footage** of the band and their entourage of screaming girls. There's a particular poignant moment when the group is interviewed after the sudden death of Brian Epstein.

The re-creations of important events are accurate and detailed, right down to the life-sized copy of the newspaper office of the *Mersey Beat* with the editor sitting with his feet on the desk while on the phone. You can listen in to his conversation with the owner of the Cavern Club, who's calling to complain that the other bands don't get a look-in because of the extensive Beatles coverage, by picking up the receiver of one of the period phones. There are similar set-ups of the **Abbey Road recording studio**, and even the plane in which they flew to America. To take in all the rooms of the Beatles Story, allow two hours.

Information/tours/guides No guided tours are conducted, nor is a guidebook available, but the video narration is very informative.

When to visit It's all indoors and open all year round so it's good to visit whatever the weather.

Age appeal Just about everyone has heard of the Beatles, so it should be of interest to most, although Beatles fans and music fans generally might enjoy it more.

Food and drink There are no refreshments or toilets on site but the Albert Dock nearby has many bars and cafés.

Shops A gift shop sells a surprisingly limited number of items: T-shirts, videos, mugs, toys and only a few CDs.

🚗 Liverpool city centre and follow the signs. ⊖ Liverpool Lime Street station, then 5-minute walk or take Smartbuses 1 or 4. ⏲ Daily 10am to 6pm, Apr to Sept; 10am to 5pm, Oct to Mar (closed 25, 26 Dec). 💷 Adult £6.95, child (under 16 yrs old) £4.95, senior citizen/student/unemployed visitor £4.95. ♿ Wheelchair accessible; lift; but no toilets.

Bekonscot Model Village

Warwick Road, Beaconsfield, Buckinghamshire HP9 2PL ☎ *(01494) 672919*
🖳 *www.bekonscot.org.uk*

Quality ★ ★ ★ | **Facilities** 🛗 🛗 🛗 | **Value for money** ££££
Highlights Great for children, model-train enthusiasts and gardeners
Drawbacks Little explanation or commentary on the history or construction of village

What's there This sizeable model village, covering 1½ acres, was started in 1929 and presents an idealised image of **rural life in the 1930s**. Consisting of six imaginary villages, it incorporates a wide range of scenes, including a zoo, coal mine, churches, fairground, harbour, football stadium, castle and racecourse. The shop windows display a range of **miniature goods from the period** (no supermarkets here), with punning names such as Dan D. Lyon (florist); Scratchett and Reckham (removal firm); and Messrs. Argue and Twist (solicitors).

Some of the exhibits have moving parts, such as the mine, funfair, watermill and windmill, while a wonderful extended **train set**, with a variety of trains serving the seven stations, covers some 455 metres of track. Most of the attraction is visual, but there are a few sound effects, such as the hymns coming out of the Minster Church and the band playing music on the pier.

Gardening enthusiasts will be fascinated by the **miniature trees and shrubs** of the village, ranging from the tiny cypress trees, Japanese maples and willows, to the little waterlilies in the pond and the small-scale version of **Hampton Court maze**. Model-makers will enjoy the detail of the buildings and their inhabitants, though it seems a shame that visitors are not invited to watch some of the process of creation. A few display boards show how the recent model of **Enid Blyton's house, Green Hedges**, was designed and constructed, and more of this sort of information would be interesting for adult visitors.

For young children, a visit to Bekonscot is rounded off by a stop at the **playground**, an attractive area offering a range of slides, climbing equipment and a 'tree house'. It is all well maintained and there are plenty of picnic tables and benches for accompanying adults.

Information/tours/guides It's easy to follow the recommended route round the village (including a raised platform for an 'aerial' view), and the models are self-explanatory, so guides are not necessary. It would add to the experience for adults if more background information were given, to put the village in a historical and horticultural context. The good-value guidebook (£1) includes photos, a map of the site and some historical background on the creation of the village, although the text may be a little cloying for some, with its Enid Blyton-style account of one girl's visit to Bekonscot.

When to visit Virtually everything is out of doors, so it's not much fun in bad weather. Any fine day would be good, but the paths can get crowded and the car park gets full at peak times, so avoid bank holidays.

Age appeal Bekonscot is primarily aimed at children, especially 3 to 10-year-olds, but accompanying parents, grandparents and so on will find plenty to enjoy in this pre-Nintendo form of attraction.

Food and drink A refreshment kiosk in the corner of the picnic area provides a limited range of good-quality hot and cold snacks, including pizza (£1.65), baked potatoes with filling (£2.75), hot dogs and a range of sandwiches (£1.30 to £1.50). Service is prompt and friendly.

The picnic area is attractively laid out with plenty of tables and benches, some under cover but most in the open air. Notices exhort visitors to keep the area tidy, but inevitably some rubbish is dropped.

Shops A disused railway carriage has been converted into a shop, which kids love, but it also means the shop is quite narrow. Most of the goods are child-oriented, including tiny animals made of china or silver, Thomas the Tank Engine trains, small pottery buildings for you to paint yourself, and printed cards from which you can construct miniature buildings. Adult souvenirs are limited, but include Bekonscot tea towels (£4.95) and mugs (£5.95).

Other facilities Toilets are provided in the picnic area, though the area could do with more at busy times. The building and fixtures are quite old, but all kept clean and tidy.

🚗 Well-signposted from M40, A40 and A355. Follow brown signs for 'Model Village'. Free car park opposite main entrance in Warwick Road. ⊖ Beaconsfield station (mainline from Marylebone, High Wycombe, Birmingham), then a few minutes' walk. ⏲ 19 Feb to 29 Oct, daily, 10am to 5pm. 💷 Adult £4.50, child (3–15 yrs old) £2.20, senior citizen/student/unemployed £3, family ticket (2 adults + 2 children) £12. Reduced rates for parties of 13 or more. Annual tickets: adult £25, child £15, family ticket £68. ♿ Exhibitions all on ground level, but some walkways narrow and awkward. Three wheelchairs available for visitors' use.

Belton House

Grantham, Lincolnshire NG32 2LS ☎ *(01476) 566116*

Quality ★ ★ **Facilities 🏛 🏛 🏛** **Value for money £££**
Highlights Boudoir ceiling; Chinese room wallpaper; tapestries and formal gardens
Drawbacks Some of the rooms are so dark (to protect contents) that the exhibits are difficult to see properly

What's there This lovely country house was built (1685–7) by Sir John Brownlow, altered by James Wyatt in the 1770s and given to the National Trust by the present Lord Brownlow in 1984. The building itself, with its succession of well-proportioned rooms, some of them with exceptionally beautiful decoration, is the main reason to visit, but particular items to look out for include **wood carvings** of the Grinling Gibbons school (especially in the entrance hall), some very fine tapestries and furniture, and an outstanding **silver** collection.

After the grand but gloomy saloon and the lighter, brighter red drawing room, containing a rare lapis lazuli cabinet, you come to the Tyrconnel room, where a design based on greyhounds (the Brownlow crest) has been painted on the wooden floor. In the chapel drawing room a remarkable tapestry depicts eastern scenes of gods and animals.

The chapel is viewed from the family gallery, facing two carved cherubs. Of the bedrooms, the **Chinese room**, with its brilliant eighteenth-century wallpaper incorporating a frieze of figures below bamboo fronds, birds and butterflies, is especially attractive. The **Queen's bedroom** contains a magnificent oak bed, surmounted by the crown of Queen Adelaide, William IV's widow, who visited the house in 1844, while the Windsor bedroom, used by the current Prince of Wales, has associations with Edward VIII, to whom the 6th Earl Brownlow was friend and lord-in-waiting.

In the well-stocked library stands an **exercise chair**, also known as a cock-fighting or a 'metamorphic' chair, with integral book-rest. Used by Sir John Brownlow's nephew, Lord Tyrconnel, late in his life when he could no longer ride, this unusual piece of furniture could also be turned into library steps.

Lady Brownlow's boudoir, perhaps the loveliest room in the house, has a wonderful plasterwork ceiling in different shades of green and gold; the green is echoed in the walls, chairs, desktop and porcelain. A large mirror (1875), flanked by gilded sphinxes, reflects light back into the room.

On the west staircase, note the **naïve painting of the house**: a giant-size image of Sir John's porter stands before the gates holding a staff that now hangs next to the picture.

The group of eighteenth-century **tapestries** illustrating the life of the Greek philosopher Diogenes has a room to itself.

Also, a room not described in the explanatory leaflet, but reached after the yellow bedroom, contains old toys and games, historical clothes for children to dress up in, and an instructive 'conservation board' showing how fabrics and wallpapers deteriorate if touched a lot by human hand (the mounted samples *can* be touched).

Before leaving the house, look into the old **kitchen**, barn-like in dimension, which displays the stern injunction 'Waste not, want not' on the far wall.

The grounds are well worth exploring. The formal **Dutch garden**, with its topiary, stone urns and sunken garden is overlooked by a fine **orangery** (1820). The small church near the orangery is packed with monuments to the Brownlow family, including a large marble statue by Canova entitled *Religion*.

Information/tours/guides The explanatory leaflet (75p) contains all you need for a short visit. An illustrated book on the house costs £4.50, and a children's guide £1.50. No tours are given but National Trust guides, on duty in every room, are happy to answer questions.

When to visit The property is open from late March to October inclusive, but only on certain days (see below).

Age appeal The House appeals mainly to adults, but the dressing-up and adventure playground outside would appeal to children. Those with children could pick up the children's guide beforehand. Special events include family days, painting/sketching events, music/fireworks concerts, book fairs, boundary walks and guided tours of the garden, as well as occasional 'lecture lunches' in the stables restaurant.

Food and drink A self-service restaurant serves lunches (12pm to 2pm) and teas thereafter. There are also tables outside. Typical dishes include carrot soup (£2.20), liver and onion casserole (£5.65), pork chop (£5.80) and fruit crumble (£2.20). Various cake and tea options are available later, including 'Her Ladyship's afternoon tea' (£2.80) and 'Gardener's tea' (£3).

Shops The shop sells a typical range of National Trust merchandise: books, tea-towels, calendars, mugs, jumpers, Head Gardener's sweatshirts, hand creams, jams and jigsaws.

Other facilities A parent-and-baby room is provided. Baby slings are provided for safe carriage within the house.

🚗 Three miles north-east of Grantham on the A607 Grantham to Lincoln road. Follow signs. ⊖ Train to Grantham, then Grantham to Lincoln bus or Grantham to Sleaford bus. ⊙ End Mar to end Oct, Wed to Sun and bank hols, 1pm to 5.30pm. *Garden and park*: all week 11am to 5.30pm. *Restaurant and shop* 12 noon to 5.30pm. Free pedestrian access to park only from Lion gates all year. 💷 Adult £5.30, child £2.60, family ticket £13.20, NT members free. ♿ Advisable to contact Belton House direct. Route avoiding cobbles in park clearly marked but access in the House is difficult. Disabled toilets.

Birmingham Botanical Gardens

Westbourne Road, Edgbaston, Birmingham B15 3TR ☎ *0121-454 1860*
🖥 *www.bham-bot-gdns.demon.co.uk*

Quality ★ ★ ★	Facilities 🏛 🏛	Value for money £££

Highlights Superb bonsai collection; good glasshouses; varied and colourful gardens
Drawbacks Inadequate information on layout of site; uninspired gift shop

What's there Birmingham's Botanical Gardens, opened in 1832, are still largely laid out as they were by the designer John Claudius Loudon. Some 15 acres of delightful, superbly maintained gardens boast an interestingly diverse collection of rare shrubs and trees, plus roses, herbs, rhododendrons, a fern walk, pinetum, and Roman, Medieval and Tudor gardens. Immune to the vagaries of weather are the four excellent **glasshouses**, which are particularly appealing to children. The rainforest climate in the **palm house** and **tropical house** should raise a sweat on even the chilliest day – look for exotica like sugar cane, cocoa, bananas, mangoes, pineapples, cardamom and ginger. The **orangery** has a touch of the Victorian conservatory, with fuchsia, coleus and colourful ornamental plants around a nucleus of citrus trees, while the **cactus and succulent house** bristles with wonderful spiky sculptures. Adjacent to the Japanese garden, the **National Bonsai Collection** has outstanding specimens, changed regularly by loans from members of the society. Apart from plants, free-roaming peacocks patrol the lawns, and the aviaries house exotic feathered creatures, including golden pheasants, hornbills and Java doves. A children's **adventure playground** is next to the **Waterfowl pond**, and the Pavilion Restaurant has a great setting overlooking the main lawn and Victorian bandstand.

Information/tours/guides Guided tours are available only for pre-booked groups. In the absence of guides, the £1.50 guidebook is good value, informative and includes a map, which was not provided in the brochure or seasonal interest supplement. Information around the gardens is rather hit-and-miss: information sheets do the basics in identifying individual plants. Some simply give the name and Latin genus, others are more user friendly and divulge details about the plant's provenance and uses.

When to visit The glasshouses are good at any time of year but the gardens are at their best when in spring and summer bloom. Monthly supplements tell visitors which plants are currently worth seeking out.

Age appeal Those of all ages can enjoy the gardens, with enough to interest children in the glasshouses, aviaries, adventure playground and wildfowl pond.

Food and drink The self-service Pavilion Restaurant has a trendy provençal-inspired décor and good ambience, which the food fails to live up to. When we visited, the choice was rather limited – sandwiches (£1.80), meat lasagne, vegetable curry (both £4.25), glass of wine (£3), and pot of tea for two (£1.40). With staff almost outnumbering customers it was surprising to see uncleared tables and food debris on the floor.

Shops A good plant centre enhances the visit, offering a wide selection of plants that feature in the gardens, as well as books, plant pots and gardening paraphernalia. A plant advisor is available from 12pm to 4pm (3pm in winter). The gift shop is rather less interesting, selling unrelated bits and pieces – mugs, candles and greetings cards.

Other facilities More toilets in convenient spots – such as near the Pavilion Restaurant – would be useful. The ones in the entrance foyer are modern and clean; those near the cottage are older and less fresh, reminiscent of public loos in a park.

From M6 junction 6, take a A38M to Birmingham centre, A456 Hagley Rd, then B4217. Follow brown signs. From M5 junction 3, take A456 to city centre. ⊖ Train to Birmingham New Street; then local buses 10, 21, 22, 23, 29 and 103 stop near the gardens. ⏱ All week 9am (10am Sun) to 7pm (dusk if earlier). Closed 25 Dec. 💷 Adult £4.30 (£4.60 on summer Sundays and bank holidays); child/senior citizen/student £2.40; family (2 adults + 3 children) £11.50 (£12.50 on summer Sundays and bank holidays). ♿ Terrain generally manageable for wheelchairs, although some hills need a strong pusher. Manual and electric wheelchairs, Braille guidebook, and large-print or tape guide available (book in advance).

Birmingham Museum and Art Gallery

Chamberlain Square, Birmingham B3 3DH   ☎ *0121-303 2834*
🖰 *www.birmingham.gov.uk/bmag*

Quality ★ ★ ★   **Facilities** 🏛 🏛 🏛 🏛 🏛   **Value for money £££££**

Highlights   Superb Pre-Raphaelite collection; elegant ironwork 'Industrial Gallery'; grand Edwardian café and restaurant

Drawbacks   Themed guided tours only, no general tour

What's there   The highlight of Birmingham Museum and Art Gallery for most visitors is its world-class collection of **Pre-Raphaelite paintings**, with works by **Rossetti, Millais, Holman Hunt** and **Ford Madox Brown. Sir Edward Burne Jones** is the local link and a whole room is dedicated to his romantic works. The rest of the art collection features British art – with works by Constable, Gainsborough, Hogarth and Turner – Old Masters and a small Impressionist collection.

The museum opened in 1885 to provide collections of paintings, sculpture, glass, ceramics, metalwork and other arts and artefacts from around the world to inspire Birmingham's manufacturers and artisans. The beautiful **ironwork 'Industrial Gallery'** is a superb collection of mainly nineteenth-century glass and ceramics. A stunning installation of stained-glass panels – some designed by Pre-Raphaelites – sits beneath an elegant gallery with art-nouveau wrought-iron balustrades. The Percy Cox gallery houses a huge silverware collection from the seventeenth to the twentieth century; the Pinto Collection is a unique and captivating collection of thousands of wooden objects. Changing exhibitions promote Birmingham's own industrial and artistic heritage, as well as contemporary work by the best West Midlands crafts-people.

Information/tours/guides   When we inspected, the museum's glossy brochure was under review, so a general guide was not available. Plasticised sheets in each gallery explain the main exhibits and their significance, and when paintings or artefacts have particular relevance to Birmingham this is made clear. An audio tour gives details on the major items and paintings concisely and informatively. The free guided tours are themed and changed periodically. On our visit, we took part in an informative, although limited, tour called 'Tea for two', which focused on the museum's teapot collection.

When to visit   Any time of year.

Age appeal Although it has wide age appeal, the art collection is probably of less interest to children than the artefacts in the museum collections. Family trail sheets are available to enhance the experience for kids.

Food and drink The atmospheric surroundings of the wonderful Edwardian Tea Room are something of an institution with city-centre office workers, so lunchtimes can get busy. The huge Edwardian galleried hall is fitted out in perfect period grandeur, with oils on the walls and glass cases of silverware. The menu offers a fine choice and good value – for example soup and roll (£2.70), beef and vegetable pie, broccoli and cauliflower cheese or lemon chicken (£4.75), and kids' meals (£1.99). Plenty of sandwiches, fresh salads and jacket potatoes are provided for lighter eaters.

Shops A spacious shop sits between the Round Room and the Edwardian Tea Room, selling quality books and prints. These are mainly on the artists and subjects in the museum's collections, with a predictable emphasis on the Pre-Raphaelites.

Other facilities Toilets are easy to find and amply provided around the galleries. They are all well maintained, but fittings are starting to show their age and a touch of wear and tear.

🚗 From M6, M5, M42 to Birmingham city centre; car parks. ⊖ Train to Birmingham New Street or Snow Hill stations, then bus to Birmingham city centre. ◷ Open all year, Mon to Thur and Sat 10am to 5pm, Fri 10.30am to 5pm, Sun 12.30pm to 5pm. 💷 Free (voluntary contributions welcome). ♿ Lifts to all levels of the museum, galleries and Tea Room.

Black Country Living Museum

Tipton Road, Dudley, West Midlands DY1 4SQ　☎ *0121-557 9643*
📠 *0121-557 4242*　🖳 *www.bclm.co.uk*　🖳 *info@bclm.co.uk*

Quality ★ ★ ★ ★ ★　　Facilities 🏛 🏛 🏛 🏛　　Value for money £££££
Highlights Costumed characters bring the houses, shops and workshops to life; family fun; good range of eating options
Drawbacks Often crowded when busy

What's there Original **historic buildings** from around the Black Country have been moved and rebuilt on a 26-acre open-air site with a canal basin and boat wharf. Friendly, costumed guides and craftsmen recreate living and working conditions in the nineteenth century, when the Black Country was the industrial heartland of Victorian Britain. The **Canal Street village** comprises a fascinating collection of shops, houses, a pub and a chapel saved from destruction when ring roads and modern development carved through the area. In the village you'll find the hardware shop, the grocer's, butcher's, baker's and the sweet shop (you can actually buy bread, cakes and boiled sweets). It's a captivating look back at life in another century. Children may be interested to sit on wooden benches in the **old schoolhouse** where a strict old-fashioned teacher tells them to sit up straight and be quiet.

In **Dickensian workshops** behind the back-to-back houses, craftsmen demonstrate traditional metalworking skills. Nails and chains are made the hard way – by hand – in the ironworks, a reminder of the early 'metal-bashing' crafts that thrived before industry was mechanised. 'Into the Thick' is an underground recreation of a **drift mine** – a display of how miners worked the 'Staffordshire Thick' coal seam in cold, dark, damp conditions. On the **narrowboat trip** into the Dudley Canal tunnel (extra £2.70 for adults and £2.20 for children and senior citizens) you can try 'legging' the boat through part of the tunnel. Allow a full day to explore the site at a relaxed pace.

Information/tours/guides The glossy colour guidebook (£1.50) provides heaps of information to accompany the visit. Knowledgeable costumed guides and craftsmen are keen to explain the sights.

When to visit The busy summer period has more atmosphere, but small buildings fill up quickly, creating bottlenecks. Fine weather is also necessary to make the most of the outdoor areas. A programme of working activities and events operates year-round, including traditional Bonfire Night and Christmas events (phone for details).

Age appeal Adults will appreciate the history and educational value of preserving the UK's industrial heritage. For children it is a fun and fascinating way to learn how people lived and worked in the Black Country.

Food and drink Hearty Black Country meals – faggots and peas (£3.65), steak and ale pie (£4.25) – as well as standard sandwiches and baguettes (£1.50 to £2.50) are available in The Stables café and tea room. In the village high street, fish and chips at the period Fried Fish shop (£2.50) are so popular that you have to queue in the street. Only old-fashioned food is sold in the authentic spit-and-sawdust setting of the Glass and Bottle pub – a pint of Holden's Bitter and a cheese and onion cob (£3). Otherwise take a picnic to eat on the benches and grassy areas around the site.

Shops The village bakery and sweet shop serve old-fashioned snacks – bread pudding (50p a chunk), jam tarts (25p) and custard tarts (40p), while pear drops, humbugs and herbal tablets go for 50p a quarter (an archaic measure of about 100g). A small rock and fossil shop sells local mineral specimens as well as geological finds from far away places. The gift shop at the entrance is a bit disappointing: apart from a good selection of history books, some on the local area, and a *Black Country revisited* video (£10.99), it's the usual selection of souvenir T-shirts (£6.95 to £7.50), mugs (£6.95), jams and preserves.

Other facilities Plenty of toilets are dotted around the site, and all of them were clean when we visited.

🚗 Three miles from M5 junction 2; 6 miles from M6 junction 10, follow signs to Wolverhampton and Dudley, then look for brown signs from around the Dudley area. **By canal**: on the Tipton branch of Birmingham Canal Navigations. ⊖ Train to Sandwell or Dudley; Tipton station (1 mile away) is on the Birmingham to Wolverhampton line; bus 126 from Birmingham centre (Corporation Street). ⏰ Mar to end Oct, Mon to Sun 10am to 5pm; Nov to end Feb, Tues 10am to 4pm, Wed to Sun 10am to 5pm; closed Mon. 💷 Adult £7.50, child (5 to 17 yrs old) £4.50, senior citizen £6.50, family ticket (2 adults + 4 children) £20, wheelchair users and carers free. ♿ Some steep or uneven ground in places and buildings with high steps unsuitable for wheelchairs. See web site or ring direct for more information. For those with limited mobility, the site is fairly flat with mostly good surfaces, and electric trams and trolleybuses transport visitors from the entrance to the village area by the canal basin.

Blackpool Pleasure Beach

Ocean Boulevard, Blackpool, Lancashire FY4 1EZ ☎ *(0870) 444 5566*
☜ *www.blackpoolpleasurebeach.co.uk*

Quality ★ ★ ★ ★ ★   **Facilities** 👜 👜 👜   **Value for money** £££££
Highlights Top rollercoasters (The Big One, Grand National); free entry; family fun and shows
Drawbacks Quite expensive rides; queues; uninspiring food; tacky shops; a bit worn in places

What's there Britain's most popular tourist attraction has a good mix of old (and generally gentler) rides that are still fun despite their age, and the new high-tech ones, but those who like scream-inducing rides will get much more out of a day here. Luckily entry is free so that it costs nothing to mooch around and watch. The rides are priced according to the thrill factor, and graded A, B or C, with A being the most exciting and so most expensive. You can pay cash for each ride, but if you are planning to go on lots of rides, the pre-payment plans are better value. The price structure is explained below.

The ten rollercoasters are the main attraction at Blackpool Pleasure Beach, and certain rides stand out from the rest. The **Big One** (best overall ride) is the world's tallest rollercoaster at 235ft. It's a must for every visitor who can face that first long drop down (at a speed of 85mph) after the anticipation of the climb up. The **Grand National** (best A ride) is a twin-track affair where two coasters run side-by-side in a race. This old-fashioned wooden ride with huge humps and turns guarantees a good time. The **Roller Coaster** (best B ride) provides a gentle introduction to rollercoasting for those who can't face the scarier rides. No safety bars are needed and stomach churning is kept to a minimum. Blackpool's **Flying Machines** (best C ride) was built in 1904 but is still inducing whoops of delight. You sit in open-air pods and get swung around in ever-increasing circles. Trauma Towers (best indoor ride) is not so much a ride as a walk through a haunted house. Fun and a little scary, it features a centrifugal ride at the end, although you can bypass that if you prefer (B-ride ticket).

Other rides worth a mention are the original Big Dipper (A ride), a real boneshaker; the Whip (C ride); and Revolution (A ride), a loop-the-loop. The newest attraction, **The Ride** – a huge mechanised, upside down bungee jump – was disappointing, not least because it's the shortest ride with the longest queue.

All the top three rides (The Big One, Grand National and The Ride) have by far the longest queues, though for the first two they move quite quickly. Go early in the day to avoid waiting as lines build up during the afternoon. There is little attempt at queue-management and you may well have to wait out in the rain/sun without protection. Height restrictions apply on many rides (mainly the A ones). The most restrictive are The Big One and The Ride, both with a minimum height of 52 inches.

For non-riders, there's mainly pay-as-you-go attractions: the **amusement arcades** are good in the wet (we particularly liked the Arabian Derby), or you can visit Ripley's Believe It or Not, or the truly scary Pasaje del Terror. Most popular are the **many shows**, which usually encompass comedy, dance, circus, ice spectaculars and magic shows. All are on two to three times a day with an evening performance, but they quickly sell out in peak periods, so book when you arrive in the morning.

Beaver Creek is especially good for toddlers and younger children. It usually closes about two hours before the main part, and has its own fare structure (see below).

The Beach is showing its age in places, with a lick of paint and new tarmac needed here and there, but given the number of visitors, it's remarkably clean and tidy, and the older rides are in great shape, even after 90 years.

Information/tours/guides The free maps are hard to read and next to useless as a way of finding your way around, but they do have discount vouchers for shops and restaurants. Signposting within the Pleasure Beach is adequate, though it can be hard to find the actual entrance to a ride in some cases.

When to visit Any time, although on sunny summer weekends it will be very busy, with long queues for rides. If you don't mind getting wet, a rainy day is a way to avoid the crowds. In March rides are usually cheaper as part of a promotion.

Age appeal All ages will enjoy this attraction, although it is most fun for those old enough to enjoy the thrills. Older non-riders can watch friends and families without paying anything, or take in one of the many shows.

Food and drink Plenty of fast-food outlets and sit-down restaurants offering cups of tea (65p) and fish and chips (£3) through to pasta and fajitas. Restaurants just outside, along Ocean Boulevard, are more varied and less hectic, though our inspection meals were rather disappointing.

Shops General low-quality seaside souvenirs available, including T-shirts (£11.99), pencils (50p) and mugs (£2.95). Better to stick to the rides and skip the shops.

Other facilities Good basic conveniences, but for choice head for the Superloo, which is superclean with mahogany cubicle doors and marble sinks.

🚗 Signposted on roads leading into town, plus on-site parking (about £5 per day midweek and £7 at weekends) and pay-and-display public car parks nearby. ⊖ Take hourly train to Blackpool Pleasure Beach from Preston (30 mins journey time) or take train to Blackpool North and catch a tram down to the Beach. ① 15 Apr to 5 Nov, Mon to Sun – phone for details of opening times (10am to midnight at height of season), which vary depending on the weather and how busy it is. Early Nov to Dec and Mar to Easter open weekends only. Closed Jan and Feb. 💷 Free entry but payment for rides, either individually or by a pre-payment plan. *Individual prices:* The Big One £4.50; A rides £2.25; B rides £1.75; C rides (and Beaver Creek rides) £1.25. *Pre-payment plans:* £22 to £25 (the unlimited ride wristband with two vouchers for shows). Beaver Creek pre-payment plans £10.50 including one show voucher. *Show prices:* variable, on average £5 to £6 for afternoon and £10 to £15 for evening shows. Children, students and senior citizens get a £2 discount. All rides during Supersaver Weekends (phone for details of dates) 80p. &. Free information guide for disabled visitors available in advance or from guest relations office on arrival. It rates all the rides on their accessibility from a wheelchair. Wheelchairs available on request.

Blackpool Tower

Blackpool, Lancashire FY1 4BJ   ☎ *(01253) 622242*

Quality ★ ★ ★ **Facilities 🏛 🏛** **Value for money £££**
Highlights View from the top of the Tower; Walk of Faith; ballroom; Dinosaur Ride
Drawbacks Queues when busy; noisy amusement arcades; grotty toilets; expensive

What's there Britain's answer to the Eiffel Tower has been dominating the Blackpool skyline for more than a century, and at night the 518-ft high edifice is lit up with a multitude of bulbs, making it even more impressive. Not surprisingly, the view from the top is the best and most popular bit, but there is enough else to make you linger a while.

Beneath the Tower itself is an acceptable selection of attractions for all ages. The first, **Undersea World,** is a series of small aquaria that kids will love. Some of the glass needs a clean but the labelling is informative and the fish delightful. More entertaining is the **Dinosaur Ride**, a gentle glide through a few million years with fibre-glass reptiles and a running commentary.

For older visitors, the **Tower Ballroom** offers a **traditional tea dance** every afternoon, accompanied by a man on a genuine Wurlitzer. The setting is very grand with gilt balconies and big chandeliers, and there's plenty of room to dance. It's worth a peek even if you don't want to shake a leg. At night there are different daily events, ranging from more dancing to cabaret and magic.

Just before you go up to the top, make a couple of stops for more fun. **The Crown Jewels** – replicas rather than the real thing – are passable imitations, although some are a bit wonky in places. The information boards are good, designed specially with children in mind. More interactive is '**Out of this World**' with optical illusions, light shows and hands-on displays.

And so to the main event. Even if there's no queue for the slow lift to the top (unlikely), take some time to read the fascinating history boards about the tower and its place in local history. Once up at the **viewing gallery**, you can admire the panorama (weather permitting). Look out to sea for something more than just Blackpool. The indoor part of the Tower is at 380 feet, and has a section of floor made of glass (Walk of Faith) so you can look down to the street below. There's also a phone box if you're desperate to talk, but no toilets. If you need to go higher, outside staircases take you up to 412 feet, but apart from feeling the wind buffet your face, the extra few feet make little difference to the view.

A extensive daily programme of events is aimed mainly but not exclusively at kids: balloon artists, game shows, children's ballet and, top attraction, **the circus**, which is on twice daily except Friday. If you want to see the circus, it's better value to buy the combined ticket as you go in.

Information/tours/guides The free map is more useful for show details than for orientation – you're better off just finding your own way by trial and error.

When to visit It's better in fine weather for the views, though most of the attractions are indoors. Go back at night for a view of all the lights. The queue for the lift can get long and boring in peak periods.

Age appeal There's something for everyone, whatever your age.

Food and drink Despite the good range of eateries on offer, the food does tend towards the chips-with-everything variety. The ballroom has the best atmosphere and you can get a sandwich (£1.75), tea and a cream cake (£1.95), or a bottle of beer (£2.50). The main restaurant serves 'traditional fayre' – prawn cocktail (£1.95), steak and kidney pie (£4.95) or scampi and chips (£5.95). Upstairs the noisy café has a choice of fast food from pizza to fish and chips, while the Jungle Café is your last resort – burger, fries and a drink (£3.99) surrounded by litter and sticky tables.

Shops The cramped displays and uninterested staff didn't help liven up the dull choice of products. Your best bet is a mini Tower (99p upwards depending on size) or a fridge magnet (£1.50). Rock is better value elsewhere in town.

Other facilities The toilets were universally awful on inspection, with a lack of soap, a broken window, cigarette butts in the urinals and a blocked toilet.

🚗 Drive to Blackpool town centre (limited parking especially at busy times). ⊖ Train to Blackpool North, then tram or walk into town centre. ⊙ 15 Apr to early Nov, Mon to Sun 10am to 11pm. Early Nov to Easter, Sat and Sun 10am to 6pm. 💷 Tower only *(with price of circus visit)* adult £7.50 (£10), child (4 to 16 yrs old) £5.95 (£7.95), child (under 4 yrs old) free. Tickets for just the circus are the same price as for the Tower. Winter: adults £5, child £3. ♿ Steps at the front entrance; the back entrance is better. Lifts to all floors.

Blenheim Palace

Woodstock, Oxfordshire OX20 1PX 📞 *(01993) 811325*
🖲 *www.blenheimpalace.com*

Quality ★ ★ ★	Facilities 👝 👝 👝	Value for money ££££

Highlights Lots of architectural and historic interest; beautiful, well-maintained grounds with plenty of walks; informative guides

Drawbacks Poor food and service in restaurants; some toilets cramped and scruffy; some confusing orientation

---

What's there Driving towards the stately baroque home of the 11th Duke of Marlborough amid 2,000 acres of parkland designed by **'Capability' Brown** is an uplifting experience. The Palace itself was designed by **Sir John Vanbrugh** for John Churchill, the 1st Duke of Marlborough, as a reward from Queen Anne for his victory over the French at the Battle of Blenheim in 1704 (look for the stone lions savaging the French cockerels, carved by Grinling Gibbons, on the clock tower).

Entry into the Palace is from the splendid **Great Court**, and the tour begins with a brief explanation of the history of the various Dukes. Other than the 1st Duke, the most notable seems to have been Charles Spencer-Churchill, the 9th Duke (1871–1934) and cousin of Winston Churchill. It was the 9th Duke who laid out the formal gardens, and tales about the antics of his two wives provide much of the human interest on the tour.

Winston Churchill was born at Blenheim and proposed to Clementine in the Temple of Diana in the gardens, and the tour takes in the room where he was born, with displays of locks of his hair as a child and copies of his letters and speeches. A series of sumptuous rooms features gilded ceilings designed by **Nicholas Hawksmoor**, family portraits by **Reynolds**, **Sargent**, and **Van Dyck**, and some splendid tapestries depicting scenes from the Battle of Blenheim. The tour finishes in the grand **Long Library,** the splendid stucco ceiling of which towers above a statue of Queen Anne and the Willis organ at the northern end.

If you want to go on a **tour of the private apartments** (available when the Duke is not in residence), buy your ticket in the Long Library. Located in the eastern wing of the Palace, the apartments overlook the formal Italian Garden but are less ostentatious than the public rooms. On show in the visitors' book from 1936 is the list of one weekend's guests, which included Edward VIII, Wallis Simpson, Diana Cooper, and Winston and Clementine Churchill.

There's no entry to the Italian Garden or other private gardens just to the south, but you can wander round the gorgeous **Water Terraces**, down to the **Lake** and through the **Rose Garden** and Arboretum to the **Grand Cascade**. Alternatively, exit the Palace and cross Vanbrugh's unfinished Grand Bridge to follow the one-mile trail past the Column of Victory.

The **Pleasure Gardens** are linked to the Palace by a narrow-gauge railway. As it's a bit of a scrum trying to get a seat at busy times, it may be preferable to walk through the Park (about 10 minutes) or drive. Note that you cannot get into the Pleasure Gardens by following the paths through the woods from the Italian Garden.

The main attractions in the Pleasure Gardens are the **Butterfly House** and **Herb Garden**. An impressive display of lavender and herbs attracts numerous insects, while multicoloured butterflies flit around tropical and sub-tropical plants in warm glasshouses. The original kitchen garden now contains the Marlborough Maze (extra charge), which features cannonballs and trumpets in its design, and various games, including pitch and putt. On the other side of the maze is a very good children's adventure playground.

If you just want to walk around the Park, admission is charged per car; if you want to visit the Palace and its gardens too, admission is charged per person (see below). Both options include entry to the Pleasure Gardens.

Information/tours/guides On entry, a map is provided, showing the layout of the site, including toilets, shops and car parks. However, the map does not make it clear that you cannot reach the Pleasure Gardens by walking through the Palace gardens.

The guides on the tour of the main rooms of the Palace are very knowledgeable, spicing up their patter with interesting facts and anecdotes about the family ancestors as well as explaining the significance of the furnishings. On busy days, the noise from other groups can sometimes be distracting (the interval between tours is 5 to 10 minutes). The tour lasts about an hour. The guide on the 30-minute tour of the private apartments continues in the same vein, conjuring up images of the family tucking into TV dinners on trays.

The guidebook (£3.50) is lavishly illustrated and provides a good historical background as well as details of the furnishings and fittings.

When to visit There is often a queue to get into the Palace just after it opens, so if you arrive early it may be best to explore the Park or Gardens first. If you want to do the grounds justice, choose a fine day. Various special events are held throughout the year, including craft fairs, a Rolls Royce enthusiasts' rally, a music and fireworks concert in the Park, and the Blenheim Horse Trials (usually in September).

Age appeal The Palace and grounds appeal mainly to adults, while the Pleasure Gardens, especially the Butterfly House, have the young firmly in mind. The adventure playground allows youngsters to let off steam.

Food and drink The Arcade Room and Indian Room Restaurant both overlook the Water Terraces and have pleasant outside seating areas.

The Arcade Room is a self-service cafeteria, with hot main courses (£5.95), such as vegetable pastizio (like lasagne) and salmon with new potatoes. An unimaginative salad bowl (£5.75) was poorer value and the soup disappointing. There was a shortage of cutlery when we inspected and when replacements finally arrived they were grubby.

The beautifully decorated Indian Room (actually more Chinese in style than Indian) is certainly elegant, although the plastic numbers on the tables and the paper napkins let the side down. A two-course lunch costs £12.95, three courses £14.95 (main courses might be wild mushroom tortelloni, cold salmon and lime mayonnaise, or hot lemon chicken and salad). Service, on the day of inspection, was slow: at 4pm we had to wait for 15 minutes to be seated, although there were only four other people in the restaurant at the time. The afternoon tea was poor value at £6.75.

There is also a small café in the Pleasure Gardens, which sells soup, pizza, and other snacks and drinks. Picnicking is allowed in the grounds.

Shops The main gift shop, on the way out of the Palace, is spacious and well laid out. As well as the usual Blenheim Palace souvenirs (china plates and bells, jam, chocolate and wine), the Churchill connection is celebrated with Winston mugs (£3), books, and CDs of famous speeches. There's also a selection of paintings and watercolours, tapestry kits, toiletries and clothes.

A separate bookshop in the Great Court sells local tourist guidebooks as well as historical books about the house and its occupants. Over in the Pleasure Gardens, the Butterfly House shop stocks herbs and lavender as well as houseplants and seeds.

🚗 On A44, 8 miles north of Oxford. Follow brown signs. ⊖ Train to Oxford, then bus 20 from Gloucester Green bus station. ① *Palace* 13 Mar to end Oct, Mon to Sun 10.30am to 5.30pm. *Park* open all year, Mon to Sun 9am to 5.30pm. *The Pleasure Gardens, Marlborough Maze and Butterfly House* mid-Mar to end Oct, Mon to Sun 10am to 6pm. 💷 Adult £9, 16- and 17-year-olds/senior citizens/students £7, child

(5–15 yrs old) £4.50, child (under 5 yrs old) free, family ticket (2 adults + 2 children) £22.50. *Entry to Marlborough Maze* adult/child/senior citizen £1. *Tour of private apartments* adult £4, child/senior citizen £2. ♿ Palace entrance and tour wheelchair accessible; adapted toilets near the cafeteria and gift shop, and in the Pleasure Gardens. The Water Terrace and Maze not recommended for wheelchair users. Disabled parking.

Bletchley Park

Bletchley, Milton Keynes, Buckinghamshire MK3 6EB ☎ *(01908) 640404*
🖱 *www.bletchleypark.org.uk*

Quality ★ ★ ★	Facilities 🏛 🏛	Value for money £££

Highlights Fascinating information on wartime code-breaking from tour guides; range of other exhibitions appealing to all ages

Drawbacks Some rooms and exhibitions rather dull and amateurish; inexperienced staff; dilapidated buildings; poor guidebooks

What's there During World War II Bletchley Park, Britain's code-breaking and intelligence base, succeeded in cracking the Germans' sophisticated Enigma code and gathered crucial intelligence. It has been estimated that the work done at Bletchley Park shortened the war by two years, saving hundreds of thousands of lives.

What remains now is a large area covered with somewhat dilapidated wartime huts (most no longer in use); the fine Victorian mansion, which houses a collection of Churchill memorabilia and the toy museum; a group of outbuildings containing old fire engines, model boats, model railways, and so on; and Faulkner House, where the bulk of the exhibitions are displayed. These displays, run by an assortment of voluntary groups, by and large have a wartime theme, such as a collection of World War II uniforms and memorabilia, engines and wreckage salvaged from crashed aircraft, and a display of wireless equipment used by the intelligence services.

You can also see a rebuilt and working version of 'Colossus', the world's first electronic computer, and follow the Cryptology Trail, which shows some of the codes used by different countries and strategies for cracking them.

However, the most interesting part of the visit is probably the guided tour, which begins in the library of the Mansion with an introduction to the work that Bletchley Park did during the war and why it was so important. The tour guide gives further information, and not a few anecdotes, about the personnel involved and the strategies used as you take a walk around the outside of the buildings. You can see where a bomb, dropped 'by accident', nearly brought Bletchley Park's work to an abrupt halt, and the Turing Bombe room, where coding information is said to have been processed 70 times quicker by mechanical means than it would be by a modern computer.

Information/tours/guides The two current publicity leaflets give basic information about dates, opening times and prices, plus a list of the displays and exhibitions. One leaflet provides a rather confusing map of the site, while the other offers a map and directions for getting to Bletchley Park itself. The guidebook (£2) includes only one page on the wartime work of Bletchley Park, plus sketchy details about the groups that run the displays. It is not a satisfying souvenir nor a helpful on-the-spot guide, but a collection of semi-promotional literature about a variety of special-interest groups.

Tours are available hourly (between 11am and 3pm), and last for just over an hour. The guide we had was excellent, telling the Bletchley Park story with a mass of fascinating detail and dry humour. There is also a daily talk about the building of the Colossus computer at 3.30pm.

Information provided in the exhibitions varies hugely as different groups run them. Most provide labels and display boards, and some (such as the exhibition run by the Leighton Buzzard Model Boat Club) offer interactive quizzes and push-button displays. There is a Discovery Trail leaflet available for children, inviting them to fill in the names of various items in the exhibitions and crack the code.

When to visit Fine weather is preferable, since the tours are mainly around the outside of the buildings. However, the exhibitions are inside, so there is plenty to see if it rains. Bletchley Park is currently open only on alternate weekends, so the choice of days to visit is limited.

Age appeal The guided tour is primarily aimed at adults and may appeal particularly to those who lived through World War II. Some of the exhibitions in Faulkner House are also concerned with the war and code-breaking but have more visual material, so will be of interest to all ages, while exhibitions such as the toy museum, model railways and model boats have a strong appeal for children.

Food and drink The canteen and bar in Hut 4 offers a range of hot and cold meals and snacks. Meals available in the canteen include ham, egg and chips (£3.50), bacon baps (£1.50), filled rolls, and a range of salads (£3 to £3.50). Children can choose egg and chips (£1.65) or sausage, chips and beans (£1.99), polished off with ice cream. The décor and furnishings are very dated and institutional-looking (unsurprisingly given the nature of Bletchley Park) and service is pleasant and prompt but not very professional. The NAAFI (in the main building) and coffee shop in Faulkner House serve just tea, coffee and snacks.

Shops The main shop is in Faulkner House, near the exit. It stocks a fairly limited range of merchandise, including books on Bletchley Park and code-breaking, plus a selection of mugs, tea towels, posters and stationery.

A range of Churchill-related items is on sale in the Churchill Rooms, including jigsaws (£10.95 upwards), key rings (85p), tea towels (£3) and Churchill's birthday cake recipe, printed on cards at 25p.

A few items are sold at the little Bletchley Park Post Office, which is being developed in the style of a World War II post office. You can buy a unique range of first-day covers and wartime memorabilia, such as duplicate ration books and ID cards.

🚗 From the M1, follow the B4034 towards Bletchley, following signs to Bletchley railway station. See Bletchley Park web site or publicity leaflets for more details or telephone in advance. ⊖ Train to Bletchley (from London Euston, Milton Keynes Central, Coventry and Birmingham New Street), then 200-m walk down the footpath opposite Bletchley railway station. Bletchley Bus Station is just a short walk from the railway station and the footpath. ⏲ Open every other weekend from early Jan to early Dec, 10.30am to 5pm (last entry 3.30pm, last tour 3pm). Telephone or see web site for a list of open weekends and other events. 💷 Adults £4.50, child (9 to 16 yrs old)/student/senior citizen £3.50, child (under 9 yrs old) free. ♿ Accessibility generally good, with most exhibitions at ground level. Ramp access into the mansion.

Blickling Hall

Blickling, Norfolk NR11 6NF ☎ *(01263) 738030*
📧 *www.nationaltrust.org.uk*

Quality ★ ★ ★   **Facilities** 👍 👍 👍 👍   **Value for money** £££
Highlights   Beautifully maintained gardens; good range of guides and leaflets,
              including children's guide; imaginative refreshments
Drawbacks   Fairly expensive

What's there   Your first glimpse of the splendid **Jacobean façade** of Blickling Hall – all curving Dutch gables and turrets, flanked by stately yew hedges – is unforgettable. Supposedly the birthplace of Anne Boleyn, Henry VIII's ill-fated second wife, Blickling Hall was largely built by Sir Henry Hobart in the early seventeenth century, although many of the apparently Jacobean features date from the second half of the eighteenth century, when John, 2nd Earl of Buckinghamshire, remodelled the house in keeping with its original style. In 1940 it became the first country house to be donated to the National Trust.

The highlights of the building's interior, which dates from Hobart's time, are the fantastic **plasterwork ceilings**, most notably in the Long Gallery and the South Drawing Room. Accounts show that plasterer Edward Stanyon was paid the princely sum of 5s 6d (27p) per square yard for his splendid pendanted handiwork. **The Great Hall**, though reconstructed in the eighteenth century, used many of the original Jacobean timbers, and a number of the unusual carved figures of soldiers on the newels of the staircase are dressed in uniforms of the 1620s. More typical of eighteenth-century taste is the **Chinese Bedroom**, with its rococo ceiling, hand-painted paper and carved ivory pagodas.

In the garden, the parterre of meticulously trimmed yews and formal herbaceous beds handsomely complements the graceful exterior of the house. From here a path leads up to the Doric Temple, with geometric avenues on either side leading off to the Orangery and Secret Garden.

Information/tours/guides   The useful leaflet you are given on entry includes a map and details of facilities. The other printed guides range from the detailed, full-colour souvenir guide to the Hall (£3.50) to a plainer leaflet (£1), as well as a free introductory leaflet to the garden. The guidebook goes into pretty exhaustive detail about the history of the Hall and its occupants, but can be a little dry. Room attendants vary in their helpfulness; the best are very enthusiastic.

When to visit   A fine day is best so that you can enjoy the gardens. For conservation reasons, light levels in the Hall are carefully controlled, so on dull days it may be difficult to pick out details of certain items. Allow at least an hour for the house, and the same for the gardens.

Special events are held throughout the year, including lakeside open-air concerts, behind-the-scenes days, wildlife family fun days, cheese and pudding tastings, guided walks and illustrated talks. For more information telephone (01263) 738049.

Age appeal An excellent children's activity guide (£1.25) provides a wealth of suggestions for things to do here – spotting family crests and matching up portrait stickers – and back at home: making marbled paper or Jacobean gingerbread. There's also a play area and picnic area, and children can enjoy playing hide-and-seek around the yew hedges in the garden.

Food and drink The Pantry serves snacks, while the Restaurant offers a wider range of dishes, largely based on Norfolk recipes from the seventeenth century and the 1930s – the imaginative menu explains their history and origins. Examples include seasonal vegetable pottage (casserole) enriched with St Peter's Ale served with Norfolk dumpling (£4.50), Norfolk Docky (a sort of ploughman's lunch; £2.75), and Norfolk shortcake and syllabub. Wine, beer and cider are also available as well as soft drinks, speciality teas, coffee and hot chocolate.

Shops The large shop, with a separate section for books, stocks the usual range of National Trust merchandise. At least all those lavender soaps are local, for once.

🚗 On B1354, 1½ miles north-west of Aylsham on the A140. Free parking. ⊖ Train to North Walsham, then Eastern Counties buses 50 and 50A Mon to Sat; buses 43 and 228 on Sun (telephone (0845) 300 6116 for more details on the Norfolk bus services) to Aylsham, then a 10-minute walk. ⏱ *Hall* 8 Apr to 31 July, Wed to Sun and Bank Hol 1pm to 4.30pm; 1 Aug to 31 Aug, Tues to Sun 1pm to 4.30pm; 1 Sept to 29 Oct Wed to Sun 1pm to 4.30pm. *Garden* 27 Mar to 31 Oct Wed to Sun (daily except Mon in Aug) 10.30am to 5.30pm; 1 Jan to end Mar, Sat and Sun 11am to 4pm. 💷 *House and garden* adult £6.50, child £3.25. *Garden* adult £3.70, child £1.85. ♿ House, shop, restaurant and parterre garden accessible to wheelchair users (lift to the first floor of the house). Disabled parking and toilets. Batri-Cars, wheelchairs and seated walking frames on loan (subject to availability).

Blue Planet Aquarium

Longlooms Road, Little Stanney, Ellesmere Port, Cheshire L65 9LF
☎ *(0930) 100300*

Quality ★★★	Facilities 🏛🏛🏛	Value for money ££

Highlights Moving walkway and glass tunnel; opportunity to touch fish
Drawbacks Very crowded; poor soundproofing

What's there Housed in a large metal warehouse-like building, this aquarium contains more than 3,000 species of fish. It's one of the biggest in the UK and divided into themed sections – for example 'Northern Streams' uses salmon and trout tanks to explain the formation of rivers from streams, and the role fish play. Others include 'Tropical Rivers', 'Lakes and Ponds', 'Mangrove Swamp' and 'Seas and Oceans'.

Throughout the aquarium most of the tanks are open-topped with painted backdrops and props to illustrate a particular theme, as well as appropriate sound effects. This allows you to observe the fish from above as well as the front – which makes you feel very close to them.

Most of the themed rooms make use of educational videos and display boards to explain what's going on. 'Lakes and Ponds' concentrates on Lake Malawi in Africa, complete with wild animal and tribal drum effects for its background, but poor soundproofing means that these noises get confused with those from other rooms, as well as the videos.

In an **interactive area**, visitors, particularly children, are encouraged to touch the fish and other aquatic life to learn about them at first hand. Divers go into the tanks to pass the creatures around and answer questions.

One of the most enjoyable parts of the attraction is the **moving walkway** that takes you through the huge main aquarium in a glass tunnel, which is all that separates you from ferocious-looking **sharks**, **stingrays** and hundreds of other fish. A visit will take about two hours.

Information/tours/guides No guided tours are provided, but the guides who wander around with microphones give background information and answer questions. A guidebook (£2.50) gives you the aquarium's history as well as facts about the fish species.

When to visit The centre is all indoors, and its exotic feel makes it an excellent rainy-day venue.

Age appeal Everyone is likely to be fascinated by the fish and the opportunity to touch some of them. There are free activities for youngsters, such as face painting and a Lego Aquazone.

Food and drink The open-plan canteen has a main counter for hot food and another selling drinks and snacks; visitors switching between the two can cause a bit of confusion. Food is standard and unimaginative, including fish and chips, jacket potatoes, and pre-packed sandwiches, but prices are reasonable, and there are special kids' meals.

Shops The goods in the spacious and brightly lit shop have a watery theme. Sharks and dolphins adorn everything from T-shirts to tea towels, posters, ornaments and jewellery, but there are also some educational books and videos.

From M53 Junction 10 follow signs to Little Stanney and aquarium. Free parking. Train (or bus) to Little Stanney (from Liverpool, Chester or Ellesmere Port), then few minutes' walk to aquarium. Mon to Sun 10am to 6pm. Closed 25 Dec. Adult £6.95, child (3 to 15 yrs old) £4.95, student/senior citizen/unemployed visitor £4.95, family ticket (2 adults + 4 children) £22.50. Wheelchair accessible; lift; disabled toilets.

Bowes Museum

Barnard Castle, County Durham DL12 8NP ☎ *(01833) 690606*
www.durham.gov.uk/bowesmuseum

Quality ★ ★ ★ ★   **Facilities** 🏛 🏛   **Value for money £££**
Highlights   Impressive collection of seventeenth-century fine art in elegant château setting; good labelling and information on exhibits
Drawbacks   Little interest to children

What's there The museum was built by Josephine and John Bowes between 1869 and 1892, specifically to house their **art collection**. Both husband and wife had a passion for art (French art in particular), and began collecting fine pieces of furniture, tapestries, porcelain and paintings to furnish and decorate the Château du Barry, near Paris, where they lived. On their return to Barnard Castle in England, near the Bowes family estate, they began building the museum to introduce 'ordinary people' to the world of art, although both died before the museum was opened to the public in 1892.

The French château, set within **wonderful grounds**, is the perfect place for such a collection. **French fine and decorative art** is dominant, seen to best effect in the tapestry collection and the furniture from the French Second Empire (1852–70). But there are also some elegant Italian and Spanish paintings, including works by **Goya**, **El Greco** and **Canaletto**, as well as some of Josephine Bowes' own works. English artists represented include **Turner**, **Gainsborough** and **Reynolds**. Prehistoric and Roman collections are found in the vaults. However, the highlight for many people is the **Silver Swan** musical automaton by the entrance, which, when operated (twice a day at 2pm and 4pm), seems to preen itself and then bend to take a fish from the water.

Information/tours/guides With your ticket comes a leaflet with basic details on facilities and a map showing the layout of each floor. Further information folders in each room highlight particular pieces and give the background to the collection's history and design.

An attractive glossy illustrated booklet is a good-value souvenir for £1, with photos of the important pieces and a bit of information on the Bowes family. For children there are free activity sheets available at reception.

In summer, Friends of the Museum provide free guided tours.

When to visit All year round, although the grounds are so impressive it would be a shame to miss them on account of bad weather. During the summer there are temporary exhibitions, and concerts are performed throughout the year.

Age appeal The museum is generally of less interest to children, though activity sheets are available, and pushchairs are allowed inside.

Food and drink Refreshments and light meals are available in the Café Bowes during opening hours. The café has a self-service canteen with hot and cold drinks, sandwiches (£1.70), scones and cake. There's usually a choice of three hot dishes, for example soup, lasagne or fisherman's pie (£3.85).

Tickets are valid all day, so if the café is not open you can have lunch in the town (Barnard Castle) and re-enter the museum.

Shops The museum shop, next to the café, sells postcards (30p), greetings cards (90p–£2), and catalogues relating to specific exhibitions. More substantial items include tapestries (£7.95–£15.95), lace items, and a book about the museum (£7.95). Sweets and soft toys are on sale for children.

Facilities The disabled person's toilet can be used for nappy changing. Non-disabled toilets are on the first floor and outside the museum.

🚗 From the A66 (Scotch Corner to Penrith road), follow signs to Barnard Castle, four miles from the village of Bowes. Free parking. ⊖ Take train to Darlington and then bus.

Alternatively take bus from Bishop Auckland or Richmond. ⊙ Mon to Sun 11am to 5pm (closed Christmas Day, Boxing Day & New Year's Day). 🖃 Adult £3.90, senior citizen/student/unemployed visitor £2.90, child £2.90, family ticket £12. ⴲ Car parking for disabled visitors, wide-access toilets and a lift. Wheelchairs available on request. All of the museum is accessible to wheelchairs except rooms 1–5.

Brighton Palace Pier

Madeira Drive, Brighton, West Sussex BN2 1TW   ☎ *(01273) 609361*

Quality ★ ★ ★ ★   **Facilities** 🛥 🛥 🛥 🛥   **Value for money ££££**
Highlights Fine Victorian Pier; tacky seaside family fun
Drawbacks Modern extension detracts from the period charm; phenomenally busy in
             summer; expensive

What's there Compared with many of the more modest piers around the UK, Brighton Palace Pier is a regal Victorian lady. Built in 1890 after a storm wrecked the original Chain Pier – immortalised in Turner's paintings – it extends over half a kilometre out to sea, sporting fancy filigree ironwork, some original kiosks and a signal cannon from the Chain Pier. The old girl is also a bit of a film star, appearing in *Brighton Rock*, mod-madness *Quadrophenia*, and more recently in *Mona Lisa* and *The End of the Affair*.

In 1995 it sprouted a controversial extension to accommodate an enlarged funfair. This has changed the pier's silhouette and character considerably, submerging the Victorian elegance further beneath modern commercial development. At the far end, the funfair offers brain-scrambling, vomit-inducing rides that spin and plummet until you scream for mercy. It includes a 360-degree looping rollercoaster, waltzers, dodgems, a spinning wheel and a rotating spinning chair which you are strapped into. For the more cowardly there's a sedate old-fashioned carousel. You can apparently see the Isle of Wight from the helter skelter on a clear day. Height restrictions apply on the wilder rides.

A vast domed hangar houses a bleeping, flashing cacophony of gambling machines and state-of-the-art video games. Kiosks selling toffee apples, candy floss, waffles and winkles sit next to side-shows, graphologists, fortune tellers and a dolphin derby. It's all loud and flashy in wonderful knees-up bad taste – but great fun. Just be warned, the various thrills and spills, games and shops can burn a larger hole in your pocket than you envisaged. The pay-as-you-ride voucher system for the funfair is not cheap – the wilder the ride, the more it costs; our £2-rollercoaster ride lasted just over a minute, dodgems were £1.50, and an electronic palm reading print-out £2.99.

Information/tours/guides A series of information plaques attached to the balustrades – the 'Heritage Trail' – gives interesting snippets of the pier's history. It would be satisfying to see more space devoted to the heritage of both Brighton's piers – perhaps a small display somewhere among the modern madness.

When to visit Sunny summer weekends have the wildest atmosphere if you can cope with crowds. Some rides close out of season and on quiet days, when the pier reverts to its original conception as a place to take a stroll or snooze in a deckchair. If you're in Brighton at any time of year, the Palace Pier is always worth a visit.

Age appeal Perennial family fun for everyone from screaming kids to septuagenarians snoring in striped deckchairs. Thrill-seekers and amusement arcade aficionados will have the most fun.

Food and drink The Palm Court fish and chip café in the old bandstand is the best bet with take-away cod and chips (£3.40) and sausage and chips (£2.15). Otherwise go for pub grub and pints in one of the three bars – Victoria's, Horatio's or Offshore (the last for karaoke victims) – or kiosks selling hot roast meat sandwiches. If you count them as food, the pier is awash with cockles and whelks, candy floss, hot-dogs, burgers, ice-cream, and all manner of nasty, sticky, smelly, greasy things.

Shops Kiosks sell Brighton rock and naff seaside souvenirs – no Yves St Laurent here.

Other facilities Toilets are clean, modern and well maintained.

🚗 M23 to Brighton, town centre car parking. ⊖ Train to Brighton station, 15-minute walk to seafront; bus to Pool Valley station, opposite Palace Pier. ⏱ Mon to Sun 9am to 2am, summer; 10am to 12 midnight, winter (depending on weather) 💷 Free; deckchairs free (see also text). ♿ Good wheelchair access; disabled toilets.

Bristol Zoo Gardens

Clifton, Bristol BS8 3HA　☎ *0117-973 8951*
🖱 *www.bristolzoo.org.uk*　🖱 *information@bristolzoo.org.uk*

Quality ★★★★　　**Facilities** 👜👜👜　　**Value for money** ££££
Highlights　Seal and Penguin Coasts; Twilight World; Zoolympics Trail
Drawbacks　Drab restaurant

What's there Imagination distinguishes Bristol Zoo Gardens from many other zoos. Among attractive gardens and walkways there is a gorilla island, various monkey islands and hundreds of other animals, from Wendy the elephant to Dacca and Indi the lion cubs, born in 1998. Where Bristol really excels, however, is in its unusual presentation of some of its smaller inhabitants. The **Twilight World**, where night begins at 10am, is cleverly designed to mimic the desert and the jungle, with tapes of buzzing insects and fibreglass rocks, trees and wood chips completing the effect. You're unlikely to hear or see any activity from the two-toed sloth, which sleeps 22 hours a day and leaves its tree only once a week, when nature calls! The blind naked mole rats, on the other hand, are in a constant frenzy, endlessly scuttling through perspex tunnels. The display of the 'House at Night', with cockroaches and other nasties lurking in dark corners, is enough to bring on the urge to spring clean a little earlier than usual.

The Reptile House takes you on a journey past all manner of cold-blooded creatures, with lots of information on diet, prey, camouflage and hibernation. It finishes by bringing humans into the equation, with a sober reminder of why some of the species are endangered. The journey continues through the underwater world to the creepy crawlies in 'Bugworld'. The **honey bee colony** with its industrious residents is particularly impressive. The most recent display is the **'Seal and Penguin Coasts'**, with underwater tunnels allowing you to come face to face with these graceful swimmers.

Information/tours/guides There is no guidebook, but the times of feeding sessions and talks throughout the day (from 11.15am to 3.30pm) are on a timetable available at the entrance. For £1.50 (and a refundable £5 deposit) you can hire an audio-guide, with commentaries matched to numbers on the cages/exhibits.

When to visit Because much of Bristol Zoo is under cover, the weather is not much of an issue. Some of the enclosed attractions could get very crowded in school holidays.

Age appeal Children will love the 'zoolympics trail', which will have them competing with members of the animal kingdom by, say, standing on one leg like a flamingo. There is also an adventure playground, an activity centre with brass rubbing and face painting as well as 'animal encounters'. Horticulturists may appreciate the rose garden and herbaceous borders.

Food and drink The Pelican Restaurant is no great shakes and feels rather like a school dinner hall, with clearing trollies scattered over the floor and lots of meals involving beans and chips. There is also a burger bar and ice cream parlour.

Shops A wide range of merchandise is available, from chocolate-covered 'monkey droppings' at £2.99 to fragrance oils and designer jewellery.

From Bristol city centre, follow the brown elephant sign. Car parking (50p when we inspected). Train to Bristol then bus 8 or 9 or open-top bus to zoo (27 Mar to 26 Sept. For more information on buses tel. Travelline 0117-955 5111.) Mon to Sun, 9am to 5.30pm (4.30pm in winter). Closed 25 Dec. Adult £8.20, child (3 to 13 yrs old) £4.60, senior citizen, young person (14 to 18 yrs old), student £7.20. Good wheelchair (and pushchair) access. Wheelchairs available for loan. Disabled parking.

Butlins Family Entertainment Resort

Roman Bank, Skegness, Lincolnshire PE25 1NJ ☎ *(01754) 765567*

Quality ★	Facilities	Value for money £
Highlights	Very large indoor swimming pool/adventure play area	
Drawbacks	Poor value for money if not using the pool all day; shamelessly commercial – extra charges and tacky merchandise for children abound; several facilities were closed when we inspected	

What's there The major selling point for non-residents is the chance to use the **Splash Sub-tropical Waterworld**, which is indoors and incorporates water rides, flumes, a wavepool, waterfalls and children's play area. An outdoor 'funpool' is nearby. The attraction also offers a small and not very exciting funfair with dodgems, roundabout, shooting galleries and a go-kart track (£3 extra charge), eight bars and restaurants (not all were open when we visited), rides for young children, 'activities' for children, and a cinema (also at extra cost).

Much of the site and facilities seems to hark back to the 1950s when such holiday centres first became popular. Even today the army-barracks ambience remains. Stretches of bare concrete are punctuated by huts emblazoned with sometimes baffling signs ('Reds – home of the Redcoats' turned out to be not a staff hostel but a venue, shut when we visited, for disco dancing and children's talent shows). No Redcoats were in evidence, but the exhortations to join an under-subscribed game of bingo evoked memories of the 'Hi-de-hi' heyday of the holiday camp.

For those to whom bingo, one-armed bandits or crazy golf do not appeal, there is a snooker/billiards hall, ten-pin bowling (extra charge) and an all-weather sports court and a bowling green. A betting shop and 'Cashino' provide further entertainment for adults, while Toyland offers gentle rides for the very young.

Information/tours/guides For the day visitor, working out what and where things are from the promotional leaflet/map, included in the admission price, and the sparse, uninformative signs is quite an effort. The location of toilets is not advertised, and the perfunctory gestures of a staff member when we enquired – much to her amusement – were misleading.

When to visit During summer and autumn.

Age appeal This holiday centre is aimed squarely at families with young children. Groups of teenagers/young adults are actively discouraged through the admission policy. Height restrictions apply for funfair rides, so little ones might miss out on some of them.

Food and drink Food is mainly of the fast-food variety, with franchise brands including Burger King. The Harry Ramsden's fish-and-chip restaurant was closed when we visited. The Pinewood Studios café served pizza (£3.95 to £4.95) and lasagne (£4.95), with tea and coffee at 80p and 90p.

Shops Numerous shops and stalls are dotted around the attraction, but apart from the supermarket they focus mainly on branded merchandise linked with the latest blockbuster movie or fictional characters such as Noddy. Items on sale include baseball caps (£5.99), picnic plates (£3.99), mugs (£4.99) and romper suits (£16.99).

Other facilities These include nursery services (3 months to 5 years) and organised entertainment for children, a medical centre, hair/beauty salon, cash machine and local tourist information.

From the north, approach on A52, follow signs. From the south ignore first Butlins entrance on right by funfair and continue to car park opening 100 yards further up A52 on left. Parking free to visitors. Train to Skegness station, then bus (destination 'Butlins') at station. End April to late Oct, 9.30am to 11pm (last entry 4pm). Times can vary so telephone ahead. Adult £9.50, child (2 to 14 yrs old), and senior citizens £6.50, child (under 2 yrs old) free, family ticket (2 adults + 2 children) £28. Under-18s must be with an adult as part of family group. No single party of four or more guests under 30 yrs old. For single parties of less than four people, guests must be over 21 yrs old. *Cinema* £3.50 (adults); £2.50 (children and senior citizens). Most areas accessible by wheelchairs (but telephone for more information). Competent swimmers only on flume rides (Waterworld).

Cadbury World

Off Linden Rd, Bournville, Birmingham B30 2LD ☎ *0121-451 4159;*
24hr-information line 0121-451 4180 🖰 *www.cadbury.co.uk/cadworld.htm*

Quality ★ ★ ★   **Facilities** 🏛 🏛 🏛 🏛   **Value for money** £ £ £
Highlights   Good history of chocolate; nostalgic Cadbury's adverts; great for kids
Drawbacks   Not enough to interest adults; none of the manufacturing process is
                visible; brochure adds nothing to the visit

What's there   If you're expecting Willy Wonka's Chocolate Factory, think
again. Cadbury World's chocolate experience starts in the **mocked-up jungles**
of Central America with the Aztecs and Mayans, where you get a taste of the
spicy drink discovered by the Spanish Conquistadores. The story of chocolate
continues in the European courts of the eighteenth century before moving on
to the more prosaic setting of Victorian Birmingham where the Quaker
Cadbury family established their global chocolate empire. The family
company intended to displace the excessive beer and alcohol consumption of
the time with more nutritious products.

Various soundtracks, videos and short films of the manufacture of Creme
Eggs and Crunchies are interesting but a disappointing substitute for choco-
holics who thought they would see vats of liquid chocolate and conveyor belts
laden with goodies. Demonstrators show how chocolates are handmade, and
you get more of a factory experience in the **packaging plant,** but this can be a
hit-and-miss event, depending on whether it is working when you visit.
Cadbury World provides a bumper box of self-promotion for Cadbury plc
with a display on the making of the Cadbury *Coronation Street* credits, and
nostalgic choccy adverts. The 'Bean Team' characters and 'Cadabra' ride are
strictly aimed at younger kids, so any adults without accompanying children
to act as cover will feel blushingly conspicuous. The experience ends in a vast
chocolate shop. As the average Briton buys 9.4 kg of chocolate a year, this may
not be a disappointment.

Information/tours/guides   This is not a guided experience – you make
your own way around a channelled route. Plenty of friendly staff are at hand to
help and answer questions. The glossy souvenir brochure is poor value at £3 –
it adds nothing to the experience, and offers no extra information. The
publicity brochure is up front about the restrictions on the packaging-plant
activity.

When to visit   Any time of year is a good time to visit, although school
holidays are, of course, peak visiting periods.

Age appeal   Chocolate is popular stuff, so chocaholics of all ages will find
something to enjoy, although couples and singles visiting without children
may feel rather out of place among all the families. There is an educational
element to the attraction, but Cadbury World is aimed mostly at families with
younger kids.

Food and drink   The self-service restaurant is spacious and modern,
and feels like a fast-food joint. The choice of cheap and cheerful dishes

won't scare children, but won't inspire adults looking for light options or imaginative offerings either: jacket potatoes (£2.35 to £2.50), steak and kidney pie (£4.55), fish and chips (£5.75), kid's meal (£2.55), coffee (90p), pot of tea (95p).

Shops Those addicted to chocolate could blow a fuse in the Cadbury World shop, which sells every conceivable Cadbury product, including 400g Dairy Milk (£1.73); 750g Mis-shapes (£2.99); Cadbury branded polo shirt (£11.99); and child's T-shirt (£7.99).

Other facilities The smart modern toilets dotted throughout are clean and well-maintained.

🚗 From M6 junction 6, follow A38 central and south, then brown signs; from M42 junction 2 follow brown signs on A441 / A4040; from M5 junction 4 follow brown signs on A38. ⊖ Train to Birmingham New Street, then connecting train to Bournville station. Alternatively, buses 83, 84 or 85 from Birmingham city centre to Bournville. ⏱ Variable. ☎ 0121-451 4180 to check. 💷 Adult £6.75, child (4 to 15 yrs old) £4.90, child (under 4 yrs old) free, senior citizen and student £5.75, family ticket (2 adults + 2 children) £20.20 (2 adults + 3 children) £24.40. ♿ Mostly flat surfaces; lift. No access to packaging plant on third floor.

Camelot Theme Park

Charnock Richard, Chorley, Lancashire PR7 5LP ☎ *(01257) 453044*

Quality ★ ★	**Facilities 🏰 🏰**	**Value for money £**
Highlights	Plenty for children to do; manageable size; rare-breeds animal farm provides a quieter spot	
Drawbacks	Tacky and expensive; poor toilets	

What's there This 'medieval' theme park contains various **adventure rides,** such as the Tower of Terror – a sort of **loop-the-loop rollercoaster** – Galleon – a swinging pirate ship – and Venom – a rollercoaster ride in the dark – as well as a rare-breeds animal farm. Other side-show stalls include coconut shies, and a jousting arena with live horseback jousting.

Sadly, Camelot is not a state-of-the-art Disneyland or Alton Towers (*qv*) with the latest computerised technology, and many of the rides are rather old-fashioned and unlikely to thrill the more sophisticated youngsters. The Camelot theme, with tatty polystyrene 'castles' and effects, is, at best, half-hearted and as such pretty unconvincing. It's a large site – there's even a hotel complex – but not a terribly attractive one, with lots of plastic on sale in the souvenir shops, along with ice cream and burger stalls, and video-game arcades.

The **jousting arena,** however, is quite authentic, and the displays entertaining. Younger children will undoubtedly enjoy the **log flume** and other rides, as well as the roller-blading hall. They might even like the **rare-breeds farm,** although in truth it consists of a few unusual-looking sheep, and very ordinary-looking pigs, cattle, goats and chickens. But, compared with the rest of the park, it is at least fairly quiet.

Information/tours/guides The free brochure has a map and details of what's at the attraction. We spotted very few attendants when we visited and getting further information was difficult.

When to visit Camelot is almost entirely outdoors, so fine, and preferably warm, weather is required.

Age appeal Younger children will love the rides, side shows and play areas, but most older people are likely to come away with a headache. Quite a lot of walking, mainly on Tarmac paths, is necessary, and some of the slopes are quite steep.

Food and drink Burger, drinks and ice cream stalls are all over the place. The main food hall in the centre of the park in a plastic tent offers Wimpy hamburgers, fish and chips, pizza, and a 'coffee shop' selling sandwiches and baguettes.

Shops Souvenir shops and stalls are everywhere, selling cheap toys, such as guns and cars, and ornaments.

Other facilities The toilets on inspection were in a sorry state, especially those in the food hall, with peeling paint, a blocked urinal and filthy fittings.

🚗 From M61 junction 8 or M6 junction 27, follow the signs. Free parking. ⊖ Train to Chorley and then taxi or C7 bus (Mon to Sat only). ⊙ Mon to Sun, 10am to 5pm Jun to mid-Aug; Sat and Sun, 10am to 5pm mid-Apr to May, Sept to Oct (open weekends only). 💷 Adult £8.99, child (under 1 yr) free, family £32 (2 adults + 2 children), senior citizen/disabled person £6.90. ♿ Wheelchairs available for hire, but steepish slopes and difficulty for wheelchair users on some rides.

Cannon Hall and Open Farm

Cawthorne, Barnsley, Yorkshire S75 4AT ☎ *(01226) 790427 (farm)*
(01226) 790270 (Hall)

Quality ★ ★ ★ ★ **Facilities** 🏛 🏛 🏛 **Value for money ££££**
Highlights Beautiful grounds and gardens
Drawbacks Crowded shop and cafés

What's there The Spencer-Stanhope family, who made their fortune from mining and furnaces, lived at Cannon Hall for 200 years. Their family home is now a museum, though much of it appears as if they still live there. Everything is in fabulous condition, from the oak-panelled rooms to the magnificent fireplaces, although some of the eighteenth-century furniture is not original to the house, much of it having been purchased from the Victoria and Albert Museum (*qv*).

Of particular note is the collection of richly decorated **William Moorcroft pottery**, along with the **Tudor-style galleried ballroom**, where it is easy to imagine elegantly dressed aristocrats swirling around. Perhaps the most striking room, however, is the **library**, with its green damask wall covering and recessed mahogany bookcases – in the eighteenth century books were so expensive that they were kept under lock and key.

Upstairs is the rather incongruous museum of the 13th/18th Royal Hussars (QMO), detailing the 300-year history of the regiment. On display are pistols, swords and uniforms from the nineteenth century to the present day, as well as a recreation of a military camp.

Cannon Hall sits amid 70 acres of **country park and landscaped gardens**. Access to the park is free (apart from a £1 parking charge), and this provides a pretty good day out in itself with its mature trees, open grassland to play football or run around in, and lake to walk round. Entry to a walled garden, dating from the 1760s, is also free. It was once famous for producing 400 varieties of pears, along with enough vegetables to feed a village – its main purpose for many years. Alongside are some wonderful landscaped gardens that make for a lovely stroll.

The **farm** is home to dozens of small and large animals, many of which visitors are encouraged to stroke and handle. Some, such as the **pygmy goats and llamas,** are so popular that small queues develop to touch them. Outside, shire horses are led around by the attendants. Children can then let off more steam in the large, nearby play area with swings and slides.

A visit to the house doesn't take more than an hour or so, and the farm takes a similar amount of time, but you could easily pass an entire day taking in the rest of the grounds and gardens.

Information/tours/guides No proper guidebook is available, but the colourful pamphlets for both the Hall and the farm give a fair amount of information. In addition, a separate leaflet called *A Short Tour of Cannon Hall* provides a bit more detail on each of the main rooms. There are occasional guided tours, but they finish for the season on 26 August.

When to visit The grounds, Hall and farm can be enjoyed all year round, but to see the colourful walled garden at its best come in summer.

Age appeal Children love the farm animals, and Cannon Hall itself may be of more interest to them if they follow the youngsters' guide and quiz 'Find out about Cannon Hall with Sammy Spider', which is available for free. Everyone can enjoy a day out in the country park, and the paths are well maintained for those with limited mobility.

Food and drink The first of the two cafés is a purpose-built affair with plenty of seating, next to the farm, and serves pre-packed sandwiches, fish and chips and jacket potatoes. The other café, which is more of a tea room, is located in what was the original kitchen next to the walled garden and provides a glimpse of what life 'downstairs' was really like. Cakes, scones and sandwiches are served.

Shops The gift shop, next to the farm, is large and packed full of goods ranging from farmyard games and plastic animals to T-shirts, nature books, tea towels and stationery. It can, however, get crowded.

Off the A635 between Barnsley and Huddersfield, then follow the road signs. Car park (£1 for 4 hrs). Train or bus to Barnsley then bus to Cawthorne (although public transport is not recommended – call (01226) 206757 for details) *Cannon Hall* Apr to Oct, Tues to Sat and bank hols 10.30am to 5pm, Sun 12 noon to 5pm. Closed Mondays. *Farm* open all year, Mon to Sun 10.30am to 5pm (4pm Oct to Mar). Closed 25 Dec.
Cannon Hall (plus extra for farm) adult £1 (£2.10), child, senior citizen, student 50p (£1.60), family ticket (2 adults + 3 children) £2.50 (£7). Full access to Farm and Hall except to first-floor museum. Disabled parking.

Canterbury Cathedral

Canterbury, Kent CT1 2EH ☎ *(01227) 762862*

Quality ★★ **Facilities** 🏛 🏛 🏛 **Value for money** ££
Highlights Site of Thomas Becket's martyrdom; good guided tours and audio tour
Drawbacks Charges for extras can add up; expensive toilets (20p)

What's there The seat of the Archbishop of Canterbury and the mother church of the Anglican community, Canterbury Cathedral became the greatest pilgrimage church in northern Europe after the martyrdom of Thomas Becket. When it was rebuilt after a fire in 1174 it became England's first major building in the Gothic style. The nave is a splendid example of Perpendicular Gothic, dating from the fourteenth century. In the north transept is the spot where Becket was killed in 1170 by knights loyal to Henry II, marked by a **modern altar of sword points**. He was originally buried in the twelfth-century Romanesque crypt.

Look up on passing into the Quire of the church to see the fine fan vaulting. From here the architecture draws your eye towards the high altar and the archbishop's simple throne. A candle marks the spot where Becket's shrine was located until King Henry VIII ordered its destruction. In the north aisle you can see some of the miracles associated with the saint commemorated in the beautiful stained-glass windows, which date from the late twelfth and early thirteenth centuries. Continue walking around the back of the altar and you will reach the **Crown Chapel**, built to hold the top of the head of Becket after it was struck off by one of the assassins – the chapel is now dedicated to martyrs of our time.

On the south side of the choir is the most famous tomb in the cathedral – that of the **Black Prince**. His effigy on top of the tomb shows him in full armour, while above hang modern copies of his gloves, shield jacket and wonderful hat topped with a lion. The somewhat faded originals are in a glass case on the wall nearby – Oliver Cromwell is said to have stolen the sword.

Information/tours/guides It is easy to miss things on the way round, as labelling is poor to non-existent, so we would recommend taking a good guidebook (the official one is not easy to use on the spot) or booking one of the audio tours or guided tours to get you started. Guided tours (adult £3.50; child £1.50; senior citizen/student £2.50) take approximately 1½ hours and run three times a day (commencing 10.30am, noon and 2–2.30pm) in summer. Tickets can be bought at the Cathedral Welcome Centre opposite the main entrance. Audio tours last 45 minutes and can be paid for (adult £2.95; child £1; senior citizen/student £1.95) inside the cathedral. There are no guided tours or audio tours on Sundays. A video about the cathedral is shown in the Education Centre (adult £1.50; child 50p; senior citizen/student £1).

When to visit The cathedral can get very busy in the summer, so avoid it if you can. Opening hours are limited on Sundays.

Age appeal An 'Explorers Guide' for children costs £2. The Black Prince's tomb may appeal to children, but little else is aimed at them.

Food and drink None is available on site.

Shops The extensive modern shop in the precincts, through which you have to exit, sells a wide range of gifts.

🚗 Cathedral not signposted; city-centre parking very difficult. Use park-and-ride scheme. ⊖ Canterbury East and West stations are about 15 minutes' walk. ◷ Easter to Sept, Mon to Sat *precinct* 7am to 9pm, *cathedral* 9am to 6.30pm; Oct to Easter Mon to Sat 9am to 4.30pm, Sun opening limited; typically 12.30pm to 2.30pm and 4.30pm to 5.30pm. *Treasury* 10.30am to 12.30pm and 2pm to 4pm (summer only). 💷 Adult £3; child (5 to 16 yrs old); senior citizen, student £2. ♿ Disabled parking (in precincts) must be pre-booked (tel (01227) 762862). Wheelchairs on loan; lift for access to Quire and north transept. Touch and hearing display for visually impaired. Disabled toilets.

Carisbrooke Castle

Newport, Isle of Wight PO30 1XY ☎ *(01983) 522107*

Quality ★★★ **Facilities** 👜 👜 👜 **Value for money** £££
Highlights Good for families; interesting display on lifestyles
Drawbacks Could do more to tell the Castle's history and improve labelling

---

What's there Carisbrooke sits at the centre of the Isle of Wight, and in the past it was believed that whoever controlled this castle would control the island – even today a walk round the battlements will make you appreciate its strategic position. The earliest castle was built by the Saxons during the eighth century and you can see the additions made over time as you walk round. Charles I was briefly imprisoned here – and made several escape bids – before being taken for trial and execution in London.

Go through the Elizabethan gateway, turn left and you can climb up to walk along the **battlement wall**. Follow the steps down and up again and you will find yourself on the top of the motte (mound) built in Norman times, topped by **the keep**. Inside here is the first well dug in the castle and a **fourteenth-century lavatory** built into the outer wall. Back at ground level you'll pass the small wheelhouse where the later well was dug. This was so deep that you need to wind a wheel to bring up the bucket. Prisoners originally turned the wheel, but in the seventeenth century donkeys were introduced – and there are regular performances of a donkey turning the wheel throughout the day. Queues here can be long, so if you see the line reduced to a reasonable length at any time, pop in. You can see some of the donkeys in their stalls, and behind this is a small exhibition describing what residents of the castle would have eaten during the various periods of history and the different jobs they would have carried out – children will enjoy this.

The original Great Hall, round to the right as you go out, has a rather dry museum on the castle and island life. Don't miss the **nightcap worn by Charles I** the night before his execution and a piece of his lace cravat worn on the day, donated by Queen Victoria. If the curator isn't too busy at the small shop he has a **suit of chain mail** that he lets children try on. Upstairs is a display of costumes and a tribute room to Tennyson. The small chapel, across the courtyard, was rebuilt in 1905 to mark the 250th anniversary of the execution of Charles I; nowadays it is a memorial chapel to those who died in the two world wars. Allow a couple of hours for a full tour of the castle.

Information/tours/guides There is a colour guidebook (£2.95) and an activity sheet for children.

When to visit Carisbrooke is best in fine weather. Saturday still tends to be changeover day on the island and can be quieter. Lots of events are held throughout the summer, such as 'knights' telling tales of their exploits.

Age appeal It's a good family attraction.

Food and drink The Castle affords a good picnic spot. Snacks can be bought at the self-service restaurant (open April to October), such as cream tea (£3.50), soup of day (£1.95), and baked potato and coleslaw (£3.35).

Shops The shop sells books, clothing, ornaments and children's items.

🚐 About 1 mile SW of Newport, signposted from city centre; free car parking.
⊖ Train to Ryde, then bus (Carisbrooke nine miles away) or bus to Newport, minibus to Castle leaves hourly 10am to 4pm Apr to Oct. Tel (01983) 827005 for bus details. ⊙ Mon to Sun, Apr to Sept, 10am to 6pm; Oct 10am to 5pm; Nov to Mar 10am to 4pm. Closed 24–26 Dec, 1 Jan. 💷 Adult £4.50; child £2.30; student, unemployed, senior citizen £3.40; family ticket (2 adults + 3 children) £11.30. Free to English Heritage members. ♿ Wheelchair access to grounds and lower levels only.

Carlisle Cathedral

The Abbey, Carlisle CA3 8TZ ☎ *(01228) 548151/535169*

Quality ★★★	Facilities 🍴🍴🍴	Value for money ££££

Highlights Good architecture and some very interesting interior detail; imaginative shop

Drawbacks Sparse interpretation

What's there Carlisle Cathedral rarely features on lists of the great cathedrals of England. In comparison with Salisbury, Winchester or York, it is provincial and unsung. But this small red sandstone building, in the centre of a town that most people happily pass by, is worth a great deal more attention than it receives.

Its setting, for a start, is reminiscent of the great foundations further south. Right next to the city centre, the **cathedral close**, with a scattering of ancient buildings and walls, is something of a peaceful haven of greenery, with useful benches from which to contemplate the stonework from Hadrian's Wall, now part of the fabric of the building.

Founded in 1122, too close to the Scottish border for comfort, the Cathedral has suffered from centuries of warfare. Much of the old Norman nave has gone, leaving the cathedral curiously unbalanced, with a long choir – most of it dating from the fifteenth century – transepts, and not much else. The interior, however, is a place of fascination – not simply because of the venerability of the slumped **old Norman arches** above the crossing, or the beauty of the **fourteenth-century stained glass**, but because of the curiosities to be found tucked away here and there, in a kind of centuries-long collection of the flotsam of provincial religious life.

Chief among them is the **Brougham triptych**, a wonderful carved Flemish altarpiece from the sixteenth century. How this magnificent example of the woodcarver's art came to the wilds of Cumbria is a story in itself – one that the guides are happy to relate. Then there are the **misericords** and the **choir stalls**, both from the early fifteenth century, and the carved capitals of the columns with their depictions of the months of the year. Battered, barely visible, medieval paintings of the lives of St Cuthbert and St Anthony hang on the walls. There are human stories too – letters from Dean Tait written while watching his daughters dying (he commissioned the great window in their memory).

Even the treasury – in most cathedrals a place of extreme tedium – is brought to life here by the stories surrounding the objects on display. There's the communion cup rescued from a sales room, and the walrus tusk that has pitched up among the silver and gilt chalices.

Information/tours/guides Resplendently robed, Carlisle Cathedral's volunteer guides provide an excellent welcome to visitors, and know their stuff as well. You do have to buttonhole them, or wait for them, if you just want one or two questions answered. A rather more detailed explanatory handout for visitors would be useful. It is probably as well to reckon on having to buy the guidebook (£2.50) in the shop if you want a clear understanding of what you are looking at. The practicalities of visiting the Cathedral are excellently outlined, both in the 'Historic Carlisle' leaflet and in the Cathedral's own leaflet, both available at the tourist office in the town centre. There are separate inserts for both the cathedral shop and the restaurant.

When to visit There is no 'best' time to visit, although the setting is at its most attractive in spring and the Christmas season brings a little extra magic.

Age appeal Children either find cathedrals fascinating or they don't. Because of the stories connected to so many of the objects here, Carlisle may appeal more than most, especially as the guides make a special effort to interest young visitors.

Food and drink The 'Prior's Kitchen' inhabits the undercroft of the medieval Fratery, originally the monk's dining hall. This is an appropriate setting for the Cathedral's catering outlet, a self-service café-restaurant popular with shoppers as well as cathedral visitors. It's an atmospheric setting, with vaulting, old tiles and a strong sense of the past, although it can get a little gloomy and steamy on a wet day. There's plenty of space, and the food is home-made and fresh. It is not cheap, however, with main courses, such as Cellarer's Sausage Casserole or Medieval beef at £4.95. Simpler dishes, such as jacket potatoes (£2.90), or soup, roll and butter (£1.85), are available too. The home-made sandwiches (£1.85) are very good. Service is swift.

Shops A tiny shop inside the cathedral, just off the entrance way, sells an extremely imaginative range of goods, although space is limited, the cashiers are volunteers (a bit prone to error when we inspected) and prices are not always clear. However, this is a shop that repays a long browse, for there is a lot of variety and some good souvenirs of the cathedral. As well as the general guidebook, specialist books on the cathedral's misericords and other aspects of interest are also on offer. There are reproductions of the misericords too (£7.75 to £9.50). Cathedral mugs are £3.90, and a cassette of the choir costs £8. Candles for Christmas (£4.30), crafts and jewellery, preserves and prints (most of them local) round out the range. Children are offered a good selection too.

🚗 From M6 junction 43 towards Carlisle city centre. Public car parks nearby. ⊖ Train to Carlisle station, then short walk. ◷ Mon to Sat 7.30am to 6.15pm, Sun 7.30am to 5pm. *Shop* Mon to Sat 10am to 5pm (4pm in winter). *Restaurant* Mon to Sat 10am to 4.30pm (4pm in winter). 💷 Free admission (£2 donation requested). ♿ Some areas accessible but steps down to restaurant. Separate disabled toilet.

Castle Howard

Nr Malton, North Yorkshire YO60 7DA　☎ *(01653) 648444*
📠 *(01653) 648501*

Quality ★★★★★　　　**Facilities 👜 👜 👜 👜 👜**　　　**Value for money £££££**

Highlights　Family house that has evolved through the years; excellent guides; wonderful grounds and rose gardens; plenty to keep you occupied for a day

Drawbacks　Toilets at Lakeside could have done with a clean when we visited; children's leaflet for the house would be useful

---

What's there　The private home of the Howard family and a fine tribute to the cult of the English amateur, Castle Howard was designed by the dramatist John Vanbrugh, who had never built a house before, and building started in around 1700 for the 3rd Earl of Carlisle. It took over a hundred years to build, and Vanbrugh's flamboyant baroque design and dramatic dome were tempered by the addition of a sober Palladian wing that leaves the house spectacularly asymmetrical. Wonderful grounds encompass woodlands, formal gardens, temples, lakes and follies.

A tour of the house starts with the Grand Staircase hung with family portraits, leading to the China Landing with over 300 pieces on display – mainly Crown Derby, Meissen and Chelsea. The bedrooms beyond were the private apartments of the family from the 1830s after the marriage of Georgiana Cavendish – daughter of Georgiana, 5th Duchess of Devonshire – and George Howard. The marriage linked the two great houses of Chatsworth and Castle Howard, and the apartments are still used by the family today when the house is closed. The Antique Passage, lined with busts collected in Italy, scarcely prepares you for the splendour of the **Great Hall** – the centrepiece of the house – with its wonderful dome, massive columns, and riot of colour and detail. Look up, and in the dome's centre you will see the moment when Apollo's son falls to earth – an illustration of the perils of ambition that gently mocked the family's own aspirations – as well as the four elements and twelve figures of the zodiac, all painted by **Giovanni Pellegrini** in the early eighteenth century. His work on other rooms was lost when a huge fire swept though the South Front in 1940, and much remains to be done to repair the damage caused.

Rooms on the west side survived, however, and here you will find some wonderful Old Masters – look out for **Holbein**'s portrait of Henry VIII in particular amongst the **Gainsboroughs** and Reynolds, as well as a fine collection of Italian works. The Museum Room is the sort of 'spare room' every family needs – it is just that this is rather grander than most – filled with old knick-knacks brought back from their travels that don't seem to fit elsewhere. The splendid 160-foot **Long Gallery**, flooded with light on a summer's day, houses portraits of family and royalty. The family chapel has a strong pre-Raphaelite presence, with stained-glass windows designed by **Burne-Jones** and three embroidered panels by **William Morris**. The chapel is still used for family occasions, and visitors can attend a short service at 5.15pm on Saturdays and Sundays, when the house is open.

When you've finished with the house the grounds will easily occupy the rest of the day. Seasonal walk guides will give a recommended route through **Ray Wood** and identify the plants you will see. If you have children there is an **adventure playground** and boat trips on the lakes in the summer – as well as the peacocks strutting the lawns trying to pinch food from al fresco diners by the cafeteria. If you're tired enough by then, pick from a number of beautiful places to sit in the walled **rose gardens**.

Information/tours/guides A map handed out on arrival gives some idea of the scale of the place. A colour souvenir guidebook, a good buy at £3.75, goes through the house room by room and will undoubtedly add to your visit. The guides in the house are simply excellent: they approach visitors and are happy to tell them about the house and answer any questions. Leaflets giving details of seasonal walks in Ray Wood cost 20p.

When to visit Come on a fine day to enjoy the grounds: May for the rhododendrons in the woods, June for the roses, September to avoid the crowds. Saturdays are tipped as the quietest days.

Age appeal This is a spectacular house, and even if you know little about architecture, the variety will enthral and the guides are very informative. Budding gardeners will want to see the roses – which are helpfully labelled. Children will enjoy the grounds and adventure playground, though you will need to keep an eye on them near the water. There isn't any information particularly aimed at youngsters, but there is a lot to see in the house and you can take it at your own pace, moving on when they get bored.

Food and drink For hot food and the widest selection go to the self-service cafeteria in the house, which has a pleasant indoor seating area and benches on the lawns outside on fine days. Sample dishes include steak pie and chips (£5), vegetable bake and salad (£4.25), cream scone (£1.20), fruit pie (£2.10). A lakeside café opens in summer and there's another café in the entrance courtyard.

Shops The courtyard gift shop has plenty of themed gifts that start at modest prices – toffee or a jar of jam for £2.50; a Castle Howard thimble for £2.99; trinket boxes for around £10. The Jorvik Glass workshop had some beautiful exhibits, starting with a heart-shaped paperweight for around £3.

🚗 15 miles north of York off the A64. Follow the brown signs. ⊖ Train to York station, then Yorkshire Coastliner (tel. (01653) 692556) to Castle Howard. ① Mon to Sun,

17 Mar to 5 Nov, 11am (grounds and gardens 10am) to 6pm, last admissions 4.30pm.
🖭 Adult £7.50; child £4.50, senior citizen, student £6.75, family ticket (2 adults + 2 children) £19.50. Adult season ticket £21. Grounds only: adult £4.50, child £2.50. ♿ The grounds, rose gardens, shops, plant centre and cafeteria are wheelchair accessible. A chairlift can take visitors to the main floor of the house but not to the private chapel. The upper floor of the exhibition wing is not wheelchair accessible. Manual wheelchairs available for loan. A land train runs every 20 mins between the car park and the house.

Chartwell

Westerham, Kent TN16 1PS ☎ *(01732) 866368*

Quality ★★★★   **Facilities 🏠 🏠 🏠 🏠**   **Value for money ££££**

Highlights Combines the feel of a family house with a keen sense of the political life of Winston Churchill; well-maintained attraction

Drawbacks Not an ideal choice for children; little to inform people who are a bit hazy about Churchill and his significance until the very end of the tour

What's there Chartwell was the family home of Sir Winston Churchill, the British prime minister who led the country through the dark days of World War II and the winner of the Nobel Prize for Literature for his history of the English-speaking people. If you visit on a sunny day, it will be easy to see why Churchill loved this house, with its beautiful views over the Weald of Kent and bright homely rooms. The National Trust has restored it to its 1930s appearance and presents it as if the family has just popped out – there are fresh flowers on the polished furniture and the day's newspapers in the drawing room.

On the ground floor are the family rooms, hung with pictures by or of Churchill – a notable exception being Monet's *Charing Cross Bridge* above the bureau in the drawing room. Family knick-knacks include small busts of Napoleon (one of Churchill's fascinations) and a Lalique crystal cockerel presented by De Gaulle.

Upstairs are displays of more famous treasures: **the 1953 Nobel Prize for Literature**, his American citizenship conferred by Kennedy, and his insignia for the Order of the Garter – alongside the badge of the Hastings Winkle Club, of which he was a member. There are evocative **photos and letters** on the walls – his telegram to General Alexander ordering him to destroy Rommel and his forces – and the phlegmatic response when this had been accomplished, concluding '*I await your further instructions*'. A **letter from President Roosevelt** to 'a certain naval person' features a touching verse that concludes: '*Humanity with all its fears / with all the hope of future years / is hanging breathless on thy fate*'.

The heart of the house is **Sir Winston's study**. Here, again, the personal touches – the cuddly toys from his children in the bookcases, the fish tank he bought after a small London boy handed him a fish in a plastic bag – rub shoulders with mementoes of great times in British history, like a Union flag that flew in Rome on its liberation in 1944. Back downstairs is the Dining Room and the exit, through a small exhibition of Churchill's life with an all too short snatch of a recording of him speaking. Allow an hour for your visit.

The grounds include a lake and swimming pool, and a water garden where in later life Churchill loved to sit and feed the fish. The roses are particularly fine, especially the **Golden Rose Walk** planted by the Churchills' children in 1958 to celebrate their parents' golden wedding anniversary – the roses are illustrated by some of the leading British artists of the day in a book on show in the dining room. In the studio are many of Churchill's paintings, and staunch patriots should pop into the back room to read the great man's scathing letter to the Foreign Office on its use of foreign place names: 'Foreign names were made for Englishmen . . . '! Allow another hour for the grounds – or longer if you just want to sit and soak up the sun and the views.

Information/tours/guides The map of the site is free, but it is well worth paying 60p for the small guide, as labelling in the family rooms is fairly sparse. There is also a colour souvenir guide for £4.50. You'll find a volunteer guide in all the rooms, and some are happy to chat and tell stories about the house. Guided tours are only by prior arrangement (contact the property secretary on (01732) 868381).

When to visit Come in June for the roses and to enjoy the gardens. This is one of the most popular National Trust sights, so try to avoid weekends and bank holidays if at all possible. Entry to the house is by timed ticket for all visitors. There tends to be a rush at the beginning of the day and a lull at lunchtime.

Age appeal The presentation of the house assumes that you know the significance of Sir Winston Churchill's life and is perhaps most enjoyed by people who lived through the times and remember Churchill. There was nothing aimed at children when we visited, although the National Trust says a quiz should be available. Pushchairs and big bags cannot be taken into the house.

Food and drink The self-service restaurant serves hot food at lunchtime – soup of the day (£2.80), Speldhurst sausages in cider and apple with vegetables (£6.75), Kentish apple cake (£2.75), as well as cold selections (tuna roll for £2.50, lemon syllabub for £2.25). There is a good selection of cakes and biscuits for tea – a pot of tea for £1, shortbread for 80p. You can picnic in the car park or the adjacent meadow.

Shops The usual range of National Trust products are on sale plus some items relevant to the house – Chartwell roses for £4.99, Chartwell jigsaws from £9.99 to £19.99, books on the war and on Churchill's sayings, and tapes of speeches.

Other facilities There are baby-changing facilities by the visitors' reception.

🚗 2 miles south of Westerham, off B2026. Follow brown signs. ⊖ Train to Bromley station, then Metrobus 246 (every hour) stops by gates of Chartwell (tel (01689) 861432). Alternatively, train to Sevenoaks station, then Chartwell Explorer bus (goes to Chartwell, Squerryes Court, Emmetts Garden and Quebec House) during summer. Tel (0345) 696996 for details. ⏰ (in 1999) *House, studio and garden* 1 Apr to 29 Oct, Wed to Sun (Tues to Sun in Jul, Aug and bank hols), 11am to 5pm. Last admission 4.15pm. 💷 Adult £5.50; child £2.75; family ticket (2 adults + 3 children) £13.75. *Garden and studio only* £2.75. Free to National Trust members. ⅊ Smooth paths but slopes and steps to the house, studio and round the garden. Path at the front of the house without steps leads to a viewpoint over the garden. Ground-floor entrance via ramps. Two steps lead to a small lift (built for Sir Winston) for the first floor. The lower floor and exhibition can only be reached by a staircase. Wheelchairs are available. Disabled parking. Disabled toilets. Braille guides are available at the house.

Chatsworth House

Bakewell, Derbyshire DE45 1PP ☎ *(01246) 565300*
🖰 *www.chatsworth-house.co.uk*

Quality ★★★★	Facilities ⌂⌂⌂⌂	Value for money ££££

Highlights Beautiful house and gardens; good choice of refreshments; range of attractions to appeal to all ages

Drawbacks All the 'extras' can make for an expensive day out; no plan of house or indication of tour length

What's there There's enough at Chatsworth to keep visitors of all ages interested for the best part of a day. However, because all the individual fees soon add up, families would be advised to buy a family pass (see below).

The house contains a fascinating **collection of art and furnishings**, displayed in a series of **grandiose state apartments**. Beneath sumptuously painted ceilings by Louis Laguerre you can admire walls covered in embossed and gilded leather, window frames covered in gold leaf (it lasted longer than paint!), Boulle furniture, and the intricate Mortlake tapestries based on Raphael cartoons. Look out for the famous **trompe l'oeil violin** behind the door of the State Music Room.

The **Scots Bedrooms** (extra charge) are where **Mary Queen of Scots** stayed while in the custody of the 6th Earl of Shrewsbury. However, the rooms were completely transformed around 1830, and are now decorated in the height of Regency style, with hand-painted Chinese wallpaper (including, in the Wellington Bedroom, a painting of the Cavendish banana, which was grown successfully at Chatsworth by Joseph Paxton).

Downstairs, you pass through the Chapel and the extraordinary **Oak Room**, the oak panels and carved heads of which, originally from a German monastery, were bought 'on impulse' by the 6th Duke of Devonshire from a London auction house. Don't miss a carving by **Grinling Gibbons** at the top of the Oak Stairs, which depicts a lace cravat of unbelievable delicacy. The gilded stuccowork of the splendid Library and Great Dining Room forms a dazzling backdrop for **portraits by Van Dyck** and the famous **Gainsborough** painting of Georgiana Duchess of Devonshire. More top-class art follows in the **Sculpture Gallery**, where marble masterpieces by **Canova** and **Thorvaldsen** are matched with paintings by **Landseer**, **Hals** and **Rembrandt**.

In the gardens the best-known feature is probably the **Cascade**, where water flows down a series of 24 steps over 208 yards, east of the house. But there is much else to see and admire, from the clipped delights of the Serpentine Hedge and Maze to the fruitful Conservative Wall, where tender figs, peaches and nectarines are cultivated, and the attractive Kitchen Garden, a stunning array of flowers and vegetables. Art, here too, has its place, including the bronze *War Horse* **by Dame Elizabeth Frink** on the South Lawn and the renowned **Willow Tree Fountain**, which still catches the unwary by surprise. The display of art does not stand still either; new works are still being commissioned – a **water sculpture** by Angela Conner was being installed when we inspected.

Information/tours/guides Visitors receive an information leaflet when they arrive, showing the locations of the house, refreshment facilities, car park and toilets (though not all of the gardens). There is no plan of the house, even in the guidebook (£3.25), so it's difficult to plan how long you might need, but allow a couple of hours. The guidebook is lavishly illustrated and not too dry, and the room attendants are always happy to fill in any gaps. The garden has a separate guidebook (£2.75) with a map.

The audio tour of the house (£2.30) is good at pinpointing unusual details, though it doesn't evoke the atmosphere as well as it might – it concentrates on the house and its furnishings rather than telling you much about the family. Neither does it include any information about the Scots Bedrooms; you need to turn the machine off and read a separate printed information leaflet about these rooms.

When to visit The gardens are well worth exploring, so it's best to visit during fine weather. Special events throughout the year include horse trials, an angling fair, a flower and garden show and a country fair. It would be easy to spend a whole day at Chatsworth.

Age appeal For children the extremely good adventure playground is likely to have the most appeal. There's an area for smaller or less adventurous children too, with swings, sandpit and small slides, as well as the main area of rope bridges, trampolines and longer slides. The collection of farmyard animals features pigs, game birds, poultry (including newly hatched chicks), donkeys, trout and cattle, with rather dry, educational information boards and a milking demonstration every afternoon. But the extra admission is pricey, especially as adults and children pay the same (£3.50).

A rather unimaginative children's guide to the house is available for £1, but youngsters will enjoy running round the gardens and Maze (some were even paddling in the Cascades when we visited).

Food and drink Full marks for the wide range of catering options (though you can still bring a picnic if you want). A refreshment booth within the grounds sells sandwiches (cheese and pickle £1.95, crab and ginger or tuna salad and mayonnaise £2.15), hot and cold drinks, biscuits and chocolate. For more substantial fare you have to go out of the grounds to the former carriage house, where you can choose between Jean-Pierre's Bar (no children) and the Carriage House Restaurant. As well as waiter service and alcoholic and soft drinks, Jean-Pierre's offers trendy sandwiches and ciabatta for about £5. Tables next to the glass walls overlook the courtyard.

The Carriage House Restaurant also has a very pleasant seating area, overlooked by portraits of Tsar Nicholas I and Empress Alexandra. The self-service queues moved rather slowly on the busy lunchtime we inspected, and the range of hot and cold food is more traditional (maybe steak and mushroom pie, pork pie salad or baked pasta (one of the three vegetarian options)), but helpings are generous. The range of cakes and desserts was extensive, and some unusual soft drinks, such as Seville orange jigger, were on offer.

A tea room in the farmyard sells ice-creams, sandwiches and drinks, and there are picnic benches up in the adventure playground.

Shops The two main shops are in the Orangery, at the exit to the house, and in the carriage house, next to the restaurant. Both stock a similar range of items, but the shop in the Orangery feels less cramped. More unusual souvenirs include (smaller) plaster replicas of the Colossal foot and Canova lions (£19.95 each), as well as china, cushions and other ornaments based on Chatsworth designs. The garden shop sells plants, and the shop in the farmyard stocks cuddly toys.

Other facilities Toilets and baby-changing facilities are situated near the information office; other toilets are found in the House and eating areas. Those at the entrance to the refreshment block tend to have the longest queues when it's busy, so it would be better to head for others if you can. There are also toilets in the farmyard.

Chatsworth is 8 miles north of Matlock off the B6012. Follow brown signs from the M1 junction 29, via Chesterfield. Parking (£1 per car). ⊖ Train to Chesterfield, then taxi to Chatsworth (30 minutes away). Alternatively, buy Midland Mainline ticket, which includes return rail fare (from London Kings Cross), coach transfer and entrance to Chatsworth (Tues and Thur, Apr to Oct, adult £30, child £16, tel. (0990) 125242.). ○ **(in 1999):** Mon to Sun, *House* 15 Mar to 29 Oct, 11am to 5.30pm; *Garden* 11am (10.30am in June to Aug) to 6pm; *farmyard and adventure playground*, 10.30am to 5.30pm. ▣ House and garden (incl Scots bedroom) adult £6.75 (£7.75), child £3 (£3.50), child (under 3 yrs) free, senior citizen, student £5.50 (£6.50), family ticket (2 adults + 4 children) £16.75 (£19). *Garden only (farmyard adventure playground only)* adult £3.80 (£3.20), child £1.75 (£3.50), senior citizen, student £3 (£3.50), family ticket £9.50. Family pass for all attractions £26. Farmyard season ticket (2 adults + 4 children to farmyard and adventure playground only plus free parking) £65. ⅊ Garden, farmyard, shops and restaurant fully accessible (but House generally inaccessible because of stairs. Ring for information). Disabled toilets; wheelchairs and electric scooters for loan in garden (book ahead).

Cheddar Caves and Gorge

Cheddar, Somerset BS27 3QF ☎ *(01934) 742343*

Quality ★★★	Facilities 🎫🎫🎫🎫	Value for money ££££

Highlights Cox's Cave; lots for children to do
Drawbacks Parking problems and crowds in high season

What's there Cheddar village was certainly at the front of the queue when they were dishing out natural beauty. Above ground, the gorge, formed over the past two million years, is an awesome reminder of the power of nature. Perhaps it is best enjoyed away from the crowds from the cliff top reached by a daunting flight of 274 steps up **Jacob's Ladder**. If you're still feeling energetic then there is a 3-mile cliff-top walk which is not for the faint-hearted. Alternatively, the **lookout tower** provides panoramic views of the surrounding countryside.

Underground, things are no less spectacular. **Stalactites** and **stalagmites** in otherworldly formations are atmospherically lit to bring out their true beauty in the two show caves. **Cox's Cave** is the most beautiful, with reflections of multi-coloured stalactites in still pools. Stone stairs lead down to the Crystal Quest in the Fantasy Grotto, a hammy, tacky addition that young children nevertheless seem to appreciate.

Discoveries within the caves have allowed experts to piece together a fascinating history of the caves over the past 13,000 years. Interestingly, in the past the caves seem to have been sought-after abodes. Recently a skeleton buried 9,000 years ago was discovered in Gough's Cave. Amazingly, DNA proved that he, 'the Cheddar Man', still had a living descendant in Cheddar. People were still living in these caves well into the nineteenth century, and there are still believed to be hundreds of undiscovered caves and passageways, and explorations are ongoing. The museum displays the finds so far, such as flint and bone tools and the **remains of ice-age animals**, such as the mammoth and woolly rhinoceros.

Adventurous types can have a go at caving and abseiling at £10 each for adults and £8 for children (11 to 17 years old) or £19 for adults and £15 for children to attempt both.

Information/tours/guides *Timeless Cheddar Caves* (£1.99) is a glossy souvenir book that gives some background on the formation and exploration of the caves. It also contains a rough map showing the layout of the gorge. The Gorge Tour bus leaves every 20 minutes from the bottom of the Gorge. There is a short commentary and the bus drops you at Gough's Cave at the top of the gorge.

When to visit If you visit in high season expect long queues and parking difficulties. There is a park-and-ride system that operates in the school summer holidays from the western outskirts of Cheddar; otherwise arrive early and park in the main car park at the bottom of the Gorge for free, or pay and display £3 further up.

Age appeal The Gorge and caves appeal to all ages. Children will enjoy the 'Fantasy Grotto' in Cox's Cave, though they may find the museum a bit dull. Elderly visitors should bear in mind that Cox's Cave is quite low in places.

Food and drink There are a lot of eateries in the village, with a choice ranging from cream teas to fish and chips to pub/bistro food. The Explorer's Café near Gough's Cave is not helped by the crowds traipsing through from the 'Cheddar Man Exhibition'.

Shops The main shop of the complex is by Gough's Cave and has some rather irrelevant stock, from fluffy bags to football car stickers. Some interesting books on Celtic mythology are also on sale.

🚗 From M5 junction 22, nr Bath. ⊖ Train to Weston Super Mare station, then bus to Cheddar. ① May to mid Sept 10am to 5pm; mid-Sept to Apr 10.30am to 4.30pm. Closed 24, 25 Dec. 💷 'Caves and Gorge Explorer' ticket: adult £7.50; child (5 to 15 yrs old) £4; child (under 5 yrs old) free; family ticket £20. Senior citizen special (Gough's Cave and a cream tea) £5. ♿ Difficult access for disabled visitors. Free but limited access for people in wheelchairs to Gough's Cave.

Chessington World of Adventures

Chessington, Surrey KT9 2NE ☎ *(01372) 727227*
🖳 *www.chessington.co.uk*

Quality ★ ★ ★ **Facilities** 👜 👜 **Value for money £££**
Highlights Some top-notch rides; activities for small kids
Drawbacks Overpriced poor-quality food; long queues; few activities for non-riders;
unsanitary toilets

What's there If you're after an adrenaline rush, then look no further. But if you hate even the thought of being shaken, stirred, twisted and turned, then stay away. Chessington has some **state-of-the-art rides**, but it doesn't offer much to those who can't or won't ride along, making it an expensive day out for them.

All the six top rides are worth going on, although there will be long queues for them, especially in the summer. When we inspected in August the average wait was 45 minutes, and the vaunted ticket system for the popular Dragon Falls wasn't in operation. But at least the queues are usually beside or even beneath the rides so the anticipation builds all the time. All the rides could do with being a bit longer to compensate for the wait.

The **Samurai**, the newest attraction, is a gut-wrenching star-shaped ride that hurls you up and around a triple 360-degree rotation while your legs dangle in the breeze (more like a mighty rushing wind). **Dragon Falls** is popular on a hot day because you get wet as you splash down in your little log flume. Expect long queues but not much excitement. **Rameses' Revenge** is rather like being in a washing machine, complete with jets of water to rinse off (don't sit in the middle if you want to stay dry). You sit as you spin and you whirl as you turn, and are then left hanging upside down as the ground careers towards you. Don't eat first. A gentler ride for those who can't face any more stomach-churning is the **Runaway Train**: it's good for first-timers but far too short. The **Rattlesnake** provides more twists and turns as you hurtle round an old mine. Good fun as you whizz through shafts and feel the need to duck, but again too short given the wait. The **Vampire** is one of the original suspended rollercoasters, but still going strong. Suspended from a monorail, you get a real buzz as you swing and fly through the leafy glades.

Of the other rides, Terrortomb is, frankly, unterrifying, but Rodeo is fast, furious fun, while Professor Burp's Bubbleworks is a very gentle option if it's raining, though you are likely to get wet anyway. And it's a shame about the litter along the way. **Toytown** offers a variety of attractions for smaller children.

For non-riders, **Animal Adventures** is the best bet, with everything from big cats to small monkeys, as well as sea lion, penguin and bird shows. Other live shows, though this time with human actors, take place periodically, such as the Mexican stunt show in the afternoons.

Information/tours/guides The hard-to-find publicity brochure has some money-off vouchers at the back (£4 in 1999, quite a big saving on the entry fee). The useful free map given out on entry lists all the rides, grading them according to the scariness, as well as giving the height restrictions. It also has money-off vouchers for Thorpe Park and Alton Towers (under the same ownership).

When to visit   It's more enjoyable in the sunshine but it can be busier then and queues are longer. Avoid summer weekends if possible. From mid-July to the end of August go later in the day, when it's much cheaper after 4pm and open until 9pm (see below).

Age appeal   Children will love it, but there are (clearly signed) height restrictions on the main rides. Those who don't like rides will be hard-pushed to enjoy themselves, with Animal Adventures the only escape.

Food and drink   The best Chessington has to offer is at Pizza Hut, McDonald's or KFC outlets. Otherwise you will end up with an overpriced, unidentifiable plate of something very greasy, fatty and distinctly unappetising. The fact that most of the outlets were also dirty and strewn with rubbish didn't help. Take your own picnic.

Shops   There are lots of shops dotted around, but most offer the usual array of cheap souvenirs. You can get a Chessington baseball cap (£5) or mug (£3), a Samurai T-shirt (£14), or any manner of toy, sweet or novelty items.

Other facilities   The toilet facilities were very poor on our inspection. We saw stained lino, a blocked toilet, overflowing bins, non-working driers, graffiti, and soggy loo roll on the floor. Hold your nose and hope for the best.

Lockers (50p) and cashpoints are available in the Market Square. Strollers can be hired at £4 per day.

Follow signposts from either the A3 or M25 junctions 9 or 10, on the A243 near Kingston. Free car parks. ⊖ Regular rail service from Waterloo, Clapham Junction or Wimbledon to Chessington South (takes half an hour), then 10-minute walk to the park. Alternatively bus 71 runs every 10–15 minutes from Kingston to the park (tel 020-7222 1234). ⊙ 5 Apr to Oct, Mon to Sun 10am to 5pm (9pm in high season). Closed Nov to end of Mar. 🎟 Adult £19.50; child (4–13 yrs old) £15.50; child (under 4 yrs old) free; family ticket (1 adult + 3 children or 2 adults + 2 children) £59 (£55 if booked in advance); disabled visitors/helpers £8.50. Reduced admission after 4pm mid-July to end Aug: adult £9; child (4–13 yrs old) £7; disabled visitors £6. Groups of 12+ can book in advance to get a discount. Season ticket: £70 gives unlimited entry to all Tussauds properties – Chessington, Thorpe Park, Alton Towers, Madame Tussauds, Warwick Castle, Rock Circus – until the end of the calendar year (depending on individual site's opening times). ♿ Leaflet for disabled visitors. Wheelchairs available if booked in advance (£50 returnable deposit) – tel (01372) 729560.

Chester Cathedral

St Werburgh Street, Chester, Cheshire CH1 2HU   ☎ *(01244) 324756*

Quality ★ ★ ★   **Facilities 🏛 🏛 🏛 🏛**   **Value for money £££££**
Highlights   Magnificent building; excellent tea rooms; very friendly staff; free entry
Drawbacks   Poor interior signs; small, old-fashioned toilets

What's there   There's been a church on the site of Chester Cathedral for over a thousand years: the original building was Saxon, and it became a cathedral after the dissolution of the monasteries in 1541. Parts of the Norman church, begun in 1092, can still be seen – most strikingly to the right of the **Great Nave**.

The majority of the cathedral was built between 1250 and 1535, and features all the major Gothic styles of those periods. Some of the medieval woodwork is among the finest in the world, most notably in the breathtaking **Quire Stalls**, carved in 1380. The intricate canopies are so delicate that they could be lace work. They curve round to form the famous **rood screen** that shields the choir from the rest of the congregation.

The ground floor of the south-west tower houses an intriguing consistory court that really is like an old wooden court room. Benches are set around a large square table with a raised canopy and additional seating behind, which is where the Bishop may still sit in judgement when a member of the clergy is accused of committing disciplinary offences.

Along the north aisle wall of the Great Nave, a series of huge mosaic murals depicts characters from the Old Testament, and behind these are the wonderful cloisters and gardens that trap the sunlight and make an ideal spot for quiet contemplation.

Depending on how long you wish to sit, rest, gaze or contemplate, either outside or in the pews, you should allow a couple of hours for a visit.

Information/tours/guides The guided tour takes place at 2.30pm from mid-May to mid-October, and in August there is an additional tour at 11.30am Monday to Saturday. Tours last 45 minutes. Just inside the main entrance an introductory video gives a detailed history of the cathedral (copies are available in the shop). The colourful and helpful guidebook is reasonably priced at £2.50.

When to visit The cathedral will look stunning at whatever time of year you visit, and even the cloisters can be enjoyed in the rain.

Age appeal Older children and adults will undoubtedly be moved by the scale and beauty of the building, although younger children may not be so impressed.

Food and drink The large tea rooms are actually in the main part of the cathedral, which provides a lovely setting. A self-service bar offers a broad choice of many home-made dishes, such as cottage pie, chilli con carne and full breakfast, as well as imaginative sandwiches, including Brie with cranberry.

Shops The modern and brightly lit shop sells a range of advent calendars in August, but also CDs featuring the choir, religious books for both adults and children, as well as cathedral wine, mugs and book marks.

Other facilities The toilets, situated near the entrance, are rather small and old-fashioned.

🚍 Chester town centre, then follow signs (NCP parking nearby). ⊖ Train to Chester, then bus followed by few minutes' walk. ① Mon to Sun, 7.30am to 6.30pm. 💷 Free (suggested donation £2). ♿ Full access (with ramps); disabled toilets.

Chester Zoo

Upton-by-Chester, Chester, Cheshire CH2 1LH ☎ *(01244) 380280*
🖥 *www.demon.co.uk/chesterzoo*

Quality ★★★★★ **Facilities 🍴🍴🍴** **Value for money ££££**
Highlights Monkey Islands; Twilight Zone; good programme of animal talks
Drawbacks Mediocre restaurant (new one due to open in spring 2000); more toilets
would be useful

What's there With large enclosures for its animals, excellent viewing areas
for visitors and an attractive garden setting, Chester is a thoroughly modern
zoo. You can get a good overview of it by taking a monorail ride (extra charge),
which also has a brief commentary about the animals that you pass. Following
the timetable of **animal talks** is a useful way of seeing the animals and getting
some interesting information – we enjoyed the talks on condors and vultures
and on the colony of coatis, a furry animal from South America. The East Zoo
has a number of interesting special enclosures, including the **Orang-utan
House** and the **Tropical Realm** with its reptiles and free-flying birds.

Two of the best set-piece exhibits are in the West Zoo. The **Monkey Islands**,
including mandrills and lion-tailed macaques, have good viewing areas both
inside and outside and include some interactive activities – such as testing
your grip compared with that of a primate. Nearby the **Twilight Zone** features
nocturnal animals, including a large hangar with free-flying bats!

As we went to press there were several development plans for 2000,
including a major extension of the elephant paddock, a new Wildlife
Discovery Centre, the Egg Centre and the new Islands in Danger exhibition.

Information/tours/guides Numerous free talks, which last about 20
minutes each, are arranged throughout the day – the timetable is posted up
near the entrance, and they are sometimes announced over the tannoy. A
canal-bus tour of lemur and tamarin islands (summer only) and the monorail
trip each cost extra (summer rates: adult £1.40, children and disabled visitors
£1.10; monorail adult £1.70, children and disabled visitors £1.30 22 July–2
Sept). The guidebook (£3) would make a nice souvenir.

When to visit Fine weather is best, as the zoo has mostly outdoor
attractions, but there are several indoor enclosures to visit if there are showers.

Age appeal There is a very popular activity centre for children with brass
rubbing, mask making and a children's farm. Of the main attractions, the
Twilight Zone and the Monkey Islands are likely to appeal most to children.

Food and drink When we inspected there were two choices for hot
meals. In the East Zoo, the Oakfield Restaurant had waiter service and was a
little pricey. Our vegetable curry (£6.25) was bland; other dishes include
minted lamb fillet (£7.95) and soup (£2.25). The Oasis Cafeteria, next to the
main entrance, was cheaper, with offerings such as steak pie (£1.35) and
sandwiches (from £2.20). A new cafeteria is due to open in spring 2000.

Shops The Ark shop at the main entrance and the Garden shop in the East
Zoo are both well stocked with books, toys, games and good-quality souvenirs.

Zoo T-shirts cost £9.99, rhino bookends £25, a penguin mug £4.99, and a tiger purse £1.50.

Other facilities The zoo could do with a few more toilets.

🚌 From M56 westbound junction 14, follow signs to zoo (further signs on A5117).
⊖ Train to Chester, then bus from Chester town hall (4, 14 or 40). Sun and bank hols take 11C or 12C bus. Combined train/bus/zoo tickets available from Merseyrail stations.
🕐 Mon to Sun, 10am opening (closing times vary with season. Tel for details). Closed 25 Dec. 🎫 Adult £9.50; child (3 to 15 yrs old) £7; student, senior citizen, unemployed, disabled visitor £7.50. ♿ Wheelchairs and electric scooters for hire (tel (01244) 650225 for details). Tape tours for visually and aurally impaired.

Chesters Roman Fort

Chollerford, Humshaugh, Hexham, Northumberland NE46 4EP
☎ *(01434) 681379* 📧 *www.english-heritage.org.uk*

Quality ★ ★ ★	Facilities 👜 👜 👜	Value for money £££users

Highlights Well-preserved Roman ruins, especially the baths; well-stocked shop; friendly staff; riverside setting
Drawbacks Little guidance; no audio tour; boring guidebook; cluttered museum

What's there Chesters Fort is unusual for a number of reasons, most noticeably that it was built **astride Hadrian's Wall**, rather than alongside it. This means that three of its four gates are actually on the north (i.e. Scottish) side of the Wall, the path of which bisects the fort. It was also a cavalry, rather than the usual infantry, outpost. But none of this would be particularly interesting were it not for the fact that some fairly **extensive remains** have been excavated, making it one of the best preserved Roman sites in Britain.

Unfortunately, visitors are left pretty much to their own devices, with very little guidance or interpretation available. Like Housesteads Fort (*qv*) down the road, there is a distinct failure to capitalise on the excellent ruins, so you are left to wander around with only minimal information boards and a dry-as-dust guidebook for help. Even if English Heritage can't stretch to an audio tour, there should at least be a succinct, suggested tour with numbered boards matching a readable guidebook. It's noticeable that at nearby Corbridge (also run by English Heritage) the ruins aren't as impressive, but are brought to life and made much more interesting by virtue of the good, free audio tour.

Little remains of the fort walls, though the ruined gates are still pretty imposing, especially the east and west ones. But the gem of Chesters is the **bath-house,** down by the River Tyne. As you walk from the changing room to the cold and hot rooms, it's possible to see how remarkable Roman engineering and design was – the underfloor heating, the sewage channels, the barrel vaulting. The most interesting feature is the seven alcoves in the changing room. Their use is still unknown, though it is presumed they housed statues representing the days of the week. Within the **main fort**, it's possible to see the stone outlines of barrack blocks and the commandant's house – very upmarket with its own bath block and hypocaust (underfloor heating).

The **small museum** is a love-it-or-loathe-it kind of place. It has been altered very little since it opened in 1903, so the two small rooms are chock-a-block with tombstones, sculptures and other artefacts found on site. While it is endearingly atmospheric, it's also incredibly frustrating. Outstanding exhibits, such as the **sculpture of Juno** with a bull, are lost in a multitude of more mediocre remains. This is all intentional, but even when the museum isn't crowded (which it invariably is in season as it's not too big) it just comes across as a jumble of bits of rock and metal with no help given to the uneducated eye.

Information/tours/guides The lack of an audio tour means you must rely on the handbook (£1.75) for any detailed information, but it's pretty hard going. It's worth persevering with the tour outlined in the handbook, even though you have to wade through the text to use it, to learn a bit more. Alternatively you can buy English Heritage's general book on Hadrian's Wall (£2.95), which in four pages manages to convey a lot more and direct you round the site.

When to visit Try to avoid rainy days, as the site is all outdoors. In peak summer months it starts getting crowded towards mid-morning, and spaces in the car park are at a premium.

Age appeal All ages, though children might get bored quickly. The English Heritage activity book covers all three main forts along Hadrian's Wall, so the Chesters section is short.

Food and drink A green wooden hut just inside the entrance serves sandwiches (from £1.90), soup, tea (50p), cakes and milkshakes, as well as sweets and drinks. There's limited seating inside (but lots more outside) so it gets very crowded if it's raining, and the service can be a bit haphazard.

Shops The entrance/ticket office is also a pleasant shop with a fairly good range of gifts, many with a Roman theme – stone column bookends (£19.99), soldier figurines (45p), walking stick mount (£1.25) – as well as 'A Scent of History' products such as lip balm and rose foam bath.

Other facilities Adequate toilets are provided.

🚗 Off the B6318, just west of Chollerford. Free car park. ⊖ The Tyne Valley line train to Hexham (roughly once an hour). From end May to end Sept the Hadrian's Wall bus (682) connects all the main sites and towns (Hexham to Chesters) along the Wall four times a day in both directions. From Oct to May bus 880 runs daily (except Sunday) from Hexham to Chollerford, a 5–10 minute walk from Chesters. ⏰ (in 1999) Apr to Sept, Mon to Sun 9.30am to 6pm; Oct, Mon to Sun 10am to 5pm; Nov to Mar, Mon to Sun 10am to 4pm. Closed 24 to 26 Dec, 1 Jan. 💷 Adult £2.80, child (5–16 yrs old) £1.40, child (under 5 yrs old) free, senior citizen, student, unemployed (with ID) £2.10, companions to disabled visitors free, English Heritage members free. ♿ Difficult terrain for those with limited mobility.

City Museum and Mappin Art Gallery

Weston Park, Sheffield S10 2TP   ☎ *0114-276 8588*

Quality ★★   **Facilities 🏛 🏛**   **Value for money £££££**

Highlights Eclectic mix of exhibits full of surprises; pleasant park next door

Drawbacks Dusty and old-fashioned in parts; lack of facilities at time of inspection

---

What's there The museum houses the city's collections of cutlery, metalwork, ceramics, clocks, stuffed animals, archaeology, history and fine art, as well as a few other assortments in between. Although some of the subject matter in this rather dusty and at times tatty museum may at first seem to be rather dull, it often turns out to be more interesting than you might expect.

The first exhibit to greet you is a wonderful nineteenth-century Japanese gold **household shrine** standing about six feet tall. The **Applied Arts room** takes in English Delft-style tiles, and explanations of different metal fusion techniques, such as electroplating, as well as some fine nineteenth-century Staffordshire pottery.

Social history and archaeology displays comprise an eccentric mix ranging from horseshoes from the Norman Conquest, medieval gargoyles and Viking swords to a truly scary Egyptian mummified head. There is also a bizarre **Ice Age room** featuring, among many other items, a 'modern wood mouse', a hippo skull and a model of a hyena.

Most of the exhibits are displayed in traditional glass display cabinets, although there is an attempt to make things a little less stuffy in the **Evolution** area, where model mock-ups and painted back-drops help recreate swamp and rainforest themes. The exit to the museum is in Weston Park, which affords an opportunity to get used once more to daylight and fresh air.

Allow a couple of hours to go round the museum.

The **Mappin Art Gallery**, which has a permanent display of eighteenth- and nineteenth-century paintings, was closed for refurbishment when we inspected, but it was due to reopen in February 2000.

Information/tours/guides At the time of our visit there was no guidebook or other literature available, although the few attendants who were present were helpful and knowledgeable.

When to visit The museum is entirely indoors and isn't a bad place to spend a rainy day, although if you want to sit in the park afterwards you should bear the weather in mind.

Age appeal There is so much on offer that there really has to be something for everyone – it is just a matter of finding it. Children will like the stuffed animals and live wood ants' nest, while older people will find plenty to reminisce about.

Food and drink The tea room offers sandwiches, jacket potatoes, toasted sandwiches, home-made cakes and crumbles plus hot and cold drinks. Sometimes there's also a daily special, such as lasagne (£2.95).

Shops A shop is due to open selling souvenirs, books, catalogues and post-cards.

From M1, take junction 33 and follow signs to the university from where museum is signposted. No dedicated parking, but street parking available nearby. ⊖ From bus and train station, 15-minute walk or catch 51 or 52 bus. Alternatively, take tram and get off at the university stop. ⊙ Tue to Sat 10am to 5pm, Sun 11am to 5pm. Closed Mon. ⊞ Free. ⅋ Entrance ramp, then all on one level. No wheelchairs available.

Colchester Castle and Museum

14 Ryegate Road, Colchester, Essex CO1 1YG ☎ *(01206) 282931*

Quality ★★★★ **Facilities 🏛 🏛 🏛** **Value for money ££££**

Highlights Lots of interactive exhibits and audio-visual presentations which help to put displays in context

Drawbacks Not always clear what order to see things in; no café facilities on site (though available nearby)

What's there The castle itself is interesting because of its Norman architecture and its Roman associations, both of which can be appreciated by taking the 45-minute guided tour of the vaults, great stairs, roof and chapel. The vaults were the original foundations of the Roman Temple of Claudius, built around AD 49, and the tour guide explains how the Temple was built and used. The Norman castle was built on the Roman foundations in about 1076, mainly using stone from the Roman ruins. Its importance is indicated by the Great Stairs, which, at 16 feet, are the broadest winding staircase in Britain. The current imposing exterior is largely an eighteenth-century reconstruction, but there are some interesting original features such as Norman graffiti on the Great Stairs and examples of medieval 'toilets', with chutes opening out on to the castle walls.

The main attraction for most people will be the **museum** within the castle. Attractively set out and full of **interactive exhibits**, it includes substantial sections on Roman Colchester, including reconstructions of Roman rooms, examples of costumes and artefacts, the opportunity to **try on a chainmail shirt and helmet**, and an audio-visual presentation about Boudicca's attack on the town. The sections on medieval Colchester are equally varied, with more reconstructions, the chance to do a brass rubbing or design your own coat of arms, and the chilling tape of 'The Gaoler's Tale' which accompanies a visit to the castle prisons. The main emphasis is on putting history in context, starting with an interesting display about the significance of archaeology and the ways we collect evidence about the past, and using a variety of different media to connect artefacts with daily life at the time.

Information/tours/guides The publicity leaflet gives an enticing taster of what the museum has to offer, and the glossy colour booklet (£2.50) makes an interesting and informative souvenir. It doesn't really operate as a guide around the museum though, and it would be helpful to have some kind of additional room-by-room information. The colour-coded map in the guidebook helps to clarify the overall structure, but there is no clear order in which to see things, so it is easy to lose the chronological thread.

Guided tours with a qualified Blue Badge Guide are available several times a day; they last about 45 minutes and cost £1.20 for adults, 70p for children. Tours are quite separate from the museum, taking you to parts of the castle that are not otherwise accessible to visitors. They may be less suitable for young children, as the interest comes more from what the guides say than from what you see. But watch out for some fascinating details, such as the oyster shell left over from a workman's lunch hundreds of years ago, which now forms part of the fabric of the vaults.

When to visit Everything is indoors, so this could be a good option on a wet day. However, the outside of the castle looks better in fine weather, and the extensive castle grounds are an attractive place to stroll or picnic. Entry tickets allow you to go in and out as much as you want during the day of issue, so you can intersperse your visit with shopping or other sightseeing if you wish. Special events take place during the school holidays, including craft workshops and 'visits' from historical characters.

Age appeal There is something here for everyone, except perhaps for very young children. Great efforts have been made to make exhibits varied, visual and interactive, with lots of activities for children to take part in. There is also a free quiz sheet that provides an additional focus of interest for children. Adults will not feel patronised by the lively presentation, however, and there is plenty for the most serious historian.

Food and drink There's no café on site, though the Castle is near a busy shopping centre, with plenty of cafés, pubs and restaurants close by. The museum itself provides a refreshment area where visitors can eat their own food, with a vending machine that dispenses hot and cold drinks (though the cold drinks were out of order when we visited).

Shops A small but attractive shop area next to the entrance offers a wide selection of books and postcards. Some substantial decorative items with a historical feel are displayed in glass cases, including sculptures and cushion covers. There are also various small items, many of them aimed at children, such as 'Roman' snake rings and coins (£1.25), card kits to make historical dolls or buildings (99p) and an assortment of stationery.

Other facilities The toilets are tucked away in a corner near the refreshment area and you have to go through the exhibition area to reach them. They are fairly well maintained but could be in short supply at busy times.

🚗 Head for Colchester town centre, then follow brown signs to Castle. Car parks in Priory Street, Osborne Street and Vineyard Street, all a short walk from Castle Park. ⊖ Train to Colchester Town station or bus to Colchester bus station, then short walk to Castle. ⏱ Mon to Sat, 10am to 5pm, Sun 1pm to 5pm Mar to Nov. Last admission 4.30pm. 💷 Adult £3.80; child (5 to 15 yrs old) £2.40; senior citizen, student, disabled visitor and carer £2.50. Saver ticket (two adults and any two concessions, or one plus three) £10.20. ♿ Access to the ground floor (no steps), lift to first floor. But tours of the castle include two sets of steep stairs. Disabled toilets.

Colchester Zoo

Maldon Road, Stanway, Colchester, Essex CO3 5SL ☎ *(01206) 331292*
🖥 *www.colchester-zoo.co.uk*

Quality ★ ★ ★ ★	Facilities 👤 👤 👤 👤	Value for money ££££

Highlights Masses to see and do, including special events and displays; excellent play areas for children, including a large soft-play adventure playground

Drawbacks Could do with a better map and a proper schedule of events through the day; walking round the large, hilly area can be tiring for young children or elderly visitors

What's there Many of the animals, of which there is a wide range, are housed in natural-style outdoor enclosures, while some smaller animals are displayed behind glass, indoors. The larger animals include lions, tigers, elephants, zebras, camels, bears and alligators; giraffes are due to arrive in 2000. The **Aquatic Zone** features penguins and sea lions (both taking part in regular displays), while the variety of small animals include lots of different monkeys as well as less familiar species such as mongooses, meerkats, marmosets and agoutis. Animal events to watch include the **elephants' bath time**, a falconry display, parrot display, reptile encounter, and **feeding sessions** for lions, chimps, otters and others. New animals and areas are being added each year, and there is a real problem finding time to visit all the displays and events you want to see.

When your legs get tired you can take a ride on the Tanganyika Road Train, which tours round the lakes and Lemur Island. Children can also ride on the Jungle Safari train. The array of different play areas for children include the wooden Noah's Ark play area and an under-cover soft-play complex at Kalahari Capers (face painting is available here too).

Information/tours/guides Each visitor receives a fold-out brochure and map on arrival, which is comprehensive but quite hard to follow. Even with the signs around the zoo it is easy to get lost and to miss some of the displays (the times are indicated on the map).

A less hilly 'Easier Route' is available for visitors with buggies or wheelchairs, and this is well signposted, enabling you to visit each enclosure in a logical order.

When to visit There are plenty of viewing areas under cover, so rain is not a complete disaster, but a visit in good weather is certainly much more enjoyable. Extra displays and events are laid on in July and August; if you go out of season it will be quieter but the number of 'performances' may be limited. Whenever you go, make sure you allow enough time – a visit can easily fill a whole day.

Age appeal The zoo has obvious attractions for children; many of the information displays and quizzes are aimed at 5- to-13-year-olds, and the range of play areas is particularly suitable for this age group. However, everyone with an interest in animals will find plenty to enjoy; the information is presented at a range of levels. There is a lot of walking involved, even if you take the 'Easier Route', so it may not be suitable for people with mobility problems.

Food and drink The two main places to eat are the Inn at the Zoo, which serves hot meals, salads and snacks, and the Treetop Food Court, which is part coffee shop, part fast-food outlet. The Inn at the Zoo offers a special breakfast menu for £2.50 (if ordered before noon), and the lunch menu includes vegetarian pasta, lasagne or stroganoff at £3.99. There is also a Sunday roast at £3.90, and a children's menu for £1.99. The Treetop Food Court offers very good-value burgers (£1.15), jumbo sausages (99p), cheeseburgers (£1.25), and chips (£1). Both eating places, with seating on the terrace, are quite light and attractive, but rubbish didn't always find its way into the bins.

Snacks and sandwiches can be bought at the various small shops throughout the zoo, and there is a covered picnic area by the Julie Ward Gardens.

Shops Several small shops dotted around the zoo sell a mix of gifts, snacks, and ice creams, as well as films and batteries. The main shop is the Ark Gift Shop, at the exit (and entrance) of the zoo. The huge selection of merchandise is aimed mostly at children – soft toys, plastic animals, jigsaws, videos, stickers, plastic snakes, cheap jewellery, snowstorm paperweights, animal pens and toothbrushes – but includes some framed animal prints, china mugs and a selection of books.

From the A12 south of Colchester follow signs to zoo, from the A1124, follow the brown elephant signs. ⊖ Train to Colchester St Botolph station, then 10-minute taxi ride. Alternatively, Eastern National buses 74 and 75 from Colchester bus station go to Tiptree and Colchester Zoo. ① Mon to Sun, 9.30am to 6.30pm (Jul and Aug), 9.30am to 6pm (Easter to Oct), 9.30am to 5pm (or dusk if earlier) (Oct to Mar). Closed 25 Dec. ⊡ Adult £8.25, child (3 to 13 yrs old), senior citizen £5.25. Disabled visitors £3.50. Advance Discount Entry Tickets: adult £6.50, child, senior citizen £4.50. Discount of 5% for groups of 3 to 8 people incl. at least one paying child. Discount rate for parties of 15 or more: adult £5.95, child, senior citizen £3.95. Annual gold card, giving unlimited access: adult £24.95, child, senior citizen £16.50.
♿ Wheelchairs available for hire. 'Easier Route' for wheelchairs and pushchairs is signposted around the zoo, and available in printed form, but hilly terrain still difficult for those with limited mobility.

Corfe Castle

Castle View, Wareham, Dorset BH20 5DR ☎ / 📠 *(01929) 480609*

Quality ★★   **Facilities** 👜 👜 👜   **Value for money** £££
Highlights Dramatic backdrop provided by ruins
Drawbacks Lack of signs and information in castle itself

What's there The impressive ruins of Corfe Castle still cast a watchful eye over the Isle of Purbeck. Founded by William the Conqueror, it was enlarged by various kings until its completion by Edward I in the thirteenth century. Its destruction came in the English Civil War, when the Parliamentarians finally destroyed the stronghold after several failed attempts.

But to condense the history of this fascinating castle into two sentences is to do it a great injustice. The small **Castle View Visitor Centre** is an enthusiastic attempt to fill in some of the gaps – since the fifteenth century, anyway, as it dismissively skims over the previous few centuries. Here you can learn about the castle's **sewerage system** and the lifestyles of some of the previous residents, and see some finds – from cannonballs to clay pipes – from the ongoing archaeological digs. The Visitor Centre concentrates on the **sieges** in 1643 and how **Lady Bankes**, who kept the castle for the King, bravely defended two attacks until she was betrayed by one of her own garrison. This is probably the one part that children will enjoy, as there are some good interactive exhibits, audio-visual displays of the siege, and even a chance to converse with Lady Bankes herself (via computer). The downside is that the centre is located 15 minutes' walk away from the castle, although there is an attractive, but hilly route between the two, through woodland past the old mill.

If you go in the summer, take advantage of the services of one of the National Trust volunteers who give guided tours around the castle and point out some things not in the history pamphlet on offer. A good example of this is the recently discovered **graffiti** on the wall of the **Outer Keep**, which is thought to have been engraved by a bored guard.

Without either a guide or a visit to the Visitor Centre, though, you will have a problem: an over-reliance on the drama of the ruins themselves has resulted in little effort to bring the castle alive in any way at all. There are no information boards, no audio tour and no signposts to guide you between the herringbone stone wall of the **Norman Hall** and the ceremonial centre of the **Keep**. The views from the lookout towers are stunning, but would be so much more meaningful with some information on hand about, for example, how the attacks were staged.

If you really want a fun day out, consider instead visiting on a '**medieval weekend**' in the autumn, when historical societies use their imagination and the history books to recreate the castle as it was in the fifteenth century. You can have lots of fun trying medieval activities from archery to scribing, stone-masonry and cookery – all at the normal admission price.

Information/tours/guides Throughout the summer, volunteers give informative tours – usually one in the morning and one in the afternoon: call in advance to check. The leaflet *Corfe Castle – 1,000 Years of History* (50p) has a handy map of the castle with some dry commentary on the bits that remain. A more detailed guidebook costs £1.95, a children's guide £1.80.

When to visit Ideally, visit during one of the 'medieval' weekends in October. Otherwise, wet and windy weather is probably best avoided as the site is high and exposed.

Age appeal You need at least a casual interest in history to enjoy the castle. The site is not brought to life at all, so there is little to appeal to children, although a study room is provided for school groups.

Food and drink The Corfe Castle restaurant has stunning castle views from the pretty garden and plenty of space inside. The simple tea-room menu includes ploughman's lunch, jacket potatoes, home-made soups, and cakes such as Dorset apple cake and Bakewell tarts. The nearby pub, the Greyhound, is one of several other options in the pretty village of Corfe itself.

Shops The shop is a typical National Trust gift shop, selling the usual selection of preserves, juices, fudge and calendars. The range of books includes children's history books and local-interest titles. Also stocked are items on a cat theme (the stars of which are real cats at National Trust properties – among them Jock III, a descendant of Churchill's cat), and musical sweatshirts. Children will like the shields, archery sets and suits of armour.

On A351 Wareham to Swanage road. Park at unsurfaced Visitor Centre car park off A351 or at pay and display car park near village square. ⊖ Swanage steam railway runs to Corfe Castle station, a few minutes' walk from castle. Nearest main line station is Wareham. Park-and-ride scheme from Norden. For details of Dorset and Wiltshire buses call (01202) 673555. ⏱ Mar to Oct, Mon to Sun 10am to 5.30pm; Nov to Feb, Mon to Sun 11am to 3.30pm. Closed 25, 26 Dec. 💷 Adult £4; child (5 to 16 yrs old) £2; family ticket (2 adults + 3 children) £10, (1 adult + 3 children) £6. NT members free. ♿.Wheelchair access very limited inside castle. Castle View Visitor Centre is accessible.

Cotswold Wildlife Park

Burford, Oxford OX18 4JW ☎ *(01993) 823006* 📠 *(01993) 823807*

Quality ★ ★ **Facilities 🐾 🐾 🐾** **Value for money £££**

Highlights Great countryside and wide-open spaces; fruit-bat colony; leaf-cutter ants

Drawbacks Lack of educational information; dated exhibits

What's there The name says it all. Take the grounds of the Bradwell Grove Estate in the beautiful Cotswold countryside, add some **exotic creatures** – including incongruous-looking rhinos and camels – in acres of grassy paddocks, season with a few reptiles, fish, insects and bats, housed in the stables and outbuildings of the nineteenth-century Gothic manor house, and top off with a **farmyard** of the usual guinea pigs, chickens and rabbits, then wait for the crowds.

But it is not exactly a walk on the wild side – more a stroll in the park (or a circuit on a narrow-gauge railway if that takes your fancy). Although the animals' presence no doubt swells visitor numbers, the **gardens** themselves have much of interest. The 130-year-old **wellingtonia tree**, towering 40 metres high, is visible for miles around, and the weathered oak near the restaurant has cast a watchful eye over the park for nearly 600 years. The walled garden, now a blaze of colour, once supplied the manor house with its greens. Today, it's home to the likes of meerkats, otters, lemurs and tamarin monkeys, who enjoy the shelter and warmth the walls provide.

Unfortunately, the rural respite is shattered every few minutes by low-flying aircraft from the nearby RAF Brize Norton.

Information/tours/guides There is little around the park to keep enquiring minds happy. The few information boards that do appear are either out of date – the exhibition on UK bat conservation, for example, dated back to the mid-1980s – or weathered and sun-bleached. Interesting displays, such as the fruit-bat colony and the impressive leaf-cutting ants, are let down by a lack of information.

The glossy guidebook (£1.50) is practically essential for any detail on the animals. The handy map, which is easier to read than the information boards scattered around the park, gives a little background on the house and the grounds. A free pamphlet called 'Wild Talk' brings you up to speed with the year's animal births, deaths and marriages and also announces details of special events, from birds-of-prey demonstrations to car rallies.

When to visit A visit on a fine summer's or a crisp winter's day would be ideal, as it's not a wet-weather venue.

Age appeal Children will enjoy the adventure playground with tree houses and slides, and the brass-rubbing centre with an animal and countryside theme (rubbings from 60p). The acres of open space will appeal to all ages.

Food and drink The Oak Tree Cafeteria does not have much choice, and most main meals are near the £5 mark or over. Even children's meals are £3.75, so a family day out could be rather pricey. There is also a rather dingy bar. A much better option is to take your own lunch and use the numerous picnic benches scattered around the park.

Shops The park's shop sells a range of merchandise, including preserves, place mats, animal print rugs and rather tasteless candles in the shape of animal heads.

Other facilities The toilets here won awards in 1997, and there are good baby-changing facilities too.

🚗 On the A361, signposted from Burford. ⊖ Not recommended. ⏰ Mon to Sun, 10am to 5pm (dusk in winter). Closed 25 Dec. 💷 Adult £6, child, senior citizen, student £3.80, child (under 3 yrs old) free. ♿ The site is flat and mostly accessible. Wheelchairs available on request.

Crealy Park

Sidmouth Road, Clyst St. Mary, Exeter, Devon EX5 1DR ☎ *(01395) 233200*
🖰 *www.crealy.co.uk* 🖰 *fun@crealy.co.uk*

Quality ★ ★ ★ **Facilities** 🏠 🏠 🏠 **Value for money** ££
Highlights Good balance of indoor and outdoor activities for younger and older children
Drawbacks The display boards on the outdoor animal paddocks were in poor condition and, in some cases, out of date

What's there This well-maintained park more or less outsmarts the unpredictable British weather with its variety of activities. Outdoors, you'll find animal paddocks, playgrounds and go-karts suitable for younger and older children (£2 per ride), an adventure course, bumper boats, and a land train. Of the two large indoor play barns, the Magical Kingdom is better suited to smaller children and includes rides, plenty of ball pools and climbing frames. The rough and tumble of the Adventure Zone (which is huge) may be too much for younger children, but their older counterparts will no doubt enjoy it.

The Animal Barn is home to cows, pigs, hamsters, rats and rabbits – friendly rangers are on hand to supervise children who want to pet the smaller animals. There is also a daily programme of activities, such as bottle-feeding lambs and hand-milking cows. The Stables next door have a lovely collection of miniature ponies and there are pony rides daily (£1.20 each).

The various rides, animal barns and playgrounds are well-kept and clean. Allow at least half a day to visit the park – longer if your charges get lost in the ball pools!

Information/tours/guides A free map of the park is included in the admission price. Visitors also receive a list of times of animal activities. Display boards dotted around the animal paddocks were in poor condition when we inspected.

When to visit There's plenty to do whatever the weather, but it might be worth enquiring about the special events put on throughout the season, including Halloween and Christmas parties. Usual admission prices apply.

Age appeal There are height and age restrictions in the outdoor adventure areas and on the go-karts. For older people or those with mobility problems, the grounds are relatively flat and the paths well maintained.

Food and drink Pirate Island Restaurant is located next door to the shop – it was closed when we inspected. Two other self-service restaurants, located in each of the indoor play areas, serve sandwiches, baguettes, pizza, sausage or chicken with chips, ice creams and hot and cold drinks. Inevitably, because of their locations, they are noisy and busy. One outdoor kiosk serves hot snacks and drinks. There are covered picnic tables located beside the snack kiosk – an area that was untidy when we inspected.

Shop The range of goods on sale is aimed mainly at children and includes cuddly toys, colouring cards, Beanie Babies, and toy cars and tractors.

🚗 Located off M5 junction 30 on the A3052 Sidmouth road. ⊖ Train to Exeter, then stagecoach 52 from the bus station (situated on the High Street). Tel. (01803) 613226 for more details. ◷ Mon to Sun, Apr to Oct 10am to 6pm; Nov to Mar, 10am to 5pm. Closed 24–26 Dec, 1 Jan. 💷 Apr to Oct, adult/child £5.50; child (under 3 yrs old) free; senior citizen £4.25; groups of 4 or more £5.25 (per person), annual ticket £23.50. Reduced winter rates available (indoor areas only). ♿ Wheelchair access throughout. Helpers admitted free.

Cricket St Thomas Wildlife Park

Chard, Somerset TA20 4DB ☎ *(01460) 30111*

Quality ★ ★ ★ ★   Facilities 💷 💷 💷   Value for money ££££
Highlights Beautiful setting; lively lemurs and falconry displays
Drawbacks Limited appeal in poor weather

What's there The beautiful wooded valley of Cricket St Thomas contains the house made famous in the hit TV comedy *To the Manor Born*. These idyllic surroundings now accommodate **animals and birds**, many of them rare and endangered, from all over the world.

The **lemurs** are particularly captivating. Three species can be seen: ring-tailed lemurs (show-offs, given to leaping kamikaze-style from the top of one tree to the next), red-fronted lemurs, and black and white ruffed lemurs (the largest). They live in two enclosures in the 'Lemur Wood'. The females are dominant, grabbing the best food and roosting positions and leading the troupe movements. All of them walk with their tails aloft, like a flag, for location purposes. They make noisy territorial calls, and although they would never attack a human being, visitors are discouraged from touching them. Joining a guided tour through the wood, or being around for feeding time, is a must.

Young **falcons** are in training here and the 15-minute display of the birds responding to the trainer's commands (as long as some edible reward is on offer) is well worth catching.

The park comprises a succession of different habitats where animals can live as naturally as possible – in the South American paddock, for example, there are rheas (large flightless birds), fallow deer, capybaras (large rodents resembling guinea pigs) and tapirs, while ostriches, zebra and lechwe (a type of antelope) roam the African paddock. The very rare Siberian **Amur leopard** lives in its own enclosure. Elsewhere, you will encounter lolloping wallabies, bison, an **otter pool**, a deer paddock, monkey island, ibis and African parrot aviaries, a tropical house and koi carp pool. The wildfowl paddock is home to a host of exotic birds, from American flamingos and South African pink-backed pelicans (which have a co-operative fishing technique, grouping together to surround shoals of fish) to whistling tree ducks and red-breasted geese from the Siberian Arctic.

More familiar species, including guinea-pigs and rabbits, can be seen – and touched – at the pets' corner and farmyard.

A **miniature railway** runs from 'Flamingo Junction' to 'Lemur Wood' stations – the length of the park, in fact – and 'Larry the Lemur' is on-hand to entertain younger visitors with stories and activities around the park.

Allow at least 3 hours to see all that the park has to offer.

Information/tours/guides Leaflets provided at the ticket booth include a map of the park, with photos of many of the animals and birds to look out for; an activities timetable indicating where and when the falconry displays, guided tours of Lemur Wood, otter and lemur feeding times and Larry the Lemur performances take place; and start/finish times for the train (last run at 3.30pm). The friendly guides explain where the animals originate from, their habits and habitats, and the park's conservation work. Also, information boards are provided for the main enclosures.

Age appeal Visitors of any age will enjoy this wildlife park. The site is family-focused, with an outdoor play area and a ball park for under-7s, as well as the children's attractions mentioned above.

Food and drink Drinks and sweets are available at the entrance. More substantial fare, again family-oriented, is available from the coffee shop and food court near the entrance, or from the Black Swan pub, located within the grounds (bar meals, coffee, ales and wines).

Shops One shop, at the entrance, sells drinks, sweets and souvenirs (cuddly toys, baseball caps, T-shirts, mugs, novelty pens and rubbers, jams and honey), plus colouring books, camera film and umbrellas. The shop near the pub sells gift items.

Other facilities A baby-changing room is provided.

Follow signs 3 miles east of Chard on the A30, or from M5 junction 25. ⊖ Not recommended. ⊙ Open all year, Mon to Sun, 10am to 6pm (or dusk if earlier). Last admission 4pm (summer), 3pm (winter). ⊞ Adult £4.95, child (4 to 14 yrs old) £3.75, child (3 yrs or under) free, senior citizen £4, family ticket (2 adults + 2 children) £16. Wheelchair users and blind visitors free, carers £3.95. Group discounts and season tickets available. Reductions in winter. ♿ Mostly negotiable by wheelchair users, though woodland paths are sometimes steep.

Dinosaur Museum

Icen Way, Dorchester, Dorset DT1 1EW ☎ (01305) 269880

Quality ★ **Facilities** 📷 📷 **Value for money ££**
Highlights Fun sheets and quizzes for children
Drawbacks Tiny; poor computer graphics; amateurish presentation

What's there From the publicity brochure with its talk of life-size reconstructions, skeletons, videos and hands-on exhibits you can be forgiven for thinking that the museum is going to be rather larger than it turns out to be. It has all of the above and more, but it is all crammed in to what looks like a converted house just off Dorchester High Street.

Within four rooms the development of dinosaurs is traced through the Triassic, Jurassic and Cretaceous periods, including information on the Big Bang, dinosaur hunters and excavations. There is lots of local interest – for example, the footprints of the Diplodocus found on the Isle of Purbeck. One display projects the evolution of dinosaurs had they not been wiped out and comes up with the Dinosaurid, which is weirdly human-like. There is also a **life-size model of a dinosaur** and lots of **interactive displays**, including Dinoenergy to illustrate the amount of energy used by a dinosaur in one second.

Overall the effect is amateurish and has the feel of a temporary exhibition. We found there was little logical order to the information, which was stuck to un-numbered display boards. Much of the information was repetitive or hard to digest. The computerised displays were very slow and had poor graphics, and the videos downstairs had terrible picture quality. Interactive flaps and buttons and a short video are upstairs.

Allow 1 to 2 hours for a visit.

Information/tours/guides There are free **fun sheets and quizzes** for children – clipboard and pencil provided.

When to visit Its small size means that the museum gets crowded easily. If you can, avoid during wet weather in the high season.

Age appeal The life-size models will appeal to younger children, as will the interactive room upstairs. The content of the museum shadows the National Curriculum to appeal to young children and school groups, but is of less interest to adults.

Food and drink No food or drink on site.

Shops The 'shop' occupies a tiny corner of one room and sells lots of relevant goods, including dinosaur masks, models and mugs as well as doodle posters (8 for £1.40).

🚗 Within Dorchester centre, follow signs from main (municipal) car parks. ⊖ Train to Dorchester station, then 10- to 15-minute walk to Museum. ◷ Mon to Sun, Apr to Oct 9.30am to 5.30pm. Nov to Mar 10am to 4.30pm. Closed 24–26 Dec. ⊞ Adult £4.25; child £2.95; child (under 4 yrs old) free; student, senior citizen £3.50; family ticket (2 adults + 2 children) £11.95. Disabled visitors free. ♿ Wheelchair access to lower level only.

Dover Castle and Tunnels

Dover, Kent CT16 1HU ☎ *(01304) 211067*

Quality ★★★★★   **Facilities** 🛈 🛈 🛈   **Value for money** £££££
Highlights Tour of wartime underground passages; battlement walks; impressive site
Drawbacks Hilly site; long queues at Keep Yard restaurant

What's there This imposing castle is presented in a way that will keep all the family entertained for the day. As you draw up at Dover you will experience a small thrill of anticipation – this looks like a proper castle, and its strategic location means that it wasn't just built to serve some noble's vanity.

You should start with the most recent additions first. The **wartime tunnels** used as a command centre and wartime hospital during World War II can be seen only on a timed tour – so get your ticket when you arrive. The atmosphere of those days is recreated as you follow the drama of a wounded airman and see the command centre where Operation Dynamo – the evacuation of Dunkirk – was directed by Vice Admiral Ramsay in 1940. A short film tells the story to children.

After this the best plan is probably to go halfway back up the hill to **Henry II's keep**, built in the late twelfth century. It was at the centre of a double ring of defensive walls, making it the first concentric medieval fortification in Europe. Check the times of when the '*Siege of 1216*' **film** is showing, describing what the soldiers must have experienced when they defended the Castle against a French attack. Children will be impressed if you can explain how the big **siege engine** outside works. Inside the keep you can see the massive thickness of the walls as you wander through to the **Great Hall**. The interior is set up to show the preparations for a visit from the ubiquitous Henry VIII, who seems to have popped into most of the sights in Kent.

These are the must-sees – what you visit next really depends on the time you have and, possibly, the weather. On a fine day you might fancy a walk along the battlements for tremendous views and a closer look at some of the castle's defences. Alternatively, you can pick up an audio tour from the Keep Yard shop and head underground again to see the network of tunnels developed under the Castle to counter any threat from Napoleon. The network was based on the system put in after the siege of 1216 to strengthen this area of the Castle. The complexity of the system is amazing – at one of the guardrooms a series of doors allowed defenders to divert any attackers into a walled enclosure where they could be shot from above. Hike up to the highest part of the Castle and discover two buildings that pre-date the fortification – the remains of a Roman lighthouse, built to guide ships across the Channel, and a Saxon church built on a cruciform plan. If you walk over to the cliff forming the Castle's southern boundary you can stand at Admiralty Look Out and see the modern-day ferries leaving from the harbour.

You could easily spend the day here – allow a minimum of 4 hours.

Information/tours/guides The tour of the secret wartime tunnels lasts 55 minutes; the audio tour of the medieval tunnels 30 minutes; the audio tour of the battlements walk 45 minutes. As well as the audio tour there is a guidebook for £2.95 – particularly useful if you want to guide yourself.

When to visit It's a large site so it's best on a fine day, out of peak times. Arrive early and go straight to the wartime tunnels. Events, such as mock battles for children, are arranged most weekends. Telephone events line (01304 202754) for details.

Age appeal There is plenty here to interest all the family.

Food and drink The main self-service restaurant by the keep suffers from slow service and long queues; cream tea platter costs £2.60, fish and chips and mushy peas £5.30. Alternatively, try the café by the secret wartime tunnels or use the picnic site by Admiralty Look Out.

Shops Lots of wartime memorabilia can be bought at the shop at the secret wartime tunnels, and a more extensive selection is available at the outlet at Keep Yard.

🚌 From M20 and Dover town centre, follow signs. Large car park. ⊖ Train to Dover Priory station, then bus or taxi to Castle (one and a half miles away). Tel (0345) 696996 for bus information. ⊘ Mon to Sun, Apr to Sept 10am to 6pm; Oct 10am to 5pm; Nov to Mar 10am to 4pm. Closed 24–26 Dec and 1 Jan. 💷 Adult £6.90; child £3.50; student, senior citizen, unemployed, disabled £5.20; family ticket (2 adults + 3 children) £17.30. Free to English Heritage members. ♿ Very hilly site. Land train stops around Castle and can take wheelchairs. Electric wheelchairs provided.

Down House

Luxted Road, Downe, Kent BR6 7JT ☎ *(01689) 859119 (for information)*
🖰 *www.english-heritage.org.uk*

Quality ★ ★ ★ ★ ★   **Facilities** 👜 👜 👜 👜   **Value for money** £££users£

Highlights Audio tour of downstairs rooms; real attempt to explain the science to all ages; welcoming staff

Drawbacks Tickets must be booked at least one day in advance

What's there Down House was the home of Charles Darwin and the place where he wrote the revolutionary *On the Origin of Species*, encapsulating his theory of evolution. English Heritage deserves an enormous pat on the back for not taking the easy route of turning it into a display on the home life of an eminent Victorian, but for explaining the scientific basis of his theories of evolution and the outcry they caused at the time.

Darwin lived in this house for over 40 years and his 10 children were born here, seven of whom survived to adulthood. The audio tour of the downstairs rooms helps you imagine it as a family home. You can see the study where Darwin worked, full of the paraphernalia with which he surrounded himself – bits of bone, a microscope, piles of books and little bottles. There's also a hip bath he used regularly, as he suffered from skin and stomach complaints after his voyages on HMS *Beagle*. The well-thought-out audio tour ends with details on the furniture and fittings.

Upstairs starts with the tale of his five-year travels to the Galápagos Islands (during most of which he was miserably seasick). In the **collecting room** you'll find some of the many **specimens** he shipped home and his journal of the voyage is there to be read. His written observations of animals help explain how he developed his theory of evolution. If you have children with you, you have the perfect excuse to go to the **hands-on room**, where youngsters are kept amused by the exhibits that explain the ideas rather more simply and in a fun fashion. Alternatively, head for the **controversy room**, which covers some of the outraged reactions to his theory, including some pretty cruel cartoons from *Vanity Fair*. The controversy did not end with the nineteenth century, either. The exhibition recounts the story of the teacher who, in 1925, was prosecuted in Daytona, Tennessee, for teaching evolution, and how the Pope did not formally accept the theory until 1996.

Outside the house itself, the **gardens** are pleasant to wander around on a fine day – you can even mimic Darwin and walk the sandwalk, his 'thinking' path, to see if any great ideas are germinated.

Information/tours/guides The audio tour is included with the entrance fee. The guidebook costs £3.95, but you really don't need it to enjoy the visit.

When to visit The number of visitors is controlled, so you have to book a time for your visit at least a day in advance. Pick a fine day to come if you want to wander around the garden.

Age appeal All ages should find something of interest here.

Food and drink The small, clean and bright café serves light lunches, home-made cakes and teas. Soup and bread costs £2.95, two scones, cream and jam, and tea £2.60.

Shops The reception area has a collection of English Heritage goods.

🚗 Off A233, follow signs. Small car park (with disabled parking). English Heritage encourages use of public transport. ⊖ Train to Orpington station, then R2 bus, alternatively train to Bromley South station then LT 146 bus (tel 020-7222 1234 for bus details). ⏲ Entry by timed ticket only. All tickets must be booked at least one day in advance in summer. Wed to Sun, Apr to Sept, 10am to 6pm; Oct 10am to 5pm; Nov, Dec and Feb, 10am to 4pm. Open bank hols. Closed 23 Dec to 6 Feb. 💷 Adult £5.50, child £2.80, student, senior citizen, unemployed £4.10, child £2.80, English Heritage members free. ♿ Disabled parking; side wheelchair access and lift and ramp to upper floors.

Drayton Manor Family Theme Park

Tamworth, Staffordshire B78 3TW ☎ *(01827) 287979*
🖰 *www.draytonmanor.co.uk*

Quality ★★	**Facilities** 🍴 🍴	**Value for money £££**

Highlights A couple of high-class rides; good value for small children; reasonable food prices; helpful guidance for disabled visitors

Drawbacks Drab zoo; overall layout is unimaginative; general lack of visitor information around the park

What's there On the former estate of the Victorian Prime Minister Sir Robert Peel – his mansion is long gone – this theme park has a varied selection of attractions, from the excellent to the mediocre. For maximum enjoyment don't miss **Stormforce 10**, a cleverly thought-out ride that simulates the excitement and danger of a lifeboat launch. Your little orange boat is plunged into the water at breakneck speed, both forwards and backwards to guarantee a thorough soaking. Bring a mac or hire one, as you *will* get wet. **Shockwave** is another unique ride and is billed as the only roller-coaster where you stand up as you hurtle round. Some of the other experiences will be more familiar, such as bobbing along in **Splash Canyon** and taking the train on **Klondike Old Mine Coaster** and **Buffalo Coaster**. We also enjoyed the **Pirate Raft Ride**, which is fun for all ages as you float past animated models of pirates wenching and drinking and fighting a sea battle. After that there are more traditional fairground rides and the chance to go out on the lake in a steamboat or around it on the railway.

The disappointments were the tatty and depressing zoo and farm, which had hardly any information boards, Cine 180 - a big-screen special-effects show that looked outdated – and Haunting, a spook-filled house that was not scary and had a long queue.

The pricing policy works well – the entrance price is low, but you can then buy a wristband for unlimited rides or pay as you go, though it is annoying that you cannot buy your ride wristband with your entrance ticket. We visited on a sunny day in September, when there were few queuing problems.

Information/tours/guides You are given a good free map with your ticket but no guide is available. There is little information about daily events when you enter the park, and no announcements about shows. Signposting could also be better.

When to visit Definitely come in warm weather, as the majority of attractions are outdoors – and you will get very wet on Stormforce 10.

Age appeal Children under the height of 90cm have free entry and rides (only five rides have height restrictions). Children's Corner offers amusements and small rides, including a giant slide and a small roller-coaster. Non-riders can watch others without having to fork out a high entrance price.

Food and drink Plenty of choice of standard fare is offered all over the park, including fish and chips, chicken nuggets (£2.35) and pasties (£1.35) at reasonable prices. A pleasant surprise was the tidy self-service cafeteria in the entrance plaza, where we had a decent beef stroganoff (£3.65); salad bowl costs £1.99.

Shops Dotted around the park are outlets selling varied merchandise related to rides: for example, Splash Canyon T-shirt (£14.99) and Stormforce baseball cap (£5.99). There is no zoo-related shop, which is a shame.

Other facilities Plenty of baby-changing facilities are available, except at Children's Corner. The loos could do with smartening up.

🚌 On the A4091, close to M42 junctions 9 and 10. 10 miles north of Birmingham, near Tamworth. ⊖ Train to Tamworth, then Network 2000 bus. ⏱ *Theme park* 25 Mar to Oct, Mon to Sun 10.30am to 5/6/7pm depending on the season. *Zoo* open all year, except winter bank holidays, 10.30am to 5pm. Closed 25, 26 Dec, 1 Jan. 💷 Adult £4, child (4 to 13 yrs old) £3; child (under 4 yrs old) free; senior citizen £3; disabled (wheelchair) visitor and helper £3. Discount for groups of 12 or more in 1 vehicle. *Ride prices:* wristband (for unlimited rides) adult £14; child (90cm or taller or 13 years and over) £10; child (under 90cm tall) free; senior citizen and disabled (wheelchair) visitor and helper £6; family ticket (2 adults + 2 children) £42. Or pay as you ride at £1 per ticket (1, 2 or 3 tickets for most rides). *Combined entrance + unlimited rides* Adult (14 yrs +) £14; child (90cm/13 yrs) £10; senior citizen/disabled visitor + carer £6. Ask also about the VIP Pass for unlimited visits. ♿ Useful care and difficulty ratings on all the rides.

Dreamland

Belgrave Road, Margate, Kent CT9 1XG   ☎ *(01843) 227011*
📠 *(01843) 298667*

Quality ★   **Facilities** 👜   **Value for money £**
Highlights Choice of paying per ride or an all-inclusive price
Drawbacks Facilities look rather dated and knocked about

What's there This traditional **seaside amusement park** is creaking a little at the seams and showing its age alongside more modern theme parks. On the plus side, its smaller size means that you can see which are the rides with the shorter queues and avoid some of the worst of the hanging around. You can pay either with a **wristband** that gives unlimited access to most of the rides (but not all – so if you have a particular ride in mind, check that the band will be valid) or by buying **tokens**. If you have younger children or only want to spend an hour here, tokens will probably be the best bet.

Thriller rides include the bungee ejector (a reverse bungee ride for which wristbands are not valid), Skymaster and the Loop, for people who enjoy turning upside down. The venerable **scenic railway** – said to be the UK's oldest wooden roller-coaster – may be preferable for those who don't want to turn through 360 degrees. There are also several tame roundabouts for toddlers.

Information/tours/guides The good free map shows the location of the rides, height restrictions and number of tokens needed.

When to visit The park is quieter out of school holidays.

Age appeal The mix of rides on offer appeals to all the family.

Food and drink Picnic benches are laid on (but why not go to the beach?) and a number of fast-food outlets serve pies, burgers and fish and chips.

Shops Novelty shops are located on the walk-through to the beach.

🚗 Follow signs throughout the town. Adjacent car park (£2). ⊖ Train to Margate station. Connex offer combined rail and admission packages, call (0345) 484950. ⊘ (1999) July to Sept (peak times: school hols, weekends) Mon to Sun 10am to 10pm; July to Sept (outside peak times), Mon to Sun 10am to 6pm; Apr to June and Oct, Mon to Fri 1.30pm to 5.30pm. 💷 (1999) *Wristbands* adult £9.99; child (below 1.35m) £6.99. Pre-paid adult wristbands ordered at least 48 hours in advance on credit-card hotline (01843) 227012 are half-price. *Tokens* 80p or £10 for 18 (most small children's rides are 1 token, bigger rides 2). ♿ Park accessible by wheelchair, though several rides are up steps.

Dudley Zoo and Castle

2 The Broadway, Dudley, West Midlands DY1 4QB ☎ *(01384) 215314*
🖰 *www.dudleyzoo.org.uk/*

Quality ★ **Facilities** 🏛 **Value for money £££**
Highlights Castle visitor centre; tropical bird house; chimpanzee enclosure
Drawbacks Poorly maintained; disappointing restaurant

What's there Dudley Zoo is not the easiest attraction to tackle. It is laid out on a wooded hillside with concentric pathways and the ruins of a castle at the top. It's best to take the tourist train to the top of the hill to start with and follow the programme of guided talks.

The better exhibits were the new **chimpanzee enclosure**, which had big clear information boards, and the **tropical bird house** next door, which simulates a rainforest with colourful birds flying about freely – it was a shame there wasn't more information on the plight of the rainforests themselves. After that, head up to the **orang-utans** and the fascinating antics of the **Sulawesi crested macaques**.

Dudley Castle consists of a gatehouse, keep and apartments, with sparse information boards. Much better is the permanent exhibition in the **visitor centre**, which has attractive storyboards about **medieval life and the Dudley family**, models and pictures. An excellent audio-visual display describes the trial of John Dudley, Duke of Northumberland, who hatched the plot to put Lady Jane Grey on the throne in 1554.

Overall our general impression of the attraction was poor with a lack of welcome and badly maintained buildings.

Information/tours/guides The signposts are not easy to follow, and the map we were supplied with was a black and white photocopy printed in 1998. Free 15-minute talks on penguins, bears, otters, apes and sea lions are given throughout the day, but those we attended were fairly basic, often with the guide reading from a sheet of paper. Information boards were inconsistent and sometimes non-existent. When we inspected, the guidebook was good value at £1, with plenty of information (due to be replaced in June 2000). The Castle guide was sold out.

When to visit Definitely come in the summer: many of the special attractions, such as the bouncy castle, chair-lift and talks, run only from Easter to September.

Age appeal Children are catered for with an adventure playground, funfair and face painting. However, the elderly or those with mobility problems may find the hilly layout a bit of a challenge.

Food and drink The Queen Mary Restaurant is the main eaterie at the centre of the zoo and has the feel of a school canteen with food to match: for example, pizza and chips (£4.25), jacket potato and one filling (£3) and coffee (80p). There is also the Grey Lady tearoom (closed on our visit) and various kiosks dotted around.

Shops The main shop is at the entrance and sells an unimaginative selection of furry animals – big lion (£12.99), small lion (£5.75) – and souvenirs like Dudley rock (35p).

Other facilities Quite a walk to some toilets. Although the main ones were presentable, those under the Discovery Centre were in dire need of a clean.

🚗 On the A461, three miles from M5 junction 2. ⊖ Bus to Dudley bus station, then 2-minute walk. Alternatively, train to Dudley Port and Coseley station, then taxi (three miles to zoo and Castle). ⏰ Mon to Sun 10am to 6pm (5pm in winter). Last admission 90 minutes before closing. Closed 25 Dec. 💷 (1999) Adult £6.50; child (4 to 15 yrs old) £4; child (under 4 yrs old) free; student, senior citizen, disabled visitor £4.50. Season tickets available. ♿ Wheelchair loan available (tel (01384) 215301 for details).

Durham Cathedral

The College, Durham DH1 3EH ☎ *0191-386 4266 (Chapter Office)*

Quality ★ ★ ★	**Facilities** 🏛 🏛 🏛	**Value for money** £ £
Highlights	Stunning Norman architecture; knowledgeable guides	
Drawbacks	Extra costs of visiting the tower and treasury can add up; not much of great interest for children	

What's there Durham Cathedral would not exist today were it not for Cuthbert, the most famous and best-loved saint of the north-east. St Cuthbert spent his life as a monk and bishop on the Holy Island of Lindisfarne until he died in 687. But it wasn't until 995 that the great saint was laid to rest, in a shrine, in Durham. In 1093, the building of the cathedral started to shelter **Cuthbert's shrine** and to house the community of Benedictine monks who took care of it.

Throughout the Middle Ages, pilgrims visited the shrine, seeking the saint's prayers and healing powers. But in 1539, at the time of the Reformation, the richly ornamented medieval shrine was destroyed, so his coffin was buried in a secret vault. Today all that can be seen of his shrine is a plain marble slab.

When construction of Durham Cathedral began as a monastery, the choir was the first part of the cathedral to be built. It was used as a place of worship while the rest of the cathedral was constructed. It is the best example of **Romanesque architecture** in England, characterised by the semi-circular arches and chevrons (zig-zag patterning on the columns). Furthermore, it boasts the **first rib-vaulted roof** in the world, exemplifying the transition of styles from Romanesque to Gothic.

In the choir, **the bishop's throne** – dubbed 'the highest in Christendom' – was built in the fourteenth century by a vain bishop to cover his tomb. The **delicate altar screen** behind, superb even without the 107 statues that once adorned it, also dates from the fourteenth century. It is worth climbing the **cathedral tower**, which soars 218 feet up. The 325 steps are steep, and the stone spiral staircase is narrow, but from the top, panoramic views stretch into the distance, making Durham look like a model city.

The monks' dormitory (built between 1298 and 1404) originally provided accommodation for up to 100 monks, but today contains part of the **cathedral library** (some 30,000 books) and a collection of stone carvings. The most striking stone works are casts, but the other segments of crosses and tomb-stones inscribed with saints, circles and plaiting are original.

A permanent exhibition in the **Treasury** displays valuables such as St Cuthbert's coffin and pectoral cross, embroidered vestments given to his shrine, illuminated manuscripts, seals and relics of bishops and kings, and the original twelfth-century sanctuary knocker from the north-west door to the cathedral.

Information/tours/guides A full colour guidebook (£3) covers the history of the saints and their shrines, and the development of the cathedral. Guided tours (donation of £3 requested – children under 16 accompanied by an adult are free) are available during the summer (27 May to 30 September, Monday to Saturday at 10.30am and 2pm) and last about one hour. The guides are all volunteers, very knowledgeable and happy to answer questions.

When to visit The cathedral is open all year round, though organised tours only operate during the summer months.

Age appeal Children would probably enjoy going up the tower, although they might find the guided tour a tad on the boring side. For less mobile or less fit visitors, the tower could be rather challenging; the rest of the cathedral is all quite accessible.

Food and drink The cathedral's Undercroft restaurant, just off the cloisters, is light and airy, with paintings by local artists adorning the stone walls. It serves hot and cold drinks as well as plenty of cakes, such as carrot cake (99p) or St Cuthbert's slice (shortcrust pastry with raisins and cherries for £1.25).

Shops The gift shop sells postcards (20p), cathedral lithographs by local artists (£9.99), heritage coins (about £42.95),and jewellery and candles. An SPCK bookshop immediately next to the gift shop has books on spirituality, art history and other related subjects.

Off the A1/ M1 follow signs to Durham city centre, then signs to cathedral (university staff car park, £1 for 2 hrs). Train to Durham station, then either bus (infrequent service), taxi or 20- to 30-minute walk (up steep hill) to cathedral. Mon to Sat 9.30am to 6pm, Sun 12.30pm to 5pm (until 8pm May to Aug). *Treasury:* Mon to Sat 10am to 4.30pm, Sun 2pm to 4.30pm. *Cathedral library:* Mon to Fri, 10am to 3.30pm, Sun 12.30pm to 3.30pm. Free admission to cathedral (although £2.50 donation requested from each visitor). *Tower:* adult £2, child, student, senior citizen, unemployed £1, family ticket (2 adults + 2 children) £5. *Treasury:* adult £2, child £1, student, senior citizen, unemployed and group rate £1.50, family ticket (2 adults + 2 children) £5. Cathedral accessible, with special routes highlighted on cathedral maps; disabled toilets.

Earth Centre

Denaby Main, Doncaster DN12 4EA ☎ *(01709) 322085*
www.earthcentre.org.uk

Quality ★ | **Facilities** 👍👍👍👍👍 | **Value for money** £

Highlights Beautiful facilities, including very pleasant restaurant and attractive shop
Drawbacks Main exhibitions confusingly presented and over-ambitious

What's there Built on the site of a disused colliery, Jonathon Smales' (a former director of Greenpeace) visionary site is intended to ensure that 'you'll never see the world in the same way again'. Unfortunately, the reality of this project, which was partly financed by National Lottery funds, falls far short of the stated aim, though only the first of three phases of development has so far been completed – perhaps the next two phases and a further £52 million will bring the attraction to life.

As the site stands it has a rather unfinished feel, with little of the ambitiously planned gardens, especially the Forest Gardens with their 'living canopies', properly established. The **Planet Earth Experience** is intended to transport visitors inside the planet, but the surreal warehouse-like interior with its rotating, monolithic glass display cases, plasticky 'fractured spheres', and multimedia effects feels more like an experimental exhibition of conceptual art. Worst of all, the bridge near the exit 'that seems as precariously balanced as our lives on this planet' has all the poignancy of a pointless little ramp in the middle of the floor.

Next door, the **Action for the Future Gallery** seeks to convey the history of the Earth Centre through a large model of the sight surrounded by various displays, but is busy and difficult to follow. The wall displays lack sufficient explanation, and many of them might seem a little self-righteous in tone – for example, the monkey trap, in which you put your hand through a narrow hole to pick up a ball and then find that you cannot remove your hand, is intended to represent greed.

Besides these two exhibitions, a number of further displays are scattered about the site, including the primary-school-like NatureWorks, the WaterWorks – with a stepped natural sewage treatment works on a scale that could be employed for entire communities – and the Rokkaku Trail, where visitors are invited to explore all of their senses by sniffing scents, putting their heads against enormous ear trumpets, and taking off their shoes to tread upon stones carefully laid in concrete. The ensemble is completed by an adventure playground with an artificial ley line, an EarthArena for presentations, the Kaki Tree grown from a cutting taken from one of three trees to survive the bombing of Nagasaki, and, surrounding it all, 400 acres of the Ecology Park.

Information/tours/guides Visitors receive a free map, and there are guided tours irregularly arranged. However, most of the site offers little in the way of information, and there is no guidebook to help explain what is intended. EarthTrail and Earth Adventures (for children) provide ways to explore the site through a series of questions; both may be appropriate for children, but we found the EarthTrail highly patronising and irritating for adults.

When to visit It might be best to wait a few years until phases 2 and 3 have been completed and the vegetation has settled in. If you do want to go now, go in summer to make the most of the atmosphere and avoid poor weather.

Age appeal Children will probably enjoy Earth Centre far more than adults, as there are lots of hands-on activities and places to play.

Food and drink A very stylish restaurant serves a range of largely organic meals, including baked potatoes with fillings (£3.45), soup (£2.55), and couscous with sautéed vegetables (£5.85).

Shops The spacious and beautifully laid out shop contains stalls from major high-street traders with environmental themes, including Oxfam, Bodyshop, and Neal's Yard. There are also stalls belonging to Dorling Kindersley and Patagonia, as well as a range of the site's own merchandise, such as mugs (£3.50) and T-shirts (£7.50). Computer terminals allow customers to find out more about the products on offer.

From A1 junction 36 follow signs through Conisbrough. ⊖ Train to Conisbrough station, then under 5-minute walk to attraction entrance. ⊙ Mon to Sun, 10am to 6pm (last entry 4pm). 💷 (1999 prices) Adult £4.95, child £3.50, child (under 5 yrs old) free, senior citizens, students, unemployed, disabled visitors £3.50. Various forms of annual membership: Earth Friend £8.50, Earth Companion (with season ticket) £22.50, Earth Family (2 adults + 3 children) (with season ticket) £48. ♿ Full access to exhibition and facilities (and most areas of the site).

Eden Camp

Malton, North Yorkshire YO17 6RT ☎ *(01653) 697777* 📠 *(01653) 698243*
🖱 *www.edencamp.co.uk* 🖱 *admin@edencamp.co.uk*

Quality ★★★★★   Facilities 👜👜👜👜   Value for money £££££
Highlights Wide appeal – makes history accessible to all; open all year; good wet-weather attraction
Drawbacks Very popular with school parties; toilets could do with smartening up; as an old prisoner-of-war camp it is not the most beautiful site

---

What's there This brilliantly conceived and executed attraction tells the story of civilian life, often with reconstructions, during World War II, all set in the huts of an original prisoner-of-war camp. This is one of the few attractions where you will wish you had taken your parents as well as your children. It is wonderfully evocative, not just capturing the look of wartime streets but using sounds and smells to equally good effect.

You will be given a plan of the site and the route is clearly labelled. All the huts have something different to offer and each one is worth a walk through, so don't miss any out – though you're bound to have your favourites. We particularly liked Hut l, with the family gathered round the TV set in the living room as they listened to **Chamberlain's declaration of war**; Hut 3, depicting a **submarine under U-boat attack** in the North Atlantic; and Hut 5 – **a street after an air raid**. If you are a more serious student of history then visit Hut 9, where, as well as hearing bomber command talking down a Halifax, you can read about the history of the **escape routes** that returned 2,803 Allied servicemen to active duty. Huts 24 to 29 also give a more detailed history of the war.

When you feel like a sit-down catch the music hall in Hut 6 – and see if you can sing along with the puppets. Hut 18 houses a large collection of newspaper headlines from the war years. Visitors who lived and fought through the war may like to attend the **forces reunion** in Hut 22, where they can link up with former comrades and record their experiences on video to add to the visual history. Or you can stir the memories with a walk around the prefab that was a major talking point when we visited. Outside is a growing collection of hardware to admire – tanks, planes and weaponry.

The site pays a fitting tribute to the people who endured the history of recent times, and is not gung-ho about war: the final hut, Hut 29, is a small chapel if you have more personal memories to consider.

Allow 3 to 4 hours for a visit.

Information/tours/guides You don't need to buy anything extra to go around the site – the plan you are given when you enter is perfectly sufficient. There is a good guidebook for £2.99, but it is the sort of thing you will enjoy taking home and reading rather than needing it as you go around.

When to visit Apart from the hardware this is all under cover, so you could visit at any time of year. It is a very popular attraction with school parties, who can swamp the place in term time, but they tend to start leaving by about 2pm. Saturday is the quietest day.

Age appeal This is an attraction to connect the generations – history is provided in bite-sized pieces so you can decide what your children would like, from puppet shows to U-boat attacks. An assault course, sensibly divided into two age groups, allows them to let off steam. Adults can dip into some social history and just tour the tableaux or top up with some of the more serious presentations in the higher-numbered huts.

Food and drink The food area is themed into the Prisoners' Canteen (lunch), the Officers' Mess Tea Room and the Garrison Cinema Bar. A blackboard lists what was happening around that date during the war, while the menu offers Churchill's pie (steak pie) or 617 Dambuster stew and dumplings (both served with chips and peas or beans for £3.99). Scone and jam costs 85p, passion cake £1.25 a slice, a cup of tea 60p. There are also picnic tables so you can bring your own.

Shops The heavily themed gift shop has a selection of books – both novels and non-fiction – tea towels from £1.50, wartime scents in bottles and Eden Camp biscuits for 99p.

🚗 From A64, follow brown signs. Eden Camp is just north of Malton. ⊖ Train to York station, then bus to Eden Camp (bus service (tel 90 01904 622 992) or Yorkshire Coastliner). Alternatively, train to local station Malton on the York to Scarborough line. ⏰ (in 1999) Mid-Jan to Dec, Mon to Sun, 10am to 5pm (last admission 4pm). Closed 24 Dec–12 Jan 2001. 💷 Adult £3.50; child £2.50; senior citizen, disabled £2.50. ♿ Exhibition laid out in series of huts, which are wheelchair-accessible. Limited loan of wheelchairs from reception. Braille sheets and tapes are available. Disabled toilets.

Elsecar Heritage Centre

Wath Road, Elsecar, Barnsley, Yorkshire S74 8HJ ☎ *(01226) 740203*

Quality ★ ★ ★ **Facilities 🏛 🏛 🏛** **Value for money £££**
Highlights Highly interactive variety of attractions; good shop and tea rooms
Drawbacks Can get crowded; old-fashioned toilets

What's there The buildings of the heritage centre date back to the time of the Industrial Revolution, and are situated on land once owned and worked by the wealthy Fitzwilliam family, who made their money from iron founding and coal. Cobbled and Tarmac streets lead visitors around a large courtyard housing an interactive science and power exhibition, working craft shops, a living history museum and a working steam train.

The **Power House,** all exposed brick and timbers, is in the old maintenance sheds, which were used to repair the Earl's private steam train and track. After a general introduction about sources of power in the home, you move on to a section called Power Laws. Here explanations and illustrations about how science works are accompanied by an assortment of **working models** – for example, you can sit in a chair and use your own strength, a set of pulleys and a rope to haul yourself six feet up in the air. **Powerdrive** illustrates the principles of electricity, again using working models. One device has a handle that you turn, and the faster you turn it, the more electricity you generate and the more household items you can stimulate to work, such as a lightbulb, radio, hairdrier and TV. **Powerplan** is a look into the future to see how our changing needs might be met by solar and wind energy – for example, using a light source to move a toy boat across a pool of water.

The **Living History Museum** displays a fascinating array of Victoriana, with everything from ration books and costumes to kitchen utensils. There's also a mock-up of a mine with an interactive video room showing different aspects of pit life.

Dozens of craft shops show artisans producing everything from wicker baskets to jewellery and furniture, while a collectors' shop and bottle museum offer for sale old cigarette cards and bottle tops. The *pièce de résistance*, however, is the **1924 Avonside Saddletank locomotive** that will transport you a mile alongside the Dearne and Dove Canal and back again, in 50-year-old carriages.

Allow three hours for a visit, as there is plenty to walk around and see and do.

Information/tours/guides There is no guidebook or specific tours, but the attendants in the Power House, museum and steam train are all enthusiasts and can answer most questions.

When to visit The main attractions are indoors, but there is walking and browsing in between, so fine weather is required. It can get busy at weekends. There is a varied programme of special events throughout the year, from classic car and bike shows to musical events and flower shows.

Age appeal The working models keep youngsters fascinated (and even adults find it an education), while much of the Victorian memorabilia will be of interest to those keen on history. The steam train can be enjoyed by all, but is particularly pleasurable for enthusiasts.

Food and drink The old-fashioned Brambles tea rooms provide a waitress service and serve jacket potatoes, sandwiches, Yorkshire puddings, pasties and scones with lashings of jam and cream, all at reasonable prices. There is also an ice cream stall and crêperie.

Shops The main gift shop in the Power House sells lots of educational books and science kits, like magnet sets, gyroscopes and other 'scientific' toys. Separate craft shops sell everything from paper dollies to beds, jewellery and ceramics.

🚗 From M1 junction 36 follow the brown signs; car parking. ⊖ Train to Elsecar station, then few minutes' walk. Alternatively, bus 227 from Barnsley. ⊕ Mon to Sun, 10am to 5pm. Closed 25 Dec–1 Jan. ▣ *Full access with Power House and train (Power House only)*: adult £5.25 (£3.25, child (under 16 yrs old) £3 (£2), student, senior citizen £3 (£2). Train only: adult £2.50, child (under 16 yrs old) £1, student, senior citizen £1. ♿ All on one level with special facility to get on the train.

Ely Cathedral

Ely, Cambridgeshire CB7 4DL ☎ *(01353) 667735*

Quality ★ ★ ★ ★ **Facilities** ⚅ ⚅ ⚅ **Value for money £££production£**

Highlights Sublime building; excellent guided tour
Drawbacks Crowded eateries at peak times

What's there Ely Cathedral was founded as a monastery in 673 by St Etheldreda, a Saxon princess from East Anglia. Work on the present building began in the early 1080s. For more than 400 years it was a Benedictine monastery as well as a cathedral, until Henry VIII's dissolution of the monasteries in 1539, it was used solely as a cathedral. But what a cathedral – different styles of architecture through the ages have blended to form a coherent, evocative whole. It is still very much a place of worship, but visitors are welcome to wander around the fine **Norman nave**, sample the **Romanesque** and **Transitional work** in the Transept, and wonder at the **Octagon**, where eight massive pillars support 200 tons of timber, glass and lead. The latter seem to hang suspended in space way above your head – a masterpiece of medieval engineering. Other highlights are the **largest Lady Chapel in England**, excellent examples of Renaissance and Victorian ceilings, Gothic ornamentation, and a large collection of monastic buildings.

The guided tours are part history lesson, part architecture lesson, part geology lesson, and are absolutely fascinating. The guides are funny and engaging, with an encyclopaedic knowledge of and love for the Cathedral. They guide you from the origins of Christianity, through Etheldreda herself, the Dissolutions and Reformation, to present-day restorations. We learnt, among many other things, that in Norman times every stone in the Cathedral was painted a gaudy colour, and they were all removed during the Reformation. Examples of Norman, early English, perpendicular, medieval and Victorian architecture are pointed out, and many amusing anecdotes are related.

Allow two hours to include the guided tour, a visit to the monastic buildings and to view the Cathedral from outside.

Information/tours/guides It is possible to get around using a guidebook (available in the shop for £1 or £2.50; the Pitkin is best) and the information boards, but we recommend the guided tour. It's free, lasts one hour, and is available Monday to Saturday. Tours in summer are at 10.45am, 11.45am, 2.15pm, and 3.15pm. There's a video in one of the cloisters covering restoration and the work of artisans, and some organised events such as brass rubbing.

When to visit The Cathedral can be visited in all weathers, but it's best to choose a fine day to wander around the exterior and the monastic buildings.

Age appeal Older children and grown-ups alike will be gripped by the guided tour.

Food and drink A small, funky café inside the Cathedral offers jacket potatoes (£2 to £3) and sandwiches (£1 to £2), but it can get busy, as can the Almonry Restaurant in the Undercroft, a short walk away in town. Here a cooked lunch, such as gammon steak and salad, costs £3.95. Arrive early for lunch to be sure of a seat.

Shops The hushed Cathedral shop has a great array of goods: cards, pictures, books on sacred Britain, CDs of classical and devotional music, candles, etc. The gift shop in town has more fun items, such as toys and children's books, to suit all pockets.

🚗 15 miles north of Cambridge. Follow signs from A10. In the centre of Ely. Free car parking (500 m from Cathedral). ⊖ Train to Ely railway station, then 5-minutes' walk or taxi to cathedral. Alternatively, bus to coach station, then walk. ⏲ Mon to Sat, 7am to 7pm (7.30am to 6pm in winter), Sun 7.30am to 5pm. 💷 Adult £4, child (with accompanying adult) free, student, senior citizen £3.50. ♿ Access possible around cathedral but not gallery around Octagon.

Eureka! The Museum for Children

Discovery Road, Halifax, West Yorkshire HX1 2NE ☎ *(01426) 983191*
🖳 *www.eureka.org.uk* 🖳 *Eureka-Museum@compuserve.com*

Quality ★ ★ ★ ★ ★ **Facilities** 🎒 🎒 🎒 🎒 🎒 **Value for money** £££££
Highlights Stimulating and exciting exhibits with lots of interaction and hands-on exploration
Drawbacks Gets very busy, especially in wet weather or school holidays (on busy days your time may be restricted to three hours)

What's there This well-designed **interactive museum** for children is aimed at 3- to 12-year-olds and will keep them entertained for hours. Every exhibit is hands on and many are larger than life. There are two floors, each divided into two sections. On the ground floor, in '**Invent Create Communicate**', children can send messages in a basket up a rope, take part in a broadcast in the television studio, or make music by bouncing on stools, dancing on coloured pebbles and manipulating giant flowers. In '**Living and Working Together**' children can experience doing the jobs that adults usually do in a supermarket, post office, garage, kitchen, bank or factory.

Upstairs, '**Me and My Body**' lets children find out about how the body works and how to look after it. Exhibits include a skeleton that rides a bike and a mouth they can climb into. They can weigh, measure and test themselves in all sorts of ways. The rest of the upper floor is taken up by the '**Things**' display – how things are made, how they are used and how they change our lives.

For pre-school children there is a jungle soft play area and ball pool, and craft activities in the classroom. The bathroom is also popular (the transparent toilet and bath let you see what happens when the toilet flushes or the bath is filled), along with the water play table.

Information/tours/guides Maps of the site are handed out at the entrance, and there is an information desk in the centre of the ground floor. Floor staff help you use and enjoy the exhibits. A list of special events, posted on the blackboard each day, might include model making with Lego or Duplo in the theatre.

When to visit During school holidays the best time to come is early morning or after midday to avoid queues. Wet days are always busy. In term time it's quieter after 2.30pm, when the school groups have left (half-price entry after 3pm during term time).

Age appeal The museum is aimed at 3- to 12-year-olds, though accompanying adults will enjoy it as well.

Food and drink The café offers a selection of good-value children's meals (£2.39), burgers, baked potatoes, sandwiches (£1.65 to £1.99), baguettes (£2 to £2.30), pastries and cakes in bright surroundings. Staff are friendly and efficient.

Shops You can buy a good range of Eureka logo novelties in the £1 to £2 price bracket but also a selection of discovery-style books and activity toys, including stencilling kits, make-and-fly-your-own kite kits (£4.50), jewellery craft, science in the garden sets (£3.65), and picture framing kits (£9.99).

Other facilities Both the children's and adult toilets are spotless. There are also good baby-changing facilities and disabled toilets. Baby backpacks can be borrowed from the shop for use in the museum.

🚗 From M62 junction 24 on to A629 to Halifax, then follow brown and white signs to Eureka. ⊖ Train to Halifax station, then under 5-minute walk. ○ Mon to Sun, 10am to 5pm. Closed 24–26 Dec. 💷 Adult (and child over 12 yrs old) £5.75, child (3 to 12 yrs old) £4.75, child (under 3 yrs old) free, saver ticket (2 adults/older children + 2 children) £18.75. *Annual ticket:* adult £15.50, child £15.50, family ticket £52. Half-price admission after 3pm in term time. ♿ Accessible and suitable for those with mobility problems. Wheelchairs (limited numbers) and dual headset audio guides available.

Exeter Cathedral

Exeter, Devon EX1 1HS   ☎ *(01392) 214219*

Quality ★ ★ ★ ★   **Facilities 🏛 🏛 🏛**   **Value for money ££££**
Highlights Architectural gem with many unique features
Drawbacks Cramped layout of refectory

What's there There has been a cathedral at the heart of this university town since 1050. The construction of the present-day cathedral began in 1270 and was completed in 1369, though additions and developments continued. The unique north and south towers are the most substantial remains of the early Norman building. An unusual image screen on the west front of the building includes figures of apostles, evangelists and Richard II.

One of the most interesting features of the interior is the **Gothic vaulting** that stretches from the west door to the east window – at 100 metres it is the longest example of its kind in the world. The most unusual of the cathedral's bosses, which depicts the murder of Thomas Becket in Canterbury Cathedral (*qv*), can be found along this stretch of vaulting. On the left, above the north porch, is the minstrel's gallery.

The **medieval screen** that encloses the Choir dates from 1325. The 13 paintings on the screen depict biblical scenes, including the Creation. Inside the Choir are **thirteenth-century misericords** – the most famous of which, the elephant, is now on display in the south choir aisle. The richly carved canopy over the Bishop's throne dates from 1315 and was made from oak from the Bishop's estate.

Other notable features include the organ case, the oak cover of the baptismal font with its eight inlaid figures of apostles, and the canopy and base that surround the black basalt effigy of Walter Bronescombe, bishop from 1258–1280. The newly completed Exeter Rondels – embroidered cushions that tell the story of the Cathedral – are displayed on the nave plinths.

Information/tours/guides The full-colour guidebook (£2.50) gives a good, comprehensive history of the Cathedral's development. A free leaflet includes a simple map of the cathedral with the highlights clearly marked. Guided tours (April to October) run at 11am and 2.30pm Monday to Friday and 11am on Saturday. The guides dotted around the cathedral are friendly and knowledgeable.

When to visit The Cathedral choir normally sings every day at 5.30pm (3pm on Saturday), except Wednesday, during term time. The cathedral library, which holds a small collection of early English manuscripts and printed books, is open Monday to Friday, 2 to 5pm.

Age appeal The Cathedral is likely to appeal to older children and adults.

Food and drink The licensed refectory serves hot lunches from midday to 2.30pm daily. A selection of sandwiches, cold snacks, good home-made scones and cakes and hot and cold drinks is available.

Shops Located off the south choir aisle, the shop's merchandise includes a reasonable selection of books, with a predominantly religious theme, as well as a small range of pottery, tapes and CDs, toiletries and foodstuffs. The official visitor guidebook (available in English, French and German) for the cathedral can be purchased here.

🚌 Situated in the heart of Exeter. Pay-and-display parking. ⊖ Train to Exeter Central station, then 10-minute walk away. ① Mon to Sun, 8am to 6.15pm, 5pm on Sat, 7.30 Sun. 💷 Adult £2.50, family ticket £5, concessions £1 (suggested donation). ♿ Full wheelchair access. Audio tour and Braille material available free from information desk.

Fitzwilliam Museum

Trumpington Street, Cambridge CB2 1RB ☎ *(01223) 332900*
📠 *(01223) 332923* 🖱 *www.fitzmuseum.cam.ac.uk*
🖱 *fitzmuseum-enquiries@lists.cam.ac.uk*

Quality ★ ★   **Facilities 💺 💺 💺**   **Value for money ££££**
Highlights Large, beautiful repertoire of exhibits; impressive building
Drawbacks Poor signs; little interpretation of exhibits

What's there The Fitzwilliam Museum at the University of Cambridge is housed in a fabulous neo-classical edifice, complete with colonnades and porticos. The interior is as ornate as the grand exterior, with galleries on two levels. The collections began in 1816, when Richard, 7th Viscount Fitzwilliam of Merrion, bequeathed paintings, prints, books, medieval manuscripts and music autographs to the University of Cambridge. Since then, further bequests, gifts, modest purchases, and divisions of antiquities from excavations have increased the exhibits to a vast array of objects from round the world, from the tiny and everyday to the monumental.

The Upper Galleries house paintings, sculptures, etchings and furniture from early Italianate through to the twentieth century – **Canaletto, Rembrandt, Monet, Cézanne, Degas, Hepworth** *et al*. The Lower Galleries have literally hundreds of pieces displayed rather dryly in glass cases: **porcelain**, coins, pots, **sarcophagi**, **statues**, miniatures, ceramics and textiles. There's also an Armoury. Allow at least two to three hours to get round.

Information/tours/guides With the aid of a free map, you can guide yourself around the museum. You can also buy glossy *Brief Guides* – one on the whole museum and one on the Greek, Roman and Cypriot Galleries. Even with these guides we found the different galleries confusing and badly signed. Also, the exhibits were poorly labelled. A guided tour is available on Sundays at 2.30pm for £3. Guides in each gallery will answer questions.

When to visit It's an all-year-round attraction. There may well be school parties during term time. Events are organised throughout the year: lunchtime gallery talks, music concerts and promenade concerts.

Age appeal It's probably best for those who appreciate old-style, 'look but don't touch' museums. Activities are organised for children in the holidays or on the educational programme.

Food and drink A small, bright cafeteria offers simple fare, such as baguettes (£2.50), cakes (£2), tea, coffee and wine. Note that the cafeteria closes at 4.30pm.

Shops The cramped shop has plenty of postcards, prints and books featuring the exhibits, and some children's items.

🚗 In Cambridge city centre, on Trumpington Street. (parking in Lion Yard, off Pembroke Street or park and ride at Madingley Road off M11 junction 13). ⊖ Train to Cambridge, then short walk. ◷ Tues to Sat, 10am to 5pm, Sun 2.15pm to 5pm. Closed on Mondays, 24 Dec to 3 Jan. 🖭 Free (suggested donation of £3). ♿ Difficult building for those in wheelchairs or with limited mobility (for more information tel (01223) 332900).

Flagship Portsmouth

Porter's Lodge, College Road, HM Naval Base, Portsmouth PR1 3LJ
☎ *(02392) 861512/722562*   📠 *(02392) 295252*   ⬦ *www.flagship.org.uk*

Quality ★★★★	Facilities 🍴 🍴	Value for money £££
Highlights	Tour of *Victory*; boat trip round harbour; Nelson museum	
Drawbacks	High entrance fees; poor food and toilets; *Victory* tour not run when busy	

What's there Portsmouth **historic dockyard** contains several maritime attractions – most famously Nelson's flagship HMS *Victory* and the remains of the *Mary Rose*, a sixteenth-century warship.

If the 40-minute guided tours of **HMS** *Victory* are running you will be given a timed ticket for one at the visitor centre. Otherwise you can pick up the free leaflet and do the tour on your own. Nelson died on this ship in 1805 during the Battle of Trafalgar. On the quarterdeck you can see a plaque marking the spot where he was hit by a French marksman. He was then taken down to the Orlop deck, where he is romantically depicted on his deathbed; nearby a barrel reminds visitors that his body was shipped home in a barrel of brandy (it was topped up with wine in Gibraltar). Nelson's cabins, where he entertained and briefed his officers, are rather fine. On the way out you pass his sleeping area, containing a replica of his cot – most officers had a cot like this, to be used as their coffin should the need arise. Wandering the decks, surrounded by the old guns and ammunication, gives you a good feel for life at sea in those days.

Go to the **Mary Rose Museum** by the entrance before the ship hall to see a short **film** of the vessel's raising and some of the artefacts found on board, including gold coins and pewter plates. The battered hull itself is right at the far end of the Dockyard, preserved behind glass in what looks like a cascading waterfall, which is actually a water-soluble wax to prevent the hull from distorting as it dries out. A recorded commentary tells you about the ship's layout.

The other ship you can clamber round is **HMS** *Warrior* – a battleship from 1860. In her time she was the largest, most heavily armed and armoured battleship in the world. More than 700 men lived on board and you can see the gun deck where the crew slept, ate and relaxed, the cramped galley where all the food was cooked, and below, on the lower deck, the officers' cabins and wardroom.

The **Nelson Museum** has been well designed, offers activities to keep children entertained while the grown-ups study the display cases of Nelson relics and memorabilia – among them his visiting card, a watch and a piece of his hair. The gallery opposite focuses on the sailing navy, explaining more about the structure of the navy and life at sea. In addition, a small exhibition called the **Dockyard Apprentice** looks at the traditional skills of shipbuilders at Portsmouth.

If the weather is fine you may enjoy the 45-minute **trip round the harbour**, with views of the modern naval base: if you are lucky you will see the Royal Navy's aircraft carriers and other modern warships in dock.

Allow at least four hours to enjoy the site.

Information/tours/guides timed ticket for a tour of HMS *Victory* is issued on entry and will normally be the next available (tours are suspended during the school holidays, when the site is very busy). Tours are conducted by retired naval servicemen, who spice them up with tales of leg irons and cats-o'-nine-tails and explain where the terms such as 'shake a leg' and 'brass monkeys' came from. An audio tour of the dockyard 'heritage trail' is included in the passport ticket. About 30 minutes long, it gives a good introduction to the history and layout of the dockyard, including the world's first dry dock, built in 1495 by order of Henry VII. A free commentary is provided on the *Mary Rose*. The audio tour of HMS *Warrior* costs an extra £1 – worth paying to find out more about shipboard life. A full-colour guidebook to the whole site (£3.50) and guides to individual ships are also available.

When to visit If you want to go on the Victory tour do not visit during school holidays.

Age appeal Excellent for children, with much to interest adults as well.

Food and drink Main Tradewinds restaurant serves meals all day. Queues can be lengthy and the food kept warm for too long. Choices include soup and roll (£2.25), roast of the day (£5.95), slice of pizza (£2.50). The Ship's Biscuit (summer only) serves snacks.

Shops Well laid-out gift shop with wide range of souvenirs and gifts, such as *Mary Rose* snowstorm (£1.99).

Other facilities The toilets were a let-down – dingy and institutional.

🚗 Follow signs on main roads (M275, M27) into city. Car park 5 minutes' walk from site (up to 2 hours £1.50; 2–4 hours £2.50; 4–8 hours £4. ⊖ Portsmouth Harbour railway station practically adjacent. ⏰ Mar to Oct 10am to 5.30pm; Nov to Feb 10am to 5pm. Closed 25 Dec. 💷 (1999 prices) *Passport for all attractions* (valid for 1 entry to each attraction over 2 years): adult £14.90; child, student, disabled, unemployed £10.90; senior citizen £12.90; family ticket (2 adults + 1 child) £35.25 (extra child £5.45). *All-ships ticket* (valid for Mary Rose Museum and Ship Hall, HMS *Victory*, HMS *Warrior*, Royal Naval Museum (valid for 1 entry to each attraction over 2 years): adult £11.90; child, student, disabled, unemployed £8.90; senior citizen £10.40; family ticket (2 adults + 1 child) £28.25 (extra child £4.45). *Season ticket* (unlimited entry to all attractions for 2 years): adult £19.95; child, student, disabled, unemployed £14.50; senior citizen £16.95; family ticket (2 adults + 1 child) £47.15 (extra child £7.25). *Harbour trip* adult £3.50; child, student, unemployed £2; senior citizen £3. ♿ No orange badge parking at all. Free wheelchairs available. *Mary Rose* and museums accessible; other ships very difficult.

Flambards Village Theme Park

Helston, Cornwall TR13 0QA ☎ *(01326) 573404*
🖥 *www.flambards.co.uk*

Quality ★★★★	Facilities 🏛🏛🏛	Value for money £££

Highlights Authentic and unique exhibition; well-kept park with a good variety of rides and attractions

Drawbacks Disappointing merchandise in shops; internal signing in exhibition area could be better

What's there A unique under-cover exhibition centre forms the core of this attraction. **'Britain in the Blitz'** combines authentic sounds and smells with subdued lighting, crackling flames, bombed houses and air-raid shelters to give visitors a taste of the hardships endured during World War II. A recreated public house – The Bull – includes life-size army-clothed personnel, wartime music, and a notice telling patrons that beer is in short supply.

The attention to detail in the lamp-lit **Victorian Village** is carried through into the interiors of the various shops. The shelves of Birch, Birch and Co. are stocked with long obsolete trademarked provisions, the tables of the Bakehouse display bread and cakes, and an organ grinder and his monkey chat to the barmaid in the **Pheasant Inn**. Upstairs, a fully furnished Victorian home gives visitors a glimpse of domestic life during this era.

The **'War Galleries'** hold a fascinating collection of old war memorabilia, including used ration books, press cuttings of the air raid on Buckingham Palace and wartime aircraft – some of which you can enter. Wedding cakes and dresses (one made from parachute silk), and other odds and ends, such as old prams and bicycles, are displayed in the **'Hall of Miscellany'**. Squint through cobweb-covered windows into the **Chemist Shop Time Capsule** to see dusty jars of chemicals, medicines and ancient equipment.

Outside there is plenty to do. Young children will love the **'Wonderful World of Gus Honeybun'** with its rabbit burrow complete with families of fully dressed model rabbits having supper or reading papers. The rides and play zone in this section of the park are also suitable for younger visitors, as are the paddocks of hens, goats and pigs in **Pets Paradise** next door.

Older children and adults will enjoy the **Hornet Rollercoaster** and the various water rides. The 'Exploratorium' with its 'Tunnel of Illusion' is fun, as is the **laser show** in the **'Space Quest Centre'**. It lasts approximately eight minutes and is shown five times daily. Aircraft enthusiasts should head for the **'Aeropark Collection'**, one of the largest privately owned aircraft collections in the country.

A parrot show takes place three times daily and afterwards visitors can have their pictures taken with the birds (£2.99). The TV Weather Forecasting Studio allows budding weather forecasters to video themselves in action (£3).

Information/tours/guides A full-colour leaflet, with a fold-out map, is available free of charge. However, you may need to ask for it when you buy your ticket. There is no great need to buy a copy of the souvenir guidebook (£2).

When to visit When we inspected there was little evidence of queues for the various rides, although the exhibitions can get crowded and noisy with school groups. Special events take place throughout the year and cost no more than the usual ticket price.

Age appeal There is something for all age groups here and everyone will enjoy the exhibition centre. Novelty buggies for small children are available for hire (£5 and a £5 refundable deposit). For those with mobility problems the grounds are flat and paths well maintained.

Food and drink The snack outlets dotted around the park sell cold drinks, sweets and ice creams. A covered patio area with plastic tables and chairs adjoins the main restaurant, which serves hot meals and snacks (for example, Cumberland sausage pie and steak and kidney pasties), a standard range of pre-packed sandwiches, cakes, cream teas and hot and cold drinks.

Shops The three separate shops sell a disappointing range of goods mainly aimed at children. A good local-books section, friendly staff, and a limited selection of wartime-related items redeem things slightly.

🚗 Situated off the A394 outside Helston. Follow brown signs. ⊖ Train to Redruth station, then Truronian T34 bus (10.05, 10.55, 12.05 and 12.50) to Flambards. ☎ (01872) 273453 for more details. ◷ Mon to Sun, 31 Mar to 18 July, 10.30am to

5.30pm; 19 July to 2 Sept, 10am to 6pm; 3 Sept to 31 Oct, 10.30am to 5pm. Closed on some Mondays and Fridays during spring and autumn (phone in advance). 💷 Adult £7.95, child (4 to14 yrs old) £6.95, child (under 3 yrs old) free, senior citizen (60 yrs plus) £5, family ticket (4 persons) £27. Over 80s free. Reduced rates from 2.15pm: adult £5.50, child £4.40, senior citizen £3.30. Parkcard Seasonal Return: visitors can return to the park at anytime during the season for £2.50 each with a Parkcard (25p per person). ♿ Fully accessible. A special route guide for the exhibition centre is available. Wheelchairs for loan (limited numbers so book in advance). Disabled parking; disabled toilets.

Flamingoland Theme Park and Zoo

Kirby Misperton, Malton, North Yorkshire YO17 6UX ☎ *(01653) 668287 Fax (01653) 668280* ☏ *www.flamingoland.co.uk*

Quality ★★   **Facilities 👶 👶 👶**   **Value for money ££**
Highlights   Mix of attractions will probably keep the family happy; zoo pleasant to wander round
Drawbacks   Same admission prices for adults and children; disappointing food

What's there   The zoo part is set in an attractive wooded setting which is pleasant to stroll around on a fine day. There is a **bird walk** with some lovely owls, some penguins (fed at 4pm) and a good selection of animals to appeal to children, such as **zebras**, **lions**, **tigers** and an old **polar bear** in a depressing concrete enclosure. In addition there is a children's farm section where younger children can meet some **tamer species**.

In the theme park section the rides are set in groups, with the rides for small children nearest the entrance. All are clearly labelled with height restrictions – there are quite a few rides that children under 4 feet high will not be able to go on. The thrill rides like **Thunder Mountain** and the **Corkscrew** have signs indicating the queuing time (if longer than 45 mins). The **Bullet** operates for only a couple of hours a day.

A sky train and cable car help you to get from one end of the park to the other – but there can be long queues even for these. There are also **shows** throughout the day, usually featuring entertainers or performing animals such as parrots.

If you take a picnic and go to a show or two, in good weather you might find enough here to spend a day at the park.

Information/tours/guides   You are given a plan of the site on entry which shows the layout and colour-codes the rides so that you can see the height restrictions. The leaflet also lists the times of the shows.

When to visit   Best in fine weather, and weekdays out of school holidays to avoid the queues. Some rides do not operate in high winds and rain.

Age appeal   Taken as a whole, the theme park is probably best suited to older children because of the height restrictions. However, there is a section for younger children too, and even toddlers in pushchairs will enjoy being wheeled around the zoo. So overall there's enough to keep a family with children of mixed ages happy.

Food and drink Lots of fast-food outlets serve Indian food (e.g. chicken tikka £3.95) or meals with chips (sausage, chips and beans is £2.95, a chip butty is £1.40). There's also a picnic field if you want to bring your own food.

Shops The best are nearest the entrance; some of the others have a high preponderance of tat arranged as if in a jumble sale. There's plenty for children to spend pocket-money on.

🚍 Off A169 Malton to Pickering road. ⊖ Train to York, then bus 90 (York Pullman (01904) 622992, return fare £5) or Yorkshire coastliner ((01653) 692556, return fare £4) from station to Flamingoland. Nearest local station is Malton on York to Scarborough line. ⊘ 9 Apr to end Oct, 10am to 5pm (6pm in high season). ▣ Adult, child over 4 £12; senior citizen £6; family ticket (2 adults + 3 children) £42. Free entry to guests at holiday village. ♿ Park is very flat with tarmacked paths. Staff will help people on to rides if needed. Disabled toilets.

Fountains Abbey and Studley Royal Water Gardens

Studley Park, Ripon, North Yorkshire HG4 3DY ☎ *(01765) 608888*

Quality ★ ★ ★ ★ ★ **Facilities** 🏛 🏛 🏛 🏛 🏛 **Value for money** £ £ £ £ £
Highlights Knowledgeable, friendly guides and good-quality tours
Drawbacks Price list in visitor centre not clear and prominent

---

What's there Founded in 1132, Fountains Abbey is the most complete **Cistercian Abbey** in Britain. The extensive remains of the Abbey include the church, cloisters and the infirmary, for the most part in the austere, unadorned style of the twelfth century. However, by the thirteenth century, Fountains was one of the wealthiest abbeys in England, and several examples of ambitious building projects undertaken still remain intact. The most obvious of these is the **perpendicular North Tower** built by Marmaduke Huby, the Abbot from 1495 to 1526. Built from limestone, it is 167 feet high – look closely and you will see Huby's initials carved on each side. The **Chapel of the Nine Altars** has excellent window carvings and from this point you can look down the nave, which is twelve bays in length, towards the west window. The west range, with its vaulted ceiling, runs 300 feet from the church on one side to the River Skell on the other.

The wooded valley of the Skell provides a dramatic setting for the **water gardens** (start your tour from the canal gates entrance). Created by John Aislabie, a former Chancellor of the Exchequer, and his son William, they cover 150 acres and are formal and geometric in design. The canal, which runs over cascades through the centre of the valley, is the backbone of the gardens. The **moon pond**, flanked on either side by crescent-shaped ponds, is overlooked by a classical building, known as the Temple of Piety. Three lead statues – Neptune in the moon pond, with Galen and Bacchus on either edge of the crescent ponds – complete the picture. The slopes of the surrounding valley, which are thickly planted with trees, such as yew and juniper, provide several imaginative vistas and viewpoints. The best views are from the **Octagonal**

Tower, which overlooks the water garden, and from Anne Boleyn's Seat, from where you get a spectacular view of the Abbey in the valley below.

The **400-acre Deer Park** provides plenty of scope for walking enthusiasts. You should also allow time to visit the **Hall and Swanley Grange** to see their exhibitions on the history of the estate, and St Mary's Church, an excellent example of High Victorian Gothic designed by William Burges. In total, it's worth setting aside a full day in order to make the most of your visit.

Information/tours/guides The full-colour guidebook (£3.25) covers the history of the Abbey and gardens and includes tours and plans of both, as well as a clear plan of the estate. Alternatively, simpler booklets on the Abbey and gardens (70p each) also include a tour and map. Excellent free guided tours of the Abbey last about an hour; a tour of the gardens lasts an hour and a half. An audio-visual show on the history of the estate is shown every half-hour during the day in the Visitors' Centre (starts 10.15am last show 4pm).

When to visit Special events take place throughout the year. Many are included in the admission price, though some need to be pre-booked. Contact the Visitors' Centre for more information. The Abbey is floodlit every Friday and Saturday evening from 25 August to 14 October.

Age appeal The excellent children's guide (£1.90) will provide a focus of interest for older children; younger children will enjoy running around the gardens and parkland. There's also a small activity centre at Swanley Grange. Paths leading up to the various monuments are extremely steep, so wear sensible walking shoes.

Food and drink The Visitors' Centre houses a large, self-service restaurant that provides hot and cold food at lunchtime, plus sandwiches, snacks, children's meals, and a selection of cakes and hot and cold drinks. The quality is good, but prices are on the high side (for example, lamb casserole £6.25, tomato quiche £5.25). There is also a tea room at the canal gates entrance to the estate.

Shops The shops offer a wide range of goods, some with local connections, such as locally produced fruit wines. Books cover everything from gardening to cooking, and standard National Trust items include jumpers, cardigans and umbrellas.

🚗 From B6265 road to Pateley Bridge, four miles west of Ripon, follow signposts. Free car parking or £2-per-car canal gates carpark (free for disabled visitors). ⊖ Train to Harrogate, then bus to Ripon, 36/36A, every 20 mins (tel 01423 566061). ⊕ Mon to Sun, Jan to Mar 10am to 5pm; Apr to Sept 10am to 7pm; Oct to Dec 10am to 5pm (or dusk if earlier). Closed 24, 25 Dec, 1 Jan and Fridays in Nov, Dec and Jan. *Deer Park:* open daily during daylight hours. *St Mary's Church:* limited opening times. Contact estate office before visiting. *Lakeside tea room:* Apr to Sept 10am to 5.30pm daily. 🎫 Adult: £4.30, child: £2.10, family ticket (2 adults + 3 children) £10.50. National Trust members and under 5s free; English Heritage members admitted free to estate. ♿ Information leaflet and map route available free from admissions. Wheelchairs and powered run-arounds available for loan. Guided tours for visually impaired can be organised. Call 01765 601005 to book above facilities. Braille and large print guides available from the Visitors' Centre. Disabled toilets. Disabled and free parking.

Frontierland

Promenade, Morecambe Bay, Lancashire LA4 4DG ☎ *(01524) 410024*
📠 *(01524) 831399*

Quality ★ **Facilities** 🏄 **Value for money ££**
Highlights One good ride (Texas Tornado); cheap prices; few queues
Drawbacks Poor catering; unkempt appearance; few worthwhile rides

What's there This is a place that needs help. The rides and wristbands are cheap, and it has a moderately successful Wild West theme, but overall it's down-at-heel and not much fun. Younger children will get the most enjoyment, but teenagers looking for cheap thrills won't find them here.

The one rollercoaster, **Texas Tornado**, is a good, old-fashioned wooden affair, with plenty of lurches and humps to get you going, but as it's the only real ride, the queues can be long, even on a rainy Sunday morning. If you have a wristband, make sure you go on this at least twice to get your money's worth. The **Runaway Mine Train** is the only other adrenaline-inducing ride, though it's on a much smaller scale – a two-person car hurtles round the tracks at break-neck speed with lots of sharp turns.

Most of the rest is fairly standard fairground stuff – a ghost train, giant swings, dodgems and the like. Some attractions are in really bad condition, with rust and peeling paint very evident, and there's little effort at prettifying the grounds. The car park is a disgraceful mess, and inside the Tarmac is quite pot-holed and patchworked.

For non-riders there are a couple of amusement arcades, both of which have seen better days, with torn, dirty carpets and unexciting games. Or you can go to the top of the **Polo Tower** for a view across the bay. Most Friday nights during the season are 'Yippee nights', with entertainment in the saloon bar.

Information/tours/guides There are few maps or signs to help you, but it's so small you don't really need them.

When to visit The park's probably best when there's a lively atmosphere, so go when it's likely to be busy in the summer months.

Age appeal Thrill-seekers will be disappointed, and there's very little for older adults.

Food and drink Refreshments are fairly dismal all round, with hot-dog stands and burger vans selling burgers (£1.85), chips (90p), or hot dogs (£1.75). The Fish Inn has a counter with plenty of seating, though it's a bit dark and dingy and the menu is limited to items such as fish and chips (£3.85), tea (80p), and baked potatoes (£2.40). Next door is a large but dirty and smelly bar. Avoid it if you can.

Shops With the Wild West theme, it should have been easy to include some inspired merchandise to liven things up. As it is, the selection includes a Viking helmet (£5.99), jumbo kipper tie (£4.99) and the usual assortment of soft toys, princess dress-up sets, sweets and pencils. Just one solitary sheriff's set at £1.

Other facilities If you need to use the loo, head for the ones near the dodgems, which are the best of a bad lot, though even the fixtures are extremely dated. The others had missing tiles, a cubicle without a door, dirty urinals and a sticky floor.

🚗 From M6 junction 34, follow signs. Car parking (£3 per day). ⊖ Train to Morecambe station (branch line from Lancaster), then 10-minute walk. ⊘ opening times vary considerably, depending on the month, so ring for details. General opening times as follows: Mar and Oct, Sat and Sun and school hols 12 to 5pm; Apr, May and Sept, Sat and Sun, bank hols, Easter week 11am to 6pm; June to mid-Jul 11am to 6pm; mid-Jul to mid-Aug 11am to 9pm. Yippee nights (Fridays from Mar to Oct except Aug) 7pm to 10pm. 💷 Free entry but charge for rides. Wristband prices based on height of the purchaser and allow unlimited access to rides in that category. Go karts (£2) are extra for everyone. Adult wristband (over 1.25m) £8.95 (covers all rides, including the Polo Tower); Junior wristband (under 1.25m) £6.95 (excludes Texas Tornado and Runaway Mine Train); Family of four unlimited pass £29.95. Polo Tower: £1.50. Individual prices: ride tickets £1 each. The bigger rides cost two tickets (i.e. £2). ♿ Access to some rides is limited. Ask at guest relations.

Galleries of Justice

Shire Hall, High Pavement, Lace Market, Nottingham NG1 1HN
☎ *(0115) 9520558* 🖱 *www.gal-of-justice.demon.co.uk*

Quality ★ ★ ★ ★ ★   **Facilities 👜 👜 👜 👜 👜**   **Value for money £££££**
Highlights   Interactive techniques bring history alive
Drawbacks   Could be a bit unsettling for children under 7 years old

What's there   The former Nottingham County Court, including two fine **Victorian courtrooms**, is at the heart of this fascinating tour through the history of law and order. There are three main components to the museum. The largest, the **Crime and Punishment Galleries**, puts visitors in the dock, with a guide/interpreter playing the role of a nineteenth-century court warden. The black-robed warden takes you (and a small group of fellow visitors) into the imposing Victorian courtroom to hear a reconstruction of the trial of one of Nottingham's Reform Bill rioters. The dimmed lighting, sound and a video presentation bring the story of the hapless defendant to life – and leave no doubt about the harshness of 1830s 'justice'. The tour moves next to the **1800 prison**. Down narrow stairs and corridors you reach the cells, including the pits – barely more than holes the ground – which were for those who couldn't afford the relative luxury of the cramped, dark and unheated cells of this early example of a private prison.

The other two elements of the Galleries are a thought-provoking 'law in action' exhibition in the **Civil Law Gallery** and a separate museum dedicated to policing, the **Police Galleries**. This is based in the Edwardian police station next door to the courts and starts with another guide/interpreter in the role of Custody Sergeant introducing you to a convincing mock-up of a modern police station – prepare to be fingerprinted.

There's plenty to do, and touch, at the Galleries of Justice – including electronic polls on contentious legal issues – plus contemporary exhibits about drugs and capital punishment, for example. Lighting effects, evocative sound recordings and video presentations complement the traditional glass cabinets of judges' wigs and the modern interactive exhibits. In an interactive police investigation you can decide the progress of the case from a touch-screen video. Consistently entertaining, the Galleries of Justice give a fascinating account of the social history of English policing and punishment.

Information/tours/guides Your entrance ticket is marked with a 'convict number'. As you proceed on the tour you will find display boards giving a brief biography of yourself – a one-time 'customer' of the Nottingham courts – the offence that brought you here, and the punishment you face. In addition to the introductory 'court warden' there are three further interpreter/guides to take you through other parts of the tour, including a recreated women's prison (also once on this site) and an exhibition on the history of transportation – the shipping of felons to Australia.

When to visit The Galleries could be busy with schoolchildren during term time. Weekends are quieter.

Age appeal Children from the age of 7 or 8 years upwards would find lots of stimulation in the evocative (but sometimes rather gruesome) story of justice. There's also a children's activity centre, where youngsters can try on a warder's uniform or investigate the contents of an escaped prisoner's suitcase. Older children and adults could easily fill the recommended four hours.

Food and drink Meals and snacks are available in the 'Judge's Pantry', a well-run café/restaurant under the barrel-vaulted ceiling of the court's basement. Main meals, such as pasta in a salmon and dill sauce, cost from £3.95, but you can also buy baked potatoes and filled baguettes (from £2.25) or a cream tea (£2.25). In summer there's also a Courtyard Café.

Shops A small boutique sells a limited range of souvenirs and leaflets on the history of Nottingham.

🚗 From Nottingham city centre, follow signs for Lace Market and Galleries of Justice. Fletcher Gate car park. ⊖ Train to Nottingham station, then 5-minute walk. Alternatively, bus (from Victoria coach station) to Broadmarsh bus station in Nottingham, then 5-minute walk. 💷 Adult £7.95, child (5 to 16 yrs old) £4.95, students, unemployed, senior citizens, disabled visitors £6.95, family ticket (2 adults + 2 children) £23.95. The ticket is valid for 12 months from date of purchase (one visit per gallery), so you can visit each of the galleries on different days. ⏱ Tues to Sun, 10am to 5pm (open bank hols). Closed 24–26 Dec, 1 Jan. ♿ Lifts and ramps give access to 80% of the museum. Disabled toilets.

Haddon Hall

Bakewell, Derbyshire DE45 1LA ☎ *(01629) 812855*

Quality ★ ★ ★	Facilities 🏛 🏛 🏛	Value for money £££

Highlights Wonderful medieval architecture and gardens; tasty home-baking in restaurant

Drawbacks Poor accessibility for less mobile visitors; car park across busy road; guidebook rather dry

---

What's there On catching sight of the castellated outline of Haddon Hall for the first time, it's difficult to believe that only 100 years ago this splendid medieval and Tudor building lay deserted and covered in ivy. It was the 9th

Duke of Rutland, father of the present Duke, who spent his life restoring it to its former glory.

After you pass the gatehouse and cross the bridge, you'll see a cottage with topiary in the shape of a boar's head and a rather stout peacock. These represent the crests of the two families who have owned Haddon for the past 800 years – the Vernons and the Manners. Little remains of the original twelfth-century construction, other than parts of the chapel, but over the following centuries, as their wealth increased, the Vernon family added the banqueting hall, kitchens, dining room and great chamber. Sir George Vernon, the last in the male line of the family, had two daughters; it was the younger of these, Dorothy, who eloped with Sir John Manners after her father disapproved of his suit. When Sir George died in 1567, Dorothy and her husband inherited Haddon – and the Manners family has owned the estate ever since. Dorothy's grandson, Sir John Manners, succeeded to the title of the Earl of Rutland in 1641 and became a Duke in 1703, when he moved to Belvoir Castle. Thus Haddon was left, unaltered, for two centuries until the 9th Duke returned.

A steep stone spiral staircase in the entrance tower leads up to the two rooms lived in by the 9th Duke while the house was being restored, while below is a **small museum** displaying objects found during the restoration – including a delicate painting of a young girl and dog on tortoiseshell, Elizabethan coins, bone combs, and rush candles. The **chapel** has some fascinating medieval wall paintings and a touching marble effigy of the eldest son of the 8th Duke of Rutland, who died when he was nine.

Modern environmental health officers would have had a fit in the **atmospheric medieval kitchen**, where the wooden work surfaces have been worn away by the constant pounding, grinding and chopping – you can also see a salting trough and the baker's stone ovens. By contrast, the **dining room** is lined with splendid panelling carved with the boar's head crest, the ceiling painted with Tudor roses and Talbot dogs: look for the carvings of Henry VII and Elizabeth of York, plus Will Sommers, the court jester, in the window recess. The hall is hung with seventeenth-century tapestries depicting the five senses.

The other highlight is the **Long Gallery**, where the combined symbols of the Vernon boar's head and Manners peacock feature in the panelling and stained glass. If you look closely at the leaded panes, you will see that they bulge in and out at different angles, ensuring that maximum daylight enters (they look particularly striking from the outside). In the state bedroom, a charming plaster relief shows Orpheus playing his lyre to the animals, including (of course) a Manners peacock.

The **gardens** are structured in a series of terraces, where springtime bulbs as well as summer herbaceous borders flank the flowering season of the **roses and delphiniums** for which Haddon is best known. From the terraces you can look down over the River Wye and the small bridge over which Dorothy Vernon allegedly ran on the night of her elopement.

Information/tours/guides The publicity leaflet gives details of opening times and admission prices, plus a location map. Roadside signs by the car park also give details of opening times but not prices – if you don't have the leaflet you won't know how much it will cost to go in until you've paid 50p to park and crossed the road to the gatehouse.

There's no map of the site, but it is fairly small and difficult to get lost. Guides greet you on entering the courtyard and point out the suggested route. A couple of other guides around the house will answer questions if asked.

The main rooms have labels giving enough information for you to grasp the significance of the main features. The guidebook (£2.50) is a little dry in style, but it gives a good account of the history of the house and Vernon and Manners families, as well as details of the furnishings and gardens.

When to visit The gardens are spectacular in early summer, when the roses and delphiniums are in full bloom. Special events like craft fairs or Elizabethan dancing displays are also held throughout the summer.

Age appeal There is a separate guide for children (90p), though some of the questions it asks cannot be answered by observation and rely on a certain level of general knowledge. There are also references to Henry VIII that should be Henry VII.

Elderly visitors may have problems with the steps if they are less mobile.

Food and drink The Haddon Restaurant, on the upper floor of the former seventeenth-century stable block, is clean and pleasant, if slightly cramped. Lunch options on the day we inspected consisted of home-made pies, such as steak and kidney or lamb and onion for £5.50 to £5.95; quiches (all vegetarian) for £2.85; and salads for £5.30 to £5.50. There was also a good range of home-made cakes and pies, from £1.10. Cream teas cost £1.95. Wine and beer are also available but only with 'substantial meals'.

Shops The tiny shop in the gatehouse has limited stock, including preserves and Norfolk lavender products, cross-stitch embroidery kits of Haddon Hall (£21), souvenir coasters (£9.99) and bookmarks (£1). Books on the Tudors and the Peak District are also available.

Other facilities The best toilets, also with baby-changing facilities, are in the courtyard next to the museum. The set of toilets in front of the gatehouse next to the cottage are characterful but a little gloomy.

🚐 From 2 miles south of Bakewell on the A6 follow the brown signs. Parking (50p). ⊖ Train to Derby, then R61 bus or Trans Peak bus, both to Haddon Hall. ⏱ Mon to Sun, Apr to Sept 10.30am to 5pm; Mon to Thur, Oct 10.30am to 4.30pm. 💷 Adult £5.75, child (5–16 yrs old) £3, senior citizen £4.75, family ticket (2 adults + 3 children) £14.75. ♿ Not recommended for visitors in wheelchairs and those who are less mobile.

Hardwick Hall

Doe Lea, Chesterfield, Derbyshire S44 5QJ ☎ *(01246) 850430*

Quality ★★★★   **Facilities 🏛 🏛 🏛**   **Value for money £££**
Highlights Two Elizabethan houses in one visit, set in extensive wooded parkland
Drawbacks Interior of New Hall can be gloomy

What's there Hardwick 'New Hall' was actually built at the end of the sixteenth century. It is a superbly well preserved testimony to the skill of Elizabethan craftsmen, and to a remarkable woman – Elizabeth, Countess of Shrewsbury, aka Bess of Hardwick, Bess the Builder, and mother to the first Earl of Devonshire – who ordered its construction and amassed the fortune to pay for it. Vast windows dominate the tall, symmetrical frontage of the Hall, and the Elizabethan adage for Hardwick, 'more glass than wall', is entirely fitting. Equally remarkable is that the once-grand 'Old Hall', which stands in the shadow of its replacement, now lies largely roofless and ruined, although completed only three years earlier. Perfectionist Bess decided that despite her extensive alterations to the older property, only a fresh start would do.

Inside her New Hall, now owned by the National Trust, a well signposted tour takes you around the main rooms of the house. Bess was a great fan of **tapestry**, and her vast collection covers nearly every inch of wall space. **Grand staircases**, the **High Great Chamber** reaching up over two floors, and the **Long Gallery** stretching 167 feet across the whole width of the house are imposing reminders that this was a house built to impress. The oil paintings, friezes and furniture are remarkably well preserved. But visit on a dull day and the inside of the house is positively gloomy, thanks to the heavy net curtains designed to keep out the tapestry-fading power of the sun.

Both Hardwick Halls sit atop a hill, commanding views across the valley (in which the nearby M1 now rumbles) There is a **large wooded parkland** too, and the biggest **herb garden** of any National Trust property.

Information/tours/guides   In the New Hall there is a 10-minute introductory talk. However, without any explanatory panels or labelling you will need to buy the beautifully illustrated, scholarly guidebook (£4.50). And although there are plenty of wardens on hand, armed with folders of back-up information and keen to answer your questions, the way the house was lived in (as indeed it was until the 1960s) is not well interpreted.

The ruined Old Hall, under the stewardship of English Heritage, does this much better. An audio tour (included in the entry price) gives enough information to help you mentally piece together the ruins, using actors giving first-person accounts from one of the Elizabethan stonemasons and one of the senior servants to bring the place to life.

When to visit   Brighter weather would be necessary to make the most of the interior of the house, and summer is the best season to enjoy the gardens.

Age appeal   There is a children's I-spy challenge in the New Hall, and a more engaging children's guide at the Old Hall. The interior of the house might not interest younger children, and steep, long staircases would put off some people, including wheelchair users.

Food and drink   Full meals and snacks are available in the original kitchen (New Hall), where the walls are lined with gleaming copper pans and seating is at big, old limed-oak tables. Choose from good-value roasts (£6.50) and hot main courses, plus salads and a vegetarian option. It's slightly hectic at peak time, but atmospheric.

Shops   A superior shop sells National Trust merchandise, including guides, calendars, and clothing, plus quality souvenirs of Hardwick (such as pewter ornaments) and a good selection of books.

🚗 From M1 junction 29, follow brown signs. Car parking (£2 per vehicle (NT members free)). ⊖ Train to Worksop, then Cosy Coaches C1 to Hall (Sun Jun to Aug only). Alternatively, Stagecoach E Midland 737, 747 Sheffield/Chesterfield to Nottingham, 48 Chesterfield to Bolsover, alighting at Glapwell 'Young Vanish', one and a half miles away. 💷 *New Hall (Old Hall only)* adult £6 (£2.60); child (under 16 yrs old) £3 (£1.30); student, senior citizen, unemployed £6 (£2); family ticket (2 adults + 4 children) £15. *Both Old Hall and New Hall (Garden only)* adult £8 (£3); child £4 (£1.60); student, senior citizen, unemployed £8 (£3). National Trust members admitted free, but there is a small charge at English Heritage events. English Heritage members admitted free to Old Hall. 🕐 *New Hall* 1 Apr to 31 Oct, Wed, Thur, Sat, Sun, bank hols 12.30 to 5pm, last admission 4.30pm. *Old Hall* Apr to Sept, Wed to Sun 10am to 6pm; Oct, Wed to Sun 10am to 5pm; Nov to Mar 10am to 4pm weekends only. *Park* open all year 7am to 7pm. *Garden* open 1 Apr to 31 Oct daily 12pm to 5.30pm. ♿ Wheelchair access only to the ground floor of the New Hall. Braille guide and large print guide available. Disabled toilets. Wheelchair visitors free entry.

Harewood House

Harewood, Leeds LS17 9LQ   ☎ *0113–218 1010*   ✌ *www.harewood.org*

Quality ★★★   **Facilities 🍴 🍴 🍴**   **Value for money ££££**
Highlights Beautiful landscapes surrounding the house, the bird garden and the lake
Drawbacks Toilets rather dated

What's there As you enter the grounds and follow the road down to the house, the rolling green fields and air of aristocratic splendour make you feel as though you've walked into a Gainsborough painting. The eighteenth-century **landscape gardens**, courtesy of 'Capability' Brown, are dotted with grazing sheep, and make an impressive sight.

The house itself is a magnificent piece of neo-classical architecture, built in 1772. The ground floor is open to the public, while the owner, George Lascelles, 7th **Earl of Harewood**, and his family still live on the upper floor. It was Edwin Lascelles (1712–1795), Lord Harewood, who used the wealth from sugar plantations in Barbados to commission John Carr of York to design a new house. **Robert Adam** took charge of the interior, and the elaborate decoration covering almost every surface in the interior – as well as the Chippendale furniture – is down to him. **Charles Barry**, architect of the Houses of Parliament, made several later alterations, most notably the addition of the **Terrace Gallery**, with its ornate parterres and marble statues and a superb view of the lake

Inside the house, visitors pass through a series of sumptuous rooms featuring intricate plasterwork, some fine inlaid and lacquered furniture by **Chippendale** (especially a commode in Princess Mary's Sitting Room), and delicate Chinese and Sèvres porcelain. Family portraits by Gainsborough and Reynolds hang against silk wallcoverings, though the personal collection in Lord Harewood's Sitting Room reveals more **eclectic tastes**, with works by Sir Sidney Nolan, Egon Schiele, Walter Sickert and Sir Jacob Epstein. Most splendid of all is the **Gallery**, with fake marble pillars and pilasters and even fake pelmets (actually carved, painted wood). Paintings by Bellini, Veronese,

Titian, Tintoretto and El Greco adorn the walls. The **Watercolour Rooms** contain an important collection of works by Turner, Girtin and Varley.

Outside, the **Bird Garden** is home to over 120 species of non-British rare and endangered birds, including well-known ones, such as penguins (fed daily at 2pm) and emus, as well as the more obscure yellow-throated laughing thrush, pink pigeon and ibis. Each bird has a display board with information about its feet and feathers. From here, the path descends further down the slope to an idyllic lakeside setting where it is possible to see migratory birds, depending on the time of year.

Kids will love using up any energy they might still have in the adventure playground on the route back to the front of the house. On the way back out of the grounds, a turning leads to the now-redundant All Saints Church, built in the fifteenth century, which features ornate alabaster carvings of the tombs of local notables.

Information/tours/guides Audio tours (available at reception, £1.50) give additional information on the Harewood family history, porcelain and furniture. Alternatively, you can buy the guidebook (£3), largely written by Lord Harewood himself. Every room in the house has a guide, all of whom are willing to give more details about the room and its contents.

When to visit The grounds and lake are really an integral part of the attraction, and are best seen in fine weather, as long periods of time are required walking outside. The gardens are known for their rhododendrons, so late spring is a colourful time. Various special events, including car rallies, concerts and theatrical events, are held throughout the year – call 0113-218 1010 for information.

Age appeal The house is most likely to be of interest to adults, but with the bird garden and adventure playground, a family could spend a day here with something for everyone.

Food and drink A café situated in the courtyard serves fresh orange juice, cakes, teas and coffees, as well as jacket potatoes and other standard dishes such as chilli con carne.

Shops There are two shops, one at the car park and one in the Stables Courtyard. These sell sweatshirts (£10) and colouring books (£4), as well as a range of ornaments, candles and pictures.

🚗 From Leeds and Harrogate, house is 7 miles away on A61. Free car park is situated within the grounds. ⊖ Bus 36 between Leeds and Harrogate passes the entrance. ⊕ Mon to Sun, 1 Apr to 29 Oct. Closed Nov to 31 Mar and 9 Jun 2000. *Grounds* 10am to 6pm (last admission 4.30pm); *house* 11am to 4.30pm (last admission 4pm); *terrace gallery* 11am to 5pm (last admission 4.45pm); *bird garden* 10am to 5pm (last admission 4.30pm). *Old Kitchens* 21 Apr to 28 Aug, Sat and Sun, bank hols 2pm to 4pm, closed 29 Aug to 1 Apr. 💷 *All-inclusive* adult £7.25; child (age 5 to 16 yrs old) £5; senior citizen £6.50; student, unwaged £5; family ticket (2 adults + up to 3 children or 1 adult + 4 children) £22.50. *Grounds only* adult £5.75; child £4.75; senior citizen, student, unwaged £5; family ticket £18. *Group rate* adult £6; child free. *Harewood Card* (gives entry to all attractions during the open season) individual £21; couple £35; family £50. ♿ A stairlift provides access to the house, all areas of which can be reached by wheelchair. The Bird Garden and other areas of the grounds are on a natural slope which could prove difficult, but staff are available to assist.

Harlow Carr Botanical Gardens

Crag Lane, Harrogate HG2 1QB ☎ *(01423) 565418*
www.harlowcarr.fsnet.co.uk

Quality ★★★ **Facilities** 🌢🌢🌢🌢🌢 **Value for money** £££££
Highlights Comprehensive visitors' guidebook and plant-labelling system; good
restaurant with friendly staff
Drawbacks Names of individual gardens not always displayed

What's there Opened in 1950 by the Northern Horticultural Society, the
gardens cover 68 acres. Their main aim is to provide inspiration and ideas for
keen northern gardeners and to assess the suitability of plants for the hardy
northern climate. To this end, all plants are clearly labelled and the results of
trials conducted are published on a regular basis.

Fruit and vegetable trials, fern houses, scent and foliage gardens, ornamental gardens, and notable collections of rare and endangered plants all have
their place here. Particularly appealing is the **scent garden**, which includes
roses, honeysuckle and other richly aromatic plants. The **foliage garden**
includes several varieties of variegated plants and a corkscrew hazel. The
National Rhubarb Collection can be found along the streamside, and just
below the scent garden is a sanctuary for **rare endangered plants**, including
varieties of hypericum and rheum.

The **model village**, sited close to the children's play area, is an excellent
example of a miniature Dales village and is built of Pateley stone and slate. A
small gardening museum displays a number of long-obsolete gardening tools,
including a collection of nineteenth-century lawnmowers. Gardening courses
are run in the study centre, and the adjoining library houses a good selection
of books on horticulture and botany.

A thorough visit will take the best part of a day to complete.

Information/tours/guides The full-colour guidebook (£1) includes a
useful map and a tour of the garden. Free quiz trails and I-spy leaflets are
available during school holidays and will keep children occupied during their
visit.

When to visit Come in late spring for the bulb garden and streamside
walk, summer for the scent garden and the orchids, and autumn for the sandstone maples. Special events throughout the year include guided walks, family
quiz trails and bee-keeping demonstrations. They are usually free. The bee-
keeping demonstration needs to be booked in advance.

Age appeal Children will enjoy the model village, well-equipped play area
and woodland trails. For older people, the grounds are relatively flat, though
there are some steep slopes, and the paths are well maintained.

Food and drink The visitor centre houses a licensed restaurant and café
bar, which serves hot food at lunchtime (such as pasta with smoked salmon
and prawns in a Stilton sauce) as well as sandwiches, a selection of cakes and
hot and cold drinks. Within the grounds, next to the study centre and library,
there are picnic tables.

Shops A wide range of goods are on sale on site, including plants, gardening tools, foodstuffs such as locally produced jams and honeys, and a good selection of books for both adults and children.

🚗 Off the B6162 (Otley Road), 2 miles from Harrogate town centre. Follow brown signs from town centre. ⊖ Train to Harrogate station then bus (Harrogate and District Travel 6/6A to Pannalash). Bus stops at Beckwith Road, then 10-minute walk to gardens. ① Daily 9.30am to 6pm, or dusk if earlier. 💷 Adult £4; child (under 16 yrs old) free if accompanied by adult; senior citizen £3; student £2. Admission free for members of Northern Horticultural Society and one accompanying guest and children under 16 yrs old. ♿ Gardens, restaurant, shop and plant centre are all accessible. Wheelchairs are available on loan and need to be pre-booked. Disabled toilet. Allocated car parking. Carers admitted free of charge.

Hartlepool Historic Quay

The Museum of Hartlepool, Jackson Dock, Hartlepool TS24 0XT
☎ *(01429) 222255*

Quality ★★★★★   **Facilities** 🏛 🏛 🏛 🏛   **Value for money £££££**
Highlights   Great for families; educational and entertaining galleries; good value for money
Drawbacks Food in quayside cafeteria rather bland

What's there Hartlepool Historic Quay is a reconstruction of a north-eastern seaport of the early nineteenth century. The highly stimulating exhibitions cover the hardships and suffering endured by seamen of the Royal Navy at the time of Nelson, explaining nearly all aspects of their lives on board ship, from how they worked and what they ate to how they fought and died.

'Fighting ships' is an **animated tour** that uses the latest technology to recreate an **eighteenth-century sea battle**. Models in darkened rooms with powerful sound effects and musty smells conjure up the horrors of life on board the fighting frigate HMS *Prosperity* as she engaged in battle with the French in 1800. Children love it – though the very young may get scared in parts!

The **reconstructed naval seaport** conveys the hive of activity of a nine-teenth-century port. The businesses of the naval architect, naval tailor and gunsmith, all painstakingly recreated here, prospered greatly while providing the huge range of supplies needed by the merchant ships and navy. By contrast, the gunport galleries convey the harsh realities of daily life for the lower ranks of the navy. 'Cutting Edge' is a gruesome exhibit portraying surgery in the days of fighting ships.

The **Hartlepool Museum** (free admission) has displays explaining the maritime heritage of Hartlepool throughout the ages. *Pressganged*, a 20-minute film, tells the story of two brothers forced to go to sea; 'Seapower', an audio-visual show with special effects, explains the history of the Royal Navy from Elizabethan times to the twentieth century.

You will need at least 3 to 4 hours if you want to see everything. Allow at least an hour to explore the historic quay, half an hour each for the guided tour, the two films and Hartlepool Museum.

Information/tours/guides The 'Fighting Ships' animated tour runs on the hour from 11am to 4pm and lasts about 20 minutes. The film *Pressganged* starts on the hour and half hour. The full-colour souvenir guide (£2) provides information on all the different exhibits and a map (with numbers relating to different galleries) to help you plan your visit. It is also a great souvenir of your day out.

When to visit The Historic Quay is best visited in dry weather.

Age appeal This is an excellent attraction for all ages, with everything on one level.

Food and drink The coffee shop on the quay has rustic-themed décor and offers traditional hot dishes, such as Cumberland sausage (£2), burgers (£2), beef hot pot (£4.95) and chilli and rice (£4.50), as well as sandwiches and cakes. There's also a council-run cafeteria on the *Wingfield Castle*, a 1934 paddle steamer, which provides more limited choice.

Shops Much of the merchandise follows a maritime theme. There's plenty of choice for children, such as books on Nelson or pirates from £3.99 to £9.99; sailor caps for £4.50, and plastic swords for 99p.

Other facilities Toilets are available on site.

Take the A19, then either the A179 or the A689 to Hartlepool. Follow brown signs to Quay from there. Free car park at museum. ⊖ Train to Hartlepool station, then 5-minute walk to museum. Alternatively, take bus (United buses) from Hartlepool town centre. ⊙ Mon to Sun, 10am to 5pm (including Bank Hols). Closed 25, 26 Dec, 1 Jan. 💷 *Historic Quay* (includes 'Fighting Ships' animated tour and the two films) adult £4.95; child, student, senior citizen, unemployed £2.50; family ticket (2 adults + 3 children) £13. Free admission to Hartlepool museum. ♿ Lifts and ramped access provided at the quay, along with ample seating round the quay. Wheelchairs available for loan. Adapted toilets. Allocated parking.

Hatfield House

Hatfield, Hertfordshire AL9 5NQ ☎ *(01707) 262823*

Quality ★★★	**Facilities 🛏 🛏 🛏**	**Value for money £££**

Highlights Grand Jacobean house with splendid woodwork, plasterwork and panelling; beautiful formal gardens, including Scented Garden and Knot Garden

Drawbacks Limited written information is a drawback for weekend visitors, who do not have the benefit of guided tours

---

What's there Hatfield House is strongly associated with Queen Elizabeth I, who spent much of her childhood here. Most of the Old Palace was demolished in 1608, but you can see the outside of the Great Hall and look inside from the doorway; it is now used for Elizabethan-themed banquets. The house that is open to visitors today was built in 1608 by Robert Cecil, Chief Minister to James I, using many of the bricks from the original palace. It is a fine example of grand Jacobean architecture, including a splendidly panelled **Marble Hall** and **Minstrels' Gallery**, the **Long Gallery** with its gilded ceiling, and **King James' Drawing Room**, named after the life-size statue of James I over the mantelpiece. The house is owned by the Salisbury family, who still live in some of the ground-floor rooms, and many renovations have taken place over the years as the house has been refurbished as a family home.

As well as its fine rooms and architecture, Hatfield contains a number of artistic and historical treasures. There are numerous **portraits of the monarchs** of the time (including two famous ones of Elizabeth), some fascinating **manuscripts** (including Burghley's draft of the order for Mary Queen of Scots to be executed) and a **collection of hats, gloves and silk stockings** that may have been left by Elizabeth when she stayed here.

Some of the gardens at Hatfield have been created very recently. Others have changed over the years, but the aim is to recreate, as far as is possible, the garden style of the early seventeenth century. Most of the gardens are formal, including the elegant Privy Garden and covered Lime Walk, the **Scented Garden** with an array of aromatic herbs and flowers, and the **Knot Garden**, with traditional plants enclosed within intricate box hedges.

Lesser attractions include the church of Etheldreda, parts of which date from the thirteenth century, and a fine collection of model soldiers and battle scenes created by the British Model Soldiers Society. There are also suggested walks and nature trails in the grounds, and a children's adventure playground with a selection of wooden play equipment.

Information/tours/guides On arrival, visitors are given a leaflet that includes a numbered plan of the park and buildings, but some more information and signs would be useful. On weekdays there are frequent guided tours of the house, full of evocative detail and historical context, but weekend visitors do not get tours, and there is little printed or other information to enlighten them. The gardens in particular would benefit from some guidance and explanation in addition to the rather dense prose in the gardens guidebook.

When to visit Fine weather is a major consideration, as the gardens and park are a big part of the attraction. You may particularly enjoy a visit when the spring bulbs come into flower, or you may prefer to wait for the summer roses. It's worth coming on a Tuesday, Wednesday or Thursday if you can, in order to benefit from a guided tour. There are also special events, such as the Living Crafts festival and Country Homes and Gardens Show, and others outside the normal opening season.

Age appeal There's not a lot here for young children, despite the adventure playground and exhibition of model soldiers. But there is plenty of appeal to anyone with an interest in history, art and architecture, or gardening.

Food and drink The light and spacious Palace Yard Restaurant provides a selection of hot and cold meals and snacks on a self-service basis. In addition to sandwiches and baguettes you can choose from pasta (£5.95) or jacket potatoes (£3.55) with a variety of toppings; cold cuts and salad (£5.80); or dishes of the day, such as steak pie with new potatoes and carrots (£6.60). The vegetable soup (£2.35) we sampled was home-made and tasty but contained unannounced meat and was extremely salty. A range of cakes, tarts and ice creams is also available. The restaurant is housed in an old L-shaped block around a courtyard with outside tables, while the inside walls are painted with *trompe-l'oeil* murals of the park and gardens.

Shops The main shop is across the lane from the restaurant, similarly housed in attractive red-brick outbuildings. Some of the goods it sells are specific to Hatfield, such as printed tea towels (£4.25), tote bags (£9), jigsaws (£14.50) and mugs (£3.95). There is a range of books and posters relating to the Tudors and Stuarts, as well as various toiletries and perfumed items.

The Garden Shop is a smaller outlet selling plants, terracotta pots, and gardening books among other horticultural things. Its wares are displayed in an enclosure just outside the car park.

🚗 Off the A1(M) junction 4. Follow the brown tourist signs (or those for Old Hatfield or Hatfield station) for about one and a half miles to Hatfield House. ⊖ Train from Kings Cross to Hatfield station. Hatfield House opposite station. ⊙ *House* 25 Mar to 24 Sept, Tues, Wed, Thur 12 to 4pm; Sat and Sun 1pm to 4.30pm; Bank Hols 11am to 4.30pm. *Gardens* Mon to Sun, 11am to 6pm (East Gardens open only on Fridays). *Park* open 10.30 to 8pm. Friday is known as Connoisseurs' Day, when the house is open only to groups on extended or specialist tours. 💷 *House, park and gardens (park only)* adult £6.20 (£1.80); child (5 to 15 yrs old) £3.10 (£90p). Visits on Connoisseurs' Days (Fridays) cost £5.20 for access to the park, East and West Gardens, or £9.20 including a tour of the house (booking essential). ♿ Wheelchair access is possible to all rooms of the house and to most areas of the park and gardens.

Hawk Conservancy

Andover, Hampshire SP11 8DY ☎ *(01264) 772252*

Quality ★★★ **Facilities 👜👜👜👜** **Value for money ££££**

Highlights Appeals across all age groups; displays are entertaining and educational while maintaining birds' dignity and welfare; high-quality facilities; helpful and committed staff

Drawbacks Could do with more information displayed in the grounds, and a printed list of events; more toilets needed at busy times

---

What's there The Hawk Conservancy is one of the largest collections of birds of prey in the world, housing more than 200 birds in its 15 acres of woodland and 7 acres of wildflower meadow. Within the many natural-style enclosures around the grounds, the birds can be observed (unless they are hiding) in a comfortable environment. Many species of wild birds also visit the park, and insect life can be seen in the picturesque Butterfly Garden and Dragonfly Pond.

The main interest of the day is focused around the three **flying displays** at midday, 2pm and 3.30pm. They are all different, so it's worth going to all three if you can. The midday and 3.30pm displays take place in the main flying arena but use a different selection of birds showing off their skills. It is definitely not a circus show, but demonstrates the natural behaviour of the birds, including swooping low over the audience, rising on the thermals, catching food on the wing, overturning obstacles to find food, running up and down a 'burrow', and attacking an artificial snake.

Madeleine the Secretary Bird is one of the highlights of the midday display, while a **group of kites** flying together often features at the 3.30pm show. The keepers obviously know and love their birds, and are not alarmed when they fly out of sight for a while; they are allowed to have their independence but will always (or almost always) return a few minutes later. In the **Valley of the Eagles display** at 2pm the birds fly even further away – up to 2 or 3 miles – then return and swoop back to their keeper. The displays are a wonderful blend of independent behaviour from the birds and careful training from the keepers. Children can hold one of the birds afterwards, and adults get the chance to 'fly' one – it sits on your glove, flies off, and then returns when called for its food.

Other high spots of the day are the **Raptor Safaris**, when small groups can go out in the tractor and trailer to watch and learn about the birds in the meadows; the **Vulture Restaurant** at 11.30am, when keepers feed the vultures in their aviaries; and the **Heron and Raptor Feed** at the end of the day, when visitors can wait in the hides and watch the birds as they return for their food.

An attractive toddlers' play area has a variety of wooden play equipment, which is also the location for ferret racing at weekends and during school holidays. The Study Centre contains displays of skeletons, eggs and stuffed birds, as well as videos, tapes of birds' calls, and interactive computer quizzes.

Information/tours/guides The publicity leaflet is enticing but fails to mention prices or give detailed directions on how to get there. The guidebook (£2) is much more successful, combining information about the origins of the Hawk Conservancy and the work it does, with details and photos of the main species of birds of prey. It is not so much a guide as a souvenir. A map of the park is available in the guidebook or on a separate sheet, but it would be useful to have a printed list of the different displays and when they are on.

Very little written information is provided on the birds' enclosures, though more is available in the Study Centre (and in the guidebook). The best source of information is the verbal commentary that accompanies the flying displays.

When to visit It's best to come in fine weather as almost everything is outside and families can enjoy the play areas and picnic sites as well. It is busy on summer weekends and bank holidays, but not excessively so. Also, it is at these times that there are usually extra events, such as country-craft demonstrations, ferret racing, and a chance to meet the shire horses.

Age appeal Most ages will enjoy a visit here; the birds have universal appeal and the commentary manages to involve both children and adults. It is less satisfactory for under-5s, however, as the birds may be too far away to focus on, or so close that they seem frightening.

Food and drink Duffy's Coffee Shop is located near the entrance; it's an attractive rustic-style building, with wooden screens between the tables. It serves a range of sandwiches (£1.50) and baguettes (£2.50), as well as various snacks and cakes. Simple meals are available from 12.30 to 2pm, such as jacket potato with beans and cheese (£3.75), various ploughman's lunches (£3.10), pasties and salad (£3.10) and soup with a roll (£2.10).

On busy days, such as summer weekends and bank holidays, there is a barbecue in the picnic area opposite the coffee shop, serving burgers and hot dogs for £2 each.

Shops The shop sells, not surprisingly, lots of books about birds (various prices), and posters of birds (£1). Line drawings of the birds by a local artist are popular at 50p, and some of her designs are used for the china mugs (£5.99) and jigsaws (£10 to £14). A range of T-shirts and sweatshirts is available (£19.99 for an adult sweatshirt, £5.70 for a child's T-shirt), along with various birds in the form of soft toys.

🚗 On the A303 London to Exeter road, 4 miles west of Andover. Follow signs from off the A303. Car parking. ⊖ Train to Andover station, then taxi or bus (via Amport village). ⏰ 19 Feb to 29 Oct, Mon to Sun, 10.30am to 5.30pm (last admission is 4pm). 💷 Adult £5.75; child (3 to 15 yrs old) £3.25; senior citizen £5.25; family ticket (2 adults + 2 children) £16.50. Discount for pre-booked groups of 15 or more. ♿ Everything is at ground level and the hard, surfaced paths are suitable for wheelchairs. Both flying grounds have special areas reserved for wheelchairs.

Heights of Abraham

Matlock Bath, Derbyshire DE4 3PD ☎ *(01629) 582365*
🖰 *www.heights-of-abraham.co.uk*

Quality ★ ★ **Facilities** 🏛 🏛 🏛 **Value for money £££**
Highlights Cable-car ride; friendly staff and good play areas for children
Drawbacks Uninspiring guides; lack of information about tours; basic toilets

---

What's there A half-kilometre **cable-car ride** rises almost 170 metres above Matlock Bath to the hills containing **former lead mines**, now landscaped as a country park. From the cable-car terminus, trails (sometimes steep) lead up to the Great Masson Cavern and down to the Nestus Mine. There's also a hilltop trail with views of High Tor cliff and former mine shafts.

The tour of the Rutland **Nestus Mine** lasts about 20 minutes. The guide gives an account of the history of the mine, including the search for galena (lead sulphide). Then the lights go out, and various tableaux and recorded voices explain what life was like underground in 1675. There are slopes within the mine but no steps, so it's possible to take pushchairs.

The 30-minute tour of the **Great Masson Cavern** starts with a 10-minute audio-visual display, relating the geological history of Derbyshire. It is followed by a walk through the former mine with the guide pointing out the various dates inscribed in the rock, which indicate the rate of mining progress. The 165 steps mean that pushchairs and wheelchairs are excluded, and less mobile visitors may find it difficult.

Tours run roughly every half an hour. When we inspected, the guides seemed to be reeling off a set text, with little effort to involve children or encourage questions – we had a feeling of just being processed through the caverns.

If you've still got the energy, you can tackle the hilltop trail that leads from the exit up to Tinker's Shaft for **views over the Derbyshire hills**. An alternative viewpoint is Prospect Tower, built in the nineteenth century to provide work for unemployed lead miners.

'Mega Rocks and Dinosaurs' is a low-key display of mineral clusters, fossils, and wooden dinosaur skeletons. The highlight is the icthyosaur fossil found at Lyme Regis in 1995.

Information/tours/guides A display board at the lower terminus of the cable car gives entry prices and times of the tours and cable-car rides. However, no information on the times and the lengths of the guided tours is given. A small map showing the layout of the park trails and environmental and geological features is provided with your ticket.

When to visit Go for a fine day so that you can admire the views from the cable car and Prospect Tower. The temperature in the caverns is always cool so take a sweater, and wear sensible shoes.

Age appeal Children love the excitement of going underground in the caverns. There is also a good play area with small slides, tyre swings and climbing frames, and the more sophisticated Explorer's Challenge. During the high season there's often children's entertainment, such as a clown show, in the afternoons.

Food and drink The main food outlets are in the Tree Tops Centre, which has some tables on the terrace with good views over the valley. Downstairs, the coffee shop offers drinks (tea 90p), hot and cold snacks (salad roll £1.95), and cakes and pastries. More substantial meals are served up in the restaurant (scampi and chips £4.80) as well as jacket potatoes and quiche. There's a bar next to the Nestus Mine, the Great Rutland Cavern, which serves beer, soft drinks and ice cream, and two picnic areas.

Shops The rather cramped shop in the Tree Tops Centre sells goods ranging from mineral samples (fool's gold, galena) and wooden puzzles to cuddly toys, tea towels, mugs and needlework kits. Expensive stained glass paperweights are also available. Another shop at the exit of the 'Mega Rocks and Dinosaurs' exhibition stocks a better collection of jewellery, fossils and other interesting geological wares.

Other facilities You can find limited toilets and baby-changing facilities in the main Tree Tops Centre; otherwise there are Portaloos scattered around the park.

🚗 From M1 junction 28, follow brown signs to Matlock Bath on the A6, 18 miles north of Derby. Pay and display car parks in Matlock. ⊖ Train to Matlock Bath railway station then short walk. ⏲ 19 Feb to 24 Mar weekends only 10am to 5pm; 25 Mar to 31 Oct, Mon to Sun 10am to 5pm (later in high season). 💷 Adult £6.50, child (5–16 yrs old) £4.50, child (under 5 yrs old) free, senior citizen £5.50 (Adult £3; child £2 if walking rather than taking cable car). ♿ The Great Masson Cavern has 165 steps with no access for wheelchairs. Steep paths also make access difficult for those in wheelchairs or with limited mobility.

Hereford Cathedral

Broad Street, Hereford HR1 2NG   ☎ *(01432) 359880*

Quality ★★★ **Facilities** 🛆 🛆 **Value for money** £££

Highlights Tower tour; free guided cathedral tour; choir stalls; Lady Chapel; Piper tapestries

Drawbacks *Mappa Mundi* poorly displayed; old toilet block with basic facilities

What's there This classic English cathedral contains all the elements you might expect – ancient tombs, fascinating architecture that dates back to 1100 and a long and varied history.

Try to time your visit to coincide with the hour-long free guided tour, run by volunteers, which takes you around the most significant features. Among the highlights are the **Lady Chapel**; the fine carvings on the **Norman font**, which dates from 1150; the choir stalls; and the shrine of St Thomas Cantilupe, which contrasts with the striking modern **tapestries by John Piper** in the south transept. The spirituality of the Cathedral is successfully maintained with a moment of prayer, held on the hour every hour, in which you are welcome to join.

If you are prepared to tackle the 218 steps the **tower tour** is very enjoyable. Among the sights are the loft space above the nave and the bell-ringing chamber – with information on the bells – and, at the top, a **panoramic view** of the Malvern and Black Hills to the east and west.

Unfortunately, the *Mappa Mundi* exhibition has a limited appeal. The thirteenth-century map of the world – Hereford's most important treasure – is difficult to see properly, especially if there are any crowds (at the time we visited there was a temporary exhibition on the history of maps). However, the seventeenth-century bookcases and chains and the 1,500 rare books in the chained library, in a separate room, are fascinating. Knowledgeable attendants are on hand to talk about the library, but it might have been useful to have a separate guided tour of this section of the Cathedral.

Information/tours/guides A Cathedral tour lasts one hour, costs £2.50, and needs to be booked in advance. Check on arrival for times of the tower tour (adult £1.50, child £1), which lasts 40 minutes. The guidebook (£2.50) is nicely illustrated and would make a good souvenir. If you want to know more about the *Mappa Mundi* there is a separate guidebook (£2.50) – again well illustrated.

When to visit Any time is a good time to visit.

Age appeal There is not much to appeal to young children, but if they can handle the stairs they will enjoy the view from the tower.

Food and drink There is a snack and tea shop, situated in part of a cloister, which can get quite busy. It sells a small selection of fresh sandwiches and some tempting cakes. Ice cream costs £1.

Shops The snack and tea shop doubles up as a small shop, selling a good choice of items. A *Mappa Mundi* jigsaw costs £6.75, a mini stone roof boss £15.50.

Other facilities There is just one block of toilets with old, basic facilities and no baby-changing facilities.

🚌 In the centre of Hereford. Pay and display car park by Wye Bridge (walk 15 mins from Cathedral). ⊖ Train to Hereford, then 10- to15-minute walk. ① Summer Mon to Sat 11am to 4.15pm, Sun 12.30 to 3.15pm; winter Mon to Sat 11am to 3.15pm. Closed Sundays in winter. 💷 Cathedral free. *Mappa Mundi* exhibition: adult £4; child, senior citizen, unemployed £3, child (under 5 yrs old) free. ♿ All parts accessible except tower.

Hever Castle

Edenbridge, Kent TN8 7NG ☎ *(01732) 865224*

Quality ★★★	**Facilities** 🏛🏛🏛🏛	**Value for money** £££
Highlights	Lovely grounds; story of Anne Bullen (Boleyn) well told; dolls' house display	
Drawbacks	Main restaurant rather institutional; guides uninterested in visitors on our inspection	

What's there This is a lovely intimate little castle which was the childhood home of Anne Bullen, more commonly known as Anne Boleyn. The Castle became politically important again in this century when William Waldorf Astor bought it and lavished money on it to entertain on a grand scale. The oldest part of the castle – a massive gatehouse and walled bailey surrounded by a moat – was built in the late thirteenth century, and a Tudor dwelling was added on about 200 years later by the Bullen family.

Pass over the drawbridge and under the portcullis into the inner courtyard, where the walls from both early periods can be seen. Inside, on the ground floors, however, most of what you see was reconstructed by the Astors, with much use of finely carved wood that fits in well with the feel of the house. The **Inner Hall** – the kitchen in Tudor times – has lovely panelling of Italian walnut and a Gallery above the stairs. On the walls is **Holbein**'s portrait of Henry VIII, plus others in his style of Anne Bullen and her elder sister Mary (Henry's mistress before he took up with Anne). The comfortable drawing room has beautiful inlaid panelling and is clearly designed for modern-day use, as is the library. The Dining Hall was once the Great Hall of the Castle – again, everything has been reconstructed, even the fireplace with the Bullen arms above it.

Up the stairs – which curve anti-clockwise, as this is a rare defensive staircase – the older residents become more apparent. In a small room that was once Anne's childhood bedchamber, two fine Books of Hours are displayed, with inscriptions from Anne clearly visible. The **Queen's Chamber** tells the story of Henry's many wives, and how he removed England from the Pope's jurisdiction to make Anne his second wife, although she still ended up beheaded. In the staircase gallery, built for Anne's father Thomas, are two portraits of Queen Elizabeth II, one of which is rather unusual in showing her in the earlier years of her reign. At the end of this gallery are two bedrooms with heavy period furniture – the first named after Anne's brother (with whom she was accused of having incestuous relations) and the second after Henry, who must have been a frequent visitor to the castle.

Up on the second floor the Long Gallery runs the full width of the castle. This was an essential part of any Tudor house and was used for social gatherings and exercise. Here life-size tableaux depict some of the events linked with the King and this house – quite useful for telling the story to children. In the painted glass windows you can see the coats of arms of all the owners of Hever. Then it's back to more recent times: past three small bedrooms is the Astor Suite, where letters on display give a feel for life here during the early twentieth century – Churchill's house Chartwell is just down the road, fuelling plenty of entertaining. You then pop back in time by walking through the gatehouse, the earliest part of the castle, where there is a small regimental museum and a collection of torture equipment to ponder. Allow about an hour for a tour of the Castle.

Outside are beautiful grounds, particularly the **Italianate garden** with statues and sculpture, and for the children an adventure playground and a **water maze** (you get wet if you take a wrong turn). Also, don't miss the **exhibition of dolls' houses** that shows the development of different styles of British architecture.

Information/tours/guides The guidebook (£3) is good and worth buying as little is labelled inside the Castle.

When to visit Choose a fine day to enjoy the gardens. Mondays and Wednesdays late in the season are said to be quietest.

Age appeal Younger children will probably enjoy the grounds best, though the house is small enough to keep older ones interested.

Food and drink Your best bet is to take a picnic. Cars are usually allowed in the grounds and you can picnic in this area. The largest self-service restaurant is down by the lake, rather institutional in feel, though there are tables outside; there's also a smaller one near the entrance. Typical dishes might be lasagne, steak and ale pie, and seafood bake (all for £4.30), or a children's meal (£2.60).

Shops There's a good gift shop with an interesting collection of items on sale plus a small plant shop.

🚘 From M25, junctions 5/6, off B2026. Follow signs to Castle. Large car park. ⊖ Train to Edenbridge Town, then bus (the 234 runs a limited service on Mon, Wed and Fri). ◷ *Castle* Mar, Oct, Nov 11am to 4pm; Mar to Nov, Mon to Sun, 12 to 6pm. *Gardens* Mar to Nov, Mon to Sun, 11am to 6pm. Last admission 5pm. 💷 Adult £7.80; child (5 to 14 yrs old) £4.20; senior citizen £6.60; family ticket (2 adults + 2 children) £19.80. *Garden only* adult £5.80; child £4; senior citizen £5.20; family ticket £16.20. ♿ Limited access (first floor of House only), hence free admission for wheelchair users. Gardens are ramped. Wheelchair hire available (£25 deposit).

Hidcote Manor Garden

Hidcote Bartrim, Chipping Campden, Gloucestershire GL55 6LR
☎ *(01386) 438333 (01684) 855370 (information line)*

Quality ★★★   **Facilities 🏛 🏛 🏛**   **Value for money £££**
Highlights Red Borders; Bathing Pool Garden; woodland walks; the audio tour
Drawbacks Lack of free information

What's there Hidcote Manor is largely the creation of Lawrence Johnston, an American who introduced the idea of garden 'rooms' profusely filled with flowers and separated by hedges and lawns. As a result, Hidcote, now run by the National Trust, is an astonishing assembly of 28 compact gardens, shielded from each other by an equally amazing assortment of hedges: beech, hornbeam, yew, copper beech, box and holly. (In high summer they also help to hide the huge numbers of visitors.)

Among Hidcote's many gorgeous 'rooms' are the **cottagey Old Garden**, with its gentle pinks, mauves and blues; the **White Garden**, with topiary doves; and the striking **Red Borders**, ablaze with dahlias, begonias, crown imperials and roses. Amid the clipped yews of the **Pillar Garden** you'll see bushes of Hidcote's own sweet-smelling lavender. The **Bathing Pool Garden** features blue Tibetan poppies and a fine magnolia tree.

On one side of the house, the exquisite **Pine Garden** surrounds a triangular pond embraced by raised beds of colourful perennials. Beyond it, double borders of old roses, phlox and penstemons sweep round to a kitchen garden-cum-orchard.

Information/tours/guides The easiest and most enlightening way to tackle the gardens is to take the excellent audio tour (£2). This has a numbered button for each section – for instance the White Garden or Bathing Pool Garden – and a lively commentary in the form of interviews with gardeners – Stefan Buczacki among others. This gives you all the detail you might need. If you are less concerned about horticultural history there is a leaflet (75p) with a map that is extremely useful. Without either of these aids you must content yourself with letting the flowers speak for themselves.

When to visit The variety of plants means that there is something of interest for the whole of the garden's open period, from spring bulbs on the Spring Slope, Fuchsia Garden and Poppy Garden through to the autumn colours in the Maple Garden.

Age appeal There is nothing specifically for children.

Food and drink The Garden Restaurant in the old manor house is licensed and has a small lunch menu, including chicken with fennel (£6.95) or poached pear and salad (£2.95), and also serves cream teas (£3.50). A tea bar is open in the plant centre.

Shops There's lots of choice and good variety in the shop, including Hidcote Manor jigsaw (£19.95), National Trust envelopes and cards (£3.75).

Other facilities There is a drab toilet block some distance from the gardens.

🚗 Off B4632, 4 miles north west of Chipping Campden. ⊖ Train to Honeybourne station then taxi to garden, 10-minute journey. ☉ Apr, May, Aug to Oct, Mon, Wed, Thur, Sat and Sun 11am to 6pm; June and July, Mon to Thur, Sat and Sun 11am to 6pm. 💷 Adult £5.60; child (5 to 16 yrs old) £2.80; family ticket (2 adults + 3 children) £14. Free to National Trust members. ♿ Limited wheelchair access with lots of steps and different levels.

Holkham Hall

Wells-next-the-Sea, Norfolk NR23 1AB   ☎ *(01328) 710227*
📠 *(01328) 711707*

Quality ★★★★	Facilities 🏛 🏛 🏛 🏛	Value for money £££

Highlights Marble Hall and Statue Gallery in the house; good audio tour
Drawbacks Poorly maintained toilets in car-parking area

What's there This beautiful eighteenth-century Palladian-style mansion set in a 3,000-acre deer park on the north Norfolk coast was based on designs by William Kent for Thomas Coke, the 1st Earl of Leicester. It was designed as a 'Temple of the Arts' to house the treasures collected by Coke in Europe, and is still very much a family home. The current Earl and Countess have a passion for preserving the house as Coke had intended it to look, even keeping specific pictures hanging where Coke had instructed. Paintings by **Rubens**, **Van Dyck**, **Poussin**, **Claude** and **Gainsborough** adorn the walls, while fine furniture (many pieces designed by Kent) fills the rooms. The **Statue Gallery** houses an impressive collection of classical sculpture, while the **grand Marble Hall** (actually made of alabaster from Derbyshire) is modelled on Palladio's designs for a Temple of Justice.

The Bygones Museum, part of the nineteenth-century stables, is a vast array of old agricultural and domestic items. This includes farming exhibits, vintage cars, working steam and diesel engines as well as recreated rooms, such as a kitchen and dairy room. Exhibits are labelled and those in the 'Farm and Country' section are more detailed.

Information/tours/guides Guided tours are by arrangement and for groups only. A real lack of information or labels in the house (except in the Statue Gallery) means that either the guidebook or audio tour are essential to get the most out of a visit, despite the friendly and knowledgeable room guides. The excellent audio tour (£2) is narrated by the Earl of Leicester. A full-colour guidebook (£4) covers the house and its history, park and grounds and family history.

When to visit Come any time, although it's not ideal on rainy days as the grassy car park gets boggy, you'll need to dash between house and museum and you won't want to walk in the park or round the garden centre. On Sundays you cannot access the formal gardens and the grand nineteenth-century fountain is not switched on (Monday to Thursday it is switched on between 3pm and 4pm).

Age appeal It's not for very young children. There are boat rides (extra charge) on the lake (weather permitting), which may appeal to children (although when we visited they had stopped running because of the amount of weeds in the lake). For those with mobility problems, once they have negotiated the steps in the Marble Hall, the state rooms are mostly on one level, so it is easy to walk around.

Food and drink The Stables Restaurant, adjacent to the Bygones Museum, is self-service, selling a selection of sandwiches (£2.25 to £3.25), salads (£5.25 to £6.95) and some hot meals, such as Lancashire hotpot (£6.25) or chicken tikka masala as well as cakes and cream teas. Meals are very much home-made but are a bit on the pricey side. The Ancient House is a second restaurant, tearoom and gift shop on the coast road at the entrance to the Hall, serving the same menu but in slightly more characterful surroundings – and with the bonus of a garden area.

Shops The Hall's shop has a wide range of pottery items from the Holkham Pottery, such as mugs (£4.20) or teapots (£15.75), lamps and plant pot holders. Other items include framed pictures and typically English toiletries. A small selection of books/information relating to Holkham and its history are also available. The Garden Centre is in the walled nineteenth-century kitchen garden and is a joy to look round, with mature plants along the walls and in the borders which help you when buying younger stock for sale.

🚗 On A149, 3 miles west of Wells-next-the-Sea (brown sign at turn-off to enter long drive). Free car park. ⊖ Train to Sheringham station, then 780 or 781 bus (only twice daily in summer, Mon to Fri) to Holkham Hall car park (bus journey an hour and a half). Alternatively, more frequent coastliner bus from Sheringham station to A30 (drops you at the bottom of the drive), then long walk up the drive. ◷ *Hall and Bygones Museum* 28 May to 28 Sept, Sun to Thur 1pm to 5pm. Also Easter, May, Spring and Summer Bank

Hols (11.30am to 5pm). Last Admission 4.45pm. *Holkham Nursery Gardens* open all year, Mon to Sun 10am to 5pm (or dusk if earlier). 🖭 *Hall or Bygones Museum (combined ticket)* adult £4 (£6); child £2 (£3). ♿ Good wheelchair access to Bygones Museum (all rooms are on ground floor). State rooms in the Hall are inaccessible to visitors in wheelchairs (flight of stairs).

Housesteads Roman Fort

Haydon Bridge, Hadrian's Wall, Hexham, Northumberland NE47 6NN
☎ *(01434) 344363*   🖥 *www.english-heritage.org.uk*

Quality ★★	Facilities 👜 👜	Value for money ££££

Highlights Excellent ruins; dramatic location; cheap entry; well-maintained site
Drawbacks Limited facilities; no audio tour; little guidance; tiny museum

What's there What a missed opportunity this is. Some of the best Roman remains in Britain in one of the most spectacular settings and you're left feeling uninformed and uninspired. Despite the quality and quantity of ruins on display, little effort is made to bring them to life and help you visualise life in this frontier fort 2,000 years ago. In comparison with other nearby sites, notably Corbridge, the lack of imagination in its presentation means you have to provide your own to understand and appreciate what you are seeing.

With its imposing walls and four gates, this is one of the most complete forts along **Hadrian's Wall**, and a must-see for anyone interested in Roman history in Britain. Owned by the National Trust but run by English Heritage (so members of both get in for free), its ruins encompass the fort walls, granaries, barracks and military headquarters, as well as good sections of the Wall itself. Its **location atop a steep crag** means that it is not ideal for less mobile visitors, and even the more able have a rough-ish walk uphill from the car park, half a mile away. But it's worth it, not least for the view from the top.

The fort itself covers an area of five acres, and was occupied during the third and fourth centuries. Just outside the massive south gate, with its neighbouring latrines, are the remains of a civil settlement that grew up beside the fort. Inside the fort, you'll find the impressive **east gate with its wheel ruts**, and the huge barrack blocks, now little more than stone outlines, which lie just near Hadrian's Wall where it joins the fort wall. This is the best place for the view down to the rough hills beyond, and it's easy to imagine how bleak life must have been up here 17 centuries ago. The most complete remains are in the centre, with the **commandant's house**, the **granaries**, the **hospital** and the **military headquarters building**. From the west gate, you can go up and on to Hadrian's Wall for the short walk west along to Milecastle 37, and then return along the path of the military way, still just visible beneath sheep-filled fields.

Information/tours/guides You have to buy the guidebook to stand any real chance of understanding what you are seeing, but though it's cheap at £1.75, it is very dry and high-brow. It's packed with information but it is hard to decipher it and get any value from it. The lack of colour photos doesn't help either.

Within the fort, the information boards, some of which are so faded and weathered as to be unusable, do help, but an audio tour or similar would be a much better way to inform, educate and entertain. The most annoying thing is the lack of guidance – the information boards are not numbered, the guidebook map has no suggested route, so you have to wade through the text to discover how best to see everything. In many ways, you're better off buying English Heritage's general book on Hadrian's Wall (£2.95), which in four pages manages to convey so much more and direct you round the site. The museum is disappointingly small and offers little more than a cursory overview of the area. The information boards at the National Trust shop at the entrance are marginally better.

When to visit Try to avoid rainy or very windy days, as the site is exposed and there is next to no protection. Even on a bright summer's day it can be chilly up on the top. It starts getting crowded towards mid-morning as coach parties arrive.

Age appeal Anyone interested in history will enjoy the fort, though children might get bored quickly. The English Heritage children's activity book covers all three main forts along Hadrian's Wall, so the Housesteads section is short but acceptable. Older visitors might find the walk up quite taxing.

Food and drink A refreshment kiosk at the car park, with rather surly staff, serves sandwiches (£1.75), cakes (90p), canned drinks (65p), tea (65p) and sweets. There are a few seats outside and inside the National Trust shop.

Shops Beside the National Park-run car park is the National Trust shop. At the English Heritage ticket office at the top there's a tiny shop and museum that sells much-needed soft drinks. The National Trust shop at the bottom is bigger, but sells lots of National Trust products (jams, tea towels, books, etc.) rather than Roman-related stuff. The smaller English Heritage shop up on the hill has a limited but more imaginative selection of goods – hand-made wooden sword (£3.99), columned photo frame (£4.99), Roman coasters (£4.50) and kids' colour-in poster (£1.99).

Other facilities There are no toilets up at the top – the only loos are those down beside the car park. Go before you walk up the hill.

🚗 Along B6318 halfway between Carlisle and Newcastle. Also accessible from A69 at Haltwhistle, Haydon Bridge and Hexham. Car parking (£1 for 3 hrs, £2 all day). ⊖ Train to Hexham, Haydon Bridge, Bardon Mill or Haltwhistle stations, connecting local bus from Hexham and Haltwhistle. From May to Sept Hadrian's Wall bus (682) connects all the main sites and towns along the Wall four times a day in both directions (30 mins journey time). Whole day rover tickets are also available at tourist information centres or on board. From Oct to May bus 185 runs twice daily (except Sunday) to Housesteads to/from Haltwhistle. ⏰ (in 1999) Apr (or Good Friday if earlier) to Sept, Mon to Sun 10am to 6pm; Oct 10am to 5pm; Nov to Mar (or Maundy Thursday if earlier), Mon to Sun 10am to 4pm. Closed 24–26 Dec, 1 Jan. 💷 Adult £2.80; child (5 to 16 yrs old) £1.40; child (under 5 yrs old) free; student, senior citizen, unemployed, disabled visitors £2.10 (helpers free). Free admission to English Heritage and National Trust members. ♿ Very difficult terrain for anyone with mobility problems.

Howletts Wild Animal Park

Bekesbourne Lane, Bekesbourne, Canterbury, Kent CT4 5EL
☎ *(09068) 800605/(01303) 264647*

Quality ★★★ **Facilities** 🕭 🕭 **Value for money £££**
Highlights Audio tour; gorillas, elephants, tigers
Drawbacks Poor restaurant; no animal talks or specific children's activities

What's there This is very much the private collection of John Aspinall, and it takes a more adult approach, providing less appeal to children than at other wildlife attractions. Visitors looking for a more 'entertaining' experience might be a little disappointed.

The park is principally about large mammals, with impressive collections of gorillas, tigers, elephants and a large variety of monkey species. You can tackle the site on a pleasant circular walk. The audio tour is excellent value and, given the inconsistencies on some of the information boards, is the best way of observing and understanding the animals. Pride of the attraction are the **gorillas** – one of the biggest collections in the world, with plenty of opportunity for visitors to watch their fascinating behaviour. That is also true of the extensive **elephant paddocks**, which are home to a large, active herd. The circular tour continues through pleasant grounds, past paddocks of deer and through a woodland section that has numerous cages housing primates such as gibbons and langurs.

Information/tours/guides The audio tour costs £1.50. A guidebook covers the work of Howletts in considerable detail (£1.95). The information boards were variable in quality and lacked imagination.

When to visit Come in fine weather as it is entirely outdoors.

Age appeal Apart from the animals themselves, there is very little to appeal to children specifically.

Food and drink The Pavilion Restaurant is an attractive low-level building surrounded by lawns. However, on inspection the food was unappetising; the poor selection included shepherd's pie (£4.95), sausage, beans and chips, sandwiches (£2 to £2.50) and coffee (90p).

Shops The main shop has a good and varied choice – for example, a leopard-print teapot (£24.99), cuddly gorilla (£7.99), penguin mug (£4.99) or dolphin pencil case. Nearby is the Cave of Gems where you can choose from a pile of coloured stones (£1.50 for a quarter pound).

Other facilities The toilets are showing their age.

🚘 Follow signs off A2, 3 miles south of Canterbury. ⊖ Train to Canterbury station then, taxi or train to Bekesbourne station and 15-minute walk. ⊙ Mon to Sun, 10am to 5pm (2.30pm in winter). Closed 25 Dec. 💷 (1999) Adult £8.90; child (4 to14 yrs old) and senior citizen £6.90. ♿ Flat site so easy access. Wheelchairs available.

Imperial War Museum, Duxford

Duxford, Cambridge CB2 4QR ☎ *(01223) 835000*

Quality ★ ★ ★ ★   **Facilities** 🍴 🍴 🍴 🍴 🍴   **Value for money** ££££

Highlights Well-designed attraction, particularly the futuristic Norman Foster building housing the US Air Museum; good facilities

Drawbacks Spread over a huge area, which can be a problem if it's raining, despite the transport

What's there Duxford Airfield was an important fighter station during the two World Wars, and much of it has been preserved as it was in the 1940s. The Imperial War Museum has its headquarters in London but houses an enormous collection here, particularly the larger exhibits, and the Museum has exploited Duxford's connection with the US Military to great effect. The site is more than a mile long, facing the airfield (which is still in use for displays and pleasure flights), with seven hangars that house the collections. A little transport truck drives around the site, dropping visitors off where they choose. Hangar 1 contains a **Concorde** as well as other large aircraft; hangar 2 houses a collection of **British and American fighters** from World War II; jets and a maritime exhibition are in hangar 3; hangar 4 features the air-defence collection; and hangar 5 has aircraft in various stages of restoration, as well as an operations room fitted out as it would have been during the Battle of Britain.

The showpiece of the whole place is the American Air Museum, in **Norman Foster's award-winning building** – a geometric, futuristic vision of a hangar, designed to be environmentally sensitive and visually spectacular. It houses collections detailing the US involvement in World War II, the Cold War and the Gulf Conflict. The last building (hangar) is the **Land Warfare Hall**, where tanks, trucks and artillery are displayed in dramatic tableaux.

An **adventure playground** keeps older children occupied, and a special play area for younger children features a hands-on exhibition called 'The Flying Machine'.

Allow the best part of a day for this attraction, and longer if you are a real enthusiast.

Information/tours/guides Guide yourself throughout the hangars, either with a simple plan (free) and the detailed boards at all exhibits, or with the comprehensive souvenir guidebook (£3). Pleasure flights are available, and you can watch an interesting video on the history of Duxford. An information office by hangar 3 is staffed by volunteers, normally only at weekends. Information sheets for children are available.

When to visit The museum is best in fine weather, as the hangars are some distance from one another, but all the exhibits are inside, so it can still be enjoyed during inclement weather if you have an umbrella (the transport vehicle does not come right to the doorway of the hangars).

Age appeal Not surprisingly, the museum is popular with boys aged 4 to 94, but it is appealing to all as the presentation simply but effectively brings to life the place, content and machinations of war. Although the park has plenty of space for children to play, and the ground is flat for those who find hills tricky, it is less good for those who tire easily as the place is very big.

Food and drink Of the three catering outlets, the Aerodrome Café between hangars 3 and 4 and the café in the Land Warfare Hall serve tea, snacks and sandwiches. The Interludes self-service restaurant near hangar 1 has hot food at lunchtime. Dishes such as chops, lasagne, beef in red wine sauce or mushroom stroganoff cost £4.95. Beer and wine are also available.

Shops Two spacious and modern shops offer all manner of things aviatory, from sheepskin US bomber jackets (£460) to model aeroplanes, books and target T-shirts.

From M11 junction 10, then on to the A505; follow signs. Car parking. ⊖ Train to Cambridge station then free bus to museum (at 9.45am, 11.15am, 12.45pm and 1.50pm). ⊙ Mon to Sun, mid-Mar to mid-Oct 10am to 6pm, mid-Oct to mid-Mar 10am to 4pm. Closed 24–26 Dec. ⊞ Adult £7.40, child (under 16 yrs old) free, unemployed, student and 16- to18-year-olds £3.70, senior citizen £5.20. � Information sheet for disabled visitors provided. Wheelchairs available for loan (book in advance). Access for wheelchairs in hangars (except some exhibits with steps) and transport truck; disabled toilets.

Ironbridge Gorge Museums

Ironbridge, Shropshire TF8 7AW ☎ *(01952) 432166*
www.ironbridge.org.uk *info@ironbridge.org.uk*

Quality ★★★★★	Facilities	Value for money £££££

Highlights Fascinating museums and a taste of living history; passport scheme means you do not have to see everything on one visit

Drawbacks Sites spread over a large area and no regular public transport, so you will need your own transport

What's there Ironbridge was the birthplace of the Industrial Revolution. In 1709 a local man, Abraham Darby, smelted iron using coke as fuel for the first time; his success meant that the first iron wheels, iron rails, cast-iron bridge and first steam railway locomotive were built in the area. Industrialisation changed the local landscape and people's lives, and the nine museums give an insight into these momentous changes.

Start by visiting the **Museum of the Gorge**, which provides an intro-duction to the gorge and describes the presence of the raw materials required for industry to flourish here. A 40-foot-long model of the gorge shows how it was in 1796, 15 years after the Iron Bridge was built. From here you can walk to the Iron Bridge itself and see the small display in the Toll House on the construction of the bridge. The **Museum of Iron** charts the development of the iron industry (make sure you visit the **Darby furnace** in the grounds too) and also the lives of the families who worked in the industry. A couple of minutes' walk from the museum are two houses owned by the Darby family restored to how they might have been in the eighteenth century. Rosehill is fully furnished with many family pieces.

Blists Hill is a recreated Victorian town, and you can easily spend half a day here. Some of the buildings are original; others were dismantled elsewhere and rebuilt here. Most of the exhibits are at the top of the hill, but the museum spreads over a site that is one mile in length. The town includes a bank where you can change your money into old currency and spend it in the workshops and shops around town. Workshops include a tinsmith, decorative plasterers, locksmith, harness maker and carpenter. You can also visit the doctor's house, school and squatters' cottage and ask costumed demonstrators about the lives of the inhabitants at the turn of the century.

Other museums include the Jackfield Tile Museum with its gallery of decorative encaustic tiles and workshops where you can see tile-making and decorating in progress; and the Coalport China Museum, in the remains of the old works which closed in 1926. The **old kiln** is the highlight. You can walk inside it and see how many fires were needed to fire the stacked clay boxes of china. There is also a display of porcelain.

Just down the road is the **Tar Tunnel**, which extends 300 yards into the hillside. In 1786 an attempt to drive a canal from the riverbank to the mines on Blists Hill was halted when miners struck a spring of natural bitumen, which was barrelled up and used commercially – traces of bitumen on the brickwork of the tunnel can still be seen.

The Broseley Pipeworks is a little further afield but worth going to. The buildings have been left as they were when they closed in the 1960s (after producing clay tobacco pipes since 1881). Demonstrators still make the pipes in original moulds.

You can easily spend a couple of days visiting all the museums – and if this is not enough the passport ticket gives you the flexibility of returning at another time.

Information/tours/guides You need to plan carefully to get the best out of the site in a limited time: get hold of the free visitors' guide in advance by ringing (0800) 590258. Separate leaflets suggest itineraries ranging from a few hours to all day, as well as giving ideas for those with young families. There is also a leaflet on special events, such as tile workshops or Coalport figurine painting. Each of the museums has its own detailed guidebook with lots of historical information and photographs. Staff at each museum are generally enthusiastic and helpful, especially the costumed demonstrators at Blists Hill.

When to visit Any time of year is a good time to visit, though some museums shut between November and March.

Age appeal All ages will enjoy Ironbridge. Blists Hill and the Tar Tunnel will particularly appeal to children.

Food and drink Blists Hill, the Museum of Iron and the Coalport China Museum have cafés or restaurants serving meals or light snacks. For full meals, the New Inn in Blists Hill serves filling fare, such as steak and ale pie and jacket potatoes, and baked apples or apple pie and custard. Close to the Iron Bridge is a choice of cafés along the road.

Shops There are shops at all sites except the Darby Houses. At the Jackfield Tile Museum you can buy tiles (seconds as well as best), while Blists Hill offers candlesticks (£5), sets of pastry-cutters (£4.50) and leather belts from the workshops in the town. Standard items found in all the shops includes cast-iron Victorian replica door stops, a wide range of books on the Industrial Revolution and Victorian life, and guidebooks on Shropshire. Other souvenirs include jars of Ironbridge jam (£2.50), Ironbridge tea-towels and chocolate, and pot-stands made of tiles (£13). At the Coalport China Museum a variety of china is for sale.

Other facilities Parking is generally free, except for the pay & display car park at the Museum of the Gorge and close to the bridge itself. Bikes can be hired in summer next to the Toll House. There are toilets at each Museum with separate disabled and baby-changing facilities.

From M54, junction 4, follow the brown and white signs to Blists Hill. Train to Telford Central station (5 miles north of Ironbridge), then bus to Ironbridge (call Telford Travel link on (01952) 200005). Bus shuttles between museums on Bank Holidays in summer only. Mon to Sun 10am to 5pm. Some museums close Nov to Mar, so check in winter. Closed 24, 25 Dec, 1 Jan. Passport ticket (valid indefinitely until you have visited each museum once) adult £10; child (5 to 18 yrs old), student £6; senior citizen £9; family ticket (2 adults + up to 5 children) £30. Disabled visitors and carers half-price. Museum of Iron has lifts to all floors and Museum of the Gorge is on one level. Blists Hill is partially accessible but galleries in the Jackfield Tile Museum are on upper floor (no lift) and the Coalport China Museum is mostly accessible but you will need help. Contact visitor information for further details (tel (01952) 432166), and for detailed access guides to each museum (also available in large print).

Jodrell Bank Science Centre and Arboretum

Macclesfield, Cheshire SK11 9DL ☎ *(01477) 571339*

Quality ★★   **Facilities** ▮ ▮   **Value for money ££**
Highlights Lots of interactive exhibits; good shop; impressive telescope
Drawbacks Old-fashioned building; unimaginative canteen; poor orientation

What's there Jodrell Bank is an **interactive science experience** that gives a comprehensive introduction to the planets, gravity, eclipses and other phenomena, as well as housing a giant radio telescope that dominates the landscape for miles around. Many of the displays, such as those on gravity and radio waves, can be pushed and pulled by visitors to make them work and illustrate their purposes. Some are highly imaginative, such as a giant sun that works in conjunction with a life-size model of Einstein, complete with video-projected 'talking lips' that explain his theory. A similar model is of Sir Isaac Newton.

What many people really come to see, however, is the **giant Lovell telescope** that is partly used to search for extra-terrestrials. This towering 90m-high construction resembles an enormous satellite dish, but you can only gaze up at it from beyond a fence.

The **Planetarium** is an audio-visual presentation in a darkened theatre that tells the story of how the sun and the planets came into being, with the galaxy displayed on the oval ceiling. A separate **arboretum** with mature trees, ponds and a maze is pleasant to walk in.

Including a walk of about half an hour, allow about 3 hours to visit Jodrell.

Information/tours/guides Two separate guidebooks are available, both costing £1.75. One is specifically on the telescope, while the other, called *Exploring the Universe*, contains more detail about the Centre's work. Both are colourful and informative, but there is no guided tour. An arboretum map and guide is available for 75p.

When to visit The centre is open all year round and is all indoors, which is good for rainy days, but the arboretum is best seen either in spring or autumn.

Age appeal The science material is quite technical, but is explained simply enough for slightly older children, while adults should find it fascinating.

Food and drink The canteen, like many other parts of the building, is rather old fashioned in style and serves standard pre-packed sandwiches, such as cheese and tomato, unappealing-looking burgers and chips, and jacket potatoes.

Shops The shop is a modern addition to the building and is bright and spacious, selling lots of science and nature books for both adult enthusiasts and children. There are science experiments and games, as well as solar wall charts and glow-in-the-dark stars, mugs and stationery.

🚗 From M6, junction 18 follow the signs. Large free car park. ⊖ No public transport to the Centre. Nearest train and bus station is at Macclesfield. ⏱ 18 Mar to Oct, Mon to Sun 10.30am to 5.30pm; Nov to Mar, Tues to Sun 11am to 4.30pm. Closed 25, 26 Dec, 1 Jan. 💷 Adult £4.60; child (under 16 yrs old) £2.30; senior citizen, student £3.30; family ticket (2 adults + 3 children) £13.50. Disabled visitors' carers free. ♿ Full access with ramps to all areas.

Jorvik Viking Centre

Coppergate, York YO1 9WT ☎ *(01904) 543400*
📠 *www.yorkarch.demon.co.uk*

Quality ★★★★ **Facilities 👜 👜** **Value for money ££**
Highlights Wonderfully detailed reconstruction of life in Viking Age York
Drawbacks Very short time ride round reconstructions; unappealing café

What's there The Jorvik Viking Centre was set up on the site of an important archaeological excavation in the heart of York, which uncovered a fabulously well-preserved part of the Viking Age settlement. The Centre, most of which lies under the present-day Coppergate shopping arcade, contains an incredibly detailed **reconstruction** of the site as it may have appeared in AD 948, as well as (very unusually) a reconstruction of the archaeological excavation itself. The reconstructions are accessed via a 'time' ride, which begins with a rapid journey back through the centuries, passing a number of statuesque grey figures intended to represent the various chronological eras, before arriving in Viking Age Coppergate. Here traders can be heard doing business above the noise of a bustling settlement. The time-car quickly turns off the main thoroughfare into a side street, proceeding through one of the houses where a family is preparing dinner, past the latrine (next door to the well!), and down to the docks on the Ouse where a boat is being unloaded to the jolly sound of an ancient sea shanty.

It is the attention to detail among the scenes that is remarkable, ranging from the inclusion of various **authentic odours** to accurate **facial reconstructions of Viking Age skulls** using modern forensic techniques. Even the language that can be heard spoken in the various scenes is a painstakingly researched version of Anglo-Scandinavian (a translation of the script can be found in the shop). The only substantial drawback is that the tour through the town is very swift (10 minutes at most), leaving you wishing that you had been given a chance to stop once or twice and really take in the surroundings.

From the town, the time-car whisks you into a **reconstruction of the excavation**, which is actually a mirror image of the street that you have just been down and contains all the original excavated timbers – even the toilet seat! Whether non-archaeologists are really able to appreciate the quality of the site remains questionable, and you might wonder whether *all* the attention to detail here is really necessary – Magnus Magnusson's commentary was spoiled at one point by *reconstructed* traffic noise! The time-car ride finishes with a quick glimpse of how finds were processed at the site. Visitors are fed through a reconstructed laboratory, where they can see some of the detailed work that went into extracting every last ounce of data from the site, into a small gallery that displays many of the **artefacts** that were discovered.

Information/tours/guides The museum gallery is extremely well presented and explained – there are even a few 'Vikings' on hand to explain aspects of their life in greater depth – and a short but informative display on York and the Vikings can be seen before entering the time ride. The time ride itself incorporates an audio commentary narrated by Magnus Magnusson; unfortunately, it is somewhat patchy and difficult to hear at times. The guidebook is colourfully presented and good value for money (£2.50). However, if you really wanted to find out more about York or the Vikings you might be better off buying one of the many books on offer in the shop.

When to visit Avoid peak season to miss large crowds and long queues (advance bookings can be made during the summer months, school holidays, and Jorvik Viking Festival and are strongly recommended).

Age appeal Jorvik would appeal to a wide cross-section of people; a few tactile displays are designed to introduce archaeology to children.

Food and drink The Nestlé Café at the Centre is extremely disappointing; it is far too small for such a busy attraction and the chocolate bars, ice-creams, packaged cakes and instant coffee machine are not at all tempting, given the range of attractive restaurants and cafés nearby.

Shops A slightly crowded shop sells a broad range of merchandise, including plenty of historical books, Viking-inspired ornaments and jewellery, reconstructed swords and a CD of Viking Age music, as well as every conceivable souvenir from post cards to key-rings. There is even a small reconstructed tenth-century shop where you can stamp your own souvenir Viking coins.

York town centre. Car parking in town. ⊖ Train to York station, then walk, taxi or bus. ⏲ Mon to Sun, Apr to Oct 9am to 6pm (last admission 5.30pm); Nov to Mar Sun to Fri 10am to 5pm; Sat 9am to 5pm (last admission 4.30pm). Closed 25 Dec. 💷 (1999) Adult £5.35; child (5 to 16 yrs old) £3.99; child (under 5 yrs old) free; student, senior citizen £4.60; family ticket (2 adults + 2 children) £17. Pre-booked group rates (2000): 15 or more adults £4.95; children £3.75; students/senior citizens £4.40. Disabled visitors' carer free. ♿ Good access for disabled visitors; parties with wheelchairs should telephone in advance to ensure that appropriate arrangements can be made.

Kenilworth Castle

Castle Green, Kenilworth, Warwickshire CV8 1NE ☎ *(01926) 852078*
🖰 *www.english-heritage.org.uk*

Quality ★★★ **Facilities** 🍴🍴🍴 **Value for money £££**
Highlights Beautiful, atmospheric ruins
Drawbacks Poor signs; inadequate toilets

What's there Parts of this evocative red castle ruin date back to the end of the twelfth century. No timber structures or glazing remain, and the lake that once surrounded the Castle, and where Elizabeth I was entertained by her lover Robert Dudley, Earl of Leicester, has been replaced by rolling fields. The Inner Court contains the **remains of the Norman keep**, the **strong tower**, the **great hall**, the three-storey Leicester's Building, and evidence of kitchens – foundations of fireplaces and ovens. All parts are open to the elements. A tour of the Outer Court leads you to a magnificent **Tudor barn**, which once housed the stables (and now contains the shop and cafeteria), the near-intact Leicester's Gatehouse (unfortunately closed to visitors) and the **Tudor garden**.

There are three suggested walks, one of which leads you to the site of Henry V's Pleasaunce in the Marsh, which was a banqueting house. Only the earthworks and moat remain.

A visit to the castle and grounds does not take long, but you need some time to soak up the sense of history, as no effort is made to bring the place to life. Allow 2 hours for the Castle, and 1 hour for a walk.

Information/tours/guides The placards by the ruins are not helpful, so the guidebook (£2.95) is necessary if you want a journey through the fascinating history of this place – from its origins as a Norman castle, through its extensions by King John, and then by John of Gaunt, to its glory days in Tudor times when Elizabeth I experienced the 'Princely Pleasures of the Castle of Kenilworth'. Also on offer are an audio tour (£1.50 adults, 75p children) lasting approximately 40 minutes, and an extremely primitive 'interactive' exhibition in the Tudor barn.

When to visit This is a fair-weather attraction, as all of it is open to the elements. It does not get crowded. There are special events throughout the year, from a Saxon/Viking battle to sheepdog demonstrations and medieval entertainment. Theatre companies perform outdoor shows – often Shakespeare – in the evenings during the summer months.

Age appeal The castle appeals mainly to grown-ups, although children have plenty of space to run around and play and there is a free children's activity leaflet. Access to the ramparts and parts of the ruins is by rickety wooden steps, so take care. The toilets have seen better days and need refurbishing, as well as better signing!

Food and drink The Tudor barn houses a simple cafeteria offering soup (£2), jacket potatoes, teas and coffees, and some pastries. Picnicking is another possibility.

Shops An attractive, pleasingly non-commercial shop sells appropriate merchandise, including minstrels' hats (£3.95), tapestries, books on Elizabeth I, murder-mystery games (£19.99) and jams (£1.95).

🚌 Off A46 in Kenilworth. Follow signposts from the town centre. ⊖ Train to Coventry, then bus (20 minutes). For more information on buses tel (01926) 414140. ⏰ Apr to Oct, Mon to Sun 10am to 6pm (5pm in Oct); Nov to Mar, Mon to Sun 10am to 4pm. Closed 24–26 Dec, 1 Jan. 💷 Adult £3.50; child (5 to 16 yrs old) £1.80; student, senior citizen £2.60. Free to EH members. ♿ Difficult access. Paths have limited access for wheelchairs and have plenty of inclines. No access to ruins. Phone ahead to organise parking close to the Castle.

Kentwell Hall

Long Melford, Suffolk CO10 9BA ☎ *(01787) 310207*

Quality ★★★★ | **Facilities** 👍👍👍👍 | **Value for money** £££

Highlights Elizabethan manor house, extensively restored; fine gardens; living history 're-creations' with costumed volunteers supplying much of the entertainment

Drawbacks Not a lot for children in the house when there are no 're-creations'

What's there Kentwell Hall is an Elizabethan moated manor house approached along a ¾-mile avenue of limes planted in the seventeenth century. The exterior of the mellow red brick building has hardly altered since the sixteenth century. In 1971 it was bought by Patrick Philips, and he and his family continue the considerable task of restoring the house and gardens to what they once were. Over the last 25 years they have funded these works by opening the house to the public and by staging Tudor and World War II 're-creations', for which the house has become renowned.

Visit when a re-creation is taking place and you will find costumed living history interpreters acting out their roles and staying in character when talking to visitors. A **World War II re-creation** may have the servants bickering in the kitchen while cooking lunch and snacking on jam sandwiches; a group of officers lunching in the dining room or taking orders in the Great Hall; and ladies in hats unpicking woollen jumpers for a forthcoming sock-knitting fest. The **Great Annual Re-creation** is a Tudor affair with around 300 volunteers in costume. All areas of the house operate as they might have done in Tudor times, with jousting, alchemy, pigs on spits, baking, brewing, farming and forging taking place as well as revelry and fun.

If you visit on a day when no event takes place you can go on a self-guided tour of the house and gardens. The route takes you through the kitchen, housekeeper's room and panelled room in the west wing to the dining room and Great Hall and drawing room, billiard room and library. Upstairs there are numerous bedrooms, a schoolroom and nursery. Although the family have their own private wing they do use the rooms in the house, and furnishings are by no means stately – the atmosphere is more domestic than grand.

The grounds include the cedar lawn to the side of the house within the moat; a walled garden with Tudor-style **herb garden** and potager; lots of fruit trees with around 20 varieties of apple; a yew walk; **bowling alley in the sunken garden**; a recently rediscovered and restored **ice house**; and a farm with a flock of Norfolk horn sheep, Tamworth pigs, goats and Suffolk punch horses.

Information/tours/guides During 're-creations' enthusiastic volunteers act out scenarios or involve themselves in the day-to-day working of a Tudor mansion (or World War II transit camp) in the bakery, brewery, forge and still room and also in the kitchens and house. When there is no 're-creation', visitors can go on a self-guided tour of the house and gardens armed with detailed information sheets (available in the shop). Also, each room has a folder on architectural features, restoration and furnishings.

When to visit For 2000 there are 11 re-creations and special events planned, each lasting from a weekend to three weeks and mostly coinciding with major holidays and feast days. The Great Annual Re-creation lasts from 18 June to 9 July 2000.

Age appeal Re-creations will appeal to everyone, and youngsters will particularly enjoy the farm animals and exploring the grounds.

Food and drink The Undercroft (down several steps) sells baked potatoes, soup, quiches, sandwiches, cakes, teas and coffees. During the Great Annual Re-creation refreshments are served in a marquee.

Shops The gift shop at the entrance gates sells all things Tudor. Books on Henry VIII and Elizabeth I, metal knights in armour (£2.20), Suffolk herbs, candles (£3.50 to £8), chutneys, jelly and preserves, and Kentwell souvenir pencils and pens.

Other facilities Toilets, including disabled facilities, are situated by the entrance gates, not in the house.

On the A134 in Long Melford (just north of Long Melford Green). Train to Sudbury station, then taxi. Variable so ring ahead to confirm. Generally, mid-Apr to Oct, Sun to Fri 12 to 5pm. Usually closed Sat. During special events open 11am to 6pm. *House and garden* adult £5.50; child (5 to 15 yrs old) £3.30; senior citizen £4.75. *Gardens only* adult £3.50, child £2.25, senior citizen £3.00. Special events have special prices e.g. Great Annual Re-creation adult £11.60, child £8.25, senior citizen £9.95. Disabled visitors' carers free. Ring for details. Access to ground floor of house only and grounds.

Kingston Lacy House and Garden

Nr Wimborne Minster, Dorset BH21 4EA ☎ *(01202) 883402*

Quality ★★★★   **Facilities** ✦ ✦ ✦ ✦ ✦   **Value for money** £££
Highlights Well-informed and enthusiastic room guides
Drawbacks Lack of signs in the gardens, which still need more work

What's there Kingston Lacy House was built by the influential Bankes family in the seventeenth century to replace their previous residence, Corfe

Castle (*qv*). Despite brave attempts by Dame Mary Bankes to defend the castle, it had finally fallen to the Parliamentarians in 1646. As a mark of respect, she was allowed to keep the keys to the Castle, which to this day hang above the chimneypiece in the library of Kingston Lacy.

Several members of the Bankes family were instrumental in creating Kingston Lacy, and throughout the house are echoes of their passions and professions from which you can piece together a picture of their lives. Sir John Bankes (husband of Mary) was an accomplished lawyer and you can see a portrait of him in his Chief Justice's robes between the windows.

But it was William Bankes who left the greatest mark, having transformed the house in the 1830s. His youthful travels took him to Spain, Italy and further afield, arousing interests which became passions in later life. The intricately carved **oak doors from the Vatican** in the saloon were acquired by William in the eighteenth century, as was the collection of pictures in the **Spanish Room**. There are also replica Italianate *palazzo* ceilings, paintings by **Titian** and the famous *Judgement of Solomon* by **del Piombo**. Egyptology was perhaps his greatest love – and the obelisk in the garden took four years to transport to Dorset, surviving a fall into the River Nile on the way. Perhaps not all the occupants after William were quite as keen on his Egyptian collection – a statue of Ramses II was recently discovered face down in the fernery!

The property was bequeathed to the National Trust in 1981 by Ralph Bankes. He had become very withdrawn and occupied just a few rooms of the house in his last few years. He slept in the State Bedroom and spent most of his day in the Audit Room, with its worn rug and comfy sofa facing the fireplace. The rest of the house was neglected and dirty, and the rooms on the top floor had suffered rain damage. The restored Tent Rooms, with sloping ceilings and a Gladstone bag by the bed, were where young bachelors would come and stay for hunting weekends. The National Trust is still restoring some rooms on the attic floor.

The **servants' quarters** are equally fascinating. You can still see the **ancient wine cellar** with its vaulted ceiling and flagstone floors, and the silver cupboard, which would have kept the butler busy. Each of the 22 bells connects to bell-pulls around the house for calling the servants from downstairs.

A lot of work is still needed in the gardens to do them justice. There are woodland walks, such as the Laurel Walk and the Lime Walk, a **sarcophagus** from a tomb in Luxor as well **obelisks**, a fernery and formal gardens. A lack of signs makes it difficult to find your way around, though. Keen walkers can take footpaths further afield to the Badbury Rings.

Information/tours/guides Pre-booked guided tours of the house run throughout the summer. For 70p you can buy a black and white pamphlet which includes a plan of the house and a guide to each room. It touches only briefly on the gardens. An excellent guide for children at £1.80 does a very good job of making the house fun for them too.

When to visit Time your visit to coincide with a guided tour. Activity days for children offer the chance to make a Victorian board game or masks or try other crafts.

Age appeal The house has a wide appeal with something for all ages. Children have their own guidebook to bring things to life in the house.

Food and drink The restaurant is in the old stable block and still maintains the layout with old wooden partitions now making for cosy, private seating areas. The food is not cheap, but is at least wholesome with hot dishes from £5.95 to £6.50, jacket potatoes at £4.25, and hot filled baguettes at £4.50. Cream teas are served in the afternoon for £3.50.

Shops It is well worth saving some time for a browse through the site shop, in the old kitchen wing. Pots and pans hanging from the rafters and flagstone floors add to the ambience. There are lots of books on Egyptology and gardening, plus books for children and games, such as cribbage and solitaire.

🚗 On the B3082 between Wimborne and Blandford. ⊖ Train to Bournemouth (11 miles away) or Poole (8 miles away), then take a taxi. ⊙ *House* Apr to Oct, Sat to Wed 12pm to 5.30pm. *Gardens* Apr to Oct, Mon to Sun 11am to 6pm (reduced opening outside peak season). 💷 *House and garden* adult £6; child £3; family ticket (2 adults + 3 children) £15. *Park and garden only* adult £2.50; child £1.25. NT members free. ♿ No access to house. RADAR (disabled) toilets available. The Lady Walk is suitable for wheelchairs.

Knebworth House

Knebworth Park, Knebworth, Hertfordshire SG3 6PY ☎ *(01438) 812661*

Quality ★★★	Facilities 🏚 🏚	Value for money £££

Highlights Combination of interesting exhibits with a sense of still being a family home; good range of play activities for children

Drawbacks Some facilities in need of maintenance; house restoration may be continuing until summer 2000

What's there Knebworth House has been the home of the Lytton family since 1490, though it has undergone many changes over the years. The current house reflects the style of Edward Bulwer-Lytton, the nineteenth-century author and statesman. He was a friend of Charles Dickens, who often visited – photos and memorabilia from the times when Dickens and Bulwer-Lytton staged dramatic productions here are on view. The grand **Banqueting Hall** is particularly fine, as are the elaborately carved **staircase** and **armoury**, the **Falkland room** with its extraordinary opium bed, and the children's nursery, full of Edwardian and Victorian toys, including a musical chair and beautifully furnished doll's house. The separate **Raj exhibition** shows photos, letters and costumes dating from Robert Lytton's times as Viceroy of India, and includes a 15-minute audio-visual presentation.

The gardens are mainly formal, including the lovely **Gold Garden** (with lots of yellow flowering plants), and the **Pets' Cemetery** with gravestones commemorating many family animals. There is a small **maze**, planted in 1995, and a **herb garden** designed by the Edwardian gardener Gertrude Jekyll.

Children will want to spend most of their time in the **adventure playground**, which offers a range of climbing equipment, astroglide and vertical-drop slides. Younger children are well provided for in **Fort**

Knebworth, with a range of wooden play equipment and the nearby bouncy castle. The small railway offers a free ¾-mile ride around part of the grounds, lasting about ten minutes.

Information/tours/guides The excellent publicity leaflet provides information on prices, times and facilities, and a free map shows what is available to see in the two main areas (playground and house/gardens). The glossy guidebook (£3) includes lots of photos of the rooms, paintings and family, though some of these are now out of date. Guided tours lasting about an hour are available every half-hour from Monday to Friday (no tours at weekends). Our guide related many details and anecdotes, without which the visit would have been less interesting. Little information is displayed in the gardens, though a leaflet is available for 10p.

When to visit Good weather is best, especially if you are coming with children and plan to enjoy the outdoor play areas. But you may encounter queues for slides and play equipment on busy summer weekends. Visit the house on a weekday if you can, in order to hear some of the background to the house on a guided tour. Special events, such as car rallies and garden shows, are often scheduled for summer weekends.

Age appeal The house and gardens will largely appeal to adults, though the maze and the old toys in the nursery are designed to be child-friendly. The main attraction for most children will be Fort Knebworth and the surrounding play areas (some of the slides have a minimum height requirement of about 3ft 6in). In theory, everyone should be happy, but there are some logistical problems, as the house and the play areas are about half a mile apart (a free bus service operates at peak times).

Food and drink The wonderful 400-year-old Lodge Barn is used for functions and also serves as a tearoom and bar. A limited range of hot and cold meals is available (e.g. filled rolls £2.50, vegetable soup £1.75, children's menu consisting of chicken dinosaur, chips and beans with a carton of juice, £2.25). We had good home-made lasagne with thick-cut chips and a selection of vegetables (£4.95). There is also a range of cakes and ice creams and hot and cold drinks. Food such as burgers (£2) and chips (£1.50) can also be purchased from the Stagecoach, stationed near the bouncy castle at Fort Knebworth. Ice creams and drinks are available here and also from the nearby kiosk.

Shops The main shop, near the entrance to the house, stocks various 'country' items, such as herb pots (£2.50), pot pourri (£3.95), wooden trays (£19.95) and jams and preserves (about £3). Books on sale include the story of restoring Knebworth and a guide to the rock festivals held here. A back door leads to a small outdoor area selling herbs, bedding plants and hanging baskets. The range is not wide and the shop could be better presented. A smaller gift shop within the house sells mainly guidebooks and postcards but also gifts such as preserves, photo frames and stationery.

Other facilities There are two main toilet blocks, one by the house and one at Fort Knebworth. Neither is very well maintained, and those by Fort Knebworth are in a poor state of repair.

🚗 Direct access from A1(M), junction 7. ⊖ Train to Stevenage, then taxi (5-10 minutes). ⏲ 15 Apr to 1 May, 6 to 21 May, 27 May to 4 June, 10 June to 2 July (closed 18 June), 8 July to 3 Sept, 9 Sept to 1 Oct, plus weekends and bank hols, (12 to 5pm for House and Raj exhibition). 💷 *House and all other areas (park, gardens and playground only)* adult £6 (£5); child (5 to 16 yrs old) and senior citizen £5.50 (£5); child (under 5 yrs old) free; family ticket (4 people) £17.50. Season ticket £25. ♿ Wheelchair access to most of ground floor in the house (some single steps). No lift to the upper floor of the house. The gardens are all on the level, but grass and gravel paths.

Knowsley Safari Park

Prescot, Merseyside L34 4AN ☎ *0151-430 9009* 🖱 *www.knowsley.com*
🖱 *safari.park@knowsley.com*

Quality ★   **Facilities** 🛗 🛗   **Value for money** ££
Highlights Close encounters on the safari drive
Drawbacks Little information about any of the animals

What's there Just 13 km from Liverpool city centre, Knowsley covers 494 acres with a pretty impressive five miles of roads looping through the various game reserves giving a chance to see **lions**, **tigers**, **elephants**, rhinos, giraffes and monkeys. The drive itself takes around an hour, and the journey through the animal world covers all areas of the globe, although it is hard to tell where you are at any one time. The 'White Man's Lake Area', for example, contains ostriches from Africa, guanaco from South America, **camels** from Asia and **bison** from North America, among others.

The drawback is that you leave each reserve none the wiser about the animals or their status in the wild – there are no information boards as you drive (your own car) around. The big plus point is that you can get close to the animals: the sight of an emu wandering nonchalantly up to your 'cage' and peering through at you inquisitively is a real thrill. You may prefer to keep your distance (and that of your car) from some of the creatures, such as the baboons, especially if you have concerns about any removable car parts. Staff advise that you keep on the move through the baboon territory (a bypass round the monkey enclosure was being built when we inspected).

Some of the additional attractions at the end are primarily designed to appeal to children. The **Lake Farm,** with a few goats, pigs and chickens, is a chance for children to pet farm animals and little else. There is also a Reptile House, and a few **rides**, including mini-dippers and roundabouts. A **mini-railway** does a brief circuit around the lake. Children also seem to enjoy the **sea lion and parrot show**, with displays including balls, roller skates and scooters, although the hosts speak so fast you can barely understand. Additional charges apply for train rides and shows.

Information/tours/guides Until some information is posted around the park you will need the Safari Route Guide (£3). It makes a nice glossy souvenir, with a few activities for children in the back, like quizzes and dot-to-dot. There is also a separate activity book for children at £1.99. The Lake Farm does have some signing, but it was very confusing when we inspected (brown calves labelled saddleback pigs!).

When to visit Expect traffic jams in high season (summer).

Age appeal Everyone will enjoy being able to get so close to the animals, although the additional attractions at the end of the safari are definitely aimed at children.

Food and drink The restaurant is supposedly safari-style, but aside from the thatched roof it seems to have taken its inspiration from a major burger chain. Plenty of fast food is available, accompanied by plastic cutlery and coffee from paper cups.

Shops The shop, with merchandise displayed in pine and glass cabinets, feels more like a department store than a souvenir shop. There are lots of toys for children, as well as ornaments and engraved beer tankards.

🚗 From the M62, exit 6, take the M57 exit 2 then follow the brown signs. Free car park. ⊖ No bus or alternative transport on the safari drive, so a car is essential. ① Mar to Oct, Mon to Sun 10am to 4pm; Nov to Feb Sat and Sun 10am to 4pm. Closed 25 Dec, 1 Jan. 💷 Adult £7; child (4 to 15 yrs old) £5. Group discounts available. *Mini railway rides* adult £1.60; child 80p. *Sea lion and parrot show* adult £1.50; child and senior citizen £1.20 for (children under 3 free). ♿ All accessible, apart from the miniature railway and rides.

Laing Art Gallery

New Bridge Street, Newcastle-upon-Tyne NE1 8AG   ☎ *0191-232 7734*

Quality ★★★   Facilities 🏛 🏛   Value for money ££££

Highlights Attractive, spacious galleries; cheerful cafeteria; children's gallery
Drawbacks Toilets could be better maintained

What's there The gallery was founded in 1901, built with money given by the local wine and spirit merchant Alexander Laing. Situated in Newcastle city centre, the classical stone façade, punctuated by a modern, bottle-green glass entrance, hints at the mixture of classical and contemporary art housed within.

The Laing's permanent collection, on the mezzanine level, comprises famous paintings such as **William Holman Hunt**'s Pre-Raphaelite master-piece *Isabella and the Pot of Basil*. **Gainsborough**, **Reynolds** and **Canaletto** are also represented, as well as twentieth-century artists such as **Henry Moore**. 'Art on Tyneside', the gallery's other permanent exhibition, gives a fascinating insight into the history of Tyneside's art and craft traditions and includes a re-created eighteenth-century coffee house, where the rich and educated exchanged ideas about nature, science and politics. The permanent exhibition takes about an hour to wander round.

There is also a range of temporary exhibitions covering subjects as varied as contemporary British photography to Fantasy Football.

Information/tours/guides The Gallery has no guidebook, but the Friends of the Laing offer a free guided tour every Saturday at 11.30am. A free leaflet gives a brief introduction to the various exhibitions and lists free Wednesday lunchtime talks and gallery activities, such as photography work-shops, and watercolour demonstrations.

When to visit The Gallery can be enjoyed whatever the weather or season, so any time is good.

Age appeal The Gallery makes a real effort to interest all ages. In the colourful and lively **Children's Gallery** under-5s can play with soft toys and puzzles (though an adult must accompany children). On Saturdays, 6- to 12-year-olds are invited to work with different artists at the Gallery (for information and booking call the education department on 0191-211 2104). Similarly, 'Art on Wheels' is an interactive session that takes place on weekends and during half-terms.

Food and drink Café Laing is a cheerful self-service coffee shop, with sunflower-yellow walls and large pieces of sculpture. It offers salads, freshly made sandwiches from £1.75, and cakes from 80p. Hot food includes jacket potatoes and soup.

Shops The gallery 'shop' is informal and located by the entrance. Merchandise includes standard gallery offerings, such as a book of postcards for £2.99, good-quality colour posters for £4.59, and children's stationery and puzzles.

Other facilities The toilets were poorly maintained, with no toilet roll or towels when we inspected.

From Newcastle city centre, follow signposts (NCP car park in Carliol Square).
Train to Newcastle, then metro to Monument station (with 5-minute walk to Gallery).
Open all year, Mon to Sat 10am to 5pm, Sun 2pm to 5pm. Closed Good Friday, 25, 26 Dec, 1 Jan. Free. Fully wheelchair accessible (ramps plus lift to second floor). Disabled toilets.

Lanhydrock House and Gardens

Bodmin, Cornwall PL30 5AD ☎ *(01208) 73320*

Quality 🏛🏛🏛🏛🏛   **Facilities** ★★★★   **Value for money** ££££
Highlights Fully furnished and beautifully presented Victorian house
Drawbacks During peak season some of the smaller rooms and the kitchen quarters can get extremely cramped

What's there Although it dates back to the seventeenth century, Lanhydrock is essentially a Victorian house. Much of the house had to be rebuilt after a fire almost completely destroyed it in 1881. In 1953 the 7th Viscount Clifden gave the house and some 400 acres of the surrounding parkland to the National Trust.

Every effort has been made to present the rooms as they would have been when the house was a family home. The **kitchen quarters** are fascinating, with all the tools and gadgets used in a Victorian kitchen on display. Sculleries and larders are fully fitted with the original equipment and implements, and the table in the wood-panelled dining room is set for dinner. The **nursery wing**, which includes the day and night nursery, a scullery, a bathroom and nanny's bedroom, is fully furnished, with children's toys scattered here and there. In the attic, the servants' bedrooms are more austere and functional.

The entrance porch and north wing, which includes the **Long Gallery**, survived the fire in 1881. The gallery is the most impressive room on the tour. The remarkable **barrel-vaulted plaster ceiling** is divided into 24 panels that depict scenes from the Old Testament such as Cain and Abel, and Noah and the Flood. Family pictures and loaded bookcases line the oak-panelled walls.

Formal gardens surround the house on all sides, and there are magnificent displays of magnolias, rhododendrons and camellias in the higher garden. Alongside the house is the **fifteenth-century church** of St Hydoc – service times are shown on the porch notice board. There is also a small museum and stables.

Allow at least two hours to see the house and ample time to visit the **gardens** and the surrounding parkland.

Information/tours/guides   The full colour guidebook (£2.95) includes a tour of the house and a history of the gardens. If you do not want the guidebook there are separate leaflets for the house (50p) and gardens (50p), which include maps and tours of each. Older children will enjoy having their own guidebook (£1.50). Room guides are friendly and happy to answer questions. Visitors must follow the well-planned tour of the house, which has 49 rooms on show to the public.

A leaflet that suggests five separate walks through the gardens and surrounding parkland is available (70p).

When to visit   Late spring/early summer is the best time to come for the rhododendrons, magnolias and camellias. A regular programme of events is held throughout the year, including horse trials and craft fairs. The kitchen quarters and certain narrow passages can get cramped on busy days.

Age appeal   Visitors are asked not to touch the contents of the house, which may prove frustrating for younger children, who are more likely to enjoy the gardens and parkland. The gardens are relatively flat although there are steps to the Higher Garden.

Food and drink   There are three separate waitress-service restaurants located in the Old Servants' Quarters, as well as the Stable Bar, which is situated opposite. Lunch is served from 12.15pm in the restaurants, which vary in size and décor. Each has a separate menu, but examples of dishes might include local trout for £7.25 and vegetable cobbler at £4.25. A selection of sandwiches, cakes, light snacks and hot and cold drinks is available throughout the day.

Shops   A large shop sells a wide range of items, including the standard range of National Trust goods, such as cards, books, clothing, toiletries and cushion covers.

🚗 2½ miles south-east of Bodmin. Follow signposts from either the A30 or A38 Bodmin to Liskeard road or B3268 Bodmin to Lostwithiel road. Car parking (600m from house). ⊖ Train to Bodmin Parkway station, then First Western National 55 (tel (01209) 719988). 🎫 *House, garden and park* adult £6.60; child (5 to 17 yrs old) £3.30; family ticket (2 adults + 3 children) £16.50. *Garden and grounds only* adult £3.20; child £1.60. Carers and National Trust members admitted free. Group rates available. ◔ *House* Apr to Oct, Tues to Sun 11am to 5.30pm (5pm in Oct). *Park and Garden* Apr to Oct, Mon to Sun 11am to 5.30pm; Nov to Feb daylight hours only. ♿ Ground and first floors of the house accessible. Ramp access to restaurants. Garden access via steps, ramp available.

Gravel paths are well maintained; some are sloping or steep in places. Information leaflet available with a suitable route marked. Indoor and outdoor wheelchairs are available (book in advance). Disabled parking adjacent to the house. Braille guides for house and garden, large-print guidebook for house and tactile route guide sheet available.

Leeds Castle

Maidstone, Kent ME17 1PL ☎ *(01622) 765400* 🖰 *www.leeds-castle.co.uk*

Quality ★★★★ **Facilities 🗦 🗦 🗦** **Value for money £££**

Highlights Lovely grounds with range of attractions for all the family
Drawbacks Setting more impressive than the largely 1920s interior

What's there Leeds is described in its publicity 'as the loveliest castle in the world' – and the aerial photographs show its beautiful lakeside location off to perfection. It was an occasional residence for a succession of medieval monarchs – most notably Henry VIII, who spent large sums enlarging and beautifying the buildings. But he was also responsible for the castle passing out of royal hands when he gave it to Sir Anthony St Leger in recognition of his sterling work in persuading the Irish to accept Henry as king. In the 1920s the castle was rescued from genteel decay by an American heiress, Lady Baillie, who left it to be run as a charitable trust.

From the car park, modern-day visitors walk through the lovely grounds past the duckery with its collection of waterfowl such as shelducks, Hawaiian geese and black-necked swans until the view opens out into the panorama of the pretty, moated castle. Start your visit by going round the castle itself, entering through the Heraldry Room showing the coats of arms of all the owners of Leeds before heading down the narrow corridor to the **Queen's Bedroom**. Much is made of the castle's royal connections, and this room is prepared as it might have been for Catherine de Valois, wife of Henry V in 1430, with rich pink and green hangings and the monograms H and C entwined with a lovers' knot on the walls. Next door is her bathroom – a simple wooden cooper's tub disguised with fine white cotton. In the fireplace of the Queen's Gallery you can see the emblems of Castile (a castle) and Aragon (pomegranates) – indicating that this was built before Catherine of Aragon, the first of Henry VIII's six wives, fell from royal favour.

The main features of the **Henry VIII banqueting suite** – an ebony floor and carved oak ceiling – were both introduced by Lady Baillie, as was the French chimneypiece. The chapel is a simple room but worth visiting to see the fine fifteenth-century tapestry of the Adoration of the Magi. Go up the staircase (another of Lady Baillie's French imports) and you can see her touch in the modern bedrooms and elegant and comfortable living rooms.

Outside in the grounds are plenty of attractions to keep the whole family amused. In summer you can wander round the **Culpeper Garden**, a re-creation of an old English cottage garden, and smell the roses and lavender. There's also an **aviary**, a **maze** if you have time to get lost, and the castle's greenhouses, where the flowers that decorate the house are grown. For a touch of eccentricity the **exhibition of dog collars** in the Gate Tower is unmissable;

the earliest spiked German ones date from the sixteenth century, and there's a rather fine Dutch brass one engraved with the owner's name and the words 'Seek him' dating from around 1700.

A tour of the house will take about an hour. Allow a couple of hours for wandering round the grounds – though you could easily make a day of it with lunch.

Information/tours/guides The guidebook (£2.50) is good and useful when going round.

When to visit Come on a fine day to enjoy the gardens. Open-air concerts are held during summer months, plus balloon and vintage-car weekends, flower festivals and Christmas celebrations. Call (0870) 600 8880 for details.

Age appeal Not much attempt has been made to interest children in the castle itself but there's plenty for them to do in the grounds. Special children's activities are laid on during half-term.

Food and drink You have the choice of a table-service restaurant (Terrace Room) or a cheaper self-service outfit (Fairfax Hall). Both are attractive beamed rooms in a converted barn. Hot dishes at lunchtime (12pm to 3.30pm) may be beef and beer casserole (£5.90), pizza (£1.60), apple pie (£2.25) and fudge brownie (£1.60). Picnics are not allowed in the castle grounds – there is a picnic area adjacent to the ticket office in the car park.

Shops The best gift shop is in the Courtyard complex, where you can browse among the collection of knick-knacks and edible goodies – jams for £2, brass bells for £6.50 and bookmarks for £1.

🚗 4 miles east of Maidstone off M20, junction 8. Follow signposts. Large car park. ⊖ Inclusive scheme combining rail travel, connecting coach transfers to and from Bearsted Station and admission to Leeds Castle operates all year round (tel Connex South Eastern on (0870) 603 0405). National Express offers combined admission and coach service from Victoria to castle (tel (0990) 010104). ◷ Mar to Oct, Mon to Sun 10am to 5pm; Nov to Feb, Mon to Sun 10am to 3pm. Closed 25 Dec, 24 June, 1 Jul. 🎟 *Castle and park gardens* adult £9.50; child (5 to 15 yrs old) £6; student, senior citizen £7.50; family ticket (2 adults + 3 children) £26. *Park gardens only* adult £7.50; child £4.50; student, senior citizen £6; family ticket £21. ♿ Minibus runs from car park to house. Leaflet available giving full details for disabled visitors (ring for details).

Leeds City Art Gallery

The Headrow, Leeds LS1 3AA ☎ *0113-247 8248*

Quality ★★★	Facilities 🏛 🏛 🏛	Value for money £££

Highlights Free entry; excellent good-value guidebook
Drawbacks Limited facilities

What's there Adjoining the Town Hall and municipal buildings, the gallery has two floors of paintings and sculpture, largely arranged in chronological order. The collection is strongest on nineteenth- and twentieth-century works, including a wide selection of **Pre-Raphaelites**, with paintings by **Lord Leighton**, **William Holman Hunt** and **John Everett Millais**. There is also the angular, cubist-inspired work of the war artists **Paul Nash** and **Graham**

Sutherland, L.S. Lowry's 'matchstick men', as well as **Stanley Spencer**'s rounded, comical figures. You can also see examples of **Bridget Riley**'s 'Op Art' with its stark lines, and a spot-painting and a print produced by **Damien Hirst**. Another surprise is *The Scream of Reason*, one of the more sedate offerings by the infamous **Gilbert and George**. The gallery also holds temporary exhibitions.

Although the collection is of a high standard, it is small, and it may be advisable to combine it with a visit to the **Henry Moore Institute**, which is located in the adjoining building.

Information/tours/guides There are no regular guided tours, but a free leaflet gives details of exhibitions and talks. The guidebook, at £1.50, is very good value, and is full of fascinating details about the artists and their work. When we inspected, a small number of paintings seemed to lack corresponding information panels, such as the large, impressive canvases of industrial scenes by Frank Brangwyn.

When to visit The venue is fairly quiet, even during term time.

Age appeal The gallery will hold little appeal for young children.

Food and drink The ground floor has a small café, but there is a wide range of bars and restaurants very close to the gallery.

Shops A range of books and stationery is sold close to the entrance.

🚍 Leeds city centre, next to Town Hall. Car parking (pay and display) at Leeds station then 5- to 10-minute walk. ⊖ Walking distance from Leeds station; well served by buses. ⊙ Mon to Sat, 10am to 5pm (8pm on Wed), Sun 1pm to 5pm. Closed bank hols. 💷 Free. ♿ Ramp for wheelchairs at the front of the building and a lift between floors.

Legoland

Windsor, Berkshire SL4 4AY   ☎ *(01753) 626111* 📠 *(01753) 626119*
🖥 *www.legoland.co.uk*

Quality ★ ★ ★ ★   **Facilities** 🏛 🏛 🏛 🏛 🏛   **Value for money ££**
Highlights Lego models; excellent facilities; good catering; friendly staff; great for young children
Drawbacks Not enough for older children or adults; long queues; expensive

---

What's there Essentially, what you'll see are over 25 million Lego bricks, most of which are used to create the impressive world-in-miniature, Miniland. But there's also quite a lot more, especially for children aged up to about 10 years old, and adults who like watching their kids have fun. It is, however, very popular, so include queuing time in any plans and expect to spend at least six hours here if it's busy. We inspected on a hot, busy August day, when queues were long.

As you walk down the hill from the entrance (or take the train that trundles down and thankfully back up), you'll see that the park is divided into seven sectors.

Imagination Centre is a combination of workshops and low-key rides. Both Sky Rider (a giant pedal cycle on raised rails) and Space Tower (pull yourself to the top and free-fall down) had an hour-long queue, and were rather disappointing after such long waits. It's more fun to play in the Building Site, where you can let your architectural imagination run riot among the tubs filled with Lego bricks.

Miniland – the best part of the park for young and old alike – has 12 different scenes from around Europe that took over 95,000 hours to create from 20 million bricks. The most enjoyable are the easily recognisable **scale models**, particularly in the British and French areas. Pride of place is London, complete with Trooping of the Colour and a working Underground station, as well as Big Ben, the Tower and St Paul's (the largest model in Miniland at 400kg and 385,000 bricks).

Duplo Gardens is mainly for the very young, with gentle rides, water fun and play areas. The new **X-treme Challenge water ride** had over an hour's wait for the giant water slide, but the relaxed Fairy Tale Brook boat ride had no queue. Willow Stage holds short but sweet puppet shows.

Expect very long queues for the immensely popular Lego **Traffic**, where kids (6–13 years old) can drive around realistic sets and earn a driving licence. There's also a learning-drivers' school for 3–5 year-olds, and boating and ballooning schools.

My Town, set around a harbour (which hosts **regular shows**), is a complex of shops and eateries. It also houses the Explorer's Institute, one of the few indoor attractions, where you can have fun looking for lost keys in Lego models of jungles, Ancient Egypt and ice caps. We thought the Ninja show was rather violent, considering how young most of the audience was, and the un-magical Magic Theatre had a fair few sharp edges and corners just at the wrong height for little people.

Wild Woods comprises three easy but fun **mazes**, a pleasant picnic area, gold panning and **Pirate Falls**, the park's most popular ride. You'll probably wait over an hour for a chance to get wet on this log flume.

In **CastleLand** you'll find **The Dragon**, the park's only rollercoaster, which had a surprisingly short line late in the day. It won't fulfil thrill-seekers, but the undemanding will enjoy the twists and turns. There's also a junior version for smaller kids (with a much longer queue).

Overall a trip to Legoland is a great day out in an almost pristine place. Younger children have a riot playing with Lego and going on the rides, but at a price. The entry fees are steep, especially for adults who get little – except Miniland – for their money. Teenagers will feel especially hard done by.

Information/tours/guides The free park guide leaflet is invaluable for planning your time, and lists all the rides' height restrictions. The colour guidebook makes a nice souvenir and has a fun activity section for kids, as well as a fold-out map. Each sector of the park is well labelled, having a large sign detailing the attractions and facilities within so that you know where to find rides, food, shops, toilets, etc.

When to visit A sunny day is ideal as most of the best bits are outside, but in peak summer months and on school holidays the queues are horrendous (over an hour at times), especially at weekends. Try to go on the most popular rides early or later on as queues are worst from mid-morning until late afternoon. Queue times are posted for each attraction, and tend to be fairly accurate, but remember that you might well have to wait outside in the blazing sun or pouring rain, so be prepared.

Age appeal This is a perfect place for children under 10 years old, but older children might get bored quickly unless they love Lego. Similarly, adults might enjoy reliving their childhood and building bridges in the playrooms, but will have to settle for watching rather than participating in most of the activities and attractions.

Food and drink It's hard to fault the catering, with a wide selection of food and excellent service. The smaller outlets serve pasta (£4.50) or pizza (£2.25 a slice) or a Legoburger meal (£3.99). For something more substantial, head for the Harbourside restaurant in My Town. Done out like a market place, it has counter-service for pizza, pasta and stir-fries (all around £4), or soup, sandwiches and a salad bar. Separate kids' meals (chicken nuggets and chips, £3.99) are available or you can get small portions of adult meals. There's a choice of indoor or outdoor seating. The only drawback was that the toilets in the Harbourside restaurant were well-used and consequently the least appealing in the park.

Shops As you might expect, there's a lot of Lego on sale here, some of it exclusive to Legoland. The Big Shop at the entrance has the best selection. Other than that you can get pricey souvenirs, such as mugs (£4.99), pens (£1.99), or backpacks (£14.99). You don't have to carry your goodies around all day – you can arrange to pick them up at the Big Shop as you leave (free of charge).

Other facilities The toilets are, on the whole, immaculate, decked out in bright, primary colours, and planned with children in mind, with lots of low fixtures. More signs would help as it's easy to walk past without spotting the entrances. Lockers (£1) and cashpoints are available at the entrance.

🚘 Follow signs from the M3 (junction 3), the M4 (junction 6) and Windsor town centre (2 miles away); large free car park. ⊖ Train to Windsor and Eton Riverside (from Waterloo) or Windsor Central (from Slough) and a shuttle bus to park (an all-in ticket from major stations, which includes the train fare, admission to the park and the shuttle bus, is available). Alternatively, daily Green Line buses from Victoria coach station. ☉ Daily 10am to 6pm or dusk if earlier (8pm mid-July to end Aug). 💷 Adult £17.50, child (3–15 yrs old) £14.50, child (under 3 yrs old) free, senior citizens £11.50, Legoworld club members £11.50. *Ticket valid for two consecutive days*: adults £22, children (3–15 yrs old) £19, senior citizens £16. *Season tickets* (for unlimited visits Mar to Oct): adults £49, children (3–15 yrs old) £39, senior citizens £30. Free advance booking service (tickets can be posted or picked up on the day). ♿ Wheelchairs provided on request; advisory leaflet available from guest services.

Lightwater Valley Theme Park

Lightwater Valley, North Stainley, Ripon, North Yorkshire HG4 3HT
☎ *(01765) 635321*

Quality ★★	Facilities 🏛 🏛	Value for money ££

Highlights World's longest rollercoaster; plenty of rides for younger children
Drawbacks Unenthusiastic staff in ticket booths; refreshments limited to fast food; poor toilets

---

What's there This long-established park features the world's longest rollercoaster – **The Ultimate**. Other rides have similarly hair-raising names (the Sewer Rat and the Voyager) although they may prove disappointing to seasoned thrill-seekers. A number of tried-and-tested family favourites here include the waltzers and dodgem cars, while the under-5s will enjoy the rides in Woody's Little Big Park, which include Whirly Copters and Flying Elephants. There is also a kiddiezone soft play area, go-karts and amusement arcades.

The park is not a thrill-seekers' paradise. However, families will be pleased that it caters for younger children. When we inspected there was little evidence of lengthy queues. However, if you do end up queuing it will be in the open air.

Information/tours/guides A free leaflet includes a useful map of the park and information on height requirements for the various rides.

When to visit As the majority of the attractions are outdoors, and queues for rides are not under cover, it is best to visit in good weather. The park is likely to be busy during school holidays.

Age appeal Admission to rides is by height, and restrictions are indicated at the entrance to each ride and on the map.

Food and drink Various outlets dotted throughout the park serve cold drinks and quick snacks. Restaurants offer little variety and stick to a standard range of fast food and baked potatoes, sandwiches and hot drinks. Home-made fudge is served at a counter in the main gift shop.

Shops The merchandise in the shops is aimed predominantly at children, with items such as Ghoulish Goo for sale in the Rat Shop.

Other facilities The main toilet block is near the entrance; additional toilets dotted around the park were rather untidy when we inspected. There is a factory-shopping village next door to the theme park.

🚌 3 miles north of Ripon on A6108. Follow brown signs. ⊖ Train to Harrogate then bus 36/36A to Ripon, then Dales and District 159 bus from Ripon bus station to park entrance (½-mile walk to ticket booths). Call (01677) 422371 for more details. ⏱ 15 Apr to 1 May, 1 June to end Aug, 23 to 29 Oct, Mon to Sun 10am to 5.30pm; 20 May to 29 May, 4 Sept to 22 Oct, Sat and Sun 10am to 5pm. 💷 Adult (over 1.3m) £11.95 (£9.95 if you pre-book); adult/child (under 1.3m) £9.95; child (under 1m) free; senior citizen £5.95; family ticket (4 people incl parent) £39 (£35 if you pre-book) and additional family member £9.75 (£8.75 if you pre-book). ♿ Reasonably flat grounds and well-maintained paths. Not all rides are accessible (particularly the Ultimate). Check with the attendants on duty for suitability. Wheelchairs available for hire (£2 fee and need to be booked in advance).

Lincoln Cathedral

Lincoln LN2 1PX ☎ *(01522) 544544*

Quality ★★★★★ **Facilities** 📷 📷 📷 **Value for money** £££££
Highlights Enthusiastic and knowledgeable guides and staff; good guidebook
written in accessible style; imaginative range of food in coffee shop
Drawbacks Toilets limited in number and draughty

What's there Lincoln Cathedral is difficult to miss: the spires soar above the city and can be seen from miles around. The only remains of the original, eleventh-century, early Norman building are the arches around the north and south doors in the west front, and part of the nave behind them. A fire in 1141 led to a partial rebuilding by the Bishop of Lincoln, Alexander the Magnificent. The splendid **Romanesque frieze** depicting scenes from the Old Testament and some of the gruesome punishments for vices such as avarice and lust dates from this time. Unfortunately, many of the scenes are badly damaged, and conservation work may mean that many may be boarded over.

After an earthquake in 1185 much of the cathedral again had to be rebuilt, under the charge of Hugh of Avalon (later St Hugh), bishop from 1186 to 1200. Rebuilding started from the east and worked west, incorporating the pointed arches and ribbed vaulting of the new Gothic style. If you stand outside St Hugh's choir by the south-east transept, you can see what were possibly the first tentative Gothic arches – hardly pointed at all – and trace the developing confidence of the builders as the arches become increasingly elaborate, incorporating tracery and pierced stonework.

As the new Gothic cathedral progressed westwards, the builders ran short of money and, rather than pull down the remaining Norman west front, decided to attach on the new to the old: from the nave you can see the asymmetrical join. In fact, much of the nave is asymmetrical: the column bases and blind arcading on the south side of the nave are lower than on the north side.

The great transept is lit by two wonderful **rose windows**. The Dean's Eye window to the north represents the devil and darkness, and the stained glass depicts scenes associated with death and resurrection, such as the funeral of St Hugh. To the south, the Bishop's Eye contains some elegant stonework tracery set with fragments of thirteenth- and fourteenth-century glass. Above, the crossing tower collapsed in the thirteenth century, but was rebuilt and later heightened to 70 metres – the tallest building in the world until it blew down in 1548!

At the entrance to St Hugh's choir, take a close look at the **stone choir screen** in Decorated Gothic style, awash with intricate carvings of fantastic beasts, flowers and figures. The arches above the aisles continue the theme: to the south, dragons eating fruit are killed and hung up to dry, while to the north the face of the 'Green Man' is spotlit hidden behind wreaths of foliage.

There's more carving in St Hugh's choir – look for the **misericords** beneath the seats of the choir stalls, and the **Victorian Gothic pulpit** designed by Sir George Gilbert Scott. Above, the 'crazy vaulting' gives a sense of movement.

Beyond St Hugh's choir is the **angel choir**, added on in 1255 to house St Hugh's remains after his death. It's named after the heavenly figures carved in the spandrels between the triforium arches, playing musical instruments or carrying scrolls. Also tucked away here is the famous **Lincoln Imp**, a cross-legged devil who was apparently turned to stone after causing havoc among the angels. The tomb of Eleanor of Castile's viscera is also here (her heart is buried at Blackfriars in London, and her body is in Westminster Abbey). Peek into the Russell chantry to see the wall paintings by Duncan Grant.

Off the north choir aisle, the treasury collection includes a seventh-century bronze hanging bowl and coconut cup from 1650. The north-east transept leads to the cloisters, worth visiting for the unusual wooden vaulting and roof bosses, and chapter house, which contains the throne of Edward I (he called one of the earliest English Parliaments here in 1301). The nineteenth-century stained glass tells the story of the cathedral from William the Conqueror to John Wesley's last visit in 1790.

Information/tours/guides A free leaflet containing a map and brief descriptions of the main features is available in several languages. However, the guidebook (£3.50) provides much more accessible detail on the history and architecture. A nice touch are the sidebars that provide information on the work of various bodies associated with the cathedral, such as the Association of Friends of Lincoln Cathedral and the Lincoln Cathedral Needlework Guild.

It's certainly worth taking a guided tour if you have time. Stewards and guides are enthusiastic volunteers, and point out things you might otherwise miss. Tours of the cathedral run daily except Sunday from May to September at 11am, 1pm and 3pm and from October to the end of April daily at 11am and 2pm. They last an hour and are free. Roof tours, which take you up into parts of the cathedral that are normally out of bounds, last 1¾ hours and cost £2. They run on Saturdays at 11am and 2pm and at 2pm only on Wednesdays (no children under 14 allowed).

The library is open by appointment for group visits and for readers wishing to consult the reference collection.

The cantilupe chantry contains a small display on the restoration of the Romanesque frieze on the west front, and paddleboards in the chapter house explain the scenes depicted in the stained glass.

When to visit The cathedral is open all year round. The stained glass is best seen on a sunny day. Try to time your visit to allow for a guided tour. During services all the area east of the great transept is roped off, but you can still visit the nave and cloisters. Allow at least an hour – longer if you go on a tour.

Age appeal Children are given 'A Guide for Young People' when they enter, which encourages them to look for carvings of animals and saints on their way round the cathedral. The shop also sells children's books and Bible stories. Undoubtedly, however, most of the history and finer architectural points are more likely to appeal to adults.

Food and drink Tucked in one corner of the cloisters, the coffee shop is a pleasant little cafeteria, with round tables, green bentwood chairs and stencilled walls. 'Coffee shop' is a bit of a misnomer, as it serves fine food at reasonable prices. On the day we inspected, the imaginative range of hot food included roast vegetable lasagne, leek and bacon bake, steak and onion pie (£4.25 each), four cheese and roast baby-onion quiche (£1.45) and Cumberland sausage in a roll (£1.40). There's also a selection of pre-packed sandwiches and home-baked cakes, including excellent scones with jam and cream. A pot of tea is 70p, a mug of coffee £1 – or try the Cloister Cloud (hot chocolate and marshmallows) for £1.35! The only disadvantage is that the small space gets very cramped when busy – though there are a few tables out in the cloisters during fine weather.

Shops The standard souvenirs range from china plates (£19.95) to videos (£12.99) and mouse mats (£4.25); more unusual memorabilia include carved gargoyles (£9.50), Lincoln Imp pendants (£11.25) and fridge magnets (£1.95), and copies of roof bosses (£16.95). There's also a selection of books on St Hugh, the choir stalls, the organ and the Imp, plus church candles and CDs of church music, as well as the generic collection of chocolates, tea, coffee, toiletries, jam and honey.

Other facilities Toilets are off the cloisters – there are only two cubicles in the ladies' toilets, and they are rather draughty – including separate facilities for disabled visitors. There are no baby-changing facilities.

🚐 Off A41, within Lincoln city centre. Free on-street parking (restricted to 2 hours) on south side of cathedral, or pay-and-display car parks about 10 minutes' walk away. ⊖ Train to Lincoln station, then short walk. ① Jan to May and Sept to Dec, Mon to Sat 7.15am to 6pm, Sun 7.15am to 5pm; June to Aug, Mon to Sat 7.15am to 8pm, Sun 7.15am to 6pm. 💷 Adult £3.50; senior citizen/student/unemployed visitor £3. If you want to take photos in the cathedral you have to buy a permit (£1). ♿ Wheelchair ramps throughout the cathedral. Disabled toilets. The roof tour involves climbing steps and is not recommended for those of limited mobility. A 'touch exhibition', featuring resin casts of some of the cathedral carvings, is in the north-east transept.

Longleat

Longleat, Warminster, Wiltshire BA12 7NW ☎ *(01985) 844400* ⌨ *www.longleat.co.uk*

Quality: ★★★★★ **Facilities** 👜👜👜👜 **Value for money £££££**
Highlights Excellent range of attractions; good-value 'passport ticket'
Drawbacks Poor catering in Berkeley Restaurant

What's there 'Longleat Lion Plan Lunatic' was the headline back in 1966, when Henry Thynne, the 6th Marquess of Bath, decided to introduce lions from Africa to the grounds of his estate. You can just imagine the opposition from local residents! But as more and more people paid to drive through the 100 acres to view the uncaged kings of the jungle, so he expanded the collection, and Longleat Safari Park achieved worldwide recognition.

Now, in the comfort of your vehicle you can meander your way past 300-year-old oaks in the Wiltshire countryside through 'Lion Country' and 'Elephant Country'. **'Tiger Territory'** is probably the highlight, as these majestic creatures come close to the cars but are completely disdainful of them.

Although the prospect of coming into close proximity with tigers and white rhinos may unsettle you, be warned that the fun-loving inhabitants of the 'Monkey Jungle' (which you can bypass) pose much more of a threat: we witnessed a car being steadily stripped of its wipers and windscreen seals on our visit as its occupants drove on helplessly! The alternative is to pay an extra £2 (£1 for children) and take the zebra-striped double-decker safari bus around the park. The drawback, of course, is that you lose the freedom to stop as you please; the bonus is that there is some commentary about the animals and the park, and your car stays intact!

The Thynnes' action in 1966 was only continuing in the family tradition: in 1949 the **stately home** of Longleat, which had been in the family for nearly half a millennium, became the first in England to be open to the public. Over time, successive inhabitants have each made their mark. The **extravagant ceilings** – for example, the Titian-inspired painting in the state dining room – can be attributed to the 4th Marquess, who had fallen in love with Venice in the late 1800s.

The **gardens** are not to be ignored either, with their manicured lawns and topiaried hedges as well as a modern sundial. The grounds are well sign-posted, which is more than you can say for the world's longest **hedge maze** – only suitable for those of a very patient disposition (signs say that some intrepid explorers take up to an hour to emerge).

The **Safari Boat** offers a 15-minute trip around **Gorilla Island** – look out for Nico the silver-backed male, who even has a TV to keep him amused. **Californian sea lions** have the run of the immense lake but still choose to follow the boat (no doubt waiting for the fish handouts), while hippos slouch around lazily at the edge. A train also departs from Longleat Central on rickety tracks for a trip around the lake.

The *Doctor Who* **Exhibition** takes you back to the days when Daleks and the Tardis were common language. With a life-size reconstruction of the time machine, along with various villains through the 26 years and a chance to reminisce over some of the opening soundtracks, it's a real blast from the past.

Other attractions include the **Needlecraft Centre** for cross-stitch enthusiasts, the **Dolls' House Emporium** for collectors, and a couple of interesting exhibitions about past occupants. 'Lord Bath's Bygones' exhibits paraphernalia as diverse as roller skates to the coins of the day, and gives you a glimpse of the character of the 6th Marquess. 'The Life and Times of Lord Bath' displays the various news clippings that brought him his notoriety.

Information/tours/guides Longleat comprises 12 attractions in all: Longleat House, King Arthur's Mirror Maze, the *Doctor Who* Exhibition, Safari Boats and Sea Lions, Pets Corner and Parrot Show, Longleat Railway, Butterfly Park, Postman Pat Village, Venturer Simulator Ride, Adventure Castle, Hedge Maze and Tethered Balloon Ride. You can either pay for entry into each of the attractions (which would cost £27 per adult and £26 for children and senior citizens), or buy a 'passport ticket', which allows one visit to each of the attractions. It costs £13 for adults and £11 for children (4 to 14 years old) and senior citizens. With a passport ticket, if you run out of time, you can come back and visit the remaining attractions at any point up to the end of October in the same year.

The Safari Bus leaves at 11am, 1pm and 3pm and costs £2 (£1 for children) with a passport ticket. The Safari Souvenir book has lots of glossy pictures as well as plenty of information about the animals in the park and handy symbols denoting their status in the wild and natural habitat. At £2.50 it is very good value and helps fill the gaps in the meagre snippets of information offered in the park itself.

Guided tours of the house are available only from October to March (every hour from 11am to 4pm), take up to an hour, and are included in the admission price. If you prefer not to be herded around, or in summer, when guided tours are not available, the guides in each of the rooms will gladly chat and answer questions. There's also a guidebook to the house (£3.50), which provides plenty of detail.

When to visit As with most attractions, if you want to avoid the crowds, do not go in high season or at weekends. Queues in high season get especially heavy later in the afternoon. The brochures advise visiting the Safari Boats, Mirror Maze, Longleat Railway and the Simulator in the morning to avoid long queues.

Special events are held throughout the year – for example, the Easter egg hunt, a hot-air balloon festival and family fun days. Telephone (01985) 845400 for more details.

Age appeal Children are certainly not neglected at Longleat. The Adventure Castle and Postman Pat Village have strict age limits of 14, unless accompanied by a child. Younger children will also love the pets corner, which has flaps to lift and buttons to press, although little information about the animals for older children to appreciate. Children of all ages will love King Arthur's Mirror Maze with a quest to find the sword and the chalice. The house and gardens keep adults happy.

Food and drink The Berkeley Suite Restaurant is unimaginative in layout, overpriced and pays little attention to service or taste. There is also a burger bar, but the most appealing option by far for a snack is the Cellar Café beneath the house, which has flagstone floors and serves coffees, home-made cakes and cream teas. It caters well for children with a peanut-butter sandwich and a chocolate biscuit for £1.20, or sausage in a bread roll for 99p. If you prefer to picnic, you can use the designated area next to the Berkeley Suite.

Shops There are many gift shops at Longleat, but our two favourite were the East African Trading Post shop, selling a range of ethnic souvenirs, and Lady Bath's shop, where merchandise included, for example, books on the Tudors and the Stuarts, antiques, countrified merchandise from smellies to notebooks – and even Longleat beer at £1.99 a bottle!

Other facilities Longleat is not short on toilet facilities – although some could definitely do with a revamp. Dogs are not allowed in some attractions, but free kennelling is provided while owners visit the Safari Park.

🚐 Just off the A362 between Warminster and Frome. Follow brown signs. ⊖ (During the Safari Park season) train to Warminster station then take the 'Lionlink' morning bus. It returns just after 5pm. Phone (01985) 844400 for details. ⏲ *Safari Park* 1 Apr to 29 Oct, Mon to Sun, 10am to 5pm (last admissions earlier in Oct). *Longleat House* open all year, 1 Apr to Sept, Mon to Sun 10am to 6pm; Oct to Mar, Mon to Sun 10am to 4pm. Closed 25 Dec. *Other attractions* 1 Apr to 29 Oct, Mon to Sun 11am to 5.30pm (last admissions earlier in Oct). 💷 *Passport Ticket* available 1 Apr to 29 Oct, adult £13; child (4 to 14 yrs old) and senior citizens £11. Some individual prices are as follows: *Safari Park* adult £6; child (4 to 14 yrs old) and senior citizen £5; *Longleat House* adult £6; child £4; senior citizen £5. ♿ No disabled access to the Hedge Maze or Simulator. The Butterfly Park, house and Safari Boats have limited access and the Railway has a special wheelchair carriage (see staff for availability). Disabled parking.

Lost Gardens of Heligan

Pentewan, St Austell, Cornwall PL26 6EN ☎ *(01726) 845100*
☎ *www.heligan.com* ☎ *info@heligan.com*

Quality ★★★★★   **Facilities ★★★★**   **Value for money ££££**

Highlights Chance to see an extraordinary restoration project come to life; excellent restaurant and shop; good information on individual gardens' restoration process

Drawbacks Route to the Lost Valley and the Jungle is not always clearly signposted

What's there Heligan is first mentioned in the twelfth century as part of an estate owned by the Arundell family. At some point the entire estate was sold to the Tremayne family and it was Henry Hawkins Tremayne (squire 1766–1829) who created the shape of the gardens as they appear today. Subsequent generations of the family built up an extensive plant collection, including samples of exotic palms and tree ferns in the Jungle. The gardens suffered extensive neglect during and after World War I and it was at this point that the Jungle was lost. A massive restoration project, which was the subject of a BBC documentary, began in 1991. Undergrowth, brambles and more than 1,500 tonnes of timber were cleared in the first four months. A full survey of the site was conducted and tree, plant and shrub experts were drafted in to compile a full species-identification list. As you walk around the gardens take the time to look at the information given on the restoration process of each garden. Heligan was opened to the public in April 1992.

The pleasure grounds (also known as the northern gardens) are a patchwork of small gardens and structures. They are home to many rare and beautiful shrubs and plants, including a **cut-leaf hornbeam** and the nausea-inducing **headache tree**. Highlights include the **fern ravine**, an **Italian garden**, a **sundial garden** with fine herbaceous borders, and the recently restored **northern summerhouse**, with its enclosed garden and lily pond. The **productive gardens**, which comprise a vegetable garden and four walled gardens, are unique and lay claim to having the country's only remaining manure-heated pineapple pits. More than 300 varieties of fruit and vegetables are now being grown here again, including glasshouses of citrus, vine and peach species.

A round trip via the **Lost Valley** to the Jungle is approximately 2 miles and should not be attempted by those with mobility problems. The **Jungle** is a steep-sided lush valley with four inter-connecting ponds and the largest collection of tree ferns in Europe. Palms, bamboo and wonderful specimen trees complete the picture. In the **Lost Valley**, charcoal burning and coppicing have been resumed and you can see the burners in action.

Information/tours/guides The guidebook (£1.99), which includes a map of the northern gardens, the Jungle and Lost Valley, provides plenty of background information on the restoration process. A separate guide lists the plants growing in the northern gardens (£1.50).

Age appeal The northern gardens will appeal to young and old alike. The paths to and through the Jungle and Lost Valley are rough and extremely steep.

Those with walking difficulties should take care. There is no access for those in wheelchairs or with pushchairs to the Lost Valley or Jungle.

Food and drink The restaurant comprises three separate serving areas – a servery for hot food, a separate area for light snacks, and a booth selling sandwiches, yoghurt and ice cream. The menus feature produce grown in the vegetable gardens (e.g. pumpkin soup and roll £2.50, chard quiche £4.95). The entire area gets extremely busy during lunchtime and seating can be difficult to find. There is also a separate picnic area.

Shops A wide variety of good-quality merchandise is on sale in the shop, such as videos and books on the gardens, local honey and preserves. More unusual gifts include charcoal produced at Heligan, lace and patchwork quilts. Plants are sold in a separate area.

🚌 Follow signposts for B3273 from St Austell. Brown signs to gardens from a couple of miles out. ⊖ Train to St Austell station, then Western National bus 26 to gardens (tel (01208) 79898 for more information). ⏰ Mon to Sun 10am to 6pm (5pm in winter). Last admission at 4.30pm (3.30pm in winter). 💳 Adult £5.50; senior citizen £5; child (5 to 15 yrs old) £2.50; child (under 5 yrs old) and visitors in wheelchairs free; family ticket (2 adults + up to three children) £15. Group rates (over 20 people) available. ♿ Large areas of the northern gardens suitable for disabled visitors. A small number of wheelchairs available for use (free). A leaflet from the ticket office indicates suitable routes for wheelchairs. No access to the Jungle and Lost Valley for wheelchairs.

Lotherton Hall and Bird Garden

Aberford, Leeds LS25 3EB ☎ *0113-281 3259*

Quality ★★★★   **Facilities 🏛 🏛 🏛**   **Value for money £££££**
Highlights Atmospheric country house full of fine furnishings that remains pretty
          much as it was when the Gascoigne family lived here
Drawbacks Guides could be a bit more forthcoming

What's there The Lotherton Hall estate was owned by the Gascoigne family for just under 150 years, until 1968, when the house and its contents were presented to the City of Leeds, together with its park, garden and art collections. These, along with some items bought especially for the house since it opened as a museum, are what visitors can see today. The park also contains an extensive bird garden with birds from all over the world, and there are marked trails to follow and lovely south-facing gardens to enjoy.

This **country house** gives an insight into the family's lifestyle up until World War I. It has an appealing lived-in atmosphere, with the rooms looking as if members of the family have just left – calling cards are left on a platter, invitations to exhibitions are propped up on a desk, and books are piled up beside armchairs. The **Oriental Gallery** on the ground floor has a collection of Chinese wares spanning the neolithic period to the fifteenth century, including the armorial dinner service acquired by Sir Thomas Gascoigne, the 8th Baronet, in the 1770s. The gallery also featured a temporary exhibition of arts and crafts furnishings on our visit.

The first room of the house you come to is the main hall, which remains much as it was at the turn of the nineteenth century and displays one of the best pictures of Sir Thomas. From there you can make your way through the drawing room, morning room, library and dining room, all of which are full of charm and house some fine furnishings and paintings. From the corridor you get a glimpse into the butler's room, its shelves full of silver serving dishes and candelabras. Upstairs, you can visit bathrooms and bedrooms and finally the **costume galleries**, which have regularly changing displays of fashions from the 1770s to the 1980s, including some Zandra Rhodes and Vivienne Westwood garments.

Information/tours/guides The Lotherton Hall guidebook which can be purchased on entry (£1) gives a floor plan and a tour of the house, supplemented in each room by a folder with further descriptions of furnishings. A 15-minute introductory film on the house and the family, including footage of one of the under-chauffeurs who worked at the house, is worth watching before you go round the house and the galleries. Guides were not forthcoming on our visit, even though it was quiet.

When to visit It is worth coming any time, but the grounds and bird garden are best in dry weather.

Age appeal The house appeals mainly to older children and adults, but the bird garden and grounds to all ages.

Food and drink Lotherton Hall café offers a good selection of meals, including home-made soup (£1.50) and home-made steak and kidney pie (£4.50), chicken Kiev, Yorkshire pudding and lasagne. Hot food is served until 2.30pm; otherwise there is a good range of cakes and pastries, including lemon meringue pie, Bakewell tart and chocolate truffle cake.

Shops Small shops beside the café and in the house sell locally made wooden toys and ornaments; in the house there's also a selection of Leeds creamware.

Other facilities Toilets are situated in the stable block next to the café.

🚗 13 miles east of Leeds city centre and 2½ miles east of the M1 Junction 47 on the B1217. Car park (£2 for single visit). ⊖ Bus 56 from Leeds city centre, hourly, Sun only in summer. ⏱ Apr to Oct, Tues to Sat 10am to 5pm (last admission 4.15pm), Sun 1pm to 5pm (last admission 4.15pm). Nov, Dec and Mar Tues to Sat 10am to 4pm (last admission 3.15pm), Sun 12pm to 4pm (last admission 3.15pm). Closed Mondays (except bank hols), Jan and Feb, 25, 26 Dec. 💷 *House* adult £2; student/senior citizen/unemployed visitor £1; child (5 to 16 yrs old) 50p. *Bird garden* free. ♿ Wheelchair access to ground floor only. Free parking for Orange Badge holders and free entry to the house for disabled person and accompanying helper. Electric scooters can be loaned (0113-281 3259 to book).

Louis Tussaud's Waxworks

89 Promenade, Blackpool, Lancashire FY1 5AA   ☎ *(01253) 625953*

Quality ★   Facilities 🍴   **Value for money ££**
Highlights Chamber of Horrors; cheap entry; 'Behind the Scenes' section
Drawbacks Poor facilities; tasteless anatomy section; tired décor

---

What's there A distant relation, and definitely a poorer cousin, of the better-known and more illustrious namesake in London. The main attraction is obviously the lifelike (and not so lifelike) waxworks of famous people. The trouble is that some are so bad you won't recognise them until you read the name tag. And in some cases the dummies are unlabelled, so you never know who you were supposed to be looking at. But there are some good set-piece tableaux and some excellent dummies, so it can provide an hour or so of not-too-expensive amusement in wet weather for the whole family.

The downstairs corridor has an excellent **Hollywood tableau** of 007, *The Terminator*, *Alien* and the like. Andrew Lloyd Webber also gets a star billing amid his *Cats*, complete with music from the show. It's just a shame that the drab décor takes the shine off these, the best displays. Upstairs, the Grand Hall is filled with royalty and politicians, though younger visitors will have trouble recognising some of the faces that haven't been in the news for a while. And some are just too bad to be recognisable. Mrs Thatcher looked particularly thin, Princess Diana rather haggard and Princess Margaret could have been a complete stranger.

The second floor has more waxworks, but the displays are ruined by the amusement arcade situated in their midst – far too noisy and distracting. Plus the bottom of the barrel was definitely scraped for some of these not-even-B-list celebrities: Eddie the Eagle and Linda Nolan are still there. You can pay an extra £1 to go through to the tasteless anatomy section (not suitable for children), where the shameless depiction of disease and injury (fancy gawping at rupturing blisters, malformed babies or a fractured arm?) is just about redeemed by the more educational cutaways of the body, from torso to foot. Pity that a naked model of the Elephant Man lowers the tone completely.

Better to head for the '**Behind the Scenes**' section, which shows you how the dummies are made and how much work goes into getting the faces right. A running commentary goes with it and, at the end of your stroll through, you'll find shelves of disused heads, such as the cast of *Star Trek* and Sarah Ferguson – though it's a mystery why some 'stars' are here when lesser-known ones are on display outside.

Zip through the football hall, full of unnamed has-beens, and head for the **Chamber of Horrors**, but if you're squeamish, you can go straight out instead. It's a great mix of fictional and factual gore, and has good, informative labelling. Scenes from famous horror films, such as *The Exorcist* and *Silence of the Lambs*, are interspersed with real-life killers like the Wests, Dennis Nielsen and the Yorkshire Ripper. The final punch is a depiction of a car crash, with an appropriately moral tale about safe driving. Follow the bloody footprints (a nice touch) up the stairs to the exit.

Information/tours/guides No leaflets, brochures or guidebooks were available when we inspected.

When to visit It's great for wet weather, as it's all indoors.

Age appeal All ages could enjoy this attraction, though there aren't enough current stars for younger children to gaze at, and they might not enjoy the Chamber of Horrors.

Food and drink You'll find a very limited selection of food and drink at the second-floor cafeteria – tea, coffee, sweets and crisps – in rather noisy surroundings.

Shops Closed on the day of inspection.

Other facilities The dirty, poky toilets need a make-over – and the whole place needs a good spring clean, as well as someone to pick up the litter around the entrance.

🚗 Follow signs for Blackpool town centre. Museum on seafront, south of the Tower (but no signposts). Car parking in town centre (with charge). ⊖ Train to Blackpool North station, then tram or walk along the promenade to museum. ① All year, Mon to Sun, 10am to 9pm (winter 10am to 4pm). Closed 25 Dec. 💷 Adult £4; child (5 to 12 yrs old) £2; child (under 5 yrs old) free; senior citizen £3; family ticket (2 adults + 2 children) £10. ♿ The floors are linked by several staircases but a lift is available on request.

Ludlow Castle

Castle Square, Ludlow, Shropshire SY8 1AY ☎ *(01584) 873355*

Quality ★ **Facilities** 👤 👤 **Value for money** ££
Highlights Panoramic views
Drawbacks Inadequate information boards

What's there Ludlow Castle is steeped in history and was one of the most important strongholds of the region for almost 500 years. It eventually became a royal palace in the fifteenth century and there is fascinating evidence of the different architectural styles through the ages. Visitors can climb up the stairs of the **garderobe** and **gatehouse towers** to enjoy the **panoramic views,** including a steep drop to the River Teme below.

Most of the castle's walls are still intact and surround a large lawn, a popular place for picnicking families. The main cluster of buildings forms the inner bailey, including an imposing gatehouse keep and the judge's lodgings next to it. These are a fine example of **Tudor apartments**, and among the ruins you can see carved fireplaces and mullioned windows. Inside the bailey a well-preserved Norman chapel boasts a circular nave and on the north side of the castle a series of buildings, including a huge Great Hall, where Milton's masque play *Comus* was first performed in 1634.

Information/tours/guides Either the audio tour (50p) or the detailed large-format guidebook (£2) are essential to understand the castle. The lack of imagination in presentation and the sparse content of the display boards are disappointing, and no exhibition space has been devoted to the story of the castle. The unhelpful staff and the lack of signs to direct you around the sight do not improve things, nor does the absence of a map, which should be included in the price of a ticket.

When to visit The attraction is mainly open-air, so fine weather would be ideal, although you'll get attractive views from the battlements all year round.

Age appeal The ruins should appeal to all ages. The children's leaflet guide (50p) will be enjoyed by younger visitors, but it isn't bad for adults either.

Food and drink No food or drink to be had on site.

Shops A small, but reasonably stocked, shop at the main entrance sells books and historically based items, such as games and jewellery. The Ludlow Castle cross-stitch kit costs £2.95.

🚍 Off A49, in centre of Ludlow town. Car parking nearby. ⊖ Train to Ludlow, then short walk. ⊙ Feb to Apr and Oct to Dec, Mon to Sun, 10am to 4pm; May to July, Sept, Mon to Sun 10am to 5pm; Aug, Mon to Sun 10am to 7pm; Jan, Sat and Sun only 10am to 4pm. Last admission 30 mins before closing. Closed 25 Dec. 💷 Adult £3; child (6 to 16 yrs old) £1.50; senior citizen/student £2.50; family ticket £8.50. ♿ Not suitable for wheelchairs. Disabled toilet.

Manchester United FC Museum

Manchester United Football Ground, Sir Matt Busby Way, Old Trafford,
Manchester M16 0RA ☎ *0161–868 8631*
🖥 *manutd.com/trafford/museum.sps*

Quality ★★★   **Facilities** 🏛🏛🏛🏛   **Value for money £££**

Highlights Trophy room; hall-of-fame memorabilia; behind-the-scenes insights into match-day routines

Drawbacks Hugely irksome if you are not a Manchester United fan

---

What's there This is an attraction of two halves: a leisurely dribble around the celebratory museum, then a guided tour passing through doorways otherwise the preserve of players, boot-room staff, or members of the press. Allow an hour for each, with extra time in the museum for die-hards.

The museum, opened in April 1998, charts the team's history, from its origins in 1878 as the Newton Heath Lancashire and Yorkshire Railway Cricket and Football Club to the latest treble-winning exploits. Kick off with a gawp at the extensive **trophy collection**, from obscure commemorative dishes to the most treasured trinity of soccer silverware: the premiership trophy, the FA Cup and the European Champion's Cup (though the FA Cup will certainly not be on display beyond May 2000, and there are no guarantees of long-term tenure on the other two).

Sections are dedicated to the club's two great managers – Sir Matt Busby and the current incumbent, Sir Alex Ferguson. The tragedy of the Munich air crash is recalled through yellowed newspaper clippings and archive news broadcasts; and the most famous players – the likes of **Charlton**, **Best**, **Law** and **Edwards** – are rewarded with individual displays of contemporary kit and caps.

The tour takes in the press conference suite, players' lounge and home **dressing room**. There are two opportunities to **run out into the stadium** – though the sacred turf is strictly out of bounds – and the dug out, with a chance to be photographed in the manager's seat. The empty stadium lacks atmosphere, and the fixtures and fittings look bland and functional, though the guides do try to liven things up by pointing out Giggs' peg in the changing room, Posh Spice's favoured position in the lounge and the importance of Jaffa Cakes in maintaining the players' stamina.

It is not worth a long journey just to visit the museum, but combining the museum and tour makes for an entertaining time – at least for an avid Man United supporter.

Information/tours/guides The souvenir guide (£1.50) is a dry and unimaginative 17-page booklet that adds nothing to the tour guide's spiel and looks more like business promotional bumf.

When to visit Check in advance about home games (telephone 0161-868 8020 to hear a recorded message giving details), as there are no tours on match days. Tours are in great demand during school holidays, so book several days ahead.

Age appeal Keen Manchester United fans of any age will be transfixed.

Food and drink A small café inside the museum serves tea, coffee, Eccles cakes and a limited range of sandwiches. The Red Café, beside the museum entrance, is actually a full-blown restaurant with banks of TV screens, a cocktail bar and wide-ranging menu from burger and chips (from £7) to various pastas (around £8) and Cajun chicken (around £9). Book a table in advance if you intend to eat there at lunchtime.

Shops The tiny museum gift shop has a very limited selection of goods (such as wallets and calendars) presumably because serious shoppers will be heading for the club Megastore, where everything from lollipops to lamp-shades is available emblazoned with the club logo.

🚗 Off the A56 south-west of Manchester city centre, prominently signposted. ⊖ Train (Metrolink) to Old Trafford station, then walk up Warwick Road past the cricket ground to Sir Matt Busby Way. For information on buses, call 0161–273 53451. On match days, trains run from Manchester Oxford Road station direct to the football ground station. ⏱ *Museum* Mon to Sun 9.30am to 5pm. Closed 24, 25, 31 Dec, 1 Jan. On match days, museum closes 30 minutes before kick-off. *Tours* Mon to Sun every 10 mins from 9.40am to 4.30pm. No tours on match days. 💷 *Museum and tour (museum only)* adult £8 (£5); child (under 16 yrs old)/student/senior citizen £5.50 (£3.50). Free entry to tour for disabled visitors. ♿ Lifts operate to the third-floor entrance of the museum and between floors within the museum. Two wheelchairs available at the museum entrance. Wheelchair access to the changing rooms, players' lounge and the side of the pitch.

Marwell Zoological Park

Colden Common, Winchester, Hampshire SO21 1JH ☎ *(01962) 777407*
📧 *www.marwell.org.uk*

Quality ★★★ · **Facilities 🏛 🏛 🏛** · **Value for money £££**
Highlights Tropical house; lemurs; giraffes; Encounter Village for children
Drawbacks Some inadequate information boards; be prepared for plenty of walking

What's there Located in an extensive countryside setting, Marwell Zoo has animals in a mixture of large paddocks and smaller enclosures in a roughly circular route. Among the sections that we liked best was the **Tropical House**, with its rainforest-style setting featuring an **ant colony** and **monkeys** on a small island. Close by is the **lemur enclosure,** with good viewing areas and lots of information about these primates that are native to Madagascar. Children will enjoy the **Encounter Village**, with its camels, ferrets and sheep and viewing tunnels under the rabbit enclosure. Other notable animals include tigers, jaguars and an attractive new **giraffe enclosure,** which has an African theme and also houses other animals, such as hyrax and monkeys.

A free road train and railway (60p single, £1 return) help you to get around the spread-out site.

Information/tours/guides Many of the enclosures have poor signs, and some are so far away you can't read them. The informative guidebook (£2) has good illustrations and is useful as there are, sadly, no animal talks.

When to visit It's mostly an outdoor attraction so stick to fine weather.

Age appeal The animal-handling sessions (£1) are entertaining and informative for all ages of children (available during school holidays and weekends February to October). There are play areas, and the Encounter Village allows you to get close to domestic animals. An entertaining activity book (£1) is also available.

Food and drink The main restaurant, Treetops, is close to the entrance. Refreshment kiosks are scattered around the site, but if you want something more substantial, you might be in for a long walk back for lunch. However, Treetops is gloomy and unattractive, serving food such as steak pie or pizza, chips and beans (£5.25), sandwiches (from £2.25 to £3.25) and tea (90p).

Shops The main Ark gift shop is huge and extremely well laid out with an excellent choice. A porcelain dolphin costs £28.50, a child's T-shirt £6.95 and an animal stencil £2.50.

Other facilities Tidy toilets, but could do with more.

🚌 Follow signposts from M27, junction 5 or M3, junction 11. ⊖ Not easy. Train to Eastleigh or Winchester station, then bus (only in summer, twice daily) or taxi. ○ Open all year, Mon to Sun 10am to 6pm (4pm in winter). Closed 25 Dec. 🎫 Adult £8.80; child (3 to 14 yrs old) £6.30; senior citizen £7.80. ♿ Fully accessible.

Merseyside Maritime Museum

Albert Dock, Liverpool L3 4AQ ☎ *0151–478 4499*

Quality ★★★★   **Facilities 🏛🏛🏛🏛**   **Value for money ££££**
Highlights Excellent presentation; imaginative food; helpful, polite staff
Drawbacks A bit dusty in parts; canteen service can be slow when busy

---

What's there One of the biggest maritime museums in Europe, offering an insight into the history of the once-great port of Liverpool, is appropriately set in the Albert Dock. It captures the nostalgic romance as well as the harsh reality of working on the docks and aboard ship, in a mostly imaginative and absorbing way.

Each of five storeys in the exposed brick building has a different sea-faring theme, including a history of slavery in the basement, which uses video, photos, interviews and life-sized display models to reveal just how appalling conditions were on the slave ships.

The ground floor stages the excellent **HM Customs and Excise exhibition**, which shows the ingenious methods that have been employed to smuggle everything from drugs to liquor and tobacco over the centuries – for example, drugs smuggled in the hollowed-out heels of shoes, endangered animals put down underpants, and heroin put in condoms and then swallowed – the method of retrieval is remarkable!

Upper floors have re-created wartime ship interiors in **'The Battle of the Atlantic' zone,** where interviews with survivors of torpedo attacks are activated by picking-up an old-fashioned telephone and listening in; video footage from the time is also shown. There's lots of paraphernalia and memorabilia that, along with appropriate soundtrack and pictures, gives a real sense of what war aboard ship was like.

Other areas are given over to displays of **hundreds of model ships** – some inside bottles, others that are 10 feet long – as well as so-called floating palaces, such as the *Titanic, Lusitania* and *Mauritania.* Allow a couple of hours for a full visit.

Information/tours/guides No guided tours are conducted, but there are occasional specific talks and workshops, such as on ships in bottles, as well as a guidebook for £1.95.

When to visit The entire museum is indoors and open all year round, and it's cosy on a rainy day.

Age appeal The museum has broad appeal because of the use of videos, soundtrack and the interactive nature of some of the exhibits, which keep children happy. Older people will remember a lot of the wartime material, and the lifts between floors will help those with mobility problems.

Food and drink There's a very good, spacious canteen on the top floor that serves a recommendable scampi and chips, as well as spinach and feta goujons, seared tuna steak and Caribbean chicken. All with lovely views to match.

Shops The shop is in the main entrance but sells only a limited range of goods – mainly ornaments, model-making kits, posters and naval history books – that aren't particularly well displayed.

🚗 Follow the signs to Liverpool town centre and then signs for the Albert Dock. Ample free parking. ⊖ Train to Liverpool Lime Street station, then 15-minute walk or Smartbus 1 or 4 to museum. ⊙ Mon to Sun 10am to 5pm. Closed 23 to 26 Dec, 1 Jan. 💷 *Eight-museum return-visit pass* adult £3; child (under 16 yrs old) free; student/ senior citizen/unemployed visitor £1.50. ♿ Full access. Entrance ramp and lift to all floors. Disabled toilets.

Monkey World – Ape Rescue Centre

East Stoke, Wareham, Dorset BH20 6HH ☎ *(01929) 462537 or (0800) 456600* ⌁ *www.monkeyworld.org* ⌁ *apes@aperescue.org*

Quality ★★★	Facilities 🏛🏛🏛	Value for money ££££
Highlights	Watching the chimpanzee antics; keeper talks; walk-through lemur enclosure	
Drawbacks	Poor catering; crowds in high season	

What's there Monkey World is not an ordinary zoo. For a start, as the title suggests, the emphasis is on monkeys – or primates to be exact. Moreover, all the inhabitants of this large wooded park have been rescued from abuse from the pet trade, circuses or their private owners since 1987. One of its most famous residents, **Trudy the baby chimp**, was rescued after being repeatedly beaten by Mary Chipperfield. Two other chimps, Cherri and Simon, were rescued from Spain – one from beach photographers and the other from a pole he was tethered to in a petrol station.

The good thing is that most of the primates that have been rescued have successfully been rehabilitated into new family groups. Not all of the chimps have been physically abused in the normal sense. Honey, for example, literally led a life of royalty, with her own room, wardrobe and nannies with the Royal Family of Dubai. Monkey World intervened, and Honey is now climbing and playing with her new adoptive family. The pig-tailed monkeys had a lucky escape from labs – each bears a number tattooed on its chest.

The park is attractively laid out, and information boards by enclosures give you some background information. It is great fun trying to recognise the animals from their photographs, and the chimps in particular seemed lively and occupied. Chimps are not bred in Monkey World – the females are fitted with contraceptive devices – but mistakes do happen: on our inspection there was baby Seamus, complete with nappy, playing happily with plastic toys in his playpen.

It is easy to miss some species, as the signposts around the park are not very clear, but don't miss the novel walk-through **lemur enclosure**, which gives its inhabitants plenty of space to climb and swing. There is also a pets' corner and an obstacle course aimed at children. The small adoption room gives some more background information about how the rescues were initiated and includes photographs and press articles. What a shame that the video was inaudible and the room was too cramped to stand and watch.

Information/tours/guides In addition to the information boards, the keepers give excellent talks every half hour from noon to 3.30pm. The *Ape Rescue Chronicle* (published three times a year, cost 75p) gives a behind-the-scenes insight into Monkey World.

When to visit It's best to visit in fine weather.

Age appeal A great attraction for all the family. Children can let off steam on the obstacle course, and enjoy the mini motorbikes, mini boats, swings and slides.

Food and drink There were three or four disorderly queues in the cafeteria and a limited choice of hot food on the menu (only hot dogs and chips) on the day of inspection. A cheese roll was dry and overpriced (£2.49). Picnic areas and plenty of benches are available if you plump for the BYO option.

Shops Lots of things on a gorilla theme, including books, posters and cuddly clip-ons (£1.99), are on sale.

🚌 2 miles north of Wool, off A352. ⊖ Not easy. Nearest station Wool, no bus connection to park. ⊙ Mon to Sun 10am to 5pm (6pm during July and Aug). Closed 25 Dec, 1 Jan. 💷 Adult £5.50, child (3 to 15 yrs old) £3.50; senior citizen and disabled visitor £4; family ticket (2 adults + 2 children) £16. ♿ Wheelchair accessible. Wheelchairs available for loan. Guide dogs permitted.

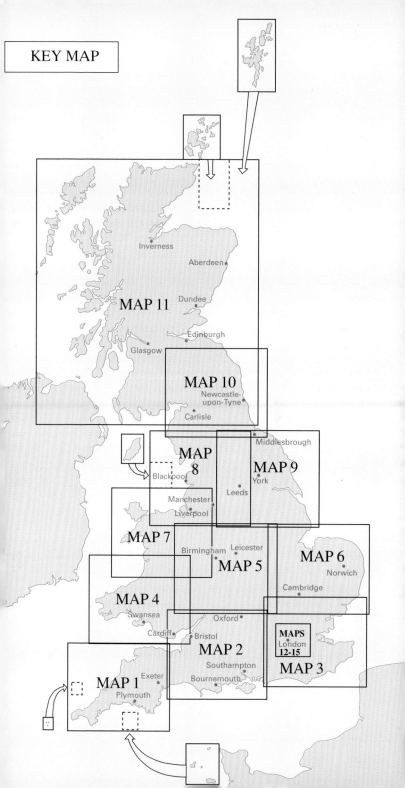

KEY MAP

MAP 11

Inverness

Aberdeen

Dundee

Edinburgh

Glasgow

MAP 10

Newcastle-
upon-Tyne

Carlisle

Middlesbrough

MAP
8

Blackpool

MAP 9

York

Leeds

Manchester

Liverpool

MAP 7

Birmingham

Leicester

MAP 5

MAP 6

Norwich

Cambridge

MAP 4

Swansea

Cardiff

Bristol

Oxford

MAP 2

MAPS
12-15

London

MAP 3

Southampton

MAP 1

Exeter

Bournemouth

Plymouth

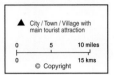

MAP 1

▲ City / Town / Village with
main tourist attraction

0 ____ 5 ____ 10 miles
0 _____ 15 kms
© Copyright

△ 4

Lundy Island

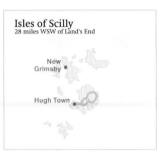

Isles of Scilly
28 miles WSW of Land's End

New
Grimsby •

Hugh Town •

Bud e
Bay

Tintagel
Tintagel Castle ▲

*Port Isaac
Bay*

Bodr

A39

Wadebridge

Bodmin
Lanhydrock Ho

Watergate Bay

A39

R. Camel

A30

Newquay

C O R N W A L

A392

A30

A39

Ligger Bay

St Austell

A390

R. Fal

Pentewan
Lost Gardens of Heligan

St Austell B

A30

A39

A390

Truro

*St Ives
Bay*

St Ives
Tate Gallery ▲

A30

A390

A39

*Veryan
Bay*

St Just •

Marazion
St Michael's Mount ▲

Penzance •

A394

Falmouth

*Falmouth
Bay*

Helston ▲
Flambards Theme Park

*Lands
End*

*Mount's
Bay*

Lizard Point

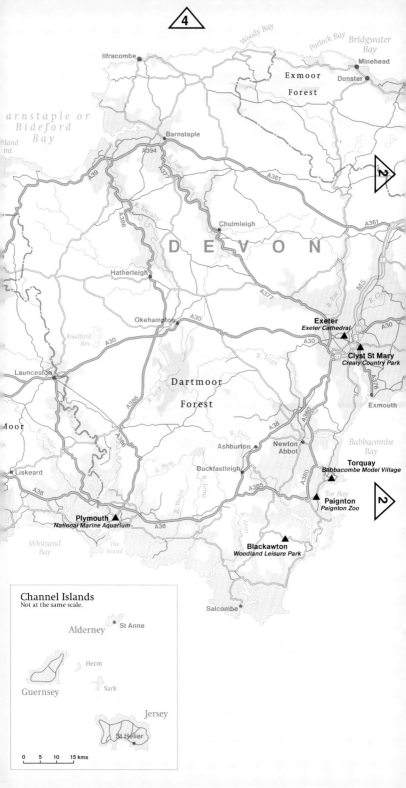

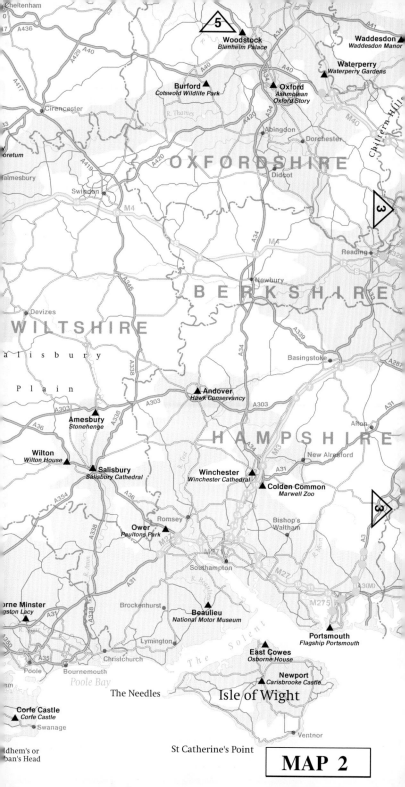

MAP 2

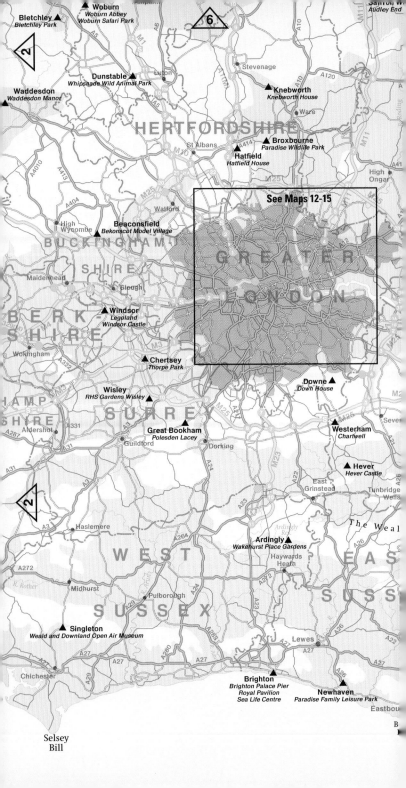

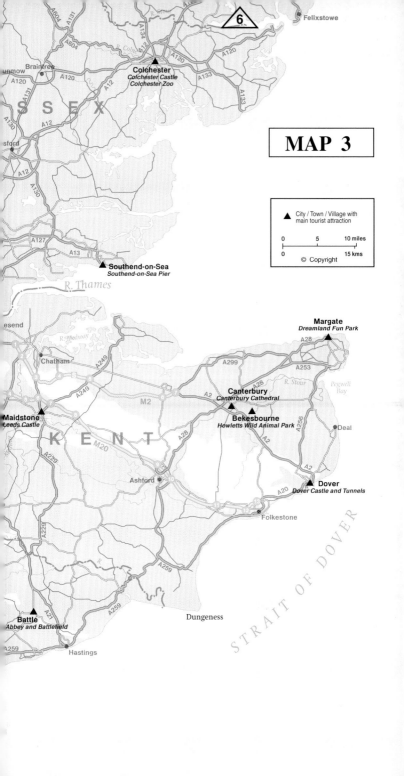

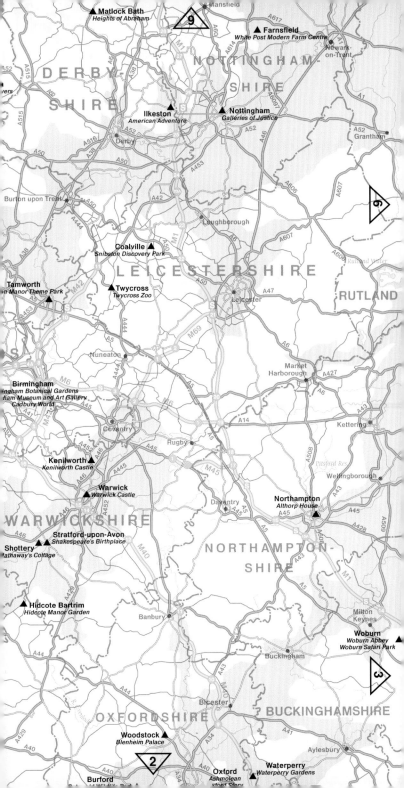

▲ **Matlock Bath**
Heights of Abraham

△ **9**

★ Mansfield

▲ **Farnsfield**
White Post Modern Farm Centre

Newark-
on-Trent

**DERBY-
SHIRE**

**NOTTINGHAM-
SHIRE**

▲ **Ilkeston**
American Adventure

▲ **Nottingham**
Galleries of Justice

Derby

Grantham

Burton upon Trent

△ **6**

Rutland Water

▲ **Coalville**
Snibston Discovery Park

LEICESTERSHIRE

RUTLAND

▲ **Tamworth**
n Manor Theme Park

▲ **Twycross**
Twycross Zoo

Leicester

Loughborough

Nuneaton

Market
Harborough

Kettering

Birmingham
ingham Botanical Gardens
ham Museum and Art Gallery
Cadbury World

Coventry

Rugby

Wellingborough

Pitsford Res

▲ **Kenilworth**
Kenilworth Castle

▲ **Warwick**
Warwick Castle

Daventry

▲ **Northampton**
Althorp House

WARWICKSHIRE

▲ **Stratford-upon-Avon**
Shakespeare's Birthplace

**NORTHAMPTON-
SHIRE**

▲ **Shottery**
athaway's Cottage

▲ **Hidcote Bartrim**
Hidcote Manor Garden

Banbury

Milton
Keynes

▲ **Woburn**
Woburn Abbey
Woburn Safari Park ▲

Buckingham

△ **3**

OXFORDSHIRE

BUCKINGHAMSHIRE

Bicester

▲ **Woodstock**
Blenheim Palace

△ **2**

Waterperry
Waterperry Gardens

Aylesbury

Burford

Oxford
Ashmolean
ford Story

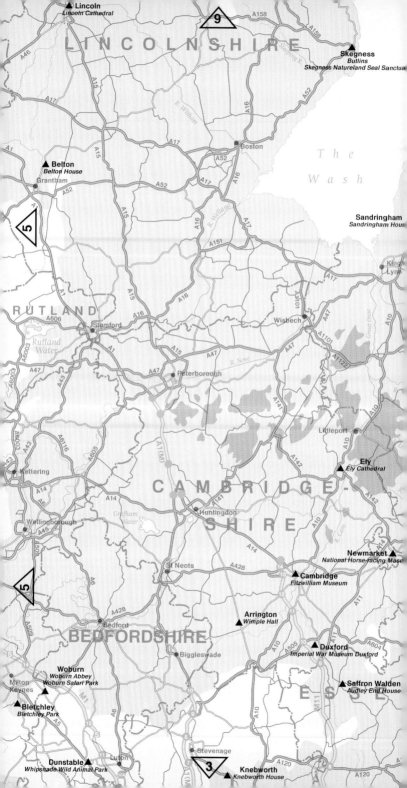

9

MAP 6

▲ City / Town / Village with
main tourist attraction

| 0 | 5 | 10 miles |
| 0 | 15 kms |

© Copyright

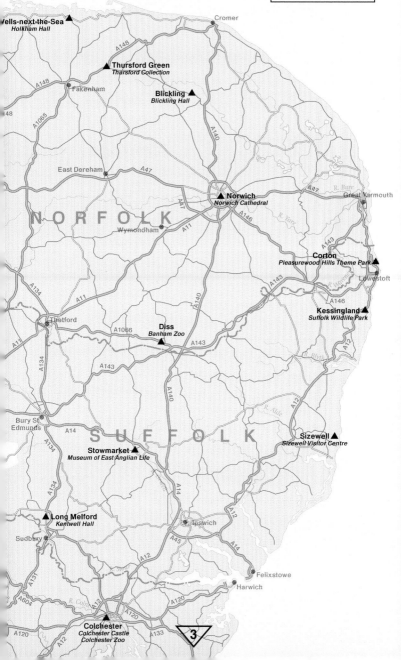

NORTH

SEA

Cromer

Wells-next-the-Sea ▲
Holkham Hall

▲ **Thursford Green**
Thursford Collection

Fakenham

Blickling ▲
Blickling Hall

East Dereham

▲ **Norwich**
Norwich Cathedral

Great Yarmouth

Wymondham

Corton ▲
Pleasurewood Hills Theme Park

Lowestoft

Kessingland ▲
Suffolk Wildlife Park

Thetford

Diss ▲
Banham Zoo

NORFOLK

Bury St
Edmunds

SUFFOLK

Stowmarket ▲
Museum of East Anglian Life

Sizewell ▲
Sizewell Visitor Centre

▲ **Long Melford**
Kentwell Hall

Sudbury

Ipswich

Felixstowe

Harwich

▲ **Colchester**
Colchester Castle
Colchester Zoo

3

MAP 7

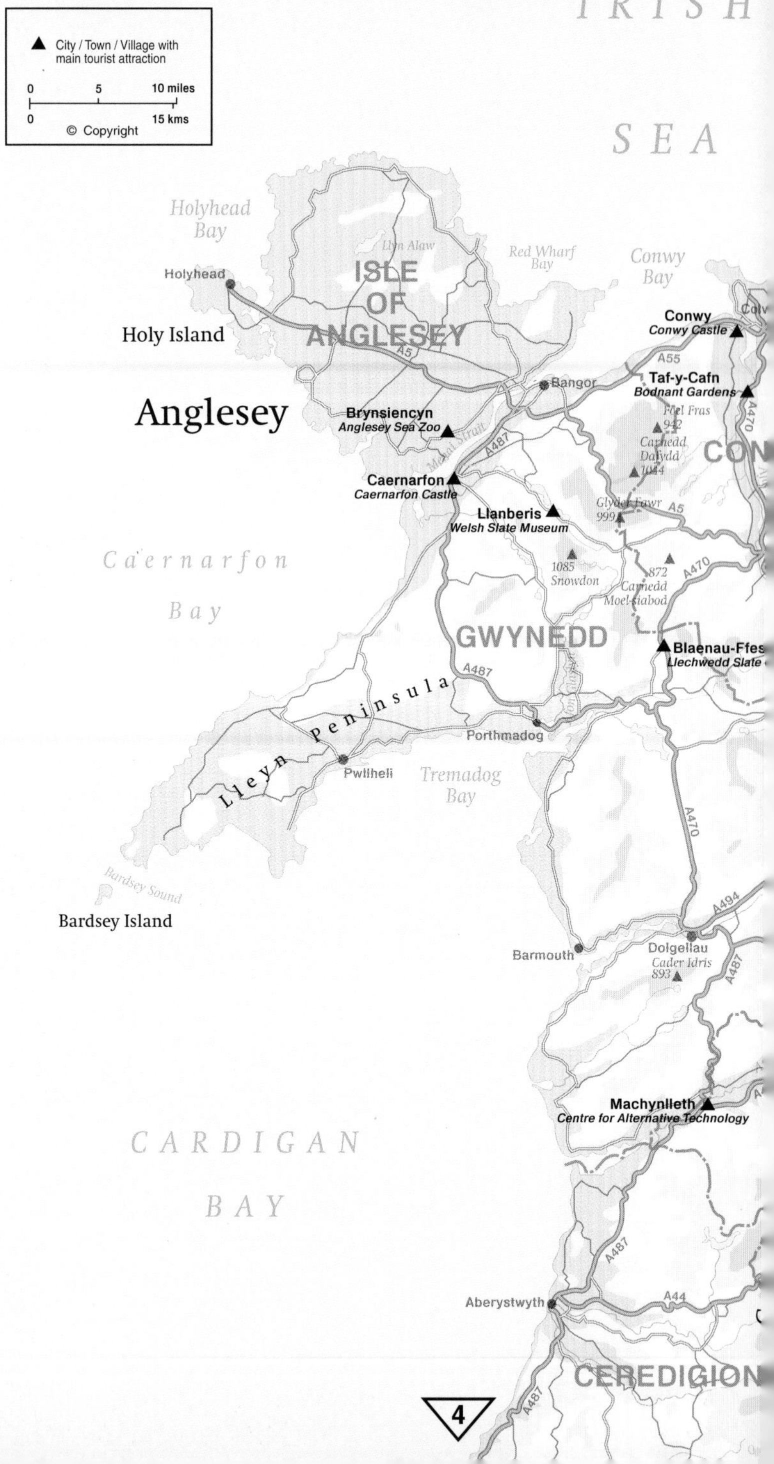

▲ City / Town / Village with main tourist attraction

0		5		10 miles
0			5	15 kms

© Copyright

IRISH

SEA

Holyhead Bay

Llyn Alaw

Red Wharf Bay

Conwy Bay

Holyhead

ISLE OF ANGLESEY

Conwy
Conwy Castle ▲   Colw

Holy Island

A5

A55

Taf-y-Cafn
Bodnant Gardens ▲

Bangor

A470

Anglesey

Brynsiencyn
Anglesey Sea Zoo ▲

A487

Ffel Fras
942

Carnedd Dafydd
1044 ▲

CON

Caernarfon
Caernarfon Castle

Llanberis
Welsh Slate Museum ▲

Glyder Fawr
999 ▲

A5

Ca'ernarfon

Bay

1085
Snowdon

872 ▲
*Carnedd
Moel-siabod*

A470

GWYNEDD

Blaenau-Ffes
Llechwedd Slate ▲

A487

L l e y n   P e n i n s u l a

Porthmadog

Pwllheli

Tremadog Bay

A470

Bardsey Sound

Bardsey Island

Barmouth

Dolgellau
Cader Idris
893 ▲

A494

A487

Machynlleth ▲
Centre for Alternative Technology

CARDIGAN

BAY

A487

Aberystwyth

A44

A487

CEREDIGION

▽4

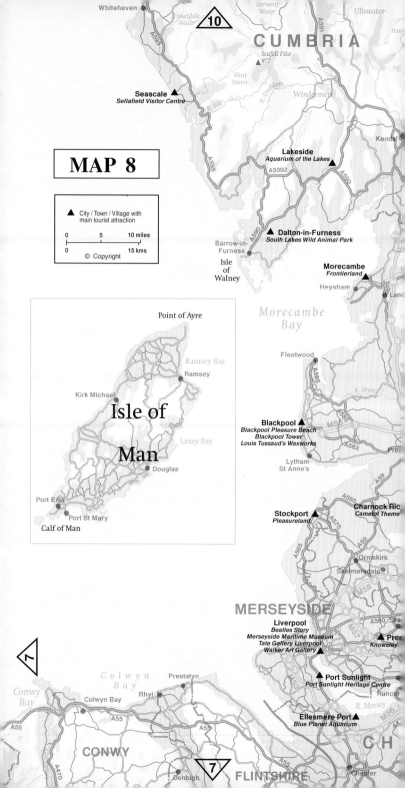

Whitehaven

10

CUMBRIA

Ennerdale Water

Derwent Water

Ullswater

Haw

Scafell Pike
▲ 977

West Water

Windermere

A595

R. Duddon

R. Esk

Seascale ▲
Sellafield Visitor Centre

A595

Lakeside
Aquarium of the Lakes ▲

A5092

Kendal

A590

MAP 8

▲ City / Town / Village with
main tourist attraction

| 0 | 5 | 10 miles |
| 0 | | 15 kms |
© Copyright

A590

▲ **Dalton-in-Furness**
South Lakes Wild Animal Park

Barrow-in-
Furness

Isle
of
Walney

Morecambe
Frontierland ▲

Heysham

Lanc

Morecambe
Bay

Fleetwood

Point of Ayre

Ramsey Bay

Ramsey

Kirk Michael

Isle of

Man

Laxey Bay

Douglas

Port Erin

Port St Mary

Calf of Man

A585

R. Wyre

M55

Blackpool ▲
Blackpool Pleasure Beach
Blackpool Tower
Louis Tussaud's Waxworks

A583

Pres

Lytham
St Anne's

A59

A565

Charnock Ric
Camelot Theme

A570

Stockport ▲
Pleasureland

A59

A565

A570

Ormskirk

Skelmersdale

A580/SFI

M58

MERSEYSIDE

Liverpool
Beatles Story
Merseyside Maritime Museum
Tate Gallery Liverpool ▲
Walker Art Gallery ▲

M57

▲ **Pres**
Knowsley

7

Colwyn
Bay

Prestatyn

Conwy
Bay

Colwyn Bay

Rhyl

A55

A55

A55

A470

CONWY

Denbigh

7

FLINTSHIRE

▲ **Port Sunlight**
Port Sunlight Heritage Centre

Runco

R. Mersey

M56

Ellesmere Port ▲
Blue Planet Aquarium

CH

Chester

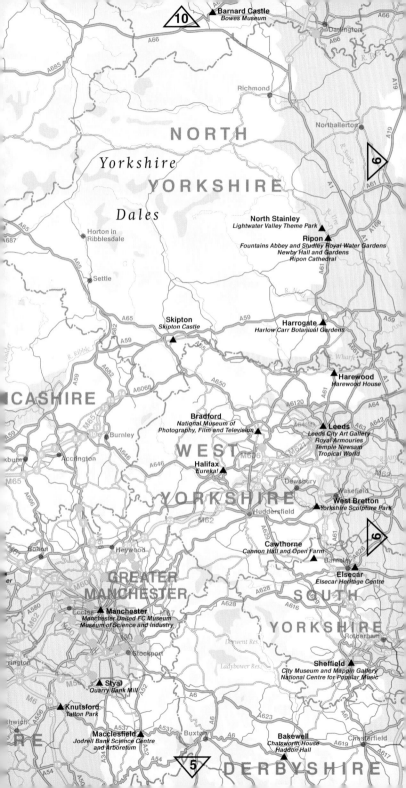

Bowes Museum

A66

A66

A66

△ **10**

Richmond

Northallerton

North York
Moors

A170

Kirby Misperton ▲
Flamingoland

△ **8**

North Stainley ▲
Lightwater Valley Theme Park

Nunnington ▲
Nunnington Hall

Ripon ▲
Fountains Abbey and Studley Royal Water Gardens
Newby Hall and Gardens
Ripon Cathedral

Malton ▲
Castle Howard
Eden Camp

N O R T H   Y O R K S H I R E

Harrogate ▲
Harlow Carr Botanical Gardens

York ▲
Jorvik Viking Centre
National Railway Museum
York Castle Museum
York City Art Gallery
York Dungeon
York Minster

Harewood ▲
Harewood House

W E S T

Aberford ▲
Lotherton Hall and Bird Garden

Bradford ▲
National Museum of
Photography, Film and Television

Leeds ▲
Leeds City Art Gallery
Royal Armouries
Temple Newsam
Tropical World

Halifax ▲
Eureka!

Y O R K S H I R E

Wakefield

West Bretton ▲
Yorkshire Sculpture Park

Huddersfield

Cawthorne ▲
Cannon Hall and Open Farm

Barnsley

Elsecar ▲
Elsecar Heritage Centre

Doncaster ▲
Earth Centre

△ **8**

S O U T H

Mexborough

Y O R K S H I R E

L I –

Rotherham

Sheffield ▲
City Museum and Mappin Gallery
National Centre for Popular Music

NOTTINGHAM-

Rampton ▲
Sundown Adventure

Worksop

D E R B Y S H I R E

SHIRE

Buxton

Chesterfield

Bakewell ▲
Chatsworth House
Haddon Hall

△ **5**

Doe Lea ▲
Hardwick Hall

Mansfield

MAP 9

▲ City / Town / Village with
main tourist attraction

0   5   10 miles
0   15 kms
© Copyright

Whitby
Whitby Abbey

A171

Scarborough

A170

A64

Yorkshire Wolds

Sewerby
Sewerby Hall and Gardens ▲

Flamborough Head

A165

A166

Bridlington

*Bridlington
Bay*

A165

A163

A1035

A165

A079

EAST RIDING
OF YORKSHIRE

KINGSTON-
UPON HULL

Kingston upon Hull

R. Humber

Barton-upon-Humber

A15

A160

LINCOLNSHIRE

...thorpe

A18

A180

A15

N.E.
LINCOLNSHIRE

A173

Grimsby
National Fishing Heritage Centre ▲

Cleethorpes
Pleasure Island Theme Park ▲

Spurn Head

A46

A16

A46

A1103

Market
Rasen

A631

A15

The Wolds

Louth

A16

Mablethorpe

A157

A158

A46

A158

A15

A158

LINCOLNSHIRE

Lincoln
Lincoln Cathedral ▲

A158

Skegness
*Butlins
Skegness Natureland Seal Sanctuary* ▲

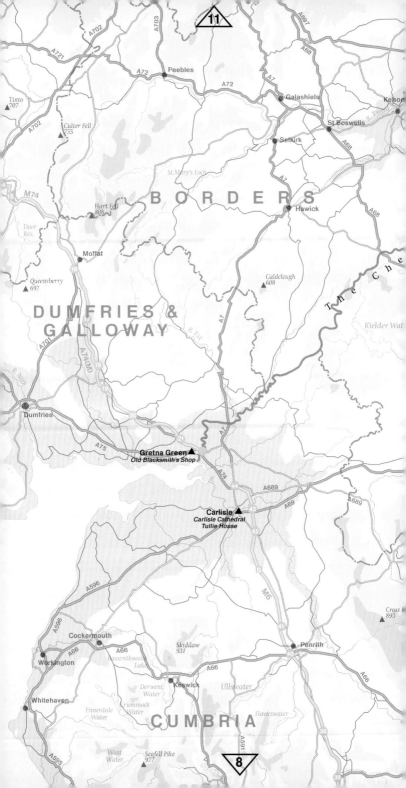

11

MAP 10

▲ City / Town / Village with main tourist attraction

0 ____ 5 ____ 10 miles
0 _____ 15 kms
© Copyright

Berwick-upon-Tweed

Holy Island

Farne Is.

▲ **Bamburgh**
Bamburgh Castle

The Cheviot
815

NORTHUMBERLAND

● Alnmouth

▲ **Cambo**
Wallington House

● Morpeth

▲ **Chollerford**
Chesters Roman Fort

Newcastle upon Tyne
Laing Art Gallery
Newcastle Discovery Museum

● Tynemouth

TYNE
&
WEAR

Haydon Bridge
usesteads Roman Fort

● Stanley

▲ **Sunderland**
National Glass Centre

● Consett

▲ **Beamish**
North of England
Open Air Museum

Durham ▲
Durham Cathedral

DURHAM

Bishop
Auckland

▲ **Hartlepool**
Hartlepool Historic Quay

HARTLEPOOL

Tees Bay

STOCKTON-
ON-TEES

● Redcar

▲ **Barnard Castle**
Bowes Museum

Stockton-on-Tees ▲
Preston Hall Museum

● Middlesbrough

REDCAR

MIDDLES-
BROUGH

● Darlington

MAP 11

Shetland Islands Not to same scale

Unst
Fetlar
Outer Skerries
Whalsay
Bressay
Lerwick
Mainland
Esha Ness
Muckle Roe
Papa Stour
Fitful Head

Orkney Islands Not to same scale

N. Ronaldsay
Sanday
Stronsay
Eday
Shapinsay
Mull Head
Westray
Rousay
Mainland
S. Ronaldsay
Brough Head
Hoy
Stroma
John o' Groats
Rora Head
Dunnet Head

Stroma
Duncansby Head

Wick

Thurso
Helmsdale

Cape Wrath

Handa I.

Ben Hope 927
Ben Loyal
Ben Klibreck 961

Ben Arkle 782
Ben Hee 873
Ben More Assynt 998
Quinag 808

Tarbat Ness

Black Isle
Dingwall

Culloden Moor
Culloden Battlefield and Visitor Centre

Ben Wyvis 1046

An Teallach 1062

Poolewe
Inverewe Gardens

Rubha Reidh

Drumnadrochit
Official Loch Ness Monster Exhibition Centre
Urquhart Castle

Sgurr Ruadh 960

Elgin
Banff
Fraserburgh
Peterhead
Buchan Ness
Rattray Head

MORAY

ABERDEENSHIRE

Huntly

ABERDEEN
Aberdeen

Inverurie

Oyne
Archaeolink Prehistory Park

Banchory
Crathes Castle and Gardens

Bennachie 528

Cairngorm
Cairngorm Mountains
Ben Macdui 1309

Aviemore

Morven 871

Ben Alligin 985

Butt of Lewis

Flannan Isles

Eye Peninsula
Stornoway

ISLE OF LEWIS

Great Bernera

Shiant Is.

HARRIS

Scarp
Taransay
Scalpay

OUTER HEBRIDES

WESTERN ISLES

Berneray

North Uist

Benbecula
Ronay
Wiay

South Uist

Eriskay

The Minch

Rubha Reidh

Rona

Rubha Hunish

Raasay
Scalpay

Island of Skye

Portree

The Old Man of Storr 719

Cuillin

HIGHLAND

North

West

Loch Ness

Ben Attow 1032

Ben Nevis 1344

Mallaig

Sound of Raasay

Soay

Canna

Rhum

Eigg

Muck

INNER HEBRIDES

The Little Minch

Blair Atholl

Grampian Mountains

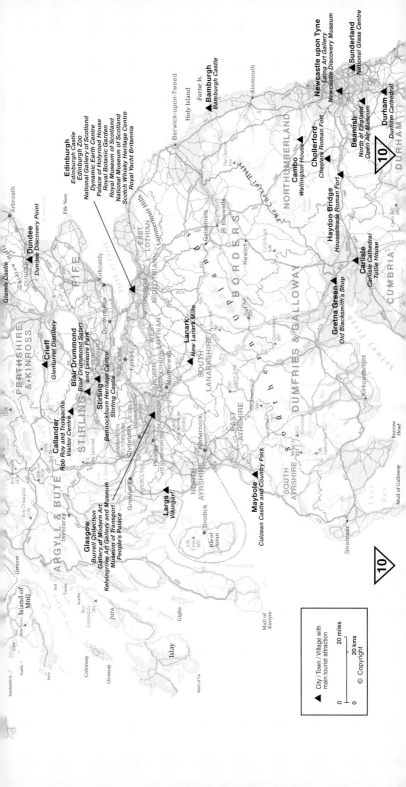

Edinburgh
Edinburgh Castle
Edinburgh Zoo
National Gallery of Scotland
Dynamic Earth Centre
Palace of Holyrood House
Royal Botanic Garden
Royal Museum of Scotland
National Museum of Scotland
Scotch Whisky Heritage Centre
Royal Yacht Britannia

Newcastle upon Tyne
Laing Art Gallery
Newcastle Discovery Museum

Sunderland
National Glass Centre

Bamburgh
Bamburgh Castle

Beamish
North of England Open Air Museum

Durham
Durham Cathedral

Cambo
Wallington House

Chollerford
Chesters Roman Fort

Haydon Bridge
Housesteads Roman Fort

Carlisle
Carlisle Cathedral
Tullie House

Gretna Green
Old Blacksmith's Shop

Dundee
Dundee Discovery Point

Crieff
Glenturret Distillery

Callander
Rob Roy and Trossachs Visitor Centre

Blair Drummond
Blair Drummond Safari and Leisure Park

Stirling
Bannockburn Heritage Centre
Stirling Castle

Lanark
New Lanark Mills

Glasgow
Burrell Collection
Gallery of Modern Art
Kelvingrove Art Gallery and Museum
Museum of Transport
People's Palace

Largs
Vikingar!

Maybole
Culzean Castle and Country Park

▲ City / Town / Village with main tourist attraction

0   20 kms
0   20 miles

© Copyright

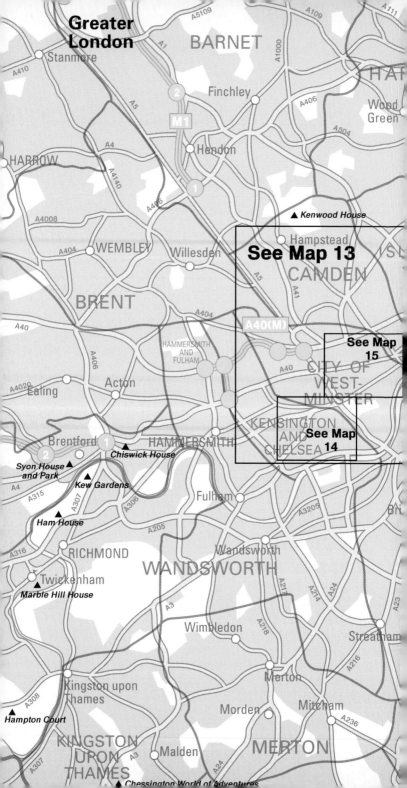

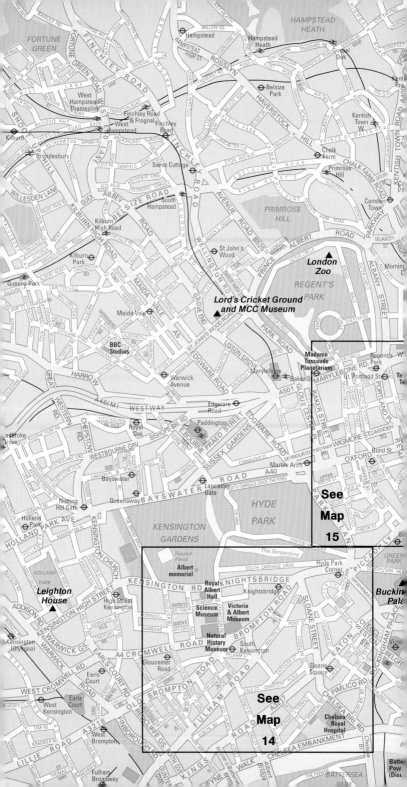

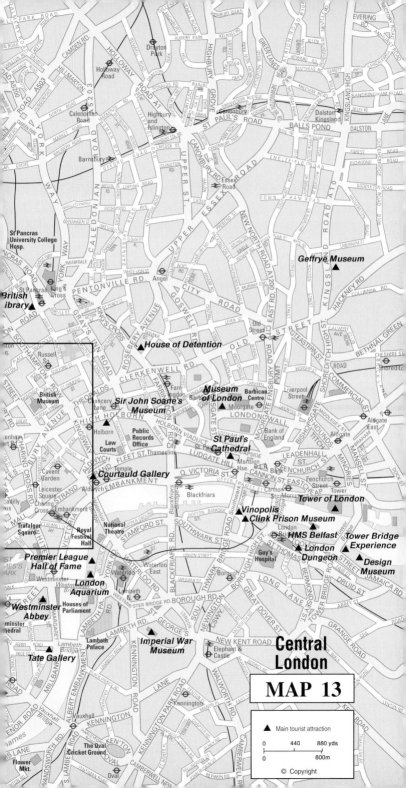

Central London

MAP 13

▲ Main tourist attraction

| 0 | 440 | 880 yds |

| 0 | | 800m |

© Copyright

Map labels

Drayton Park

Holloway Road

Caledonian Road

Barnsbury

St Pancras University College Hosp.

St Pancras

King's Cross

British Library

House of Detention

British Museum

Sir John Soane's Museum

Museum of London

Barbican Centre

Liverpool Street

Geffrye Museum

Holborn

Public Records Office

Law Courts

St Paul's Cathedral

Bank of England

Aldgate East

Courtauld Gallery

Covent Garden

Leicester Square

Charing Cross

Embankment

Blackfriars

Tower of London

Vinopolis

Clink Prison Museum

HMS Belfast

London Dungeon

Tower Bridge Experience

Design Museum

Trafalgar Square

Royal Festival Hall

National Theatre

Waterloo

Waterloo East

Guy's Hospital

Premier League Hall of Fame

London Aquarium

Westminster

Houses of Parliament

Westminster Abbey

Lambeth Palace

Imperial War Museum

Tate Gallery

Elephant & Castle

The Oval Cricket Ground

Flower Mkt.

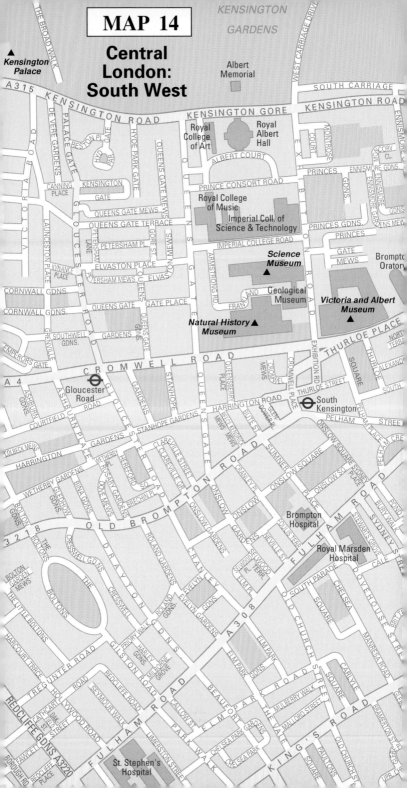

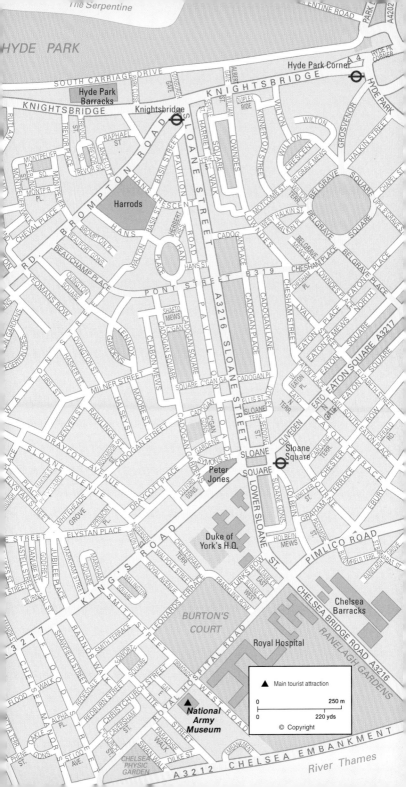

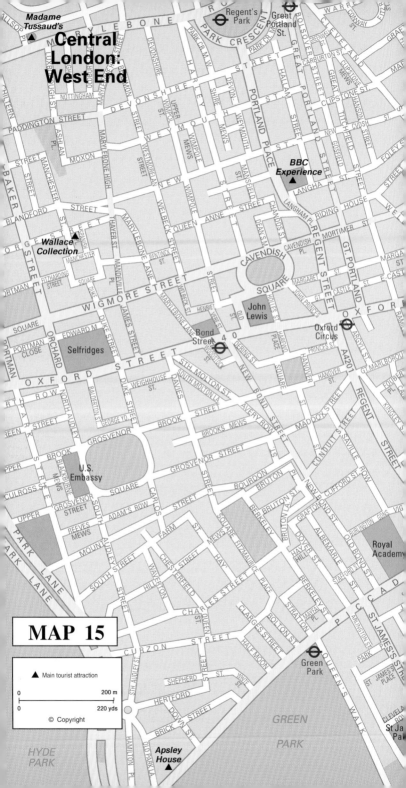

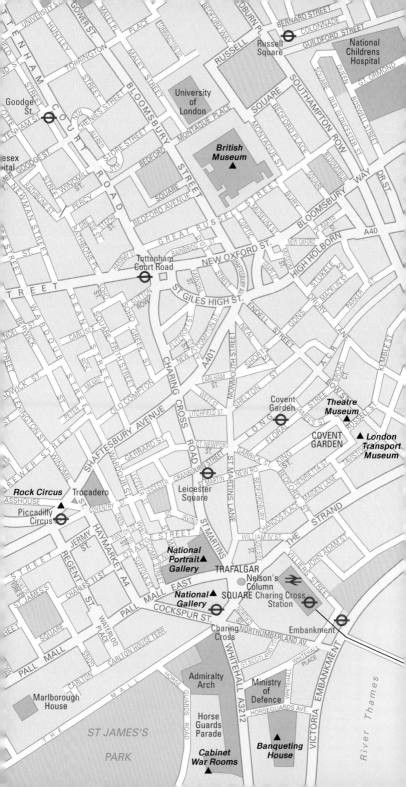

Some of our award winners

(For a full list see pages 16–17.) Clockwise from right: Lost Gardens of Heligan; Royal Pavilion, Brighton; Chester Zoo; National Museum of Photography, Film and Television, Bradford

Museum of East Anglian Life

Stowmarket, Suffolk IP14 IDL   ☎ *(01449) 612229*
www.suffolkcc.gov.uk/central/meal

Quality ★★★★   **Facilities 🏛 🏛 🏛**   **Value for money ££££**
Highlights   Enthusiastic, helpful staff; plenty of special events and demonstrations of
              past crafts
Drawbacks   Some exhibits need freshening up

What's there   The museum is based on a 70-acre site that is part of the former Abbot's Hall estate. Abbot's Hall itself is still a private house and not open to the public. The **historic buildings** include a medieval timber-framed farmhouse, a watermill and miller's house (complete with Victorian privy), windpump, blacksmith's forge and industrial workshop. Housed in barns and outbuildings, the various exhibitions give an insight into the diverse aspects of domestic, agricultural and industrial life. 'Domestic Life 1890–1910' and 'East Anglia at work' are re-creations of room settings, such as a parlour, bedroom, school room, shops and a dairy. A **thirteenth-century tithe barn** contains carts, wagons and hand tools to make up 'The Farming Year' exhibition. Grundisburgh Smithy and the Boby building (originally housing part of a nineteenth-century engineering works) covers the old industries of East Anglia.

Craft workshops include basket, rope, brush, harness and barrel making. There is also a printing press and a steam gallery with traction and ploughing engines. Craftsmen and museum staff give occasional **demonstrations.** Livestock at the museum include black pigs, goats and Remus the Suffolk Punch.

A visit to the site takes between 1 and 2 hours, but you could easily spend the best part of a day if demonstrations are taking place. On a fine day you can enjoy the paths along the river and extensive grounds.

Information/tours/guides   An interesting and well-presented guidebook, with a map and detailed information about the exhibits, is available from the ticket office for £1. Attendants are laid-back, chatty and friendly, successfully communicating their own enthusiasm for and knowledge of the exhibits.

When to visit   It's best to visit in dry weather – although exhibits are mostly under cover, you have to walk from area to area. Umbrellas are available for hire (£10 deposit). It can be busy with school parties in term time. Special themed events are organised, such as rare breeds and craft days, donkey derbies and 'Muscle to Motor Power' and fire-fighting weekends.

Age appeal   A good museum for all ages, but school-age children will particularly enjoy the demonstrations, the playground and watching the machinery, such as the watermill, in action. Younger children are likely to prefer the goats, pigs and chickens.

Food and drink   Brambles is a privately run café-style food outlet. It is small, with only seven tables inside, although there are picnic tables outside in the summer. Because of its size, it can feel claustrophobic and suffer from unpleasant frying smells. The service can be off-hand, but the café is clean and the food good value. The menu includes full English breakfast, homemade lasagne (£3.25) and kids' meals (£1.25). Tea comes properly made in a pot for 65p.

Shops   The wide range of goods include books, postcards, videos and gifts. The well-displayed, colourful children's corner has badges for 20p and cut-out models for £1.15.

🚌 In the centre of Stowmarket, opposite Asda supermarket. Signposted from the main A14 trunk road and the B115 to Great Finborough. Large pay-and-display car park by museum. ⊖ Train to Stowmarket station, then 10-minute walk. Local buses stop nearby. ⊙ 2 Apr to 29 Oct, Mon to Sat 10am to 5pm, Sun 11am to 5pm; Nov to end Mar, Mon to Fri 10am to 3pm. 🎫 Adult £4.25; child (4 to 16 yrs old) £2.75; student, senior citizen £3.75; family ticket (2 adults + up to 3 children) £13.75. Group rates (10 or more people) available. Entry £1.50 for all during Nov to Feb. By joining the Friends of the Museum, you get free access to the site all year: adult £8; couple £12; family ticket £15 per year. ♿ Paths are gravel but may get muddy in wet weather. Some buildings have restricted access on upper floors. Disabled toilets. Two wheelchairs available to borrow.

Museum of Science and Industry in Manchester

Liverpool Road, Castlefield, Manchester M3 4FP   ☎ *0161-832 1830*
📧 *www.msim.org.uk/*

Quality ★★★   **Facilities 👍 👍 👍**   **Value for money ££££**
Highlights   Magnificent and historic machines beneath stylishly renovated architecture
Drawbacks   Refreshments in very short supply at the time of our inspection, during
                 ongoing building work

What's there   Looms still chatter, pistons whistle, and gas mantles wink in the heart of the world's first industrial city. But they do so now for the purposes of illumination and the preservation of our heritage, rather than for the profit of industrial magnates. The museum is a homage to the inventions that have warmed, clothed and transported us since the earliest days of the Industrial Revolution, with the exhibits housed in parts of nineteenth-century iron and brick warehouses and the **oldest railway building** in the world.

The main entrance leads into an exhibition on textiles, with **working looms**, fashions through the ages, and hands-on levers and buttons to demonstrate the properties of threads and fabrics. Across the inner courtyard, the Power Hall houses the workhorses of the Industrial Revolution – **steam engines** with variously angled pistons and flywheels. **Vintage cars** and railway engines are under the same roof.

Along the railway tracks (traversed by a steam engine on Sundays, from Easter 2000) you come to the 1830 station building and the neighbouring warehouse. Among the various arches and lofts, you can study the origins of Manchester from Roman times; track the development of gas and electric power (with past appliances as curiosities); and let the children loose on all manner of safe scientific experiments with water, mirrors and electricity.

The Air and Space Gallery, across the street from the main entrance, is a vast hangar for all manner of **aircraft**, from biplanes to shiny jets to a model of the *Mir* space station.

Allowing about an hour to do justice to each section, the museum could easily swallow a whole day – particularly if you read all the panels, turn and press all the available handles and buttons, and schedule in the demonstrations. Even if you skim through some of the sections of less personal interest, set aside at least three to four hours.

Information/tours/guides The guidebook (£1.50) is a glossy taster for the museum, with snaps of many of the more photogenic exhibits. It is reasonably priced as a souvenir, but doesn't add anything to your appreciation as you go round. A site plan is available for free on admission.

When to visit Virtually all the exhibits are indoors. School holidays are the busiest times but the site is large enough to avoid feeling crowded at most times.

Age appeal Younger schoolchildren should enjoy the hands-on science exhibits in the **Xperiment!** area and the creative activities (e.g. aeroplane modelling or making fabric collages) supervised in the school holidays; older visitors might get nostalgic about the appliances in the gas and electricity galleries, while anyone with a soft spot for a steam engine will be in their element.

Food and drink A 200-seat restaurant in the main entrance building is planned to be open in early 2000; on inspection there was only the café in the Air and Space Gallery, selling tea (75p), coffee (90p), soft drinks, burgers, pizzas and a limited range of sandwiches.

Shops The temporary shop (until the development work is finished) was a chaotic jumble of books, sweets, mugs and science-related books and toys – such as chemistry sets (£9.99), crystal growing sets (£7.99) and Airfix kits (from £3.99).

🚗 In the city centre, look for brown signs. Limited parking available in the central forecourt (£1.50); on-street parking with meters just outside, and several large municipal car parks (£5 per day) within walking distance. ⊖ Train to either Deansgate or G-Mex Metrolink stations, then a 5- to 10-minute walk. Bus No 33 from Piccadilly bus station stops outside the Museum on Liverpool Road. ⊙ Open all year, Mon to Sun 10am to 5pm (last entry 4.30pm). Closed 24–26 Dec. 💷 Adult £6.50; child (under 18 yrs old) free; student, senior citizen, unemployed £3.50. ♿ 90 per cent of the site is accessible via smooth paths, ramps and lifts, and several locations have disabled toilets. Some staff are trained in the Sympathetic Hearing Scheme and sign language. Leaflets in Braille can be supplied if requested in advance.

National Centre for Popular Music

Paternoster Row, Sheffield, Yorkshire S1 2QQ ☎ *0114-296 2626*

Quality ★★★   **Facilities 📽 📽 📽**   **Value for money £££**
Highlights Highly visual, futuristic building; good toilets and shop
Drawbacks Poor soundproofing can cause confusion; unimaginative food

---

What's there This history of popular music, starting in the 1950s and leading up to the present day, is set in a highly futuristic building near the heart of Sheffield city centre. Four gleaming, giant steel-clad drums resemble curling stones, each housing a different theme to do with music.

Soundscapes is an enclosed, circular 16-speaker theatre that was the world's first 3-D surround-sound auditorium, which immerses you in music from around the world. A narrator takes you through the various musical elements, such as rhythm, harmony, melody and pitch, but it is loud and not as instructive as it might be.

Perspectives is a walk-through drum that itself is divided into sections, each with its own theme, the best of which is the **'love' room** with its heart-shaped design and velvet-style bench seating. A video features different artists dealing with love, while other darkened rooms illustrate religion and political protest in music, with extensive use of specially commissioned films. Again it is loud, and poor sound-proofing makes some of the narration difficult to hear.

The **Making Music zone** is the most interactive, with its hands-on approach to making your own noise by activating everything from Hammond organs to electric guitars and drums, either by selecting buttons or by standing on particular coloured panels in a mock-up of a 1970s dance floor. This is a great room for children.

Turning Points theatre has a giant wall of video screens showing images and indigenous sounds from around the world, including a native American Indian reservation and Senegal village. There is also a *Guinness Rockopedia* that contains every piece of pop trivia you are never likely to need.

If you can tolerate the noise – and of course youngsters love it – you should allow about two-and-a-half hours for a full visit.

Information/tours/guides At £3 the guidebook is good value and goes into a lot of detail about the different elements of music within the centre, as well as the background and history of the building. There is an information desk, which is helpful, but no regular tours.

When to visit All of the centre is indoors and makes a good rainy-day venue, although in fine weather local bands occasionally play outside in a small square.

Age appeal It will appeal mainly to teenagers and those old enough to remember the 1950s and 1960s.

Food and drink The centre has a diner-style café on the ground floor in the same space-age design as the rest of the building. Food is standard burger and chips, pizzas and jacket potatoes, along with hot and cold drinks.

Shops It's easy to browse in the bright and spacious shop area which has helpful and efficient staff. On sale is an extensive range of goods to do with all things pop, including T-shirts, books, posters, CDs, and even boxer shorts with musical motifs.

Other facilities Toilets are ultra-modern, all chrome and high-tech with foot-operated wash basins, and very clean.

🚗 From M1, junction 33, follow brown guitar and town centre signs. No separate parking, but several nearby pay parks. ⊖ Train to Sheffield station, then 5-minute walk. Alternatively, 5-minute walk from Sheffield bus station. ⏱ Open all year, Mon to Sun

10am to 6pm (last admission 3.30pm). Closed 25 Dec, 1 Jan. 🖼 Adult £5.95; child (under 16 yrs old) £4; student, senior citizen, unemployed £4.75; family ticket (2 adults + 2 children) £18. ♿ Full wheelchair access by lift between ground and first floor. Disabled parking.

National Fishing Heritage Centre

Alexandra Dock, Grimsby DN31 1UZ ☎ *(01472) 323345*

Quality ★ ★ ★ ★ **Facilities 🎣 🎣 🎣** **Value for money ££££**

Highlights Imaginative use of different media; lots of interactive exhibits for all ages; clear orientation

Drawbacks Poor maintenance in toilets and some exhibits

What's there The National Fishing Heritage Centre recreates 1950s Grimsby, when it was the world's largest fishing port. Within the centre lies *Perseverance*, a shrimper and the last sailing vessel to work out of the port, surrounded by **reconstructed period shops and businesses**, such as a ladies' outfitters and the Grimsby Rubber Company.

An imaginative mixture of **recorded oral histories**, reconstructed tableaux – often with sound and even smells – interactive activities, and traditional display panels bring home the hardships of life in those times. You can go from the whistling Arctic winds on deck down to the boiler room, marvel at the amount of food consumed by the crew in a day, and experience the boat lurching from side to side as the dripping catch is winched on board. A deckhand could gut enough fish in one hour to feed 1,600 people ashore – he was paid 'liver money' for the livers removed, which were boiled down to produce cod-liver oil. Down in the galley, the cook had to ensure that he cooked enough to keep energy levels up, baking bread every day and coping with pots of scalding water in the roughest seas. The couple of days spent ashore between fishing trips were spent catching up on gossip, collecting pay – and often spending it on drinking and gambling.

The **guided tour of the *Ross Tiger*** trawler is given by a genuine gruff ex-trawlerman who explains what life on board was like – 12 men away for 18 days out of every 20, washing only once on every trip, standing on board a freezing deck gutting fish for 48 hours without sleep. Down in the engine room you can experience the deafening racket given out by the main engine, winch and generator, and you can compare the relatively palatial captain's quarters (complete with pantry stocked with alcoholic necessities) with the cramped bunks below deck.

Information/tours/guides Guided tours of the *Ross Tiger* trawler start every 30 minutes or so and last 45 minutes – when you pay your admission fee you'll be given a ticket with the time of the next tour on it. There is no map or guide to the main heritage centre, but the route is very obvious (follow the painted white footprints) and the displays are clearly numbered. A full-colour booklet (£1), summing up the hardships of life on shore and on board, is more of a souvenir than a guide. Staff on the ticket desk were reasonably friendly but did not know much about the 'certificates of competency' – fun 'qualifications' ranking from ship's cat to skipper.

It may be more problematic to get information on temporary exhibitions. At the time of our inspection, the exhibition 'Trawlers at War' was run by volunteers, so staff at the heritage centre could give no definite opening times and dates. Their best advice was to ring the morning of the day you were thinking of visiting – not very satisfactory if you were travelling a long way. Two out of nine of the TV monitors showing a video of life on board a trawler were also out of action.

When to visit Everything is under cover (apart from the decks of the *Ross Tiger*), so it's ideal for wet weather. Allow at least a couple of hours. There are also various special events throughout the year, but call for details.

Age appeal Plenty of hands-on interactive activities appeal to all ages – you can try your hand at different knots or even net-making, guess how many supplies are needed for a three-week trip, and have a go at puzzles or rubbings. The recorded oral histories and reconstructed shops and interiors may be of more interest to older visitors.

Food and drink The Ice Barrel Café serves a limited range of cold snacks: rolls and baps (£1.30) plus chocolate, ice creams and cakes. Filter coffee is 80p, tea 60p, hot chocolate 70p. There are a couple of tables (gritty with spilt sugar on inspection) next to the serving counter as well as a bigger adjoining room.

Shops The shop takes up a large part of the entrance lobby and sells a selection of traditional toys such as wooden-handled skipping ropes, tin buckets, jack-in-the-boxes (£16.95) and wooden boats. The maritime theme is continued in items such as painted wooden sailors and cats (£3 to 4), piscine china, bathmats (£17.95), and trawler prints (£19 to £25). Souvenir mugs and baseball caps cost £2.95. There's also a good selection of books on fishing.

Other facilities Lots of free parking. Toilets are attractively designed, with modern fittings, but were poorly maintained on inspection: of the four cubicles in the ladies' toilets, two had no paper and one door had no lock.

🚗 Take A180 to Grimsby. Follow the brown signs through Grimsby – the heritage centre is in Alexandra Dock, next to Sainsbury's. Plenty of free parking. ⊖ Short walk or bus ride from Grimsby bus station or town centre. ⊕ Mon to Thur 10am to 4pm, Sat and Sun 11am to 5 pm (10.30am to 5.30pm Jul, Aug, Sept). Closed Fridays, 25, 26 Dec, 1 Jan. Admission fees (without *Ross Tiger* visit): adult £4.95 (£3.85), child £3.85 (£2.75), student/senior citizen £3.85 (£2.75), family ticket (2 adults + 4 children) £16.50 (£11), Skipper's Ticket (a year's unlimited visits) adult £6.60, £5.30 for a child/concession ticket. ♿ Full wheelchair access to heritage centre; lift; disabled toilets. The *Ross Tiger* trawler is unsuitable for those of limited mobility or children under 5.

National Glass Centre

Liberty Way, Sunderland SR6 0GL ☎ *0191-515 5555*

Quality ★★★★★	**Facilities** 👜👜👜👜👜	**Value for money £££**

Highlights Imaginative and informative displays; chance to see glass-making process; impressive restaurant

Drawbacks Publicity leaflet gives no admission prices

What's there The National Glass Centre is dedicated to the development and promotion of glass in both industry and art. Housed in a modern glass building, the centre comprises a glass-making factory, a permanent exhibition on the history and function of glass, and some temporary design exhibitions.

'**Kaleidoscope**', the permanent exhibition, is an interesting exploration of glass and how the discovery of glass-making 4,000 years ago (the outcome of heating sand and lime) created a material so fundamental to our lives. The exhibition also describes the birth of flat glass production in the form of stained glass in Wearside (one of the earliest glass-making centres in the country) over 1,300 years ago. Creative information panels and touch-sensitive computer screens and displays help visitors to explore the properties and function of glass.

Admission to the glass-making factory is possible only on a guided tour. Here visitors can **observe glass-making** first hand, from the initial stages of blowing to the final techniques of polishing, etching and engraving. At the end of the tour there is an optional **demonstration by the Phoenix Hot Glass Studio** of techniques such as blowing air bubbles into red molten glass and introducing different colours into clear glass.

A full visit would probably take at least a couple of hours.

Information/tours/guides Guides are very knowledgeable and happy to answer questions. There is no separate guidebook.

When to visit The museum is open all year round and all the exhibits are housed indoors, so any time of year is suitable for a visit. There is also an extensive programme of talks and workshops for both adults and children (call for full details).

Age appeal The glass centre is of interest to all ages. The interactive displays and factory tours are great for children, as are the children's activities on Saturdays, such as butterfly sand-casting and glass painting.

Food and drink Throwingstones Restaurant, which looks out directly on to the Wear, is a spacious, modern eating area. The décor is fashionably mini-malist with neutral stone walls and glass-topped tables. Open sandwiches (from £3.75) and simple dishes such as pan-fried salmon and salad (£4.95) make a good lunch. The service is highly efficient.

Shops The shop is strategically situated as you leave the final demon-stration of the factory tour. Objects such as vases, bottles and mirrors (£12 upwards) are attractively presented in glass display cabinets. Less expensive souvenirs for the children include glass marbles (£3.95) and T-shirts (£9). A range of books on glass are also on sale.

From M18, then A1231, or off the A183 Weardale Way. Signposted from major roads through the town. Free car park. ⊖ Train to Sunderland station, then 26 bus (which leaves 8 min, 28 min and 48 min past the hour) stops outside centre. ⊙ Open all year, Mon to Sun 10am to 5pm (last admission to the glass tour is 4pm). Adult £5; child (5 to 18 yrs old) £3; child (under 5 yrs old) free; senior citizen, unemployed £3; family ticket (2 adults + 3 children) £12. Mon, Fri no glass blower: adults £3.50; child, senior citizen, unemployed £2; family ticket £10. Free admission for disabled carer. ♿ Wheelchair accessible throughout with lift access to both floors. Disabled toilets. Guide dogs are welcome and Braille translations are available (if requested in advance). Guided tours for the visually impaired (if requested in advance). Disabled parking.

National Horse-racing Museum

High Street, Newmarket, Suffolk CB8 8JL ☎ *(01638) 667333*

Quality ★★★ **Facilities** 🐎 🐎 🐎 🐎 **Value for money £££££**
Highlights Some fascinating exhibits; good guided tour; practical gallery is fun
Drawbacks Slightly old-fashioned presentation

What's there The museum stands appropriately close to the Jockey Club, Tattersalls' thoroughbred sales and the National Stud in the heart of Newmarket racing country. A beautiful **statue of Hyperion** outside the Jockey Club next door sets the scene. Inside, various galleries take you through the history of horse-racing, the early importation of stallions, royal involvement, stories of famous jockeys and owners, racecourses, races and patrons, the horses themselves (you can see Eclipse's skeleton and Persimmon's stuffed head), and tales of villains nobbling and doping.

A 'practical gallery' has an **ex-jockey** on hand to answer questions and give visitors a thrilling ride on a **racehorse simulator**. You can see what the horses eat, put on some colours, weigh up, and tack up a model horse. Upstairs, an exhibition of **sporting art** features paintings, photos and bronzes. The final gallery houses display cases of famous jockeys through the ages as well as famous meets.

Allow one and a half hours, and make sure you time your visit to coincide with the free guided tour at 2.30pm every day, as this really brings the place alive.

Information/tours/guides The exhibition is self-guided, but to get the best in terms of human anecdote and humour, go on the guided tour, which is excellently led. The guide will pick out faces from the many photographs covering the walls and relate them to the display cases and boards, creating a sense of history and place you can't get if you're not an enthusiast. The guidebook (£4.95) is well presented and a useful supplement to the visit.

We were disappointed that a tour of a racing yard was not intrinsic to the museum; if you want to see live horses, book one of the tours available. There's a comprehensive list of events and tours available throughout the year (call (01638) 560622 for details). On offer are daily Newmarket tours (£15 adults, £12.50 child, senior citizen, student) for two hours which include visiting a training yard and seeing horses on the gallops and involved in activities such as swimming in the pool. Tours leave at 9.20am daily except Sun; minibuses adapted to take wheelchairs; pre-booking preferred. One tour is called 'Scandal! Racing Frauds and Betting Coups'. There are also Dick Francis tours, visits to a forensic dope-testing laboratory, and demonstrations by equine photographers and artists.

When to visit The museum is a worthwhile destination in all weathers.

Age appeal This museum is best for those with some interest, or potential interest, in horses and horse-racing. It is not suitable for young children.

Food and drink A wonderful mural of lots of contemporary jockeys, most of whom have signed their likenesses, decorates the airy cafeteria. On fine days tables and chairs are set out in the garden. Food is cheap and cheerful: a ploughman's lunch costs £3.95, lasagne is £2.75, soup is £1.95. There is also the usual array of hot and cold drinks.

Shops   The gift shop is in the reception, and doesn't have a huge variety of merchandise. Most of it is themed around horses, so you could pick up some snaffle bit cuff links, horsey tea towels, or a couple of postcards.

🚗 Follow signs to Tattersalls car park (300m from museum) in the centre of Newmarket for free parking (not available on bloodstock sale days). ⊖ Train to Newmarket from Ipswich and Cambridge, or bus from London Victoria, Stansted, Cambridge or Great Yarmouth. Rail and bus stations are about 20 minutes' walk from museum or 5 minutes by taxi. ① Apr to Oct, Tue to Sun 10am to 5pm; July and Aug, Mon to Sun and bank hols 10am to 5pm. 💷 Adult £3.50; child (5 to 15 yrs old) £1.50; senior citizen £2.50. ♿ Fully accessible for wheelchairs.

National Marine Aquarium

Rope Walk, Coxside, Plymouth, Devon PL4 0LP   ☎ *(01752) 600301*

Quality ★★★★ **Facilities 🐟🐟🐟🐟🐟** **Value for money £££**
Highlights   Excellent layout; informative display boards for each exhibit
Drawbacks   Poorly signposted from city centre

What's there   Opened to the public in May 1998, the National Marine Aquarium is a stunning building with an excellent waterside location. Displays are staggered over three levels – visitors begin at the top and work their way down.

The sequence of displays begins with a **moorland stream** and ends in the impressive **shark theatre**. Along the way you encounter displays on the **estuary**, the **shore and shallow sea**, the **deep reef** and the **coral seas**. Each section has wonderful exhibits of fish and plant life, and you can get a closer look at crabs, starfish and anemones in the **discovery pools**. Clearly illustrated boards make it simple to identify the fish in the various tanks.

The most impressive sections include the coral seas display and the shark theatre. The **world of seahorses** features the largest collection of seahorses in Europe and a unique seahorse breeding programme.

Set aside a full morning or afternoon to visit.

Information/tours/guides   A full-colour souvenir guidebook (£2) gives in-depth descriptions for every display. A free leaflet with a map is included in the admission price. Children's activity leaflets are available free of charge from the enquiry desk in the arrival area. Guides are normally dotted around the aquarium (although we saw only one when we inspected). They are enthusiastic and happy to answer any questions visitors may have.

When to visit   Fish are fed daily in the deep reef (on Monday, Friday and at weekends divers go into the tank to do this) and on Monday, Wednesday and Friday in the shark theatre. Daily talks are held around the discovery pools, and themed talks take place every day in the shark theatre, the shoreline and the deep reef auditorium – check the noticeboard in the arrival area for times.

Age appeal Children of all ages will enjoy a visit, especially if it includes one of the daily talks or feeding sessions. There are no steep stairways or corridors for those with walking difficulties to negotiate.

Food and drink A large, modern café is situated beside the aquarium. Hot lunches (including fish of the day) are served until 4pm. A standard range of sandwiches, a selection of cakes, and hot and cold drinks are also on offer.

Shops The route around the aquarium exits into the large shopping area. Merchandise has a distinctly marine theme and includes everything from cuddly fish toys and colouring books for children to beautiful artwork for adults.

🚗 Situated by the harbour. There is a large pay-and-display car park located nearby. Follow town centre signs to the Barbican – brown signs for the aquarium are almost non-existent. ⊖ City Bus 25 from Plymouth rail station to the Barbican. ◷ Apr to Nov, Mon to Sun 10am to 6pm; Dec to Mar, Mon to Sun 11am to 5pm. 💷 Adult £6.50; child (4 to 15 yrs old) £4; senior citizen, student £5; family ticket (2 adults + 2 children) £19; carer for disabled visitor free. Friends of the Aquarium admitted free. ♿ The entire building is completely accessible with a lift available if required. A small number of wheelchairs are available free of charge and should be pre-booked.

National Motor Museum, Beaulieu

Beaulieu, Brockenhurst, Hampshire SO42 7ZN   ☎ *(01590) 612345*
🖥 *www.beaulieu.co.uk*

Quality ★ ★ ★ ★   **Facilities 👜 👜 👜**   **Value for money ££££**
Highlights Wide-ranging appeal, with motor museum, house, abbey and grounds; plenty of activities for children
Drawbacks Old-fashioned presentation techniques; dated and slightly shabby facilities; no prices on publicity leaflets

---

What's there The attraction divides into three parts: the National Motor Museum, the Abbey and the Palace House. **The National Motor Museum's** main collection, displayed in a large, two-storey hangar, is roughly grouped by themes, such as vintage cars, sports cars, record breakers, motorbikes and commercial vehicles. Enthusiasts will make a beeline for their own interests, but there are enough unusual exhibits to keep general spectators happy. Examples include the 1964 Peel P50, 'the only production car made in the Isle of Man', which has a grab handle at the back rather than reverse gear; a **1962 BMW bubble car**, which had a maximum speed of 50mph; **Donald Campbell's Bluebird**, which set the land speed record of 403.1 mph in 1964; a 1972 Mini in the shape of an Outspan orange; and a 1926 Eccles caravan.

Each individual car in the Motor Museum has a typed label with a short history of its importance and development, but there are few modern interactive displays or presentations. Many of the vehicles are in full working order and you can look down into the workshops and see restorers at work. There's also a small interactive section where you can find out how the clutch and gearbox work and investigate the principles behind internal combustion and suspension.

The main emphasis is on the **technical developments** rather than the social context – for example, there is no mention of the current environmental concerns about traffic – but there is a **reconstructed historic garage**, complete with forecourt petrol pumps, piles of tyres and cycle repair section. 'Wheels' is a quaint, gentle ride past tableaux depicting the history of motoring. A small selection of works from the **Shell Art Collection** is also on display, including posters from Shell lorries in the 1920s and 1930s.

Next door is a **collection of 'rides'**: mini-bikes for children (free); radio-controlled cars (50p a go); Fast Trax, an arcade of video-racing games (£1 a game); and the Vauxhall Driving Experience, a simulator that takes you from a sedate 1920s potter through off-the-road thrills and spills to a racing spin (£2.50 extra).

From the Motor Museum it's a five-minute stroll through the gardens to the Abbey or Palace House, but many people prefer to take the high-level monorail, which passes through the roof of the Motor Museum, or the open-topped veteran bus (both free).

Beaulieu Abbey Church was founded in 1204 and was once the largest Cistercian church in England, but little is left of it now save part of one wall and the pillar bases. The main remaining structure is the Domus, which was once the living quarters of the lay brothers, who carried out the cooking and maintenance tasks around the Abbey. It now houses an exhibition on monastic life. Recorded Gregorian chant echoes off the plain white vaulting, adding to the atmosphere. Upstairs, a series of modern wall hangings tells the story of the founding of the monastery. The herb garden in the cloisters is particularly attractive, and a tranquil place to escape the crowds.

From the moment you enter the **Palace House**, you're in no doubt that this is a family home. Ancestral and contemporary Montagu portraits grace the walls, and family memorabilia are dotted about. The current Lord Montagu's personal memories of growing up in the house feature on typed labels and in the guidebook. There are no tours or guides as such, but staff in the Palace House, dressed as a Victorian maid, cook and housekeeper, act out their parts accordingly, with great gusto and enthusiasm, chastising visitors for their dress sense – 'Look, she's come out in her drawers!' – and predicting that the fad for automobiles won't last. Highlights include the **Upper Drawing Room**, a former chapel that still has the piscina where the priest washed the altar vessels, and the **fan-vaulted Dining Room** and Lower Drawing Room, with splendid stone fireplaces.

Information/tours/guides A leaflet on arrival provides a detailed map and information on facilities and services. Because of the competent labelling and straightforward orientation you don't really need a guidebook or tour. The mini-guide (50p) is perfectly sufficient. However, separate full-colour guide-books to the National Motor Museum and Palace House and Abbey (£2 each) provide much more wide-ranging information and are good-value souvenirs.

When to visit Most of the main attractions are all under cover, so Beaulieu is a good wet-weather choice. Throughout the year there are various events, including car rallies on summer weekends, autojumbles, veteran car auctions, and motorbike displays.

Age appeal This attraction provides wide appeal across the age range. Younger children can have a go on mini-bikes and veteran cars; older children can follow the Time Trail, where they scratch off the letters of correct answers to multiple choice questions. Teenagers may be happiest in the arcade of racing video games in Fast Trax and on the Vauxhall Driving Experience. Adults and non-car enthusiasts may prefer the gentler pursuits of the Abbey and Palace House.

During the school summer holidays, Fun Workshops (extra charge) offer activities such as medieval calligraphy, spinning and making stained-glass windows.

Food and drink The light and airy Brabazon Food Court provides hot and cold food and drinks on a self-service/canteen basis. Pre-packed sand-wiches include egg and cress (£1.65) and cheese and tomato or pickle, and ham and mustard. Hot dishes, such as fish and chips, lemon and pepper chicken, and cottage pie, cost around £5. You can picnic anywhere in the grounds except around the Palace House.

Shops The Motor Museum shop, in the entrance building, sells a wide variety of car memorabilia, from books and scale model cars to branded bags and hats. The Victorian Kitchen Shop in the Palace House is much smaller and concentrates on food and kitchenware, some of which is home-produced (for example Palace House jams and chutneys £1.99), and the rest is generic (Jacksons tea, Walkers shortbread, etc.). The third outlet, between the Abbey and the Palace House, sells luxurious toiletries.

Other facilities There are baby-changing facilities in the Motor Museum. The main toilets are beneath Brabazon Food Court.

🚗 Follow brown signs from M27 junction 2 to Beaulieu. Free parking. ⊖ From Brockenhurst railway station, take a taxi to Beaulieu (six miles). Alternatively, catch train to Lymington Town, then bus no 112 to Beaulieu. ⏰ April to Sept 10am to 6pm; Oct to Mar 10am to 5pm (closed 25 Dec). 💷 Adult £9, child (4–16 yrs old) £6.50, senior citizen, student £8, disabled person £5.30 to £8 (depending on age). Family ticket (2 adults + 3 children or 1 adult + 4 children) £29.50. Free re-entry tickets, valid for six days following your first visit. ♿ Motor Museum, Abbey and restaurant wheelchair accessible (but only the entrance hall and picture gallery in the Palace House). Leaflet gives further details of access for wheelchairs and pushchairs; disabled parking; disabled toilet in the Brabazon restaurant complex; free wheelchairs on loan.

National Museum Of Photography, Film and Television

Bradford, West Yorkshire BD1 1NQ ☎ *(01274) 202030*
🖰 *www.nmpft.org.uk*

Quality ★★★★★ **Facilities** 👜👜👜👜👜 **Value for money £££££**
Highlights Thought-provoking captions; variety of activities
Drawbacks Very expensive souvenir guidebook

What's there It may not have the snappiest of names, but this recently revamped museum provides a concise and entertaining **history of the**

camera, and life as seen through its lens. Developments from the first hazy portraits to the latest in digital technology are charted, high (and low) points in broadcasting archived, and the social and psychological impacts explored.

The **Kodak Gallery** on the lower ground floor has an extensive collection of cameras through the ages, from cumbersome nineteenth-century contraptions to the latest miniature devices, and details the changes using period settings. In **Wired World**, digital TV and interactivity are explained, and you can paint a bedspread with live images.

Things get rather technical on Level 3, where assiduous adults can study the insides of film cameras, and the kids can monkey about on a **magic carpet** (demonstrating the blue-screen effect used for manipulating television images). News-gathering is also explored, with thought-provoking comments on the presentation of information.

The top floor is devoted to **advertising**, highlighting the subliminal messages behind the most popular ads, and to the power of **popular TV**. Once you are sitting comfortably in your private booth in **TV Heaven**, you can revisit one of your favourite moments from a video archive of around 300 programmes.

The museum also has three **cinemas** – two devoted to movie classics, arthouse films and mainstream releases, and the third housing a giant screen for showing the large-format **IMAX** films, which usually concentrate on visually spectacular landscapes.

Information/tours/guides The free floor-plan leaflet lists the exhibitions on each of the four levels. At £9.95, the guidebook is a pricey but a comprehensive souvenir. However, although fascinating histories and insights are captured among its 100 colour pages, the book is certainly not essential to your enjoyment of the museum.

When to visit You could visit the museum any time – especially given that all the attractions are indoors – though at weekends and school holidays it gets very busy.

Age appeal The extensive library of past TV programmes from *Blue Peter* to *The Borgias*, assorted antiquated photographic equipment and hands-on optical and electrical experiments should offer something to appeal across the board. Families can create their own TV programmes at regular workshops (£10 for adults; up to 3 accompanying children free) and supervised fun days are put on during the school holidays.

Food and drink The foyer café is large and ambitious, offering a good range of fast food (sausage, chips and beans, £3.50) and healthier options, such as a vegetable stir fry cooked in front of you (£3.95). Fresh pasta dishes, pre-packed sandwiches and cakes are also on sale. A separate room is set aside for those bringing picnics.

Shops The foyer shop is well stocked with film stills of the stars, available on postcards, posters and movie calendars. A generous selection of film and photography books, both academic and more lightweight, and assorted TV and film spin-off toys are available. A small children's toy shop is tucked away off the main foyer.

🚗 Well signposted in Bradford city centre; plenty of car parks within walking distance. ⊖ Bradford Interchange railway station, with rail, bus and taxi services, is a 5-minute walk. Bradford Forster Square station (10 minutes' walk) has intercity rail services. ☉ *Museum* Tue to Sun, bank hols 10am to 6pm; *café* 10am to 9pm; *cinemas* 10am to late; *IMAX* 10.30am to 5.30pm on the hour. Closed 24, 25 and 31 Dec; 1 Jan. 💷 *Museum* free (donations welcome; suggested amount £2); *cinemas* adult £4.20; child (5 to 15 yrs), student, senior citizen, disabled, unemployed £2.90; *IMAX* adult £5.80; child/concession £4; saver ticket (1 adult + 2 children) £11. ♿ Special parking; museum fully accessible; tactile and Braille guides; IMAX and cinemas have wheelchair spaces.

National Railway Museum

Leeman Road, York YO26 4XJ ☎ *(01904) 621261; 24-hour information (01904) 686286* 🖥 *www.nrm.org.uk*

Quality ★★★★   **Facilities** 👤👤👤👤   **Value for money ££££**

Highlights Well thought-out displays that bring the history of the railway alive for enthusiasts and general public alike

Drawbacks Some displays slightly confusing; disappointing restaurant

What's there Reputedly the world's largest railway museum, this museum is trainspotters' heaven: occupying two vast halls and a new £4 million extension (The Works), it is packed with fascinating exhibits on every aspect of railway travel.

Visits usually start in the **Great Hall**, a huge hangar in which beautifully maintained classic engines radiate outwards from a central turntable like the spokes of a vast wheel (regular demonstrations show how the turntable operates). Among and around the engines is a series of well-presented **exhibitions on the history of the 'permanent way'** (the technical term for the rail track), including the story of early locomotives, the development of Eurostar and the Channel Tunnel. Many of the displays make good use of **multi-media devices** such as videos and computers, and children especially will enjoy the hands-on presentations – among them a chance to sort some letters for a section on the history of the Royal Mail.

An extensive **model railway** complements the full-size versions on display.

Above the Great Hall a row of **balcony galleries** allows you to look down on to the engines below; here you can also see an exhibition of **railway paintings** and a short **film** on the changing liveries of trains, following the history from private ownership, through nationalisation after World War II, to re-privatisation in the 1990s.

The Works, accessed from the Great Hall, is the latest addition to the museum. In its Workshop you can watch engineers carrying out **conservation and restoration** work on various vehicles, while the Warehouse is an enormous, sprawling treasure trove of railway **memorabilia**. In addition, an extensive display entitled 'The Working Railway' looks at signalling and communication (it even has a live link to York's signal box), and you can match the electronic display with actual trains at the trackside balcony.

The **Station Hall** (formerly a working station) is devoted mainly to carriages, and you can wander along the platforms peering in through the windows at the reconstructed interiors from different eras. At one end of the hall the **Palaces on Wheels** exhibition charts the history of royal trains; a model Queen Victoria can be seen in one of her restored railway carriages. Beyond the main buildings an interactive **learning centre**, **miniature railway** and a **steam train** (seasonal, and not every day) complete the collection.

Information/tours/guides Tickets include a map of the museum, while all of the displays are well labelled and explanations are supplemented by videos and models where appropriate. Guided tours of The Works (about 15 minutes) are offered twice a day. The guidebook is beautifully presented, packed with information, and very good value (£3.50).

When to visit Any time, but more is going on in summer (including the steam railway).

Age appeal This museum should appeal to a broad range of visitors, with plenty of hands-on, interactive displays for children.

Food and drink A restaurant, Brief Encounter, is situated in the Station Hall and serves full meals and light snacks; prices are higher than the quality of the food, and the ambience is marred by the smell of oil and the continuous playing of the national anthem in the nearby royal train exhibition. The Whistle Stop café in the Main Hall serves lunches and light refreshments and there is a barbecue in the South Yard (these two are open only in the holiday season).

Shops The gift shop sells a reasonable range of souvenirs, from the complete range of Thomas the Tank Engine toys to old railway posters, videos, books, sweets and soft toys. Real train aficionados could be disappointed.

🚐 Follow signs provided on all approaches to the city of York, including A1. Long-stay car park (extra charge). ⊖ 5 minutes' walk from York rail station. A road train runs to museum from Minster every 30 minutes (10am to 6pm Apr to Oct). ⊙ 10am to 6pm. Closed 24 to 26 Dec. 🎫 Adult £6.50; child (under 17 yrs old), senior citizen free; unemployed, student, disabled person £4 (essential carer for disabled admitted free). ♿ Ramps and chairlifts provide access to most parts; lift to balcony gallery. Wheelchairs available at entrances. Free disabled parking by city entrance.

National Waterways Museum

Llanthony Warehouse, Gloucester Docks, Gloucester GL1 2EH
☎ *(01452) 318054* 📠 *(01452) 318066* 🖥 *www.nwm.demon.co.uk*

Quality ★★★★	Facilities 🏛🏛🏛	Value for money ££££

Highlights 'Canal mania' exhibition is a clever interpretation of the historical information

Drawbacks Boat trip is rather dull

What's there The museum is located in a tall warehouse in the historic dock area of Gloucester. Around it are several other museums and attractions, as well as the docks themselves, which constitute the most inland port in the UK, now undergoing something of a renaissance as a tourist attraction.

The **museum** proper is on three floors, taking the visitor, self-guided, through the history of 'canal mania' from 1793 to the pleasure-boat industry of today. All sorts of media are used to present the facts, from boards, videos, audio displays and soundtracks to old newspaper cuttings, waxworks, computers and anecdotes – sometimes hilarious – about the people involved. Featured in the museum are engineering achievements including tunnels, locks and aqueducts; boat-building and canal-building; tolls and transported goods; life onboard the boats; the passing of the canal age and the rise of the railways; pulleys and winches; folk art, and much more. There are some fascinating interactive exhibits – don't miss the chance to put on a diver's helmet and see real fish swimming in a **model lock**.

Outside the museum you will find four old **working boats** to clamber on and peer inside, a traditional blacksmith at work, and various complicated wooden **models** of boats in differing stages of completion.

Visitors can take an optional boat trip along a fairly dull stretch of navigation, with a commentator providing anecdotes and historical quips.

Allow up to two hours for the museum, and half an hour for the boat trip. You could allow a little extra time for a wander round the docks, too.

Information/tours/guides Self-guided throughout. A map of the dock area is provided, but no museum guidebook is necessary. Guided tours of the whole dock area are offered several times each afternoon during the summer except Sunday (2.30pm only). The boat trip costs £2.50 for adults, £2 for children, students and senior citizens – less if you buy a combined ticket. The trips run at weekends before Easter, then daily until the end of October.

When to visit All year round for the museum itself, but fine weather is preferable for the boat trip. There are several courses on offer, for example blacksmithing and tug-driving, and special themed events at weekends.

Age appeal All ages are catered for here.

Food and drink A small cafeteria on the waterfront offers basic fare such as Gloucester sausage baguettes (£2.50), home-made soup and bread (£1.80), baked potatoes (£2.75), tea, coffee and soft drinks.

Shops The shop's range is rather uninspiring – soft toys, luminous rubbers, Beanie toys for children, and a small collection of books on waterways for adults.

🚗 From M5 follow brown signs to Gloucester's Historic Docks area. Ample car parking (pay and display) in dock area. ⊖ Museum is 10-minute walk from Gloucester's bus and railway stations. ① Daily 10am to 5pm. Closed 25 Dec. Last admission 4pm. 💷 *Museum only* adult £4.75; child/senior citizen £3.75; family tickets (1 adult, 2 children) £11; (2 adults, 2 children) £12; (2 adults, 3 children) £13. *Museum and boat trip* adult £6.50; child/senior citizen £5.25; family tickets (1 adult, 2 children) £16.50; (2 adults, 2 children) £19; (2 adults, 3 children) £22. ♿ Full access (except floating exhibits).

Newby Hall and Gardens

Newby Hall Estate, Ripon, North Yorkshire HG4 5AE ☎ *(01423) 322583*
☏ *www.newbyhall.co.uk* ☏ *info@newbyhall.co.uk*

Quality ★★★★★ **Facilities 👆 👆 👆 👆** **Value for money £££**

Highlights The house itself, designed by Adam and containing period furniture; superb gardens

Drawbacks No prices on publicity leaflet or outside main gates

---

What's there Newby Hall is an excellent example of a house altered and redesigned in neo-classical style during the eighteenth century – by Robert Adam, among others. Much of the décor dates from the tenure of William Weddell (1736–92). A member of the Dilettanti Club, he returned from a Grand Tour in 1766 full of ideas for altering and enlarging the house to display his collection of classical sculpture. Another wing was added during Victorian times by Robert de Grey Vyner, great-grandfather of the current owner, Robin Compton.

The house is full of impressive Adam designs, most notably in the **tapestry room**, which features Gobelin tapestries on the walls as well as tapestry-upholstered Chippendale chairs and sofas. The **statue gallery**, which is Roman in style, provides a sympathetic environment for Weddell's sculpture collection, including the **Barberini Venus** and a **Roman bath** of Pavonazzetto marble. Other striking rooms include the **entrance hall**, complete with martial trophy panels, the **circular room**, which features painted 'grotesque' work, and the **library**, containing an apse flanked by Corinthian pillars. By contrast, the **Victorian billiards room** is all dark wood panelling, while the **chamber pot room**, displaying the unusual collection of Robert de Grey Vyner, adds a humorous touch.

The grounds cover 25 acres and are made up of a patchwork of individual **formal gardens** including the autumnal garden, a wonderful rock garden, a species rose garden and a tropical garden. Rare and interesting plants can be seen here, together with an impressive herbaceous border that sweeps down to the banks of the river Ure. Gardeners may like to know that the National Collection of Cornus is held at Newby. The grounds also offer a **woodland discovery walk**, a **miniature railway**, and **paddling pond** and play area for children.

A visit to the house will take at least an hour. You should set aside at least three hours for a comprehensive tour of the grounds.

Information/tours/guides The purpose-built visitor centre next to the car park houses a small display on the history of the estate as well as a gift shop. Two full-colour guidebooks, one for the house, one for the gardens (£2.50 each or £3.50 for both), suggest comprehensive tours. Leaflets on shorter seasonal garden walks (20p each) and for the woodland discovery walk (40p) are also available. Guides in the house are friendly and happy to answer questions.

When to visit Seasonal highlights in the gardens include Sylvia's garden in spring, the rose pergola during midsummer, and the autumn garden in August and September.

Age appeal Children will enjoy the gardens, the miniature railway and the play area.

Food and drink A self-service restaurant serves hot food at lunchtime (e.g. lasagne, Cumberland sausage casserole and chicken and broccoli bake), as well as soup, a standard range of sandwiches, a selection of desserts and cakes and hot and cold drinks. Picnic area.

Shops Goods include foodstuffs (biscuits, jams), toiletries, and a good range of books for adults and children.

🚗 On the B6265 off the A1(M): follow signs. Free parking next to visitor centre. ⊖ Bus: Harrogate and District Travel 142 Ripon-Skelton-on-Ure (long walk from bus stop to house). Call 01423 566061 for more details. ⊙ *House* 12 to 5pm Tues to Sun and bank hols 1 Apr to 30 Sept. Last admission 4.30pm. *Gardens and restaurant* 1 Apr to 30 Sept 11am to 5.30pm Tues to Sun and bank hols. Last admission 5pm. 💷 *House and gardens* adult £6.50; child £4 (under-4s free); disabled £4; senior citizen £5.40; family ticket (2 adults + 2/3 children) £20/£24. *Gardens only* adult £4.30; child £3.20 (under-4s free); disabled £3.20; senior citizen £4; family ticket (2 adults + 2/3 children) £14.80/£18. *Ride on miniature train* £1. *River cruise* £1.50. ♿ Gardens, ground floor of house, restaurant and shop accessible. Wheelchair available (ring ahead to book). Wheelchair route signposted in gardens. Disabled toilets and parking.

Newcastle Discovery Museum

Blandford Square, Newcastle NE1 4JA ☎ *0191–232 6789*

Quality ★★ **Facilities 🏛 🏛** **Value for money £££**
Highlights Free admission; good signing
Drawbacks Rather old-fashioned design, except in the Science Factory

---

What's there Spread over three floors in a vast Victorian building, these eclectic galleries focus on discovery, both literally (as in the **Maritime Gallery**, with its numerous model ships) and metaphorically (as in the **Pioneers Gallery**, which pays homage to inventors of Tyneside and traces the history of Newcastle and its people).

Themes of other galleries include **A Soldier's Life**, which describes a soldier's daily routine through stories, models, photographs and war memorabilia, and **Fashion Works**, which explores the history of fashion from Victorian times.

Turbina, the world's first ship driven by steam turbine, is over 100 feet in length: although you cannot go on board, computer touch-screens provide virtual tours and further information.

The **Science Factory** is the gallery with the greatest appeal for children and makes the rest of the museum feel sombre by comparison. Here you will encounter a ball that floats on air, concave mirrors that invert reflections, and a teasing game called 'sound fix' which emits rather unpleasant human sounds, much to the delight of young visitors. Also on display is a **zoetrope**, built in 1868, a popular Victorian amusement before photography was invented. However, apart from its appeal to children, the gallery is not overly impressive.

The museum is large, with ten galleries in total (including the Science Factory): allow about half an hour per gallery.

Information/tours/guides No guided tours or guidebooks. Free map of the galleries.

When to visit Any time: the museum is open all year round and everything is inside.

Age appeal Broad, but children will get most fun out of the interactive Science Factory.

Food and drink Tucked at the back of the Power House gallery is a small self-service canteen offering a fairly limited choice of sandwiches (£1.40), jacket potatoes (£2.35) and slices of cake (60p to £1).

Shops A few items are on sale by the entrance, most of them pocket-money purchases (pencils, rubbers etc.), but you can also buy a Lady Anne dress-up doll for £5.95 and books on local history.

🚗 From A1/M1, join A184, cross Redheugh Bridge and follow city signs to museum in west Newcastle, close to Central Station. Pay-and-display car park in front of museum (80p for 2 hours). ⊖ Metro to Central Station, then 5-minute walk. ⊕ Mon to Sat 10am to 5pm, Sun 2 to 5pm. Closed Good Fri, 25 to 26 Dec, 1 Jan. 💷 Free. ♿ Good, with disabled toilets, lifts and ramps.

Norwich Cathedral

62 The Close, Norwich NR1 4EH   ☎ *(01603) 764385*

Quality ★★★★★   **Facilities 💺 💺 💺 💺**   **Value for money ££££**

Highlights Nave with Romanesque arcading; 1,106 roof bosses depicting Bible scenes; Cathedral Close

Drawbacks Variable quality of guided tour

What's there This fine **Norman cathedral** was founded in 1096 by Bishop Herbert de Losinga. The unimposing entrance, at the west front, belies the splendour of the arcaded **nave** inside, with its intricately carved **roof bosses** depicting scenes from the Old and New Testament. Here, a well-positioned mirror allows you to see some of these clearly, but binoculars could also be useful. The choir, dating from the fifteenth century, has 64 beautifully carved **misericords**. A recently added feature of the choir, reminding us that Norwich Cathedral is an ongoing part of community life rather than a museum, is a concentric circular arrangement of benches made of Norfolk oak.

The **treasury** (entry free but donations welcome), in the reliquary arch, was once used for displaying holy relics but now houses the historic plate of the parishes of the diocese. Be sure to look up at its **ceiling** to see the largest expanse of medieval wall paintings to have survived in the cathedral. The tranquil two-tier **cloisters** boast further examples of intricate roof bosses.

Outside, take a walk around the **Close** (the largest in England), with its elegant, historic buildings, to the river's edge and Pull's Ferry, the former watergate to the Close.

Information/tours/guides Free guide/plan on entry. The full-colour guidebook (£2.50) effectively describes the cathedral's history and highlights. From June to October free guided tours are offered several times a day, beginning at the west end by the information desk – check there for times. Quality of guides is variable. Restaurant houses an exhibition (informative but rather dry) about the history of the cathedral.

When to visit Any time.

Age appeal Mainly of interest to adults and older children although younger children might enjoy the 'animal hunt' (ask for the free leaflet).

Food and drink The small but atmospheric restaurant in the upper tier of cloisters serves a rather limited selection of sandwiches and rolls (£1.80 to £2.95) and light lunches such as soup, baked potatoes or quiche with salad. It can get crowded at lunchtimes, and too few tables and chairs mean visitors have to squash together on the pew-style seating. Opening times are Monday to Saturday 10.30am to 4.30pm.

Shops Attractively presented shop, although walkways are rather narrow. Merchandise comprises gifts and souvenirs such as spoons, paperweights, tea-towels, shortbread and chocolates as well as a large selection of Christian books, local history books and greetings cards.

🚐 Signed from city centre. Park in one of the nearby public car parks. ⊖ Norwich station; 5-10 minute walk. ⊘ Daily 7.30am to 6pm (7pm mid-May to mid-Sept). Cathedral library open Wed 10am to 1pm and 2 to 5pm (entrance in south walk of cloister). ⊞ Free – but suggested donation of £3 per adult. ♿ Disabled parking at south door. Ramp at south transept entrance. One disabled toilet available – ask staff. Restaurant not accessible to wheelchair users.

Nunnington Hall

Nunnington, York, North Yorkshire YO62 5UY ☎ *(01439) 748283*

Quality ★★★ Facilities 🏛 🏛 🏛 Value for money £££
Highlights Friendly, knowledgeable room guides; pleasant outdoor picnic area
Drawbacks Cramped toilets

What's there As a Crown property during the reigns of Elizabeth I and James I, this fine country house has had its share of illustrious owners including William Parr and Robert Huicke, doctor to Elizabeth I. The present building, which dates from the sixteenth and seventeenth centuries, was modernised in 1921 by Colonel and Lady Fife, who bequeathed it to the National Trust in 1952.

A well-organised tour route allows visitors to wander through the Hall at their own pace. Notable rooms include the **stone room**, the **oak hall**, and **Mrs Fife's bedroom**, complete with an unusual bed painted in the neo-classical style of the late eighteenth century. Excellent examples of period furniture survive, along with splendid tapestries and paintings. An extensive **collection of Victorian toys**, including a baby house, is displayed in the nursery.

The **Carlisle collection of miniature rooms** is housed on the top floor of the Hall. One-eighth of their 'real' size, these contain such scaled-down accessories as a set of tiny playing cards and a minute copy of *The Times*.

The **walled garden**, though not extensive, is remarkable for having escaped the eighteenth-century tendency to open up the landscape surrounding the house. A pleasant picnic area overlooks the duck pond.

Set aside at least an hour to see the Hall and another hour to visit the gardens, with their strutting peacocks (allow longer if you plan to picnic).

Information/tours/guides A full-colour guidebook (£2.50) covers the history of house and gardens and suggests a tour of the property. A separate guide for children costs £1 and a house quiz leaflet costs 50p. Room guides are knowledgeable and happy to answer questions.

When to visit High summer for the hybrid roses on the Hall's east front. Special events, including art exhibitions and open-air performances of Shakespeare, take place throughout the year. Extra charges apply in some instances.

Age appeal The children's guide will help older children to get value from their visit; younger children will enjoy the ducks and peacocks in the garden.

Food and drink The Hall's former sitting room is now a table-service tea room offering hot and cold food at lunchtime as well as a good selection of sandwiches (Wensleydale cheese with cucumber chutney, cream cheese with grated carrot and nuts, etc.), cakes, cream teas and hot and cold drinks. Picnic tables overlook the duck pond.

Shops A reasonable range of good-quality merchandise is available in the shop including a range of children's books and 'musical' jumpers.

🚗 4½ miles south-east of Helmsley off B1257 Malton-Helmsley road. ⊖ Yorkshire Coastliner 94 Malton-Helmsley from Malton railway station (tel. (01653) 692556). Otherwise Scarborough & District 128 Scarborough-Helmsley (passes close to Scarborough railway station) (tel. (01609) 780780). ⏱ 1 Apr to 29 Oct daily exc. Mon & Tue 1.30 to 5pm (4pm during Apr and Oct). Open Tue 1 June to 31 August and bank hols. 💷 *Hall and gardens* adult £4; child £2; family ticket (2 adult + up to 3 children) £10. *Gardens only* adult £1.50; child free. Group rates (15 or more) available. NT members and disabled carers admitted free. ♿ All rooms on ground floor of Hall accessible, as are tea room and gardens. Wheelchair available if pre-booked. Disabled visitors can be dropped at Hall entrance by arrangement. Disabled toilet. Braille guide.

Osborne House

York Avenue, Isle of Wight PO32 6JY   ☎ *(01983) 200022*

Quality ★★	Facilities 🍴🍴	Value for money ££

Highlights	Well preserved royal home; durbar room; horse-drawn carriage ride; Swiss cottage for children's collection
Drawbacks	Little interpretation so guidebook essential; shabby café by front entrance; off-hand staff

What's there Osborne House was much loved by Queen Victoria, and visitors today will get a feel for the family life of this enduring monarch, who died here in 1901. The house, built to an Italianate design, was used as a holiday home by Victoria, Albert and their (large) family. Today its rooms, preserved much as they were then, offer an endearing mix of the personal and the grand, and visitors who have seen the film *Mrs Brown*, which was shot here, may recognise much of the property.

The central room of the main wing is the **council room**, for meetings of the Queen's Privy Council. Look up at the ceiling at the Badge of the Garter and other royal emblems, and notice, at either side of the door, the portraits of the Queen and Prince Albert. Having learned how to handle a billiard cue while at Osborne, the Queen used to play against the ladies of the household after lunch in the richly decorated **billiard room**, adorned with columns of imitation marble. In the similarly grand **drawing room** are some family mementoes – life-sized statues of Victoria's nine children, carved in the 1840s and '50s and representing characters such as Peace and Plenty.

In the **dining room**, which contains a surprisingly small table, are displayed family portraits including a copy of the family group painting by Winterhalter. (Children filling in the youngsters' activity sheet will be astounded to discover that young Prince Alfred was dressed just like a girl.) It was in this room that the Queen's body lay in state before being taken to Windsor – a fact commemorated by a brass plaque on the floor.

Upstairs is the **nursery suite** with small furniture for the children – contemporary records tell of it being full of toys, but today it looks rather bare. Moving into the private apartments, you pass through the **Prince Consort's bathroom** – with a rather grand shower cubicle – and his combined dressing room and study, preserved by Victoria after his death. In the **Queen's sitting room** two desks stand side by side; she would work on her despatch boxes at the one on the left while Albert sat at the other one (notice that the drawers are shallower to allow for the Prince's higher chair) in his capacity as her private secretary.

The **Queen's bedroom** is dominated by a large plaque above the bed marking her death. Below it you can see the pocket for Albert's pocket-watch and on his side of the bed a posthumous portrait of him displayed by the Queen in all the royal residences.

Down the corridor on the right is the **horn room**, decked out with a set of furniture made out of antlers; on the wall is **Landseer**'s sentimental portrait *The Queen Called Sorrow,* showing her at Osborne on her pony Flora with John Brown, her Highland servant, wearing the mourning tartan she designed for him.

The last room on the tour, the **durbar room**, is quite stunning – a vast state banqueting hall, Indian in style, with heavily embellished white walls. The theme is echoed in the display cases, which contain many Indian presents given to the Queen on her jubilees of 1887 and 1897.

Allow about one hour for the tour of the house.

In the grounds you can ride in a **horse-drawn carriage** to the Swiss cottage and the royal children's play area. Here you may encounter long queues of visitors keen to see the individual **gardens** the children were encouraged to work on, their **kitchen**, with its small-scale range and dresser stacked with utensils, and their **collections** of items such as stuffed birds and Egyptian artefacts. The Victoria fort and Albert barracks still look fine for playing at soldiers. Victoria's **bathing machine** is also on display.

Allow one hour for the grounds – and another hour in summer for queues and getting there and back.

Information/tours/guides The colour guidebook (£3.95) is essential, and there is a good free activity sheet for children.

When to visit Best on a fine day. Saturday still tends to be change-over day on the island so it may be quieter then.

Age appeal Good for all ages.

Food and drink Unfortunately the attractive table-service tea room in Swiss cottage serves only full teas (£4.35). There is also a shabby self-service café by main gate, with children's adventure playground nearby.

Shops The shop in the reception area sells Victoriana and a typical English Heritage range of souvenirs.

🚗 1 mile south-east of Cowes, well signposted. Good car park. ⊖ Rail: 7 miles from Ryde Esplanade. Bus: for details tel. 01983 827005. ☉ 1 Apr to 31 Oct 10am to 5pm (grounds close at 6pm); 1 Nov to 17 Dec and 4 Feb to 31 Mar 2000 Sun, Mon, Wed, Thur 10am to 2.30pm on pre-booked guided tour only. Closed 18 Dec to 31 Jan. 💷 *House and grounds* adult £6.90; child £3.50; student, senior citizens, unemployed £5.20; family ticket £17.30. *Grounds only* adult £3.50, child £1.80, concessions £2.60. Free to EH members and disabled visitors' carers. ♿ Grounds and ground floor only. Disabled visitors can be dropped at the house.

The Oxford Story

6 Broad Street, Oxford OX1 3AJ ☎ *(01865) 728822*

Quality ★★ **Facilities** 👜👜👜 **Value for money ££**
Highlights Europe's longest 'dark' ride
Drawbacks Tacky 'Student Life' video

What's there 'You need a key to unlock the door of Oxford. The Oxford Story attempts to provide that key.' The carefully chosen words of Lord Jenkins, Chancellor of Oxford University, writ large at the beginning of the official guide to this sight, make one wonder whether it succeeds. Given that the Oxford Story does not hold any material from the university and is not even set in a university building, there is a good chance that the whole experience may leave some visitors with a rather hollow feeling when they come out.

Occupying the three-storey former Blackwell's book warehouse, what the Oxford Story does offer is Europe's longest **'dark' ride**, in which visitors can follow the 800-year history of the university through a series of **tableaux and pictures**, while listening to a commentary narrated by Magnus Magnusson over the headphones. Displays feature some of the university's most memorable events – such as the St Scholastica's Day massacre of 1355 in which 63 scholars were killed – and most famous students, from Roger Bacon to T.E. Lawrence. Lasting about half an hour, the ride is certainly interesting and far less fantastic than the ten-minute introductory video depicting the idealised life of an undergraduate, which could have come straight out of a university publicity pack and bears little resemblance to reality – spot the difference on a Saturday night after the pubs shut!

Information/tours/guides An audio commentary is provided in six languages, while a smart guidebook (£1.95) imparts a little additional information; however, it reads like an undergraduate prospectus in parts.

When to visit Avoid the peak season, as it is likely to become extremely crowded.

Age appeal A separate commentary is provided for children, but the sight has little of interest for them. Special children's events take place during most school holidays, involving competitions, face-painting and mask-making.

Food and drink None is available on the site.

Shops A smartly presented shop forces visitors to wander through twisting displays of university-themed souvenirs, including teddies sporting Oxford sweaters, cards, mugs and bits of jewellery; there is also a book section proudly displaying the works of famous former students, in particular J.R.R. Tolkien.

🚗 Close to the city centre and difficult to access directly by car; park-and-ride facilities around the city. ⊖ Within walking distance of Oxford railway station and bus station and fairly well signed (follow signs for Broad Street or Oxford Story). ⏰ Apr to Oct, Mon to Sun 9.30am to 5pm (Jul & Aug 9am to 6pm); Nov to Mar, Mon to Sun 10am to 4.30pm (Sat and Sun 5pm). Closed 25 Dec. 💷 Adult £5.70; child £4.70; concessions (students, senior citizens) £4.70; family ticket (2 adults + 2 children) £17.50; discounted rates available for groups of 20 or more and for those holding valid rail tickets and Guide Friday and Classic Oxford bus tour customers. ♿ Suitable for most disabled visitors; if you want to do the 'dark' ride, ring in advance (01865) 790055 to check on the restrictions.

Paignton Zoo Environmental Park

Totnes Road, Paignton, Devon TQ4 7EU ☎ *(01803) 527936*
📧 *www.paigntonzoo.demon.co.uk*

Quality ★★★★★ **Facilities** 👛👛👛👛👛 **Value for money** £££££
Highlights Great for families; logical layout; good educational information
Drawbacks Some steep areas may be difficult for prams and wheelchairs

What's there Paignton has an all-encompassing approach to zoo-keeping, with a big emphasis on conservation issues and education. The park is divided into various zones – **Wetland, Forest, Savannah** and **Desert** – and the animals live in the one that accords most closely with their natural habitat. So the Sumatran tigers are in the Forest, the cheetah in the Savannah and so on. The Marie le Fevre **Ape Centre** is home to orang-utans and gorillas, its windows sensitively camouflaged to allow for reasonably discreet viewing. The big glasshouse containing the Desert environment accommodates lizards dodging around the cacti and colourful finches and parrots plucking mealworm from artificial termite mounds. In each area visitors learn from the information panels about the threats posed to the animals in the wild as their habitats are destroyed.

There is a chance to find out about various species under threat closer to home, too, from moths to red-billed choughs, and the **Clennon Gorge Nature**

Trail is a pleasant 700-metre walk on which, if you are lucky, you may spot buzzards, water voles and grass snakes.

The park also offers some imaginative and fun ways to keep youngsters entertained. The **Ark** is an interactive zone for children, where they can try to match, on an exercise bike, the speeds at which various animals move, or to test their reaction times on hearing a lion's roar. For an extra 50p per person the **Jungle Express** will zip you around the **Gibbon Islands**.

Information/tours/guides As well as information boards, 'audio' points, with buttons to press for a commentary, are placed throughout the park. The guidebook (£2) is good value and has a useful map as well as lots of information on the animals and conservation efforts. Children's activity sheets are also available (£1.50/£1.60). The 'Feathered Feats' parrot show is one of several scheduled events along with snake encounters and various feeding sessions throughout the day.

When to visit Best enjoyed in fair weather. Arrive early and allow a whole day.

Age appeal Very broad and especially appealing to children.

Food and drink The light and airy restaurant has extra seating outside overlooking Gibbon Island. The food ranges from salads to burgers, with a decent choice of children's meals – though not cheap at £3.95 for a child's roast. For fast food, the 'kids' meal deal', comprising burger, sausage, nuggets, chips and a soft drink for £2.75, is good value.

Shops The gangways are rather narrow for buggies and pushchairs. Merchandise includes lots of fluffy toys and ethnic craft items, including banana natural paper and African carvings. Books and children's activities are also well represented. Gardeners may appreciate the 'jumbo-enriched zoopoo' (£3).

Off A385 Totnes Road. Follow brown signs from Paignton. ⊖ Stagecoach services from Torquay and Paignton. ① Daily 10am to 6pm (summer), dusk in winter. Closed 25 Dec. 💷 (1999) Adult £6; child (3–15) £4.90 (under-3s free); students/senior citizens £5.40; family ticket (2 adults + 2 children) £21.80. Disabled carers free. ♿ Site is steep in places. Tracks without wheelchair access are clearly marked; access map available at entrance.

Paradise Family Leisure Park

Avis Road, Newhaven, East Sussex BN9 0DH ☎ *(01273) 512123; 24-hour information (01273) 616006* 📠 *www.paradisepark.co.uk*

Quality ★	Facilities 🎫 🎫	Value for money £

Highlights Botanic garden
Drawbacks Superficial museums; boring presentation

What's there Paradise Park is a garden centre with various attractions tacked on in order to expand the enterprise into what is intended as a family leisure park. The **botanic garden** is the best part of an otherwise poor attraction; it houses cacti, a fernery and themed areas with Australian, Mediterranean and South American flora in a series of unimpressive modern greenhouses. Boardwalks lead visitors around the uninspiring water gardens next to the **Sussex in Miniature** display, which features models of the county's historic buildings, such as Brighton Pavilion and Chichester cathedral. Unfortunately, the grounds are close to busy A-roads, so traffic noise intrudes.

Indoors, the **Living Dinosaurs** and **Treasures of Planet Earth** exhibitions might entertain children, but are too superficial and unimaginatively presented to be of interest to adults. **Rides** and **amusements** in the pleasure gardens will also appeal largely to children, as will the miniature railway and crazy golf.

Information/tours/guides The brochure raises expectations too high for what the park offers. Information consists largely of prosaic boards and labels, supplemented by the odd video and buttons to press. Botanic garden worksheets are available for children.

When to visit Best in fine weather, although the garden centre and some displays are indoors.

Age appeal Attractions are aimed mainly at children; adults will find little to entertain them.

Food and drink A restaurant with green plastic garden furniture adjoins the garden centre; an outdoor patio overlooks the miniature railway, but indoors you are surrounded by lawnmowers and barbecue equipment. Food is unexciting, but reasonably priced: cooked breakfast £2.99, toasted sandwiches £2.35, steak and kidney pudding £4.99.

Shops A huge garden centre is at the heart of the set-up. Otherwise, a tacky gift shop sells odds and ends, most of which have nothing to do with the attractions; for example, cuddly toys £1.99-£4.99; plastic dinosaurs £5.29, £6.19.

Other facilities Large toilet block in car park is modern, clean and well-maintained.

🚌 From A27 Brighton-to-Lewes bypass, take A26 or A259 to Newhaven. ⊖ Train to Newhaven; bus to Denton Corner – contact East Sussex county busline (01273 474747). ⏱ Daily 10am to 6pm. Last admission 4.30. Closed 1 Jan. 💷 Adult £4.25; child (3–13) £3.99; senior citizen £3.99; family ticket (2 adults + 2 children) £15.99. ♿ Site mostly flat and obstacle-free; some pathways narrow. Space to manoeuvre inside Planet Earth and dinosaur displays limited.

Paradise Wildlife Park

White Stubbs Lane, Broxbourne, Hertfordshire EN10 7QA
☎ *(01992) 470490*   🖰 *www.pwpark.com*

Quality ★★★	Facilities 🏛🏛🏛🏛	Value for money ££££
Highlights	Really close proximity to (and sometimes interaction with) the animals; good play areas	
Drawbacks	Rather too commercial and circus-like; more detailed information and a guidebook would increase adult appeal	

What's there The main attraction is the **animal park**, featuring lots of wild animals which are highly visible and remarkably close, rather than lurking at the backs of cages. As well as lions, tigers, camels and zebras there are more unusual but very sociable animals such as **meerkats** and **coatis** which participate in regular 'meet the meerkats' and 'feed the coatis' events. Farm animals can be encountered in **Old MacDonald's Farmyard**, and you can visit the reptiles, ride a pony, and watch the rabbits frolicking in the painted 'village' of Bunny Town.

A crowded schedule of events running throughout the day includes the very entertaining, circus-style **Wild West Parrot Show**, in which parrots rollerskate, have a 'horse race' and demonstrate their 'counting' skills. A less flamboyant display by the English School of **Falconry** gives visitors the opportunity to hold a bird of prey. Dr Do and Dr Little perform their **Egyptian Adventure** in the jungle theatre, and regular **Big Cat Talks** take place outside the cages of the lions and tigers, outlining the background of each animal.

In addition to all the animal activities, **play facilities** such as crazy golf, various machines to ride on, old fire engines converted to slides, a woodland railway, and **Pirates' Cove** (offering climbing equipment and the chance to pan for gold) will keep children amused. Under-5s can play in an **indoor soft playground** and a large outdoor **paddling pool**, while older children will enjoy the **roller racers** (a sort of go-cart). Some of these play activities are free, but many involve further payment, which could add substantially to the cost of a day out.

Information/tours/guides Visitors are given a leaflet on arrival which includes a map of the park (in need of an update) and a schedule of events. Clear and eye-catching signs by each animal's enclosure give simple information about its origins and eating habits. These are, however, aimed mainly at young children and are rather superficial. A more detailed guidebook with information on the animals and the work of the park would be appreciated by adults. Plenty of park staff are in evidence – some very approachable and knowledgeable, others much less so.

When to visit Good weather is preferable as most of the activities are outside. Weekends and holidays are the busiest times, but extra events may be provided; during quiet periods some of the regular activities are not available.

Age appeal Aimed mainly at children, though accompanying adults will enjoy the animals and birds of prey. Many of the play areas are intended for children up to about eight or nine years old. Height restrictions apply for pony rides (4 feet 10 in) and the soft play area is restricted to under-5s.

Food and drink The Zu Café, a large room decorated with jungle designs but somehow rather cheerless, offers standard fare such as burgers (£2.05), chips (£1.20), hot dogs (£2.05) or chicken nuggets, chips and beans (£3.50). Our cheeseburger was disappointing – hot but with a poor-quality burger and served in a cold bun. Picnicking is permitted.

Shops The Jungle Trading Post is a bright and spacious building containing all manner of animal-related merchandise, mostly toys (soft toys, jigsaws, puppets at £2.99–£4.99, etc.) but also a range of posters, books and videos. Painting sets (£3.99), tiny silver animals and jewellery are also available and prices are very reasonable. Attractive Paradise T-shirts cost £9.99.

Other facilities The toilets near the café are somewhat basic; those in the animal park and near the entrance to the birds of prey area are much better.

🚗 Well signposted from A10 and from Junction 25 of M25 (about 6 miles from the motorway). Plenty of free parking. ⊖ Free bus to Broxbourne Station runs every half-hour. Broxbourne is served by trains from Liverpool Street. ⏲ Dec to Feb 10am to 5pm; Mar to Nov 10am to 6pm. 💷 Adult £7.50; child (2 to 15), senior citizen £5.50; adult season ticket £37.50; child season ticket £25. Discount for groups (10+). ♿ Good paths. Several disabled toilets.

Paultons Park

Ower, Romsey, Hampshire SO51 6AL   ☎ *(01703) 814455 or (07000)*
PAULTONS   📠 *(01703) 813025*

Quality ★★   **Facilities** 🏛🏛🏛   **Value for money ££**
Highlights Pleasant gardens; bird collection; friendly staff
Drawbacks Next to nothing for older children or adults without children; poor shops

---

What's there The **miniature train**, Kids' Kingdom **activity park**, **rabbit ride**, **magic teacups**, **runaway train**, (smelly) **pets' corner**, **whirly copters** and **flying saucers** will delight younger children, but some attractions, such as the Astroglide **giant slide**, have a minimum height restriction, so visitors who get in free because they are under 1 metre tall may not be able to go on them.

Otherwise, children have plenty of open space in which to run around and enough to keep them busy all day, even if it rains – the indoor **animatronics** of *Wind in the Willows* are good, though the story is not explained at all.

For teenagers, it is a different story. The new **Raging River Ride** is wet and quite fun, and the **maze** is a laugh, but that's about it. You can pay extra (£2 for one person, £3 for two) for the go-karts but you have to be over 16 and 5 feet tall or more to drive. The **Land of the Dinosaurs** is about as lifelike as pre-*Jurassic Park* sci-fi films, while some of the outdoor attractions like **Crazy Golf** and **Crazy Snooker** need a lick of paint to cover up the wear and tear.

Grown-ups and children alike should enjoy the two museums, which are as educational as they are entertaining. **Village Life** has plenty on cottage industries, crafts and trades, while the **Romany Experience** has an extensive collection of gypsy wagons and carts, some decorated in gold leaf. The huge **bird collection** is also impressive, with 250 species, from hornbills to owls and pelicans, dotted around the gardens. Horticulturists will relish the **landscaped gardens**.

Information/tours/guides The signposting within the park is excellent, so it is easy to find your way round even without the free map (also good). The guidebook (£2) makes a nice souvenir but is not necessary for your visit.

When to visit A lot of the best bits are outdoors, so sunny days are better, but there is enough indoors to occupy a showery spell.

Age appeal Although this is billed as somewhere for 'all the family to enjoy' with 'plenty to do' for 'children of all ages', this is not a place for teenagers. On the other hand, younger children (under-10s) will love it, as most of the attractions are aimed specifically at them. The small price differential (only £1) between adult and child entry prices is irksome, and the prices are quite high in relation to the content. However, free admission for those under 1 metre tall is a bonus for those with toddlers.

Food and drink   Despite the motorway service station ambience of plastic seats and loud canned music, the main eatery (Wagoner's Rest) is a reasonable cafeteria, with daily specials such as chicken curry or vegetable lasagne (both £5.50), a salad bar (£4.90) and all-day breakfasts (£4.35) in addition to the chips-with-everything options. Kids' portions and baby food are also available. Smaller food outlets around the park sell the likes of hot dogs, drinks and ice creams.

Shops   Aimed at a young market (but with too much within reach of tiny hands), the shops sell a wide range of toys and trinkets. Very little is linked to the park itself, but if you want a glow-in-the-dark ring (£1.99), fridge magnet (99p), fake flowers (£2) or assorted Teletubby goodies then this is the place to come.

Other facilities   The toilets were clean enough but basic – more like being in a portable loo at the seaside than anything. Baby-strollers can be hired for £2.50 per day, or for £5 you can get a 'Stroll-a-saurus' – a green plastic dinosaur stroller.

🚗 From M27, take junction 2 west of Southampton and follow signs. Free car park.
🚌 From Southampton, catch bus X7 or X71 to Ower. It runs once an hour Mon to Sat, takes about half an hour and drops you off at the entrance to the park. ⏰ 11 Mar to 29 Oct, Mon to Sun 10am to 6.30pm (rides, attractions and catering close at 5.30pm); 30 Oct to 24 Dec, usually Mon to Sun 10am to 5pm – ring for details. Nov, Dec until Xmas; Sat and Sun last admission 4.30pm. Closed 25 Dec to 10 Mar. 💷 Adult £9.50; child (under 14) £8.50 (child under 1m tall free); senior citizen £8.50; disabled person £5.50; family ticket (up to 3 adults + 1 or more children) £25.50 for 3 people; £33 for 4; £40 for 5. *Season tickets* (valid 1 year; unlimited visits exc. Santa's Winter Wonderland, open Dec weekends and 18–24 Dec): adult £43.50; child, senior citizen £40.50 (photo required). No dogs except guide dogs. ♿ Good, though some rides not accessible. Free pre-booked wheelchairs available.

Pleasure Island

Kings Road, Cleethorpes, Lincolnshire DN35 0PL   ☎ *(01472) 211511*
🖥 *www.pleasure-island.co.uk*   ✉ *pleasure-island@compuserve.com*

Quality ★★	Facilities 🎫🎫	Value for money ££
Highlights	Rides and shows for young and pre-teen children; no litter; plenty of picnic areas	
Drawbacks	No cover for queues on wet days; poor information about shows	

What's there   Pleasure Island is loosely divided into six 'lands' grouped around a central lake, though the borders are somewhat blurred. It combines **theme park rides** with old-fashioned **fairground games** and low-key shows.

Old England, Kiddies Kingdom, Spain and Africa, which are the lands nearest the entrance, contain most of the **gentle rides** aimed at younger children. Of these, the Falls of Fear in Africa is a **water slide** where you can get very wet, while the **Para Tower** hoists you up in a balloon-like basket before you float back down to earth. For more stomach-churning kicks, head for **White Knuckle Valley** and **Morocco**. The **Boomerang**, though short, takes you through a couple of loops first forward and then backward (which is much worse), while on the **Terror Rack** you constantly revolve through 360 degrees, often hanging upside-down in mid-air, for what seems like an eternity but is really just over three minutes. The **Crazy Loop** is a more traditional roller-coaster ride, but as its carriages carry only eight people at a time its queue is one of the longest. Over in Morocco, **Dream Boat** also turns you upside-down as the boat turns full circle.

The **shows** last 10–20 minutes (times are chalked up on the board outside). Some involve live animals (performing sea lions and parrots), others are child-size animated puppets (Billy Bob's Rockafire Show, Talking Chimp Show). The **Big Top Circus** features juggling, clowns and balancing acts. While in the **Magic Water Theatre** spotlit fountains waltz to popular classics.

Some of the buildings are rather basic but the site is very tidy, with plenty of litter bins provided and staff wandering around picking up litter.

Information/tours/guides The publicity leaflet has details of opening times, admission prices and how to get there, plus the height restrictions for the different rides (worth knowing before you go). When we inspected the map had not been updated to include the Para Tower, which opened in 1999, but shows the location of toilets, eating outlets, and baby-changing facilities. However, as it has no scale it is difficult to know until you arrive how big the park is. And although the leaflet gives the times of the shows, it does not say how long they are or what they involve. Get your ticket stamped if you are leaving the park but intend to return later the same day.

When to visit The longest queues form during school holidays; arrive early if possible. Very little shelter is available for queues on rainy days; some rides may be closed during bad weather.

Age appeal All the rides are colour-coded according to height restrictions, which are strictly enforced (platform-soled trainers will fool no one). Five are coded red, excluding those under 1.4 metres tall. However, most rides are aimed at young and pre-teen children; only two or three rides in White Knuckle Valley will keep teenage and adult thrill-seekers happy. Shows such as the Sea Lion Show and Big Top Circus are short enough to keep children of most ages amused. Senior citizens, who will find less to interest them, pay a lower entry fee.

Food and drink Plenty of outlets all round the park sell a variety of fast food such as burgers, hot dogs, baked potatoes, popcorn and ice cream – the longest queue was near the carousel in Kiddies Kingdom. The best option is Fatima's Fish and Chips, in Morocco, which offers crisp, chunky chips for 90p and hefty portions of battered fish with chips for £3.50. The Food Arcade, in Spain, shares its premises with various video games, and disco music blares constantly. Many families prefer to bring their own food and picnic outside on the grass by the lake (several picnic tables are provided, too). McCormack's Family Bar outside the park (no restrictions on children) serves up more solid fare: mixed grill (£7.75), beef and ale pie (£5.25), cream cheese and broccoli bake (£5.75) and lasagne (£5.25). If you leave the park to visit McCormack's, get your ticket stamped so you can return later.

Shops The Tinkaboo Sweet Shop, at the exit of the Tinkaboo Sweet Factory Water Ride, majors on edible items but also offers souvenir baseball caps, mugs, T-shirts and sweatshirts, mouse mats and so on. The saccharine, irritatingly catchy song that plays throughout the ride continues in the shop, which may discourage adults from lingering.

🚍 Follow signs from M180, A46 and A180. Plenty of free parking. ⊖ Cleethorpes railway station is quite a walk from the park; buses 9X or 17 (seasonal), take 5–10 minutes. ⏰ 16 Apr to 10 Sept, Mon to Sun, then weekends to end Oct plus 23–29 Oct, 10am to 5pm (later in high season). Phone for details. 💷 Adult £9; child £9 (under-4s free); senior citizen £5; family ticket (any 4 people) £30. ♿ The site is all fairly flat. Wheelchairs can be booked in advance. Disabled toilets around park. Access to rides depends on level of disability, but most rides and attractions can be stopped to allow disabled visitors to board as long as enough staff are on hand.

Pleasureland

Marine Drive, Southport, Merseyside PR8 1RX ☎ *(01704) 532717*
📠 *(01704) 537936* 🖥 *www.pleasureland.uk.com*

Quality ★★★ **Facilities** 🏛 🏛 🏛 **Value for money £££**
Highlights Two great rides (Traumatizer, Cyclone); good range of food; fun for kids
Drawbacks Dated and tatty in places; not enough for non-riders; poor car park; mediocre shops

---

What's there The opening of **Traumatizer**, the UK's tallest, fastest suspended looping roller-coaster, put Pleasureland back on the thrill-seeker's map, but it still has a way to go to catch up with its big brother up the coast. The **theme park** is half the price of Blackpool Pleasure Beach but also half the fun. Its saving grace is the two top rides, both worth a trip on their own.

Entry is free, though you must pay for each ride individually or buy a wristband at the entrance. The latter is better if you want unlimited access to rides. Rides are categorised and priced according to their excitement value – either White Knuckle or Pink Knuckle – and there are gentler rides for young children (Ali Baba).

You cannot escape **Traumatizer**, even if you do not go on it, as it towers over the whole area and the screams of delight (or terror) can be heard over the thunder of the coaster itself. Just under two minutes long, the ride is one of the most nerve-racking you are likely to experience (and not for the faint-hearted), mainly because you are suspended beneath the tracks and constantly looping upside down. Sixty years older, **Cyclone** is a rather rickety wooden coaster that is just as much fun in its own way. No high-tech twirling here – just old-fashioned humps and drops that push your stomach into your mouth. Half the thrill is never being entirely sure whether the track will hold together.

The rest of the park is less exciting, though **Wild Cat** is fast and furious, and **Big Apple** the best of the Ali Baba rides. Elsewhere, peeling paint and rust on some attractions make them less than attractive, and the much-mended Tarmac makes the place feel like a council car park. The Arabic theme does not quite work, though it is the only attempt at landscaping or beautification. Overall, the park is faded, jaded and crying out for a good paint job and some upgrading.

Those not tempted by the rides will find just enough to entertain them for an hour or so; the array of **fairground-style stalls** includes a camel race, shooting gallery and hoop-la, as well as **palmists**, **ten-pin bowling** and **amusement arcades**.

Information/tours/guides It is easy to find your way around this small park. The map is more useful for its discount vouchers than for orientation.

When to visit Likely to be busy on sunny summer weekends but would still be fun on a wet weekday.

Age appeal Limited appeal for those who do not like rides.

Food and drink The eating options range from candy floss and burger vans to sit-down restaurants. In the fast-food Mustapha diner a quarter-pounder will set you back £2.99, pizza £3.75, a cup of tea 70p. The most upmarket option is Casablanca, offering BBQ ribs (£6.25), prawn stir-fry (£6.95), salads (£3.75) or chicken Marrakech (£8.25). Children's meals are £2–£3.

Shops The souvenirs are the usual seaside nonsense, but you can buy a photo of yourself on Traumatizer for £3.95, a Pleasureland baseball cap (£4.99) or kid's T-shirt (£2.99).

Other facilities The toilets are badly signposted, but fine once you find them.

🚗 Follow signs from motorway (M62, M57 or M58). On-site car park leaves a lot to be desired, with its pot-holes and muddy patches, but costs only £2.50 and is close to the entrance. ⊖ Direct trains to Southport run from Liverpool (45 minutes) and Manchester (1 hour). ⊙ Check ahead if you are going outside July/Aug. Midday to 5pm or 7pm Easter to end Oct (mainly Fri/Sat/Sun during Apr, May & Oct); 11am to 9pm Sat & Sun June to Aug. Closed Nov to Easter exc. Sat/Sun in March. Eves May to Oct Wed to Fri 5 to 9pm. 💷 Free entry. Rides charged. Wristband prices, based on height of visitor, allow unlimited access to rides in that category. Extra charge for go-karts (£3 for 4 minutes) and waltzer (£1). *White Knuckle wristband* (over 1.2m; all rides): £12.99 . *Pink Knuckle wristband* (1–1.2m; excludes most of top rides): £8.99. *Ali Baba wristband* (under 1m: rides for small children): £5. *Super Saver* (any 4 wristbands): £40. *Individual ride tickets* : £1, from entrance or vending machines inside. Most adult rides cost 2 tickets (i.e. £2) except Traumatizer (4 tickets). Ali Baba rides mostly 1 ticket. ♿ Ask for free guide either in advance or from guest relations on arrival.

Pleasurewood Hills Theme Park

Leisure Way, Corton, Lowestoft, Suffolk NR32 5DZ ☎ *(01502) 508200*
🖳 *www.pleasurewoodhills.co.uk* 🖳 *info@pleasurewoodhills.co.uk*

Quality ★★★ | Facilities 🎫 🎫 | Value for money ££££
Highlights Good range of rides, amusements and shows for families
Drawbacks Tatty and old-fashioned in parts

What's there This **family leisure park** on the fringes of Lowestoft offers a generous range of amusements and activities. As well as '**thrill rides**' it provides fairground-style rides including **roller-coasters**, **water flumes**, **miniature trains** and **waltzers**, plus a **chair-lift**, **canyon rafting**, **mini-golf**

and an indoor **soft play area**. **Woody's Little Big Park**, aimed at 4- to 9-year-olds, contains smaller versions of the adult rides. Shows and special events include a **sea lion show, Cine 180** and **parrot shows**. These take place at advertised times throughout the day.

Allow a whole day: there is plenty to occupy all ages, and all rides are included in the price of admission.

Information/tours/guides The free map shows all the rides, colour-coded to show which are suitable for different ages. Visitors also receive a show plan listing timed events throughout the day. Rides display warnings if they are unsuitable for pregnant women, young children or epilepsy sufferers. Assistants on the rides are helpful and polite.

When to visit To avoid the crowds, aim to visit during term time rather than in the summer holidays.

Age appeal Not suitable for the very young or very old. Children aged 4 upwards will enjoy the Little Big Park and are encouraged to identify with the Woody Bear character, whose image and name recurs throughout the site. Size restrictions operate: visitors must be over 1.3 metres (4ft 3in) for some thrill rides.

Food and drink Good choice of food and drink including a bacon kiosk, although little in the way of fresh food. Smokey Joe's Restaurant (licensed bar and barbecues), Chip 'n' Dip (ice cream and hot dogs), Giovanni's Pizza, Hungry Bears, Waffle House and Coca-Cola Express. Cheap fast food domi-nates: burger meals (£3.75), Kids' fun boxes (£2.75), large pizzas (£9.95), coffee/tea and Danish pastry (£1.75). Gas-lit barbecues are available for hire. Picnic areas provided.

Shops Various outlets sell souvenirs and sweets, including Woody's Emporium, a general store, joke shop and a pocket-money shop. Colourful displays of goods include cuddly toys (£1.55), notepads (75p) and baseball hats (£5.99); marketing focuses adroitly on children's tastes and pockets.

 Off A12 between Lowestoft and Great Yarmouth (follow brown signs). Large, free car park next to entrance. Eastern Counties buses run from Lowestoft Bus Station to Tesco on A12, from which park is a 5- minute walk. Weekends and school hols 16 Apr to 31 Oct (phone above tel. no. for details). Gates open at 9.30am. Rides close at 4, 5 or 6pm depending on time of year. Visitor over 1 metre tall £10; visitor under 1 metre free; senior citizen £7.50; disabled visitor/carer £7.50; group bookings (20+): £7.50 (booked at least 1 day in advance) or £8.50 (on day) – 1 free ticket for every 20 purchased. Repeat visits are discounted on production of voucher stamped on leaving park. Level paths for wheelchairs. Most rides suitable. Wheelchair hire £2 per day.

Polesden Lacey

Great Bookham, Nr Dorking, Surrey RH5 6BD ☎ *(01372) 458203*
 www.nationaltrust.org.uk

Quality ★★★   **Facilities**   **Value for money £££**
Highlights Fascinating insight into Edwardian upper-class social scene; lovely gardens and views from Long Walk; good children's activity book and quiz
Drawbacks Too few toilets for number of visitors; expensive guidebook

---

What's there Situated on the North Downs, Polesden Lacey is best known as the home of Edwardian society hostess Mrs Ronnie Greville, although its most famous resident was the playwright Richard Brinsley Sheridan. The house is now in the care of the National Trust. Friends and acquaintances might have described Mrs Greville as a 'collector of royalties'; the less enamoured, notably Cecil Beaton, considered her 'a galumphing, greedy, snobbish old toad who watered at the chops at the sight of royalty . . . and did nothing for anyone but the rich'.

Mrs Greville was also an ardent collector of art, and the house is filled to the brim with Dutch Old Masters, Italian majolica, Chinese porcelain, and English and French furniture and *objets d'art*, to say nothing of a Roman sarcophagus. Photos of the royal guests who attended her celebrated house parties are everywhere – Edward VII and his mistress Mrs Keppel, Queen Mary (who used to invite herself for tea at short notice), and the Duke and Duchess of York (later George VI and Queen Elizabeth), who spent part of their honeymoon at Polesden Lacey – along with assorted prime ministers, viceroys, chancellors and ambassadors. The finest rooms are the extraordinary **saloon**, the dazzling carved and gilded woodwork of which was removed *en bloc* from an Italian palazzo; the delicate white **tea room**, with its dinky writing bureau and tables; and the panelled **picture corridor**, which runs around three sides of the central quadrangle and contains the best of the **Dutch paintings** as well as **porcelain** and **furniture**. At one end of this corridor stands a full-length **portrait** of Mrs Greville herself, by Carolus-Duran.

Outside, the formal **Edwardian gardens** to the west of the house are planted with roses, peonies, irises and lavender, enclosed by hedges and walls and flanked by a superb herbaceous border. The **pets' graveyard** is the resting place of Mrs Greville's favourite Pekes, Cho and Lokai. From the south terrace, the majestic **Long Walk,** originally laid out by Sheridan, provides splendid views over the wooded valley to the south. A small open-air theatre nearby is used during the Polesden Lacey Festival in summer.

Suggested circular **walks**, from one to three miles long, all start from the car park and are clearly marked (a leaflet can be obtained from the shop). Admiral's Walk, the shortest and easiest, can be tackled by wheelchair users with a strong companion; the other walks are hillier and can be muddy in wet weather.

Information/tours/guides The excellent leaflet supplied on entry contains a map and details of facilities, including the price of admission to the house – not revealed on the board at the entrance to the grounds. The main guidebook, a pricey £4.50, describes the rooms and furnishings in a rather dry manner, but the account of Mrs Greville's life and social activities provides a vivid insight into her social milieu. A basic leaflet with room descriptions costs 50p, and the children's activity book and quiz is £1. Also available are a small booklet on the gardens (60p), a children's garden quiz and a free walks leaflet. Guides in the rooms are friendly and generally helpful.

When to visit Viewing the house will not take very long, so it is best to visit on a fine day to make the most of the gardens and walks. The gardens are open all year round, and there is something of interest in most seasons, including irises and peonies in late spring, roses and lavender in summer, and aconites and snow-drops in winter. Occasional summer events feature Morris and Scottish country dancing, croquet coaching and lace-making demonstrations, and classic cars.

Guided walks with the warden are also offered. For details tel. (01372) 452048. Concerts and plays are given in the open-air theatre during the three-week festival in June/July (tel. (01372) 451596/457223/455052 for details).

Age appeal The activity book and quiz gives children a focus of attention in the house. They will also enjoy many of the special events, such as Greville Day, and guided walks or 'countryside capers' for children in the summer.

Food and drink The Tea Room is in the former stable block, leading off the central courtyard (the old stalls are still visible). Modern photos of the countryside and black and white reprints of Edwardian house parties and the Queen Mother on honeymoon hang on the walls. A few tables and chairs are provided outside. The food is mostly home-made, often from local ingredients. When the house is closed, a limited menu of soup, salad and sandwiches is on offer. On other days, two or three main courses such as locally produced sausage casserole or poached salmon, plus a vegetarian option, are available, along with various salads. Main courses range from £4.50 to £6.95 for Sunday roast. Cream teas (£2.70) feature jam made by a local farmer from his own fruit. Beer and wine are also available. Picnics are allowed in the park.

Shops Although the shop offers little of direct relevance to the house, it has a range of accessories for country pursuits, including shooting sticks, tracker stools and clothing, as well as the usual fudge, chocolates and preserves, and books on gardens and walks. Plants are also on sale.

Other facilities With only four women's toilets, queues are common at busy times. Baby-changing facilities are provided in both the men's and the women's toilets.

🚗 Off A246 Leatherhead-Guildford road, 5 miles north-west of Dorking, 2 miles south of Great Bookham. Plenty of parking about 200 metres from house. ⊖ The nearest railway station is Boxhill & Westhumble (2 miles). Surrey Hills Leisure Bus no 433 runs from Guildford railway station on Sun (May to Sept). Arriva Surrey & West Sussex no. 479 runs between Guildford and Croydon – alight at Great Bookham, 1½ miles away. Tel. 01737 223000 for details. ⊙ *House* 27 Mar to 29 Oct daily exc. Mon and Tue (but open bank hol Mon), 1pm to 5pm (bank hol Mon 11am to 5.30pm); last admission 30 minutes before closing. *Garden* 10am to 6pm or dusk if earlier. 🎫 *Garden, grounds and walks* £3; family ticket (2 adults + up to 3 children) £7.50. *House* adult £3; child (5 to 17 yrs old) £1.50; family ticket £7.50. NT members free. Dogs are allowed if kept under strict control. ♿ Disabled visitors may be dropped at front door of house. Toilets, shop and tea room all accessible. Most of the gardens are accessible (some gravel and paved surfaces), except for the rock garden and sunken garden, reached via stone steps. The Admiral's Walk, the shortest of the designated walks, can be negotiated by wheelchairs and pushchairs, although part is uphill on gravel. Wheelchairs and a self-drive batricar are available for loan if booked in advance.

Port Sunlight Village

95 Greendale Road, Port Sunlight, Wirral CH62 4XE   ☎ *0151–644 6466*

Quality ★★★★   **Facilities 🏛 🏛 🏛**   **Value for money £££££**

Highlights Unusual example of living heritage; splendid pre-Raphaelite collection
Drawbacks Pricey gallery guide

What's there This picturesque **garden village** on the Wirral was founded by

William Hesketh Lever in 1888 to house the workers in his soap factory (the name comes from Sunlight soap). A forward-thinking man, Lever realised that a happy, well-fed and well-housed workforce would be more productive than one that was not, and he used some of the profits from his company to pay for the maintenance and upkeep of the village, as well as building a church, technical institute, hospital and the Lady Lever Art Gallery. Today, Port Sunlight is a conservation area, and although residents no longer have to work for what is now Unilever to live in the village, and the houses can be bought on the open market, the company was until recently responsible for the maintenance of the village environment and landscape. The site changed hands, however, as we went to press.

The **heritage centre** is a small two-room building housing an exhibition on the history of Port Sunlight. An introductory video, display boards and old photographs show the housing and working conditions around 1900.

A village trail map (50p) identifies, among other **buildings**, the still-working Gladstone theatre, the Lyceum, which had a dual role as church and school, the former women's dining room of Hulme Hall, and the Lady Lever Art Gallery. As Port Sunlight remains a working village, most of the handsome red-brick houses can be viewed only from the outside.

The **Lady Lever Art Gallery**, opened in 1922, is the jewel in the crown, with its neo-classical, pillared frontage and glass-domed roof. It houses one of the finest pre-Raphaelite and Wedgwood collections in the world, along with an awe-inspiring art and pottery collection and an amazing display of eighteenth-century furniture.

The trail around the village, taking in most of the main sights, will take about 1½ hours; the art gallery will take about the same again. The roads are all flat and everything is signposted.

Information/tours/guides Guided tours of the village (1½ hours) take place every Sunday from 12 April and bank holiday Mondays until the end of September at midday and 3pm: adult £2.50; child £1; concession £2. Gallery has free audio guides, and its own very detailed guidebook costs £7.95.

When to visit The art gallery is open all year, but fine weather is preferable for exploring the village.

Age appeal Sunlight involves quite a lot of walking, so anyone who tires easily, including young children, might find it taxing, although you can stop for refreshments at the garden centre and pubs. No child-focused guides are available.

Food and drink Cream teas and pre-packed sandwiches are available at the garden centre, and a variety of hot food at the two pubs.

Shops A very small gift area in the heritage stocks prints of the village, postcards and coasters. There is also a post office.

Junction 4 of the M53, along the B5137 (follow the signs). Street parking available. Θ Services to Port Sunlight rail and bus station run from Liverpool, Birkenhead and Chester. ⊙ *Gallery* Mon to Sat 10am to 5pm, Sun 12 to 5pm. Closed 23–26 Dec and 1 Jan. *Heritage centre* Apr to Oct, Mon to Sun 10am to 4pm; Nov to Apr, Mon to Fri 10am to 4pm, Sat and Sun 11am to 4pm. *Heritage centre* adult 60p; child 30p; student, senior citizen 50p. *Gallery* £3; student, senior citizen, unemployed £1.50. ♿ Good.

Preston Hall Museum

Yarm Road, Stockton-on-Tees TS18 3RH ☎ *(01642) 781184*

Quality ★★ **Facilities** 🍴 🍴 **Value for money** £££
Highlights Cheap admission; enough activities to entertain the children
Drawbacks Rather old-fashioned

What's there Preston Hall, built in 1825, is a **country house** set in over 100 acres of parkland overlooking the river Tees. Today it serves as a museum, housing **period rooms** and a reconstructed **Victorian cobbled street** complete with recreated shops.

The museum's main exhibition, **Life in the Home**, is an eclectic and rather old-fashioned collection of costumes and period room settings, evoking domestic life from the 1820s onwards. Other displays include 'Dig for Victory', depicting the campaign to encourage people to grow their own produce during the two world wars; 'Toy Box', a quirky collection of toys dating back to the 1930s, including dolls' houses and model farmyard animals; and a giant game of snakes and ladders which takes up an entire room.

The real highlight of the museum is the reconstructed cobbled street of the 1890s with its recreated Victorian shops and resident craftspeople at work, such as the blacksmith and cabinet maker. The chemist's has mirrored shelves of ointments and tinctures, while the old sweetshop displays jars of brightly coloured boiled sweets.

Allow 1–2 hours to see the museum exhibitions and 20–30 minutes to explore the Victorian street. In addition to the museum, children can enjoy, outside, **Butterfly World**, a **narrow-gauge railway**, **river cruises** on the *Teesside Princess* (tel. 01642 608 038: cruises twice daily in summer, Wed, Sat and Sun) and **rowing boats** (weekends only). However, all these cost extra.

Information/tours/guides No guidebooks or guided tours of the museum are available, but there is a free A4 factsheet on the history of Preston Park. Labelling is variable: some displays provide detailed information, while others, particularly the costume collections, say very little.

When to visit It is preferable to visit in fine weather, in order to enjoy the outdoor activities such as rowing (weekends only) or woodland walks.

Age appeal Suitable for families with young children, who will enjoy the Toy Box, Victorian street, rowing boats, train ride or river cruise. Preston Hall is also popular with elderly visitors who come on organised day trips.

Food and drink The museum has a simple cafeteria, close to the car park. The décor is rather dated, but the staff are friendly. The menu is dull but extensive: sausage and chips (£2.50), jacket potatoes (£2), burgers and chips (£1.50–£2). Sandwiches cost £1.20, scones and cake from 30p.

Shops A few items relating to the museum exhibitions (sepia postcards at 25p, children's colouring books depicting scenes of Victorian life for 60p, and pamphlets entitled *Life in Victorian Britain*, £2.99) are supplemented by child-oriented merchandise and knick-knacks such as key-rings.

🚗 Follow signs from the A135, north of Yarm. Free car park. ⊖ Nearest railway station is Eagles Cliff, 5 minutes' walk away. Tel. 01642 781184. ⊙ Apr to Sept, Mon to

Sun 10am to 5pm; Oct-Mar, Mon to Sat 10am to 4.30pm, Sun 2pm to 4.30pm. Last admission 45 minutes before closing. 🖼 Adult £1; child, senior citizen, student 50p; family ticket (2 adults + 2 children) £2.50; (1 adult + 2 children) £1.50. ♿ Disabled parking. Good wheelchair access.

Quarry Bank Mill

Styal, Cheshire SK9 4LA ☎ *(01625) 527468* 🖰 *www.quarrybankmill.org.uk*

Quality ★★★★ **Facilities** 🗲🗲🗲🗲 **Value for money ££££**
Highlights Authentic working mill; tasty, home-made food; wonderful river walks
Drawbacks Noisy when machines running; prices at entrance could be clearer

What's there This 'dark satanic mill' built in red brick is one of the largest historic working cotton mills in Britain, containing authentic weaving machines, a water wheel and a working steam engine. In 1939 the mill, along with the surrounding estate and Styal village, was donated to the National Trust by Alec Greg, great-great-grandson of its founder Samuel Greg. It is located within a 284-acre country park offering woodland and riverside walks.

Arranged over five storeys, the **working museum** illustrates the entire production process, from women **spinning** the cotton on wooden wheels, to the **weaving** shed, where great old clattering machines cause the floor to vibrate, and the **mule room** and finishing process. A great iron **water wheel** has been restored to working condition, as has a Boulton and Watt-type **steam engine**.

The **Apprentice House**, in a separate building up a cobbled street, gives an insight into the draconian and dangerous conditions in which the child workers lived and laboured. The house, built in 1790, was home to 100 children who began work at 6am and finished at 8pm, after which they got some rudimentary schooling before going to sleep in hard wooden beds.

You can happily spend half a day at Quarry Mill if you include a walk by the river.

Information/tours/guides The Apprentice House can be visited (accompanied by a knowledgeable costumed guide) only by timed ticket, but numbers are limited to 30, so it is advisable to book early. Tours begin at 11.30am and run every half-hour except in the school term, when they start at 2pm. The excellent guidebook is priced at a reasonable £2.50.

When to visit The centre is open all year, but to enjoy a walk it is best to visit in fine weather.

Age appeal The mill, especially the working machinery and water wheel, will fascinate visitors of all ages.

Food and drink The traditional-style tea rooms are situated in a lovely old building that was once the stables, serving a good variety of home-made food – for example, vegetable hot-pot and chilli with rice (£3.90 each), as well as sweets and savouries.

Shops The gift shop is spacious and easy to browse. Its fine range of merchandise includes cotton goods made in the mill, such as dressing-gowns and tea-towels, as well as locally produced jams and preserves.

Follow signs from Junction 5 of M56. Plenty of parking. ⊖ Not advisable: no direct access. ◷ Apr to Sept 11am to 6pm; Oct to Mar 11am to 5pm exc. Mon. *House* 2pm to 5 pm in school term exc. Mon, otherwise 11am to 5pm. £ *Mill and house* adult £5.80; child (under 16) £3.60. *Mill* adult £4.40; child, student, senior citizen, unemployed £3.10. *House and garden* adult £3.60; child, student, senior citizen, unemployed £2.60. ♿ Good, but some steepish ramps on approach to mill and limited access within it. Wheelchairs available.

RHS Garden, Wisley

Woking, Surrey GU23 6QB ☎ *(01483) 224234; (01483) 211113 (shop and plant centre)* *www.rhs.org.uk*

Quality ★★ **Facilities** ☕☕☕☕ **Value for money** ££££

Highlights Splendid variety of gardens and habitats, beautifully maintained; popular plant centre and shop; good provision for wheelchair users

Drawbacks Orientation not very clear; lack of information in garden itself

What's there Wisley is a huge site – 240 acres – and the jewel in the crown of the Royal Horticultural Society. The variety of habitats provides something of interest for everyone, be they vicarious vegetable growers or woodland walkers.

Near the entrance are the most formal parts of the garden – the **Canal**, scattered with water lilies, some beautiful examples of intricate carpet bedding, and the Walled Garden. The **Mixed Borders** are a splendid sight in summer; to the left, rhododendrons blaze in spring; to the right, behind hornbeam hedges, lie the **Rose Garden** and the new **Country Garden**, designed by Penelope Hobhouse. On the other side of Battleston Hill, a terraced Mediterranean Garden slopes down to Portsmouth Fields, where the RHS carries out trials of different cultivars. It is interesting to compare the species for yourself, though noise from the A3 is rather intrusive in this corner of the garden.

The route continues through the **Jubilee Arboretum** and the **Fruit Field**, which contains some attractive espaliered fruit trees. The **glasshouses** are divided into sections by temperature: the beautifully lush warm section, complete with flowing stream, air plants, orchids and ferns, is the most exotic. The adjoining **Model Gardens**, on a scale more comparable to the average garden, provide visitors with ideas for their home plots: maybe some Japanese touches in the form of gravel, acers, rocks and bonsai; a gazebo formed from whitebeam trees; container gardening, including vegetables in pots; or climbing plants on arches and pergolas. There are also Model Herb and Fruit Gardens.

The **Rose Borders** on Weather Hill lead through to the **Alpine Houses**, Monocot Borders and **Model Vegetable Garden** – a decorative as well as productive site. North of here, small pools and streams cascade down the magnificent slopes of the **Rock Garden** to the Long Ponds at the bottom, crossed by small bridges. Following on is the **Wild Garden**, the oldest part of Wisley, now a series of attractive wooded glades planted with hostas and bamboo. Beyond, Seven Acres is a grassy landscaped area with a couple of lakes, leading on to the restaurants. Finally, the **Pinetum** consists not just of conifers but also acers, witch hazels and dogwood, plus **the National Collection of heathers** in Howard's Field.

Most of the plants are well labelled, but otherwise the emphasis seems largely to be on education by inspiration. There is little practical follow-up information on site about how visitors might apply some of the techniques and ideas to their own gardens, even in the model gardens and vegetable garden – presumably those interested enough can go and browse through the volumes available in the shop. However, you can look up individual species in the Reading Room, and there are also demonstrations on subjects such as flower arranging, lawn maintenance, and pests and diseases, as well as courses leading to professional qualifications.

Allow at least half a day if you want to see all the gardens, although real enthusiasts could easily spend a whole day.

Information/tours/guides Guided tours run once a day Monday to Friday, lasting 1½ hours (£1.20). They cover the main highlights of the gardens, but can be adapted to the needs and interests of people on the tour. Visitors are also given a free leaflet with details of plants of seasonal interest.

The good-value guidebook (£2.95) provides some background information and plenty of colour photos. It also has a map, but this is small and rather tricky to use. Close study of the text shows that there is a recommended route around the garden, but this is not marked on the map; nor are the features that are numbered on the map numbered in the text. Without a guidebook, you are likely to be even more disorientated: maps are few and far between, though there are plenty of signs to different parts of the garden, toilets and restaurants.

When to visit The garden is open year-round, so it depends on your area of interest. Most visitors, of course, go for summer splendour, but spring is the time for rhododendrons and azaleas and you will find plenty of autumn colour. With relatively little under cover, however, it is easier to visit when the weather is dry.

Age appeal Only the chance to run around and stretch their legs will appeal to children, although some areas are restricted and no ball games or radios are allowed. Family Fortnight, held during the school summer holidays, provides more structured activities, such as basket-making and flowerpot painting, as well as entertainers (you many need to book in advance for some of these).

Food and drink The self-service Conservatory Café can be a bit of a scrum at lunchtime. Its straightforward fare includes a range of sandwiches, (£2–£2.50), jacket potatoes with various fillings (£4.50), and soup and roll (£2.25). Hot options (about £6.15) may include vegetable lasagne, steak and kidney pie, and seafood mornay. Afternoon tea costs £2.20. The indoor conservatory-style seating area can get a bit stuffy on sunny days, but the pleasant terrace will provide a shaded table and chairs. Service at lunchtime on the day we inspected was suffering under the strain. The pricier, waiter-service Terrace Restaurant offers two courses for £17, three courses for £19.50. The style is modern European, taking in leek and coriander broth with parmesan croûtons alongside chargrilled swordfish niçoise with garlic and herb sauce. For something less formal, the Car Park Chalet and Garden Chalet sell a range of sandwiches, baguettes, drinks, cakes and ice cream. A woodland picnic area is provided next to the car parks (picnics are not allowed in the grounds).

Shops The large plant centre is extremely popular for its huge range, including some more unusual species. In the shop, you can buy books and videos on every conceivable aspect of horticulture. In addition, it sells the usual range of tea-towels, china, crystal, glass and toiletries (RHS hollyhock body balm at £6.95). Staff are cheerful, polite and obliging, queues only in plant centre.

Other facilities Large, free car park organised along one-way lanes. Toilets next to the entrance and near the glasshouses are clean but dated and a little cramped. Those in the restaurant are better and brighter, and also have baby-changing facilities.

🚗 20 miles south-west of London and 7 miles north of Guildford on the A3. Follow brown flower signs on A3 and from M25, junction 10. ⊖ Train to Woking station then organised bus to gardens. Tel. (01483) 224234 for details. Alternatively, take train to Kingston-upon-Thames or Guildford and Arriva bus 415 to gardens (Mon to Sat). ⊙ Mon to Fri 10am to sunset (6pm during summer); Sat and Sun 9am to sunset (6pm during summer). Closed on Sun (except to members and their guests, although shop and plant centre open on Sun) and 25 Dec. Note that glasshouses close at 4.15pm, Nov to Feb and at 4.45pm, Mar to Oct. 💷 Adult (including senior citizen): £5; child (6–16 yrs old) £2; child (under 6 yrs old) free; Affiliated Society Garden Entry Card holder £3.50; disabled visitor's carer free; RHS member free (plus one adult guest or two children). ♿ Free map with suitable routes for wheelchairs and pushchairs available from the ticket office. To pre-book wheelchairs tel. (01483) 211113. Disabled toilets.

Ripon Cathedral

Ripon, North Yorkshire HG4 1QT   ☎ *(01765) 603462*
🖰 *www.riponcathedral.org.uk*

Quality ★★★★   **Facilities 👜 👜 👜**   **Value for money £££**
Highlights   Excellent audio tour; friendly and knowledgeable guides
Drawbacks   No mention outside of requested £2 donation; not much to amuse children

---

What's there Ripon holds the distinction of being the oldest cathedral in England. In 672 St Wilfrid built the first church to stand on this site. The crypt is the only remaining feature of the original church to have survived unscathed. Today, no fewer than five styles of architecture are represented in the cathedral, among them Early English for the imposing west front.

Notable features in the **nave** include the bronze art nouveau-style **pulpit** and the Tudor **font**, still used for baptisms. The stained-glass window above the font is the only example to survive the destruction inflicted by Parliamentary soldiers in 1643.

The **misericords** beneath the seats of the choir stalls date from 1494 and some like the griffin catching a rabbit are reputed to be the inspiration for Lewis Carroll's *Alice in Wonderland* – his father was Canon of Ripon

(1852–68). The choir stalls themselves were also completed in 1494, although some of the canopies are nineteenth-century copies replacing those damaged by the fall of the spire in 1660.

The **treasury** houses a selection of valuable artefacts that belong to parishes within the dioceses of Ripon. The **Ripon Jewel**, discovered near the cathedral in 1976, dates from the earliest period of the cathedral's history, and the **charter** of 1604, by which James I reinstated Ripon as a collegiate church, is also on display.

Information/tours/guides Free leaflet. Full-colour guidebook (£2.50) covers the history and layout of the cathedral. Better still is the Sound Alive audio tour (£2), which lasts for about an hour and really brings the cathedral to life. The cloaked guides dotted around the cathedral are extremely knowledgeable and happy to answer questions.

When to visit Choral evensong is normally at 5.30pm (exc. Wed); see *The Daily Telegraph*, *The Independent* and *The Yorkshire Post* for details. Special events, including recitals, take place all year (purchase tickets in advance).

Age appeal Likely to appeal to older children and adults. An activity leaflet for younger children, who will not appreciate the audio tour, would be useful. Steps leading into and out of the crypt are extremely steep and uneven.

Food and drink None.

Shops A small but good-quality range of merchandise with a mainly religious or Celtic theme is available in the compact cathedral shop. The range of books and videos includes a selection of material of local interest.

🚗 In centre of Ripon (follow signs from A1). Pay-and-display car park nearby. ⊖ Nearest rail station is Harrogate. Harrogate and District 36 or 36A bus goes to Ripon. Tel. 01423 566061 for details. 🕐 7.30am to 6.30pm. Guides available 10am to 5pm. 💷 Suggested donation of £2 for cathedral, 50p for treasury. ♿ Full access apart from crypt. Ramped access at west door.

Roman Baths

Pump Room, Stall Street, Bath BA1 1LZ ☎ *(01225) 477785*
📠 *(01225) 477743* 🖥 *www.romanbaths.co.uk*

Quality ★★★★	Facilities 👜👜👜👜	Value for money ££££

Highlights Excellent complex of ancient baths; free guided tours; good audio tours
Drawbacks Not enough for children to do; over-priced restaurant; orientation sometimes confusing

---

What's there If you are expecting just a giant, steaming bath, you will be surprised at how much there is to see here. This is one of the best Roman sites in Britain. Once a sacred place for local Britons, the natural hot springs were transformed by the Romans into a huge leisure complex that became the focal point of the town Aquae Sulis.

But it is not the Roman bits you see first, as most of those are 20 feet underground. Instead you come upon the attractive **Georgian and Victorian superstructure** built when the baths were rediscovered and became a 'must-see' for royalty and nobility alike. The star attraction of this part is the **Pump Room**, an elegant, colonnaded room opened in 1795 and now home to the site's restaurant. It is very Jane Austen, with chandeliers and heavy drapes, starched white napery and formal waiters. You can still drink a glass of spa water (disgusting) from the fish fountain, and look down into the Great Bath.

The layout is a little confusing but you will eventually find the main entrance to the baths. Take a walk around the **terrace**, graced by statues of Roman figures that are actually Victorian, before you head down into the extensive **museum** and Roman remains. Make sure you use the hand-held audio tour to get the most from the exhibits – it explains all about the building of the baths and the significance of the finds. The exhibits are all well-laid out and labelled, but it can get crowded around the most popular items, among them the **Gorgon head pediment** and the life-size gilded bronze **head of Minerva**. Parts of the temple steps and courtyard are also visible.

After the museum, if you have timed it right, you can join a guided tour of the **baths** themselves, or carry on using the hand-held guide. Both are informative, although we preferred the real guide for enjoyment and interest. As you walk around the baths, remember you are walking on flagstones that were laid nearly 2,000 years ago, and that the lead lining of the **Great Bath** is still the original one.

The water, which contains 43 minerals and is heated to 46°C, flows from the spring into the steamy Great Bath, where it is coloured green by algae growth. Do not overlook the surviving piece of Roman lead piping set into the stone floor. In adjacent areas are large bath complexes, with changing rooms, steam rooms and Roman equivalents of saunas. All are remarkably preserved with original mortar and underfloor heating, although little remains above floor level. The **East Baths** are more impressive, but the **West Baths** have a cold plunge pool filled with water containing an amazing array of foreign currencies thrown in for luck, including soggy dollar bills.

The last stop is the **King's Bath**, a Norman creation over the original sacred spring. Look out for the wall niches that provide seating and the iron rings for hauling yourself out of the water, which was much higher in Norman times – notice the tide mark around the walls.

Information/tours/guides All the exhibits and remains are well explained. The guidebook (good value at £3.50) is packed with colour photos and information and makes a good souvenir, but is not essential to your visit. Conversely, without the free, hand-held audio tour (lasting about an hour) you will not appreciate the full history and significance of the sight, but its numbering system is illogical and confusing, so be careful not to miss anything out. The tone is a little dry and earnest, but you will learn a lot. More animated and enjoyable is the free guided tour (of the baths only, not the museum) which leaves every hour on the hour between 10am and 4pm, lasts about 30 minutes, is full of anecdotes and trivial but interesting facts – and gives you the chance to ask questions. It starts at the end of the museum but is badly publicised, so ask about it on entry.

When to visit In summer, the baths are packed with tour groups. In

July/Aug a visit early in the day could be advisable; alternatively, try the evening, when it is pleasantly quiet and atmospherically torchlit. Only a short section is outdoors, so the baths are ideal for rainy days.

Age appeal Very few people will find the site boring, but little is done to liven it up for children. Some activity sheets and more hands-on displays would not go amiss.

Food and drink Above the baths, the Georgian Pump Room (run by Milburns) is a lovely spot for tea, or a full meal, served by immaculately dressed waiters and accompanied by piano music. Unfortunately the prices are exorbitant and the food hit-and-miss: our inspection dinner (£18.95 for three courses; a greasy Caesar salad and a disappointing spinach frittata, thankfully followed by a divine chocolate mousse) was distinctly mediocre and marred by lacklustre service. Lunch options include soup and salad (£7.95), and steak and potatoes (£13.25). Tea for two, with sandwiches and cake, costs £16.95; pot of tea £1.95.

Shops The main shop opens on to the street, so you can go in without paying the entrance fee. It has an imaginative range of products, although not all are 'Roman' in theme: many relate to Bath or capitalise on the foreign market. Among them are a pseudo-Roman pottery vase (£15.50), postcards (30p), replica Roman coins (99p) and Bath tablemats (£16.50) as well as Wedgwood china, jam and books. Overall the goods are upmarket and expensive, with not enough for children (a blessing for some parents, perhaps).

Other facilities Three out of the four toilets were rather average and need a make-over. Lucky ladies get the spanking new ones if they go to those beside the Pump Room.

🚗 Access is limited as the baths are in the centre of town, much of which is pedestrianised. No parking on-site, but plenty of pay car parks within easy walking distance. ⊖ Bath's rail and bus stations are 5 minutes' walk away. ◷ Oct to Mar 9.30am to 5pm; Apr to Sept 9am to 6pm (Aug 9am to 10pm). Closed 25, 26 Dec. £ Adult £6.90; child (6 to 18 yrs old) £4; senior citizen (over 65) £6; family ticket (2 adults + up to 4 children) £17.50; disabled visitor/carer free to terrace; Bath/north-east Somerset resident free with proof of residence; groups of 20+ receive discount but must pre-book. No pushchairs allowed but child carrier available. ♿ As the baths are underground and the floor is very uneven, there is no wheelchair access. The viewing terrace offers free access, and disabled guests are given free spa water in the Pump Room. No disabled parking.

Royal Armouries Museum

Armouries Drive, Leeds, Yorkshire LS10 1LT ☎ *0113–220 1999*
🖥 *www.armouries.org.uk*

Quality ★★★   **Facilities 👜👜👜👜👜**   **Value for money ££££**
Highlights Appropriate use of interactivity and modern technology will fascinate children and adults alike
Drawbacks Relatively expensive

What's there Opened in 1996 as an extension to the collection of arms held in the Tower of London, the **museum** is housed in an impressive, castle-like glass and steel structure situated in Leeds' scenic redeveloped canalside. Inside, the three floors, each with a mezzanine level, are divided into galleries covering different aspects of weaponry and combat throughout the ages.

However, the museum is not simply about warfare – the top floor houses a gallery covering **hunting throughout the centuries,** from its original purpose as a necessary means of procuring food to the pastime many types have become today. Whaling, wildfowling and big-game hunting are represented, with videos explaining the role of hunting in culling animal populations. An interactive monitor lets children identify creatures from their food and habitat, and highlights the issue of endangered species. This gallery houses a vast collection of hunting weapons ranging from medieval spears and clubs to modern rifles.

The **Oriental gallery** presents military costumes and arms used by the great civilisations of Asia, including the fearsome Mongol and Hun mounted archers and Samurai warriors. Such was the level of craftsmanship in the exquisite **Japanese armour and swords** that during restoration X-rays were used to gain a better understanding of the original construction. A video demonstrates the skills of the *Yabusame* horse archers, still practised today. The gallery also contains the largest piece of armour in the collection, the only surviving set of **elephant armour** in the world, donated to Clive of India in 1801, which weighs in at a total of 142kg – a truly impressive sight.

Another gallery deals with **self-defence**, and ways in which individuals have sought to fend off attack. A video describes the art of duelling by means of a story of two naval officers committed to duel according to the nineteenth-century code of honour simply as a result of a fight between their pet dogs. Other videos tell of gunfighting in the Wild West, and the weapons and tactics used by police forces in countering crime. A superb interactive 3-D exhibit of modern weapons reveals, for instance, the mechanisms of a machine gun and a pistol.

The **tournament gallery** deals with heraldry, jousting and armour in medieval times. Children will be enthralled by the demonstration of two knights in full armour walloping away at each other while explaining the techniques used, in accordance with a medieval manual on foot combat.

A final gallery covers **modern warfare**. Another interactive screen allows you to 'role-play' the Battle of Pavia, the first battle in which fire-arms had a decisive impact. There is also a **mini-cinema** showing a fascinating film on the Battle of Agincourt. Also worth seeing is the **Hall of Steel**, the architectural centrepiece of the museum, which is a curious creation of art from weapons of war – an arrangement of 3,000 shields and weapons along the inside of the stairwell.

The realities of war are not glamorised or glossed over in any way. One exhibition, for example, mocks the pomp and glory of war; another film focuses on the dark, inhuman side of war, with footage of the Iran-Iraq War and the destruction in the Gulf.

It is certainly worth checking out temporary **exhibitions** and daily **demonstrations**. Examples at the time of inspection were Buffalo Bill's Wild West and the Hiroshima and Nagasaki exhibitions. In summer, reconstructions of **jousting** can be seen on the Tiltyard, and in the **Craft Court** weapons are made and maintained.

Information/tours/guides No gallery guides but it is worth buying the glossy guidebook (£2.95), which is well written and full of interesting details. Each day demonstrations of various types of combat and famous battles are provided (phone in the morning for times and locations).

When to visit This is very much on the school-trip circuit. Tiltyard and other outdoor exhibitions are usually held in summer months.

Age appeal Definitely geared to entertaining children, but of interest to all ages.

Food and drink The Nelson Bistro on the ground floor serves, for example, cold meat salads (£4.95), gammon steak and chips (£6.25) and beef-burger and chips (£5.50); a café on the mezzanine offers tea and coffee (£1.50) and sandwiches (£2.50).

Shops The large shop stocks a massive variety of goods, mostly designed for children, including T-shirts (£6) and videos (£20).

🚗 Follow signs from city. Car park to the front of the building (£3 for whole day).
⊖ From Leeds rail station, follow signs for a pleasant 10-minute walk along canal.
🕐 Nov to Mar 10.30am to 4.30pm; Apr to Oct 10.30am to 5.30pm. Closed 24, 25 Dec.
💷 Adult £4.90; child (3 to 15 yrs old), senior citizen, student £3.90; family ticket (2 adults + up to 3 children) £14.90. ♿ Wheelchair access by lift to all areas.

Royal Pavilion

North Street, Brighton BN1 1EE ☎ *(01273) 290900*
⁊ www.brighton.co.uk

Quality ★★★★★	Facilities 🏛🏛🏛🏛🏛	Value for money £££££
Highlights	Opulent oriental fantasy palace built by eccentric monarch; wonderful Regency furniture and antiques; Queen Adelaide tea rooms; excellent guidebook and guided tour; broad appeal	
Drawbacks	Lack of space means that excellent introductory video is shown at end of visit; busy on summer weekends	

What's there Brighton's Indian-style fantasy is unique among British palaces and royal buildings for its flamboyance and eccentricity. George IV, the 'Prince of Pleasure', had the Pavilion built by John Nash for dirty weekends in Brighton with Maria Fitzherbert, whom he married illegally. George liked to spend vast amounts of money; possessing superb taste and no concept of restraint, he mingled eclectic styles to amazing effect. In a jaw-dropping contrast with the Moghul-influenced domes of the exterior, the inside is over-the-top Chinese opulence, all red and gold, hand-painted bamboo wallpaper, serpents and dragon motifs.

It is difficult to imagine a British monarch enveloped in so much *chinoiserie* and sensual excess: Queen Victoria hated the Pavilion and thought Brighton an immoral town. During her reign the magnificent rooms were stripped and left in a dilapidated state. The town of Brighton bought the building in 1850 and Victoria later relented, returning much of the original **art** and furniture; Queen Elizabeth II also returned a substantial **collection of antiques and furniture**.

Among the many splendours are the dramatic **banqueting room**, over which a silver dragon dangles a magnificent chandelier, and the **music room**'s dome of gilt cockle shells – like a dragon's scales – above an immense hand-knotted carpet. Beneath cast-iron palm trees, the **great kitchen** displays lavish menus that hint at the decadent scale of entertainment that went on here.

Information/tours/guides Free floor plan offers basic information on the highlights; expanded information on boards in each room; excellent guided tours (11.30am and 2.30pm; great value at £1.25); attractive glossy guidebook (£3.25) recommended for in-depth story, fascinating insights and great pictures.

When to visit Any time, but summer weekends are busiest. Free-access days might save you money, but the place will be bursting at the seams.

Age appeal The Pavilion's eccentricity and flamboyance appeals to virtually all ages, except possibly under-8s.

Food and drink The Queen Adelaide tea rooms ooze period character (try a £4.95 Pavilion cream tea) and overlook the restored Pavilion Gardens and Dome. Various coffees £2.10, tea £1.30. Limited selection of light lunches: ploughman's (£4.95), home-made soup (£2.50), patisserie (£1.15–£1.95). Seconds away are Brighton's Lanes, where dozens of restaurants cater to all tastes.

Shops The upmarket shop sells pricy ceramics, from Wedgwood candle-sticks (£25) to rose jars (£299), reproductions of the Pavilion's wallpapers and fabrics and books on art and architecture relevant to the Regency and Victorian periods. Prints from Pavilion collection come framed (£39.50) or unframed (£3.50–£12).

Other facilities Toilets are not easy to spot: they are on the upper floor. If the Pavilion is busy there could be a lot of people between you and relief! One is sensibly located next to the tea rooms. All are clean with adequate fittings.

🚗 Follow signs from M23. Use a town-centre car park (e.g. NCP Church Street). Avoid on-street parking. ⊖ 10-minute walk from Brighton rail station. Bus to Brighton Pool Valley a couple of minutes' stroll away. ⏲ Oct to May 10am to 5pm; June to Sept 10am to 6pm. Closed 25, 26 Dec. 💷 Adult £4.90; child (under 16) £3; student, senior citizen, unemployed £3.55; family ticket (2 adults + up to 4 children) £12.80; (1 adult + up to 4 children) £7.90. Brighton residents enjoy cheaper admission (£2) Oct to Mar. ♿ Ground floor accessible; 3 steps up to tea rooms.

Salisbury Cathedral

Salisbury, Wiltshire SP1 2EJ   ☎ *(01722) 555120*
🖰 *www.salisburycathedral.org.uk*

Quality ★★★★ **Facilities 💷 💷 💷 💷** **Value for money £££**

Highlights Fine medieval structure; tombs; stained-glass; chapter house carvings and Magna Carta

Drawbacks Restoration of the exterior continues, which means some of building may be shrouded in scaffolding and protective coverings

What's there Built between 1220 and 1258, with few later additions, this cathedral is a pure example of one architectural style: Early English Gothic. Reaching up to over 400 feet and added half a century after the rest of the cathedral was finished, the tower and spire are the tallest in Britain. The cathedral's exterior has inspired many artists over the centuries – most famously, John Constable and J. M. W. Turner. Inside, the slender, soaring arches of the **nave** and huge windows draw the eye upwards, and the overall impression is light, airy and elegant. None the less, the huge weight of the tower and spire, despite strengthening devices, has caused the elegant columns to twist under the strain, which you will notice if you stand, for example, at the base of those at the corner of the south transept and look up.

The church is dedicated to the Virgin Mary, and religious services have been held here daily since 1225. Some of its contents, such as the remains of St Osmund, cousin of William the Conqueror and builder of the first (Norman) cathedral at Old Sarum, are even older. Osmund died in 1099, and his modest, undecorated tomb has double holes each side to enable pilgrims to touch the top of the grave. Other interesting **tombs** around the cathedral include that of William Longspee, Earl of Salisbury and half-brother to King John. Longspee, a military and naval commander, was one of the advisers on the Magna Carta, the signing of which he witnessed; he died in 1226 and was the first person to be buried in the church, in the **Trinity Chapel.** Another tomb, in the north aisle, is that of Sir John Cheney, who survived the Battle of Bosworth Field in 1485; other noble warriors buried here fought in the Crusades and at Agincourt and Crécy.

But the **Mompesson tomb** could not be more different: Sir Richard and Dame Katherine Mompesson, who lived in the cathedral close in the seventeenth century, have a tomb of many colours, their clothing depicted in vivid three-dimensional detail. However, because the tomb was formerly on the other side of the aisle the couple are facing the wrong way (west rather than east).

In the morning chapel is part of the original thirteenth-century stone screen that used to separate quire and nave, and, in a niche, a revolving engraved glass **prism** (1985) by Laurence Whistler, depicting the cathedral. This is one of several fine examples of contemporary art here: note also the **prisoners of conscience window** (1980) in the Trinity Chapel by Gabriel Loire of Chartres and the striking **embroidery** on the altar cloth here and on the high altar.

Other items to look out for within the main body of the cathedral are, in the quire, the **Bishop's throne**, designed by Gilbert Scott in about 1870; the nearby misericords (under the tip-up seats) in the back two rows of the choir stalls – beautifully carved and, incidentally, an indication of how much shorter people were in the thirteenth century; the bulky **medieval clock**, of about 1386, which is the oldest in England and the earliest mechanical clock in virtually complete working order in the world (it has no face, but strikes the hour on a bell in the triforium); and the wonderfully detailed **model** of the cathedral while it was being built, surrounded by blacksmiths', glaziers', carpenters' and masons' workshops, stables, a lime kiln, a treasurer's office, and even a graveyard for the craftsmen and labourers.

Just off the adjoining cloisters – the largest in England, although this cathedral was never monastic – is the **chapter house**. Dating from the latter half of the thirteenth century, this fine octagonal building is supported by a central column that rises to meet the fan vaulting above. Here the clergy would meet to discuss church business and listen to a chapter of the Bible being read. They sat on the stone bench that surrounds the room, no doubt gazing from time to time at the marvellous **bas-relief frieze** above them that recounts the stories of Genesis and Exodus – Adam and Eve, Noah's Ark, the Tower of Babel and the exploits of Abraham, Isaac and Jacob – and at the **carved heads** on the arches. These warts-and-all medieval sculptures are almost certainly of people who were around at the time when the chapter house was built.

This building also houses a copy of the **Magna Carta** (1215), one of only four surviving from 42 that were made. Written in colloquial English, rather than Latin, this 'great charter' has been the basis of many nations' constitutions, including the 1688 English Bill of Rights. Salisbury's copy is on calfskin.

Information/tours/guides A leaflet, with map, is included in the entry price, and information boards are situated around the cathedral. Tours of the ground floor, including chapels, cloisters and chapter house, take place 9.30am to 4.45pm Mar to Oct, 10am to 4pm Nov to Feb, also evenings (Mon to Sat June to Aug 6.30 to 8.15pm), and last about an hour. Sun tours 4 to 6.15pm May to Sept. Tower tours (1½ hours, 330 steps) take place at 2pm all year (Mon to Sat), and also at 11am and 3pm Apr to Sept (Sun 4.30 May to Sept). Tours of the craft workshops (book in advance) focus on the building, stone, lead, glass and craft areas: Mon to Fri. Tours and access are restricted during Dec owing to special events. Souvenir guidebook costs £2.50.

When to visit Any time, but avoid visiting while a service is in progress unless you wish to take part.

Age appeal Children may like the model of the cathedral under construction and the chapter house's stone carvings, especially if they have one of the educational booklets (*Look at Salisbury Cathedral*, 75p, or *The Story of Salisbury Cathedral*, £1.99).

Food and drink Coffee shop offers tea and coffee (95p), soup (£2.50 – e.g. carrot and orange), savoury tart (£4.75 – e.g. cheese and onion) and main courses (£4.95) such as shepherd's pie; filled jacket potatoes £3.75; flapjack or shortbread 75p, cheddar/chive scone £1.05; spicy bread pudding £1.25.

Shops Broad range of goods stocked: books, posters (including copies and translations of the Magna Carta), greetings cards and stationery, plus gift items such as hand-made bookmarks (£2.50), tea-towels, mugs (£3.50 and £6.99), T-shirts (£13.95) and sweatshirts (£26.50).

🚗 Follow signs from Salisbury ring road. Centre of city is very compact: unless you are prepared to pay £5 to park within the cathedral close car park, use a public car park (one is just off Milford Street) and walk. 🚇 5-minute walk from Salisbury railway station. 🕐 June to Aug 7.15am to 8.15pm; Sept to May 7.15am to 6.15pm. 💷 Adult £3; child (5 to 18 yrs old) £1; senior citizen (over 60), student £2. *Tower tour* adult £3; child £2. *Craft workshop tour* adult £1; child (under 18) 50p. ♿ Phone ahead to arrange for disabled visitors to be dropped at west front and parking will be made available in the cathedral close car park. Wheelchair access to ground floor is good. Touch-and-hearing model of cathedral in nave.

Sandringham House

Sandringham, Norfolk PE35 6EN ☎ *(01553) 772675*

Quality ★★★	Facilities 🛠🛠🛠🛠	Value for money ££££

Highlights A personal insight into royal life; friendly, knowledgeable room guides; fine grounds

Drawbacks Museum design rather old-fashioned

What's there One of the Queen's private country homes, Sandringham House was rebuilt in neo-Jacobean style in 1870 in accordance with the wishes of Prince Edward (later Edward VII) and Princess Alexandra. Many of the furnishings from that period remain, particularly some splendid **tapestries**, **bronzes** and **porcelain**. The house contains more homely touches than some of the grander royal residences, such as a half-finished jigsaw and a video recorder in the stately **saloon** overlooked by the **minstrels' gallery**.

The **museum**, converted from the coach houses and stable block, houses an eclectic collection ranging from **Queen Victoria's wheelchair** and **Minton** porcelain to **big game trophies** and **royal cars** of various ages (including a miniature copy of the Aston Martin featured in the James Bond film *Goldfinger*, made for Prince Andrew in 1966).

The 600 acres of **grounds** are splendidly landscaped, incorporating woods, lakes and streams. The formal **North Garden** is hedged with box and flanked by avenues of pleached limes. The small church contains an exquisite aluminium and ivory **figure of St George**, made by Sir Alfred Gilbert as a memorial to the Duke of Clarence.

A visit to the house does not take long, but the extensive grounds provide plenty of scope for walks and picnics in fine weather. Allow half a day overall.

Information/tours/guides A full-colour guidebook (£2.50) covers the gardens, the house and its history, the museum and the church. Room guides are knowledgeable, helpful and happy to supply titbits about the domestic life of the Royal Family as well as information on the furnishings and history. Tractor-and-trailer tours of the park take 45 minutes (adult £2; child £1; senior citizen £1.50).

When to visit Early summer for the rhododendrons, high summer for the roses and herbaceous beds in the North Garden. Special events throughout the year include craft fairs, driving trials, firework concerts and flower shows (extra charges apply).

Age appeal The Family Fun Quiz (50p) gives older children a focus of interest when visiting the house; younger children are more likely to enjoy running around the grounds (also containing an adventure playground, near the visitor centre). Free land train providing transport between ticket office and house could be a boon for some elderly people.

Food and drink The purpose-built visitor centre houses a self-service restaurant, serving hot food at lunchtime as well as rather unimaginative sandwiches (cheese and tomato, tuna and cucumber, ham, smoked salmon, egg), good scones with generous helpings of cream and jam, cakes, and hot and cold drinks. Also provided are a waitress-service tea room and an ice-cream kiosk. Within the grounds, next to the museum, another (self-service) tea room offers scones, cakes and hot and cold drinks. Picnic tables are provided next to the visitor centre.

Shops Wide range of goods, some with royal connections (e.g. Sandringham wine, place mats and a video narrated by Prince Edward), others less so (shortbread and fudge, china animals, jewellery). Range of books also somewhat eccentric – gardening and wildlife books along with discounted books on rock stars.

🚗 Off A148, 8 miles north-east of King's Lynn (follow signs for last 2 miles or so). Free parking next to visitor centre. ⊖ Buses from King's Lynn railway station and bus station leave every hour Mon to Sat 9am to 4pm, dropping you at visitor centre (allow 30 minutes); service slightly less frequent on Sun and bank hols. For more information tel. 0500 626116. ① *House* 15 Apr to 18 July (closed Good Friday), 3 Aug to 8 Oct 11am to 4.45pm. *Museum* 15 Apr to 22 July (closed Good Friday), 3 Aug to 8 Oct 11am to 5pm. *Grounds* As museum, 10.30am to 5pm. 💷 *House, museum and grounds* Adult £5.50; child (5–15) £3.50; senior citizen, student £4.50 family ticket (2 adults + up to 3 children) £14.50. *Museum and grounds only* Adult £4.50; child £3.50; senior citizen, student £4; family ticket (2 adults + up to 3 children) £12. ♿ Ground floor has good wheelchair access (carers admitted free). A small number of wheelchairs are available on loan on a 'first come, first served' basis. Free land train carries visitors to house from visitor centre.

Sea Life Centre

Marine Parade, Brighton BN2 1TB ☎ *(01273) 604234*
🌐 *www.sealife.co.uk*

Quality ★   **Facilities** 💺   **Value for money ££**
Highlights Seeing marine life up close and personal; flexible re-entry system allows you to come and go throughout the day to see scheduled talks and activities; Victorian vaulted building
Drawbacks Inadequate explanation; poor facilities; no family ticket

---

What's there This **aquarium** houses mainly native marine life in a vaulted subterranean building in the Victorian arches of Brighton's sea front. The attraction relies on the novelty of close-up encounters with marine life to provide entertainment – even cod and plaice look exciting when they are swimming in front of you rather than encased in batter. The fish are the stars here, let down by the uninspired layout, presentation and interpretation. The best parts are a **shark tunnel**, a **seahorse exhibit**, **rays** and **touch tanks**. A disappointing 'Adventures at 20,000 leagues' feature consists of a mock-up of Jules Verne's imaginary *Nautilus* submarine with a short **film** loop recounting part of the *Twenty Thousand Leagues under the Sea* story in an auditorium overlooking the shark pool. Little evidence of the Sea Life Centres' marine environmental programmes can be seen here.

Information/tours/guides The information and interpretation at this attraction need a lot of improvement and a more committed approach. Opportunities to give visitors more insight into what they are seeing are constantly lost: a tank of wonderful rays, for example, lacks any explanation as to what exactly they are, their diet, habitat etc. The sharks are probably the no. 1 crowd-puller, but you will not discover even what sort of sharks they are. Some tanks lack any explanation at all. The souvenir guide (£2.50) is poor value, with four pages devoted to advertising other Sea Life Centres; the rest is sketchy, superficial and adds nothing to the visit. The guide who explained the seahorse display seemed knowledgeable, but the head-microphone she used distorted her voice and gave off feedback, while visitors milled chaotically around.

When to visit Any time, but as this is an indoor attraction it is best seen on a rainy day. Space inside is limited and can become too crowded for comfort. For a crush-free experience, avoid main holiday weeks and busy summer weekends, when Brighton is too popular for its own good.

Age appeal Who can resist the novelty of seeing fish (especially sharks) close-up? Children in particular find this exciting, but adults who want to learn something more serious about marine life will probably be disappointed. The 'FinZone' trail is aimed at children, as are various touch-screen computers and CD-ROM games.

Food and drink The depressing café with its peeling walls is not inviting. The poor selection of unappealing self-service items is not worth the bother when the excellent cafés and restaurants in Brighton's Lanes are just over the road. If you are desperate, you will find here sandwiches (£1.80), cheese bagels (£1.25), unappetising-looking hot-dogs (£1.95) and instant coffee (99p). During our visit one overworked young woman struggled to serve ice-cream cones and take money from a growing queue.

Shops The poor merchandise includes little to enhance the visit, other than a limited selection of books on marine life. Otherwise New Age CDs and tapes cost £8.99–£12.99, fluffy sea creatures such as dolphins (£5.25–£16.99) and sweets in lurid colours (pick & mix 79p per quarter) are typical items. Two uniformed girls on the cash desk were more interested in chatting to one another than being helpful.

Other facilities The single toilet next to the entrance was completely inadequate for the number of visitors; the Formica-and-lino décor and an overflowing waste bin (when we visited) did nothing to improve matters.

🚌 Follow signs from M23. ⊖ 15 minutes' walk from Brighton railway station to sea front (Sealife Centre is opposite Palace Pier). ① Apr to Oct 10am to 6pm (last admission 4pm); Nov to Mar 10am to 5pm. Closed 25 Dec. £ Adult £5.95; child (4–14), student £3.95; senior citizen £4.25. ♿ Raised areas around tanks prevent wheelchair users getting close and invite other visitors to stand between them and exhibits; steps are also a problem; limited space to manoeuvre.

Sellafield Visitors Centre

Sellafield, Seascale, Cumbria CA20 1PG ☎ *(019467) 27027*
🖥 *www.bnfl.com*

Quality ★★★★★   **Facilities** 🍴🍴🍴   **Value for money £££££**
Highlights Highly interactive, hi-tech and educational
Drawbacks Out-of-the-way location

What's there This ultra-modern site tells the story of nuclear energy in a highly interactive, hi-tech and informative way. Your opinion of it – either as an educational visit or cynical manipulation – is likely to be influenced by your personal views on nuclear power.

Nuclear power produces 16 per cent of the world's electricity. Sellafield's job is to generate small amounts of it and, more importantly, dispose of and recycle the waste products. The centre has a walk-in re-creation of the **inside of a power station**, with a **giant model of the Earth** and representations of the amount and types of pollution with which we poison it.

Throughout the centre are touch pads that activate **video and audio displays** about how energy is created and used, along with space-age chairs from which to watch interactive video presentations. A **music hall theatre**, complete with stage curtain and pop-up characters, is used to tell the story of the splitting of the atom in an easy-to-understand and very imaginative way.

A state-of-the-art **auditorium**, designed to resemble the inside of a nuclear reactor, uses banks of video screens and stunning sound systems, along with moving 'fuel rods' that descend from the ceiling, to tell you what happens there. Similarly, a walk-in **model of a recycling chamber** takes you through that process.

Sellafield has stacks of **working models**, including one that allows you to create your own tornado and put your hand inside it, with lots of handles, levers and dials to twist and pull. You can also take a coach tour of the actual **nuclear site**. Allow about three hours in total.

Information/tours/guides Strangely, no guidebook is available, but many leaflets and information desks are provided from which you can find out anything you want to know. The coach tour (30 minutes) with guide leaves every half-hour (Apr to Oct 10.30am to 1 hour before closing).

When to visit Everything is indoors, but to get the best views on the coach tour you need clear weather.

Age appeal Of wide appeal owing to the interactive and hi-tech style of the presentation, and a story that is likely to fascinate. Not too much walking.

Food and drink A modern self-service coffee shop with good views across the site serves drinks along with a limited menu of pre-packed sandwiches, jacket potatoes, and hot baguettes.

Shops The small gift shop sells items that mostly have no relevance to the centre, including scented candles, Beatrix Potter books, mugs, ornaments and grow-your-own crystals.

🚌 From M6 take junction 40 and follow A66, then A595. Ample free parking. ⊖ Train to Carlisle, then to Sellafield. You will be bussed to the centre from the nearby police reception area (trips not timed). ⊙ Apr to Oct 10am to 6pm, Nov to Mar 10am to 4pm. Closed 25 Dec. ⊞ Free, including coach tour. ⅙ Good. Ramps and toilets provided. Wheelchairs and induction loop available. Coach tour not accessible.

Sewerby Hall and Gardens

Church Lane, Sewerby, Bridlington, Yorkshire YO15 1EA   ☎ *(01262) 677874*

Quality ★★★	**Facilities 🍴 🍴**	**Value for money £££**

Highlights A variety of attractions rolled into one, including the Museum of East Yorkshire, gardens, a land train and golfing green

Drawbacks Museum layout confusing due to lack of internal signposting; mediocre children's zoo

What's there Sewerby Hall contains the Museum of East Yorkshire, which features a variety of exhibitions. Displays of local, regional, national and international material hang in the **East Yorkshire Photographic Gallery** and the **Yorkshire Showcase Gallery**, while the changing face of the surrounding area is traced in the well-thought-out **East Yorkshire Journeys** display, which will appeal to young and old alike. A varied array of souvenirs, trophies and mementoes presented to Amy Johnson, the pioneering female aviator, is displayed in the **Amy Johnson room**. On the ground floor examples of period rooms are to be found, though these lack any real atmosphere or character. The **oak room** is the most impressive, thanks to some beautiful panelling and good views over Bridlington Bay.

The 50 acres of grounds include the splendidly landscaped **Pleasure Garden**. The towering monkey puzzle trees are reputed to be among the oldest in England, and the peaceful Old English and Rose **walled gardens** provide plenty of wooden benches for relaxing on. The Marie Curie **daffodil walk** supplies colour in spring. There is also an indifferent children's zoo, a playground, some animal paddocks, a pitch and putt golf course and a bowling green. A **miniature land train** runs along the scenic clifftop to Limekiln Lane.

A visit to the hall and the various museums will take between one and two hours. The grounds, together with their many attractions, provide plenty of scope for walks and picnics in fine weather. Allow at least half a day for house and grounds.

Information/tours/guides Poor internal signing can make a tour of the various museums and galleries rather confusing: a well-planned tour of the hall would improve the visitor experience significantly. Room attendants are extremely thin on the ground. A simple guidebook (£1) includes a very sketchy plan of Sewerby Hall and provides a brief history of the hall and gardens, but is not particularly good value for money. There is no guide to the gardens, and children are not well served as no activity leaflets are provided.

When to visit Go in high summer for the roses in the walled gardens, or in spring for the Marie Curie daffodil walk. Special events take place throughout the year, including concerts, vintage car rallies and medieval jousting pageants (extra charges may apply). For details tel. (01262) 673769.

Age appeal Younger children are likely to enjoy running around the gardens, visiting the zoo and playground and taking a ride on the miniature train. The museums and galleries are likely to appeal to older children and adults. Those with mobility problems should be able to cope with the flat grounds and reasonably well-maintained paths.

Food and drink The clock tower houses a cramped waitress-service tea room, which serves hot snacks (burgers, chips and sausages) at lunchtime and a standard range of sandwiches (egg mayonnaise, cheese and tomato, smoked salmon), as well as cream teas, ice cream and hot and cold drinks. There is also a terraced area and a licensed bar. The picnic area situated in front of the hall has stunning views over Bridlington Bay.

Shops The small range of goods includes a selection of books on the local area, and the official guidebook.

🚗 On B1255, off A165, 2 miles from Bridlington. Car park is second left after Leys House. ⊖ Train to Bridlington station (3 miles away), Bus: tel. (01262) 673142 for details. East Riding of Yorkshire bus 10 from Quayroad Side (near station). ○ *Hall* 19 Feb to 28 Mar, Sat to Tue 11am to 4pm; 3 Apr to 29 Oct, Mon to Sun 10am to 6pm; 30 Oct to 17 Dec, Sat to Tue 11am to 4pm. Closed 2 Apr, 18 Dec to 18 Feb. *Gardens and zoo* Mon to Sun, 10am to 6pm. 💷 *House and gardens* Adult £3; child (5 to 15 yrs) £1; senior citizen £2.20; family ticket (2 adults + 3 children) £7. *Land train* Adult: one-way 80p, return £1.50; child: one-way 50p, return 70p. *Golf* 12-hole: adult £2.50; child £2; senior citizen 50p. 18-hole putting: adult, child £1; senior citizen 50p. *Golf season pass* Adult £65; child £45; senior citizen £33. *Bowling* £1 per hour. ♿ The gardens, tea rooms, zoo, hall and museum are all accessible to disabled visitors.

Shakespeare's Birthplace

Henley Street, Stratford-upon-Avon, Warwickshire CV37 6QW
☎ *(01789) 204016*   ☝ *www.shakespeare.org.uk*
☝ *info@shakespeare.org.uk*

Quality ★★★	Facilities 👜 👜 👜	Value for money £££
		(£££££ if visiting all the Shakespeare houses)

Highlights Beautiful house; good attempt at a characterful exhibition in separate Visitor Centre

Drawbacks Can get ridiculously crowded; design of exhibition makes for much frustrating elbowing

---

What's there The house where the Bard was born in 1564 stands on a pedestrianised street in the centre of Stratford. It is an impressive Tudor building, beautifully restored and maintained, surrounded by a small garden filled with plants and herbs mentioned in Shakespeare's plays.

The modern Visitor Centre adjacent to the birthplace houses the **Shakespeare's World exhibition**, which makes a valiant attempt to give a picture of the poet's life and times – from information about his **parents** and his **will**, to drawings of Stratford and London, furniture, seals, documents, **models of the Globe Theatre** and a copy of the **first folio** of **collected works**. The exhibits are interesting and well presented – it is the design of the place that is at fault. Some exhibits are viewed as if through the windows and doorways of a stylised Elizabethan village, along a winding route. As a result, if the place is crowded, people push to see through the too-small openings.

The cramped nature of the attraction is evident in the **Birthplace** proper too. The beamed and flagged house is a treasure trove of **period furniture** and fascinating **oddities** – such as a baby-walker and a room arranged as it might have been at the time of the Bard's birth – but frustrating bottlenecks can take the shine off this self-guided tour. There are no placards or boards to explain any of the pieces.

Allow 40 minutes for the exhibition, and 30 minutes for the house.

Information/tours/guides There are no guided tours. Guides in the house can answer questions. The guidebook (£2.50) gives limited information on each room and covers all the Shakespeare houses: the Birthplace, Anne Hathaway's Cottage (*qv*), Hall's Croft (see directory at back of this book), New Place and Nash's House (counted as one sight), and Mary Arden's House (both in the directory).

When to visit Good all year round. You will need an umbrella to get from the Visitor Centre to the house if it is raining. Expect crowds virtually all the time, especially during school holidays.

Age appeal Probably best for adults and older children. Those who find stairs difficult will not be able to see upstairs in the house.

Food and drink The cafeteria, across the street, was refurbished in early 2000.

Shops A shop at the end of the tour offers all sorts of Shakespearean paraphernalia: scripts, tea-towels (£4), books, aprons, models of Anne Hathaway's Cottage (£57.95), and books on woad and wattle and daub. Staff are helpful but the shop is too small to cope with the summer crowds.

🚗 Nearest pay-and-display car park of several in central Stratford is on Windsor Street (3 minutes' walk). ⊖ From station, birthplace is 5 minutes' walk. ⊙ 20 Mar to 19 Oct, Mon to Sat 9am to 5pm, Sun 9.30am to 5pm; 20 Oct to 19 Mar, Mon to Sat 9.30am to 4pm, Sun 10am – 4pm. 💷 Adult £5.50; child £2.50; senior citizen, student, unemployed £5; family ticket (2 adults + up to 3 children) £14. *Inclusive ticket for all 5 houses* Adult £12; child £6.50; senior citizen, student £11; family ticket £29. *Inclusive ticket for 3 central houses* Adult £8.50; child £4.20; senior citizen, student £7.50; family ticket £20. ♿ Ground floor of house accessible to wheelchair users. Full access to Visitor Centre, exhibition and garden.

Sizewell Visitor Centre

Nr Leiston, Suffolk IP16 4UE ☎ *(01728) 653890*
🌐 *www.british-energy.co.uk*

Quality ★★★	Facilities 💷💷💷	Value for money £££££

Highlights Free admission

Drawbacks Can be frustrating if walking tours of Sizewell A are not available; poor catering

What's there Two nuclear power stations are based on a 10-hectare site on the Suffolk coast. The older of the two, **Sizewell A**, is a Magnox twin reactor station owned by BNFL Magnox which has been producing electricity 24 hours a day since 1966. On a typical day, the station can supply more than 10 million kWh of electricity, enough to serve the needs of a third of East Anglia.

Sizewell B, which sports a distinctive 'golf-ball'-shaped dome, became operational in February 1995, having taken nearly eight years to build at a cost of £2 billion. Owned by British Energy, it is Britain's first pressurised water reactor. It generates electricity for up to 1.5 million people and, at full capacity, can light over 20 million light bulbs.

A visit to the site starts at the **Visitor Centre**, where a small but impressive exhibition hall explains the history of electricity, beginning with Michael Faraday's pioneering work in 1831. From here visits are organised to the power stations. You can choose between a 40-minute minibus tour of Sizewell B or a 1½-hour tour on foot to Sizewell A (unavailable on day of inspection). The latter follows a set route and may be altered or cancelled according to what is happening within the station.

Information/tours/guides Plenty of information comes free of charge – although some of it is so technical as to be rather mind-boggling for first-time visitors. However, a bevy of approachable and down-to-earth guides, both in the exhibition hall and on the tours, are on hand to explain the power stations in layman's terms. It is advisable to book Sizewell A tours 24 hours in advance. You cannot book minibus tours of Sizewell B in advance, but if you phone ahead staff will advise you on the best time to come.

When to visit Good weather preferable if you want to do the walking tour (if it is running), otherwise this is a mainly indoor attraction.

Age appeal Not suitable for young children. School-age children will enjoy the high-tech nature of the Visitor Centre exhibition and the walking tour of Sizewell A. However, it is probably best suited to adults who want to learn more about the nuclear fuel industry.

Food and drink Minimal facilities: vending machines stock uninspiring sandwiches, chocolate bars and crisps. Tea, coffee and hot chocolate are also machine-produced. Although items are cheap (sandwiches are 55p, drinks 20p), the standard of refreshment is low.

Shops A glass-fronted display sells a selection of Sizewell souvenirs such as a glossy book (£3.50) as well as pens, pencils, T-shirts, sweatshirts and notebooks.

🚗 From Leiston (off A12), follow brown signs to Sizewell. ⊖ Not advisable: nearest rail station is Saxmundham, a 20-minute taxi ride away (also bus service, but this is irregular). ⊙ Easter to 31 Oct, Mon to Sun 10am to 4pm. Closed Nov to Easter. 💷 Free. ♿ Sizewell A not accessible, but Visitor Centre is. Minibus for Sizewell B tour has wheelchair lift.

Skegness Natureland Seal Sanctuary

North Parade, The Promenade, Skegness, Lincolnshire PE25 1DB
☎ /📠 (01754) 764345

Quality ★★★   **Facilities ★★★**   **Value for money £££**
Highlights Interesting animals; a refreshing lack of commercialism
Drawbacks Facilities, especially off-season, are rather limited, so do not make plans to eat here

What's there The sanctuary is about much more than seals – it is really a miniature zoo, giving children (in particular) a good overview of all members of the animal kingdom and how they live. As well as the adult **harbour seals** in their big concrete figure-of-eight pool, there is a separate (seal) **baby-rearing pool** and a seal hospital, built in 1990 after an epidemic killed many North Sea seals: rescued animals are brought here for treatment.

You will also see, in other pools, jackass penguins, koi carp and, on their own central island, chipmunks. The sheep, goats, turkeys and small, **tame domestic animals** in the Pets' Corner enclosure can be fed by visitors (appropriate food is on sale at the shop). A small aviary contains budgerigars, peach-faced lovebirds and a golden pheasant.

Indoor environments include a **Tropical House**, with **Nile crocodiles**, an iguana, terrapins, a royal python, a tegu, scorpions, locusts, tarantulas and giant snails, and the **Floral Palace**, where butterflies (birdwings, monarchs, swallowtails) and tropical birds (waxbills, doves, finches, nuns, blue-winged sivas and spice birds) fly free. Chilean flamingoes with bright pink knees paddle in their own pond. Cacti, yucca, hibiscus, fuschias and palm trees flourish in the humid rainforest atmosphere of this glazed building, which also contains a goldfish pond.

Another warm place to retreat to if the weather is cold is the **Aquarium**, which has a wide variety of fish – including the bulbous-eyed gourami and some innocent-looking piranhas – and other sea creatures, from anemones to crabs, in its tanks. One section features native marine tanks containing creatures from the nearby beach and shallows. 'Fishy facts' on the walls highlight points of interest (for example: you are seven times more likely to win the Lottery jackpot than to be killed by a shark).

Many of the animals have been given names and adopted by local people.

Information/tours/guides This is a small site, easy to navigate and clearly labelled on signs that incorporate identification photographs. The souvenir booklet (£1.50) includes a plan, colour photos and descriptions of the animals and conservation work. An audio commentary in that area describes the seal hospital's activities. At the exit a board contains helpful reminders of some of the items you might have missed, so you can backtrack if you wish. Seals and penguins are fed at 11.30am and 3pm; baby seals at these times and 2pm (feeding times are announced over the PA system). Dogs are allowed on a lead, except in the Floral Palace.

When to visit Any time of year, though the butterflies in the Floral Palace stop flying about in the colder months and refreshment options are limited off-season.

Age appeal The exhibits offer children entertainment and education combined. They can also feed the tame animals (food is sold at the gift shop) and make animal brass rubbings (paper and wax cost 30–50p). Adults will find much to enjoy too.

Food and drink Light refreshments are available in summer from a booth alongside a covered seating area. Off-season, a drinks machine sells tea (55p), coffee (65p), chocolate, and tomato soup in a cheerless room provided with tables and chairs.

Shops A gift shop sells cuddly toys, brass-rubbing and educational materials, souvenirs and packets of food for feeding the tame animals.

Other facilities The toilets, though not lavish, are well maintained and have won an award. A separate loo for wheelchair users and baby-changing is provided.

🚗 From A52 or A158, enter Skegness and follow signs to sanctuary, on sea front. Public car park and on-street parking nearby. ⊖ Train to Skegness, then taxi (no specific bus service). ⊙ Apr to Sept, Mon to Sun 10am to 5pm; Oct to Mar, Mon to Sun 10am to 4pm. Closed 25, 26 Dec, 1 Jan. 💷 Adult £4.10; child (3–16) £2.70; senior citizen £3.30; family ticket (2 adults + 2 children) £12.20. Group rates (for 10 or more visitors) available. ♿ Most parts accessible to wheelchairs. Disabled toilet.

Skipton Castle

Skipton, North Yorkshire BD23 1AQ ☎ *(01756) 792442*
🖥 *www.skiptoncastle.co.uk*

Quality ★★ **Facilities** 👛 👛 👛 **Value for money** £££
Highlights Excellent example of medieval castle; pleasant picnic area
Drawbacks Lifeless interior

What's there Skipton Castle is one of the best-preserved and most complete examples of a medieval castle in England despite having endured a three-year siege during the Civil War. The history of the castle is closely linked with that of the Clifford family, who were granted the property in 1310 by Edward II. Still fully roofed, the fortress stands virtually unaltered since its modernisation more than 300 years ago.

However, the interior is lifeless and the visitor needs to work hard to imagine what daily life would have been like for the Clifford family. A guided tour or audio tour and some illustrative displays would go a long way towards improving the visitor experience.

Visitors begin their tour in the **shell room**, which doubles as the ticket office. Located in the east tower of the gatehouse, it is one of only two such grottoes in England and was made for Henry Clifford between 1626 and 1629. Its shell-studded walls are an impressive display of craftsmanship.

The castle is accessed via Lady Anne's steps. The **banqueting hall**, which would have been a hive of activity in the medieval castle, lacks atmosphere – it is empty except for a pair of nineteenth-century **naval cannons**. The kitchen, despite a fine flagstone floor, is similarly disappointing – no effort whatsoever has been made to give visitors a feel for what once must have been been a bustling and noisy room. The new kitchen, created in the sixteenth century, still has its original **charcoal burning stove** as well a newer cast-iron range. Smaller rooms on the tour sheet include a ladies' parlour, where Mary Queen of Scots was allegedly held prisoner, beer and wine cellars, and a curing room.

The **dungeon** is every bit as dank as you would imagine it to be, while the **watch tower**, as one might expect, offers good views. Other points of interest are the **medieval font** in the twelfth-century chapel of St John the Evangelist, and the **yew tree** planted in 1659 by Lady Anne Clifford in Conduit Court (the castle's central courtyard).

Information/tours/guides A full-colour guidebook (£2) covers the history of the castle and gives a short description of each room and what it was used for. A very basic black-and-white leaflet, which suggests a tour route, is included in the admission price, as is a castle explorer's badge for children.

When to visit Any weather conditions will do, as the castle is fully roofed. A limited number of special events take place during the year – admission is included in the normal ticket price (phone for details). Parking can be difficult to find on market days (Mon, Wed, Fri and Sat).

Age appeal A family quiz (20p) gives older children a focus of interest when visiting the castle. Younger children and infirm people may find the steep steps to the watchtower and dungeon difficult to manage.

Food and drink A small tea room serves light meals (soup, french-bread pizza and baked potatoes), a standard selection of sandwiches, cream teas, a selection of cakes and hot and cold drinks. Picnic tables are provided on the chapel terrace.

Shops The castle gift shop, next door to the tea room, sells a reasonable range of goods including adults' and children's books, ice creams and cold drinks.

🚗 From A59 or A56, head for Skipton town centre. Pay-and-display car parks nearby (no on-site parking). ⊖ Train to Skipton station, the Pride of the Dales bus 72 (phone 01756 753123 for details). ① Mar to Sept, Mon to Sat 10am to 6pm, Sun 12pm to 6pm; Oct to Feb, Mon to Sat 10am to 4pm, Sun 12 to 4pm. Closed 25 Dec. 💷 Adult £4.20; child (5 to 18 yrs old) £2.10; senior citizen, student £3.60; family ticket (2 adults + up to 3 children) £11.50. ♿ Not suitable for wheelchair users or those with walking difficulties.

Slimbridge Wildfowl and Wetlands Trust

Slimbridge, Gloucestershire GL2 7BT ☎ *(01453) 890333*

Quality ★★★★★ **Facilities** 🏛🏛🏛 **Value for money £££££**
Highlights Flamingoes; Peng Observatory; Tropical House
Drawbacks Basic facilities (due to be revamped, with a new Visitor Centre, in 2000)

What's there The Trust was founded here in 1946 by **Sir Peter Scott** and now supports the world's most comprehensive collection of wildfowl. It has large **wetland areas** for wild geese, ducks and swans, as well as **lake enclosures** for permanent collections of clipped birds, including the only place in Europe where you can see all **six types of flamingo**. The **Peng Observatory** is the best place from which to observe the wild geese and swans. But this is not just a twitcher's paradise: the well-organised programme of events, for both adults and children, and the attractive setting mean that Slimbridge appeals to a very wide audience.

A free map of the extensive site suggests walks of one, two or three hours or even for a whole day, but a handy way of getting an overview of what's here is to join the hour-long free **tours** that are usually available at weekends. These are fairly informal and you are free to come and go as you wish. Your guide can helpfully point out things like flamingo chicks – not that easy to spot – and **rare species**.

The wild birds can be observed from large hides (binoculars can be hired), while the permanent collection is divided into regions of the world, such as Asian, Australian, and Tundran, with helpful information boards. The **Tropical House** recreates the conditions of the rainforest, where the birds flying free, but Slimbridge also concerns itself with **local wildlife and plants**, providing information on these as well.

Information/tours/guides Free tours take place from 11am at weekends (times are posted on a noticeboard at the entrance). Check in advance for the times of craft demonstrations and talks (for example, on flamingoes, or on the Tropical House) held around the site. One-off events held each month may include wildflower walks or duck decoy demonstrations. In winter, until the last weekend in February, the wild birds can be viewed out-of-hours by floodlight (adult £3.50, child £1.50, no advance booking required). The guidebook (£1) is superb value, with plenty of pictures and information about birds and the work of the Trust.

When to visit All year round. Birds display their mating colours at the start of the year, and build nests in spring. From the end of May, and throughout the summer, plenty of young can be seen. In autumn geese and ducks fly in from the north, while in the winter the Bewick swans are in residence.

Age appeal Numerous weekend events are held for children, from storytelling to badge-making (phone for times or check at the main entrance). Play area also provided.

Food and drink The old restaurant is to be replaced in 2000 by a modern Lottery-funded Visitor Centre. The food on inspection was straightforward, but tasty. Main dishes include roast pork (£4.95) and cheesy cabbage and leek bake (£3.95). Sandwiches are £1.85-£2, coffee 75p.

Shops Situated at the main entrance, the shop has everything you might want to buy connected with birds, e.g. a wildfowl tea tray (£24.95) or duck mug (£5.75).

Other facilities Toilets are not well distributed through the site.

From M5 between Gloucester and Bristol, take junction 13 or 14 and follow signs. ⊖ Train to Cam and Dursley station then taxi to Trust (phone 0345 484950 for information). ◷ Summer (26 Mar to 29 Oct), Mon to Sun 9.30am to 5pm; winter (29 Oct to 24 Mar), Mon to Sun 9.30am to 4.30pm. Closed 25 Dec. Adult £5.75; child (4 to 16 yrs old) £3.50; senior citizen, student, unemployed, single parent £4.75; family ticket (2 adults + 2 children) £15.50. ⑉ Easy access, with wheelchairs available for loan. No guide dogs. Talks and tactile exhibits can be organised by prior arrangement.

Snibston Discovery Park

Ashby Road, Coalville, Leicestershire LE67 3LN ☎ *(01530) 510851; information (01530) 813256*

Quality ★★★★ **Facilities** 🏛🏛🏛🏛 **Value for money** £££££
Highlights Great hands-on scientific experiments; full consideration for children
Drawbacks Inexperienced staff in café; Sheepy Magna's wheelwright workshop open only on request

---

What's there The park was created on the site of the former **Snibston**

Colliery, where the Stephenson brothers (of *Rocket* fame) sank the first shaft in 1832. The pit heads are still there, and a fascinating surface Colliery Tour is on offer for exploring this area fully. A huge modern exhibition hall houses an eclectic mixture of galleries on the theme of discovery, whether scientific, historical, engineering or historical in nature. You can walk through a **mini tornado** and experiment with wind power in the Science Alive! gallery, or **make your own rainbow** in the Science of Light gallery. Transport, Extractives and Engineering galleries are crammed full of large, bright exhibits, while a Textiles and Fashion gallery displays examples of **underwear through the ages**. These last four galleries are of local historical import, as they are based on Leicestershire industries.

The Discovery Park as a whole is closely linked with the local community: some of the huge sculptures on display have been made by local schools and artists, and in the **Universities Showcase** gallery you can explore genetic fingerprinting or create your own earthquake courtesy of the local centres of academe.

Outside, the colliery provides the backdrop to an innovative and accessible **outdoor science play area**. Huge exhibits have been designed to let you experiment with levers, water and heat, as well as secret messages. **Sheepy Magna,** an authentic wheelwright's workshop, can reputedly be opened on request but remained closed on our visit.

Ten minutes' walk away are the **nature trail** and **carp lake,** with more sculptures, masses of wildlife, and plenty of quiet, secluded places for picnicking or relaxing.

You could spend the whole day here enjoying a happy balance of indoor and outdoor activities. It is advisable to bring a picnic, as the cafeteria serves only simple food.

Information/tours/guides The guidebook is simple, informative and good value at 50p, but is not essential as a free site plan is provided. Friendly staff are on hand to assist if necessary. The colliery tour starts every half-hour (from 11am until 1½ hours before closing) and lasts an hour (adult £1; child 50p). The tour is worth taking – the guides, all ex-miners, are both funny and knowledgeable. However, it is perhaps not suitable for very young children, as there is lots of walking and standing around.

When to visit Ideally, go in good weather, as a fair bit of the attraction is outside, but even in wet weather the park has enough to keep children and adults occupied for a couple of hours. Special events throughout the year feature, for example, kite-making, theatre, technology challenges, jazz evenings and steam rallies. You may run up against large groups of school-children during term time.

Age appeal Most galleries have been designed to be interactive, so the park is fun – and fascinating for children and adults alike – although adults on their own have to be willing to 'learn through play'. Plenty of space is provided for playing and picnicking. Top marks for the younger children's play areas in the more adult displays, which help to keep toddlers occupied.

Food and drink The open-plan exhibition hall houses a good-value if limited self-service cafeteria – food includes sandwiches, baked potatoes (about £2) and hot baguettes, as well as standard hot drinks, cans of pop and cakes. Service by the youthful staff was a little erratic when we inspected.

Shops A great little shop perfectly complements the attraction with something for everyone. Fossils range from 25p to £20, while you can also purchase books, science games, kites and examples of gemstones from around the world.

🚗 From M1 take junction 22 and A511 to Coalville then follow signs. Free parking. ⊖ Train to Leicester or Loughborough (Snibston is equidistant from both). *From Leicester* buses 117, 118, 119; *from Loughborough* buses 125, 126, 127 (45 minutes from both towns). Alternatively, 25-minute taxi ride (about £10). ◷ Apr to Sept, Mon to Sun 10am to 6pm; Oct to Mar, Mon to Sun 10am to 4pm. Closed 25, 26 Dec and 1 week in Jan for maintenance (phone for details). 💷 adult £4.75; child (5 to 15 yrs old) £2.95; senior citizen, student, disabled, unemployed £3.25; family ticket (2 adults + 3 children) £13.50. *Season tickets* Adult £12; child £9; senior citizen, student, disabled, unemployed £10; family ticket £35. ♿ Parts of Colliery Tour inaccessible, otherwise good access.

South Lakes Wild Animal Park

Crossgates, Dalton in Furness, Cumbria LA15 8JR ☎ *(01229) 466086*

Quality ★★   **Facilities** 🏛 🏛   **Value for money** ££
Highlights Access to the animals
Drawbacks Poor facilities and maintenance

What's there This rather motley **collection of animals and birds** is themed according to country, and a trail leads you from one to the next. Africa is the first in the series, but sadly seems to comprise a couple of zebras and two rhinos in one rather barren-looking field, two apparently listless cheetahs in another, and a few porcupines, all with a busy main road for a background.

The wildlife generally has plenty of space, but although the **monkey and gibbon enclosures** have ropes and wooden frames for the primates to climb on, the other animals do not have very much to occupy themselves with. Looking through a fence at a tiger or lion lying on ground overgrown with weeds and nettles is not very entertaining – for either species. Presumably as an attempt to enhance the country theme, loudspeakers hidden in trees pump out appropriate soundtracks. The **Australian zone**, for example, has bush noises echoing through it, but the only real purpose it serves is to drown out the noise of the traffic.

The Australian area is, in fact, very unusual in that it lies within a fenced area that can be walked through, thus allowing the visitor to 'mingle' with such creatures as **emus**, **kangaroos**, **wallabies** and **storks**. However, a rather worrying sign tells people that some of the animals are 'dangerously aggressive' and will bite. Another sign tells you not to 'get close to the peacocks', which is difficult to avoid when they are wandering around. The country theme starts to break down after a while, as animals of various origins are kept in the same area.

A large pond is a central focal point in the park, but it is unattractive and dirty-looking, despite having a collection of ducks and swans on it. A toy

children's train can be ridden a short distance and back again through part of the zoo. Allow about two hours for a visit.

Information/tours/guides A guidebook is available at a reasonable £2, and continues the 'country' theme with lots of colour pictures and brief details about the animals. The book also contains a map, but there are no guided tours. Daily talks are given on the apes and monkeys (12.30pm) and rhino conservation (1pm) between Easter and September. Feeding times are between midday and 3pm.

When to visit It is all outside, so fine weather is required. At colder times of the year, many of the animals are more likely to stay inside their covered enclosures.

Age appeal Children should like looking at the animals. Quite a lot of walking is involved, some of it a little on the rough and steep side.

Food and drink A small self-service café has unimaginative décor and food, some of which was left lying on the floor when we visited. Pie and beans, jacket potatoes, and standard pre-packed sandwiches are about the extent of the range.

Shops A separate gift shop in an exposed breeze-block building sells animal calendars, T-shirts, stuffed toys, and a few books and videos.

From M6, take junction 36 and follow signs. ⊖ Train to Dalton, then bus to park gates (phone park for details). ⏲ Mar to Oct, Mon to Sun 10am to 6pm; Nov to Feb, Mon to Sun 10am to dusk. Closed 25 Dec. 💷 Adult £6.50; child (3 to 15 yrs old), senior citizen £3.25; disabled person free with full-price carer; family ticket (2 adults + 2 children) £17. *Half-price admission* Nov to end Feb. ♿ No specific facilities. Some steep, rough ground. Wheelchair available for loan.

Southend Pier

Western Esplanade, Southend-on-Sea, Essex SS1 1EE ☎ *(01702) 215620*
⌨ *www.southendpier.co.uk*

Quality ★ | **Facilities** 🏛 🏛 | **Value for money** ££
Highlights A historic landmark; fun to take a trip to the end on a sunny day
Drawbacks Not much to see; mainly a collection of shops, cafés and arcades

What's there Southend Pier is the **longest pleasure pier in the world** at about 1.3 miles, and the train ride (or walk) out to the end of the pier is a large part of the attraction. At the far end you will find an assortment of cafés, bars, shops and arcades, including the **Pavilion**, where live music is on offer at certain times during the summer season. It is pleasant enough on a sunny day, with visitors strolling around and fishermen trying their luck, but there's not a lot to see. Apart from eating and shopping, the limited attractions include having your fortune told by Madame René, visiting the **Southend lifeboats**, feeding money into the arcade machines and seeing the charred remains of the timbers devastated in the 1976 fire.

Back at the shore end of the pier is a more extensive amusement arcade as well as the **Pier Museum**, which puts the whole experience into a historical context. The largest items are examples of the old pier trains, including one of the so-called 'toast-rack trams' dating from 1890, and a reconstructed pier **signal box**, complete with working levers. One of the train carriages shows videos about the history of the pier, and has a selection of **old slot machines** that can be operated using old pennies, available from the desk.

Information/tours/guides A leaflet gives details of opening times, prices and special attractions, but it is not something you need on the spot. There is also a history of the pier on offer (60p), but it is quite dry and all in black and white. The volunteers who run the Pier Museum are enthusiastic about their work, and may be able to answer questions.

When to visit The pier really needs fine weather, and crowds bring it to life. Go on a summer weekend during a special event and it could be good fun (though parking will be difficult). Out of season or in bad weather the place can be bleak and depressing, with little going on and everyone huddling indoors.

Age appeal Young children will enjoy the trains, and there are a couple of rides for them at the pier head, but they will be more interested in the nearby adventure playground and beach. Older children may take more of an interest in the lifeboats and museum, and are bound to be fascinated by the amusement arcades.

Food and drink There are various places to get a drink, snack or meal at the pier head, including a couple of cafés, a wine bar in the Pavilion, and McGinty's Café Bar, which the publicity leaflet claims to be famed for its fish and chips. We found the cod and chips (£4.20) heavily battered and somewhat greasy. Also available is a range of dishes such as mussels (£4.90), steak and kidney pie (£3.80), burger and chips (£3.30), and a seafood platter (£9.70 for two).

Shops The Pier Emporium is not the most upmarket of shops, but it offers a good range of seaside trinkets and knick knacks to take home. Children will delight in the range of seaside rock and candy floss, as well as cheap toys and joke products. There are various predictable mugs, tea towels and seaside hats, plus a more unusual array of shells and shell products, including mobiles (from around £6).

Other facilities The public toilets at the pier head are of rather functional steel design, and on our visit were not particularly clean or well maintained.

🚗 From M25, take junction 29 then A127 to Southend; follow brown signs to seafront. Pay and display parking along the esplanade. ⊖ Train to Southend Central, then 10-minute walk to pier. ⊙ Apr to Oct, Mon to Fri 8am to 9pm, Sat and Sun 8am to 10pm; Nov to Mar, Mon to Fri 8am to 4pm, Sat and Sun 8am to 6pm. Closed 25 Dec. *Pier train* every 30 minutes when pier is open. *Pier museum* May to Oct, Tue, Wed, Sun and bank hols 11am to 5pm. 💷 *Pier train* adult £1.50 one-way, £2 return; child (3 to 13 yrs old) 75p one-way, £1 return; family ticket (2 adults + up to 3 children) £3.50 one-way, £5 return. Single tickets only cover journey back from pier head. ♿ Trains are accessible and most shops and cafés are at ground level or accessible by ramp. The Pier Museum is reached via a flight of steps. Disabled toilet.

St Michael's Mount

Marazion, Nr Penzance, Cornwall TR17 0EF ☎ *(01736) 710507*

Quality ★★★★ **Facilities 🎫 🎫 🎫 🎫** **Value for money ££££**

Highlights Wonderful location; well-thought-out visitors' route
Drawbacks Admission poorly displayed; more room guides would be helpful

What's there Dedicated to St Michael the archangel who, according to old Cornish legend, appeared here in 495, St Michael's Mount has been in turn a church, priory, fortress and a private house. It was given to the National Trust in 1954 and is reached from the mainland via a cobbled causeway.

The **granite castle**, which dates from the twelfth century, is a steep ten-minute climb from the little village of Marazion. Visitors enter through the west doorway where audio tours can be collected (£1); an audio-visual show on the history of the castle and the Cornish legend of Jack the Giant Killer is included in the admission price. A circular route ensures that visitors see the castle in its entirety, although some rooms can become crowded during peak season.

A collection of **sporting weapons and military trophies** including bugles, drums and steel helmets is displayed in the Armoury. Chevy Chase, so called because of the **plaster frieze** that consists of a series of hunting scenes, is the most impressive room on the tour. The painted enamelled windows were brought to the Mount early in the nineteenth century – note the two **roundels depicting Heaven and Hell** at the bottom of the central window. The beautiful oak table dating from 1620 was what the former community of monks ate their meals on – the room was originally their refectory.

Further along are the **blue drawing rooms**. With their rococo interior, Chippendale furniture and vaulted ceilings, they are a complete contrast to the rest of the castle. The northern and southern terraces give visitors splendid views of the surrounding area and the impressive **terraced gardens**.

Information/tours/guides A full-colour guidebook (£2) contains a comprehensive history of the Mount and a description of the main rooms seen on the tour. Leaflets are available on the castle and the village, with maps and plenty of useful information (50p each). There is also a children's quiz book with a fold-out colouring section (50p). The one room guide we encountered during our inspection was enthusiastic and knowledgeable, despite being swamped with visitors' questions. The entrance to the audio-visual cinema is via the shop, which can get crowded just before a show. Privately operated boat trips run from the pier in Marazion (adult £1, child 50p).

When to visit The Mount is open all year round, though visitors should telephone before embarking on a trip between November and March. The terraced gardens are open on weekdays during April and May and certain weekends throughout the year.

Age appeal Young children and those with walking difficulties will find the steep cobbled paths to the castle difficult to manage. Children of all ages will enjoy the audio-visual show and boat trips around the island.

Food and drink The waitress-service licensed Sail Loft restaurant serves hot and cold lunches – such as seafood pancakes, crab salad or Stilton and mushroom flan – from 12.15pm to 2.30pm daily, as well as a limited selection of sandwiches, plus cakes, cream teas and hot and cold drinks. The Island Café (not NT-managed) in the village serves snacks, hot and cold drinks and ice creams.

Shops A quality range of merchandise appeals to young and old alike, and includes foodstuffs (e.g. jams, fudge, chutneys and fruit wines), an interesting book section and some wonderful Celtic jewellery.

🚗 From A394, Marazion is ½ mile south. Public car parks. ⊖ First Western National buses 2, 2A (Penzance-Falmouth), 17A (Penzance-St Ives) and 32 (Penzance-Cambourne) pass Penzance railway station, 3 miles away. Call (01209) 719988 for details. ① Apr to Oct, Mon to Fri 10.30am to 5.30pm (last admission 4.45pm); Nov to Mar, variable – phone in advance to check exact times. 💷 Adult £4.40; child £2.20; family ticket (2 adults + up to 4 children) £11. Deaf or blind visitors and their carers admitted free. Group rates available. Free admission for NT members except on charity event days. *Ferry fares* adult £1 each way, child (under 15 yrs old) 50p each way. Tel (01736) 710267/710507 for tide and ferry information. ♿ Unsuitable for wheelchairs: steep site, cobbled causeway and paths. Braille and tape guides available.

Stonehenge

Amesbury, Wiltshire ☎ *(01980) 624715* ⌕ *www.english-heritage.org.uk*

Quality ★   **Facilities 🚹**   **Value for money ££££**

Highlights These ancient stones will always inspire awe and provoke more questions than they answer about what our ancestors intended

Drawbacks Visitors are kept well away from the stones (you can see almost as much from the roadside); lack of interpretation, both at the start of the visit and on site; poor facilities

What's there The purpose for which this very ancient monument was built remains a matter of speculation, but this World Heritage Site continues to exert a fascination and attract visitors in considerable numbers, despite the fact that the famous stones can currently be viewed only from a distance.

The site, dating from 3050 BC, is surrounded by a circular ditch and bank (a 'henge'), 100 metres across. Within this area was built, about 2500 BC, a wooden structure. The enclosure originally comprised six concentric rings of wooden posts, and may have had a roof: the antiquarian John Aubrey, exploring the site in 1656, found 56 holes (now known as 'Aubrey holes') made to hold wooden posts. The wooden monument was to be replaced, during the next 1,000 years, with the stone monument, a circular structure aligned with the sun's rays at the sunrise of the summer solstice. Not all of it survives: stones have been plundered for other buildings over the centuries, or to make farm tracks. What can be seen today is about half of what originally stood here.

The **circle of stones** comprises 6-metre-high sarsens (sandstone boulders) connected by stones forming a continuous lintel, and a circle of smaller (4-metre-high) **bluestones** within it, encircling a **horseshoe of 'trilithons'** – the giant archways constructed using two tall upright stones with a shorter one laid across the top. The stones were shaped for their purpose, and held firm by means of a mortice and tenon joint.

While the sarsens came from the Marlborough Downs, 30 kilometres away, the bluestones were hauled an astounding 385 kilometres from the Preseli mountains in Pembrokeshire, South Wales. Why this should have been done is a mystery, though it is known that the Welsh mountains were on the trade route from Ireland – the first landmark after Rosslare.

The builders would have been hunter-gatherers living nearby. They were the first farmers, and they reared domestic animals, the bones of which were used for digging out the ditch; deer antlers were used as pick-axes. The area would have been thickly wooded, with pine and hazel trees, turning to downland, so the site would perhaps originally have been in a clearing.

Various theories have been proposed as to why those ancient Britons should have gone to the trouble of building this site. It may have served as a temple – perhaps to a sun god – as there is an altar stone in the centre and, outside the ditch/bank circle, a 'heel stone' over which the sun's rays pass at sunrise. The site very probably has astronomical significance, and may have been an observatory. Whether the purpose was scientific, religious or both, the circle may have served as a calendar, created by priest-astronomers. Certainly the site was used for burials: two barrows are to be found within the ditch/bank circle, and 345 within a 4-kilometre radius, arranged in a linear pattern. People were buried in pits with pottery and other possessions, some of which can now be seen in the museums at Salisbury and Devizes.

Unfortunately, over the years, a combination of road-building and mass tourism have robbed Stonehenge of much of its atmosphere. At the moment it stands in a field between the A360 and the A303. English Heritage and the National Trust (which owns the land) have plans to redirect the A303 through a tunnel and then re-route the A360, as well as construct an exhibition centre from which visitors would approach the site by walking across the fields, rather than funnelling beneath a dreary underpass as at present. However, the centre is unlikely to open before 2004.

Information/tours/guides A leaflet is included in the entry price but contains minimal information. Guided tours are publicised as taking place when weather permits, though none was available when we visited. When they happen, they last 30 minutes. Audio tours are provided, in six languages, but seemed to be in short supply (they are 'subject to availability'). If ever a site needed interpretation, this does. A video explaining, in particular, the alleged astronomical significance of the arrangement of the stones would be of great help, as would more interpretative boards on the route around the site.

When to visit The site is extremely exposed, and the wind can be biting. Try to go on a warm, calm day.

Age appeal Children may wonder what all the fuss is about unless they have been very fully prepared. Those who can use the audio tour will find links to stories and legends about the site that may amuse them.

Food and drink The Stonehenge Kitchen is an outdoor refreshment stall (no seating) between the car park and entrance turnstile serving tea (85p), coffee (£1.05), ices, sweets, Stonehenge 'heel-stone sticks' (£2.85), sandwiches (£3.65), 'trencher' (open) sandwiches (£2.45) and 'sarsen' pies (£2.05 to £2.30). 'Megalithic' rock cakes are £1.35, scones £1.25.

Shops The shop has a large central counter with goods around its periphery. Several of the books available are relevant to the site (factual ones such as *The Story of Stonehenge, Mysteries of the Stones and Landscape*, and novels such as *Stonehenge* by Bernard Cornwell, *Old Sarum* by Edward Rutherfurd and *Tess of the D'Urbervilles* by Thomas Hardy). Also sold here are gift items including pencils, rubbers, stationery and postcards, posters, mugs, sweatshirts and T-shirts, Stonehenge-design silk scarves (£34.99), jams and chocolates, umbrellas and camera film.

Other facilities The main toilets, like the main entrance area, have all the allure of a wartime concrete bunker. When we visited they were smelly and had broken fittings, temperamental hand-driers, and bins overflowing with paper towels. The other toilets, in a wooden hut, were padlocked.

🚗 2 miles west of Amesbury on junction of A303 and A344/360. ⊖ Nearest rail station Salisbury, 9½ miles. Wilts and Dorset bus 3; tel. (01722) 336855. ⏰ Mon to Sun,16 Mar to 31 May 9.30am to 6pm; 1 June to 31 Aug 9am to 7pm; 1 Sept to 15 Oct 9.30am to 6pm;16 Oct to 15 Mar 9.30am to 4pm. Closed 24–26 Dec, 1 Jan. 💷 Adult £4; child (5 to 15 yrs old) £2; senior citizen, student, UB40 card-holders £3; family ticket (2 adults + 3 children) £10. ♿ All parts accessible, but disabled visitors' toilet at far end of car park was locked well before site closed. Main toilets not accessible. Hearing loop.

Stourhead

Stourton, Warminster, Wiltshire BA12 6QD   ☎ *(01747) 841152*

Quality ★★	Facilities 🏠🏠🏠🏠🏠	Value for money £

Highlights Beautifully laid-out and maintained gardens, village and estate
Drawbacks Disappointing house interior with some overbearing room guides

What's there This magnificent **landscape garden** was begun in the eighteenth century by Henry Hoare. Centred on the **lake**, it shows plenty of classical influences, with features such as the Temple of Flora and the Pantheon to draw the eye. The mature and extensive collections of **azaleas** and **rhododendrons** are especially splendid and provide splashes of vibrant colour in late spring and early summer.

The eighteenth-century **house** is a grand Palladian villa and is undeniably impressive from the outside. However, the interior is somewhat disappointing, with poorly lit rooms, a lack of labels and several intimidating room guides to police visitors.

The house and garden are at the centre of a 2,650-acre estate and you are free to wander the woodland and open countryside. You can walk (or drive) from the gardens the 2 miles or so to **King Alfred's Tower**, a striking triangular red-brick folly. Climb the 205 narrow, spiral steps for excellent views.

Information/tours/guides The free map of the garden and walking routes is good for orientation, so the full-colour guidebook to the garden (£1.75) is worth buying only if you want a pictorial souvenir. The 50p leaflet on the house summarises its history and highlights items such as the seventeenth-century 'Pope's Cabinet' and fine Chippendale furniture. The full-colour guidebook to the house (£3), although detailed, is rather dry.

When to visit Spring/early summer is the best time to visit for the rhododendrons and azaleas (making weekends in May and June rather crowded) or autumn for maple trees. Avoid going to Stourhead in wet weather, as the gardens are the real draw here, and the house does not merit a visit in itself.

Age appeal Stourhead will appeal mainly to adults (especially gardening enthusiasts). The very useful children's guidebook (£1.65) provides a focus of interest in the garden and the house – although the latter is probably a bit too stuffy for most children's tastes.

Food and drink The Village Hall is a self-service tea room (open daily March to end October, 10.30am to 5.30pm) offering a selection of sandwiches (£1.65 to £3.25) and light lunches (such as ploughman's at £3.60) and soup of the day. Some prices seem steep for what you get, and the tea room is geared more to tea and cakes than meals. The Spread Eagle Inn opposite is open all year round and serves sandwiches as well as hot meals/pub fare.

Shops The National Trust shop is attractively set out. It sells a range of children's games and books, in addition to the usual National Trust gifts – calendars, greetings cards, biscuits, fudge, pottery and tea-towels, etc. A small plant centre sells shrubs grown at Stourhead (open daily, April to October).

In village of Stourton, off B3092, 3 miles north-west of Mere (off A303). 50p charge for car park. ⊖ Train to Gillingham (Dorset) then 58 bus (Mon to Sat twice daily; 25-minute journey). ① *Garden* Mon to Sun 9am to 7pm (or dusk if earlier), except 20 to 22 July 9am to 5pm (last admission 4pm). *House* 1 Apr to 29 Oct, Mon to Wed, Sat and Sun 12pm to 5.30pm (or dusk if earlier; last admission 30 minutes before closing). *King Alfred's Tower* 1 Apr to 29 Oct, Tue to Fri 2pm to 5.30pm (or dusk if earlier); Sat, Sun and bank hol Mon 11.30am to 5.30pm (or dusk if earlier). ⊞ Mar to Oct *garden or house* adult £4.60; child (5 to 16 yrs) £2.60; family ticket (2 adults + 3 children) £10; *garden and house* adult £8; child £3.80; family ticket £20; Nov to Feb *garden* adult £3.60; child £1.50; family ticket £8; *King Alfred's Tower* adult £1.50; child 70p. Free for NT members. ♿ Special parking; entrance via Bristol Cross, by Spread Eagle Inn; wheelchair and 1 powered vehicle (not bookable) on loan. *House* stairclimber by arrangement (01747 840348); *garden* path steep in places; more than 1 strong companion for wheelchair users essential; *King Alfred's Tower* inaccessible. Disabled toilets. Braille guides to garden and house. Bookable touch-tour guide to house.

Sudeley Castle and Gardens

Winchcombe, Cheltenham, Gloucestershire GL54 5JD ☎ *(01242) 602308*
🖰 *www.stratford.co.uk/sudeley*

Quality ★★★★	Facilities 🍴🍴🍴🍴🍴	Value for money ££

Highlights Immaculate gardens and romantic ruins of the banqueting hall
Drawbacks Poor toilets; audio tour is a bit too long and sometimes confusing

What's there This small-scale castle is most notable historically for being the home of Henry VIII's sixth wife, Katherine Parr (who is buried in the Chapel of St Mary in the gardens). During the Civil War, Sudeley became a

Royalist headquarters and a refuge for Charles I. After its fall, Oliver Cromwell made the owner, Lord Chandos, pay dearly, sending in troops to vandalise it. The remains of what must have been a very impressive **banquet hall** in the south quadrangle still stand as Cromwell's men left them in 1649. The castle was left in ruins for 180 years, until it was bought by the Dent family, who reversed the process, turning it back into a family home, as it still is today. The Emma Dent Exhibition features a collection of the belongings of the woman who was seen as the driving force behind the revival of Sudeley in the nineteenth century.

The contents of the castle apartments emphasise the royal connections, housing items such as Elizabeth I's christening robes and a wonderfully elaborate carved four-poster bed slept in by Charles I. The grounds have been laid out as a delightful series of separate **gardens**, the jewel being the **Queen's Garden**, which is full of old-fashioned roses.

There is also a small adventure playground for children, with a wooden fort and plenty of space to dash around.

Information/tours/guides The free map of the grounds is useful, but it has no plan of castle rooms. The full-colour guidebook (£2.50) contains plenty of beautiful photos and a long history of the castle, but very little information on the rooms you can visit and their contents. Some rooms have information leaflets in them and room guides who are happy to answer questions, and many exhibits are labelled. There is also a separate colour guidebook to the gardens (£2.50), which is very detailed and worth buying if you are an enthusiastic gardener. (You can buy both guidebooks for £4.) The audio tour (£2) tries to bring the history of the castle to life, but it suffers from being rather long and confusing at times, especially in the garden, despite signs showing you where you should be in relation to the commentary.

When to visit Any time is good to visit Sudeley, but avoid rainy days because you should walk around the gardens, which are a big attraction. From May onwards the 800 roses in the Queen's Garden are in impressive full bloom.

Age appeal The sight has something for all ages – the small adventure playground will please children, although the house and gardens will hold less appeal.

Food and drink The characterful and professionally run self-service Stableyard Restaurant and Tea Rooms are open 10am to 5pm, and lunch is served from noon to 2pm. Flagstone floors and a beamed ceiling ensure an atmospheric medieval-style setting in which to enjoy the high standard of food on offer. There is a good choice of sandwiches and rolls with fillings such as chicken and cranberry (£2.75), salads, soup, jacket potatoes, etc. Hot meals are very good and local produce is often used, Gloucester sausages with roast potatoes and fresh vegetables (£5.25) being a typical choice. Good selection of cakes and biscuits also available. Picnic area in the adventure playground section.

Shops The attractively laid out shop offers a large selection of jams, marmalades (£2) and biscuits plus gift items and plenty of Sudeley memorabilia (e.g. pens, pencils, frisbees). It also has a good choice of gardening books, greetings cards and Dents gloves (£33 to £44 a pair). A small plant centre specialises in old-fashioned roses, herbs and perennials.

🚐 Follow brown signs in village of Winchcombe (8 miles north-east of Cheltenham) on B4632. 10 miles from M5 Junction 9. Free car park. ⊖ From Royal Wells bus station in Cheltenham (Bay 13) Castleways bus runs Mon to Sat, at 60–90-minute intervals to Winchcombe. Very limited Sunday service. ⊕ **(1999)** *Ground, gardens, Emma Dent Exhibition, shop and plant centre* 4 Mar to 29 Oct 10.30am to 5.30pm. *Castle apartments, church and restaurant* 1 Apr to 29 Oct 11am to 5pm (last entry 4.30pm). 💷 *Castle, gardens and exhibition* adult £6.20; child (5 to 15 yrs old) £3.20; student, senior citizen, unemployed £5.20; family ticket (2 adults + 2 children) £17. *Gardens and exhibition only* adult £4.70; child £2.50; concessions £3.70. *Connoisseur's choice (incl adult ticket to castle, gardens and exhibition, audio tour, guidebook and coffee)* £10; *enthusiast's choice (as above but excl guidebook)* £8. ♿ Very limited access – castle and Emma Dent exhibition not accessible for wheelchair users. Parts of the gardens are flat for wheelchair users but would be difficult in wet conditions over grass. No disabled toilets. Steep steps to the Emma Dent exhibition.

Suffolk Wildlife Park

Kessingland, Lowestoft NR33 7SL ☎ *(01502) 740291*
🕸 *www.banham-zoo.co.uk*

Quality ★★★ **Facilities** 👜👜👜 **Value for money** £££target£
Highlights Wide range of animals with an interesting safari theme
Drawbacks Poor catering facilities

What's there This large (100-acre) site on a sloping hillside has a **variety of animals** in large enclosures. The area includes lakes, rivers and grassy islands. The zoo is promoted as an African **safari adventure**, with lions, giraffes, cheetahs, zebras, ostriches, Congo buffaloes, hyenas and monkeys, a farmyard corner and a walk-through wallaby enclosure. A wildfowl lake contains plenty of water birds, and paddocks house donkeys and Cameroon sheep.

In addition to the animals a **playground** offers a small helter-skelter, slide and two-seat carousel as well as a newer area containing attractive wooden climbing frames set on wood-chip safety surfaces. Crazy golf and a bouncy castle cost an extra 50p each. An indoor area offers 'family entertainments' in the form of slot machines. Animals can be handled in the 'Discovery Centre'.

Information/tours/guides No guidebook was available on the day of inspection, but a useful map (25p) gives feeding and talk times, as well as information on first aid and lost children plus directions to the toilets. The map includes three different trails to follow: Livingstone's Trail (the longest), Stanley Trail and Baker Trail (the shortest). The Kilimanjaro Safari road train trundles around the park at regular intervals, taking around 25 minutes.

When to visit The site is outdoors, so visit in dry weather. Inevitably, the zoo is more crowded during holiday times, but there is enough space to absorb large crowds. Out of season, the park can be bleak, with certain attractions, such as the crazy golf and bouncy castle, closed. Feeding and talks take place at specified times throughout the day. Special events include an Easter Eggstravaganza, birds of prey display and children's entertainments.

Age appeal The wide range of animals will appeal to all ages. Young children will enjoy running around the park as well as the bouncy castle, events such as face-painting and handling the animals. The playground suits older children, who will also enjoy following the trails.

Food and drink The Explorers' Food Pavilion, a self-service canteen-style outlet serving coffees, lunches and teas, is sorely in need of redecoration. It is a large, neon-lit, barn-like room with dingy brown Formica tables and plastic banquette seating. The noisy air-conditioning system and the pervasive smell of fried food are not conducive to an enjoyable experience. Food on offer includes lasagne (£4.50), salads (£2.99), children's safari meals (beefburgers/sausages/sharkbites and chips at £1.99), teas and a selection of unappetising cakes.

Shops The souvenir shop in the ticket office is brightly lit and well laid out with predictable items ranging from badges (50p) to more expensive soft toys, books and plastic animals.

🚗 On the A12, south of Lowestoft. Free car parking next to site. ⊖ Bus from Lowestoft bus station stops at entrance to the drive. 🕐 (1999): 27 Mar to 30 Jun 10am to 5pm; 1 Jul to 30 Sept 10am to 5.30pm; 1 Oct to 26 Mar 10am to 4pm (last admission 1 hour before closing time). Closed 25, 26 Dec. 💷 Adult £6.95; child (3 to 14 yrs old), student £4.95; senior citizen £5.50; family ticket £22. 1 Nov to 31 Dec; adult £5.50; child, student £4; senior citizen £4.50; family ticket (£2 adults + 2 children) £17. Annual season ticket adult £22; child £17; senior citizen £19; group rates available. ♿ Most areas are accessible, although ground can get boggy. Road train covers all areas. Special toilets and ramps. Wheelchairs available for loan (pre-booking necessary).

Sundown Adventureland

Rampton, Nr Retford, Nottinghamshire DN22 0HX ☎ *(01777) 248274*

Quality ★★ **Facilities** 🏛🏛 **Value for money** £££
Highlights Good for families with very young children
Drawbacks Quite a remote location; single admission price for adults and children

---

What's there A range of **themed areas and rides**, including a Wild West Street, Pirate Adventure Land and an indoor Nursery Rhyme Land. The Boozy Barrel boat ride is a sedate version of a water-rapids ride, while a gentle rocky-mountain train ride is the nearest Sundown gets to motorised excitement. Each of the brightly coloured sets offers a slightly different activity – for example, listening to a recorded fairy story in the miniature cottages of Storybook Village, or crawling about inside the houses in Smugglers Cove.

Quite a lot of the attractions involve peering into glass cabinets at mechanised puppets and twee fantasy scenes. But there are good **outdoor play areas** with climbing frames, swings and slides, plus a large, clean sandpit.

Information/tours/guides A leaflet shows the layout of the small park, and signposting is reasonable.

When to visit It is certainly at its best in fine weather – some attractions are under cover, but would not be worth the journey on a rainy day. In the run-up to Christmas the park is open later at weekends and has special entertainment as well as a Santa Claus house.

Age appeal This attraction is aimed exclusively at families with children under 10 years old – indeed, even kids towards the top of this range might not be occupied for long. There is a special play area for the under-5s. Height restrictions apply on some of the rides and in the Junglemania play area. Children must be accompanied by an adult on all rides and attractions.

Food and drink Three low-key fast-food outlets serve freshly cooked food at reasonable prices amid functional but brightly coloured seating and décor. A bacon butty costs £1.50, chicken nuggets and chips £1.85.

Shops The shop sells a wide variety of toys, from miniature figures through to model trucks.

🚗 5 miles south-east of Retford. Signposted from Dunham on Trent crossroads, A57. Free parking. ⊖ Train to Retford, from which coaches occasionally run to park. ☉ Summer 10am to 6pm; winter 10am to 4pm (open for 6 pre-25 Dec Christmas Spectacular weekends till 7pm). Closed 25 Dec to 1 Jan; weekdays in Jan. 💷 Adult and child over 2 yrs £4.75; group rates (20+) available. ♿ Level access in most areas. Some rough surfaces – the Wild West Street, made of woodchips, would be impossible for wheelchairs (or pushchairs).

Tate Gallery Liverpool

Albert Dock, Liverpool L3 4BB ☎ *0151–702 7400*

Quality: ★★★ **Facilities** 👍👍👍👍 **Value for money** £££££
Highlights Cutting-edge modern art; very good facilities
Drawbacks Not to everyone's taste

What's there The Tate Gallery Liverpool is home to the only **national collection of modern art** in the north of England and is the largest of its kind outside London. It is housed in a superbly converted warehouse in the historic Albert Dock, in an ultra-modern, minimalist-designed building, and has a collection of works entirely by twentieth-century artists. Much of the art is meant to be shocking or thought-provoking, depending on your point of view. Many of the paintings and exhibitions will not to be everyone's taste.

Damien Hirst's main contribution is a glass display cabinet with shelves full of large sea shells. **Andy Warhol**'s 'Electric Chairs' from his celebrated, or denigrated, Death and Disaster series is prominently displayed, as is work by **Francis Bacon**. Some of the more obscure exhibits include a video of people doing horse impressions, a silver-plated teapot that has been thrown off the White Cliffs of Dover, and an entire room (not recommended for young children) given over to depictions of violence in art.

The exhibitions do change, and not everything is meant to be disturbing: you will find lovely pieces by **Henry Moore** and **Barbara Hepworth**, for example, as well as some by **Lucian Freud**. The building itself is spacious, light and bright and provides a wonderful background and environment for displaying the art.

If you enjoy modern art, allow about 2½ hours for a visit; if you don't, you will be in the fabulous coffee shop with views of the dock in about 15 minutes.

Information/tours/guides Occasionally, artists give talks about their work (phone for details). An informal talk is given daily by one of the attendants at 2pm, which is free, lasts half an hour and is engaging and easily understood. A souvenir guidebook is available at £2.95; this is colourful and gives a lot of background about the history of the gallery, what's in it, and why. Daily events are advertised on monitors throughout the gallery; leaflets are also available on workshops and other activities.

When to visit The Tate is all indoors and can be visited all year round.

Age appeal It's unlikely to appeal to young children or those with conservative views on art, but teenagers and younger adults should get something out of it.

Food and drink The modern licensed café has great views of the Albert Dock and is stylish and bright, with some imaginative dishes such as farfalle pasta as well as fish and chips (both £5.95) and daily specials. There is also a children's menu, and excellent cappuccino.

Shops As you'd expect, the shop is crammed with art books on just about every subject under the sun, many of which are expensive coffee-table tomes. However, you will also find calendars, mugs, mouse pads and videos.

From M62 or M57, follow signs to Liverpool town centre and then Albert Dock. Huge free car park. ⊖ A 15-minute walk from Liverpool Lime Street station, or Smartbuses 1 and 4. ⊙ Tue to Sun 10am to 5.50pm. Closed Mon (exc. bank hols), 24 to 26 Dec, and 1 Jan. £ Free (charge for special exhibitions). ♿ Full, with lifts to all floors, which are level. Wheelchairs available.

Tate Gallery St Ives

Porthmeor Beach, St Ives, Cornwall TR26 1TG ☎ *(01736) 796226*
🖱 *www.tate.org.uk*

Quality ★★★★★   **Facilities 🏛 🏛 🏛 🏛 🏛**   **Value for money £££££**
Highlights Good guided tours included in admission price; lovely rooftop café
Drawbacks Unclear and insufficient signposting from town centre

---

What's there The Tate St Ives opened its doors to the public in June 1993. Built on the site of the town's old gasworks, it has wonderful views over the beach and the Cornish coastline. The gallery has no permanent collections, but displays feature pieces from the Tate Gallery's collection of **British and modern art**, private collections and loans from the public. All the work displayed is connected in some way with Cornwall. Exhibits are changed once a year in November.

The building is on four levels. An introduction to the building and its displays can be found on the wall to the left of the **Patrick Heron window** on level one. The five interconnecting galleries and the information desk are situated on level three. The galleries are airy and bright, with stark white walls and wooden or tiled floors. Wall texts introduce the theme in each gallery and labels provide more in-depth information on each individual piece of work.

A visit to the gallery will take at least two hours, and a ticket that includes admission to the Barbara Hepworth Museum and Sculpture Garden is available.

Information/tours/guides A full-colour guidebook (£2.95) is sold in the gift shop. A free leaflet, which includes a map of the gallery, is available to visitors. There is a room guide in each gallery. Guided tours take place at 2.30pm on weekdays when the Tate is open and at 3pm on Saturdays and bank holidays. They give a general introduction to the building and its collection. Guides are knowledgeable and tours last approximately one hour.

When to visit A variety of special events take place throughout the year, including artist-led studio visits and special talks and workshops aimed at children. Extra charges apply in most cases, although some events are free with admission. The gallery's web site lists a full programme of events. Avoid November, as the Tate is closed then.

Age appeal A family activity pack, which is available free of charge from the information desk, will give children a focus of interest when visiting the galleries. However, each pack focuses on one gallery only, and they might prove too difficult for younger children. A series of talks and storytelling sessions aimed specifically at children takes place throughout the year.

Food and drink A waitress-service coffee shop (licensed) with an outdoor seating area and stunning views is situated on level four. It offers a good variety of reasonably priced dishes (e.g. chicken and avocado salad, Thai fishcakes), and the team of young staff is smartly attired and efficient. Cakes, cream teas, sandwiches and hot and cold drinks are also served.

Shops A wide range of merchandise is offered, including posters, calendars and a good, if somewhat expensive, selection of art books.

🚗 Parking is available close by. The park-and-ride system (see below) is a better alternative than trying to negotiate the narrow streets of St Ives. ⊖ A park-and-ride system operates 1 May to 25 Sept. Park at Lelant Saltings rail station and take the bus into St Ives for an all-inclusive ticket (£7.50). Out of season, purchase your parking ticket and travel ticket separately. ⊙ Dec to Oct Tue to Sun 10.30am to 5.30pm. Closed Mon (except bank hols, Jul & Aug); Nov for rehanging of paintings. 💷 *Tate only* adult £3.90; student, senior citizen, disabled visitor, unemployed £2.30; child free. *Tate and Barbara Hepworth Museum* adult £6; student, senior citizen, disabled visitor, unemployed £3; child free. ♿ Ramped access, adapted toilet and lift available. For visitors with mobility problems there are lifts between floors.

Tatton Park

Knutsford, Cheshire WA16 6QN ☎ *(01625) 534400* 📠 *(01625) 534403*

Quality ★★★★	Facilities 🏛🏛🏛🏛	Value for money £££

Highlights 1,000 acres of parkland; appealing to all ages; helpful, knowledgeable staff

Drawbacks Requires a car to get round; toilets a bit old-fashioned

What's there This estate with 1,000 acres of parkland, woods, lakes, deer, children's play area, picnic spots, mansion and Tudor Old Hall has been inhabited for centuries, and the buildings and courtyards ooze history.

The neo-classical **mansion** has lavish state rooms that are fabulously well preserved and decorated largely in bright, bold colours, often with damask on the walls. The card room, designed by Samuel Wyatt in the 1790s, is buttercup yellow and contains open armchairs and other antiques from the seventeenth and eighteenth centuries, while the music room uses cherry-coloured silk damask to set off the natural wood of the instruments. The drawing room has some fine masterpieces on the walls, including works by Canaletto, Van Dyck and Poussin, and a pair of splendid giant mirrors. Many of the rooms have ornate fireplaces and chandeliers and make heavy use of giltwood.

The **Tudor Old Hall**, a sixteenth-century house a few minutes' drive away on the other side of the park, has been lived in for 500 years, originally by the gentry when it was a substantial farmhouse and from the mid-nineteenth century by humbler estate workers. The Great Hall dates from when masters and servants ate and slept in one large room, and the Stuart bedrooms from when the class structure became more rigid. There is also a gamekeeper's cottage from the turn of the nineteenth century.

The 50-acre **gardens** are said to be among the finest in the UK, and come in a variety of themes. Beauty awaits at every turn, from the Italian terrace to the glass fernery, the enclosed rose garden and the simpler Japanese garden. You will also find a pond with lilies, a topiary display, a pergola and a well-concealed maze.

Laid out and set in the same style as it would have been in the 1700s, the **Home Farm** includes a chopping shed, piggeries, stables, a blacksmith's store and a slaughterhouse – but now the animals, such as the shire horses, rare breed cattle and piglets, are there to be fed and stroked.

You could easily spend a whole day at Tatton, with the mansion and gardens taking at least an hour apiece and the Tudor Old Hall and Home Farm slightly less. There are also plenty of walks and picnic tables for fine weather.

Information/tours/guides Separate guidebooks are available for the gardens at £2.50, Home Farm at £1, and the mansion at £3.50, while a free leaflet informs you about the Old Hall. Each is thorough and informative, but the attendants in the mansion really bring it alive.

When to visit The park is open all year round and the different seasons each have their own beauty, but early summer is best for the rhododendrons and high summer for the roses. A host of special events is held throughout the year, from concerts and car rallies to flower shows and Christmas craft festivals.

Age appeal The park will appeal to people and children of all ages. The farm will keep the children happy and the mansion and Old Hall are quite informative. The gardens can be enjoyed by everyone.

Food and drink Much of the food in the spacious self-service café is home-made. You can have, among other things, delicious soup (£2.50), haddock and chips (£5.25) and ploughman's (£4.25). Seating is provided both inside and out in the courtyard. Just opposite, the Housekeeper's Store sells estate produce, including wine, rabbits and pheasants, as well as rolls, cheese and pies for picnics.

Shops The gift shop is large and airy with plenty of room to browse, and has a wide selection of goods, from books on World War II and gardening to polo shirts, tea-towels and colouring books for the youngsters. A garden shop sells plants and flowers.

🚗 Follow signs from M6 junction 19 or M56 junction 7. Car parking (whole day) £3.50. ⊖ Bus or train to Knutsford and then a taxi or 2½-mile walk – no local buses. ⏲ Apr to Oct (closing times 1 hour earlier in last week of Oct) *park* Tue to Sun 10am to 7pm; *gardens* Tue to Sun and bank hols 10.30am to 5pm; *Mansion* and *Home Farm* Tue to Sun and bank hols 12pm to 4pm; *Tudor Old Hall* guided tours 3pm & 4pm Tue to Fri and hourly 12pm to 4pm Sat, Sun and bank hols; Nov to Mar *park* Tue to Sun 11am to 5pm; *gardens* Tue to Sun 11am to 4pm; *Home Farm* Sun 11.30am to 3pm; *Mansion* and *Tudor Old Hall* closed. 🎫 *Gardens* adult £3; child (5 to 15 yrs) £2; family ticket (2 adults + 3 children) £8; *Mansion* adult £3; child £2; family ticket £8; *Home Farm* adult £2.50; child £1.50; family ticket £8; *Tudor Old Hall* adult £2.50; child £1.50; family ticket £8; *Discovery Saver ticket (valid for 1 visit to any 2 attractions)* adult £4.50; child £2.50; family ticket £12.50. ♿ Full access except to first floor of the mansion. Wheelchairs available for gardens.

Temple Newsam

Temple Newsam Road, off Selby Road, Leeds LS15 0AE ☎ *0113-264 7321*

Quality ★★★★ **Facilities 💰💰💰** **Value for money £££££**
Highlights Collection of decorative arts showing stylistic developments from sixteenth to nineteenth century
Drawbacks You need to go on a guided tour to get the most from your visit

What's there Temple Newsam house dates back to the Tudor period and has been altered, extended and elaborated on by its numerous owners. With connections to the Knights Templar in the twelfth century and to the family of Henry Lord Darnley, whose marriage in the sixteenth century to Mary Queen of Scots resulted in his subsequent murder, it has had a varied history.

In 1922 the house was handed over to Leeds Corporation by its then owner, the Earl of Halifax, who had many of the contents sold at auction and dispersed in a seven-day sale. Since then, original pieces have been returned to the house and other items brought in. The collections now include **fine furnishings**, **silver**, **porcelain** and **pottery** plus nearly **400 Old Master and British paintings**. Each room is a period piece showing stylistic developments in the decorative arts from the sixteenth to the nineteenth centuries. For example, the **Edwardian Library**, with its peacock-green and gold colour scheme, is one of the treasures of the house, featuring a library writing table made by Thomas Chippendale for Harewood House (*qv*) in the late eighteenth century. Next door, the **Chinese Drawing Room** reflects the taste of a former resident, Lady Hertford, who had the room hung with hand-painted Chinese wallpaper given to her mother by the Prince Regent in 1806. It was restored and replaced in the 1990s – restoration work continues throughout the rest of the house.

Although information on each room is detailed, if you can go on a tour do so. Otherwise, the sheer scale of the house and everything in it means you may well be running out of steam well before you reach the final rooms. Guided tours lasting about an hour run at intervals and are free. Phone for further details of these and special exhibitions.

A walk in the **parkland** re-landscaped by 'Capability' Brown in the eighteenth century and still retaining many features from its history will revive those who are house-weary, and the farm with its rare breeds will entertain younger visitors.

Information/tours/guides   In addition to the guided tours (see above), a guidebook (£2), detailed room guide (75p) and picture list (50p) are all available at the ticket desk. Folders in each room also have details of all the furnishings.

When to visit   Any time, though the extensive grounds and farm are best in dry weather.

Age appeal   Mainly adults, though everyone will enjoy the rare breeds farm and the grounds.

Food and drink   A café in the stable block serves light meals and snacks. It closes 45 minutes before the house.

Shops   There is a small shop in the house selling gifts and books.

🚐 4 miles from Leeds city centre off A63, close to M1 Junction 46. ⊖ Metro buses go up to the house only in summer. Contact Metro on 0113–245 7676. ◷ Oct to Dec, Tue to Sat 10am to 4pm; Sun 12pm to 4pm (last entry 3.15pm). Mar to Oct, Tue to Sat 10am to 5pm, Sun 1pm to 5pm (last entry 4.15pm). Closed Jan and Feb, Mon except bank hols. 💷 Adult £2; child (under 14) 50p; student, senior citizen £1. ♿ Ground floor of house, and grounds.

Thorpe Park

Staines Road, Chertsey, Surrey KT16 8PN   ☎ *(01932) 562633*
📠 *(01932) 566367*

Quality ★★★ | **Facilities 🏛🏛🏛** | **Value for money £££**

Highlights   Free entry for children under 1m and good ride section for pre-schoolers; pool and farm for relaxing on hot days

Drawbacks   Not much for teenagers who want to be terrified

What's there   This theme park, now managed by the Tussauds group (which owns Chessington World of Adventures, *qv*, and Alton Towers, *qv*), is perhaps best suited to families with younger children (say, under-12s) and particularly good for pre-schoolers.

The park is divided into various sections. The **pre-schoolers' rides** are sensibly near the entrance. Here you will find gentle roundabouts and rides, which tend to get much quieter towards the end of the day.

For those seeking a thrill there is **X: /No Way Out** – a rollercoaster backwards in the dark, which is disorientating, though the anticipation is worse than the actual ride. Probably the most well-known ride is the **Loggers Leap**, a steep drop into water (yes, you will get wet). These two rides tend to have the longest queues.

Rangers County has two gentle rides – Miss Hippo's jungle safari and the boat ride of Mr Rabbit's tropical safari. The Chief Rangers Carousel does not usually have much of a queue, so head for it if you just want to get on a ride. Over on the far side of the park is Thunder River, a fairly gentle water ride.

As you wander back you can have a look at a **model world** showing some of the world's architectural highlights in miniature. Tucked away by the crazy golf near the entrance are the dodgems, and there is another chance to get wet at the **Depth Charge** water slide. Do not forget to smile while you are screaming – you can buy your photo afterwards.

The park has been experimenting with virtual queuing (you log in electronically and are told what time you will get on the ride) to try to cut down the queues on the most popular rides. Something new is usually introduced every year. In 1999 it was the **4D pirate film**, where the screen seems to come alive, and creatures have a tendency to spit at the audience. For 2000 it will be a water splash ride called **Tidal Wave**.

When you want a break from the rides you can catch a boat or train across to the **farm**, where there are plenty of small animals to watch and pet, and a restaurant that is a bit removed from the bustle of the main park. If you choose a day with good weather, you can also benefit from the artificial beach and paddling pool with small water slides. It does get crowded, so keep an eye on your children (and don't kid yourself that you will be able to stay dry!).

Information/tours/guides You are given a map when you enter the park – hang on to it, because the signposting is fairly minimal.

When to visit Try to get there in good weather to enjoy the pool, and avoid school holidays to beat the crowds. Firework displays are held in October, and the park is open late over the August bank holiday.

Age appeal The park is best for families with children under the age of 12.

Food and drink There are a number of fast-food outlets, including Burger King and KFC, and a self-service restaurant by the farm. Opportunities to buy fizzy drinks and doughnuts abound. Alternatively, you could take a picnic.

Shops Several shops are scattered around the park selling lots of branded Thorpe Park merchandise.

Other facilities Not surprisingly, the park has good baby-changing areas and quiet rooms for feeding.

🚗 Off M25 junctions 11 or 13; follow signs. Large car park. ⊖ Trains from London Waterloo to Staines and then a bus (tel. (01737) 223000 for details of buses). ⊙ Apr to end Oct, Mon to Sun 9.30am to 6.30pm. 💷 Adult £18.50; child (over 1m, under 14 yrs) £14.50; senior citizen £14; disabled visitor £11; family ticket (2 adults + 2 children) £56. Discounts for pre-booked tickets apply. Tussauds annual season ticket (for all attractions) £70. ♿ Special parking; wheelchairs for loan; disabled toilets.

The Thursford Collection

Thursford Green, Thursford, Nr Fakenham, Norfolk NR21 0AS
☎ *(01328) 878477*

Quality ★★★　　　　Facilities 🍴🍴🍴　　　　Value for money £££
Highlights　Unique collection of lovingly restored steam engines
Drawbacks　Extra charge to go on the rides once inside

What's there This eclectic collection of **steam-powered machines**, including organs, steamrollers and fairground rides, in a small rural village in north Norfolk was started by a local man, George Cushing (now in his mid-nineties), who developed a love of steamrollers while employed as a road-mender with the district council. He bought his first roller for £225 in 1930.

The collection is housed in former farm buildings that have been converted and extended to create a vast barn, a clutch of small shops and a handful of food outlets. The barn contains the collection of shiny engines and gaudy organs. In the centre is a 1,308-seat area where audiences can listen to the **Wurlitzer** – one of the highlights of the collection. This 1,339-pipe organ was bought from the Paramount Cinema in Leeds. It is played twice a day (1.30 and 3pm) by Robert Wolfe, who has been resident organist since 1981. The other big attraction is the **Gondola**, a magnificent nineteenth-century round-about, so called because of the shape of its richly carved cars which circle around a central pipe organ on a switchback. Rides on the Gondola cost an extra 60p per person. There is also a **mini-roundabout** with painted horses for children to ride on at 20p a time.

The collection will take a couple of hours to see, but the visit can easily be extended to fill an afternoon – starting with lunch at the restaurant and including two Wurlitzer concerts and a browse around the shops.

Information/tours/guides The full-colour guidebook costs £2 and covers the history of the collection, with interesting photographs and information on each machine. The site is compact, and clear signposting means there is no need for a map.

When to visit Avoid school holiday periods and aim for off-peak weekdays when the crowds are at their lowest. Special children's entertainments are organised at half-terms. The attraction is open for Christmas shopping from the end of October to mid-November. The Christmas Spectacular Show runs from 18 November to 23 December (two performances daily, 2.30 and 7pm, £15 per person for 3 hours of entertainment).

Age appeal This collection is a nostalgia trip that is especially good for older people who remember the steam age. Children will enjoy the fairground rides, and a good adventure playground caters for young children and teenagers.

Food and drink The large self-service restaurant in a converted barn retains original beams, flints and tiles and is sectioned off with stable-style partitions. Hot food such as soup (£1.85) is served until 3pm, as well as teas, pasties, hot dogs and chips. There is also a separate tea shop; good home-made ice cream is sold from another outlet. Picnic tables are provided next to the playground.

Shops Three small 'Olde Worlde' shops line the 'street' which leads to the collection. These are high-profile and obviously designed to be a major part of the visiting experience. One sells gifts, another food and the third potpourri, soaps and cards. Apart from the nostalgia element, they seem to have little to link with the collection itself.

🚗 North of A148, 6 miles to the east of Fakenham. ⊖ Buses are infrequent. Taxis available in Fakenham. ⊙ **(1999):** Good Friday to 24 Oct, Mon to Sun 12pm to 5pm; Christmas shopping 20 Oct to 15 Nov; Christmas shows 18 Nov to 23 Dec 2.30pm & 7pm. 💷 Adult £4.70; child (4 to 14 yrs) £2.20; senior citizen £4.40; student and group rate (over 15 people) £3.95. ♿ Paths are mostly flat. Ramps provided where necessary. One disabled toilet.

Tintagel Castle

Tintagel, Cornwall PL34 0HB ☎ *(01840) 770328*
📶 *www.english-heritage.org.uk*

Quality ★★★★ **Facilities 🏛 🏛 🏛 🏛** **Value for money ££££**
Highlights Splendidly dramatic site; clearly marked route
Drawbacks Steepness of site makes access difficult for less mobile visitors; children's
activity leaflet available only in summer

What's there Tintagel is the legendary birthplace of King Arthur, and there has been a settlement on this site since the third or fourth century. The current ruins, now managed by English Heritage, date from the thirteenth century, when Tintagel was a stronghold of the Earls of Cornwall. The location, on a dramatic windswept **headland**, is stunning – but it does mean that there are steep steps to reach the castle.

Take time to see the small but interesting **history exhibition** in the shop before visiting the **castle** itself. The ruins are divided between the mainland and what is known as 'the island'. The most straightforward way to visit the site is to follow the numbered waymarkers, which correspond to the numbered symbols (complete with descriptions) in the guidebook. The first of these is at the head of the path beside the shop. Following this, you pass through the ruined gate tower into what would once have been the mainland courtyards of the castle. From here you descend one set of steps and then ascend an equally steep set that takes you on to the island.

The route then continues past the ruins of the island courtyard, Dark Age houses, a chapel and what is thought to have been a medieval garden. Spectacular **views** are to be had from the northern and southern cliffs.

Allow at least two hours to see the site and wear sensible walking shoes.

Information/tours/guides Although there are display boards, the full-colour guidebook (£2.95) is indispensable if you want to get the most out of your visit – it includes a tour that corresponds to the waymarked visitors' route, a history of Tintagel and a chapter on the legend of King Arthur.

When to visit Time your visit for fine weather – this is not the place to be on a stormy winter afternoon! Special events including battle re-enactments, music and drama take place from April to October. Admission is normally included in the standard ticket price.

Age appeal Young children and those with walking difficulties will find the steps and steep paths difficult to climb. A guidebook or activity leaflet for children would increase their enjoyment and understanding of the site (this is provided during the summer months only).

Food and drink A basic café (not EH-managed) sells snacks, cakes and hot and cold drinks.

Shops A small shop sells a good variety of merchandise that will further enhance your visit. The range of literature available includes books of local interest as well as plenty on King Arthur. Beautiful (but expensive) tapestry hangings are displayed on the walls.

🚗 Follow signs for Tintagel off A39. Ample parking available in village. A ½-mile uneven and steep track leads to the entrance of the site. A Land Rover service (£1 per person) operates during the summer months. ⊖ First Western National's bus125 from Bodmin Parkway Rail Station (Sat only). Alternatively, the 122 bus operates from Weybridge to Tintagel, Mon to Sat. Tel. (01840) 212954 for details. ① 1 Apr to 10 July, Mon to Sun 10am to 6pm; 11 July to 21 Aug Mon to Sun 10am to 8pm; 22 Aug to 30 Sept Mon to Sun 10am to 6pm; 1 to 31 Oct Mon to Sun 10am to 5pm; 1 Nov to 31 Mar Mon to Sun 10am to 4pm. Closed 24 to 26 Dec, 1 Jan. 💷 Adult £2.80; child (5 to 16 yrs old) £1.40; student, senior citizen £2.10; groups (11 or more) 15% discount. EH members free. ♿ Unsuitable for wheelchairs, steep site. Braille and tactile guides available free from shop.

Tropical World

Roundhay Park, Leeds LS8 1DF ☎ *0113 266 1850*

Quality ★★★ **Facilities** 🍴 🍴 **Value for money** ££££
Highlights Having a large butterfly land on your arm; spotting a colourful bird swooping through the foliage
Drawbacks Display boards are often tatty and information very limited

---

What's there Opened in 1988 by Leeds City Council in Roundhay Park, Tropical World has one of the largest collections of **tropical plants** in the UK outside Kew Gardens (*qv*), according to the brochure. At first sight it looks like one rather grubby glasshouse; however, it consists of several interlinked houses. Unfortunately, there is little information displayed about what you might see in each house, but the staff are knowledgeable. A gentle walk along a path takes you through the temperate, tropical, desert and nocturnal habitats, and if you look carefully you may catch a glimpse of a brightly coloured bird or butterfly, a tree shrew or an iguana.

Coronation House, the first house you enter, has flowering plants and a pool with carp. The **Butterfly House** contains various species of butterfly which settle on plants and – if you are still – may land on your arm. You can see butterfly eggs on a banana leaf and the chrysalises hanging in the warm breeding box by the entrance. In the **Aquatic House** a few cases of tropical fish, piranhas and enormous catfish are on display. Next comes the **South American House**, where lush shrubbery and trees are home to colourful birds and iguanas sitting high up on the bark-covered beams. Pass through the rather claustrophobic **Nocturnal House** and some rather sad-looking monkeys and bush babies to the **Cacti House**, where some splendid spiky plants are well displayed. Finally, you go through the **Asian House**, which has lush planting, orchids and forest plants, before you emerge into the shop.

Allow an hour or two for your visit.

Information/tours/guides No guided tours are conducted, and little information is available. However, the staff are enthusiastic.

When to visit This is an attraction that is ideal for those wet, cold days when little else can be done, as it is indoors and warm.

Age appeal Children of all ages and adults will enjoy Tropical World.

Food and drink The Canal Gardens Tea Room, in Roundhay Park, serves light meals and snacks.

Shops The shop stocks plenty of souvenirs and small plastic animals (£1 to £2), including butterflies and frogs, and stickers of butterflies, beetles, frogs and snakes.

🚌 Follow signs to Roundhay Park, 3 miles north of Leeds city centre. ⊖ Bus routes 2B, 10, 12, 12B, 19, 19A and 21 from city centre. ⊙ May to Sept, Mon to Sun 10am to 6pm; Oct to Apr, Mon to Sun 10am to 4pm. 🎫 Adult £1.50; child (8 to 15 yrs) 75p; Leeds Card holders free. ♿ Full access for wheelchairs. Electric scooters for loan. To book call 0113–266 1850.

Tullie House Museum and Art Gallery

Castle Street, Carlisle, Cumbria CA3 8TP ☎ *(01228) 534781* 📠 *(01228) 810249*

Quality ★★★★   **Facilities 👜👜👜👜**   **Value for money ££££**
Highlights Revamped local museum with some excellent displays; good for children
Drawbacks Confusing layout; plenty of school parties

What's there Tullie House is a local museum that has been given the full 1990s makeover. At a cost of over £5 million, the worthy old glass cases have been replaced by galleries full of interpretative exhibitions, whispered voice-overs, panoramas, models and interactive displays. There aren't even any rooms – just **themed areas**.

It is wonderful, especially for children, at whom the displays are chiefly directed, but the modernisation is done to excess, which can cause problems. Chief among these is the historical confusion that could result from taking a wrong turning and finding yourself listening to platform announcers from the railway era when you thought you were in the Dark Ages. Also, the voice-overs have to be muted so as not to interfere with each other, leading to inaudibility in some instances, and a general background whispering, like a cathedral full of ghosts. A great deal could be done to solve the first problem by daring to use old-fashioned signs, rather than expecting visitors to refer to the floor-plan hand-out all the time.

However, the frustrations of finding your way around are more than compensated for by the **imaginative displays**, especially if you have children. The museum is especially strong on the **Roman period**, with plenty of artefacts from nearby Hadrian's Wall. The turbulent centuries of cross-border warfare are covered by a surrealistic and impressive audio-visual show about the **Border reivers** (cattle rustlers), while the **siege of Carlisle** during the Civil War is brought to life by narrated passages from a journal kept by a person from that era. All in all, the historical coverage is excellent. Dioramas about Cumbria's environment and landscape are rather more conventional and less immediately striking.

The main museum is on the first floor. Downstairs are the shop, Garden Restaurant, **art gallery** (with changing exhibitions) and the toilets, together with the large reception desk. It is all somewhat functional, but staff are helpful, if not particularly welcoming.

Next door, **Old Tullie House** provides a break from modernity. Here, in a silent and rather beautiful old house, collections of children's toys are ranged beside portraits and paintings.

Information/tours/guides Information about prices and opening hours is clearly displayed, and the floor plan that all visitors receive has further details. The museum caters well for school parties, with worksheets and workshops (which also take place during school holidays) available. There are no guided tours as such, but groups can telephone in advance to make particular arrangements.

When to visit This is an all-weather sight, open all year. It is popular with school parties, so go in the holidays if you have the choice.

Age appeal It is specially good for children of all ages, with plenty to see and do.

Food and drink The Garden Restaurant is a big, bright, cheery room that opens off the lobby. The range of food is reasonably wide, with specials written up on the blackboard. Toasted, filled baguettes (£2.50), salad (£2.20) and soup and roll (£1.75) form the staples, backed up by some impressive home baking (65p to 95p). A small play corner for children is a thoughtful touch.

Shops The museum shop is spacious and offers a wide range of gifts and souvenirs, many of them directed at children and well within pocket-money price range, such as the fridge magnets (£1). A major effort has been made to sell things relevant to the museum's displays, so there is a wealth of books and games on historical themes. Of special interest is the corner given over to the reivers.

Tullie House is a short walk from Carlisle city-centre car parks. ⊖ Close to Carlisle railway station; follow signposts. ① *Tullie House* Mon to Sat 10am to 5pm; Sun, 26 Dec and 1 Jan 12pm to 5pm. Closed 25 Dec. *Old Tullie House* Mon to Sun 12pm to 4pm. ⊡ *Tullie House* adult £3.75; child (5 to 16 yrs) £2.75; student, senior citizen £2.25 to £2.75. *Art gallery* and *Old Tullie House* free. *Tullie Addict card* (unlimited entry for a year) £12. *Early bird* (10am to 11am Mon to Sat) half normal price. Local ratepayers free. ও Very good; lift to upper floors; plenty of space between exhibits.

Twycross Zoo

Twycross, Nr Atherstone, Warwickshire CV9 3PX　☎ *(01827) 880250*

Quality ★★★　　　　　**Facilities** 🏛 🏛 🏛　　　　**Value for money** ££££
Highlights Plenty of primates
Drawbacks Layout quite confusing; talks and animal-feeding in public restricted to
　　　　　　　summer season

What's there In the 1970s Twycross became a conservation charity, and most of the animals (several of them endangered species) here have been bred in captivity, either in Twycross itself or in another zoo.

The zoo is famous for its **primates**. It has one of the largest zoo populations in the UK of noisy gibbons, who shriek and whoop excitedly when startled or frightened – the cacophony can be heard all over the zoo. The orang-utans take centre stage in their large outdoor enclosure, nonchalantly performing on ropes and tyres while paying attention to their audience's reactions. Other popular features include the Gorilla House, which can get packed with people depending on what the gorillas are doing at the time, and the ape nurseries, where young primates pad around playing with boxes and blankets as in any human nursery. The Chimpanzee House has some bonobos (man's closest relative), two of whom were born at Twycross, while in the Langur House some very active langurs race around in an unruly game of chase. Other animals include penguins, seals and Patagonian sea lions, tapirs, camels, cassowaries (large flightless birds from Australia), lions, tigers, giraffes and elephants.

You could easily spend a full day at the zoo. Other diversions come in the form of donkey and miniature train **rides** (50p a ride), a good adventure playground and a soft-play centre.

Information/tours/guides The information office was not open on our visit on a very busy day in the autumn half-term holiday. The guidebook (£2) has a plan of the zoo and information on a selection of animals as well as an eight-page activity section for children. It names some individual animals, but they are difficult to spot unless a keeper is standing by. Talks and feeding times open to the public take place in summer only, so if you want to know more about the animals at other times you will have to ask the keepers while they are busy cleaning or preparing the animal's meals.

When to visit The best time to go to the zoo is in the summer, when talks are held and you can see the animals being fed. Most animals have under-cover shelter as well as outdoor space.

Age appeal All ages will enjoy the zoo, although the adventure playgrounds and miniature rides are a bonus for younger children.

Food and drink There are two busy but functional self-service cafeterias (one licensed) and a snack bar. The selection of meals includes pasties, quiche and cottage pie (£4.50), lasagne and baked potatoes (£2.20). Children's meals are of the sausage/fishfingers, beans and chips variety (£2.20).

Shops Plenty of animal-related gifts are sold here – for example, soft toys (ranging in price from £8 to £30), plastic animals (£1 to £2), an endangered species jigsaw (£3.50) and a *World Atlas of Wildlife* (£9.99).

On A444, within easy reach of M42 and M1. ⊖ None. ◷ Mar to Oct, Mon to Sun 10am to 6pm; Nov to Feb, Mon to Sun 10am to 4pm. ⊡ Adult £6; child (3 to 14 yrs) £4; senior citizen £4.50. ♿ Most of the animal houses are accessible to wheelchairs. Disabled toilets.

Waddesdon Manor

Nr Aylesbury, Buckinghamshire HP18 0JH ☎ *(01296) 651226*
📠 *(01296) 653208* 📧 *www.waddesdon.org.uk*

Quality ★★★★	Facilities 🏛🏛🏛🏛🏛	Value for money ££££

Highlights Superb collection of eighteenth-century art; immaculate house and grounds; good choice of places to eat; excellent shop

Drawbacks Poor signposting on approach roads to Waddesdon

What's there The main attraction is the wonderful honey-coloured manor, built by Baron Ferdinand Rothschild at the end of the nineteenth century in the style of a French château, and now a National Trust property. It is decorated and furnished with **treasures** bought mainly from royalty and the aristocracy, and houses a superb collection of **French works of art**. There are particularly fine displays of decorative dinner services and vases, an extensive collection of prints and drawings which have only recently been put on view, many beautiful cabinets and desks with inlay work, and numerous paintings including works by Reynolds, Gainsborough and Boucher.

The **Bachelors' Wing** is open only on certain days, but is well worth a visit, being more intimate and 'domestic' than the main parts of the house. It was traditionally used by the gentlemen on hunting or shooting weekends, and contains the billiard room, smoking room and armoury.

In the many acres of grounds, the most notable features are the seasonal bedding-plant displays of the **parterre** and the splendid nineteenth-century **aviary** (under restoration at the time of inspection). There are also many wilder areas, such as Daffodil Valley and the Woodland Walk, which can be explored independently or as part of a guided walk.

The Rothschild **wine cellars** contain thousands of bottles dating back to the nineteenth century, including some signed by presidents and prime ministers in commemoration of significant events.

Information/tours/guides The 'Waddesdon Diary' (free) includes information about opening times, charges and facilities as well as many special events. Various other leaflets and guidebooks are available, many of them free, including the fold-out sheets presented to you on entry, which give updates on recent exhibitions, a plan of the grounds and masses of practical information for your visit. There are two main guidebooks for sale, one on the house (£3.50) and one on the gardens (£4.50). Both are full-colour glossy publications; the house guide gives details of the main exhibits in each room, but the gardens guide is more of a history of the creation of the gardens, with little detail of what to see. The aviary guide (£1) combines historical background with details of the birds, and a Children's Garden Trail containing puzzles and quiz questions is available for 50p. A tour of the house begins with an introduction to the history of the Rothschilds and Waddesdon by one of the guides, lasting about ten minutes. After that you are free to look around at your own pace, either referring to the guidebook and written display boards, or hiring an audio guide for £1. Wardens at many points along the tour can direct you or answer questions.

When to visit To explore the beautiful grounds you need good weather. At busy times, such as summer weekends, you may need to wait for entry to the house, as numbers are limited and a system of timed tickets operates. Special events, such as wine tastings, lectures and connoisseur tours, take place throughout the year.

Age appeal Under-5s are not allowed in the house, and the house tour is unlikely to interest many children. Children will enjoy attractions in the grounds, however, notably the aviary, a new Children's Garden with climbing frames and swings, and the Children's Garden Trail. Adults with an interest in fine arts, history and gardens will find plenty to enjoy at Waddesdon, and provision is made for visitors with impaired mobility.

Food and drink There are three main options for refreshments at Waddesdon. The attractive Manor Restaurant, with courtyard terrace, offers a selection of hot and cold starters, main courses and desserts, as well as interesting sandwiches. A range of coffees and teas and various home-made biscuits and cakes are available throughout the day. The Stables, a short walk from the Manor, serves simpler food, but the salad buffet incorporating fresh salmon, beef, ham, roast vegetables with couscous and all manner of accompaniments is superb. The informal Summerhouse, an open area with tables and benches near the aviary, has a selection of baguettes, focaccia and other high-quality sandwiches, as well as some simple pasta dishes.

Shops The Manor Shop is notable for the diversity and quality of its goods, and for its attractive presentation. In addition to Waddesdon and National Trust merchandise a wide range of other products at all price levels is offered, such as china, porcelain, enamel work and jewellery, books, art posters and toiletries. A separate section of the shop is dedicated to Rothschild wines and wine accessories.

🚗 Waddesdon is about 20 minutes' drive from junctions 7 (northbound) and 9 (southbound) of M40, off A41 between Bicester and Aylesbury. ⊖ Aylesbury is the nearest station; bus and taxi services run from Aylesbury and Bicester. ⏱ *House* and *wine cellars* Mar to Oct, Thur to Sun (plus Wed and bank hols in July and Aug) 11am to 4pm (last admission 2.30pm). *Grounds, garden, aviary, shops* and *restaurant* Mar to 24 Dec, Wed to Sun (plus bank hols) 10am to 5pm. *Bachelors' Wing* July and Aug, Thur and Fri (plus Wed in July) 11am to 4pm. Closed Nov and Dec. 💷 *House* and *grounds* adult £10; child (5 to 16 yrs old) £7.50. *Grounds* adult £3; child £1.50. NT members free. ♿ Special car parking area; wheelchairs and Braille guides for loan; all areas except wine cellars, Bachelors' Wing and some parts of the grounds (around the South Terrace) fully wheelchair-accessible; no powered wheelchairs or guide dogs allowed in the house.

Wakehurst Place Gardens

Ardingly, West Sussex RHA7 6TN ☎ *(01444) 894067* 📠 *(01444) 894069*
📧 *www.rbgkew.org.uk/wakehurst*

Quality ★★★★★   **Facilities** 🏛 🏛 🏛 🏛 🏛   **Value for money ££££**

Highlights Superb gardens combined with a major botanical institute; exemplary
signs and information; knowledgeable guides and good tours; year-
round colour and interest

Drawbacks Less obvious appeal for children than for adults

What's there Wakehurst Place is an outstation of Kew Gardens (*qv*), chock
full of collections of important plants that thrive better on the High Weald of
Sussex than at Kew. It combines the function of an important **botanical
institute** with the sensual attraction of a **private ornamental garden**.
Wakehurst is big: with over 170 acres to explore, you should start with the exhibition in the sixteenth-century Tudor mansion for an overview of the garden's
aims and importance. Count on at least half a day to appreciate the highlights.
Woodland collections are arranged geographically to reproduce walks through
the world's forests; Horsebridge wood has Californian redwoods and re-creates
the spectacular autumnal colours of New England; the Southern Hemisphere
woodlands have beeches from Patagonia and New Zealand; you can imagine
trekking into the Nepalese mountains in the Himalayan Glade. There are also
extensive water gardens and cottagey plantings in the walled gardens.

Information/tours/guides The glossy colour guidebook is excellent,
informative and a snip at £1.50. Do not miss the introductory video, presented
by David Attenborough, in the superb exhibition in the mansion. A good map
with information on how to enjoy Wakehurst and details of month-by-month
seasonal features are included with the entry fee. There are clear site maps, useful
information boards and labelling of individual specimens around the gardens.
One-hour guided tours with experts leave at 11.30am and 2.30pm on Tuesdays,
Thursdays and at the weekends and cost £1 per head (children under 12 free).

When to visit The gardens are open all year and planted to provide year-
round interest. April to August is best for the flowering displays, including
Chilean fire bushes in May, Himalayan lilies and blue poppies in June, and
Japanese irises in July. Stunning autumn colours are to be seen in the woodlands in October and November.

Age appeal Wakehurst has a serious botanical mission, so the focus for
children is educational rather than fun. Woodland walks and native wildlife
provide interest for children of all ages. Those with mobility problems will
appreciate the well-kept paths, but some are long woodland walks or have
steep gradients.

Food and drink A large and airy conservatory-style self-service
restaurant is in the former stables; outdoor seating is in a courtyard behind the
mansion. The staff are cheerful, the décor is modern with exposed stone pillars
and the food is generally good value – sandwiches cost £1.95 to £2.95, the oven
bake of the day £5.35, and soup with a roll £2.05.

Shops The smart, attractive shop inside the mansion offers rather pricey merchandise, much of which has a gardening theme: examples include poppy sweatshirts (£28.99), aprons (£8.99) and garden-design greetings cards (£6.99). A good range of horticultural books and guides is available. A garden shop (March to October) sell plants, seeds and pots.

🚗 On B2028 south of Turner's Hill and north of Ardingly; free parking. ⊖ Nearest train station (6 miles away) is Hayward's Heath; take bus 82 from station. ⏰ Apr to Sept, Mon to Sun 10am to 7pm; 1 Oct to 30 Oct, Mon to Sun 10am to 6pm; 31 Oct to 31 Jan, Mon to Sun 10am to 4pm; Feb, Mon to Sun 10am to 5pm; Mar, Mon to Sun 10am to 6pm. Last admission to gardens ½ hour before closing; shops and restaurant close 1 hour earlier than gardens. Closed 25 Dec and 1 Jan. 🎟 Adult £5; child (5 to 16 yrs) £2.50; senior citizen, student £3.50; family ticket (2 adults + 4 children) £13. NT members, blind and partially sighted, disabled and their carers free. ♿ Generally good; wheelchair users need a strong companion; wheelchair loan available at entrance kiosk.

Walker Art Gallery

William Brown Street, Liverpool L3 8EL ☎ *0151-478 4199*
📠 *0151-478 4190*

Quality ★★★　　　　　　**Facilities** 👜👜👜　　　　　**Value for money** £££users
Highlights Variety of modern and classical art
Drawbacks Displays a tad old-fashioned

What's there One of the largest public exhibitions of contemporary painting in the UK, housed in a grand, classical building, the Walker Art Gallery was founded in 1957 by Sir John Moores of Littlewoods Pools fame.

A majestic staircase leads from an impressive entrance hall with an atrium to more than a dozen rooms displaying **art from many different periods** and schools, which together form an extensive and satisfying collection. The **sculpture gallery** is the only exhibition room on the ground floor, and is a dazzling presentation of a large collection of white marble statues and sculptures, including a replica cast of the Elgin Marbles.

The twentieth century is represented by work from such luminaries as **Ben Nicholson**, **L.S. Lowry** and **Lucian Freud** (including his famous *Interior at Paddington*, 1951), along with more obscure work by the brothers **Gilbert and George** (their painting *Dangling* is probably not one for the children), and a picture of a giant hamster cage by Dan Hays.

In the Impressionists' room, you will find work by **Degas**, **Monet**, **Matisse** and **Cézanne**. Medieval and Renaissance art is well represented, especially by pieces from northern and southern Europe, as are the seventeenth and eighteenth centuries. Pre-Raphaelites, too, have a strong showing. Adding to the eclectic mix are fine Henry Moore bronzes and French and German furniture.

Depending on your level of appreciation a visit could take anywhere between two and four hours.

Information/tours/guides A very useful free map and pamphlet is available, as well as a lavish guidebook at £7.95.

When to visit The gallery is all in one building and open nearly all year, so any time is good.

Age appeal A lot of the gallery is rather serious and presented in an old-fashioned museum style, which will not appeal to everyone. However, children will enjoy the colouring corners and free quizzes.

Food and drink Situated in the main entrance hall, the coffee shop has a lovely setting, but food is limited to cold dishes and cakes – more a snack or light lunch stop. Pie and salad, sandwiches and bagels are served.

Shops A few items, such as jewellery, greetings cards, posters and art books, are available by the entrance desk.

🚗 In Liverpool city centre follow signs to gallery. Pay and display parking in William Brown Street and at Liverpool Lime Street station. ⊖ 10 minutes' walk from bus station. Trains to Lime Street and Liverpool bus station, and a few minutes' walk. ⏱ Mon to Sat 10am to 5pm; Sun 12pm to 5pm. Closed 23 to 26 Dec and 1 Jan. 💷 Adult £3; child (under 16 yrs old) free; student, unemployed £1.50; senior citizen free. ♿ Full access, with ramps, lift and toilets.

Wallington House

Cambo, Nr Morpeth, Northumberland NE61 4AR   ☎ *(01670) 774283*

Quality ★★★★   **Facilities 🏛 🏛 🏛 🏛**   **Value for money ££££**

Highlights Interesting house with fascinating history; lovely garden and woodland walks

Drawbacks Souvenir guidebook essential; some muddy paths; public transport very difficult

---

What's there Wallington House started life as a castle and was then transformed into a comfortable neo-classical abode for a series of Northumberland squires. Under the ownership of the Trevelyan family in the nineteenth century it became a hotbed of radical politics and a home-from-home for the leading intellects of the time, among them Ruskin, the artist and critic, and Macaulay the historian.

Wallington is now a National Trust property, but it is the lasting impact left by its previous owners which makes it such a fascinating place to visit. Public access has not brought a neat sterility in its wake – the house has seen a great deal of earnest activity and eccentric behaviour, and something of this still lingers in the fabric.

It is also a house full of curiosities. Chief among them are the **pre-Raphaelite murals** of Northumbrian life which surround the colonnaded two-storey Central Hall. They were painted by William Bell Scott between 1850 and 1861 and transform the room into a place of almost Italian splendour. Elsewhere, portraits, paintings, books, sepia photographs and political mementos abound, but it is the bizarre objects scattered among them which catch the eye. Most eye-catching of all, perhaps, is the '**cabinet of curiosities**' assembled by a Lady Wilson in the eighteenth century, and now given a room of its own at the top of the house. Visitors can also admire a huge case of nearly 4,000 lead soldiers, much played with in childhood by the future historian G.M.Trevelyan, not to mention a collection of magnificent dolls' houses (not originally from the house). A special **children's room**, almost inaccessible to adults, contains further strange items and toys.

The grounds and estate of Wallington are extensive, and lengthy walks are possible. The one essential walk is to the **walled garden**. This, most unusually for a walled garden, follows the contours of a small valley and creates a sheltered paradise full of shrubs, herbaceous plants and gravel paths. There is also an attractive pool and a large glasshouse with scented exotic plants.

Information/tours/guides To put what you are seeing into context, and to learn about the characters who inhabited Wallington, it is virtually essential to buy the engagingly written guidebook. At £4.50 this adds considerably to the cost of a visit, but the room guides (70p) just do not do the same job. A child's guide is available too. A leaflet with a map of the grounds is given out at the entry kiosk, and is useful for shorter walks, although somewhat deceptive in its scale. The kiosk also has lists of the many events which take place at Wallington. National Trust volunteers in the rooms of the house are well briefed about the history and the items on display. Guided walks through the garden are held on seven Sundays during the year.

When to visit Wallington needs at least half a day to be properly enjoyed, and certainly offers sufficient diversity and interest for a full day out in fine weather. Throughout spring, summer and early autumn the walled garden is ablaze with colour, while the landscape is probably at its best in early summer – the time for longer walks.

Age appeal Children will find plenty to entertain them in the grounds. An adventure playground reasonably close to the house is a further draw. Inside the house, a real effort is made to interest young visitors, and even those normally bored stiff by stately homes ought to find the soldiers, the amazing dolls' houses and the tiny 'children's room' entertaining.

Food and drink The main tea room, situated in the stable block, is a long narrow area under the open rafters. A broad range of food is on offer, with afternoon tea for £3.75, soup and roll at £2.65 and hot lunches at £4.95. Specials are chalked up on a blackboard. The food is good, and it is served by a bevy of very friendly and efficient staff.

Shops A small shop sells the usual high-quality ware typical of the National Trust, but includes a number of items unique to Wallington. Among these is a limited edition of prints by a local artist at £39; there are also cards with views of the house for £1. Other items range from potpourri and jars of preserves to furniture polish (£2.99).

Take B6342 to Cambo; parking free in season; £1 to non-NT members out of season. Bus from Newcastle's Metro Centre at weekends, Jun to mid-Sept. For information, call 0191–213 3000. *House* Apr to Sept daily except Tues 1pm to 5.30pm; Oct daily except Tues 1pm to 4.30pm (last admission 30 minutes before closing time). *Garden* Apr to Sept, Mon to Sun 10am to 7pm; Oct, Mon to Sun 10 am to 6pm; Nov to Mar, Mon to Sun 10am to 4pm (or dusk if earlier). *Grounds* all year during daylight hours. *Shop* and *tea room* Apr to Sept daily except Tues 10am to 5.30pm; Oct, Mon to Sun 10.30am to 5pm; Nov to mid-Dec Wed to Sun 12pm to 4pm. *Estate walks* Jun to Oct. *House, garden and grounds* adult £5.40; child (5 to 14 yrs) £2.80;

family (2 adults + their children) £13.50. *Garden and grounds* adult £3.90; child £1.95. NT members free. ♿ Wheelchair access to the ground floor of the house, shop and tea room. Wheelchairs on loan; also a self-drive powered vehicle (booking needed). Braille guide available.

Warwick Castle

Warwick, Warwickshire CV34 4QU ☎ *(01926) 406600*
📠 *(01926) 401692* 🖳 *www.warwick-castle.co.uk*

Quality ★★★★★	Facilities 🏛🏛🏛🏛🏛	Value for money ££££

Highlights Top marks for bringing history to life; beautiful grounds; impressive castle
Drawbacks Bottlenecks in one of the exhibitions

What's there This spectacular stone castle has been the backdrop to centuries of history. William the Conqueror held a strategic post at Warwick in 1068, but it was in the Middle Ages that Warwick Castle saw its most bloody political intrigue. An excellent, inspired exhibit called the **Kingmaker**, detailing the chequered existence of the Earl of Warwick, sets an example of how best to bring history to life. Waxworks, costumed players, music and smells create a sense of place almost theatrical in its intensity. There is humour too, which continues throughout the castle: skilled actors show you to the grim dungeon, the torture chamber, the armoury, the towers and ramparts. The opulent **State Rooms** show what life was like in the seventeenth and eighteenth centuries, with knowledgeable guides to answer questions. A **Royal Weekend Party** is a themed exhibition set in 1898, using waxworks of Daisy, Countess of Warwick, and the then Prince of Wales, to illuminate the activities of the aristocracy of the Victorian era. Bottlenecks may occur here, as some of the rooms can be seen only through narrow doorways.

During the summer months fascinating **outdoor presentations** are on offer: a Red Knight on horseback discoursing on the horrors of heraldic battle, as well as hilarious displays of medieval hand-to-hand fighting, an archer and a jesting minstrel. On River Island you can see medieval craftsmen at work, and participate in medieval games (extra charge).

Splendid **grounds** offer ample places for picnicking or walking. The river is full of fish, ducks and geese; you can also admire the peacock garden, the rose garden and the eighteenth-century conservatory.

The sense of progression through history, the use of actors and themed exhibitions, the superlative attention to detail and the legendary nature of the castle itself mean that this is an attraction where history really comes alive.

The entrance fee is not cheap, but you can easily spend a whole day here.

Information/tours/guides An interesting and well-presented glossy guidebook costs £3.50. Costumed players are on hand to help with orientation and fill you in on historical fact. Well-informed and friendly guides are present in the State Rooms and Great Hall. An audio tour costing £2.25 provides about an hour of commentary (your tour will take longer as you walk from exhibition to exhibition) on the areas of the castle not peopled with waxworks or actors, and more historical detail. The Red Knight, archer and fighting knights (only in summer) give insightful short talks.

When to visit Although it is probably best to visit in the summer, when the outdoor presentations make it a great family attraction, it can get very crowded. There is still plenty to see indoors if the weather is inclement, but bring an umbrella for crossing the huge courtyard and exploring the grounds.

Age appeal Children will enjoy the Kingmaker exhibition, the dungeon and all the outdoor presentations, especially the jesting minstrel and the fighting knights. Adults will also appreciate the grounds, the State Rooms and the castle itself. The grounds are rolling rather than flat, but the paths are well maintained.

Food and drink There are various catering outlets around the castle, ranging from an Undercroft restaurant (done out in medieval style), where a roast dinner will cost around £5, to cafés and hot-dog stalls.

Shops Outlets at the end of each part of the castle sell a wide and appropriate range of goods – books on medieval life and history, tapestries, teddy bears wearing medieval costume, pewter jewellery made on site by the craftsmen, as well as standard souvenirs and trinkets.

In Warwick town, 2 miles from M40 junction 15. Well signposted. Several pay and display car parks, which get very busy in the peak times. ⊖ Ten-minute walk from Warwick railway station (or about £3 by taxi). Chiltern Railways (08705 165165) offers a combined rail ticket and entry package from London Marylebone. ⏰ Apr to Oct, Mon to Sun 10am to 6pm; Nov to Mar, Mon to Sun 10am to 5pm. Closed 25 Dec. 💷 Adult £9.75; child (5 to 15 yrs old) £5.95; senior citizen, student £7; family ticket (2 adults + 3 children) £28. ♿ Very limited – only the grounds and armoury are accessible.

Waterperry Gardens

Waterperry, Nr Wheatley, Oxfordshire OX33 1JZ ☎ *(01844) 339254*
📠 *(01844) 339883*

Quality ★ **Facilities 🏛 🏛 🏛** **Value for money £**
Highlights Lovely Saxon parish church within grounds
Drawbacks The gardens seem to play second fiddle to the garden centre

What's there Waterperry Gardens began to take shape in 1932, when a Miss Beatrix Havergal moved to the area, taking with her six students and establishing a centre of learning with the aim of educating women in all things horticultural. From the very outset ornamental and utilitarian aspects were to be found side by side, and this dual character is still very much present. Day courses continue to be run for amateurs, but much of the site, including the lovely **walled kitchen garden**, has now been given over to a **garden centre**. Even the gardens themselves contain large areas devoted to well-regimented beds of stock plants and rank upon rank of apple orchard. In fact, many of the ornamental elements are quite new – for instance, the celebrated **formal garden** with its Tudor knot, wisteria walk and pagoda was developed in 1986, while the rose gardens were planted in 1991 – and the whole garden hangs together rather uncomfortably as a tourist attraction.

Other features of the garden include a pretty little **rockery** and a short woodland walk along the banks of the Thame (a tributary of the Thames); most impressive are the two stretches of wall around the former kitchen garden, which harbour a collection of shade-tolerant plants along the secluded **Virgin's Walk** and a classic **herbaceous border**, glorious in summer. Overall, however, the gardens remain unimpressive in terms of scale or grandeur, and – most disconcertingly, perhaps – give little sense of having been landscaped, seeming, rather, to have been set down on former parkland (which can be seen stretching away beyond the limits of the orchards).

Outside the gardens there is a beautiful little **church** with a wooden tower which dates back to Saxon times. Within the whitewashed interior, you can trace various stages of Romanesque architecture as you wander between the box pews and marvel at the original stained-glass in the thirteenth-century lancets.

Information/tours/guides The advertised free tour on Sunday afternoons at 3pm failed to take place on our inspection visit. Otherwise, the gardens offer little in the way of information or signs, and the only map is displayed some distance from the entrance. An attractively presented guidebook is reasonable value (£1.50) and does include a useful map, but it is not always available at the ticket office. Groups can pre-book a tour: phone for details.

When to visit It is almost certainly best to visit in summer, when the gardens are in full bloom; outside peak season the gardens can appear bleak and windswept. However, large numbers of summer visitors could make the gardens feel very claustrophobic.

Age appeal Very little in the gardens will appeal to children.

Food and drink The Pear Tree restaurant serves a range of good-quality lunches prepared using local ingredients, as well as some very tasty cakes, though the prefab building and twee décor do not make for a pleasant ambience.

Shops A large garden centre, selling everything from seedlings to sundials, seems to be the main attraction at the Waterperry Gardens. In addition, a small gallery in an eighteenth-century barn sells some lovely bits of art and crafts, including paintings, hand-thrown ceramics and designer jewellery.

🚗 Turn off A40 at Wheatley and follow signs; Waterperry is 2½ miles away. ⊖ Nearest bus stop is in Wheatley. ⊕ Mon to Sun, Apr to Oct 9am to 5.30pm; Nov to Mar 9am to 5pm. Closed 25, 26 Dec and 1 Jan and 15 to 18 Jul. 🎫 Apr to Oct adult £3.40; child (10 to 16 yrs old) £1.90; senior citizen £2.90; Nov to Mar £1.60. ♿ Complete access, including ramp to restaurant and disabled toilets.

Weald and Downland Open Air Museum

Singleton, Chichester, West Sussex PO18 0EU   ☎ *(01243) 811348*
☞ *www.wealddown.co.uk*

Quality ★★★★	Facilities 🏛🏛🏛	Value for money ££££
Highlights	Beautifully maintained, well-planned collection of unusual buildings; plenty of detailed technical information; live demonstrations	
Drawbacks	More social context would be useful for non-specialist visitors	

What's there Over 40 buildings from around south-east England have been saved from destruction, dismantled and re-erected on this attractive rural site. Carefully clustered in small groups spread over 50 acres of downland, woodland and farmland, they include a watermill and wind-pump as well as a farmhouse moved from the site of the Eurotunnel terminal in Folkestone in 1992.

Many of the buildings are empty, but you can still sense atmosphere in, for example, the smell of wood-smoke and blackened walls of the medieval house from North Cray in Kent. Buildings that have been furnished include a tiny **Victorian school** from West Wittering in Sussex, Whittaker's cottages from Ashstead in Surrey, and Bayleaf Farmstead from Kent – a medieval **Wealden house** with a reconstructed garderobe, or overhanging toilet. Elsewhere on the site you can discover a charcoal-burner's hut, surrounded by turves of grass, and a **shepherd's hut** with a brief description of the strange counting system for sheep: 11 was 'yan-a-dik'; 15 was 'bumpit'. A limited number of livestock, including pigs, sheep and horses, are also kept on the site and managed in a traditional way. Live demonstrations may include building with flints or smithing.

Some of the buildings contain detailed exhibitions: the Barn from Hambrook houses an introductory exhibition on building techniques, while in the Court Barn from Lee-on-Solent you can learn all about plumbing, masonry and glazing. Upstairs in Bayleaf Farmstead another exhibition describes how the replica furniture, garden, and equipment were created. Although most of the information given concentrates on technical details, occasional push-button recorded commentaries provide more social context – for example, in Whittaker's Cottages.

Information/tours/guides The museum is staffed by (mostly mature) volunteer stewards, who are chatty and helpful. The free introductory leaflet includes a map of the site with a numbered key identifying the buildings, and two suggested colour-coded routes (one long, one short). The guidebook (£2) provides exhaustive, rather dry detail on the technical aspects of each of the buildings in the museum, with plans and cross-sections. There are few sign-posts on site, so you need the leaflet to check where you are. Some buildings simply have small boards explaining where they came from and the historical context.

When to visit Fine weather is best. Neither the buildings nor the refreshment hall are very large, and there is a lot of walking between groups of buildings. Various special events are organised throughout the summer, such as medieval cookery demonstrations, rare and traditional breeds shows, children's activity weekends, and historical re-enactments. Allow at least half a day if you want to see everything.

Age appeal An activity book for children (95p) provides ideas and activities for both during and after the visit. In the Joiner's Shop the 'Getting to Grips' exhibition also allows children to have a go at working with roof peg tiles, sifting aggregates and using timber joints. Youngsters can also enjoy feeding the ducks and seeing other animals such as pigs and sheep. The buildings are widely spread over the 50-acre site, and many of the paths are rather bumpy and uneven. Visitors who tire easily face long stretches without any seats or benches to rest on.

Food and drink The cafeteria next to the lake sells a limited range of hot food such as home-made pizza (£1.95), Cornish pasty (£1.25), flan with new potatoes and salad (£4.75), and a selection of cakes and pastries plus hot and cold drinks. Limited indoor seating is available at refectory tables in a fifteenth-century house from Kent. Alternatively, the geese and ducks are always happy to welcome picnickers (there are several tables by the lake, or you can picnic anywhere in the open areas of the site).

Shops The shop has plenty of books on various aspects of building and architecture, from brickmaking to timber frames, tithe barns and tools. You can also buy stoneground flour from the mill (£1 for 1kg), and local produce such as apple juice (£1.95 a bottle), beeswax candles, jam and chutney. Some plants are for sale.

From A286, follow brown signs to museum (5 miles north of Chichester). Free parking. ⊖ Take Stagecoach buses 60/60A between Midhurst and Bognor Regis (every half-hour Mon to Sat 9am to 6pm and every hour Sun); get off at Horse & Groom in Singleton. Combined travel and entry tickets available (adult £5.50 adult, child £2.75) – call Traveline (0345) 959099 for details. ⊙ Mar to Oct, Mon to Sun 10.30am to 6pm (last admission 5pm); Nov to Feb, Wed, Sat and Sun 10.30am to 4pm (daily in Feb half-term holidays); 26 Dec to 1 Jan, Mon to Sun 10.30am to 4pm. Closed 25 Dec. 🔳 Adult £6; child (5 to 16 yrs old) £3; senior citizen £5.50; family ticket (2 adults + 2 children) £15. ⅙ Access to the site is via an automatic gate, with reserved parking next to the entrance. Disabled toilets.

Westonbirt Arboretum

Tetbury, Gloucestershire GL8 8QS ☎ *(01666) 880220*

Quality ★★★★★   **Facilities** 🏛🏛🏛🏛🏛   **Value for money** ££££
Highlights Old arboretum, maple tree collection and autumn colour; friendly, approachable staff
Drawbacks Poor picture quality on introductory video; outdoor café in cold weather; tatty toilets

What's there The 600 acres of beautifully landscaped countryside are planted with 18,000 specimens of 4,000 species of trees and shrubs, and are now managed by the Forestry Commission after passing to the Crown in 1956.

Established in 1829 by **Robert Holford**, the collection brought together exotic species from temperate climes worldwide, with specimens from countries such as China, Japan, India, Australia and America. Robert's son George inherited his father's passion and after his father's death in 1892 George continued adding to the arboretum. The Holfords also experimented with propagation and hybridisation of species, many of them new Britain.

The Arboretum as it stands today encompasses 17 miles of pathways – so don't aim to see everything in one visit! The most manageable section is the **Old Arboretum**, which incorporates Savill Glade and Circular Drive – the best areas for viewing rhododendrons, azaleas, cherries and camellias in spring. Also in this part are the Old Acer Glade (planted between 1850 and 1875) and the New Acer Glade (planted in the early 1960s), providing dramatic colour in autumn. On the opposite side of the car park and Visitor Centre, **Silk Wood** covers a larger area and is usually less crowded. There is a small Japanese maple collection here (still rather immature at present) as well as the Hillier cherry tree collection and an area devoted to native species. In spring the array of wild-flowers here is impressive, especially the display of bluebells.

Information/tours/guides The well-designed free map (from the Visitor Centre) clearly shows paths and routes and is divided into grids. Each square represents 100 metres, which should take about five minutes to walk slowly; steep hills are also marked. The guidebook tells you more about Westonbirt. Most trees and shrubs are clearly labelled, and those which are not can be identified in a master atlas in the Visitor Centre. Dogs are welcome in two-thirds of the grounds, but are not allowed in the Old Arboretum, the Visitor Centre or café.

When to visit Go in spring for rhododendrons, azaleas, magnolias, camellias and wildflowers in Silk Wood (peaking in May). Autumn is best for leaf colour, especially maple trees (which excel in October) but the site can be very busy on October weekends, so go mid-week if you can. There is an extensive programme of events and guided walks for an extra charge (phone for details).

Age appeal Something for all ages – but keep an eye on small children, as some leaves and berries are poisonous.

Food and drink The outdoor Courtyard Café is a small, self-service kiosk offering sandwiches and baps (£2.50), hot bacon rolls (£2.50), hearty soup with a roll (£2.75), quiche and salad (£4.95), and cakes from £1.30. Several benches are arranged at tables under an awning, but most are exposed to the elements – lovely in fair weather, not so appealing in winter. There are also two picnic areas (one dog-free) adjacent to the car park.

Shops The attractively laid out, spacious shop in the Visitor Centre has an appealing selection of goods. Plenty of books related to gardening are to be found, as well as some on trees and wood (e.g. *The Complete Woodmaker's Annual*). Lots of good-quality wooden objects are on sale, some quite pricey, such as a footstool (£85), bookends (£45), a letter rack (£20) and bowls (£40). An unusual selection of jams and marmalades also features, such as Earl Grey marmalade. Plenty of items will appeal to children, such as books, rubber insects (75p), pencils (50p) and soft toys. A garden centre is also on-site.

From M4, take junction 18 and follow signs from A46 to arboretum on A433 (3 miles south-west of Tetbury). From M5, take junction 13 (Tetbury is 20 minutes south-east). Free car park. Limited bus services only from Tetbury: X55 stops outside the Arboretum and F152C, 620 stop at Hare and Hounds. For details call Tetbury Tourist Information Centre (01666) 503552. Mon to Sun 10am to 8pm (or sunset if earlier). *Visitor Centre, café and gift shop* Mon to Sun 10am to 5pm. Closed 24 Dec to 3 Jan. Jan to Sept, adult £4; child (5 to 15 yrs old) £1; senior citizen £3. Oct to Nov, adult £4.50; child, disabled visitor £1, senior citizen £3.50; 27 Nov to 23 Dec, Free. Life or corporate membership plus membership of Friends of Westonbirt Arboretum available, which allows unlimited access. For further details tel. (01666) 880148. The old arboretum (to the right as you enter car park) is level, has hard paths and is suitable for wheelchairs or those with walking difficulties. The Courtyard Café, Visitor Centre/shop and plant centre are accessible; disabled toilet nearby. Wheelchairs, including electric, may be borrowed from the Visitor Centre if pre-booked.

Whipsnade Wild Animal Park

Dunstable, Bedfordshire LU6 2LF ☎ *(01582) 872171*
Information 0990 200 123 📠 *(01582) 872649* 🖳 *www.whipsnade.co.uk*

Quality ★★★ **Facilities 🏛 🏛** **Value for money £££**
Highlights Animal demonstrations; hippos, chimpanzees and lemurs
Drawbacks Extra charge to take in a vehicle

What's there The main part of the park stretches over a wide area with numerous enclosures. To see it you can choose from driving your car around the park for an extra £8, hopping on and off the free safari bus, or taking a long walk.

The main activities take place around the demonstration arenas near the main entrance. Visitors hear three interesting and informative talks, starting with a demonstration on birds, which shows how the creatures catch food in the wild. This is followed by a sea-lion show.

Nearby is a **children's farm**, where you can learn more about domestic animals, and a **discovery centre** which houses cages of smaller animals, including snakes and monkeys, but provides rather variable amounts of information. The penguins are fed daily at 2pm. You can take a train ride around open paddocks populated by various species of **deer** from the Asian plains – a free leaflet is supplied to help you identify the animals.

The best enclosures are the hippos (which occupy the hippo house in winter and the paddocks in summer), and the ring-tailed lemurs and chimpanzees (both species are located near the main gate).

Information/tours/guides The talk on birds and the sea-lion show are free and last about 20 minutes. Times of these events are on a leaflet given to you with your ticket. Train rides round the deer paddocks depart on the hour (adult £2, child £1). The guidebook (£2) is reasonable value. Not all the animal cages display decent information boards, but the hippo, lemur and chimpanzee enclosures feature plenty of signs and graphics.

When to visit This is mostly an open-air attraction (even the talks are held outdoors), so think twice if there is a chance of rain.

Age appeal Talks are aimed at both adults and children, but otherwise the farm is the only feature specifically intended for children.

Food and drink The unexceptional cafeteria offers limited choice, but has helpful staff. A typical main course might be chicken and mushroom pie with chips and vegetables (£5.75), while snacks include sandwiches (£2.25 to £2.95) and coffee (£1).

Shops The main shop at the entrance sells a variety of animal products including cuddly seals (£12), mugs (£2.50) and sweatshirts (£28).

Other facilities It is a long walk to the toilets from some parts of the park.

🚗 From M1, follow signs from junctions 9 and 12. Parking outside, £2. ⊖ Train to Luton or Hemel Hempstead. Bus from Luton and Dunstable tel. (0345) 788788 or Green Line Bus from London Victoria (summer only). ① Mon to Sat 10am to 6pm (7pm Sun and bank hols). Closed winter bank hol Mons. 💷 Adult £9.90; child (3 to 15 years); senior citizen £7.50; disabled person £8.50, carer admitted free. £8 to take car into park. ♿ Accessible. Disabled toilet. Free car parking.

Whitby Abbey

Whitby, North Yorkshire YO21 4JT ☎ *(01947) 603568*
🖰 *www.english-heritage.org.uk*

Quality ★★★	Facilities 👜👜👜	Value for money £££

Highlights A small but informative exhibition provides visitors with a clear picture of the Abbey's history

Drawbacks The shop, which doubles up as an arrival area, can become congested on busy days

What's there Founded by St Hilda, Whitby Abbey has occupied its dramatic clifftop position since AD657. Although none of the early buildings survives, the foundations of the earliest monastery have been revealed by excavation. The ruins that are visible today are largely the product of rebuilding undertaken by the monks during the thirteenth and early fourteenth centuries, and include examples of **Gothic and Early English architecture**.

A small but interesting **exhibition** traces the development of the Abbey and describes the daily round of its inhabitants. Replicas of the tools used by the community to spin, weave and write are also displayed.

Allow at least an hour and a half to see the Abbey and the exhibition.

Information/tours/guides A full-colour guidebook (£1.50) includes a tour of the Abbey and covers its origins and development. Plans are afoot to introduce an audio tour, which should improve visitors' experience significantly, and a new museum, which will feature computer-generated images of the Abbey in its heyday, is due to open in 2001.

When to visit This is an outdoor attraction and is best seen in dry weather. Special events, including Viking and medieval pageants, take place throughout the year (call for details). Admission is normally included in the standard ticket price.

Age appeal A good-quality children's guidebook (99p) explains the Abbey's history in an accessible manner and is packed full of practical activities. Steps from the main car park to the arrival area (combined with the shop) are relatively steep, so visitors with mobility problems should park in the south car park. The site is relatively flat.

Food and drink Apart from a drinks cabinet, no refreshments are available on-site.

Shops A good selection of quality merchandise is available, including reading material that will further enhance your visit.

🚌 From Whitby town centre, follow brown signs east to Abbey. ⊖ Train to Whitby station, then 20-minute walk. Buses from Longborne Road (2 minutes from rail station). Tel. (01947) 602674. ① Apr to Sept, Mon to Sun 10am to 6pm; Oct, Mon to Sun 10am to 5pm; Nov to March, 10am to 4pm. Closed 24–26 Dec. 💷 Adult £1.70; child 90p; student, senior citizen, disabled, unemployed £1.30. Free entry for EH members. ♿ South car park has disabled spaces. Path to Abbey is bumpy/roughly mown and not suitable in wet weather.

White Post Modern Farm Centre

Farnsfield, Nottinghamshire NG22 8HL ☎ *(01623) 882977*
www.whitepostfarmcentre.co.uk

Quality ★★   **Facilities** 🏠🏠🏠   **Value for money ££££**
Highlights Opportunity to see and handle animals in an authentic farm setting
Drawbacks Less appeal for older children

What's there This working farm has been converted from various barns and outhouses into a very authentic theme park and amateur natural history museum. The sights, sounds and smells of the farmyard are here in abundance. Children will love the chance to see a wide variety of familiar **animals** (sheep, chickens, pigs and horses) and some more exotic ones (including pygmy goats, various reptiles and chipmunks) at close quarters. Handling of some of the animals is encouraged, with supervision from the staff, and feeding is allowed, with inexpensive food available at the entrance.

Particularly impressive is a long, low barn which is kept dark to trick its **resident owls** into thinking it is night. As you walk through, owls oblige by flying across your path just feet away.

The hand-written, slightly amateurish signs and information boards serve as a reminder that this is farm first, museum second. But although this slightly scruffy collection of farm buildings is not a slick modern museum experience it benefits from the realistic feel and lack of commercialism.

Entertainment is also on offer – a very effective and scarily dark **haunted house** had been made in one of the barns at Hallowe'en. Also available are a large indoor soft play area, structured play activities and a bouncy castle.

Information/tours/guides School visits are guided and content is aimed at meeting curriculum targets. The public are left to their own devices, although staff are on hand to answer questions. The level of explanation of what you see – for example, the information boards describing a sow's time in the farrowing barn, or how eggs are hatched – is good.

When to visit A few of the activities and facilities – feeding animals, a duck pond and a play area – are outdoors, so fine weather would be ideal but not essential.

Age appeal The farm is aimed squarely at younger children. Adults will enjoy the experience too, but take children to get the most out of the visit.

Food and drink Visitors have a choice of two places to eat at – a restaurant with a pleasant conservatory facing a garden, and a lunch barn which doubles as an indoor play area. Both offer friendly service and no-frills café food at reasonable prices (baked potatoes from £1.50 and toasted sandwiches from £1.85).

Shops A small souvenir shop sells some attractive children's books on animals. Also on sale are reptiles from the vivarium barn and pet-care products from the Pet Centre, which adjoins the farm.

🚗 12 miles north of Nottingham. Well sign-posted from A614. Follow Robin Hood signs from M1 junction 27. ⊖ Main Nottingham-to-Doncaster bus route runs past farm. ☉ Mon to Fri 10am to 5pm; Sat and Sun 10am to 6pm. 💷 (1999) adult £4.50; child (3 to 16 yrs old) £3.50; senior citizen, adult with special needs £3.50; child with special needs £2.65. ♿ Level access for most areas; not all smooth surfaces.

Wigan Pier

Wallgate, Wigan, Greater Manchester WN3 4EF   ☎ *(01942) 323666*

Quality ★★★   **Facilities 🏛 🏛 🏛**   **Value for money £££**

Highlights   Highly informative displays, with imaginative use of videos and historic buildings

Drawbacks   Poor toilets in mill; uninspiring food; some repetition in displays

What's there   Wigan Pier is not a pier in the conventional sense, but a long dock alongside the Leeds-Liverpool Canal where boats used to tie up to load and unload. Both an exploration and an exhibition of the twentieth century, this heritage centre is spread over two sites.

The **Way We Were** experience is housed in a historic warehouse on the pier made famous in a ditty by local boy George Formby and in the writings of George Orwell. The museum takes you on a journey through the past, starting with the seaside at the end of the nineteenth century, complete with 'What the Butler Saw' peep-shows and penny slot machines contained in a re-creation of a **seaside pier**. Life-sized figures in appropriate costume pose in front of painted and model backgrounds to create an authentic ambience that is enhanced by a mood-evoking soundtrack.

From here, you pass through into a 'back to work' theme, which for most Wigan people in the early twentieth century meant the pit. A convincing mock-up of life down a **mine** shows how dangerous and cramped the conditions were, and how and why disasters occurred.

The theme of **daily life** is explored via re-creations of homes belonging to a middle-class vicar and a miner, complete with rats living in the roof! Plenty of authentic Victorian household items and memorabilia are on show, as well as audio telephones that allow you to listen to people who lived through the times recounting their lives.

Most impressive of all, perhaps, is the construction of a three-storey **Victorian marketplace** with shops, warehouse, pub and school, all of which can be entered and explored. Costumed actors also act out scenes from everyday life.

From here, you can choose to walk or take an electric boat ride along the canal to **Opie's Museum of Memories**, which, appropriately, is in a more modern building, as it covers the period from the 1930s to the 1990s. It makes use mainly of shops and cafés from the era, such as a 1970s groove record shop, a 1960s 'flower power' boutique and a 1940s corner shop, along with items of popular culture, like Raleigh Choppers, flares and jukeboxes. Next door to the museum is a huge working steam engine and weaving shed.

You should allow between three and four hours for a complete visit.

Information/tours/guides   No guided tour or guidebook is available, but several free leaflets give a good idea of what is going on and where.

When to visit Both sites are under cover, as is the boat ride, but should you wish to enjoy a walk along the canal basin you will need fine weather.

Age appeal The interactive nature of some of the exhibits, as well as the costumed actors, help to bring the place alive for younger visitors, and there is plenty to interest adults.

Food and drink The canteen opposite Opie's Museum is let down by the rather tatty condition of the building and unimaginative food (burger and chips, fish and chips, and beans on toast), though the prices are reasonable.

Shops The large and bright shop, next to Opie's, has a good range of modern history books to complement your visit, as well as classic children's books, mugs and old-fashioned toys, such as skipping ropes and gyroscopes.

🚗 Signposted from all major roads leading to Wigan town centre. Free parking. ⊖ Both Wigan North Western and Wigan Wallgate rail stations are a 5-minute walk. ⊙ Mon to Thur 10am to 5pm; Sat and Sun 11am to 5pm. Closed Fri (except Good Friday); 25 and 26 Dec. 💷 Adult £6.95; child (5 to 16 yrs old) £5.25; student, senior citizen £5.25; family ticket (2 adults + 3 children) £19.50. *'The Way We Were'* adult £3.95; child, senior citizen, student £3.25. *Opie's Museum* adult £4.95; child, senior citizen, student £3.50. ♿ Full access with lift and toilets, but not on to the boat.

Wilton House ☺

Wilton, Salisbury, Wiltshire SP2 OBJ ☎ *(01722) 746729*
🕸 *www.wiltonhouse.com*

Quality ★★★★★   **Facilities**   **Value for money** £££££
Highlights Double cube room with impressive collection of Van Dyck paintings; adventure playground for children
Drawbacks Bottleneck queues as people leave film theatre and funnel through rest of visitor centre at end of introductory film

---

What's there This splendid seventeenth-century **Palladian-style mansion** in 21 acres of landscaped parkland, still the family home to the 17th Earl of Pembroke, was built using plans designed by Inigo Jones. The interior is stunning, in particular the single and double **cube rooms** – the latter houses a specially commissioned collection of **Van Dyck** paintings and a painted *trompe l'oeil* ceiling. The immaculate grounds include a Palladian bridge across the River Nadder, rose garden, woodland walk and a fun whispering seat near the water garden. The extensive outdoor **adventure playground** will appeal to most children.

The **visitor centre** in the converted riding school has a central display which changes yearly and a cinema seating 67 for the showing of the very good introductory film. You can also see re-creations of a Tudor kitchen and Victorian laundry, and the popular Pembroke Palace Dolls' House. Also featured is the Wareham Bear collection – 200 miniature teddy bears dressed in clothes and in tiny houses, stables and other scenes.

Information/tours/guides Visitors are given a free map and plan for the house and grounds, and will find the introductory 15-minute film narrated by Anna Massey very useful as it gives a potted history of the house.

The excellent full-colour guidebook (£3) covers the visitor centre, the house and its history, the grounds and the family. A leaflet (20p) picks out highlights to see in the house and its history in brief. The guides in each room are knowledgeable and very friendly. *Meet the Wareham Bears* (£1.50) is more of a story book than a guidebook.

When to visit Any time is good to visit, but fine weather is necessary for children to enjoy the adventure playground. Special events – such as the Children's Fun Day, the flower and craft show, and classical concerts with fireworks – are held throughout the year (extra charges apply).

Age appeal Children of all ages will love the well-designed adventure playground, which has a separate area for the under-fives. The free treasure-hunt quiz sheet given out to children will keep them interested in the house, and items like the Wareham Bear collection and the dolls' house will also appeal.

Food and drink The large, open-plan self-service restaurant (open 10.30am to 5pm – hot lunches served 12pm to 2pm) offers good hot food such as chicken curry (£5.25) or leek and potato bake (£4.95). It also has a range of sandwiches and a salad bar plus various cakes and biscuits. There is a picnic area with tables and benches near the adventure playground.

Shops An attractive shop sells up-market gifts such as Spode and glassware as well as the more usual selection of biscuits, fudge and jams. It has a wide choice of teddy bears and soft toys. The Wilton House Garden Centre nearby on Salisbury Road is well stocked.

🚌 3 miles west of Salisbury on A30, brown signs in village of Wilton. Free car park. ⊖ From Salisbury buses 60, 60A or 61 from outside Marks and Spencer in the New Canal. ⏰ Mon to Sun 10 Apr to 29 Oct, 10.30am to 5.30pm (last admission 4.30pm). 💷 *House and grounds* adult £6.75; child (5 to 15 yrs old) £4; senior citizen £5.75; family ticket (2 adults + 2 children) £17.50; *grounds* adult £3.75; child £2.50; senior citizen £3.75. *Season ticket for grounds* individual (holder + 1) £19.50; family (holder + 3) £39.50. ♿ Full wheelchair access; grounds largely level. Disabled toilets. Special parking. Guide dogs admitted.

Wimpole Hall and Home Farm

Arrington, Nr Royston, Cambridgeshire SG8 0BW   ☎ *(01223) 207257*

Quality ★★★★   **Facilities 🏛🏛🏛🏛🏛**   **Value for money £££**
Highlights Plenty to entertain all the family – stately home, animals, walks
Drawbacks Not good in bad weather

What's there The building of Wimpole Hall was started by Sir Thomas Chicheley in 1640 and has been much extended and remodelled by its subsequent owners. It was bequeathed to the National Trust by Mrs Bambridge (daughter of Rudyard Kipling) in 1976. The house itself is relatively small, although it has an impressive façade, but it is surrounded by hundreds of acres of rolling and wooded grounds.

Filled with furniture collected by Mrs Bambridge, the **red-brick house** is presented in a way that reflects the character and penchants of her family. There is a huge library, several memorable paintings, and fine examples of rooms by Sir John Soane – note the impressive ceilings. Soane also built a bath house in neo-classical style, in stark contrast to the baroque chapel which features *trompe l'oeil* walls.

The thatched **Home Farm**, reached via the gardens along a pretty walk, was also built by Soane. It now houses all manner of rare breeds of sheep, pigs, cows, horses, goats and poultry – breeds which would once have been commonplace at Wimpole Hall.

Visitors can walk for miles through old forest and parkland. Capability Brown created serpentine lakes and meandering belts of trees, as well as the ruined gothic tower on a hill. The grounds feature parterres, a rose garden and a Dutch garden.

At least half a day is needed to take in the hall, gardens and Home Farm.

Information/tours/guides A glossy guidebook gives details of the history, architecture and contents of the hall and gardens (£4.50). A free leaflet contains enough information for you to make a self-guided tour of the house. Friendly NT volunteers are on hand in each room to answer any questions you may have.

When to visit Wimpole Hall is best visited on a fine day, otherwise you cannot really explore the grounds. Many events are organised throughout the year, from lambing weekends to jazz in the stables and open-air concerts in the gardens.

Age appeal Kids will love Home Farm. Adults will appreciate the house and gardens.

Food and drink The spacious Old Rectory Restaurant in the gardens serves up Victorian-style food such as hodge podge (soup) and freshly made bread for £2.50, farm workers' docky (meat, cheese, apple, celery, pickled cabbage, onion and soda bread) for £4.50, and lemon posset and strawberries for £3. The cafeterias in the Stable Block and Home Farm offer better-than-average sandwiches and ice creams.

Shops The shop in the Stable Block offers classic NT merchandise, such as lavender-scented candles, books on gardening and stately homes.

🚌 Off A1198, near Cambridge. Large car park. ⊖ Train to Royston, then taxi (approx £7 each way). ○ *Park* Mon to Sun sunrise to sunset (sunrise to 5pm 8 and 9 Jul, 19 and 20 Aug). *Hall* 18 Mar to 31 Oct, Tue to Thur, Sat and Sun 1pm to 5pm; bank hol Sun and Mon 11am to 5pm; Good Fri and Fri in Aug 1pm to 5pm. *Home Farm* 18 Mar to 31 Oct, Tue to Thur, Sat and Sun, Good Fri, bank hol Mon and Fri in July and Aug 10.30am to 5pm; Nov to Mar, Sat and Sun 11am to 4pm; closed 25 and 26 Dec. *Shop and restaurant* 18 Mar to 31 Oct same days as Hall 11am to 5.30pm; Nov to Mar, Tues to Thur, Sat and Sun 11am to 4pm. 💷 *Hall, farm and gardens* adult £8.50; child (5 to 16 yrs) £4.20; family ticket (2 adults + 2 children) £21; *hall* adult £5.90; child £2.70; *farm* adult £4.70; child £2.70; *gardens* adult £2.50; child free. NT members free. ♿ Hall has 12 steps up to front entrance; some gravel paths in the park, gardens and grounds.

Winchester Cathedral

Winchester, Hampshire SO23 9LF ☎ *(01962) 857200*

Quality ★★★ **Facilities** 🛋 🛋 🛋 🛋 **Value for money** ££££
Highlights Breathtaking building and the great screen
Drawbacks Unless you take a tour, you could find it quite difficult to interpret what is on view

What's there This mighty medieval edifice is a symbol of Christianity, an architectural wonder and a treasure-store of art. The history of the building is complex, the original 'Old Minster' having been established in the seventh century, when Winchester became the royal and ecclesiastical centre of the Saxon kingdom of Wessex. In the ninth century a 'New Minster' was built alongside, on Alfred the Great's instructions, and completed by his son, but this was relocated to the suburb of Hyde in 1110.

The Norman cathedral was begun by Bishop Walkelin in 1079, and by 1093 its east end and transept were ready to receive the remains of St Swithin – a local saint remembered today mainly for his alleged connection with weather conditions – and tombs of the Anglo-Saxon kings and bishops. The cathedral we see today retains some Norman/Romanesque (1079–1150) features, but the soaring expanse of its west front (where you enter) and the nave are Perpendicular (1346–1525) and a good deal of the chancel is Early English (1200–60).

Inside the church, besides the glorious architecture (ideally, bring binoculars so you can view the detail of the sculpted **vault bosses** and corbels), points of interest include the great **screen** of 1470–6, supporting a phalanx of statues of the saints; the twelfth-century black marble font; the colourful thirteenth-century **tile floor** of the retrochoir; the grave of Izaak Walton, author of *The Compleat Angler*; the **carved animals** nestling in the choirstalls; the wall paintings of the Lady Chapel; the various chantry chapels, where masses were said for the souls of the dedicatee; the stained-glass **windows**; and **Jane Austen's grave** (1817), located in a side aisle and bearing an inscription that praises her character but makes no mention of her literary achievements.

The famous twelfth-century **Winchester Bible** is in the seventeenth-century Bishop Morley bookroom (the cathedral library): you can tour this and the triforium gallery for a small fee. It is also possible to visit the **tower**, rebuilt in the twelfth century and supported on huge arches above the choir. Apart from marvellous views of the city and surrounding area, the tower tour gives access to the bell-ringing chamber and the nave vault.

The crypt, under the eastern end of the church, reveals the plan of the Norman cathedral. However, it often floods in winter, leaving the modern statue *Sound II* (1986) standing in water.

Outside the building is Dean Garnier's garden, entered via a thirteenth-century doorway. Here on the site of the former monks' dorter (dormitory) of St Swithin's Priory you can see where a passage used to lead directly into the cathedral's east end – and also how subsidence has affected this end of the building. Interpretative panels throw light on the cathedral's structural history.

On the lawns at the cathedral's west front you will see the site of the Old Minster marked out in brick, and more explanatory panels describing the buildings' history.

Information/tours/guides A free leaflet that includes a map showing where the main points of interest are sited can be picked up near the entrance, but to appreciate the building better it is worth joining one of the free tours of the cathedral (these last about 50 minutes), starting near the main entrance. Failing this, voluntary guides wearing red badges and vergers (wearing black cassocks) are usually on hand to answer questions. Crypt tours are also free. Tower/roof tours take about 75 minutes (weekdays at 2.15pm, Saturdays 11.30am and 2.15pm), and cost £1.50. Tours of the cathedral library and triforium gallery (containing treasures including medieval statuary) cost £1 for adults (50p for senior citizens) and £2 for families. General tours for school and adult groups can be pre-booked. Note that there are *no tours on Sundays*. The souvenir guide of the cathedral costs £2.50.

When to visit Visitors are asked to avoid times when services are taking place, and Sundays. It is advisable to complete your visit before evensong starts at 5.30 (weekdays inc. Saturdays).

Age appeal The main appeal is to adults, but children's booklets sold in the shop are designed to arouse the interest of younger visitors (for example, the humorous carvings on the misericords).

Food and drink The splendid refectory is open daily. Besides tea and coffee (95p), you can find home-made cakes, buns and pastries, soup (£2.30), 'trenchers' (open sandwiches, £3.85), salad (£5.50), chef's specials (£5.25 to £5.95), puddings (£1.95) and cream teas (£3.85).

Shops The shop sells many items connected with the cathedral and the city, from Bibles, guidebooks and books on Jane Austen to framed (£38) and unframed (£25) prints; prints of illuminated medieval manuscripts range from £60 to £75. There are also CDs of choral music, educational packs for children and a host of gift-shop items from jams and mustards to tapestry cushion covers (£36), pens and bookmarks, calendars and greetings cards, mugs, keyrings, candles and ceramics.

Other facilities Lavatories cost 10p (no baby-changing facilities) unless you are a refectory patron.

🚐 Winchester has several park-and-ride car parks on its outskirts. ⊖ Rail to Winchester station, then park-and-ride bus. ◷ Mon to Sat when no service is being held. 💷 Adult £2.50; child 50p; senior citizen/student £2; family ticket (2 adults + children under 18) £5. ♿ Ramps into cathedral and up to shop, toilets and refectory. Stairlift available in north transept; touch-and-hearing model located in nave.

Windsor Castle

Windsor, Berkshire SL4 1NJ ☎ *(01753) 869898* ⌖ *www.royal.gov.uk*

Quality ★★★　　　　　**Facilities 🏛 🏛 🏛**　　　　　**Value for money £££**
Highlights Fantastic restoration work; good orientation leaflet; friendly, helpful staff
Drawbacks No refreshments; no admission prices on publicity leaflet; audio tour detailed but rather dry

What's there It was William the Conqueror who first established a castle at Windsor in 1080 and it has been in continuous use since that time. The form and proportions of the main rooms in the State Apartments date largely from the time of Charles II, who reinstated Windsor as his main non-metropolitan palace after the Restoration in 1660. However, much of the baroque ornamentation was removed when the rooms were remodelled during the reign of George IV (1820–30).

Queen Mary's Dolls' House, designed by Sir Edwin Lutyens (with a garden by Gertrude Jekyll), is an extraordinary feat of miniaturisation, on a scale of 1: 12. Every detail is perfect: the doors lock, the lifts go up and down, the toilets flush, the cellar is stocked with bottles of vintage wine. Unfortunately the low lighting level necessary for conservation doesn't allow you to see anything close up, but you can still appreciate the craftsmanship involved.

In the Gallery is a small exhibition describing the restoration work required on the castle after the disastrous fire of 1992; then you enter the **State Apartments** proper. As well as the magnificent art collection there are some fascinating curios, including an Indian ivory throne presented to Queen Victoria in 1851. The Waterloo Chamber, built by George IV specifically to commemorate the defeat of Napoleon, is filled with portraits of the statesmen and commanders who contributed to the victory.

The highlight is undoubtedly **St George's Hall**, damaged by the 1992 fire and splendidly restored in modern Gothic style. The hammerbeam roof, designed by Giles Downes, is once again adorned with the shields of every Knight of the Garter. Behind the Hall is the new Lantern Lobby. This was previously the site of the Private Chapel, and was the spot where the fire started (an inscription commemorates the fact). It's now a beautiful, rib-vaulted octagonal space, gloriously modern Gothic.

The state rooms that follow (some open only during the winter months) were also badly damaged, but have been restored to the gilded splendour of George IV's time – seen to particularly dazzling effect in the **Grand Reception**.

From the exit of the State Apartments the route leads back through Middle Ward and down to Lower Ward, past the neat terraced cottages of the Military Knights, who represent the Knights of the Garter at Sunday services in **St George's Chapel**. This, their spiritual home, is a first-rate example of Perpendicular Gothic, with stunning vaulting and fascinating side chapels.

From the Dean's Cloister you enter the **Albert Chapel**, which also dates from 1240 but was completely reworked (and how!) by Queen Victoria after her beloved husband died in 1864. Gold mosaics glitter on the ceiling, marble intarsia panels illustrating the Prince's virtues such as steadfastness, purity and justice cover the walls, and the floor is richly patterned in marble.

Information/tours/guides The publicity leaflet for 2000 gives opening times, location map and transport details, but unfortunately lacks admission prices. When you buy your ticket you are given a useful orientation leaflet with a map showing the recommended visitors' route and the location of toilets, shops and disabled access.

The main guidebook (£3.95) is largely a listing of fittings and furnishings, with plenty of glossy photos. Separate guides are sold for Queen Mary's Dolls' House (£2.50), St George's Chapel (2.50) and the Albert Chapel (£1).

An audio tour, covering the State Apartments, St George's Chapel and all the areas of public access, costs £2.50 – considerably cheaper than buying all the guidebooks – though its rather dry tone provides little atmosphere and lacks human interest. For that, you could try chatting to one of the wardens, who are generally friendly and approachable.

When to visit The castle is a good year-round attraction, as the grounds are limited, and most of it is under cover. The Changing of the Guard takes place at 11am every other day except Sundays. The State Apartments are closed at various times of the year, so do check before you visit.

The queue to see Queen Mary's Dolls' House can take over 45 minutes on busy days, so during the summer try to arrive early. Allow a couple of hours for Queen Mary's Dolls' House and the State Apartments, and another hour or so for St George's Chapel.

Age appeal Queen Mary's Dolls' House is fascinating for all ages and children as well as adults enjoy the spectacle of the Changing of the Guard. The State Rooms, however, hold less appeal for youngsters. St George's Chapel has a special guide for young people (£1).

Food and drink No refreshment facilities are available in the castle (though the Middle Ward shop sells cold drinks). You can get re-entry permits from the Lower and Middle Ward shops.

Shops The castle has three shops. The main shop in Middle Ward is the largest and has the widest range of goods, from traditional toy soldiers (£8.95) and Windsor Castle biscuits (£3.75) to porcelain costume dolls (£149 to £165) and tapestry cushions (£99). The Engine Court Shop and Lower Ward Shop are much smaller. St George's Chapel has a separate shop; there's also a small stall outside the Albert Chapel.

🚗 20 miles from central London, M4 junction 6 or M3 junction 3. Pay-and-display council-run car parks (castle is well sign-posted). ⊖ Regular train service from London Waterloo to Windsor; also from London Paddington via Slough; rail enquiries (0345) 484950. Regular coaches from Victoria Coach Station – telephone 020–8668 7261. ⏰ Mon to Sun, Mar to Oct 9.45am to 5.15pm (last admission 4pm); Nov to Feb 9.45am to 4.15pm (last admission 3pm). Closed 1 Jan, 16 Feb, 23 May, 19 June, 25, 26 and 31 Dec. St George's Chapel closed Sun. All arrangements subject to change. Advance booking tel. (01753) 869898. 💷 Adult £10.50; child (5 to 17 yrs old) £5; senior citizen £8; family ticket (2 adults + 2 children) £25.50. ♿ All parts except Queen Mary's Dolls' House accessible. Disabled toilets. Carers admitted free.

Woburn Abbey

Woburn, Bedfordshire MK43 0TP　☎　*(01525) 290666*

Quality ★★★	Facilities 🏛 🏛 🏛	Value for money £££
Highlights	Many fine paintings by well-known artists; superb collections of porcelain, gold and silver	
Drawbacks	Not much to see in the grounds, though the deer park is an attractive setting	

What's there The main attraction is the abbey itself, the home of the Russell family since 1619, but with origins dating back to 1145. You can visit some 18 rooms, including the sumptuous **state dining room**, with its beautiful Meissen dining service, the elegant Blue Drawing Room and Queen Victoria's Bedroom, used by various visiting royals over the years, but most recently used by Queen Victoria and Prince Albert in 1841. Many of the rooms are hung with **paintings** by artists such as Gainsborough, Van Dyck, Vélasquez and Reynolds. Most of the Canalettos are displayed in the Venetian Room (still in regular use by the family and sometimes closed to visitors), while the Breakfast Room contains some fine portraits by Joshua Reynolds. In the Racing Room is a collection of horse-racing memorabilia, and the Flying Duchess's Room tells the story of the dynamic 11th Duchess of Bedford, who took up flying in 1925 and was eventually killed in a flying accident. Down in the **crypt** are some remarkable collections of porcelain, gold and silver, mainly dating from the eighteenth and nineteenth centuries.

Other attractions include the Antiques Centre, where over 50 shops display all kinds of antiques for sale, some of them behind authentic eighteenth-century shopfronts. A small pavilion houses a working potter, whose wares are displayed for sale next door. You can walk through some attractive natural-style gardens. The formal gardens and maze are open to the public for a few days each year. Around the abbey are some 3,000 acres of deer park, inhabited by nine species of deer; there are no designated walks or trails, but visitors can park on the grass in the picnic area and wander freely in the grounds.

Information/tours/guides The beautifully presented colour guidebook serves both as an on-the-spot guide and also a souvenir of the visit. It includes room-by-room information, family history and photos, details of recent acquisitions and a map. An audio guide is available for hire (£1) which gives you a detailed commentary on each room. The guide is introduced by the current owners, the Marquis of Tavistock and his wife, which gives a personal dimension to some of the descriptions. Laminated cards describing the exhibits are also provided in each room, and room wardens are on hand to answer questions.

When to visit The tour of the house can be enjoyed in any weather, though the exterior and park look best in sunshine. Several special events (such as craft fairs, doll fairs and car rallies) are scheduled during the year; garden enthusiasts may wish to visit during the few days when the private gardens are open to the public.

Age appeal This is not really an outing for children, who will be much happier at the Safari Park (*qv*) next door. Anyone with an interest in art, architecture or history will enjoy Woburn, and elderly people who cannot walk far will find that it suits them too.

Food and drink The Flying Duchess Pavilion serves a range of home-made cakes and pastries, as well as hot meals and salads. Choices include several dishes of the day, such as lasagne or lamb casserole (£5.75), baked potatoes (£4.25 to £5.75), home-made soup and a roll (£2.20) and various salads. The Chinese-style pavilion is an attractive place for coffee or lunch, with glass walls looking out over the grounds and more tables out on the terrace. Prices seem on the high side, though, and the service was somewhat slow.

Shops The main gift shop is by the entrance to the grounds, while a smaller shop is located inside the abbey, accessible at the start or end of a tour. The merchandise includes some items specific to Woburn, such as place mats (£22.50), framed prints (£17.50), jigsaws of the rooms (£14.99 or £19.99), T-shirts (£15.50) and printed shopping bags (£6.99), but plenty of more general items, including lots of books (many at reduced prices), CDs, china, porcelain dolls and toiletries, are also on sale. Visitors can also buy fresh Woburn venison.

🚗 Well-signposted from M1 junction 13; alternatively, turn off A5 at Hockliffe on to A4012. ⊖ Nearest stations Flitwick and Leighton Buzzard, 10 to 15 minutes away by taxi. ☉ Mon to Sun, late Mar to late Sept *park* 10am to 5pm; *abbey* 11am to 4pm (5pm Sun and bank hols); Jan to Mar and Oct, Sat, Sun and bank hols *park* 10.30am to 3.45pm; *abbey* 11am to 4pm. 💷 *Abbey and park* Adult £7.50; child (4 to 16 yrs old) £3; senior citizen £6.50; family ticket (2 adults + 2 children) £19; *park* £5 per car. *Annual season ticket to abbey and park* £35. ♿ Ground and first floors of abbey accessible to wheelchairs (lift does not operate between 1 and 2pm). Crypt cannot be accessed in a wheelchair. Gardens are on the level, but have gravel paths so can be hard work.

Woburn Safari Park

Woburn, Bedfordshire MK17 9QN ☎ *(01525) 290407*
🖰 *www.woburnsafari.co.uk* 🖰 *WobSafari@aol.com*

Quality ★★★   **Facilities** 🏛 🏛 🏛   **Value for money** ££

Highlights Safari drive; feeding lorikeets; Monkey Business enclosure; animal talks; children's facilities

Drawbacks Quite expensive; some long walks between attractions; no access without a vehicle

---

What's there This is really an animal theme park rather than a traditional zoo, with plenty of activities suitable for children. You should probably start by doing the **safari drive** through extensive grounds, where at times your car appears to come perilously close to Woburn's pride of **lions**. After parking the car head to the central courtyard where a timetable of daily events is posted. These include talks on penguins, a demonstration of birds of prey – including a Harris hawk catching food in mid-air – an elephant show and a tacky 'Wild West' sea lion show, which is a contrived attempt to show off the animals' skills.

Some wild animals are housed in innovative enclosures: enter **Monkey Business** and you can watch tiny squirrel monkeys leaping about in the trees above you and running around between your legs; **Rainbow Landing** is a large hangar containing a simulated rainforest with lorikeets flying about. If you buy some nectar (60p) the birds will feed from your hand – remember to wash your hands afterwards! At the far end of the complex is a less interesting traditional zoo and a farm area where you can encounter sheep, goats and hens.

Information/tours/guides It is worth getting the guidebook on its own (£3), or the guidebook pack (£5) if you have children as this contains an audio tape, narrated by Christopher Biggins and Linda Bellingham, which can be played during the drive around the safari park, and a small puzzle book. In addition look out for the activity book (£1) which is fun and informative for children and is in an attractive format.

When to visit Make sure you go to Woburn in fine weather, as most of the activities and sights are in the open air.

Age appeal The emphasis is very much on children, who will find plenty to keep them occupied – a lake with swan boats, a train, an indoor and outdoor adventure playground, and a play area for toddlers. Older children might enjoy the computer room, which has some interesting information on animals and their natural habitat.

Food and drink The Safari Lodge restaurant has the feel of a fast-food outlet and is unattractive, but our pasta with meatball sauce (£3.95) was fine. Other hot meal options include steak and kidney pie (£5.65). You can also have sandwiches (from £1.95) and apple pie (£1.95), or purchase refreshments from stalls around the attraction.

Shops The Jungles gift shop concentrates on toys, games, furry animals and children's books.

🚌 Take M1 junction 13 or leave A5 at Hockliffe for A4012. ⊖ No access without a vehicle. ⊕ Apr to Oct, Mon to Sun 10am to 6pm (6.30pm during summer hols) or dusk, last admission 5pm; Nov to Mar, Sat and Sun 11am to 3pm (4pm during Feb half-term; last admission 3pm). 💷 Apr to Oct adult £12/£12.50 school hols; child (3 to 15 yrs old) £8.50/£9 school hols; senior citizen/student £9/£9.50 school hols; disabled person/carer £5.50 all year; Nov to Mar adult £6.50; child £5; senior citizen/disabled person £5.50. Family ticket and annual pass available. ♿ Largely accessible although movement can sometimes involve a steep gradient. Pre-book wheelchairs on (01525) 290826. Leaflet available for disabled visitors.

Woodland Leisure Park

Blackawton, Totnes, Devon TQ9 7DQ ☎ *(01803) 712598*

Quality ★★★ **Facilities** 📣 📣 **Value for money** £££
Highlights Three fun water rides
Drawbacks The appearance of the park grounds and the quality of the restaurant facilities could be improved

---

What's there Visitors will make a beeline for the water rides at this adventure park. **The Twister**, which has a 150-foot corkscrew tunnel, is the best of the three. The **Sidewinder** plunges riders into an underground tunnel before they splash into a pool below. Best described as the original water-slide (you jump into a pod at the top of the orange slide and whiz to the bottom), the **Rapids** is also good fun, as are the **bumper boats**.

If you prefer to stay dry, try the **Alpine Dash**, which is on a par with the water rides, explore the numerous **climbing frames**, or put yourself on a **combat course**. Indoor play areas are a good option for wet days and during the summer months jugglers perform tricks in the **Circusdrome**. The **Falconry Centre** is home to birds of prey such as buzzards, owls, falcons and kestrels – the birds take part in flying displays daily. The very young will enjoy the **toddlers' play area** and scrambling through the wooden buildings in **Golden Bear City**.

On the whole, the rides and play areas are in reasonably good condition although some appear very weathered. The ground surrounding them can become rather muddy (as can the verges of the paths) despite the use of wood chippings. The **animal barn** in Honey Farm smelt overpoweringly unpleasant when we visited.

Information/tours/guides A simple leaflet, which has a map of the park and activity quizzes, is included in the admission price. Falconry displays take place Sun to Thur at 12.30pm and 3pm and on Fri and Sat at 2.30pm only. In the Circusdrome, juggling displays take place throughout the day during summer and on weekends only during the winter months.

When to visit The indoor play areas are ideal for wet afternoons. Some rides may close on wet days. Themed events and fireworks displays take place throughout the year. Entertainers appear every day during July and school holidays.

Age appeal Height restrictions apply on certain rides, including the popular trio of water rides.

Food and drink The park has two restaurants: the main one is situated beside the information centre and the other, Loves Grove Café, is situated beside the water rides. Neither was particularly comfortable and Loves Grove Café was bare and untidy. Both concentrate largely on fast food, although options such as quiche and broccoli and cheese bake were on the menu in the main restaurant. Hot and cold drinks are served at both.

Shops The merchandise, aimed predominantly at children, includes plastic swords, masks, dolls, T-shirts and miniature ceramic ornaments. A small bookstand offers a limited selection of local-interest material.

🚗 Off A3122 close to Dartmouth. Follow brown signs for A38. ⊖ First Western National X89 from Totnes rail station (bus departs from Station Road). ⏰ Mid-Mar to 7 Nov 9.30am to 6pm; 7 Nov to early Mar weekends and Devon school holidays only 9.30am to 4.30pm. Closed 24, 25, 26 Dec. 💷 Adult £5.95; child £5.40; senior citizen £3.25; family ticket £20.95 (2 adults + 2 children); disabled visitor £3.20 (carers free). Group rates available. ♿ Flat Tarmac paths throughout park, with moderately steep slope leading into activity area. Guide dogs admitted.

Wookey Hole Caves

Wookey Hole, Wells, Somerset BA5 1BB ☎ *(01749) 672243*

Quality ★★★★ **Facilities 🏛🏛🏛🏛** **Value for money ££££**
Highlights Pretty site and stunning caves; legend of the witch; good use of lighting
Drawbacks Lack of background information on the Celts; slightly dull museums

What's there Wookey Hole leisure complex developed from a series of spooky caverns that were chiselled out of the limestone slopes of the Mendip Hills by the River Axe a million years ago. A scenic woodland path leads up to the entrance of the caves, where visitors queue for guided tour. Over the next hour or so, you will marvel at the beauty of the **caves**, the atmospheric **underground lake**, the huge **caverns** enhanced by clever lighting and **life-size models** of the divers who first explored the caves. But the tour is brought to life by the legend of the **witch of Wookey Hole**, enthusiastically recounted by the guide.

The lush greenness of the vegetation at the exit of the caves alongside the river really makes you appreciate life above ground as the trail continues past the prehistoric **Hyena Den**, where digs have exposed rhino, bear and mammoth bones as well as prehistoric flint tools. Next you pass the last surviving **paper mill** in the UK and have a chance to see a demonstration of paper-making (and buy some in the adjacent shop).

The **Magical Mirror Maze** comprising about 40 mirrors is an illusionist's dream, where images loom before you, then vanish as you try to escape – shielding your nose with your hand usually prevents injury! Children love it nearly as much as the distorting mirrors, which are always a source of hilarity. Some **slot machines** from Victorian times can be played with nearby.

The two small **museums** focus on the caves and the mill respectively. The former includes some of the archaeological finds, but touches only briefly on the many fascinating topics, such as paganism and Celtic rituals, that come up during the tour itself.

Alllow two hours to see everything.

Information/tours/guides The compulsory guided tours are excellent; they run every 15 minutes in summer and on demand in winter, and take up to 60 visitors at a time. The tours take 30 minutes. The guidebook costs £2.25.

When to visit The caves close in extremely wet weather and sometimes when it snows.

Age appeal Very broad – equally popular with children and adults.

Food and drink The Galloper family restaurant has unexciting décor but a good selection of reasonably priced hot dishes (12 to 2.30pm). Ice cream parlour also available. Picnic tables are provided on a grassy verge.

Shops The Paper Mill shop is very well laid-out and specialises in sets of hand-made notepaper. One interesting item is the Table of Descents (£1.99), on to which you can insert your own family tree.

🚗 Near Wells and Shepton Mallet. Exit M5 at junction 22 and take A38. If heading south from Bath, take A367 or follow signs for A37 from A303. ⊖ Hourly bus service to Wookey Hole from Wells bus station. ⊘ 9.30am to 5.30pm in summer; 10.30am to 4.30pm (last admission) in winter. 💷 Adult £7.20; child (4–16) £4.20. Group rates available. ♿ Wheelchair access to paper mill but not caves.

York Castle Museum

Eye of York, York YO1 9RY ☎ *(01904) 653611*
🖰 *www.york.gov.uk/heritage/museums/castle*

Quality ★★★★	Facilities 🍴🍴🍴	Value for money £££
Highlights	Full-scale reconstruction of an entire Victorian street complete with the sounds of daily life	
Drawbacks	Disappointing restaurant	

What's there The York Castle Museum occupies the former prison buildings on a site in the very heart of modern York. It began life in 1938, when the city of York acquired a collection of artefacts belonging to a man named Dr John Kirk, who, during the 1890s, had decided to keep a record of a way of life that he could see was coming to an end. While the museum still retains a gallery devoted to Dr Kirk, it has gone on to amass a vast collection of tools, clothing, and furniture that records life over the last 400 years.

The museum's display is based around a one-way tour taking in six floors over two huge buildings as it winds its way through an extensive series of galleries. Among the highlights are the two **reconstructed streets**, especially Kirkgate, the Victorian street, where visitors can see historical artefacts displayed in a realistic setting as they wander from shop to shop or stop to inspect the hansom cab, the horse-drawn Victorian answer to our taxis. The second reconstructed street, Half Moon Court, is Edwardian. More traditional displays include 'Every Home Should Have One', showing the history and development of some of the labour-saving devices that we usually take for granted, such as the vacuum cleaner; the **Hearth Gallery**, with a beautiful example of an inglenook fireplace; and the **Barn Gallery** with its wealth of nineteenth-century agricultural implements.

In **'Great Yorkshire Battles'**, visitors can follow some of the most important events of the English Civil War – including the siege of York and the subsequent Battle of Marston Moor that broke the back of the Royalist cause – through a fictitious Royalist diary and plenty of war-like accoutrements.

Youngsters will enjoy the **children's gallery**, which has a large collection of dolls – although they may prefer the arms and armour upstairs. In an exhibition devoted entirely to **chocolate**, you can learn not only about how cocoa (or cacao as it was known to the Aztecs) reached Europe, but also, and rather disturbingly, just how saturated your mind has become by advertising. One of the absolute gems of the entire collection is the **Coppergate helmet**, which was recovered from the same excavations that produced the Jorvik Viking Centre (*qv*) and is the only complete example of Anglo-Saxon armour yet found.

Information/tours/guides There are no guided tours, but plenty of boards tell you all about the objects on display – far more information than can be absorbed in a single visit. The attractive guidebook is good value (£2.50) and is a useful companion, although you could probably manage quite well without it.

When to visit Avoid the peak season to avoid overcrowding and a feeling of being herded through the museum.

Age appeal This museum will appeal to people of all ages, with several displays (such as Exploring Armour) aimed specifically at children, while adults will find plenty to interest them too.

Food and drink The restaurant, with a cafeteria-like ambience, has a limited menu that ranges from jacket potato with beans (£2.29) to sausage or quiche and chips (from £2.50); baguettes provide an alternative option (£2.69 for bacon, lettuce, and tomato), but it is just as easy to find a much better restaurant in town.

Shops The smart and spacious shop offers a range of good-quality merchandise that includes plenty of greetings cards, books (including a host of classics), Victorian sweets, a game designed for antiques aficionados, and some lovely period-inspired jewellery.

🚗 In centre of York. Two nearby car parks offer limited-time pay-and-display parking, but three hours is not enough to do the museum justice and have lunch or tea; a better bet is to make use of one of the park-and-ride facilities that can be found close to the A64, A19, A1079, and A166 main roads into York. ⊖ The museum is just a 10-minute walk from York train station (follow signs to the castle area); regular bus services run into the city centre from the surrounding area. ⏲ Apr to Oct, 9.30am to 5pm; Nov to Mar, 9.30am to 4.30pm. Closed 25 & 26 Dec; 1 Jan. 💷 (1999) Adult £4.95; child £3.50; concessions (students, senior citizens, unemployed) £3.50; family ticket (2 adults + 2 children) £14.80; free for residents of York and disabled people. ♿ Wheelchair access to the ground floor only.

York City Art Gallery

Exhibition Square, York YO1 7EW ☎ *(01904) 551861*
🖥 *www.york.gov.uk/heritage/museums/art*

Quality ★★★★   **Facilities 🏛 🏛 🏛**   **Value for money £££££**

Highlights Expansive collection encapsulating the development of Western art from the Renaissance to the present day; free entrance

Drawbacks Lack of internal signing

What's there The York City Art Gallery was originally opened in 1879 to house the second Yorkshire Fine Art and Industrial Exhibition. Since its inception, the collection has expanded, thanks largely to three benefactors, to become one of the UK's best representations of artistic development from the Middle Ages to the present day outside the capital. The collection revolves around four main galleries; a special exhibitions gallery is used for temporary displays.

The ground floor, devoted to work predating 1800 and going back to the fourteenth century, houses the **Old Master paintings**, an incredible collection made possible largely by a single generous bequest in 1955. Although it does not contain work by any very famous artists, it nevertheless possesses examples from the Italian, Dutch and German schools and includes such beautiful paintings as *The Martyrdom of St Clement* (from the altar in the church of Santa Maria dei Servi in Siena) by Bernardino Fungai, the *Interior of the Church of St Bavo, Haarlem* by Isaak van Nickelen, and *the Piazza San Martino, Lucca* by Bernardo Bellotto, whose style is very similar to that of his uncle, Antonio Canaletto. The second ground-floor gallery displays work by **British artists** – concentrating on the development of portraiture under the influence of Van Dyck as Elizabethan formalism was replaced by greater stress on individuality – and houses a large selection of paintings by William Etty, a contemporary of Turner and Constable, particularly noted for his depictions of nudes (considered rather daring in his own day).

The first floor contains a gallery exhibiting work from the nineteenth and twentieth centuries, with plenty of chocolate-boxy Victorian scenes of family life. More avant-garde contributions include examples by Albert Joseph Moore from the Aesthetic Movement and Philip Wilson Steer, who was influenced by the French Impressionists. The twentieth century's artists are represented by Lowry and Nash, among others, and there is a wonderfully understated painting by Gwen John, entitled *Young Woman in a Red Shawl*. The last of the galleries displays a collection of **Pioneer Studio Pottery**, principally focusing on works by Bernard Leach, Shoji Hamada and William Staite Murray, all of whom were reacting against mass-production and took their inspiration from a combination of oriental and traditional sources – Leach's *Tree of Life* motifs are particularly appealing, with their emphasis on rural simplicity.

Information/tours/guides There are no guided tours, but the pictures are all well labelled and an attractive guidebook (£2.75) offers additional information on the collection. Some of the pictures in the guidebook, however, are no longer on display.

When to visit You could visit the gallery at any time; various special exhibitions are held throughout the year and are detailed in a special brochure, *Gallery News*.

Age appeal The gallery does not contain much that is easily accessible to children, though special exhibitions have included such topics as children's book illustrations.

Food and drink No food and drink is available in the gallery, but the attractive St William's College Restaurant is very close.

Shops A reasonably spacious shop sells a range of art-related merchandise including postcards, greetings cards, calendars, posters and books, as well as the odd mug.

🚌 The gallery is right in the city centre, very close to the Minster. There are several long-stay car parks within walking distance. ⊖ It is walking distance from York train station. ⊙ daily, 9.30am to 4.30pm. Closed 25 Dec. 💷 Free. ♿ Wheelchair access to all areas.

York Dungeon

12 Clifford Street, York YO1 1RD ☎ *(01904) 632599*
☞ *www.yorkshirenet.co.uk/yorkdungeon*

Quality ★★★ | **Facilities 🍴🍴** | **Value for money £££**
Highlights Well constructed and unpleasantly realistic display on the plague
Drawbacks Too frightening for the audience it is primarily aimed at

---

What's there A spin-off from the famous London Dungeon, the York Dungeon certainly has plenty of grisly horrors all of its own, including a recent extension devoted to the **plague**. The one-way unguided tour begins with a recreation of the burning Clifford's Tower, where York's Jewish population was massacred in 1190, before moving on to the plague-ravaged streets of the fourteenth century. Visitors can learn about the spread of the disease and witness its gruesome effects before being shown into a medieval doctor's surgery, where a frighteningly masked physician reveals the dreadful treatments that were employed in the fight to control it.

From there it's on through the plague pits, past the Daneskin (the skin of a Viking nailed to a church door), gibbet (York's version was a precursor to that of the French Revolution) and stocks, and into a cellar where a local man was recently terrified by a patrol of ghostly Roman soldiers – unfortunately, the rather two-dimensional projection on the back wall is unlikely to scare anyone else. The **dungeon** proper comes next, replete with a whole range of horrifyingly inventive methods for maiming and murdering, all brought to life in glorious Technicolor with sound effects and moving blades thrown in. Whether this is truly as edifying as the owners would have us believe is questionable, but it certainly won't bore anyone to death.

From the torture chamber visitors are taken into a room where they can sit down and witness the unfolding story of the **Gunpowder Plot** (Guy Fawkes was born and educated in York) before discovering the torture that Fawkes was subjected to before his eventual execution. After that it's the **Dick Turpin** story, in which the notorious highwayman narrates the events of his own life from his cell in York Castle before being hanged in the chamber behind.

Information/tours/guides All of the exhibits are fairly well explained (at least their gruesome aspects) and the guided sections of the tour are lively and entertainingly presented for children. The glossy guidebook (£1.95), however, contains very little that cannot be gleaned from the sight, partly because the text is repeated in French and German.

When to visit The Dungeon is likely to become very crowded in peak season, which will reduce the impact of some parts of the display.

Age appeal The Dungeon strikes a rather curious balance. Although it is primarily aimed at children, the brochure warns that it is not recommended for those of a nervous disposition or for very young children; children under 15 must be accompanied by an adult.

Food and drink No refreshments are available at the site, although there is a slush machine in the shop.

Shops A small shop sells a variety of tricks and jokes (such as severed hands), as well as books on such charming topics as torture. It also has a range of its own merchandise (including mugs, T-shirts, and baseball caps), and a selection of jewellery normally associated with fantasy and heavy-metal magazines.

🚌 In York city centre. The castle car park is nearby. ⊖ 10 minutes' walk from York Station and 5 minutes' walk from the bus station in Rougier Street. ⏱ Apr to Sept 10am to 6.30pm (last entry 5.30pm); Oct to Mar 10am to 5.30pm (last entry 4.30pm). Closed 25 Dec. 💷 Adult £6.50, child £4.95, senior citizen/disabled person/student £4.95, family (2 adults + 2 children) £19.90. ♿ A number of stairs may make access awkward, but there is a disabled toilet.

York Minster

Deangate, York YO1 7HH ☎ *(01904) 557216* 📠 *(01904) 557218*

Quality ★★★★ **Facilities** 👜👜👜 **Value for money ££££££**

Highlights One of England's most beautiful cathedrals; free entrance; enthusiastic guided tours

Drawbacks Gets busy; limited numbers allowed up the tower

What's there Work was started on this site in 1220, with the aim of building on a scale to rival Canterbury. The cathedral took about 250 years to complete, and you can see how architectural style in England developed over that period as you wander around. The stained glass is also wonderful – some 60 per cent of the UK's surviving medieval **stained glass** is here. All this, and the welcoming feel for visitors – evidenced in the very reasonable pricing policy – means that the visitor experience here is certainly superior to that at Canterbury.

Do take one of the free **guided tours**, run every half hour by enthusiastic volunteer guides as an informative introduction. The arcading down the wide Gothic nave is decorated with the coats of arms of the knights who fought with Edward I against the Scots. If you walk forwards to the transepts you can see four of the great main windows. In the north transept, Early English in style, is the 'Five Sisters' window, decorated in grey 'grisaille' glass. It was built in 1250 when coloured glass was made only overseas and would have been too expensive to import. The great West Window incorporates the shape of a heart in its stonework tracery and has thus been called the 'Heart of Yorkshire' – it has had to be replaced recently as the original became badly corroded. The south transept houses the Rose Window, built to commemorate the end of the Wars of the Roses. Although this was the area damaged by the fire in 1984, the lead in the glass held out, so none was lost. Finally, behind the altar is the great East Window, about the size of a tennis court and one of the largest areas of medieval stained glass in the world. At the top, God the Father, alpha and omega, presides over saints and prophets.

Most standard services nowadays take place in the choir. The screen separating it from the nave shows the kings of England from William I to Henry VI. After Henry's death people began to worship his statue, so it was taken away until 1810, when another one was put back. The choir itself is all Victorian, as it had to be rebuilt after yet another fire.

Once you have seen the main body of the cathedral there are a number of other smaller areas to explore. Downstairs is the twelfth-century **crypt**, which has some early sculptures. Go to the **Undercroft Treasury** if you are interested in the development of the cathedral on this site – it takes you through the different underground levels of the building, including the crypt, and shows you Roman remains of the original fortress and the early Norman cathedral.

The beautiful chapter house dates from the thirteenth century and is still used today as the meeting place for the dean and chapter, the governing body of the cathedral. If you have the legs for it you can also climb the 275 steps of the **tower**, which opens every half hour. The Minster library and archives can be seen only Monday to Thursday, by appointment.

Information/tours/guides The guided tours, which are free, last approximately an hour (£15 fee for groups of over 20 people, who must book 10 days in advance). Go to the reception desk at the west end of the cathedral to find out when next tour runs. The guidebook (£2.50) is good. Various free leaflets are available.

When to visit Access is limited on Sundays as services are held then; sung evensong is 5pm weekdays, 4pm weekends.

Age appeal Children will find little to interest them apart from the intrinsic beauty of the place.

Food and drink St William's Restaurant is open from 10am. Housed in an attractive building, it serves food and snacks throughout the day (e.g. pan-fried chicken breast in chunky tomato sauce, new potatoes and sweetcorn £6.75; cream tea £3.25). There is no disabled access into the restaurant, but if the weather is fine you could use the tables outside.

Shops The shop sells a range of religious artefacts, books and cards.

🚗 In York city centre. Parking is difficult, consider park-and-ride schemes.
⊖ 10-minute walk from York railway station. ⊘ Apr, 7am to 6.30pm; May, 7am to 7.30pm; June to Aug, 7am to 8.30pm; Sept, 7am to 8pm; Oct, 7am to 7pm; Nov to Mar, 7am to 6pm; limited opening Sun because of services. 💷 *Cathedral and guided tours* free; donations welcome. *Undercroft Treasury* adult £3; child (6 to 16 yrs old) £1; senior citizen, student £2.60; family ticket (2 adults + 4 children) £6.50. *Tower* adult £3; child £1. *Chapter house* adult £1; child free, senior citizen, student 80p. ♿ Ring in advance for parking. Ramps into cathedral and choir; wheelchair available. Touch and hearing centre. Large print and Braille books and acoustic fingerprint guide cassette for the visually impaired.

Yorkshire Sculpture Park

Bretton Hall, West Bretton, Wakefield, West Yorkshire WF4 4LG
☎ *(01924) 830642*

Quality ★★ **Facilities 🏛 🏛 🏛** **Value for money ££££**
Highlights The natural setting provides an interesting way of looking at sculpture
Drawbacks Difficult to reach by public transport; orientation within the park itself is tricky

---

What's there Situated on a gently sloping area of grassland just outside the scenic village of Bretton Hall, the park features a changing collection of sculpture. In fact, the bracing Yorkshire air and rolling, green landscape make the attraction worth visiting in their own right. When you enter the park, take the path that leads down to the information centre, where you can pick up a map which will help you get your bearings as you go around.

The **Access Sculpture Trail**, suitable for wheelchairs and pushchairs, leads off the car park. The path winds in and out of the trees, past sculptures hidden in clearings and framed by trees. Children will find this more interesting than a traditional gallery, as it removes some of the mystique associated with looking at sculpture. The 'installation' aspect of the pieces is enhanced by the fact that you can touch the metal, concrete and wooden shapes, ranging from monolithic blocks and Brothers Grimm-style characters carved from trees, to what look like curious, disused steam boilers.

From the end of the trail you can head over to **Bretton Country Park**, a 98-acre hillside dotted with distinctive rounded Henry Moore sculptures which sit unceremoniously on the grass, sheep nibbling at their bases. (It is also possible to park by the Bretton Country Park Visitor Centre – open weekends only – and enter the park by various trails from the south-eastern corner.)

North-east of Bretton Hall the enclosed **Bothy Garden** contains the Pavilion Gallery, a small collection of smaller, abstract pieces.

Information/tours/guides There are no guided tours, and it is best to call in advance for information on events and exhibitions. Navigation can be a problem given the lack of adequate signposting and the fact that the map has no scale. A photocopied leaflet (£1) gives details of some of the sculptures in the permanent collection.

When to visit It is best to avoid the park in bad weather, as the rough ground becomes muddy and difficult. Talks, public sculpture workshops and theatrical performances are held throughout the year – call for more details.

Age appeal The park will appeal mainly to adults; children will find plenty of space to run around.

Food and drink A small café in the Bothy Garden serves a range of sandwiches and cakes. There are picnic areas near the car parks.

Shops Inside the Bothy Garden a shop sells artwork, ranging from £10 to £150.

🚗 1 mile from M1 Junction 38. ⊖ From Wakefield catch 441 bus to Westgate/West Bretton. Tel. 0113-245 7676 for bus times. ⏰ Seasons determined by when clocks change. Summer *grounds* 10am to 6pm; *information centre* 10am to 5pm; *galleries/café/shop* 11am to 5pm; winter *grounds* and *information centre* 10am to 4pm; *galleries/café/shop* 11am to 4pm. 💷 Free (though there may be a charge for some activities). ♿ The Access Sculpture Trail is suitable for wheelchairs and pushchairs, but access to the Bothy area is limited. Free electric scooters are available for loan – call (01924) 830302 to book.

SCOTLAND

Archaeolink Prehistory Park

Oyne, Insch, Aberdeenshire AB52 6QP ☎ *(01464) 851500*
📠 *(01464) 851544* 🖱 *www.archaeolink.co.uk*

Quality ★★   **Facilities** 🏕🏕🏕🏕🏕   **Value for money** £££
Highlights   The Iron Age farm was the hub of activity during our visit
Drawbacks   Visitors need to draw information out of demonstrators to get the most
out of their visit

What's there   Archaeolink sits at the heart of an area with over 7,000 ancient monuments such as stone circles, forts, marching camps and Pictish carvings. The hub of the 40-acre site, which opened in 1997, is an award-winning **building of earth mounds**, with grassed-over roofs and glass walls which blend into the landscape. Around it on the sloping fields of Berryhill are reconstructed historical scenes, from a hunter-gatherer settlement to a Roman marching camp. You can talk to **costumed demonstrators** involved in activities including basket weaving, dying cloth with herbs grown locally, or making pottery from local clays.

It is best to get an introduction to the site by seeing the 20-minute video. This follows the transportation of children through time as they get glimpses of life in the past, from the Mesolithic period up to the Roman advance on Scotland in AD83. Other indoor presentations reveal myths and legends of the times. Outside the reconstructions are still being developed, and there is a lot of empty space. The **hunter-gatherer settlement** is in a corner of the field closest to the road and car park, and consequently lacks realism. On our visit the sole demonstrator was weaving baskets dressed in sackcloth, the look completed with modern spectacles. The main activity was in the **Roman marching camp** and in the **Iron Age farm** with its animals, wood turners, clothes dyers and wicker-building displays. Further up the hill is a **prehistoric tree trail** and the original foundations of an Iron Age house and fort, on which archaeologists are still working. If all this has whetted your appetite for other pre-history sights, then you can devise your own tour of the area using the **ArchaeoQuest computers** to find out further information.

Information/tours/guides   The guidebook is £1.50 and, although glossy, it is light on information. Display boards around the reconstructions are minimal, so you need to rely on the demonstrators for information to bring them alive. Many are archaeologists, and their depth of knowledge is good, but you may need to ask lots of questions to unfold it. Some staff were more involved with their own discussions than with enlightening visitors about what was going on. That said, others were very informative.

When to visit   Come on a dry day, as most of the attractions are outdoors.

Age appeal   Children and adults alike will enjoy the reconstructions. Some activities for children, such as making clay pots or paper, take place at weekends and during holidays, in the activity room or outdoors.

Food and drink   The coffee shop is stylish and appealing, with a range of open sandwiches (£1.35), chips, home-made soup, salads and a decent selection of pastries and cakes.

Shops For children there are Roman coins and soldiers, and Pictish stones with pictures. There is a good range of publications on the Romans, Picts and local historical sights, and various souvenirs of stone or wood – including an executive house for a hedgehog.

🚗 On the A96 from Aberdeen to Huntly, take the signed exit to Oyne village north of Inverurie. ⊖ Train to Aberdeen station, then bus (change at Inverurie) to Oyne village (sporadic service). Buses to Oyne junction (1¼ miles away) are more frequent but less convenient. ⊙ Apr to Oct, Mon to Sun 10am to 5pm. Closed 31 Oct to 31 Mar. ▣ Adult £3.90; child (5 to 16 yrs old) £2.35; all concessions £2.35; family ticket (2 adults + 3 children or 1 adult + 4 children) £11. Season tickets: adult £10; child £5.95; family £25. ♿ Access to all areas, although the path up the hill is quite steep and only for the energetic.

Bannockburn Heritage Centre

Glasgow Road, Stirling FK9 0LJ　☎ *(01786) 812664*

Quality ★★★　　　　　**Facilities 🏛🏛🏛🏛**　　　　　**Value for money £££**
Highlights Symbolic sight for all Scots
Drawbacks Not a great deal to see; some interpretation looks dated

---

What's there The defining battle of Scottish history was fought in June 1314 in boggy ground beside the River Forth, a few miles from Stirling. In contrast to the many battles which the Scots lost through dissension or bad generalship during their 400-year struggle against English domination, Bannockburn represents a rare triumph against the odds. It was the crowning achievement of King **Robert the Bruce**, a victory which unified the country, netted a booty of approximately £50 million in today's money, and led to eventual (if temporary) peace with England.

The site of Bannockburn is therefore a symbol of huge importance to most Scots, and much of it was gifted to the National Trust for Scotland (NTS) in 1932. Its merits as a place to visit are, however, limited, for this is not the most inspiring of battlefields. Much of the ground where the battle was fought has been drained and built on, and even the immediate surroundings are suburban. Genuine relics are non-existent, apart from the remains of the '**borestone**' where Robert the Bruce supposedly raised his standard. In the face of these difficulties, the NTS's efforts at interpretation are certainly sufficient to give you an idea of what happened where, but fall a little short when it comes to atmosphere or background.

The **heritage centre** itself, an unobtrusive, white, well-maintained building, contains a shop, a new café, a small auditorium lined with heraldic banners, and space for a few displays. Audio-cassettes are available for both the interior and to take out on to the battlefield. The exhibitions are, frankly, passé. Posed waxworks of Scottish nobles signing the **Declaration of Arbroath**, combined with the kind of wall-posters usually seen lining history department corridors in Scottish secondary schools, don't really pass muster in this day and age. The audio-visual display is much better, although on the short side, and gives a helpful run-through of the course of the battle.

The part of the **battlefield** preserved by the NTS is reached by a 100-metre walk along a surfaced path (wheelchair available). The centrepiece is the '**rotunda**', a curious 1960s mix of stone circle, Stalinist war memorial and a giant flagpole. Beyond stands the famed equestrian statue of Robert the Bruce, which was erected in 1964. Everything else is neatly cut grass, trees, and views over to Stirling Castle.

The audio-cassette, which you can take with you, attempts to put a bit of life into it all through a dramatised narrative spoken by one of the Bruce's foot-soldiers. It's a little too reminiscent of radio drama for comfort (background noises of whinnying horses and swords being bashed together), but it does help to inspire a setting that otherwise feels uncomfortably like a public park. Battlefields, especially ones as ancient or symbolic as this, are definitely a problem for our heritage organisations. Right now, Bannockburn is an uncomfortable mix of shrine and history lesson, and doesn't quite succeed at either – but not for want of trying.

Information/tours/guides The souvenir guidebook (£2.95) is excellent, with clear narrative and good illustrations. The publicity leaflet you pick up from tourist offices doesn't have a sufficiently detailed map with which to navigate your way to the sight, and printed an incorrect opening time in 1999.

When to visit Views are good from the battlefield, and a clear day is necessary to see all the places where the battle was fought.

Age appeal There is some attempt to interest children – notably the audio tour, and a small booklet entitled *Young Person's Guide to Bannockburn*. Replica brasses (none with any obvious connection to the battle) can be rubbed in the Heritage Centre.

Food and drink A new café serves light snacks and a few 'specials' such as haggis and neeps (mashed turnips) (£4.10). A clean, bright, open-plan room with pleasant wooden furniture and friendly waitress service, it makes a good spot to relax in, especially since there are newspapers to read (an excellent touch). On inspection, a slightly stale baguette was the only disappointment – apart from the prices. Coffee (£1.10), soup and bread (£2.35), panini (£3.65) and filled baguettes (£3.65) were on the menu when we visited.

Shops A small shop opposite the entrance to the café holds a rather smaller range than many other National Trust shops, but there is some very high-quality stuff for sale, including the most expensive souvenir we found in Scotland: a sculptured chess set inspired by Nigel Tranter's *The Bruce* trilogy, for a mere £1,595 (no, they haven't had any impulse buys yet). The same author's work is available on three CDs (£9.95 each). More usual items include postcards at 25p and 38p, jam and whisky marmalade (from £2.25) or a cashmere scarf in NTS tartan for £55.

🚐 From M9 motorway, follow well-marked signs to Stirling. Ample free parking. ⊖ Train to Stirling, then bus 24, 39 or 81 to Bannockburn from the bus station (beside the train station). ⊕ Mar, Mon to Sun 11am to 4.30pm; Apr to Oct, Mon to Sun 10am to 5.30pm; Nov to 23 Dec, Mon to Sun 11am to 4.30pm. Closed 24 Dec to 1 Mar. 💷 Adult £2.50; concessions £1.70; child under 18 free; family ticket (2 adults + 2 children) £6.70. ♿ Access for disabled visitors is good, with separate spaces in the car park, well appointed toilets, and no unduly steep slopes or difficult walking surfaces.

Blair Castle

Blair Atholl, Pitlochry, Perthshire PH18 5TL ☎ *(01796) 481207*
📠 *(01796) 481487* ✎ *blair@great-houses-scotland.co.uk*

Quality ★★★★ **Facilities** 🏛 🏛 🏛 **Value for money £££**
Highlights Some fascinating collections of curiosities; smartly run baronial castle;
lovely grounds
Drawbacks Disappointing catering

What's there This rambling, white Victorian **baronial castle** on the
southern fringes of the Highlands is a most pleasing stately home. It is smartly
run, has lovely and extensive grounds, and is full of family clutter (and some
nobler things) stretching back for at least four centuries. It does not take itself
in the least bit seriously but just sets out to give visitors a memorable day, and
this is one of the chief factors in its success.

The self-guided tour takes in 32 rooms – enough to satisfy the keenest of
castle-visitors. A good cluster of these are found in the old service wing down
in the basement. Here, among the old kitchens, there are display cases full of
intriguing objects – Victorian umbrellas and reticules, fine china, **Jacobite
relics** and much more. Even the **nursery display** is composed of objects
'discovered at different times throughout the castle' – and it's easy to imagine,
even today, an Edwardian doll being found beneath a cushion somewhere and
added in.

There are grand rooms and interesting things to see, too. The wall decorations in the entrance hall are entirely composed of pistols, muskets and pikes.
The **Georgian section** is where Blair Castle goes suddenly elegant, with
splendid plasterwork and fine furniture. Several rooms have their own stories:
the bedroom where **Bonnie Prince Charlie** is supposed to have stayed; the
Atholl Highlanders room which commemorates the Duke's own private
army (the only one sanctioned in Britain); and the huge ballroom, lined with
stags' antlers and resembling a Gothic tithe barn.

It's a long trek through it all, upstairs and downstairs and in and out of
numerous chambers, but there are good room notes to help you through it
and uniformed room guides to point out anything of interest. A particularly
useful touch is the family tree appended to many of the portraits – invaluable
for showing how all the sitters fitted in to the dynasty. Look out in particular
for **Sir Henry Raeburn**'s portrait of Niel Gow, who was fiddler to the 2nd, 3rd
and 4th Dukes of Atholl.

Outside the castle, the grounds are spruce and well kept. The car park is
only a short walk away. Here there is a map showing the main points of interest
in the grounds, which include a **formal water garden**, an old chapel and
woodland paths. All are a short distance, although more extensive walks are
possible through the estate.

Information/tours/guides The introductory brochure carries most of
the hard information necessary to plan a visit, while the well-designed,
engagingly written guidebook (£2.95) picks out the highlights of the castle
without going into laborious detail. There are too few staff for each of the 32

rooms, but they are placed at strategic intervals, and most of them know their stuff. Guided tours are available only for tour groups and must be pre-booked.

When to visit The castle shows itself at its best at any time in summer when the weather is fine. There is usually a piper playing outside during high season. The last weekend in May sees the Atholl Highlanders go on parade, followed by traditional Highland Games. There are international horse trials in August – phone for details.

Age appeal Some of the splendours and oddities of the castle ought to interest older children, and there is a play area in the grounds too. On the whole, this is not a sight for young children or those who find stairs difficult.

Food and drink Blair Castle has recently re-vamped its catering area, which is situated on the ground floor at the end of a long, straggling wing of the building, with a separate entrance for visitors who have bought tickets for the grounds only. Well-planned architecture allows a nice, airy feel and some exhibition space in the restaurant's foyer, but the eating space is rather too crammed with tables. There is a little outdoor terrace for fine days. When inspected, the food did not do justice to the new layout, with a rather uninspiring selection of sandwiches (£2), bakery and desserts, and hot dishes (£5.25 to £5.75), such as chicken à la king, which had been allowed to develop an unattractive crust under the infra-red lamps. Staff were on the casual side, too.

Shops Close to the restaurant, and conveniently located at the end of the tour, Blair Castle's shop is bright and spacious, with good lighting. There's a somewhat pricey selection of Scottish souvenirs and produce, though all are good-quality. A high proportion have been branded with the Blair Castle logo, such as the teddies (£5.95), jigsaws (£13.99) and ashtrays (£5.90). There's a nice cross-stitch kit for £10.50 and a fair range of cheaper items, too, but nothing much out of the ordinary.

🚗 From A9, follow signs to the castle. ⊖ Train from Edinburgh or Inverness is best option (relatively frequent service) to Blair Atholl railway station, then walk to castle (1 km). Alternatively take bus 87 from Pitlochry to Castle (sporadic service). ◷ Apr to June, Mon to Sun 10am to 6pm; Jul and Aug, Mon to Sun 9.30am to 6pm; Sept and Oct, Mon to Sun 10am to 6pm; last admission to castle 5pm. Closed 27 Oct to 1 Apr. 💷 *House and grounds* adult £6; child £4; student, senior citizen £5; disabled £2; family ticket (2 adults + 5 children) £18. *Grounds only* adult £2; child £1; concessions £2; family ticket £5; disabled free. ♿ Disabled access to the castle is difficult, although access is possible to some of the ground-floor rooms, the shop and restaurant.

Blair Drummond Safari and Leisure Park ☹

Near Stirling FK9 4UR ☎ *(01786) 841456*

Quality ★   **Facilities** 🏛🏛   **Value for money £££**

Highlights   Safari drive to see monkeys, camels, rhinos and lions; boat safari to see chimpanzee island

Drawbacks   Unappetising restaurant

What's there The attraction is split between a small zoo, pet farm and amusement area on one side, and a boating lake with shop and snack bar on the other. In between is the **safari drive** route. This takes about 40 minutes and leads you past some lively rhesus monkeys running between the legs of the camels, and takes you up close to a pride of lions and some rare rhinos. Sadly, however, you are not supplied with any information about the animals as you go past, unless you buy a guidebook. At the boating regular trips are on offer out to see four **chimpanzees** who live on an island. It takes about 20 minutes and there is an opportunity to see the animals as they hurry down the bank to niftily catch food as it is thrown by the boatman; the boat passengers are also thrown a few facts.

Over at the main sight – an unattractive collection of buildings – are an **amusement arcade** and dodgems. The small **zoo** next to this has penguins, meerkats, otters and monkeys, and a separate **pet farm** where you can stroll past llamas, rhea, wallabies, pigs and goats. Four times a day a **sea-lion show** at an indoor pool puts the animals through a series of circus tricks, such as playing with balls and rings and waving their flippers. Unfortunately there is not much information on the habits and life of these animals in the wild. During the regular **falconry displays**, members of the audience don a glove while a harris hawk swoops down for food.

Information/tours/guides No formal tours are arranged – the attraction relies on basic notice boards. The guidebook (£1.50) is light on information, but does include a useful map of the sight, which is not available elsewhere.

When to visit Visit in fine weather, as most of your time will be spent outdoors (except for the safari drive).

Age appeal There are a number of activities for children, including a giant astraglide, pedal boats, adventure playground and, for older children, a cable slide. Other activities not included in the price are face painting, dodgem cars, a bouncy castle and remote-controlled boats.

Food and drink Frankly disappointing. The main self-service restaurant was draughty and dismal and served burgers, baked potatoes and hot meals. Our beef biryani (£3.25) was one of the worst meals we have tasted. There is also a barbecue area (available in summer) and a snack bar by the boating lake (sandwiches £1.35).

Shops A range of cheap souvenirs is sold in the Trading Post in the main area and in another shop at the boating lake. You can purchase furry animals, mugs (£2.50) and toys (inflatable animal £1.35, elephant hand-puppet £6.90), but no books.

Other facilities Toilets are generally clean and well maintained.

🚌 From M9, junction 10, then A84 to Callander. ⊖ Buses 569, 359, 59 from Stirling tel. (01786) 450039 for details. ⏰ Apr to Oct, Mon to Sun 10am to 5.30pm; last admission 4.30pm. 💷 Adult £8.50; child (3 to 14 yrs old) £4.50; senior citizen £4.50; disabled visitor £3.50 (carer free). ♿ The site is flat, although the boat safari might be difficult for wheelchair users. Disabled toilets available.

Burrell Collection

2060 Pollokshaws Road, Glasgow G43 1AT ☎ *0141-287 2550*
📠 *0141-287 2597*

Quality ★★★★   **Facilities 🛗 🛗 🛗 🛗**   **Value for money £££££**

Highlights   Brilliant all-round art collection in a wonderful setting; very good restaurant

Drawbacks   Not great for children

What's there   The Burrell Collection is the result of one wealthy man's lifetime passion for art. Sir William Burrell was a steamship owner, who made his money by the shrewd timing of his shipping sales and purchases and then spent it on amassing one of the most interesting collections to be seen in Britain. He donated it to Glasgow in 1944, but surrounded the gift with various conditions – notably that the collection should be exhibited in a purpose-built gallery in a rural setting away from Glasgow's polluted atmosphere. It took the city until 1966 to find a suitable site in what is now **Pollok Country Park**, and it was 1983 before the new brick-and-glass gallery built for the collection was opened to the public.

It was worth the wait, for the building and its leafy surroundings form a wonderful setting for the collection. Architectural features from old houses and castles are built into its interior walls, and the **artefacts and sculptures from the Ancient World** are exhibited against a background of foliage. Almost 20 years on, the building still looks magnificent, but some of the interior fittings – notably carpeting – are in bad need of renewal. This slight air of shoddiness is a pity, for the Burrell Collection is in other respects the flagship among Glasgow's museums.

Burrell's buying was eclectic, and the collection ranges from Ancient Egypt and China through furniture, glassware, silverware, tapestries and stained glass, to the paintings and drawings which are its backbone. There is no single work of art that you would travel miles to see, but the variety and quality of the collection as a whole is outstanding. The collection is strongest in the fields of **medieval furniture**, **glass and woodcarving**, and nineteenth-century **French painting**.

The collection is arranged on two floors, with most of the decorative arts on the ground floor, and the paintings on the floor above, shielded a little from the light that pours into the building through its glass walls. There are no formal rooms such as you find in conventional galleries, but rather a series of spaces where the works of art are grouped together. This can make finding your way around a little confusing, but the gallery is small enough for it not to be much of a bother.

Recent attempts at providing themed areas of the 'life and times' kind are probably a mistake. The gallery has been conceived and laid out in a style where the charm of the objects can make their own impact, so display panels and interpretative explanations are apt to distract attention from the objects rather than illuminate them. Such attempts are few and far between, however: for the most part, this is a gallery where you are left to contemplate beauty in peace.

Information/tours/guides Visitors receive a map of the gallery, with the display areas and facilities clearly marked. There is little further internal signage, and none is necessary. Staff are smart, knowledgeable and very approachable, and the information desk has all necessary information to hand. There are worksheets for children.

Tours are run by volunteer guides, and so follow no fixed pattern: sometimes there are none, sometimes two or three. Ring the gallery in advance to check. Specialist tours and lectures also take place, and are publicised in the Glasgow Museums' events guide (available here and at other museums).

When to visit This is an excellent sight at any time of year, but the setting is at its best when the surrounding trees are in leaf.

Age appeal A sight for adults really, despite the gestures made towards younger visitors. There are many objects which will certainly interest children, and much that could be useful for school projects, but once their attention span is exhausted, families would be better outside in the country park, where there is masses of space for children to play.

Food and drink The Burrell has one of the best restaurants we came across among our Scottish sights. It is situated on the lower ground floor, away from the main gallery, but sharing the glass walls and the view of the outside world. Medieval stained-glass panels are built into the windows. In this setting, the smoked trout (£3.75) or steamed mussels (£3.95) followed by baked salmon (£5.75) or crêpe stuffed with goats' cheese and vegetables (£5.25) go down very well. There are speciality sandwiches (£5.25) and a wide range of desserts (from £2.75). The restaurant is not cheap (a Coke costs £1.15) but given the setting and the standard of cooking, it is good value. Service is friendly and willing if not always prompt. The adjacent café shares a similar setting and is rather cheaper and equally good value, with sandwiches from £2.95, pastries (£1 to £1.85), quiche (£2.95), and coffee (£1.10). The quality is again high.

Shops Two small shopping spaces in the main entrance passage form the Burrell's retail outlet. They both sell a range of similar items. Most are art-related to some degree, with a particularly good selection of books for children. Branded goods include small badges (£1.25) and chocolate (£1.25). There are posters (£3) and arty postcards (£1.25) from the collection, and a few reproductions of some of the more beautiful or popular objects, including a cat statuette (£35). Small souvenirs for children are well-chosen.

🚌 Follow signs from the M8 south of the Clyde (no sign at the M77 exit). Pay-and-display car park (£1.50) 60 metres from building's entrance. ⊖ Not within easy walking distance of the city centre. Suburban train to Pollokshaws West station, then free shuttle bus (every 20 mins) from the gates of Pollok Country Park to the Collection. Buses 45, 47 and 57 run down Pollokshaws Road. ⊕ Sat, Mon to Thurs 10am to 5pm; Fri, Sun 11am to 5pm. Closed 25–6 Dec, 1–2 Jan. 💷 Free. ♿ Access is good, with plenty of space on the ground floor and a lift to the upper floor.

Crathes Castle and Gardens

Banchory, Aberdeenshire AB31 5QJ ☎ *(01330) 844525*

Quality ★★★★ **Facilities** 🏛🏛🏛🏛🏛 **Value for money** £££££

Highlights A well-preserved sixteenth-century tower house with remarkable painted ceilings and beautiful walled gardens

Drawbacks Turnpike stairs in castle can make it tricky for those who have mobility problems

What's there Crathes Castle is one of the highlights of a visit to Deeside and Aberdeenshire. The sixteenth-century **tower house in fine Scottish baronial style** has exuberant decoration in the form of round towers with conical roofs and overhanging turrets at the top. Owned by the **Burnett of Leys** family for 350 years, the house was handed over to the care of the National Trust for Scotland (NTS) in 1951.

Each room is presented as it may have been when it was inhabited by the family. Family portraits and furnishings decorate the rooms: in the **Green Lady's Room** (named after the castle ghost) there is a group of Scottish sixteenth- and seventeenth-century children's chairs, a Jacobean cradle and an antique babywalker. Above the fireplace in the High Hall sitting room is the **Horn of Leys**, said to have been given to the first Burnett of Leys by Robert the Bruce. Several of the rooms have painted ceilings dating back to the sixteenth and seventeenth centuries. In the stair chamber they are unrestored, but others, restored in the nineteenth century, are easier to read and have more vibrant colours – look out for those in the **Room of the Nine Nobles** and the **Muses Room** (a leaflet gives all the verses painted on the ceilings). The family room contains the family archives and information on Burnetts all over the world. If you want to find out more about the Lairds of Crathes, an exhibition in the visitor centre traces the history of the Burnett of Leys family from the fourteenth to the twentieth centuries.

The grounds are extensive, with beautiful walled gardens. Yew hedging metres thick surrounds the gardens on the upper level, which have fountains and blue borders. The walled gardens were redesigned in the 1920s by Sir James and Lady Sybil Burnett, and later by NTS gardeners. Herbaceous and white borders and the golden, red and rose gardens are just some of the highlights of this section. There is also a woodland garden, croquet lawn and numerous marked trails through the woodland, including one designed to be accessible to wheelchair users.

Allow around an hour or so for the castle and half a day for the walled gardens and grounds.

Information/tours/guides Forthcoming and informative guides occupy most of the rooms. The guidebook (£2.95) gives a room-by-room description. Visitors who enter the castle on the last admission may find themselves chivvied along, despite plenty of time for a more leisurely tour.

When to visit The gardens are lovely in good weather. There are lots of events throughout the summer, including craft fairs, ranger walks and exhibitions (mostly at weekends). Telephone for details.

Age appeal There is a children's workbook for the castle, and youngsters will enjoy the woodland trails (there are some special ranger walks for children, such as 'Paws and Poos – finding the clues') and the adventure playground in the woods. Turnpike stairs can be tricky for those with walking difficulties.

Food and drink The pleasant licensed restaurant serves meals and snacks for breakfast, lunch and afternoon tea. There is a decent range of local produce and home-made dishes. Breakfast includes smoked salmon with scrambled egg on toast (£2.85). Other dishes throughout the day include filled hoagies (£3.85), baked potatoes (£3.85) and daily specials. Afternoon tea includes a scone with jam and cream and a cup of tea (£2.85).

Shops The spacious shop sells some Scottish items including woollens, fleece hats and scarves, as well as high-quality postcards and the usual chocolates and soaps, plus a good selection of books.

Other facilities Public toilets with baby-changing facilities.

From A93, 15 miles west of Aberdeen, turn off to Banchory. Parking charge £1. Aberdeen to Braemar bus 201 stops outside the castle gates (the driveway is ¾ mile long). ⊙ *Grounds and gardens* Mon to Sun 9am to sunset. *Castle, visitor centre, shop and restaurant* Apr to Sept,10.30am to 5.30pm (last entry to castle 4.45pm); Oct, 10.30am to 4.30pm (last entry to castle 3.45pm). Closed Nov to Mar. Grounds free except walled gardens. *Castle and walled gardens* adult £6; child (under 18 yrs old) free; students, senior citizens, unemployed £4; *castle only* adult £4; child (under 18 yrs old) free; concessions £2.50; *walled gardens only* adult £4; child (under 18 yrs old) free. Disabled person's carer admitted free of charge. Free entry for National Trust for Scotland and National Trust members. & Limited to ground floor for wheelchair users. Wheelchairs available on loan. Most of the walled garden is accessible for wheelchairs and there is a hard-surfaced trail through the woodland. Disabled parking by the restaurant, shop and disabled toilets.

Culloden Battlefield

Culloden Moor, Inverness IV2 5EU ☎ *(01463) 790607*
📠 *(01463) 794294* ✆ *rmackenzie@nts.org.uk*

Quality ★★★★ **Facilities** 🏛 🏛 🏛 **Value for money** ££££
Highlights Atmospheric battlefield, with good interpretation
Drawbacks Can be very bleak in bad weather

What's there On this barren stretch of ground high above Inverness was fought the last battle on British soil. It marked the end of the 1745 Jacobite uprising against the Hanoverian dynasty, the end of **Bonnie Prince Charlie**'s hopes, and the beginning of a savage repression of the Highland way of life.

The contestants were the **Duke of Cumberland**'s professional army, relatively fresh and well supplied with artillery, and those **Highland clans** who had thrown in their lot with the Prince. Twice in the previous year, the Highlanders had routed the forces sent against them. Now, exhausted after an abortive night attack, drenched by the April sleet, and on utterly unsuitable ground, they had little chance of repeating their success.

The Battle of Culloden was a last moment of desperate bravery for a cause that was already lost. It was also a massacre, and one which was followed by bitter reprisals. It was to be many years before the fear of further Jacobite plots turned into the kind of romantic regret with which Bonnie Prince Charlie, Flora Macdonald, and Culloden are seen today.

Many visitors find the **battlefield** curiously moving, for a place whose notoriety is now sinking into the distant past. Over the years, the National Trust for Scotland has cleared it of the trees that once covered much of it, and has restored it to something approaching the state it was 250 years ago. Flags marking the positions of the armies flutter over the flat stretch of boggy moorland, while the **burial mounds of the clans** are plainly labelled, and are often marked by bunches of fresh flowers left by visitors. One well-trodden path leads across the battlefield, but you can explore wherever you like.

The **Visitor Centre** is carefully dovetailed into the landscape to give the appearance of a low farm building, and behind it stands **Old Leanach Cottage**, which dates back to the time of the battle. This is the setting, during the summer, for short 'living history' presentations – with costumed actors running through short scripted pieces designed to bring aspects of the battle to life – the work of the dressing station where the wounded were brought, for example. Very good these are too.

Inside the Visitor Centre itself, there is a display room with well-mounted and presented material on the 1745 rising, a collection of **small arms** of the types used in the battle, and an excellently narrated audio-visual which fills in the background to the battle itself.

Information/tours/guides Tours of the battlefield (adult £3.50, child £2.50) run four times a day during the summer season, and take approximately an hour. They are detailed and interesting. There are small panels or signs at important points on the battlefield, and a useful map at the start of the path. The guidebook (£2.95) contains a sketch map of the battlefield, and much useful background material.

When to visit The battlefield is at its most atmospheric in April – the month when the battle was fought – but if you are not prepared for the cold, go later in the season.

Age appeal This is not, perhaps, a sight for everyone, but it is less a question of age than of interest. The exhibition material and the living history performances should appeal to older children.

Food and drink The restaurant in the Visitor Centre is rather a bleak room, despite some attempt to give it atmosphere, and was not helped, when we inspected, by a slight smell of staleness. However, there's a good range of food at reasonable prices, including sandwiches (£2 to £2.30), home-made venison or Aberdeen Angus burgers (£4.50) and baked potatoes (£3.50 to £4.75). Breakfast is served until 11.30am, and you can get picnic lunch boxes for children (£3.75). Staff are friendly and engaging.

Shops A smart, square shop lies off the entrance to the Visitor Centre, done up with black shelving and bright lighting. There's a decent range of things to browse through, especially the books, which include detailed and interesting works on the Jacobite period, such as *Culloden* (£10.99) and *Jacobite Spy Wars* (£19.99). Small souvenirs include model cannon (85p), National Trust for Scotland rubbers (50p) and postcards (38p).

Other facilities The toilets are clean enough, but cold and old-fashioned.

🚌 From outskirts of Inverness or A9, follow signs to battlefield. ⊖ From Inverness, take open-topped tour bus from Bridge Street. Bus 12 goes every hour from outside post office in Queens Gate to Culloden Moor. On the whole, though, a car is the most sensible way of reaching the battlefield. ① *Battlefield* Mon to Sun 9am to 6pm. *Visitor Centre* Feb to Mar, Mon to Sun 10am to 4pm; Apr to Oct, Mon to Sun 9am to 6pm; Nov and Dec, Mon to Sun 10am to 4pm; last admission 30 minutes before closing. Closed 24–26 Dec. 💷 Adult £3.50; up to 3 children with adult go free; students, senior citizens, unemployed and disabled £2.30; group rates available. Free entry for National Trust for Scotland and National Trust members. ♿ Access is possible to the Visitor Centre and most of the battlefield, although the path has wet and bumpy places. Wheelchairs are available. A raised map is provided for visually impaired visitors.

Culzean Castle and Country Park

Maybole, Ayrshire KA19 8LE ☎ *Castle (01655) 884455*
Country Park ☎ *(01655) 884400*

Quality ★★★★   **Facilities** 🏛🏛🏛🏛   **Value for money ££££**

Highlights Excellent combination of interesting house with extensive, amenity-packed country park; splendid views and good walks

Drawbacks A little bit anonymous

What's there Culzean was offered to the National Trust for Scotland in 1945, and has been its flagship country property ever since. It combines a large and dignified **Robert Adam house** with an extensive **country park**, cliffside walks, views over the sea to the Isle of Arran, and numerous opportunities for shopping and eating. There's certainly enough here for a full day out. The only obvious disadvantage is the location, Culzean not being within easy reach of anywhere except Ayr.

This does not stop it being a popular sight, and the facilities are well up to coping with visitor numbers of over a quarter of a million per year. Recent renovation of the castle stonework and various buildings within the grounds has left it looking spruce and clean, while the old stable block has been turned into a roomy **Visitor Centre**, complete with an exhibition room, shop and restaurants.

The house, which is the centrepiece of the attraction, is a mix of castle and stately home. From the outside, it is not the most beautiful of buildings, but the interior shows distinct flashes of genius. These culminate in Robert Adam's magnificent **oval staircase** (which filled in an interior courtyard). This leads to the best room in the house – the **circular saloon** where you look straight down on the sea and across to the misty hills of Kintyre in the distance. In addition, there is an entrance hall decorated with **Napoleonic-era armaments**, several Adam ceilings, and a variety of bedrooms, all full of interesting paintings and furniture. The kitchen was in the process of restoration when we inspected and should be open in time for the millennial season.

One wing of the house was given to **General Eisenhower** for his own use after World War II, and this is now set out with mementoes, photographs and old newsreels which commemorate his wartime leadership. They sit a little oddly with the dignified eighteenth-century air of the rest of the house, but are most certainly part of its history.

The country park is extensive enough to need a stiff 40 minutes' walk from end to end (although you can cut it short by driving). By following the seashore as far as possible you get the best of the views, although you miss out some of the other landmarks. At one end of the walk stands the **Visitor Centre** with its various facilities; its counterpart at the other end is the artificial lake known as the '**Swan Pond**'. Here there is shelter, an adventure playground, an aviary and an ice-cream kiosk in season. There's also an extensive field of mown grass for children to run free on. Between the two are the New Stables and shop and the Walled Garden with a plant sales outlet.

The grounds are scattered with further buildings, any of which can serve as a destination for a walk. Among them are the **old gas house** by the sea shore, the **ice house**, the **powder house**, and several others, most of them belonging to the fashion for Picturesque landscaping which marks the transition between the formal eighteenth-century garden and the wilder, Romantic planting which followed. You can also walk in the deer park and on the small, semi-circular beach.

The only real downside is the slight sense of anonymity, perhaps inescapable in a place which performs so much of a public function. In other words, it is much more like a rather grand and efficiently run public park than a much-loved private home.

Information/tours/guides The level of information is excellent. The Visitor Centre contains a large map of the grounds, duplicated in a leaflet, which also contains some background detail on the various things you may see on the walks. There is a ranger service (which runs many events and activities, especially for children), an exhibition about the estate and its wildlife, and ample, but unobtrusive signing. Free guided tours (about 1 hour) of the castle by volunteers take place twice daily in the summer months (11am and 3.30pm), and once a day off-season (3.30pm). Otherwise, the room guides will provide further information and the well illustrated guidebook (£2.95) contains good back-up.

When to visit Exploring the Country Park is half the fun of visiting Culzean, so choose a fair day when walking will be a pleasure, not a pain. Spring and early summer are the times when the landscape is at its best. Some of the facilties (such as the Old Stables restaurant) may only open at weekends outside the high season.

Age appeal The castle itself does not have a lot to offer small children, but there is plenty in the Country Park to keep them happy, ranging from the deer in the Deer Park to the aviary at Swan Pond and the small beaches and rock pools along the coastal strip.

The rangers run a series of activities for members of the Young Naturalists' Club (ages 6 to 12) and the Ecos Club (ages 13 to 16). Membership of both costs £4 per year, and visitors can participate in the clubs' two-hour activities by joining on the spot.

Those who find walking difficult can get close to the main centres of activity by car, and electric buggies are also available. Most of the paths are gently sloped.

Food and drink The Home Farm restaurant, part of the Visitor Centre complex, is an old farm building turned into a self-service eatery. The room is lovely, with glassed-in stone arches and a tiled floor, and the range of food is fair, with a choice of hot meals (not very attractively presented) from £4.95 to £5.50. Cold food includes meat with a salad (£3.95) or chunky sandwiches (£3.95). Coffee is expensive at £1.40. The Old Stables waitress-service restaurant is close at hand.

Shops Three shops, as well as the plant sales outlet at the walled garden, are on hand to waylay visitors. The Country Park shop, halfway between the castle and Visitor Centre, is the most extensive, with ranges of country crafts, fabrics, books and ceramics. At the Visitor Centre itself, the Castle Shop has general gifts and souvenirs, while the Home Farm Shop at the same location sells edible produce of all kinds, including cheese, smoked meats, biscuits and shortbread. You are encouraged to put together your own picnic here, which is likely to end up rather a lavish one. Typical gifts you might come home with are ceramic bird feeders (£15.95), fleece tops (£29.95) or the Culzean Castle address book (£2.95).

Other facilities There are four separate car parks within the grounds, well located not just for the Castle and Visitor Centre, but for the most popular walks too.

🚗 Off A77, then A719, 12 miles south of Ayr. ⊖ A car is something of a necessity, given the extensive nature of the Country Park. ⏰ *Castle and Visitor Centre* Apr or Easter to 31 Oct, Mon to Sun 10.30am to 5.30pm (last admission 5pm). *Country Park* Mon to Sun 9.30am to sunset. Groups can visit the castle by arrangement in winter. 💷 *Castle and Country Park* Adult £7; accompanied child (up to 17 yrs old) free; students, senior citizens £5. *Country Park only* adult £3.50; child free; students, senior citizens, £2.50; group rates (20 or more people) available – call (01655) 884500. ♿ Access is good, with a lift inside the castle. Exhibition spaces in the Visitor Centre are being made fully accessible for the year 2000. Disabled toilets. Self-drive powered buggies available (book two days in advance (01655) 884400).

Discovery Point

Discovery Quay, Dundee DD1 4XA ☎ *(01382) 201245*
🖰 *www.rrs-discovery.co.uk* 🖰 *info@dundeeheritage.sol.co.uk*

Quality ★★★★	Facilities 🏛🏛🏛	Value for money ££££

Highlights Excellent interpretation of historic voyage; fascinating restored ship to explore; extensive hands-on display on Antarctica; excellent for children

Drawbacks Limited range of food available; crowded with children from school outings

What's there The Royal Research ship *Discovery* was the vessel in which **Captain Scott** first voyaged to Antarctica in 1901, some years before his ill-fated expedition to reach the South Pole. Commissioned from a Dundee shipyard that had experience of building the wooden whalers necessary for voyages deep into the southern oceans, the *Discovery* had a long and eventful life after her first, most famous voyage. At the end of service, she was returned to Dundee, and now lies tied up at a berth on the banks of the Tay, close to the town centre.

With the ship itself as the central focus, a multimedia exhibition in an adjacent modern building takes visitors through the story of the voyage, from its conception in the heyday of **Antarctic exploration** to the reality of spending two long winters locked in the pack ice. This is followed by exploration of the ship itself, which has been restored to the condition she was in when she set sail. The final stage of the visit is an interactive exhibition – Polarama – located in a large room, usually full of schoolchildren. Here preconceptions about Antarctica are challenged and the facts imaginatively explained with jigsaws of prehistoric continents, experiments into conductivity and magnetism, and a machine that allows you to experience the effects of wind chill.

The various elements to the visit form an engaging whole, and what might have been a dry-as-dust factual display is given massive added value by the careful use of different media and the dramatic scripting of voice-overs. The focus is primarily on the personalities behind the expedition – not just Scott and Shackleton, but the president of the Royal Geographical Society, Sir Ernest Markham. The building, launching and stocking of the ship are explained through models, sound, and well put-together film. The research work undertaken by the crew, and their difficulties, is outlined on display panels, while something of the drama of the ship's land-locked winters is conveyed via a full-screen audio-visual presentation.

The tour of the ship (self-guided) necessarily involves steep stairways and narrow passages. Restoration of the interior is complete enough for visitors to have a real sense of the conditions under which the crew and scientists had to live and work. All that is missing is the icy cold.

Information/tours/guides Discovery Point's web site is a useful starting point for information, giving opening times and a brief but enticing outline of what there is to see. There are no tour guides as such, but the entry desk has a good range of information. Entry prices are made unnecessarily complex by the plethora of different family prices for different numbers of children, and they are not prominently displayed either. This is very much a self-guided site, although there is usually someone available on board the ship to answer technical questions.

When to visit This is a good all-weather attraction, as almost everything is under cover, and is ideal for bored children on a wet day. (The Arctic winds that can assault the Tay estuary may even add to the realism of the experience!) You'll need at least two hours to explore properly – more if everything in Polarama is going to be test-driven.

Age appeal The main appeal of this riverside attraction is the way it brings the story of the ship and its voyage to life for children. Very small visitors may not find much here, but anyone over seven years old is bound to enjoy it, while the hands-on experience of Polarama will interest slightly older children.

Elderly people may find the passageways of the ship itself hard going, but the exhibition is easily accessible, and there are seats for watching the films.

Food and drink The café within the complex is an irregularly shaped room, with exposed ducting, creating strange shapes under the high ceiling, and walls often used for art exhibitions. Although the range of food is limited (don't expect much more than a snack), it is good value, serving tea at 85p, toasted sandwiches and jacket potatoes from £1.65, and pie and beans at £1.60. The quality is average; the room is kept spotlessly clean by hard-working staff.

Shops A single, large shop by the entry desk serves the complex. The large selection of books sold here has Antarctica as the common theme, and you can find both glossy, illustrated books about the continent together with more serious accounts of travel and exploration. The most memorable link to the *Discovery* expedition is provided by reproductions of artwork by the ship's naturalist (prints for £12.99). The wide range of branded goods includes medallions (£3.39), plates (£9.99), thimbles (£1.99) and mugs (£2.99), plus smaller souvenirs affordable for those with pocket money.

🚗 From Perth take A90 to Dundee; at Swallow roundabout take 3rd exit signposted Dundee airport. At Riverside roundabout take 3rd exit into Earl Grey Place to municipal car park. ⊖ Train to Dundee station, Discovery Point lies directly opposite. ⊙ (in 1999): Mon to Sun, Apr to Oct, 10am (11am Sun) to 5pm, Nov to Mar, 10am (11am Sun) to 4pm. 💶 Adult £5.50, child £3.25, concessions £3.75, family ticket (2 adults + 1 child) £13, (2 adults + 2 children) £16.50, (2 adults + 3 children) £18.25, (2 adults + 4 children) £20.75. Group rate (tel. for further information) £4.95 each. ♿ Exhibition area, shop and café accessible to disabled visitors. Only the deck of *Discovery* is wheelchair accessible.

Dynamic Earth Centre ☺

Holyrood Road, Edinburgh EH8 8AS ☎ *0131-550 7800*
📠 *0131-550 7801* 🖥 *www.dynamicearth.co.uk*
🖥 *enquiries@dynamicearth.co.uk*

Quality ★★★★   **Facilities 👤👤👤👤👤**   **Value for money ££££**
Highlights Wide-screen film presentations and off-screen special effects
Drawbacks Toilets are available only at start of tour – there's no going back!

What's there The *avant garde* architecture of the Dynamic Earth Centre at the foot of Salisbury Crags in Edinburgh houses an ambitious series of exhibits and films that aim to take the visitor on a trip through time from the 'Big Bang' to the present day.

The displays are a mixture of interactive exhibits, question-and-answer boards for children, and photos and video footage. The first three main zones explain the origins of the earth and how the physical landscapes were formed, using wide-screen films, **hydraulic floors** to simulate earthquakes, clever lighting and sound effects. After these presentations you are free to wander at leisure through **recreations of different climatic zones** on the planet, including an ice zone and a tropical zone with simulated rainfall, and information about indigenous animals and species, including humans. The last feature is a **seatless cinema** where you lie on your back and watch a succession of images projected on to a domed ceiling with an accompanying commentary about what influences the future of life on the planet.

The attraction is very well put together and is a highly entertaining mixture of geography, sociology and history that teaches you about the planet and the various species living on it. An easy one-way system means you can't get lost, and there is lots to keep adults and children involved. Allow two hours.

Information/tours/guides Groups of visitors stay together for the first few wide-screen presentations (7–8 minutes), then take their own time to examine various exhibits and showcases. The accompanying booklet detailing all the zones costs £4. Translated recordings in handsets are available in French, Spanish, Italian and Japanese.

When to visit Everything is indoors, so it is ideal for a rainy day. Weekdays are less fraught than weekends.

Age appeal There is certainly lots to do and see for adults and children, though it is not really suitable for very young children (four years and under).

Food and drink The rather spartan Food Chain restaurant lacks atmosphere, though the food on offer can be quite adventurous, such as artichoke, sun-dried tomato and parmesan salad (£3.75), and fresh rolls with brie and red onion marmalade (£2). Teas, coffees and snacks are also available (£1 to £3). There is also the licensed Polar Bar.

Shops Items on sale include posters (£5.99), model kits (£12.99), jigsaws (£20) and globes (£27.50) alongside assorted stationery and postcards (40p to £2), T-shirts (£6.99) and a selection of books (£5 to £10).

🚗 Follow signs from central Edinburgh. Car parking £2 for 1 to 3 hours, then £1 for each subsequent hour. ⊖ The centre is 10 to 15 minutes' walk from the bus and rail stations; buses 1 and 6 pass the centre. ⊙ Easter to Oct, Mon to Sun 10am to 6pm (last entry 5pm); Nov to Easter, Wed to Sun 10am to 5pm (last entry 4pm). Closed Mon and Tue and 25–26 Dec. 💷 Adult £6.95; child (5 to 16 yrs old) £3.95; senior citizen £3.95; student £4.40; disabled adult £3.95; disabled child £2.95; family ticket (2 adults + 3 children) £21; group discount 20% (groups of 12 or more). *Season tickets* adult £16.95; child, senior citizen £9.95; student £7.95; disabled adult £5.95; disabled child £5.95; family ticket £48.95. ♿ The centre is fully accessible to visitors in wheelchairs; carers are admitted free. Three wheelchairs are available for loan.

Edinburgh Castle

Edinburgh EH1 2NJ ☎ *0131-225 9846*

Quality ★★★★   Facilities 🏛 🏛 🏛 🏛 🏛   Value for money ££££

Highlights The Crown Jewels; the one o'clock gun; views from the battlements
Drawbacks Crowding in the Crown Jewels exhibit and some of the smaller rooms
          and apartments

What's there Edinburgh Castle is one of the most potent symbols of Scotland, and one of the capital's most popular tourist attractions. First fortified in the Iron Age and constantly rebuilt over the centuries, it is more a citadel than castle, with many different buildings enclosed within the formidable walls. There are spectacular views to be had if the weather is kind.

It can be difficult to pick out the different stages of the building, and the best way for a casual visitor to see what is on offer is to take one of the guided tours from the entrance gate up to the highest part – Crown Square. From here you can take in the **Scottish National War Memorial**, the **Scottish Crown Jewels**, the **Great Hall** with its ancient hammerbeam roof, and the **Royal Palace**, which was home to the later Stuart kings and queens of Scotland.

A leisurely stroll back down will take you past the oldest building in the castle – **St Margaret's Chapel**, which dates from the twelfth century and was apparently built in memory of Scotland's saintly queen who died in 1093. There are also three regimental museums: those of the **Royal Scots** and the **Royal Scots Dragoon Guards**, whose detailed presentation enhances fascinating exhibits such as battle standards, silverware and an armoured car, and the **Scottish United Services Museum** (see also 'Regimental Museums of Edinburgh Castle' in the Scotland directory at the back of the book). After a visit to the **French prisons** and marvelling at the biggest cannon ever built – **Mons Meg** – you can catch the firing of the famous **one o'clock gun**, an Edinburgh tradition since 1861. Allow at least three hours for your visit.

Information/tours/guides Points of interest and historical significance are marked on placards along the cobbled road that winds up from the castle esplanade up to Crown Square. A full-colour souvenir guide (£2.50) highlights the main parts of the castle and outlines its history in even more detail than the guided tour.

Informative, free and often witty guided tours are available from the entrance gate and last approximately 35 minutes. Check information board by the gate for details. Audio guides are also available if you prefer to go at your own pace.

When to visit Avoid high season if you don't like crowds, but try to pick a clear day as the views are a major attraction. Changing of the guard occurs at the gate on the hour during the summer. The military tattoo, held during the Edinburgh Festival every year, is a popular event – for details call 0131-225 1188.

Age appeal There is plenty for young and old alike. Children will love the changing of the guard, and the firing of the one o'clock gun.

Food and drink The main café has tables inside and out in summer, and superb views over Princes Street and the Firth of Forth. The buffet-style set up offers dishes such as chicken breast with plum sauce, or venison sausage with onion marmalade (£4.95), as well as scones and jam (£1.90), bottled beers (£2.40), and teas, coffees and cakes (£1 to £2). Another café on Crown Square has plenty of space but serves no hot food.

Shops The main shop on two levels is well stocked with a large range of touristy items such as clan crests (£7.95), keyrings (£10.50), hip flasks (£34.95), jerseys (£29.95), fleeces (£34.95), jewellery (£10 to £365) and a selection of Scottish music (£10) and confectionery (£1 to £2).

🚗 Within central Edinburgh; nearest parking is on the Esplanade (£3 for up to two hours). ⊖ Walk up the Royal Mile. ① Apr to Oct, 9.30am to 6pm; Nov to Mar, 9.30 to 5pm. Closed 25, 26 Dec. 🎫 Adult £7; child (5 to 15 yrs old) £2; senior citizens, unemployed £5. Free entry to carer. ♿ Most of the castle, except for the French prisons, is accessible to visitors in wheelchairs. A courtesy car provides transport from the Esplanade to Crown Square. Two wheelchairs are available for loan (first come, first served).

Edinburgh Zoo

Corstorphine Road, Edinburgh EH12 6TS   ☎ *0131-334 9171*
🖰 *www.edinburghzoo.org.uk*

Quality ★★★   **Facilities** 🛋 🛋 🛋   **Value for money £££**
Highlights   Hilltop Safari; Magic Forest primate house; penguins; chimpanzees and gorillas
Drawbacks   Hilly site; talks scheduled April to August only

What's there As the zoo is on ground that rises 300 feet, the best idea is to start your visit with a trip on the Hilltop Safari trailer. The driver gives an interesting talk about some of the animals, and you are dropped off at the highest point, from where there is a fine view. Nearby is the **African Plains** section with a viewing platform out into a paddock. Here you can see scimitar-horned oryx, zebra and ostrich. Next, head down the twisting paths to the **Magic Forest**, with its collection of small monkeys, such as marmosets and tamarins, which has some fascinating information on rainforests and the threats to these animals. Close by is the striking **Darwin Maze**, an ambitious attempt to illustrate evolution via a series of information boards around the pathways – perhaps a regular guided tour would be helpful, as it requires a measure of concentration on the part of visitors.

Other animals not to miss are the **chimpanzees** and **gorillas** and the **pygmy hippos**; lots of detail is provided about individual animals. There is also a large **penguin pool** hosting several different species of these birds.

Information/tours/guides Between April and August there are animal talks at regular intervals throughout the day. They last 15 to 20 minutes, and the times are posted up at the main entrance. Animal-handling sessions (£1) take place every day in July and August and on selected dates from April to June. The Hilltop Safari trailer costs an extra 50p. The guidebook (£1) is informative and useful, as is the Darwin Maze booklet (£2).

When to visit For the best value, visit between April and August, when the talks are scheduled. At other times of year the same admission is charged, despite there being no talks. The lack of indoor attractions means the sight is best in fine weather.

Age appeal Apart from the universal appeal of the animals, the Darwin Maze and the adventure playground are the main draws for children. The hilly site might not be suitable for those with mobility problems.

Food and drink There are two main eateries – Stripes, which can get crowded, and the more spacious Den. Stripes has a wide choice of food, including hot meals such as ham and cheese crêpes (£4.95) or fish and chips (£5.85), as well as sandwiches (£1.95) and coffee (98p).

Shops There's an attractive shop close to the main entrance selling a good selection of items, including clothes, games and books. Gifts include penguin T-shirts (£8.99), cuddly lions (£15) and zoo keyrings (£1.65).

Other facilities There are plenty of toilets with baby-changing facilities.

🚗 From city centre head west on A8, follow signs to the zoo. Parking £1. ⊖ From Princes Street, red LRT buses 2, 12, 26, 31, 36, 69, 85, 86 and green SMT buses 16, X16, 18, 80, 86, 274 stop nearby. ◷ Mon to Sun 9am to 6pm Apr-Sept; Oct-Mar to 5pm; Nov-Feb to 4.30pm. 💷 Adult £6.80; child (3 to14 yrs old) £3.80; student £4.80; senior citizen £4.30; unemployed £4.30; disabled visitors £3.80 (carers free). ♿ Zoo is on steep slope. All enclosures and animal homes are accessible. Ramps available. Free wheelchair loan – ring in advance.

Gallery of Modern Art

Queen Street, Glasgow G1 3AZ   ☎ 0141-229 1996   📠 0141-204 5316

Quality ★★★★   **Facilities** 🏛️ 🏛️ 🏛️   **Value for money ££££**
Highlights Intriguing collection in a beautiful building; good for children
Drawbacks Toilets let the place down

What's there Few modern art galleries have premises as magnificent as the old Glasgow Royal Exchange. A minute's walk from George Square at the very hub of the city, this neo-classical building used to be a temple to business, and its massive portico suggests wealth and grandeur in equal proportions. The ground-floor interior is equally lavish, with gilded Corinthian pillars, high windows and a beautiful ceiling.

This building is now the unlikely setting for the most recent of Glasgow's ground-breaking exhibitions (since 1996), and the place which best exemplifies the concept that art should be accessible and fun. This gallery is not another assemblage of big names or fleetingly fashionable 'installations'. For one thing, only living artists are represented; for another, the buying has been single-mindedly dedicated to assembling a collection whose impact depends on fundamental artistic skill. Within those two principles, however, there is a lot of room for manoeuvre, and the collection is eclectic both in the media and in the geographical range. The four floors are named after the four elements of **earth**, **air**, **fire** and **water**, but the themes are loose enough to serve as no more than a frame for the works on show.

The ground-floor exhibition has the most impact. A superb **kinetic sculpture**, somewhere between a bicycle and a flying machine, draws groups of silent onlookers waiting for the performance to begin. This is echoed, at the far end of the room, by a grotesque collection of flying papier-mâché dragon devils (the **Seven Deadly Sins**), which in turn is placed close to *Altar au Chat Mort*, violent and blood-spattered. The dominant painting is Howson's *Patriots*, one of the most disturbing portrayals of our times.

It is not all showmanship and gore, however. Gentler works, curiously vivid photographs, strange working anti-communist contraptions, a clay floor and a fibreglass caricature of the Queen are all to be found. The basement is full of **interactive art** – panels of movable steel pins, a neon-sheathed tunnel that lights up as you run through, and a kind of do-it-yourself mixing desk where you can play with sound and video clips.

It's an inspiring gallery for children, because there is so much that is unexpected, and quite a lot that can be played with, too. Not all the art can stand the strain, however, and four years into the run, some of the do-it-yourself gadgets are looking a bit worn, while the computers where you could surf the Internet for inspiration are often either out of order or apparently monopolised by all-day chess players. The fact that the downstairs toilets are closed at weekends because of 'undesirable characters' merely goes further to show that even modern art has to live with the real world.

Information/tours/guides Information and signing are adequate: one nice touch is that many of the works of art have personal notes by the artist to explain them, rather than the usual biographical details.

A lavish souvenir guidebook (£9.50) provides a useful and carefully written reinforcement to your gallery visit. Otherwise there is only the usual Glasgow Museums floorplan. The best sources of information on the ground are the smartly uniformed attendants, who are very knowledgeable about the works on display. Free guided tours are run by volunteers at weekends (usually 11am and midday – check in advance). Pre-booked group guided tours are available (£1 per head).

When to visit The gallery makes an ideal wet-weather sight at any time of year. Special exhibitions or themes are publicised in the *Glasgow Galleries Guide* and in the widely available *Preview* magazine.

Age appeal The Gallery of Modern Art is one of the best art galleries around for children. High spots are the kinetic sculptures and the hands-on exhibits in the basement gallery. However, some of the violent paintings could be disturbing to youngsters.

Food and drink Murals by Adrian Wiszniewski enliven the split-level rooftop café, making it an interesting place to have a snack, although space can be limited at weekend lunchtimes. There is a reasonably wide range of food, although it is not cheap. Mackerel pâté, chutney and toast (£2.50), followed by a main course (£4.50 to £6.75) such as Cajun chicken would be a typical offering. Sandwiches are lavish but expensive at £4.95.

Shops A small gallery shop by the entrance hall sells high-quality craft souvenirs, notably silverwork (jewellery up to £60) and objects in Glasgow Style, including Charles Rennie Mackintosh drawer liners (£4.95). There are several gallery-related items, including Beryl Cook calendars (£7.99), and a range of posters. Cheaper gifts and small souvenir items for children provide decent choice.

🚌 Within central Glasgow. Several fairly expensive car parks within a ½-mile radius. ⊖ Train to Queen Street station, then 200-yard walk. Also, short walk from George Square (centre of Glasgow's bus network). ⏲ *Gallery* Mon to Thurs, Sat 10am to 5pm, *café* Mon to Thurs, Sat 10am to 4.30pm, Fri and Sun 11am to 4.30pm. Closed 25–26 Dec, 1–2 Jan. 💷 Free. ♿ Access is good, with a large central lift between floors. Generally there is room for manoeuvre, although the rooftop café may pose problems.

Glamis Castle

Glamis, Angus DD8 1RJ ☎ *(01307) 840393*
🖱 *www.great-houses-scotland.co.uk/glamis*
🖱 *Glamis@great-houses-scotland.co.uk*

Quality ★★★★	Facilities 👜👜👜👜👜	Value for money ££££

Highlights Welcoming and highly efficient attraction; interesting tours; good balance of things to see and do

Drawbacks Difficult to get to by public transport

What's there Among the rolling hills of lowland Angus, 12 miles from Dundee, this ancient mix of palace and tower house rises over its sheltering woodland like a curious pink sugar sculpture. It is as close as you will come to a Scottish version of the classic stately home, and direct connections with both Macbeth and the Queen Mother (an unlikely pair) ensure that it pulls in added numbers of visitors.

The history of Glamis goes back to the fourteenth century, and throughout the tour you find yourself shifting from medieval halls to vast Edwardian drawing and dining rooms, from suits of armour to billiard tables. The high spots are the **drawing room**, with its furniture arranged exactly as shown in a tinted sepia photograph and a portrait of the 3rd Earl of Strathmore wearing curious 'transparent' armour; **the chapel** with its painted ceiling panels; and the various **rooms where the Queen Mother grew up**. Towards the end of the guided tour, the guide mentions the Macbeth connection, but strongly plays it down. The visitor is left with the impression that the reality of Glamis' story is far more interesting than anything Shakespeare came up with. It runs from a sacked jester to an underpaid artist, with ghosts, secret chambers and a stolen watch along the way.

There is a great deal to see by way of portraits, old furniture, massive silverwork and arms and armour. They are all made more interesting in their context of family possessions, rather than museum objects. Photographs, ancient and modern, are everywhere, and there is a strong sense that Glamis is a real home, not a museum. This does a great deal to humanise the royal connection, and the Queen Mother comes across as just another member of the extensive family.

Possessions and history that cannot be included in the tour are presented in two **separate exhibition rooms**, which visitors are free to walk around. There is much information here about the building of the castle and the estate, and it is good to find a private stately home putting some of it in context for children, through use of interactive touch-screen, role-playing computers.

The **gardens and grounds** are extensive, and well worth a wander. A huge **baroque sundial** is the main talking point, but there's also a charming Italian garden, a nature trail and a picnic area.

Information/tours/guides As a tourist sight, Glamis is exceptionally well run, cleverly managing its visitors so that neither the fabric of the house nor the welcome are damaged by excess numbers. This cannot be easy, given that the house is full of small rooms and narrow corridors. Yet waiting times for tours are short, and guides are relaxed and approachable.

Standards of information are very high. The brochure gives you all the information you need, and the Glamis web site is equally useful.

A free map of the grounds is handed out to visitors, and entry times and prices are prominently displayed. Tours run every 10 to 15 minutes, even out of high season, and guides are welcoming and relaxed. A nicely produced and good-value (£3.50) souvenir guide fills in any gaps in the tour itself, and explanations in the display rooms are also of a high standard. Staff are uniformed in a smartly casual fashion as if they were much-valued family retainers (which perhaps they are).

When to visit More plus points to Glamis for extending its season to the end of October – an ideal month to visit, with the trees turning colour and little risk of overcrowding. The castle and grounds, however, can be seen to advantage at any time of year, and rain will not spoil it too much.

Age appeal A good stately home for older children, with a very fair effort made to interest them, both during the tour and in the exhibition rooms. A small play park is situated not far from the picnic area. There are unavoidable staircases inside the castle, but those who might have difficulty are given plenty of warning, and are allowed to wait in peace if they don't wish to tackle them.

Food and drink A somewhat cavernous room (the old kitchen) is now the restaurant. Distinct efforts have been made to make the room an interesting place, with portraits on the walls, the old Victorian equipment left in place, and a large collection of copper utensils. The quality of the food is high, and most is home-made, including the bread-and-butter pudding (£2.50). There's a sensible choice of quiche and salad (£4.50), pizza (£3.70), and hot dishes such as broccoli bake. Soup and roll goes for £2.12 and toasties for £2.80. Waiting staff are efficient and smart, if not quite so cheery as elsewhere in the castle.

Shops There's not enough room in the castle for more than one shop, so Glamis has supplemented its interior gift shop by providing three others in wooden pavilions between the car park and the main entrance. They do look rather out of place, it has to be said, but they allow the range of goods to be expanded into books, clothing and kitchen produce. Cheerfully run and well laid out, the shops sell quality, branded goods, ranging from Glamis sweat-shirts (£11.95) to mugs (£2.99) and tea-towels (£4.49).

🚗 Off the A94 between Aberdeen and Perth, 12 miles north of Dundee. Free parking. ⊖ Difficult to arrange. Train to Dundee then bus. Alternatively, take public bus from nearby town of Forfar to Castle (you can get back again the same day). ⊙ (in 1999): Mon to Sun, 2 Apr to 12 Nov, 10.30am (10am in Jul and Aug) to 5.30pm (last admission 4.45pm; closes at 4pm in Nov. Groups are welcome during the winter by appointment. 💷 Castle and grounds (grounds only) adult £6 (£3); child (5 to 16 yrs old) £3 (£1.50); student, senior citizen £4.50 (£1.40); family ticket £16.50. Free entry for visitors in wheelchairs. Season tickets are available. ♿ Very limited access inside Castle. Access to grounds, exhibition and shops possible.

Glenturret Distillery

Crieff, Perthshire PH7 4HA ☎ *(01764) 656565* 📠 *(01764) 654366*
📠 *www.glenturret.com* 📠 *Glenturret@highlandDistillers.co.uk*

Quality ★★★ **Facilities 📖📖📖📖** **Value for money £££**

Highlights An efficiently run and friendly sight; good but expensive shop; wonderful toilets

Drawbacks A little thin on activities; not brilliant for children

What's there Glenturret claims to be Scotland's oldest distillery, its legal establishment dating back to 1775 but with a long history of illicit distilling recorded on the same site before that. Like many of its competitors, it has thrown its doors open to the public, and though it is neither the biggest nor the most famous of the distilleries, the advantages of its location on the southernmost edge of the Highlands make it one of the most visited.

The formula for distillery visiting is by now well-established. From the Visitor Centre, tour groups are taken around the various processes involved in distilling, subjected to a schmaltzy audio-visual, given a dram and then left to enjoy the delights of the shop and anything else the distillery has put in place for them. Glenturret sticks to this formula, and does it well. The smartness and efficiency of the operation in no way smothers the **small-scale, family firm atmosphere** of the place, and visitors will feel personally welcome, even on crowded days. The low white buildings of the oldest parts of the distillery blend in well with modern adjuncts such as the restaurant. Staff are smartly casual in kilts and white shirts, wear name badges, and are friendly and approachable.

From the Visitor Centre, tours move to the buildings where the various distilling processes take place. They pass the statue of **Towser**, one-time distillery cat, who still holds the Guinness record for the best mouser ever. Inside the distillery, explanations are clear and coherent, and questions are encouraged. Everything is on a small scale, so tours do not take long – about 30 minutes. During the tour you peer into huge vats full of frothing liquid smelling of beer, see the fresh whisky running through the 'safe' where it is tested for quality, and gaze at rows of slowly maturing casks.

In the **Tasting Bar**, the full range of Glenturret's produce is on display. Complimentary drams are served, and miniatures are available for drivers. Visitors are prodded very gently towards the shop – no unpleasant pressure is applied.

Information/tours/guides Glenturret's web site is a good one, with a direct-buy facility, gift vouchers, competitions and bags of information. The brochure suffers from rather too much hype and not enough solid information, although it does include a sample menu from the restaurant and a useful map. The souvenir guide is not strictly necessary but good value (99p), and provides useful back-up for what you learn on the tour itself.

Tours run every 15 minutes, so there is little hanging about. In January, when the distillery has its 'silent' month, they are free.

When to visit The distillery is not really extensive enough to be worth a full day's outing, and a visit here is best built into a general tour of the area or as an excursion from Perth. It is open all year, but at its most attractive in summer or autumn.

Age appeal Children too young to be whisky connoisseurs may wonder what all the fuss is about. Distilling does not involve enough moving machinery to be attractive to the mechanically minded, and apart from the curious smells, the technicalities of whisky-making are not readily accessible to young visitors. The world-champion mousing cat is more likely to appeal, and Glenturret bases its appeal to children on the said feline (there is an activity sheet for youngsters).

Food and drink Two restaurants are on hand for the hungry. The Pagoda Room is upmarket, with waitress service and pricey food such as venison (£9.25) and chops cooked with Glenturret whisky and honey (£8.50). Main courses start at £6.50. The self-service restaurant is located in the same area, and, despite its extensive size (it is rather barn-like) feels a little cramped. Service is friendly and willing, but there were a few defects on inspection, such as the prices for main courses not being listed. The menu makes a commendable effort to be Scottish, including haggis and neeps among its offerings (£4.95). Quality is reasonable. Sandwiches cost £2.20, and palatable home-baked cakes and biscuits in the region of 85p.

Shops The gift shop is big and smart; presentation is immaculate. Branding is relentless, and almost every item carries a Glenturret logo (usually very tastefully done). You can even get clothing in the Glenturret tartan. The range of goods is extensive. Bottles (full), glasses and decanters form the most prominent display, but there's a fair range of clothing and preserves as well. Some thought has been given to children, with pencils (75p and 50p) and items associated with Towser the cat. Clothing in particular is expensive but high-quality, ranging from a Glenturret tartan kilted skirt (£75.50) or a monogrammed woollen jersey (£44.95) to T-shirts (£6.90). Aged whiskies sell from £24.99 a bottle upwards, and include some rare and extremely expensive offerings.

Other facilities Special mention should be made of the toilets – by far and away the best we saw among our Scottish sights, and worthy of a five-star hotel, even down to the piped music.

The grounds of the distillery are relatively small, but there are one or two sunny spots to sit in. A nature trail/walk is being created across the River Turret and into the woods and fields beyond. Still in its early days, this will be a pleasing additional facility for visitors when finished, since at the moment there is not much to do apart from the tour, eating and shopping.

From A85 Crieff to Comrie road, follow signs to distillery (about three minutes' drive from Crieff town centre). The neatly kept car park is on the small side for popular days. ⊖ 15 bus from Perth to Comrie passes the distillery, but only really dedicated public transport users would prefer this to car or coach. Coach tours with Glenturret on the list of stops run from Perth and Edinburgh (ask the Tourist Office). ⊙ Feb to Dec, Mon to Sat 9.30am to 6pm (last tour 4.30); Jan, Fri 11.30am to 4pm (last tour 2.30). Closed 25, 26 Dec, 1–1 Jan. 🎟 Adult £3.50; child (12 to 17 yrs old) £2.30; senior citizens £3; family ticket (2 adults + 4 children) £9; group discount for groups over 40 (10%). 🚻 Access is possible to the facilities, but only about a third of the tour (and not the most interesting third) can be undertaken without confronting a flight of stairs.

Inverewe Garden

Poolewe, by Gairloch IV22 2LG ☎ *(01445) 781200*

Quality ★★★★   **Facilities** 🏛 🏛 🏛 🏛   **Value for money £££**
Highlights   Magnificent setting; rhododendrons; woodland walks
Drawbacks   No public transport; disappointing restaurant

What's there   Inverewe is the most famous of the gardens on the west coast of Scotland. This is partly because of its unique ability to grow sub-tropical exotic plants on a latitude north of Moscow, partly because of its wonderful setting, and partly because of its remoteness and the unexpected impression it makes upon visitors.

Osgood Mackenzie, author of *A Hundred Years in the Highlands*, started carving the garden out of a barren peninsula when he and his mother bought the estate in 1862. The exceptionally mild climate worked in his favour, but the salt-laden gales which lash the peninsula did not. It took years of experimental planting of shelter belts before the garden could be established. But the venture succeeded, and in the century since Mackenzie commenced his labour, it has developed into something entirely without comparison in Britain.

Inverewe's appeal is twofold. Primarily it is a plantsman's garden, especially for rhododendron lovers. The list of exotic shrubs and trees contains specimens from all over the world, including large numbers of Chilean plants and varieties from New Zealand and South Africa, as well as China and the Himalayas.

For those not interested in the minutiae of plants, however, the aesthetic appeal of the garden is almost as strong. Mostly this is because of the setting: after several hours of driving across a landscape of mountain and moorland where scarcely a tree thrives, Inverewe Garden seems a foretaste of paradise. Woodland paths wind between glades and banks of flowering shrubs, while the **walled garden** is full of herbaceous perennials and glossy vegetables. The sea and the mountains lie all around, as if to emphasise the contrast. The garden itself is, as is usual with the National Trust for Scotland (NTS), beautifully kept and maintained. No dogs are allowed in the garden (except guide dogs).

Information/tours/guides   The general standard of information and publicity is high – as it should be for a major sight – although prices ought to be displayed rather more prominently, in a position other than the reception desk. Signing in the garden is kept to a minimum, but is sufficient to guide you round; the system becomes clear when you use the little map handed out to visitors as a supplementary aid.

The welcome is friendly, and expert knowledge is usually at hand if you need it. Detailed information about the plants themselves is not so easy to come by. All gardens have problems with label thieves, but at Inverewe they must be a particular plague – too many plants lack any indication of their names. A good plant list would go some way to compensate, but currently none is available.

Walks with one of the gardeners or a volunteer take place between April and mid-September at 1.30pm on weekdays. Pre-booked tours of the garden with one of the gardeners are available for groups at any time during working hours. They cost £12 per guide on weekdays and £20 at weekends. A separate guide is needed for every 20 people.

When to visit Weather plays an important part at Inverewe. 'Go on a fine day' is obvious advice – but may not be easy to follow in this notoriously rain-swept part of the world (bring an umbrella). The garden is at its most colourful in spring and early summer, when the rhododendrons flower, but is also well worth seeing in autumn. Mid-August is its least colourful period, although the NTS does its best to provide interest in the walled garden and around the house.

Age appeal As gardens go, this is a good one to visit with children, for the paths lead to interesting glades and nooks, and out to a stony beach. There is ample opportunity for smaller children to run free, while teenagers will find the odd corner to be alone in. Paths are mostly gentle enough for pushchairs. It is an extensive layout, with a good deal of mounting and descending for those who find much walking difficult, but there is a great deal to see on the flatter ground immediately round the house.

Food and drink The smart restaurant 100 yards from the Visitor Centre is a beautiful modern building, with high ceilings, glass walls and a clever star-shaped layout. A pity, then, that we were disappointed by the catering: on inspection, there was a smell of stale cooking, while the range of dishes on offer was rather poor and not very attractively presented. The prices did nothing to compensate for this, with main dishes about £6.95, jacket potatoes at £3.45, and soup at £1.55.

Shops One large gift shop serves Inverewe. This has been carefully designed with three separate wings, so that shoppers for books, food and clothing have separate areas to browse in. Goods are high-quality and attractive, and there is an enticing range. Any real individuality has, however, been sacrificed. In its previous incarnation, the gift shop held racks of seeds from the garden; now there is a much smaller, bought-in range. Souvenirs of the garden are limited to large and small postcards (38p and 25p) and branded goods in the shape of items such as mugs (£3.25), boxed pens (£1.95) and badges (£1.50). There is a selection of general horticultural books (from £1.99). Ceramics and outdoor clothing are worth looking out for, as is the range of herbal lotions and balms, such as seaweed soap (£1.50).

🚌 Follow signs from A832, six miles north of Gairloch. ⊖ Public transport is non-existent unless you want to stay the night nearby. Most coach tours of the north-west Highlands have Inverewe as one of their destinations. A car is the only other realistic way of reaching Inverewe. ① *Garden* mid-Mar to Oct, Mon to Sun 9.30am to 9pm; Nov to mid-Mar, Mon to Sun 9.30am to 5pm. *Visitor Centre and Shop* Mid-Mar to Oct, Mon to Sun 9.30am to 5.30pm. *Restaurant* Mid-Mar to Oct, Mon to Sun 10am to 5pm. 💷 Adult £5; child free; senior citizens £3.50; family ticket £13.50. Free entry for NTS and NT members. ♿ Wheelchairs with carers are available for the garden (pre-booking advised), and there is a useful map of suitable routes to take.

Kelvingrove Art Gallery and Museum

Kelvingrove, Glasgow G3 8AG ☎ *0141-287 2699* 🖷 *0141-287 2690*

Quality ★★★★   **Facilities** 🏛 🏛 🏛   **Value for money ££££**

Highlights Extensive collection; fine paintings; beginning to be transformed by some imaginative interpretation

Drawbacks Some displays still dry and dusty; a lot of walking

What's there This is the largest and one of the oldest of the Glasgow museums and galleries. The huge red building at the foot of the hill below Glasgow University was purpose-built to house the city's collections, and was opened in 1901. By today's tastes it is vastly impractical as a museum, dignified as it is by a cathedral-sized, echoing central hall complete with organ, and what seems like miles of colonnaded stone galleries (originally designed for musical promenades) and lofty exhibition rooms.

Museum collections and art galleries do not always sit together easily under the same roof. Here they do, perhaps because they are rigorously separated. The main museum is firmly downstairs; if you want the pictures, they are on the upper floor. Both the museum and the gallery have collections of terrific range and quality, and the chief problem for the visitor lies in judging how best to split the time available between them. The **museum** is particularly strong on arms and armour, archaeology (chiefly Scottish), ethnography and natural history. The **art gallery** is notable for its British and French painting of the nineteenth century, but has fine Italian and Flemish works from earlier periods too.

Given the nature of the building, the displays could be as cold and dry as this factual summary might suggest. But there is a lot of good work going on at Kelvingrove to make the objects and pictures exciting and relevant to the general visitor. It does not always work, true. But there are moments of inspiration, such as the full-sized **Imperial trooper** straight from the *Star Wars* set, who is displayed alongside a suit of late medieval armour. The similarities between the two are enhanced by notes and diagrams highlighting the parallels.

Another idea that works is the '**Picture Promenade**' in one of the long galleries upstairs. Here, the walls are completely covered by paintings not normally on show owing to space restrictions, which have been drawn from the gallery's storerooms. The effect of these massed artworks, split into periods and styles, is to demonstrate at once what techniques or fashions the different periods have in common. Careful descriptions, and the opportunity for visitors to choose their 'painting of the month', are additional interesting touches.

There are many other clever ideas. Even the serried rows of butterflies in glass cases are made interesting by explanations of why such research collections are needed and how they are used.

All in all, this is an excellent collection in the process of being made more accessible to visitors by some imaginative thinking. Temporary exhibitions are usually interesting, and there's even a special space for small children, with curious objects and paintings, building blocks and mini-chairs. Access for pushchairs is good.

Information/tours/guides As with the other Glasgow museums, publicity is not the strong suit here. Visitors get a useful floor plan, but between that and the massive, erudite and expensive guidebook (£7.95) there is nothing much available, except for descriptive panels by some of the displays (all admirably coherent). It is about time there was a web site too. On the other hand, the permanent staff are skilled, and knowledgeable on the whereabouts of particular paintings. There are tours by volunteer guides, running at no set frequency. If you're interested, telephone before visiting.

When to visit An all-year attraction which can be combined with a visit to the Transport Museum across the road to provide sightseeing for half a day or more.

Age appeal The increasing number of imaginative displays make this an ever-better sight for older children. The arms and armour and the natural history sections should appeal, and there is the odd dinosaur too. Small quizzes and worksheets are also available.

Food and drink Metallic sculptured trees, bright colours and scrubbed wooden flooring transform a sombre Edwardian room into a Caribbean diner. Food is presented on three separate serveries, which break up the square shape of the place and even create a slight sense of privacy. There's lots of space between tables too – very appealing. Food is fresh and looks and smells good. Filled baguettes are about as arty as it goes (£2.25), but the steak and sausage pie (£3.95) is tempting, and tea (85p) and coffee (95p) are good value.

Shops A small enclave in the immensity of the main hall, the shop is not quite large enough for everything to be displayed to advantage, but there is a good range of imaginative gifts and souvenirs. Postcards from the gallery are to be found from 25p, and branded umbrellas at £8.25.

There's a variety of interesting stuff for children, ranging from a miniature Roman cooking set (£1.50) through Viking warriors (£2.25) to Victorian-style scrapbooks (£2.25) and packets of scraps to cut out and paste into them (75p).

🚗 Poorly signed from Glasgow's major roads – you'll probably need a street map. Small free car park behind the museum. ⊖ From city centre, the museum is within easy walking distance of Partick suburban railway station and Kelvin Hall subway station. ⊙ Mon to Thur and Sat 10am to 5pm; Fri and Sun 11am to 5pm. Closed 25, 26 Dec, 1, 2 Jan. 💷 Free. ♿ Access is surprisingly good, given the unpromising nature of the building. There is a lift to the first floor and an automatic entrance door.

Museum of Transport

1 Bunhouse Road, Glasgow G3 8DP　☎ *0141-287 2720*

Quality ★★	Facilities 🍴🍴	Value for money £££
Highlights	Very comprehensive collection; of interest to enthusiasts	
Drawbacks	Lack of enough money and imagination to make it really interesting; facilities in need of a face lift	

What's there In the cavernous space of Glasgow's one-time exhibition centre – the **Kelvin Hall** – ranks of vehicles of all kinds stand witness to the city's transport and manufacturing through the centuries. It is a huge and comprehensive collection, and herein lies the museum's problem.

Large numbers of bulky metal objects arranged in rows are difficult to accord with today's fashions for interpretation and interactivity. This is especially true when they are vehicles too fragile or historic to be climbed on or touched, and when none of them can be started up and driven around. There is the additional fact that cars, trains and trams are fascinating to the enthusiast, but hard to make of interest to the uninitiated.

In trying to solve these problems, the Museum of Transport has fallen badly between two stools, perhaps lacking the funding to do anything really interesting. There are attempts at interactive displays, and small interpreted, themed areas shoehorned in between the trams and locomotives, but their effect is minimal when compared with the rows of stationary vehicles minimally labelled and garnished with 'do not touch' notices.

The first part of the museum is the best, with a display of proposed solutions to city congestion, and some **futuristic pedal cycles** (which you long to ride, but can't). There is also a street scene from 1938 and a reconstructed Glasgow subway station. Thereafter, the main hall contains separate areas for Glasgow's famous **trams**, a couple of locomotives and a coach from a royal train, and a car 'showroom' where family and sports cars of all kinds stand in rows. There are also commercial vehicles and examples from Glasgow car manufacturers of the past, and many truly venerable machines. In an upstairs gallery, motorcycles lurk, together with a long gallery full of **model ships** in glass cases (almost all Clyde-built ships).

The attempts at interpretation and interactivity are spasmodic and curious. There's a kind of sculpture among the bicycles, a corner display about the Lockerbie air disaster (the only item to have anything to do with flying) and a good display on the dangers of speeding cars, with a test-your-own-reflexes machine. With a curious lack of sensitivity, a video car-racing game is positioned close to a home-made and moving patchwork collage commemorating road victims. There are further arcade machines up by the motorbikes, and a themed area about how ordinary people used to travel, as well a Pathé News-style film about Clyde shipbuilding and an accompanying exhibition, which somehow makes the rows of model ships in their cases seem very sad.

Information/tours/guides Information comes in the form of a fold-out map, which is useful for finding your way to the sections that most interest you. Details of special exhibitions are in a general guide to Glasgow museums. The souvenir guidebook is good value at £2.95, nicely laid out and interesting. If anything will make sense of the collection for you, this will.

Volunteer guides run occasional tours – check with the museum for the times. However, compared with other Glasgow museums, we found the staff lacking in enthusiasm and not exactly going out of their way to welcome visitors. A heated dispute about a till receipt in the shop during inspection showed a lack of pride and dignity.

When to visit Any time of the year is suitable. School groups are not likely to be a problem, since there is so much space. Everything is under cover, so it is a useful destination for rainy days.

Age appeal The museum is not made as interesting to the young as it could be, but there is nevertheless plenty to hold children's attention – although the lack of things to climb on or play with may shorten their attention span. Anyone from an older generation in search of their first car or motorbike will find plenty to jog their memories here.

Food and drink The café, overlooking the roofs of trams and trains, has been refurbished fairly recently in art deco style, and contains a small exhibition of 'Food on the Move' – a nice touch. There's a strong smell of chips, but it's a fresh smell. The offerings are cheap and cheerful, with a portion of chips for 75p, tea for 75p, a kid's lunch box for £1.95 and sandwiches from £1.55. The food is well presented and the café is kept clean.

Shops The small shop opening on to the foyer is a little cramped, and certainly not state-of-the art, but sells a fair range of items admirably focused on transport. Most of the goods are aimed at children, with model cars (from 99p), packs of stamps (£2.35), and pencils (35p). Enthusiasts will find some useful books of relevance to the collection.

Other facilities Don't use the toilets behind the café (an unrefurbished experience) – go downstairs instead, where they are much more pleasant, and have nappy changers. Access for pushchairs is good.

🚗 On-street parking is possible, but there's not a great deal of it in the immediate area. ⊖ From city centre, the museum is within easy walking distance of Partick suburban railway station and Kelvin Hall subway station. ⏰ Mon to Thur and Sat 10am to 5pm, Fri and Sun 11am to 5pm. Closed 25 Dec, 1 Jan. 💷 Free. ♿ Access is good, with a separate entrance avoiding the front steps and internal lifts.

National Gallery of Scotland

The Mound, Edinburgh EH2 2EL ☎ *0131-624 6200*

Quality ★★★★ **Facilities 👜👜👜👜👜** **Value for money £££££**
Highlights Central location; lovely architecture; elegant galleries and wonderful art
Drawbacks Rather cramped shop

What's there The National Gallery of Scotland is the flagship of a group of six galleries that comprise the National Galleries of Scotland. The others include the Scottish National Portrait Gallery, the Scottish National Gallery of Modern Art, the Dean Gallery (all in Edinburgh), Paxton House in Berwickshire, and Duff House in Banff.

The size of the collection means that it can easily be enjoyed over a period of a few hours. In the lofty and impressive Princes Street galleries, visitors can stroll past and examine paintings by the likes of Raphael, Titian, Reubens, Rembrandt, Poussin and Velázquez. The majority of galleries are on the ground floor and are arranged in hexagonal form, each one leading on to the next in an easy-to-follow, logical progression. Among the seventeenth-century exhibits are the *The Feast of Herod* by **Rubens** in Gallery 6, and **Poussin**'s series *The Seven Sacraments* in Gallery 5. The **Impressionists** are well represented in Galleries 2 to 6 upstairs. Works by Monet, Van Gogh, Degas, Renoir, Seurat and Cézanne all feature in the display, as well as paintings by the Italian artist Canaletto.

Gallery A1, the only one not accessible to wheelchairs, houses a display of early Italian paintings from 1400–1550 which features the work of Raphael. The eight galleries in the basement house the **Scottish Collection**, which covers artwork from the seventeenth to the twentieth centuries by native artists such as Allan Ramsay, Sir Henry Raeburn, Alexander Nasmyth and Sir David Wilkie.

Information/tours/guides Hand-held audio sets provide information on some of the paintings in the collection (£2 or £1 concessions). The guidebook to the gallery covers several affiliated galleries as well, including the Scottish National Gallery of Modern Art, the Dean Gallery and the Scottish National Portrait Gallery (£9.95).

When to visit Go at any time of year.

Age appeal The gallery is not ideal for young children, but there's plenty here for anyone looking for a bit of culture.

Food and drink None.

Shops The merchandise on offer is understandably heavy on art books (£5.99 to £50), prints (£5.95), calendars (£10.95) and postcards (95p). The shop is rather small, but is well stocked and has friendly and helpful staff.

🚗 Centrally located on Edinburgh's main shopping street and thoroughfare (the Princes Street Gardens side of the road). Car parks nearby. Not the building closest to the road, but the one behind it. ⊖ Take all buses with Princes Street on the front to the gallery. ⏰ Mon to Sat 10am to 5pm; Sun 2pm to 5pm. Closed 25, 26 Dec. 💷 Free (donations welcome). Charge for specialist exhibitions (about £3).
♿ Gallery A1 is not accessible, but the rest of the gallery is.

National Museum of Scotland – *see* Royal Museum of Scotland

New Lanark Mills

Lanark ML11 9DB   ☎ *(01555) 661345*   📠 *(01555) 665738*

Quality ★★   **Facilities** 👜 👜   **Value for money £££**
Highlights Riverside setting; decent shopping; interesting history
Drawbacks Some exhibits are on the scanty side

What's there New Lanark is an eighteenth-century complex of cotton mills and stone-built workers' housing on the banks of the River Clyde in one of its wildest and most appealing stretches. This early (1785) industrial settlement was saved from demolition in 1975, and is now a World Heritage Sight. It is far more than an industrial museum, for it was the scene of a pioneering piece of benevolent capitalism in an age which by and large regarded the workforce as cannon fodder for the production process. Ideas such as the Co-operative Society, the responsibility of the employer for his workers, and the undesirability of child labour can all be directly traced to what happened at New Lanark.

David Dale, the founder of the enterprise, and his son-in law Robert Owen were determined to create an ideal industrial community. Their elegant Institution for the Formation of Character, the School for Children, and the village store, where goods were bought in bulk and sold at cost price, remain as witnesses to this idealism. Many visitors – the Japanese in particular – visit New Lanark out of a kind of historical reverence.

There is plenty here, too, for those less interested in the past. Not much machinery remained in the huge spaces of the old mills (one is now a hotel), but a modern carding set and an old spinning mule have been brought in and can be seen hard at work turning out the woollen yarn which is on sale in the shop. A new ride linking New Lanark with the New Millennium was due to open at Easter 2000.

A mammoth **steam engine** is on view, and occasionally runs (by electricity only, alas). Additionally there is a period village store, a house furnished as it would have been in the 1820s, and Robert Owen's School for Children to look at. The New Lanark Conservation Trust has sensibly let some of the plentiful remaining space to craft shops and to a branch of the Edinburgh Woollen Mill.

Even if the exhibitions and the machinery are a little thin on the ground for a full day out, there are other attractions. The setting of the old village is very beautiful, down at the bottom of a gorge beside the rough waters of the Clyde, and a nature reserve stretches along both banks. So not only is there plenty of opportunity to contemplate the massive **water wheel** which used to power the mills, but there are also some attractive walks up the river towards the dramatic waterfalls which lie half a mile away.

Restoration of New Lanark has been a long, slow process, and is still continuing. Conservation is the priority, and the tourist attraction side of things has grown slowly, whenever there was any spare cash. So this is not a planned, super-smooth sight, and there are still a few rough edges. The passport system, whereby you have to get your ticket stamped for each separate building, is irritating, and there has been such a build-up of signs, framed awards, explanatory panels and posters over the years that it is at times difficult to see what is important and what is not. It would be a great benefit (and inexpensive) to rationalise the interpretation, bring it up to date and give it a unifying style.

Information/tours/guides Four separate booklets on different themes are available to guide you around. Their total cost is £5, but if you just want one guide, the *New Lanark Heritage Trail* is the most useful. Guided tours are available for groups only (book in advance). You can also go on guided walks through the nature reserve with the Scottish Wildlife Trust, which manages it (wear sensible footwear, preferably wellies). At £2 for an hour's walk, these are excellent value. Maps are situated at strategic points in the buildings and grounds, and help to make some sense of the complex. Staff are very friendly and helpful, and do a lot to make a visit a pleasure.

When to visit Summer is the ideal time: temperatures in the shelter of the gorge can rise to sunbathing level on a good day. Weekends are apt to be a bit crowded. There are various events on at weekends – phone for details. There's always something on around Christmas, and a Victorian fair on the first Sunday in September.

Age appeal   There is enough working machinery to provide some interest for children, and we hope that the new ride will interest both the young and the old. Trekking around the shops may prove less fascinating for very small children.

Food and drink   The Mill Pantry is a big, echoing room on the ground floor of a mill. Once packed with machinery, it now has plain wooden tables ranged round it. The self-service counter provides a fair range of home-cooked light snacks and meals. The baking is especially good, with biscuits, scones and so on selling for around £1. Baked potato with a choice of fillings (£3) or soup and a roll (£1.35) are typical of the kind of food on offer. On crowded days, tables are slow to be cleared, and the décor isn't wonderful.

Shops   There's a village shop, a gift shop, a big branch of the Edinburgh Woollen Mill and several different craft shops within the complex. Especially worth looking out for is the spun-on-the-premises wool, which is packed on huge spindles on the shelves (£12 to £14 per kilo). There's a wide range of branded souvenirs, such as New Lanark mugs (£3.99), plus a mass of small items for children. The Edinburgh Woollen Mill contains lots of bargain bins full of jumpers and cardigans, while the crafts range from kilts and cashmere to wrought iron. Poking around the various outlets is a pleasurable way to extend your visit, particularly as there's no slick merchandising and no great pressure to buy.

Other facilities   The toilets could be cleaner and would benefit from up-to-date equipment.

🚗 From M8 or local routes, follow signs. The car park is high up above the gorge, so there is a very steep walk down. ⊖ Take train from Glasgow, or bus from Edinburgh and Glasgow. A local bus runs at roughly once an hour from Lanark to New Lanark. There may be combined travel and entry tickets from stations in the Strathclyde Transport area. ⊘ Mon to Sun, 11am to 5pm. Closed 25 Dec, 1 Jan. 💷 Adult £3.75; child (3 to 16 yrs old) £2.50; senior citizens, students, unemployed £2.50; family ticket (2 adults + 2 children) £9.95 (2 adults + 3/4 children) £12.50. ♿ People with mobility problems are allowed to drive down to the village. The organisers do their utmost to help wheelchair users. Call for an explanatory leaflet.

The Official Loch Ness Monster Exhibition Centre

Drumnadrochit, Inverness-shire IV63 6TU   ☎ *(01456) 450573*
📠 *(01456) 450770*   🖰 *www.lochness.scotland.net*
🖰 *Info@lochness.co.uk*

Quality ★★★★ **Facilities 🏛 🏛** **Value for money ££**
Highlights   Good use of multi-media and special effects; objective and interesting; fun shop
Drawbacks   Expensive entry fee; lack of good on-site facilities

---

What's there   'From the dawn of time to the dawn of the third millennium' is the promise conveyed by the Loch Ness 2000 leaflet. A rather severe stone building on the outskirts of the tiny Highland village of Drumnadrochit seems an unlikely setting to embrace such a lengthy period, but where the Loch Ness Monster is concerned, anything goes.

It has to be said at once that this is an engrossing sight, whatever the hype used to sell it. Drumnadrochit is the capital of 'monster' tat, and makes its living on visitors' willingness to countenance the existence of a 'beastie' in the nearby loch, so it is something of a surprise to find an exhibition here which is objective, sober and downright interesting on the subject.

It is very well conceived and designed, too. A sequence of rooms – imaginatively clad and atmospherically lit – comes to life one after another as you enter. In each there is an **audio-visual display**, supplemented on some occasions by laser effects, outlining some aspect of the environment of Loch Ness, and the hunt for the monster. You learn a lot – not just about the curious habitat down in the dark depths, but also about the clear scientific reasons why the existence of a monster is improbable, at best. There are excellent explanations of the methods – sonar, fixed cameras, fleets of boats – used to try to track down the monster, and illuminating suggestions about the actual origins of the more famous photographs.

The display is marred only by the somewhat rushed and garbled quality of the commentary on the audio-visuals, while some of the technicalities need further explanation for non-scientists. For this reason it would be useful to have the audio-visuals supplemented by some old-fashioned display panels, or for there to be an accompanying guidebook. As it is, the tour is on the short side, given the high price of entry.

This may be because the sooner visitors reach the shop, the happier everyone is. The shop is a truly 'monstrous' operation, and when combined with further outlets and a hotel a few paces away makes clear what the rationale for the sight's existence is.

Information/tours/guides The publicity brochure for Loch Ness 2000 could do with a little less breathy enthusiasm and a little more hard information. It is equally difficult to dig solid information out of the web site, which was still under construction at the time of writing. However, it already has a plethora of links to other sites, including a link to a live camera overlooking Loch Ness.

This is a self-guided sight, and small enough for it to be obvious where to go, but staff at the entry are helpful if you have particular queries.

When to visit This is an all-year sight. Traffic is obviously a lot less heavy out of season. Refurbishment happens in winter, so check the exhibition's status before setting out in the blizzards.

Age appeal The colourful effects will appeal to children, even where the technicalities are above their heads. School packs are available by prior appointment, which individuals can also obtain on the same basis (free of charge). A CD-ROM is in prospect.

Food and drink On site, there's only a tiny hole in the wall, which sells drinks and ices in season. The nearby hotel serves lunches. Items from the bar snacks or full menu include soup (£2.75), sandwiches (£2.20) and hot dishes (up to £6.75).

Shops The shop attached to the exhibiton is a huge Z-shaped, split-level affair, with the first two sections given over to souvenirs, and the third to tartan and outdoor wear. In the first two sections, approximately 80 per cent of items are monster-related, with small plastic plesiosaurs (£2.75), little cuddly Nessies (£1.95) and key-rings (between 95p and £2.50). The clothing section has more serious goods and more serious prices, with tartan travelling rugs (£24.95) and deerstalker hats (£22.50). In the shop as a whole, the range is wide, even if the theme is limited, and it is a fun place to prowl round. Smarter uniformed staff would be a help.

Other facilities The sight's surroundings are worn and fairly scruffy, although a landscaped pond provides some relief. Toilets, round the back, are better not described, as the third millennium has not dawned here.

🚗 Signs to the 'Official' Loch Ness Monster Exhibition Centre are not helpful, and are easily confused with signs to the 'Original' Exhibition, not far away. Parking space is adequate, but apt to be swamped by buses. ⊖ Inverness to Drumnadrochit bus (approximately four times daily) is the only public transport available. Better to seek out one of the coach tours from Inverness that have the sight as a stop. ⊕ Easter to May, 9.30am to 5pm; June and Sept 9.30am to 6pm; July and Aug 9am to 8pm; Oct 9.30am to 5.30pm; Nov to Easter 10am to 4pm. 💷 Adult £5.95; child (7 to 16 yrs old) £3.50; students, senior citizens £4.50; disabled people free; family ticket (2 adults + 3 children) £14.95. *Groups* (10+ people) adult £4; child (7 to 16 yrs old) £2; concessions £3. ♿ Access is good. A side door avoids the entrance steps, and everything is on the ground floor.

Old Blacksmith's Shop Centre

Headless Cross, Gretna Green, Dumfriesshire DG16 5EA 📞 *(01461) 33822*
🖥 *www.gretnagreen.com* 📧 *Info@gretnagreen.com*

Quality ★★★ **Facilities** 🏛 🏛 **Value for money £££**
Highlights A genial stop-off point on a long motorway journey; shopping; romance
Drawbacks Overcrowding; facilities under pressure; designed for tour groups rather than individuals

---

What's there Gretna Green would merely be a rather muddy village on the Scottish border if it had not been for an eighteenth-century legal difference between the marriage laws of Scotland and England. This meant that couples could be legally married in Scotland simply by asserting their desire in front of witnesses, unlike in England.

So Gretna became a haven for eloping couples, and the village blacksmith was often called in to officiate as the 'anvil priest'. Marriage records going back to 1772 supply historical backing to the village's reputation.

All the same, if it were not for the draw created by romantic fiction, it is doubtful that the Old Blacksmith's Shop would be able to pull in the half-million visitors it achieves each year. For while the sight has done its utmost to gather together relevant material, there is, in comparison to an old house or great castle, virtually nothing of historic interest to be seen.

A small walk-through exhibition prettily outlines the history of Gretna marriages; there is a splendid collection of **coaches and carriages**, one or two reconstructions of cottage interiors, and an intriguing array of fading newspaper cuttings and old photographs – which is all there is to see. However, sightseeing is not really the point of the place. The point is perhaps better summed up by the thousands of romantic graffiti left by visitors, demonstrating that for many people a wedding or renewal of vows at Gretna Green is an act of self-evident importance.

The other act of importance is to have a memento of a visit here, and so the floor space devoted to **shopping** easily outstrips that of most other Scottish sights. The shops and other facilities are arranged around two pleasant courtyards filled with curious sculptures, where there are plantings of heather, and benches to sit on.

The space and the facilities are currently not up to the number of visitors taking advantage of them, especially when numerous tour coaches converge. Litter also accumulates rapidly in difficult-to-get-at spots.

Information/tours/guides Surprisingly for such a popular sight, there is no glossy souvenir guide to the Old Blacksmith's Shop. Instead, there's a sheet of paper with a brief history. It is very much a self-guided sight, although tour groups can have a guide and a 'fun wedding' as part of their experience. Information packs on how to get married at the Blacksmith's Shop are available on request, and are very clear. The web site gives reasonable background information and will soon have a direct shopping facility.

When to visit Popular all year, the Old Blacksmith's Shop is at its best on a sunny day off-season, when the tour coaches are fewer on the ground. If it rains this means a soaking between shops and nowhere much to sit.

Age appeal Gretna should appeal to romantics of any age. There is a small playground by the car park for those too young for the first flush of love.

Food and drink The large restaurant and coffee shop are designed to cope swiftly with large numbers, and the catering, which offers a limited range, is of decent quality, fairly priced and efficient. Tea (85p) and sandwiches (£1.45) are good value. Full meals (salad £4.45, steak pie £4.95) are reasonable, especially since the hot food is well presented and fresh. Cold food and snacks can run low if you are late for lunch.

The décor (plastic tablecloths, tartan carpet and dim lighting) is gloomy, but the restaurants are kept very clean, and there are few signs of wear and tear. The Conservatory Bar is brighter and more appealing. Drinks and ice cream are on sale here, and you can bring your food through from the main restaurant. Staff remain friendly at the busiest times.

Shops A tiny newsagent's shop sits oddly alongside its companions: a big souvenir shop, a bigger tartan shop, one outlet for decorative glassware and another for ceramic 'collectables'. There is also a Tourist Information Centre. Within the categories of 'souvenir' and 'Scottish produce' the range of goods for sale is huge and runs from replica broadswords to pens (60p), branded keyrings (£2.99), car stickers (£1.25) and notepads (£1.25). Distinctive mementos are not hard to find, such as a brass anvil (£5.95) and a glass sculpture of a wedding couple with an anvil (£24.99).

The shops are staffed largely by local people who are unfailingly helpful, even under pressure.

Other facilities The toilets in particular suffer from the pressure of numbers: queues develop, and cleanliness is affected.

🚗 From M74 ten miles north of Carlisle or local roads, follow well-marked signs. ⊖ Train to Gretna Green from Carlisle (they run roughly every two hours, buses every hour). ⊙ July and Aug, Mon to Sun 9am to 8pm; June and Sept, Mon to Sun 9am to 7pm; May and Oct, 9am to 6pm; Nov and Mar, Mon to Sun 9am to 5pm. Closed 25, 26 Dec, Jan 1. 🖼 *Exhibition* adult £2; child (10 to 16 yrs old) £1.50; senior citizens, students, disabled £1.50; group rate £1.50. ♿ Access is good, with spaces in the car park and special toilets. Things to see and do are on the ground floor; there are ramps where needed and help is on hand from the staff. There's a slightly hazardous road crossing between shops.

Palace of Holyrood House

The Royal Mile, Edinburgh EH8 8DX ☎ *0131-556 7371*

Quality ★★★★ **Facilities** 👜👜👜👜 **Value for money £££**
Highlights Mary Queen of Scots' Apartments; the Great Gallery; friendly staff
Drawbacks No guided tours in summer and an expensive guidebook to replace them

What's there The Queen's residence in Edinburgh provides a good introduction to the rich history of royalty in Scotland over the past five centuries. James IV made the first additions to the original abbey, whose ruins can still be explored on the site, though James V oversaw the most significant expansion of the Palace between 1528 and 1536. Many of the most dramatic events of the reign of his successor, **Mary Queen of Scots**, including her marriage to Lord Darnley and the murder of Rizzio, her secretary, took place within the Palace walls.

The rooms open to the public include the dining room, throne room, drawing rooms, King's Bedchamber and Mary Queen of Scots' living quarters. The latter are both the culmination and the highlight of a tour by a guide whose stentorian delivery swoops through the octaves in an operatic way. Only in Mary's chambers (the scene of Rizzio's frenzied stabbing) is the interior emphatically Scottish, thanks to a wonderful **painted ceiling** and specimens of the doomed queen's needlecraft.

Visitors can also marvel at the **Great Gallery**. This contains a series of paintings of the real and legendary kings of Scotland, from Fergus I to Charles II, painted by **Jacob de Wet** the Younger in 1684. There is also a small exhibition of objects and artefacts such as necklaces, brooches and pendants, as well as some more portraits of regal figures of the period. Finally, the **ruined abbey** and the gardens are pleasant to stroll around to finish off your visit.

Allow one hour for your tour of Holyrood House.

Information/tours/guides Guided tours between November and March leave every 15 minutes and last approximately 45 minutes. Price is included in the entry ticket. From April to October there are no guided tours, and visitors have to make do with the official guidebook (£3.70) which, although immaculately presented and extremely detailed, is a very poor substitute for actually hearing the history and stories from someone who knows. The attendants in the rooms are always happy to help with information and are very knowledgeable, but having a guide will make all the difference to a visit to Holyrood House.

When to visit During the winter, when the guided tours run.

Age appeal Appeals to adults and children alike, though children will be quickly bored if not on a guided tour.

Food and drink None.

Shops A rather mediocre range of items is on sale in the shop by the entrance gate. Visitors can choose from cards (£3), kilt pins and brooches (£10.50), pens, pencils and stationery (£1 to £2), jewellery (£10 to £100) and comestibles such as oat cakes (65p), chocolate and shortbread (£1 to £2.75).

🚗 Within central Edinburgh. Car park next to the Palace (pay and display). ⊖ Easy walking distance from the base of the Royal Mile. ① Apr to Oct, Mon to Sun 9.30am to 5.15pm; Nov to Mar, Mon to Sun 9.30am to 3.45pm. Closed 21 Apr, 16–27 May, 24 June–8 July, 7 Aug, 30 Nov, 25–6 Dec. 💷 Adult £6; child (6 to 17 yrs old) £3; senior citizen £4.50; family ticket (2 adults + 2 children) £13.50; group discount 10% (groups of 15 or more). ♿ Mary Queen of Scots' apartments are inaccessible to wheelchairs, but all the main state rooms are accessible.

People's Palace

Glasgow Green, Glasgow G40 1AT ☎ *0141-554 0223*

Quality ★★★   **Facilities 🍴**   **Value for money £££**
Highlights Quirky exhibits; good for children; excellent local history; very friendly
Drawbacks Not well signed or publicised

What's there Opened in 1898 in one of the most overcrowded and unhealthy areas of Glasgow, the People's Palace started life as a kind of Edwardian cultural resource centre. Over the years it has transformed itself into a museum of Glasgow, assembling histories and artefacts from the lives of the Glaswegians and setting out to tell the story of the city through the eyes of the people who live there.

The bulky red sandstone building now standing on its own on a corner of Glasgow Green looks rather isolated and forgotten, and its future has been in doubt on more than one occasion over the past decade. However, the recent upgrading of the exhibition space has given the place a new lease of life, turning the interior into a modern and accessible local museum. Local, because this is very much a museum for the Glaswegians themselves. It is not widely publicised to the outside world, and not easy to find for anyone who does not know the city. It does, however, repay the effort of getting to it, for not only is it full of fascination, but done with that mix of pride and ironic humour that is Glasgow's own.

The story of Glasgow unfolds on three floors, with separately themed areas carefully integrated into a coherent whole. The themes range from Glasgow's political idealism, as in '**The People's Vision**,' with its collection of Trade Union banners and sepia photographs of suffragettes, to the down-to-earth life of **old Glasgow**, with the 'Steamie', the 'Wally Close' and the 'Single End' featuring prominently. There's a very careful mix of nostalgic appeal to the elderly and hands-on interest for the young, with imaginative use of sound dovetailed in. Sit on the bench from an Italian café, for example, and you are immediately aurally encased by a gossipy conversation which seems to be taking place at the next-door table. The section entitled '**The Patter**' carries video clips from Stanley Baxter, Billy Connolly and Rab C Nesbit taking a dig at the Glasgow dialect and explaining to the uninitiated the meaning of 'Razza burdoora hairywullie?' A talking parrot plays a prominent part.

For all the modernity of the presentation, there are not many bells and whistles where facilities are concerned. Some of the building still looks and feels like a damp public library, and will continue to do so, at least until the beautiful and extensive glasswork of the attached **Winter Gardens** is fully restored following a fire and decades of neglect (due for completion by Easter 2000).

Information/tours/guides The all-round excellence of the smartly uniformed staff – relaxed, friendly, and never too busy to come up with information when you need it – goes some way to counter the dearth of publicity or printed information reaching the outside world. The booklet *The People's Palace*, for example, now sells for a discounted £1 because it is not only abominably printed but has not been rewritten to fit the new exhibition. A helpful map to guide you round is on hand.

When to visit Go at any time except (currently) meal times. The museum is open all year and ideal for a wet Sunday morning

Age appeal The revamping of the museum's exhibition space has done a lot to make it of interest to children. For older people, the place is full of memories, and there is much here for anyone old enough to remember the war, whether they are Glaswegian or not.

Food and drink At present, only light snacks are available from a small counter, such as cakes (90p), juice (65p), coffee (£1.10) and biscuits (30p). There are a few tables and stools to sit at, but since they were actually designed for children, adults will not relax in comfort.

Shops A small shop is attached to the ground floor exhibition rooms, selling a fair, but not very extensive, range of Glasgow-related goods. There's little directly related to the People's Palace apart from postcards of the Ken Currie murals which adorn the top floor (40p). Glasgow playing cards (£2.50) or a set of Glasgow table mats (£24.99) are imaginative. For children, there are a few small items, such as flying gliders (20p).

Other facilities The toilets – their tiles with Shakespearean scenes still more or less intact – ought to be wonderful. They aren't.

From city centre, signs to the Palace are sporadic and wayward at best, and a street map is the only answer. Some parking spaces in front of the museum, and on-street unrestricted parking is usually available nearby. ⊖ Not easy. Guide Friday Tours have a stop at the People's Palace, if you are doing a more general tour of Glasgow. Otherwise, local buses 62 (a, b, c), 18 or 64 will get you within easy walking distance. ⊙ Mon to Thur and Sat 10am to 5pm; Fri and Sun 11am to 5pm. Closed 25 Dec, 1 Jan. 💷 Free. ♿ Access is reasonable with a ramped entrance, central lift and disabled toilet. Two wheelchairs are available.

Rob Roy and Trossachs Visitor Centre

Ancaster Square, Callander, The Trossachs, Perthshire ☎ *(01877) 330342*

Quality ★★   **Facilities** 📷 📷   **Value for money** £££
Highlights Friendly staff; good use of media; wet weather refuge
Drawbacks Not a lot to see

What's there Callander is the main stopping point for tourists on the scenic route around the Trossachs, an area of Scotland first popularised by **Sir Walter Scott**, and still a major draw for coach excursions today. The Rob Roy and Trossachs Visitor Centre is a purpose-built attraction, carved out of a redundant church in the very centre of the small town. Bereft of any visible historical remains worth a mention, Callander has capitalised on the romantic myths surrounding the figure of the outlaw Rob Roy McGregor, and sells the surrounding landscape as 'Rob Roy Country'.

The attraction is somewhat meagre in terms of things to see and do, consisting as it does of a series of small displays centred around Rob Roy and his times. It doubles up as Callander's Tourist Information Centre. But as the town's single tourist sight, it makes a useful stop-off point, or refuge from the rain.

There's a craftily mounted initial show, with the animated face of Rob Roy projected on to a static model, and a relatively coherent script to go with it. You then move through further rooms, where different media (display boards, models, videos) introduce you to the politics of Rob Roy's time, the trade of cattle droving, and the hardships of Highland life. Finally there is a mock-up of a **Highland house**, such as Rob Roy might have inhabited, with various farmyard implements, clothes for children to dress up in, and a box bed which they can try out for size. The children's play area mentioned in the sight's flyer turns out to be just a ball pit by the reception desk.

Downstairs in the auditorium, the joys of 'Rob Roy Country' are lovingly dwelt on in a short, nicely shot Scottish Tourist Board film. This may be replaced shortly by a film or audio-visual more relevant to Rob Roy.

The sight is definitely on the thin side, and you would be hard pressed to spend more than three-quarters of an hour here. It is clearly aimed at foreign visitors to Scotland (masses of multi-lingual material), and coverage is correspondingly somewhat superficial. It's a friendly place, however, with smart, welcoming staff keen to answer visitors' queries.

Information/tours/guides Apart from some confusion over prices in the 1999 edition, the Visitor Centre's flyer is comprehensive in the information it gives, but somewhat over-sells the joys of the attraction. The tour is entirely self-guided, but reception staff are knowledgeable if you have questions.

When to visit The centre is best visited on a wet day (it is a fair alternative to sitting in a café gazing at the drizzle).

Age appeal The display is carefully pitched to embrace young as well as old.

Food and drink None on site, but there is a range of pubs, cafés and restaurants within a couple of minutes' walk.

Shops The shop is a typical Scottish Tourist Board shop, bright and well-displayed, with a good range of reading matter on Scottish subjects. It boasts several branded items, such as Rob Roy Country mugs (£2.25) and clotted cream caramels (£1.60). Rob Roy T-shirts cost £9.95, and a McGregor tartan tie costs £6.99. There are a few souvenirs for children, particularly a nice series of animal posters (75p).

🚌 A84 to Callander, follow signs. Car parks nearby. ⊖ Coach tours of the Trossachs that stop at the Visitor Centre are found in Edinburgh and Glasgow. Local bus from Stirling (approximately every two hours) to Callander. ⏲ Jan and Feb, Sat and Sun 11am to 4.30; Mar to May, Mon to Sun 10am to 5pm; June, Mon to Sun 9.30am to 6pm; July and Aug, Mon to Sun 9am to 10pm; Sept, Mon to Sun 10am to 6pm; Oct to Dec, Mon to Sun 10am to 5pm. Last admission to show 30 minutes before closing. Closed 25 Dec, 1 Jan. 💷 Adult £2.75; child (5 to 16 yrs old) £1.25; senior citizens £2; students £2.25; family ticket (2 adults + 2 children) £6. ♿ Disabled access is reasonable for such an inconvenient building, with a lift to the first floor and disabled toilets.

Royal Botanic Garden, Edinburgh

Inverleith Row, Edinburgh EH3 5LR   ☎ *0131-552 7171*   ⌨ *www.rbge.org.uk*

Quality ★★★★★   **Facilities** 👜 👜 👜   **Value for money** £££££
Highlights Hothouses; Chinese Garden; Rock and Heath Gardens; Exhibition Hall
(children's displays); Inverleith House Art Gallery
Drawbacks Poorly organised catering facilities

What's there The Royal Botanic Garden is located just north of Edinburgh city centre, and comprises 70 acres of lawns, gardens, trees and water features, as well as a number of huge glass houses which replicate arid and tropical climates and their flora and fauna. It is primarily a scientific research institution: the laboratories are not open to the public, but the beautifully landscaped gardens themselves are, and they are a great favourite with locals and visitors alike, who can wander freely, with friendly squirrels and ducks to amuse the children.

The Garden is split up into specific areas. The **Ecological Garden** displays Scottish flora in a range of typical habitats, while the Demonstration Garden has themed plantings on different topics such as herb beds and medicinal plants. The **Rock and Heath Gardens**, made up of a series of mounds and gullies with a scree slope and stream, are home to 5,000 different plants from rocky or Arctic habitats. Exotic trees such as the Caucasian wingnut, dawn redwood and swamp cypress surround the Pond Lawns. The 165-metre-long **Herbaceous Border** is at its vibrant best between May and October, while the **Winter Garden**, planted with snowdrops, witch hazels and winter-flowering honeysuckle, provides interest when other plants are dormant. The sloping **Chinese Garden** features oriental plants that flourish at different altitudes as well as a lovely stream and mini pagoda. Routes and walks are suggested in the guidebook, and each plant and tree is carefully labelled should you want more information on it.

The **Exhibition Hall** is a must for children, with its hands-on microscopes and different flowers to identify by smell, while **Inverleith House** in the centre of the garden is a good stop for art lovers as it presents exhibitions throughout the year. The **Hothouses**, constructed in the 1890s, are home to a myriad of exotica, including orchids, cycads, ferns and palms, and cost over £100,000 a year to heat, so donations are welcome.

Information/tours/guides There are guided tours twice daily, starting from the West Gate in Arboretum Place. They last between 1 and 1½ hours (£2). A full-colour booklet is available with an excellent map of the gardens and details of all they have to offer (£3.50).

When to visit Spring and summer are best for the flowers, though winter hothouse visits are fun too. Families with small children flood in at the weekend.

Age appeal There's something for everybody. The children will love the microscopes and toys in the Exhibition Hall.

Food and drink The Terrace Café has seating indoors and out, though the staff struggle to cope with numbers at weekends. The food available is a very standard selection of teas and coffees (£1 to £1.50), cakes and pastries (£1 to £1.50), and baked potatoes and filling (£2.50). There is another, smaller outlet called Dill's Snack Bar located by the West Gate which is open during the summer.

Shops The excellent shop here is full of high-quality and varied merchandise. Items include a selection of books on gardening (£5 to £20), including a children's section, vases (£9.99), garden mobiles and wind chimes, candles (49p), toys (£5 to £10), writing paper and stationery (50p to £5), picture frames (£8.99), packets of seeds (£2.49) and small pot plants (£3 to £10).

🚗 Off A902. On-street parking is by the West Gate. Gardens are one mile north of the city centre. ⊖ Regular bus services from Hanover Street stop at the East Gate (numbers 23, 27, 37). ⏰ Mar and Sept, Mon to Sun 9.30am to 6pm; Apr to Aug, Mon to Sun 9.30am to 7pm; Feb and Oct, Mon to Sun 9.30am to 5pm; Nov to Apr, Mon to Sun 9.30am to 4pm. Closed 25 Dec, 1 Jan. 💷 Free (donations welcome). ♿ Fully accessible.

Royal Museum of Scotland and National Museum of Scotland

Chambers Street, Edinburgh EH1 1JF   ☎ *Royal Museum 0131-247 4219*
National Museum 0131-247 4422   ✆ *www.nms.ac.uk*

Royal Museum	**Quality ★★★★**	**Facilities 🏛 🏛 🏛**
National Museum	**Quality ★★★★★**	**Facilities 🏛 🏛 🏛 🏛 🏛**
Value for money (both) £££££		

What's there The Royal Museum of Scotland was the original Chambers Street Museum, which now plays second fiddle to the brand new, architecturally innovative National Museum of Scotland. These two museums are next door to one another, and a single admission fee covers entry to both.

The **Royal Museum of Scotland** is a taxidermist's Utopia, with scores of representatives from the animal world stuffed, mounted in glass cases and labelled for easy identification. Elephants and elephant seals compete with parrots, tigers and spider crabs for your attention. Eclectic galleries come thick and fast one after the other, covering everything from Norwegian dress, souvenirs of the twentieth century, ancient Egyptian artefacts, the world of fish, European art 1200–1800, ceramics and glass, to arms and armour. The problem with this is that there seems to be little logic or cohesion, which leaves the visitor somewhat bewildered by the range and scope of what is on offer.

This is not the case in the **National Museum of Scotland**, though, where the history of Scotland and the Scots is laid out thoughtfully and imaginatively, with over 10,000 objects on six levels. The story begins on the first level with the formation of the land that is now Scotland, and moves through its early people, agrarian farming and the Roman invasions. Further galleries and levels cover the land and the people, monarchy and power, the Renaissance, the medieval church, trade and industry, the Industrial Revolution and the advances of the twentieth century. It concludes on the top floor with a series of displays from the 1980s and 1990s, in which the public were asked to pick items from the twentieth century that have made a significant impact on life in Scotland. Exhibits include Highland dirks, early banknotes and an entire steam locomotive. Interactive touch-screen technology is used throughout the museum to give more information on items of interest.

Allow at least half a day for your visit to either museum, or a whole day if you want to do both.

Information/tours/guides The National Museum of Scotland has daily tours which leave from the information desk (Mon and Thur to Sun 2.15pm and 3.15pm; Tue 2.15pm, 3.15pm and 6pm; Wed 3.15pm). Royal Museum of Scotland Highlight Tours leave from the information desk (Mon to Wed 2.30pm; Fri and Sat 2.30pm; Sun 3.30pm). Tours are free in both musuems and last up to an hour.

Themed tours – for example, on Chinese dress or the Jacobites – are also available on specific days.

When to visit The museums are ideal for rainy days, and the buildings are so huge they very rarely get crowded.

Age appeal Very broad – there's certainly something for all age groups to enjoy.

Food and drink Two cafeterias in the Royal Museum of Scotland offer a range of light lunches and sandwiches (£2 to £3), children's lunch boxes (£2.20) and even baby food (60p), along with coffees, teas and cakes (£1 to £2).

The Museum of Scotland boasts The Tower restaurant, a very upmarket establishment offering high-quality food. Main courses are dishes such as braised pheasant with caramelised apple sauce, or baked cod (£6 to £15). Reservations recommended.

Shops One shop serves both museums, and is located between the two. A wide range of merchandise is on offer, from greetings cards (£1.50 to £3.50), pens (£4.50), picture frames (£12.50), aromatic creams and soaps (£2 to £5) to chemistry sets (£24.99) and a selection of stationery and toys for pocket-money buys.

🚗 Off the Royal Mile along George IV Bridge, in the old town. Parking in Crichton Street. Walking is the best option. ⊖ Take buses 3, 31 and 33 from Princes Street. ⊙ Mon to Sat 10am to 5pm, Tue 10am to 8pm, Sun 12pm to 5pm. Closed 25 Dec. 💷 Adult £3; child (up to 18 yrs old) free; senior citizen, student, unemployed £1.50. Free admission on Tue for all visitors between 4.30pm and 8pm. ♿ Fully accessible.

The Royal Yacht *Britannia*

Leith Docks, Leith, Edinburgh EH6 6JJ ☎ *0131-555 5566*

Quality ★★★★★ · **Facilities** 👜👜👜👜👜 **Value for money £££**
Highlights Dining room and Royal Apartments
Drawbacks Surrounded by an unattractive industrial estate; bottlenecks at busy times

What's there The Royal Yacht *Britannia*, built on the Clyde at John Brown's Shipyard and launched in 1953, has now been decommissioned and is open to the general public, as well as being available for private functions. *Britannia's* interior was designed and furnished by the Queen and Prince Philip, which, according to the Prince, 'was rather special because all the other places we live in had been built by predecessors'. She saw 44 years' service and was used for state visits to the Commonwealth as well as for family holidays and honeymoons.

The tour begins in a specially constructed exhibition building on the quayside. The centrepiece is the **Royal Launch**, which brought dignitaries to and from the yacht, but there is also some excellent interactive touch-screen technology that tells you all about the mechanics and crew, and gives plenty of relevant nautical statistics. Several five-minute films show *Britannia* in action in various parts of the globe, including footage of the Hong Kong hand-over, and Charles and Diana in Venice. A selection of family photos is on display, alongside a wide range of historical *Britannia*-related memorabilia.

Visitors board the boat from a four-storey gantry before touring the bridge, the ward-room, the Queen's and Duke's bedrooms and the **Royal Apartments**, terminating at the sparklingly clean engine rooms. The most impressive rooms are the Royal Apartments and the **Dining Room**, the latter laid out as if for one of the many state banquets that were hosted on board. Some of the more unusual sights on the ship are the signs on the 'Royal Cold Larder' and the 'Royal Cold Room', while you pick up snippets of information such as the fact that Prince Philip prefers blankets to a duvet, and doesn't like lace borders on his pillowcases.

A visit to *Britannia* will take about one-and-a-half hours.

Information/tours/guides An expensive, glossy guidebook (£7.95) covers everything in great depth. A free audio tour allows you to go at your own pace and explains what you are looking at, as well as providing stories and history as you pass through. Handsets are also available in German, Spanish, Italian and French.

When to visit It is advisable to book in advance, as on busy days admission cannot be guaranteed. To book, call daily between 9am and 5.30pm, or call in person at the Edinburgh Tattoo Office (33–34 Market Street) daily between 10am and 4.30pm. For group bookings of 15 or more, call 0131–555 8800.

Visitors are allowed through in groups every 20 minutes, from which point each visitor picks up an audio handset and goes at his or her own pace. Try to avoid weekends, as on busy days the route through the ship can be very cramped, and there can be severe bottlenecks at the more interesting exhibits.

Age appeal Ideal for anyone curious about royalty, or who just wants to follow in the footsteps of some very famous visitors like Sir Winston Churchill, Nelson Mandela, Rajiv Gandhi, Boris Yeltsin, Ronald Reagan and Margaret Thatcher among others.

There is a small play area in the Visitor Centre, but the sight is not really suitable for very young children, as you have to listen to the handset for all your information.

Food and drink A very limited selection of teas, coffees and snacks is available in the modern, airy buffet and cafeteria area in the Visitor Centre (between £1 and £3 per item).

Shops There are a number of high-quality items on sale in the gift shop, such as T-shirts (£15.95), preserves and shortbread (£2 to £5), stationery (50p to £2), and a range of crystalware (£15.95 to £125).

🚗 From Edinburgh, follow yellow signs. Free parking on dockside. ⊖ 'Guide Friday' or Lothian Regional Transport (X50 bus) dedicated bus service from Waverley Bridge, opposite the station in town centre. One bus to the dock leaves every 20 minutes after 10.10am. The last bus back is at 6.03pm. Regular service buses to the area are the 10/10A, 16, 22/22A and 88. ◷ Mon to Sun 10am to 4.30pm. Closed 25 Dec, 1 Jan. 💷 Apr to Sept adults £7; child £3.25; senior citizen £5.25; student £3.25; Jan to Mar and Oct adults £6.75; child £3; senior citizen £5; student £2.75. ♿ Fully accessible, with ramps.

Scotch Whisky Heritage Centre

354 Castlehill, The Royal Mile, Edinburgh EH1 2NE ☎ *0131-220 0441*
📧 *www.whisky-heritage.co.uk* 📧 *enquiry@whisky-heritage.co.uk*

Quality ★★★★★　　　**Facilities 🏛🏛🏛🏛🏛**　　　**Value for money ££££**
Highlights Short lecture from member of staff and chance to ask questions
Drawbacks Tricky layout for disabled or elderly people

What's there The Scotch Whisky Heritage Centre provides an hour-long themed tour covering the history of Scotch whisky, how it is made and where it comes from. The tour takes visitors through various stages, ending up at the bar, where they can **sample the Scotch of the day**.

After an introductory film about an American tourist talking to a barman and wondering about his Scotch-drinking Scottish great-grandfather, one of the members of staff talks visitors through the malt whisky manufacturing process using a **scale model of an actual distillery**. You learn about the various ingredients of the whisky manufacturing process, see and touch the peat that is used and smell small samples of Scotch at various stages of maturity. The different regions of Scotland where whisky comes from are also highlighted using an overhead projector, and the advances made in whisky distilling are explained.

After this short lecture and the chance to ask questions, a clever holographic display featuring the resident '**ghost**' talks visitors through the process of blending whiskies, as 90 per cent of all whisky consumed worldwide is blended from a range of different single malts that are 'married' together before bottling. This is followed by a ride in a **whisky barrel-car** through the history of the spirit over the last 300 years, which uses displays, mannequins and different smells to create effects.

The tour ends with a free dram in the bar for those over 18 who wish to partake, followed by a short tour of the shop.

Information/tours/guides Tours start every 12 minutes and take approximately 1 hour. A free leaflet summarises the exhibition in the lobby before the tour commences. Tours can be taken in English, French, Spanish, Italian, German, Japanese, Dutch and Portuguese.

When to visit Aim to visit in the quieter tourist months (between October and March), or try to arrive earlier rather than later. Everything is indoors so weather is not a factor.

Age appeal Ideal for anyone with an interest in whisky, and best value for the over-18s as the entry price includes a shot of whisky denied to younger patrons. Not really suitable for under-5s.

Food and drink There is a bar with a spectacular range of whiskies and a seating area downstairs in the buffet restaurant area. The choice of foods is fairly good but a bit pricey – quiche and filo parcels (£5.50), baked potatoes (£4.50), cakes and pastries (£1 to £1.50), and tea and coffee (£1 to £2).

Shops The shop is at street level and sells all manner of whisky-related material, from miniatures to Scottish quaichs (£15), hip flasks (£15), glassware (£2.50 to £4.99) and reference books.

🚌 Entry is just by the Castle Esplanade, at the top of the Royal Mile. NCP car park on Castle Terrace 5–10 minutes' walk. ⊖ Walk up Royal Mile (the area is pedestrianised for much of the year). ⊘ Mon to Sun 10am to 5.30pm. Closed 25 Dec. 💷 Adult £5.50; child (5 to 17 yrs old) £2.75; senior citizens, students, disabled £3.85; family ticket (2 adults + up to 4 children) £13.50. ♿ Fully accessible.

Stirling Castle

Stirling SK8 1EG ☎ *(01786) 450000*

Quality ★★★★	Facilities 🏛 🏛 🏛	Value for money ££££

Highlights Splendid Renaissance buildings; good restoration; fine views
Drawbacks Occasionally overcrowded in summer

What's there Stirling Castle, like Edinburgh Castle, is built on a plug of rock rising above the River Forth, at the point where it was first possible to bridge the river in medieval times. This made the castle one of the most strategically significant strongholds in Scotland, and for a great deal of the Middle Ages it was the focus of much of the conflict between Scotland and England. Both the Battles of Stirling Bridge and of Bannockburn were fought virtually under its walls.

It was also a royal residence until the Union of the Crowns, and the scene of much fine building during the reigns of James IV, V and VI. Thereafter it was abandoned to the military for approaching 300 years, until finally being decommissioned in 1964. Now, in one of the most ambitious restoration and reconstruction programmes being undertaken in Scotland, the magnificence of Stirling as the focal point of the Scottish Renaissance court is gradually re-emerging from the utilitarian clutter left behind by the army.

One building – the **Great Hall**, built for James IV around 1503 – has been restored after 35 years' work. Somewhat garish as yet in its peach-coloured cladding, this building has been authentically put back together after years as a barrack block. Now, the entirely new hammerbeam ceiling crowns a room of lofty proportions, complete with wall hangings, embroidery, stained glass and thrones. It looks and smells new, but then so it did 500 years ago. The only modern touch is to be found in the five great fireplaces that still heat the hall. Hot air is now blown down the chimneys.

Next in line is the Palace, built for James V around 1538. This building has many French touches to its architecture, particularly in the statues that garnish the outside walls. The interior once held a panelled ceiling embossed with carved roundels, the '**Stirling Heads**' – wonderfully sculpted and lifelike faces – which are now on display behind glass.

The chapel royal has also been restored – or rather, re-designed, for this now has a distinctively modern interior, with a wooden vaulted ceiling and new oak floor. But the **frieze** painted for Charles I's visit in 1633 still remains.

Apart from these three great buildings, there is much else. Some of it – the wall walks, the batteries of cannon and the various defensive walls – is military in origin, but much, such as the sunny bowling green or the nicely restored kitchens, belongs to Stirling's time as a palace. Within one of the old buildings is the **Regimental Museum** of the Argyll and Sutherland Highlanders, very well laid out, and with its own stories to relate. This part of the castle is also where James II is reputed to have murdered the **Earl of Douglas** and to have thrown his corpse from the window.

In nooks and crannies of the castle, Historic Scotland has laid on various displays, illustrating, for example, the lifestyle of castle artisans in the sixteenth century using models and sound effects. Beneath the Great Hall, an audio-visual display picks through the whole elaborate story of the restoration.

All in all it is a fascinating place, with some magnificent views to go with the history and architecture. It is well run too – very much Historic Scotland's showpiece – and guides are expert and approachable.

Information/tours/guides Guided tours run every 30 minutes during the summer season, and approximately four times daily in winter. They last about an hour, and serve as an excellent introduction, although you cannot hope to see everything during that time. There are two guidebooks, the more expensive (£15.99) probably being more elaborate than most visitors will need. The ordinary guidebook (£2.50) is well designed and very clearly written.

When to visit A clear day is needed to take best advantage of the views. Otherwise, out of season there are many fewer visitors, and parking on the castle esplanade is free.

Age appeal There is nothing much specifically aimed at younger visitors, but there are endless places to explore, and very few of them are out of bounds.

Food and drink A modern café with a small roof terrace for fine days has been craftily inserted among the vaulting of old military storerooms. It makes for an atmospheric, if somewhat corridor-like, place for a quick snack. Filled baguettes (£3.80) and baked potatoes with a variety of fillings (£3.25) are the staples, supplemented by a small range of hot dishes (£3.50 to £4.80).

Shops Stirling Castle has a small gift shop by the entrance, with many of the items branded either for the castle, or for Historic Scotland. Top of the range is a replica broadsword (£250). At the other end, a Stirling Castle tax disc for your car is £1.25. Clan mugs are expensive at £6.95, and Historic Scotland baseball caps (£7.95) are unlikely to be the rage on the streets of the Bronx. However, the Historic Scotland 'Mary Queen of Scots' line of perfumes and pot-pourris (£2.95) is beautifully packaged, and not too outrageously priced. Parents may wish to steer offspring away from the well-crafted and authentic-looking bows and arrows (£5.95) and towards something more appropriate, such as a Stirling Castle eraser (50p).

🚌 From M9 or edge of town, follow signs. Car park on the Esplanade (£2 in summer) may be full in high season at peak hours. Limited on-street parking (metered) available nearby. ⊖ Bus and train connections to Stirling. From town centre, castle is five minutes' walk up a very steep hill. ⊕ April to Sept, Mon to Sun 9.30am to 6pm; Oct to Mar, Mon to Sun 9.30am to 5pm. Closed 25, 26 Dec. 💷 Adult £6; child (5 to 16) £1.50; senior citizens, unemployed £4.50. ♿ Reasonable, considering the nature of the buildings. The restored parts are very good, with suitable ramps, etc., but some of the fortifications and underground parts are not so easy. A new courtesy adapted vehicle runs all day for wheelchair users to get up steep hills.

Urquhart Castle

By Drumnadrochit, Inverness-shire IV63 6XJ　☎ *(01456) 450551*
🖰 *www.historic-scotland.gov.uk*

Quality ★★　　　　　　　**Facilities** 🏛　　　　　　　**Value for money ££**
Highlights Beautiful setting; romantic ruin
Drawbacks Very primitive facilities

What's there After Edinburgh and Stirling, Urquhart is the third most visited castle in Scotland. Its chief draw is its setting, on a promontory thrusting out into the dark waters of Loch Ness. Coincidentally, or not, this is the part of the loch where the **Loch Ness Monster** has most frequently been sighted, and it is fair to say that more visitors are probably drawn to Urquhart by the loch's reputation than by the intrinsic interest of the castle.

Indeed, in comparison to Edinburgh and Stirling Castles, there is little of the fortress left. The crumbling remains of walls, towers and a gatehouse form a romantic foreground to the loch and the hills beyond, and most visitors, military historians excepted, will find the picturesqueness of the site a good deal more interesting than the ruins themselves.

Urquhart does, however, have a long and bloody history. It may have been a stronghold as far back as Pictish times; it most certainly played a leading part in the Scottish Wars of Independence. Later in history it acted as a bulwark against the powerful Lords of the Isles on their periodic invasions from their territories in the west. It finally featured during the first Jacobite rebellion in 1690. Thereafter it was partially destroyed by an explosion and by a storm. What was left was used as a stone quarry.

Despite many additions over time, the castle shows its medieval origins clearly. Entry is over a drawbridge and through a gatehouse, with upper and nether baileys beyond. A portion of the **tower house**, the best preserved part of the ruins, probably dates from the late fourteenth century, although later work transformed the old strongpoint into a more comfortable residence, once the threat of invasion had subsided.

Outside the castle, on a relatively flat piece of ground, where archaeological work is still going on, there is a **model trebuchet** (siege engine) to provide a bit of added interest.

The facilities at Urquhart Castle were swamped by the growing number of visitors years ago. While the protracted process of getting the go-ahead for a total revamp went on they were left in their primitive state, and our ratings reflect this. At the moment, the car park is the worst and most dangerous aspect of the place, with an inadequate number of spaces and a dangerous exit on to a main road. Work on a new Visitor Centre and a proper car park was due to start in December 1999, with a projected completion date of 2001. Disruption during the building works will be kept to a minimum, we are told.

Information/tours/guides There are no guided tours of the castle as such, although there is always at least one custodian on hand willing and able to answer questions. Discreet signs point out the various parts of the castle, but for any in-depth information you will need the souvenir guidebook (£2.50). This provides useful background information about what you are looking at, but is somewhat on the dry side.

When to visit At present, avoid high summer. The sight itself has plenty of room, but the car park and other facilities are likely to be overcrowded.

Age appeal Those who find walking difficult should avoid the castle. The entrance path is steep and long, and there is nowhere pleasant to while away time while more able members of the family are visiting. This is not the best of sights for children either: the trebuchet provides a moment's interest, but there is nothing else in place for a younger audience. There is also a lot of deep water around.

Food and drink Currently a mobile van stationed in the car park is the only catering outlet. It dispenses hot and cold snacks (Lorne sausage £1.50, baked potato and cheese £1.85) and drinks, but the range is inevitably narrow and there is nowhere, apart from your car, to sit down to eat.

Shops Tucked into a corner of the ancient ruins (and doing little to enhance their ambience), Historic Scotland's shop was apparently brought in by helicopter. The limitations of this form of transport mean that the shop is small and a bit cramped. It does, however, have a very wide range of goods for its size. Much is branded, such as the Castle Urquhart sweatshirt (£22.95) or T-shirt (£9.95), and you can buy a model of the building, too (£22.75). Otherwise there is a good range of books on historical subjects (£2 to £5), craft items, and packaged Scottish produce such as clootie dumpling (£3.99), as well as jams and preserves.

🚗 A82 and follow signs. The car park is dangerous. An overflow car park with a shuttle bus was operating when we inspected. ⊖ Most coach tours with a route including Loch Ness will stop at Urquhart Castle. Otherwise a car is the only practical way of getting there. ⊙ Apr to 3rd week Jun, Mon to Sat 9.30am to 6.30pm, Sun 9.30am to 6.30pm; last week Jun to 1st week Sept, 9.30am to 8.30pm; Oct to Mar, Mon to Sat 9.30am to 4.30pm, Sun 9.30am to 4.30pm. Closed 25–26 Dec, 1–2 Jan. 💷 Adult £3.80; child (5 to 15 yrs) £1.20; senior citizens, unemployed £2.80; group discount 10% (groups over 11). Entry free for holders of the Scottish Explorer Ticket issued by Historic Scotland. Free to disabled people. ♿ Disabled access is very difficult, with an extremely steep path down the hill to the castle. Access to the toilets (ironically, equipped for disabled people) is nearly impossible, as a steep flight of wooden steps is involved.

Vikingar!

Barrfields, Greenock Road, Largs, Ayrshire KA30 8QL ☎ *(01475) 689777*
📠 *(01475) 689444* 💻 *www.vikingar.co.uk*

Quality ★★★★ **Facilities** 🏛 🏛 🏛 **Value for money £££**

Highlights Good, imaginative multi-media historical experience; very enjoyable for children

Drawbacks A primary-school hotspot; not enough here for a full day out

---

What's there Largs is a seaside resort on the Ayrshire coast, known for its bracing climate and its excellent ice cream. It also happens to have been the site of a crucial battle between the Scots and the Norsemen in 1263, which proved decisive in settling the question of which nation was to dominate the western seaboard of Scotland. This far-off battle is the excuse for this attraction's location.

Like its closest relative, Jorvik in York, Vikingar! is more of an experience than a museum. Tours are conducted by costumed guides, and move through a series of rooms where **different aspects of Viking society** are brought to life. Vikingar's appeal is directed mainly at primary-school parties, but this is not to say that adults cannot benefit too. The experience is carefully planned, using props (helmets and spears), sound, light and models very effectively, and culminating in a dramatically narrated audio-visual presentation. The final room on the tour is a kind of **interactive museum**, where visitors are left to answer for themselves the questions about the Vikings that the rest of the experience may not have touched on. Home life, religion and the Vikings' impact on Scotland are the main themes. While Vikingar! pitches its material carefully at the level of the primary-school project, there is enough of it, in a sufficiently dramatic context, for almost anyone to find enjoyable.

This is a relatively small sight, and the tour itself lasts less than an hour, even if you spend time in the museum. But it is good for a morning or afternoon's diversion, especially if you have primary-age children with you. Tours run every half-hour during the summer months, and every hour during the winter.

Vikingar! is part of a complex that also includes the local cinema, fitness centre and swimming pool, so the surroundings and facilities belong in the municipal-leisure-centre class rather than to anything grander. Everything is housed in a modern building tacked on to an old cinema – pleasant enough, but not outstanding.

Information/tours/guides The brochure for Vikingar! is attractively produced and packed with information, including maps and entry prices. There is also a very good-value souvenir guide for £1.50, which is exceptionally well designed and illustrated, even if you do not actually need it for the tour. The web site, too, is worth a visit for only slightly over-the-top tasters of what the attraction is like.

Vikingar's guides put in a polished performance, not allowing the repetitive nature of the job to show in their delivery, and taking time to get children to respond.

When to visit Visiting in summer means less hanging about waiting for a tour, and means too that the location on the edge of the Firth of Clyde will show up to best advantage. If you go too far out of season, either there will be hordes of schoolchildren, or else you may be on your own (which could be an embarrassment on a personally guided tour). Summer is also the time of the Largs Viking Festival, with a Viking Village, fireworks and many other events. Telephone for details.

Age appeal The chief appeal is to children from eight upwards, but any adult should find enough to interest him- or herself here.

Food and drink The Winter Garden Café is too grand a title for a few tables and chairs cordoned off from the rest of the world by some large potted palms. That aside, this is a plain, no-frills snack bar with reasonably priced food, such as a bacon roll (£1) or baked potatoes (£1.30 to £2.20). There's no sign of the Viking 'themed cuisine' promised in the leaflet, but perhaps that's just as well. (At the time of going to press the café was closed and vending machines were on site instead.)

Shops The shop is a small display area directly opposite the exit from the Experience. It is not large, and not brilliantly lit, but it has an interesting range, and makes a worthy attempt at linking many of its souvenirs and gifts to the Viking theme. Thus there is good imitation Viking pottery (about £10.50) and jewellery (£4.99). Figurines retail for £3.10. As well as these special items, there are plenty of branded goods, such as mugs (£2.99). As is to be expected, there are plenty of souvenirs and small gifts for children, some of them worthy and educational, others just fun.

🚗 In Largs, follow signs (signs are scarce outside town). Large car park outside the building. ⊖ Train to Largs from Glasgow, then 10-minute walk (or take local bus or taxi). ⏲ Apr to Sept, Mon to Sun 10.30am to 5.30pm; Oct and Mar, Mon to Sun 10.30am to 3.30pm; Nov to Feb, Sat and Sun 10.30am to 3.30pm. Closed 23 Dec–3 Jan. 💷 Adult £3.75; child (4 to 15 yrs old) £2.85; senior citizen £2.75; family ticket (2 adults + 2 children or 1 adult + 3 children) £10.50; group discount 10% (pre-booked groups). ♿ Access is good, with ramps where needed, separate access away from the revolving doors, and everything on one level.

WALES

Anglesey Sea Zoo

Brynsiencyn, Isle of Anglesey LL61 6TQ ☎ *(01248) 430411*
📠 *(01248) 430213* 🖥 *www.nwi.co.uk/seazoo*

Quality ★★★★   **Facilities** 🏛 🏛 🏛 🏛   **Value for money £££**
Highlights Innovative presentation; very educational for children
Drawbacks Not much for adults unaccompanied by children

What's there The Sea Zoo sets out to present information on the marine life around the Isle of Anglesey through a series of imaginative and innovative themed exhibits with a strong emphasis on the environment and conservation. A well-organised route begins between the pier, where you can watch dogfish playing beneath your feet, and the **ray pool**, before passing through the bone-free zone (devoted to invertebrates), and a breeding/conservation area (where **sea horses and lobsters** are reared as part of a captive breeding programme).

The next stop is the **shipwreck**, where you can wander among the tanks and timbers in search of conger eels as though you were exploring one of the myriad wrecks surrounding the island.

Following the shipwreck are wave pools, in which regular breakers dramatically re-create a shoreline habitat; **touch pools** for a hands-on feel of life in the rock pools; and a **'fish forest'** behind a single huge acrylic pane, where you can sit and listen to ambient music while watching teeming multitudes of wrasse and pollack glide among the kelp. In addition, a huge shallow pool allows you to walk just inches above the water on a series of walkways while the fish swim freely about.

There are several educational sections designed for children, where they can learn, for instance, about environmental pollution. Outside are remote-controlled boats, an Aquablasta, an adventure playground, a picnic area, and, in summer, children's go-karts.

Information/tours/guides Plenty of information boards explain the significance of the displays, many of which incorporate audio commentaries by David Bellamy. There is also an attractively presented and reasonably priced guide (£2.50) that expands on the display boards – in both English and Welsh – and includes a pull-out activity section aimed at young children.

When to visit All year, as all the exhibits are under cover. The sight is too well-organised to become very overcrowded in summer.

Age appeal With its simple presentation the Sea Zoo is designed very much with children and families in mind.

Food and drink The tropically themed and attractive Blue Island Coffee Shop offers a wide selection of high-quality snacks, such as New Covent Garden soup with cheese-and-onion bread (£2.50), and more substantial fare such as jacket potato with chicken, bacon and sweetcorn (£2.95) – as well as an excellent cup of coffee (95p) – against a backdrop of clown fish and piranha.

Shops A well-laid-out gift shop has a range of gifts, including fish-inspired ceramics (£3.50 to £16.95), soft toys and confectionery, as well as plenty of books. There is also a pearl shop where you can select your own oyster (guaranteed to contain a pearl) for £12.95, or have the pearl set in gold or silver while you wait (£19.95 to £39.95).

From the A55, cross the Britannia Bridge on to Anglesey, then follow the brown lobster signs from there towards Brynsiencyn. The Zoo is about 10 minutes from Llanfairpwll. ⊖ Bus from Bangor to the Sea Zoo throughout the year (ring zoo for details). Buses also run to the nearby village of Brynsiencyn (about 20 minutes' walk). ⊙ Mar to Oct, 10am to 6pm (last admission 5pm); Nov to Feb, 11am to 4pm (last admission 3pm). Closed 25 and 26 Dec, 1 Jan and some of Dec; phone for details. 💷 Adult £5.50; child (3 to 16 yrs old) £4.50; senior citizen £5.50; family ticket (2 adults + 2 children) £17.95, (2 adults + 3 children) £19.95, (1 adult + 2 children) £12.95, (1 adult + 3 children) £14.95; unemployed visitor £13.50. *Season tickets* adult £16.50, child £13.50, senior citizen/student £15.50, family ticket (2 adults + 2 children) £53.85, (2 adults + 3 children) £59.85. ♿ The zoo is entirely on one level and provides disabled access throughout.

Big Pit Mining Museum

Blaenafon, Gwent NP4 9XP ☎ *(01495) 790311*

Quality ★★★★★ **Facilities** 🎫🎫🎫 **Value for money** £££££
Highlights Underground tour; vivid, informative exhibitions on the coal-mining industry in South Wales
Drawbacks Indifferent catering

What's there The scarred hillsides and sculpted spoilheaps of the Lwyd Valley near Abergavenny provide a vivid record of the scale and importance of coal-mining and ironstone-working in this part of south-east Wales. The Big Pit is a real colliery, opened as a tourist attraction when coal production stopped in 1980. This imaginative venture gives one of the most authentic 'industrial heritage' experiences anywhere in Wales.

The highlight of a visit is an **underground tour** through the old mine-workings, escorted and colourfully anecdoted by former colliers. Visitors don helmets and lamps, then descend more than 300 feet in the original pit-cage for an hour-long trudge through tunnels and coal-faces. Back up top, there is much to see in the old colliery buildings and surface machinery. You can wander freely through the winding engine-house (try to see it working when the tour parties are lowered or lifted), the blacksmith's workshop and the **pithead baths,** where an excellent exhibition evokes the reality of a fascinating but grim and dangerous industry.

The original buildings still retain much of their starkly uncompromising appearance: the miners' canteen has been converted to a café and the fitting shop cleverly remodelled into a reception block and gift shop.

Allow at least half a day to do this compelling attraction full justice.

Information/tours/guides The excellent full-colour guidebook costs £1.50, although a simpler visitor guide with a numbered site plan costs 50p. Education packs are also available. The worthwhile exhibition on coal-mining in the pithead baths uses display boards, touch-screen information and audio-visual presentations. The underground tour with ex-colliery workers, included in the ticket price, is well organised, informative and thoroughly entertaining. Expect plenty of unflattering remarks on Tory governments of yesteryear! Wear warm clothing and sturdy footwear for the tour. Tours run from 10am to 3.30pm. All dry-cell watches, mobile phones and tape recorders are banned underground and must be handed over for safe keeping. Points of interest above ground are numbered for easy reference.

When to visit Weather isn't a major factor for this mainly underground attraction, though you will need to spend some time in the open air. Summer holidays are the busiest periods.

Age appeal All age groups will be fascinated by this attraction. Special efforts are made to interest children, but there's a height restriction of 1 metre for safety reasons (visitors must be able to carry a hefty 5kg safety pack and wear a helmet). Children should be supervised as the winding gear and rusting, disused machinery could be dangerous. The underground tour is not especially arduous or alarming, but may be unsuitable for those who suffer from claustrophobia.

Food and drink The rugged miners' canteen is now a café serving snacks, sandwiches and drinks, and in the self-service restaurant in the pithead baths you'll find a basic range of hot food (chicken, chips and peas; apple pie). The range and quality of catering could be vastly improved – our inspection meal was very disappointing, though the staff are very welcoming.

Shops The light, attractive gift shop near the ticket entrance sells a good range of souvenirs, many geared towards industrial heritage: local guidebooks and history books, models of coal-miners and machinery carved from coal, tapes and calendars. You can even buy a mini-sack of coal for 75p.

🚗 From M4 junction 26 eastbound, or junction 25 westbound, take A465 to Blaenafon. From town follow pictogram sign (pithead winding gear). Car parking available. ⊖ Take bus (Phil Anslow Travel) from Newport to Big Pit (runs roughly every 2 hrs from 8.50am in the summer, Mon to Sat). Alternatively, take bus from Abergavenny to Big Pit (at 10.30am on Tues, Fri, Sat, returning at 4.55pm). ◷ End May to Nov, daily 9.30am to 5pm; Dec to Feb by arrangement only (maintenance work may make access impossible). 💷 Including underground tour (without underground tour): adult £5.75 (£2), child (5 to 16 yrs old) £3.95 (£1), senior citizen £5.50 (£1.75), family ticket (2 adults + 2 children) £17. Discounts available for groups of 10 plus. ♿ Wheelchair users can take the underground tour, but should ring in advance for further advice. Parts of the site may require assistance (steep in places). Disabled toilets.

Bodnant Garden

Tal-y-cafn, Colwyn Bay, North Wales LL28 5RE ☎ *(01492) 650460* 📟 *www.oxalis.co.uk/bodnant.htm*

Quality ★★★	Facilities 👍👍👍👍	Value for money £££

Highlights Beautiful stepped Italianate terraces with views over the Conwy Valley to the Snowdon Mountains

Drawbacks Suggested route around the gardens not clearly signposted

---

What's there In their present form the gardens at Bodnant are largely the inspiration of two men – the wealthy chemist Henry Davis Pochin, who purchased the estate in 1874, and his grandson, another Henry, the late Lord Aberconway (the title was originally granted to Charles McLaren MP who had married Pochin's daughter and heiress). The extensive gardens, which take full advantage of their dramatic situation on sloping ground overlooking the River Conwy, as well as the more distant peaks of the Snowdonia range beyond, are made up of two principal parts: the upper garden, consisting of the Terrace Gardens and informal lawns, and the lower garden, or 'Dell', containing the Pinetum and Wild Garden. Lord Aberconway firmly believed in using plants well adapted to their conditions, and it is this philosophy that underlies Bodnant's varied collection.

The highlight of the upper gardens are the formal **Terrace Gardens** developed by Lord Aberconway in Italian style, and it is from here that the magnificent views of the mountains to the west are to be had. Part of the success of the five terraces, with their immaculately tended flowers and hedges, is due to the fact that they were designed to incorporate important existing features, such as the two beautiful cedars that now flank the lily pond. At the bottom of the sequence, the **Canal Terrace** contains a long rectangular pond that lies between a relocated pin mill at one end and an open-air stage flanked by wings of clipped yew at the other.

The **Dell** occupies the low-lying ground around the River Hiraethlyn, a tributary of the Conwy, and is reached from the terraces via a path running through the dramatically landscaped Rockery, which makes good use of plentiful running water – as you descend, it is worth pausing to admire the view of the elegant, Italianate Old Mill. The Dell itself derives its unique character from the enormous conifers planted by Pochin on both banks – their bare trunks rise from well-maintained lawns and convey a secluded and majestic air.

Information/tours/guides A beautifully designed full-colour guidebook offers a suggested tour through the garden with descriptions of all the plants, as well as a potted history of Bodnant and a map. Otherwise, there are no guides or explanations, though a simple wander may be enjoyable if there is plenty of time.

When to visit Obviously the garden changes throughout the year, but Bodnant's substantial collection has been designed to ensure colour and interest at all times. A particular feature to look out for in late May and early June is the Laburnum Walk, where cascades of fiery blossom plummet through the arched frames.

Age appeal The garden has nothing specifically aimed at youngsters, although, with 80 acres to explore, it provides plenty of space to stretch legs and run about.

Food and drink A tastefully designed, cedar-shingled refreshment pavilion offers hot drinks, light lunches and afternoon teas from a menu of locally prepared food. Lunches include filled jacket potatoes (£2.95), Welsh steak pie (£4.55), quiche (£4.55) and a cold buffet with sandwiches (£1.95) and salads (£4.45). Sweets, ices and cold drinks are available from an adjoining kiosk.

Shops A first-class garden shop sells many of the plants at Bodnant, enhancing the visit of any keen horticulturalist. The shop also does mail order, which can be accessed through the Bodnant web site.

🚗 From the A55, take the A470 and follow signs to the garden (eight miles south of Llandudno and Colwyn Bay). ⊖ Take train to Llandudno Junction, then branch line to Tal-y-Cafn (1½ miles from the garden). Alternatively take the Arriva Cymru bus 25 from Llandudno, which also passes Llandudno Junction railway station (tel (01492) 575412 for details). ⏰ 1999 prices: Adult £4.60; child (5 to 16 yrs old) £2.30; free entry to National Trust members. ♿ Several wheelchairs are available free of charge and the guidebook contains an alternative route avoiding steps and steep slopes. Braille guidebooks are also available. A specially adapted toilet can be found adjacent to the Refreshment Pavilion, and there are ramps at the entrances to the Garden, Plant Centre and Refreshment Pavilion.

Caernarfon Castle

Castle Ditch, Caernarfon, Gwyneth, North Wales LL55 2AY
☎ *(01286) 677617* 🖥 *www.castlewales.com/caernarf.html*

Quality ★ ★ ★ ★ ★ **Facilities 🏠 🏠 🏠 🏠** **Value for money ££££**
Highlights Beautiful castle; fascinating regimental museum
Drawbacks Internal signs are slightly confusing in places

What's there Caernarfon Castle was built by Edward I after the defeat of Llywelyn in 1283 as part of his 'iron ring' of castles intended to pacify North Wales. The castle was designed by Master James of St George, who was also responsible for Edward's other Welsh castles (*see* Conwy Castle). Construction on Caernarfon began quickly (in 1284), although the work, which took place in two phases separated by the Welsh revolt of 1294, continued until 1330. This magnificent castle, one of the very finest examples of **medieval military architecture**, was built as the administrative capital for the three new shires of Gwynedd. It was intended to be a monument to the power of the English king, echoing the grandeur of Rome in its colour-banded walls and unique polygonal towers, which were inspired by the walls of Constantinople.

From the first, the castle has played a considerable role in British history. In 1284 it was the birthplace of Edward I's son, the Black Prince, who in 1301 became the first Prince of Wales. The traditional link between the two has continued to the present day – the current Prince of Wales was invested at Caernarfon in 1969. The castle has also withstood five sieges since its completion, two of them by Owain Glyn Dwr and his French allies in 1403 and 1404, and the other three during the Civil War.

The castle's indomitable walls and towers have remained largely untram-melled by the ravages of time, and the site received considerable attention from restorers during the nineteenth century, when Caernarfon played a significant part in the booming slate industry. Today, besides the stupendous towers and battlements, visitors can see several exhibitions in refurbished towers. In the Queen's Tower the **Regimental Museum of the Royal Welsh Fusiliers** offers a fascinating and colourful insight into the history of Wales's longest serving infantry regiment, with plenty of uniforms, flags, medals and arms, as well as first-hand footage from the Boer War. The Tower of the Eagles houses an exhibition on the ground floor entitled 'Chieftains and Princes', which looks at Welsh history from the earliest human habitation to the present day. On the first floor an evocative audio-visual presentation, the 'Eagle and the Dragon', which is primarily aimed at children, narrates the story of Caernarfon.

Information/tours/guides Information boards with diagrams and reconstructions reveal the most important aspects of the castle, while the audio-visual show offers more details about its history. There are also guided tours for those who prefer a more personal, interactive approach. The exhibitions are both clearly and informatively presented. The good-value guide (£2.75) is packed with details.

When to visit The castle is most enjoyable in fine weather, although the indoor exhibitions do help to make a visit rewarding at all times. Stairwells may become congested in high season.

Age appeal This classic castle will appeal to all ages and the various displays on offer are designed to inform adults and children alike.

Food and drink No drinks or food available.

Shops The small shop, housed just inside the main gate, is attractively arranged, selling a range of historical merchandise, including Welsh love spoons, ceramics, jewellery, model soldiers, books and prints.

🚐 On A55 to Caernarfon, follow signs. ⊖ Train to Bangor station, then bus. ① Mon to Sat, 27 Mar to 26 May and 2 to 29 Oct, 9.30am to 5pm; 27 May to 10 Oct, 9.30am to 6pm; 2 Nov to 26 Mar, 9.30am to 4pm; Sun 11am to 4pm. 💷 Adult £4.20, senior citizen/student/child (5 to 16 yrs old) £3.20, family ticket (2 adults + 3 children) £11.60, child (under 5 yrs old) and member of the Heritage in Wales free. ♿ Very limited access for wheelchairs.

Cardiff Castle

Castle Street, Cardiff CF10 3RB ☎ *029-2087 8100*

Quality ★ ★ ★ ★ **Facilities** 🏛 🏛 🏛 **Value for money ££££**
Highlights Superb neo-Gothic interiors; excellent guided tour
Drawbacks Poor shop; no parking facilities

What's there This eye-catching council-run amenity in the heart of the city offers a variety of attractions: a **medieval fortress** on Roman foundations, a magnificent example of High Victorian decorative style, tranquil grounds and two Welsh regimental museums. The oldest surviving parts are the moated Norman keep, and a 10-foot-thick stretch of the original Roman wall, visible from an underground viewing gallery decorated with modern sculpture friezes. Most of the present castle, however, is the result of ambitious remodelling work undertaken by the inconceivably wealthy 3rd Marquess of Bute, who inherited the castle in the mid-nineteenth century.

Teaming up with the Gothic Revival architect William Burges in 1865, Lord

Bute transformed Cardiff Castle (which was for him a mere holiday home) into one of the most extraordinary buildings of the age, a **neo-Gothic extravaganza** of dazzling colours and patterns. A dozen or so of these astonishing interiors can be visited on a guided tour, and these, more than anything else, justify the entrance charge. Each room seems more startling than the last: highlights include the **Arab Room**, the **Summer Smoking Room**, the **Banqueting Hall**, the **Library** and **Lord Bute's Bedroom**.

After the tour, the rest of the castle is something of an anticlimax. There are some points of historic interest in the **two military museums** dedicated to the Welch Regiment and the Queen's Dragoon Guards, whose battle honours read like a roll-call of Britain's finest military hours – Blenheim, Ramillies, Oudenarde, Malplaquet, Waterloo and El Alamein. Notice the winsomely carved **Animal Wall** that surrounds the castle grounds on the street side.

Allow half a day to see everything, including a guided tour, a walk round Castle Green (mostly mown grass with spring bulbs and strolling peacocks), the museums and Roman wall, a battlement walk and a climb up the keep.

Information/tours/guides Guidebooks are on sale at the gift shop or information point near the main entrance – the best one costs £2.75. Interiors are accessible only if you go on a conducted tour lasting 50 minutes; you may have to wait at busy times, but you can find plenty else to see if there is a queue. Check the time shown on your ticket, and the time of the last tour (an hour or so before closing). The tour we experienced was excellent – lively, informative and well organised, with a most helpful guide.

When to visit Summer weekends and bank holidays can be very crowded. Not all sections are open every day; civic functions may mean some of the castle rooms are inaccessible from time to time. Ring ahead to check and also ask about special events.

Age appeal Cardiff Castle should be popular with all the family, but there's quite a lot of walking with many steps (no lifts), so it is not ideal for very young children or visitors with limited mobility. The keep tower steps are particularly steep and could be dangerous in wet or icy weather. Children should be supervised near the moat and battlements.

Food and drink The self-service tea rooms are in the basement of the Bute Tower, a pleasantly traditional setting of lacy cloths and bentwood chairs. Tables are set outside in summer. A limited range of sandwiches, cakes, scones, ices, pasties and drinks is available. Staff are agreeable, but the choice of fare is not riveting. A few local specialities include Welsh cakes, bara brith (fruit tea bread) and elderflower spritzer.

Shops The small gift shop near the entrance gate (accessible without paying the entrance charge) is cramped and unsuitable for the large number of visitors the castle receives. Products on sale are mostly of the 'Made in Wales' variety – lovespoons, fudge, dragons, Celtic mug mats, Welsh gold rings, 'Horrible History' books on the more lurid aspects of medieval life, and CD recordings of 'Land of My Fathers'. If you want a guidebook or some postcards, buy them here or at the information office rather than at the ticket kiosk. The regimental museums have their own little shops selling military mementoes.

🚐 Cardiff city centre, follow signs. No car parking at castle. Park at multistorey in Westgate (£3.10 for 3 hrs; 5 mins walk to castle). ⊖ Train to Cardiff Central station or National Express coach to main bus station, then 15 mins walk, or a local bus ride (tel: Cardiff Bus on 029-2039 6521). ◷ In 1999: *Castle Green, Roman Wall, keep, museums* Mar to Oct, Mon to Sun, 9.30am to 6pm; Nov to Feb, Mon to Sun, 9.30am to 4.30pm. *Castle interior (tours)* Mar to Oct, Mon to Sun, 10am to 5pm (every 20 mins); Nov to Feb, 10.30am to 3.15pm (5–6 per day). Closed 25 and 26 Dec; Welch Regiment Museum closed Tuesday; Queen's Dragoon Guards Museum closed Friday. 🎟 *Castle tour and grounds* (separate fee for just *grounds, wall, keep, museum*) adult £5 (£2.50), child (5 to 16 yrs old) and senior citizen £3 (£1.50), student £4 (£2), family ticket (2 adults + 3 children or 1 adult + 4 children) £14 (£7). No charge for wheelchair users. Group discounts available; reduced admission charged if parts of interior are inaccessible and only a short tour is possible. ♿ Wheelchair access to Castle Green only. A video presentation of the castle tour can be watched free of charge (ask for details at information point). Disabled toilet.

Centre for Alternative Technology

Machynlleth, Powys SY20 9AZ   ☎ *(01654) 702400*   ⓨ *www.cat.org.uk*

Quality ★★★★	**Facilities** 🗲🗲🗲🗲🗲	**Value for money ££**

Highlights   A great demonstration of how sustainable energy can work in practice; especially valuable for children; excellent shop

Drawbacks   Much of the sight is designed to function rather than to be viewed and understood; probably works much better for residential courses

What's there   Established in 1975 on the site of an abandoned slate quarry, the Centre for Alternative Technology explores and researches methods of providing sustainable energy. In its seven acres of grounds, the centre allows visitors to see those 'alternative' technologies in operation, as well as demonstrating ways in which we can all choose to lead more ecologically balanced lifestyles.

As the centre is perched high up on the cliff face, most visits are likely to begin with a ride on the **cliff railway** that ascends at a 35 per cent incline, powered by nothing but tanks of water. (However, the railway is closed during the winter and entry fees are, accordingly, lower.) At the top there is a short video introducing the centre and its aims, closely followed by a range of examples of **self-build constructions** and **high-efficiency insulation systems**, including a house built entirely from straw bales. Nestling among these buildings are the 'whole home' and 'whole garden' exhibits, which seek to explain through a series of information boards how the homes we live in and the food we eat must be seen in terms of their total 'embodied energy'.

The visitors' route goes on to explore a host of variations on the themes of solar power, water power and wind power, with meters displaying how much energy the various methods on trial are producing. Interactive displays include an opportunity to produce the waves to power a generator and to see how clouds directly influence solar energy.

The grounds also include abundant **organic gardens** with plentiful ideas about making compost, a fishpond, a lake to feed the cliff railway, and a small-holding where visitors can meet the chickens, ducks, geese and goats.

Of particular interest to children will be the **Mole-Hole**, a large tunnel in which visitors can imagine that they have been shrunk down to meet the denizens under the ground, including ants, bacteria and a very savage-looking mole – children can even poke their heads out through the ground. There is also an adventure playground built from natural resources and a **transport maze** where children can learn about the benefits of cycling and public transport.

Information/tours/guides There are no guided tours, but the knowledgeable staff are happy to talk about any aspect of the centre. The sight also includes plenty of explanatory boards, while the useful guidebook is packed with information about the various displays, as well as ideas to tackle planetary enemies ranging from the hole in the ozone layer to global inequalities of wealth.

When to visit The centre is spread over a large, open area and few of the exhibits are under cover, so it is best to visit in fine weather. Crowds are unlikely to be a problem.

Age appeal Although the sight has reasonably good general appeal, most of the displays are specifically targeted towards children, and many adults are unlikely to find much that is new to them here.

Food and drink A spacious and leafy restaurant offers vegetarian meals prepared from fresh, unprocessed, largely organic ingredients. Main dishes all cost £4.50, come with a salad, and include such wholesome offerings as butterbean crumble, quarry pie and pasta bakes. For dessert you can have strawberries and cream (£1.50), and an enticing range of fruit wines to accompany your food (£6.75 a bottle or £1.75 a glass) is available. However, there is no coffee – not even organic!

Shops Far more than just a place to purchase souvenirs, the shop has a huge range of eco-products – from a device to make burnable logs out of old newspapers (£29.95), to savaplugs designed to minimise energy consumption (£29.99) – as well as a fantastic selection of books that provides an A-Z of how to go about embarking on an alternative lifestyle. The shop also does mail order. Well worth a visit.

🚗 From A487 or A484 to Dolgellau, follow signs. Centre is 3 miles north of Machynlleth. ⊖ Train to Machynlleth, then taxi or bus to centre. Alternatively hire a bike from the bike shop in the centre of town. ⊙ *Centre* 1 Nov to end May, 10am to 4pm; 1 Apr to end Oct, 10am to 5pm. Closed 3 days at Christmas, 3 weeks in January. 💷 *Summer* Adult £6.90; child (5 to 16 yrs old) £3.50; student £4.30; senior citizen/unemployed visitor £4.90; family ticket (2 adults + 4 children) £19.50; discount for visitors walking or cycling more than 2 miles to get to the centre. *Winter* Adult £4.90; child £2.50; senior citizen/unemployed visitor £3.40; family ticket £13.40. ♿ Full access. Disabled visitors are permitted to use the drive to the left of the car park and park at the top when the cliff railway is not working (it is closed from 31 Oct to end Mar).

Conwy Castle

Rosehill Street, Conwy Borough LL32 8LD ☎ *(01492) 592358*
☞ *www.cadw.wales.gov.uk*

Quality ★ ★ ★   **Facilities** 📷 📷 📷   **Value for money £££**
Highlights   Well-preserved classic medieval castle
Drawbacks   Badly maintained and very basic toilet facilities; no on-site refreshments

What's there Conwy Castle was built by Edward I at the end of the thirteenth century as part of his 'iron ring' of castles around Snowdonia following the defeat of the Welsh prince Llywelyn in 1283. The castle was designed by Master James of St George, a military architect from Savoy, and is one of the finest examples of medieval fortification. Founded on a substantial outcrop of rock, the castle consists of two more-or-less separate parts – the inner and outer wards – surrounded by eight identical and magnificent towers. Following a complex history, including involvement in the Civil War, the castle has lost all of its internal refinements – including the once-gleaming white plaster – but still retains an imposing air in its formidable stone walls.

Although bypassing the site of the original drawbridge, the modern entrance via the west barbican still takes visitors through the **main gate**. As you pass through, even a casual glance cannot fail to take in the enfilading arrow loops, 'murder holes' and the original siting of a whole series of doors and portcullises that would have brought intruders' lives to short and brutal conclusions. Once inside, you can explore the two wards, including what remains of the great hall and royal apartments. It is also possible to climb to the tops of six of the eight towers and wander round the battlements. The towers forming the corners of the inner ward are surmounted by additional turrets, atop which you will find fantastic views of the surrounding coast and mountains. The most interesting towers are the **Prison Tower**, which contained a secret dungeon accessible only via a trapdoor, and the **Chapel Tower**, where a refloored chamber with some surviving plaster leads to the remains of a beautiful little chancel.

There is also a small exhibition in the reception outside the castle that examines the strategy behind Edward's 'iron ring' of fortifications, as well as looking at the sources of labour and the building methods of the time. A life-size reconstruction shows labourers working on the unusual spiral scaffolding that was used to construct the towers.

Information/tours/guides Information boards are scattered throughout the castle, providing descriptions of most of the important aspects, as well as reconstructions of how it might have looked. There are also informative guided tours, but the excellent-value guidebook (£2.75), packed with photographs, reconstructions and history, contains its own tour of the site.

When to visit Irregular special events, such as storytelling tours, may be worth finding out about; otherwise, the castle is more enjoyable in dry weather. Stairwells may become cramped during high season.

Age appeal The castle has no specific age appeal, and although there is nothing aimed particularly at children, they may well find the imposing façade of a classic castle more than enough.

Food and drink No drinks or food available on site.

Shops A small but pleasantly organised shop by the reception sells a range of historically themed souvenirs, including ceramics, jewellery, books and model knights.

Other facilities The toilets are not well maintained.

🚗 From the A55 or B5106, follow the signs. Pay and display parking adjacent. ⊖ Train to Conwy station (request stop), a minute's walk to castle. ⊙ Mon to Sat, 29 Mar to 21 May, 9.30am to 5pm; Mon to Sun, 22 May to 3 Oct, 9.30am to 6pm; Mon to Sat, 4 to 31 Oct, 9.30am to 5pm; 1 Nov to 28 Mar, 9.30am to 4pm; Sun, 11am to 4pm. Closed 24–26 Dec, 1 Jan. 🎫 Adult £3.50, senior citizen/student £2.50, family ticket (2 adults + 3 children) £9.50, child (under 5 yrs old) and members of Heritage in Wales free; discount for English Heritage members. ♿ Access to the wards is possible, but short flight of steps separating the inner ward; access to towers and battlements very difficult as steep flights of stairs.

Erddig Hall

Wrexham LL13 0YT ☎ *(01978) 355314*

Quality ★★★ **Facilities 🏚🏚🏚🏚🏚** **Value for money £££**

Highlights Beautiful antiques; fascinating insight into life at the turn of the nineteenth century; lovely grounds

Drawbacks A slightly herded feel in the house; no information in the interior

---

What's there Erddig was originally built in the 1680s for Joshua Edisbury, High Sheriff of Denbighshire, but it was not long before crippling debts forced him into bankruptcy. In 1716 the house was bought by John Meller, a wealthy London lawyer, who was responsible for adding the two wings, extending the gardens and filling the house with the finest furniture of the period. The house eventually passed to John's nephew, Simon Yorke, in 1733 and remained in the possession of the Yorke family for over 200 years. It suffered considerable neglect during the second half of the twentieth century and was offered to the National Trust in 1973. Since then it has been painstakingly restored and now offers a fascinating glimpse into the life of a self-sufficient country house at the turn of the nineteenth century, when Erddig was last a family home.

Reflecting an emphasis on social history, the visitors' entrance winds through various yards, in which much of the day-to-day functioning of the estate would have taken place – in the **kennel yard**, a whole kitchen was devoted to feeding the estate dogs. Before you enter the house itself, there is an engaging 10-minute audio-visual presentation on the restoration process, as well as an exhibition on the Yorke family in the former dairy.

The tour of the house begins with the '**below stairs**' section of the lower ground floor, which includes the kitchen, agent's office, housekeeper's room and the remarkable servants' hall, where two sets of **portraits** from the 1790s and 1830 preserve the likenesses of various members of staff – each painting also contains a scroll bearing illuminating doggerel verses recording the duties and character of the particular individual.

To continue 'upstairs', you need to have purchased an all-inclusive ticket. It is worthwhile doing this, as the house is packed with beautiful examples of early eighteenth-century and Regency furniture, as well as family portraits and all sorts of rather kitsch but fabulous ornaments, such as the mother-of-pearl model of the ruins of Palmyra. There is also a striking four-poster **State Bed**, bought by John Meller in 1720 – now kept behind a protective glass panel – but you will need to be small to see the carved bird beneath the canopy. Near the exit, a small exhibition in the Tribes Room is devoted to Philip Yorke III and his struggle to preserve Erddig.

To the east of the house is a lovely, well-regimented garden designed for John Meller. It is a rare example of the Dutch-influenced formal style fashionable in Britain around 1700 that, with its emphasis on simplicity and horticulture, stood in marked contrast to the grander gardens of Italy and France.

Information/tours/guides There are no guided tours, but visitors are directed through the house by a host of room stewards, who are more than happy to answer any queries and discuss aspects of the house in greater depth. Most of the staff are volunteers, who, like the servants of old, work at the house for its pleasant atmosphere rather than financial reward.

The weighty guidebook (£4.50) is packed with information about the house, but a much cheaper and perfectly adequate alternative is the fold-out pamphlet (20p), which contains maps of the building, as well as descriptions of the rooms and a brief history of the sight. A second fold-out pamphlet is devoted to the garden and contains full descriptions and a large map on the reverse (80p).

When to visit Erddig is suitable to visit throughout the year, though the gardens are best enjoyed in fine weather and some parts of the house could become quite congested in high season.

The Tapestry Room and Chinese Room are open only on Wednesdays and Sundays.

Age appeal Children are unlikely to find much to interest them in the house, but will probably enjoy the grounds.

Food and drink A tasteful self-service restaurant decked out in seasoned pine serves 'simple Georgian and Welsh fare' and makes extensive use of recipes from the Yorke family archives. Offerings range from a carrot and vegetable soup (£2.35) to such mouthwatering main courses as Welsh Lobscouse – lamb casserole with leeks served with soda bread (£5.85) – and Tatws Llaeth – potatoes with buttermilk served with trout and parsley tart (£3.95), while puddings might include 'Sir Watkin Williams Wynne's Steamed Lemon Pudding' or Snowdonia traditional ice cream. You can follow the restoration process through a series of arty black-and-white photos arranged around the walls. Service is polite and efficient.

Shops The carefully arranged shop sells a range of merchandise loosely tied in with the stately home theme, such as period-style jewellery, silk scarves and ties (£20 to £50), smart mugs (£5.99 to £10) and an array of literature. There is also a garden shop.

🚗 From A483 and A525, follow signs to house (2 miles south of Wrexham). ⊖ Train to Wrexham Central (½ mile from house) or Wrexham General (1 mile from house), then walk via Erddig Road and footpath. Alternatively, bus from Wrexham bus station to Felin Puleston (to avoid walking) – tel. (01978) 266166. ⏰ *House* 25 Mar to Sept, Sat to Wed 12pm to 5pm; Oct, Sat to Wed 12pm to 4pm. Closed Nov to late Mar. *Garden* 25 Mar to June, Sat to Wed 11am to 6pm; July and Aug, Sat to Wed 10am to 6pm; Sept, Sat to Wed 11am to 6pm; Oct, 11am to 5pm. Closed Nov to late Mar. 💷 *All-inclusive* adult £6; child (5 to 14 yrs old) £3; family ticket (2 adults + 3 children) £15; group rate (15 or more people) £5. *Below Stairs* adult £4; child £2; family ticket (2 adults + 3 children) £10; group rate £3.20. Free entry for National Trust members. ♿ The house has not been adapted for disabled use. Beyond the lower ground floor there are lots of stairs to ascend, making it very unsuitable for wheelchair users.

Folly Farm

Kilgetty, Pembrokeshire SA68 0XA ☎ *(01834) 812731*
🖰 *www.folly-farm.co.uk*

Quality ★ ★ ★	**Facilities 🏛 🏛 🏛 🏛**	**Value for money £££££**

Highlights Demonstrations, including bottle-feeding young animals and the birds of prey displays

Drawbacks Barns get crowded during demonstrations

What's there This old dairy farm has been in the Williams family for 50 years and in 1988 was opened up to tourists. Visitors can feed the penned-up farm animals in the barns, stroke and pat the animals, and play on the adventure playgrounds in the barn or outside. There are some pet animals in the pet centre, including a chatty mynah bird, birds of prey, pigs and their piglets and many other farmyard animals.

The **demonstrations** and presentations throughout the day are well worth seeing. You can watch the goats being milked, hand-milk one of the cows or see how cows are mechanically milked in the milking parlour. Twice a day the younger animals are bottle-fed and everyone, including the smallest children, gets a chance to have a go. Visitors sit in lines on straw bales and pass the bottle along the line with a young goat or lamb hanging on firmly to the teat – sometimes wrenching it out of children's hands. The **birds of prey display** (twice a day but not on Saturdays) is entertaining as well as informative, and visitors can take part – lying side by side in a line on the grass as the birds swoop low overhead.

The tractor-trailer ride is dull by comparison but suits 3-year-olds with a penchant for big wheels. You can take the 15-minute ride to the nature trail over the fields and have a walk, or just do the return trip (not in wet weather). The indoor and outdoor adventure playgrounds and the pedal tractors are all good entertainment for small children, while older visitors will enjoy the vintage funfair in the afternoons. Several old restored rides, such as a carousel, ghost train and waltzer, are in one of the barns . You have to pay extra for these (50p).

Allow at least half a day for your visit.

Information/tours/guides There are a couple of worksheet/quizzes for children. A map and a timetable of events are given out with your tickets.

When to visit It's best in good weather, although there are lots of things under cover as well.

Age appeal Younger children will particularly enjoy a visit; adults will appreciate the demonstrations and displays.

Food and drink The Hungry Farmer Café offers full meals to cream teas. Lasagne and steak and kidney pies are typical fare (£5.50), or jacket potatoes with fillings (£2.99) for a lighter dish. Children's meals are fast food – fish fingers and chicken nuggets with chips (£2.50). The café gets busy with pushchairs and highchairs but staff are happy to help. Alternatively, there is a snack bar outside and lots of picnic tables.

Shops The shops sell a good selection of gifts, from plastic tractors (£2.99) to stylish pottery and bright jumpers and good-quality children's sweatshirts. If you're after gifts with animal motifs you won't be disappointed.

Other facilities The animal barns have hand-washing facilities. There are also separate disabled and baby-changing areas.

🚗 A477 Tenby to Kilgetty road, then A478 to Narberth. Follow signs. ⊖ Train to Haverfordwest, then bus 381 to Tenby (runs hourly throughout the day). Alternatively, train to Kilgetty then 15 minutes' walk. ⏱ Mon to Sun, Mar to Sept, 10am to 5.30pm, Oct 11am to 5pm. 💷 Adult £3.75, child (3 to15 yrs old) £2.75, child (under 3 yrs old) free, senior citizen £3.00. Season tickets (Mar to Oct) adult £16, child and senior citizen £12. ♿ All areas level or ramped. Disabled toilets.

Llancaiach Fawr Manor

Nelson, Treharris, Caerphilly CF46 6ER ☎ *(01443) 412248*

Quality ★★★★   **Facilities 🦮🦮🦮🦮**   **Value for money ££££**

Highlights   Servants' tour with costumed actors gives a real flavour of living history; attractive Visitor Centre

Drawbacks   Inaccessible to anyone who can't manage stairs; rather tacky sign by entrance gate

---

What's there This fine Tudor manor house has been restored to resemble its appearance in 1645, a significant date for the Puritan Prichard family who once lived here. Now owned by Caerphilly Council, it has become a popular, award-winning attraction. Before you enter the house, the audio-visual presentation and exhibition of the family's history in the context of the Civil War is worth seeing.

Though sparsely furnished, the building is full of interest. The highlight of a visit is a tour of the house conducted by **costumed actors** using seventeenth-century language, who purport to be the household servants (e.g. Jenkin the ratcatcher). The style is deliberately light-hearted, with plenty of audience participation, especially if children are present, but it is also informative. Topics include privy and bedroom arrangements, the clothes and food of the age and how to load a musket. You can find out what a scold's bridle, a stomacher or a truckle bed was, and the origin of phrases such as 'bite the bullet', 'flash in the pan' and 'taking stock'.

The gardens and grounds are landscaped in period style too, containing typical herbs and flowers of the seventeenth century. Additional attractions include regular summer **falconry displays** and a varied programme of special events (such as ghost tours, mock battles and murder mysteries).

Allow half a day for a visit, including a tour.

Information/tours/guides The full-colour guide is £1.95. In the Visitor Centre, a good audio-visual presentation and a mini-exhibition with storyboards set the house in its historical context. The hour-long tour is not obligatory, but is included in the price of the admission ticket and is great fun. You can join in at any point and catch up later with any rooms you missed. The costumed steward-guides are enthusiastic and thoroughly entertaining, with a convincing mastery of seventeenth-century speech patterns. Visitors are shown from room to room by several different actors. 'Beware if you are of stout or tall stature' – doorways and beams are low and floors uneven.

When to visit Primarily a fine-weather venue, the house gets busy on summer weekends and bank holidays, though you may encounter school parties in term-time too. Special events are very popular.

Age appeal The sight is entertaining for any age group, but unsuitable for anyone who can't manage spiral stairs.

Food and drink There is an attractive conservatory-style restaurant and lounge bar in the purpose-built Visitor Centre by the entrance. After you place your order at the bar, waitresses deliver it to tables. Fare ranges from simple snacks, cakes and teas (95p to £2.45) to more substantial meals, such as spaghetti bolognese (£5.75) or chicken tikka (£4.95). Special children's menus are available (such as turkey 'jetters' with chips, and chocolate mousse for £2.50), and beverages include beers, house wines and soft drinks. Picnic tables are outside.

Shops A spacious, well-laid-out shop near the reception sells attractive souvenirs of the 'Past Times' variety, such as prettily wrapped sweets and preserves, scented candles (50p), moth-repellent herbs and potpourri sachets (£1.90), jewellery (£2.25 to £45.99), toys, lovespoons and bookmarks. Some gifts nod at history in the shape of Welsh tales, Welsh history rulers (95p), wallcharts and surname scrolls (£1.75), and there is an unusual line in leather drinking vessels (£14.99 to £24.99). A Stuart Crystal factory outlet shop lies just beyond the ticket desk.

🚗 From M4, take junction 32 then A470 as far as Nelson exit; follow signs. ⊖ Bus X38 from Cardiff Central bus station. Nearest rail station Pengam (3 miles). ⊙ Mon to Fri (including Bank Hols) 10am to 5pm, Sat and Sun 10am to 8pm (Oct to Mar) 12pm to 6pm. Last admission 3.30pm (4.30pm weekends). Closed 24 Dec to 1 Jan, Mons mid-Oct to mid-Feb. 💷 Adult £4.50; child (3 to 15 yrs old) £3; senior citizen, student, unemployed, disabled person £3; family ticket (2 adults + 2 children) £12; school parties £2.60; group discount available (20 or more people). Free entry for Friends of Llancaiach Fawr accompanied by paying guests. Extra charge for some special events (e.g. ghost tours, which include refreshments). ♿ Only the ground floor of the house is accessible to wheelchairs. A taped commentary and photo album of the tour is available free on request. Braille maps are available for the formal gardens. Disabled toilet.

Llechwedd Slate Caverns

Blaenau Ffestiniog, Gwynedd LL411 3NB ☎ *(01766) 830306*
🖰 *www.llechwedd.co.uk*

Quality ★★★ **Facilities 🛇 🛇 🛇** **Value for money ££**
Highlights Spectacular underground locations on both rides
Drawbacks The cost of a single ride is rather high – a combined ticket is better value

What's there Llechwedd Slate Caverns, still part of the largest working slate mine in Wales, revolve around two underground rides through a series of caverns that tell the story of the mining operation and the community surrounding it. Visitors can choose either of the rides or purchase a double ticket at a reduced fee.

The **Miner's Tramway** is the more straightforward of the two rides. Set in the vast excavated caverns, it explores the skills and working environment of the miners in the nineteenth century through a series of **tableaux** accompanied by recorded commentaries – including a reconstruction of one of the tiny, slate-built *cabans* where the miners kept their minds active with topical debate during their short lunch breaks. The appalling conditions are really brought home when, in one cavern, the lights are extinguished except for the precious candle of the quarryman working high overhead, who is barely visible in the darkness. In the last cavern, the guide demonstrates how the miners bored holes into the slate using long, chisel-like steel 'feathers' in order to blast chunks of the slate away from the seam with gunpowder – it took hours of repetitive labour to drill to a sufficient depth. At the end of the ride, you are treated to a display of **slate-working**.

The second ride, the **Deep Mine**, begins on Britain's steepest underground passenger railway, which takes you down into the heart of the mountain, where you are led through a sequence of 10 caverns by the 'ghost' of a Victorian miner, Siôn Dolgarregddu. *Son et lumière* presentations in each of the caverns tell the story of Siôn's life from his first day of work in the mine at the age of 12, while at the same time revealing the character of the close-knit mining community to which he belonged – there is even a recording of Lloyd George explaining the nature of the boom-bust cycle to the miners when he visited Blaenau Ffestiniog at the very start of his political career.

The emotionally charged tour finishes at the beautifully lit **underground lake**, which has been used in the making of two Hollywood films – *The Black Cauldron* and *Prince Valiant*.

In addition to the two rides, a small free museum houses an exhibition entitled 'Slates to the Sea' exploring the transport infrastructure surrounding the industry, and there is a tiny restored Victorian village, **Pentre Llechwedd**, containing several shops, a pub, a smithy, the *Herald* office and some river-flushed Victorian privies. You can visit a bank where you can buy Victorian pennies to spend in the sweet shops and pub – prices are in old and new currencies. The home and birthplace of **David Francis** (1865–1929), the celebrated Blind Harpist of Merioneth, can be found in the village.

Information/tours/guides All the guides on the Miner's Tramway are knowledgeable and happy to discuss any aspect of slate mining, while the 'Slates to the Sea' exhibition contains plenty of information boards. The guidebook (£1.25) is well presented and forms an interesting supplement to the information available at the sight.

When to visit All year. Although the temperature inside the mine stays fairly constant throughout the year, it is cold, so visitors in summer would be advised to make sure they have a coat or thick jumper.

Age appeal All ages; the underground rides are particularly exciting for children.

Food and drink There are three places to eat. The Caverns Café offers a range of good-value canteen meals, almost universally served with chips and peas, including steak and mushroom pie, and cheese and vegetable bake (both £3.95). Jacket potatoes and toasted sandwiches are also available. In the Victorian village, the Miners Arms serves more traditional pub fare, ranging from a Miner's Lunch of pork pie or cheese, bread and salad (£3.90 or 9¼d) to Welsh chicken in a honey and mustard sauce (£4.50 or 11¼d). Alternatively, the Plaswaenydd Restaurant has a selection of salads (£3.95 to £4.75) and main dishes such as grilled gammon or deep-fried scampi (£3.50 to £5.95).

Shops A rather crowded gift shop sells a range of slightly tacky merchandise with an emphasis on slate products; the shop was gearing up for Christmas when we inspected in mid-September.

From A55 North Wales Coast Expressway (25 miles away) or A5 at Betws-y-Coed (10 miles away), take A470 from Betws-y-Coed to mid Wales and Cardigan Bay; caverns are beside road. ⊖ Train from Llandudno Junction to Blaenau Ffestiniog station, then bus from Blaenau Ffestiniog station to Llechwedd. Buses also run from Llechwedd to the picturesque narrow-gauge Ffestiniog Railway at Blaenau Ffestiniog. ① Mar to Sept, Mon to Sun 10am to 6pm (last tour 5.15pm); Oct to Feb, Mon to Sun 10am to 5pm (last tour 4.15pm). Closed 25, 26 Dec, 1 Jan. ⬛ Adult £6.95 per ride; child (5 to 15 yrs old) £4.80 per ride; senior citizen/student/unemployed/disabled person £6 per ride. Reduced rate for both rides adult £10.50, child £7.20, senior citizen/student/unemployed/disabled person £9.50. ♿ Most of the sight is accessible, but the Deep Mine ride involves a long, steep flight of stairs.

Museum of Welsh Life

St Fagans, Cardiff CF5 6XB ☎ *029-2057 3500*

Quality ★★★★ **Facilities** 🏛🏛🏛🏛 **Value for money ££££**
Highlights Wide range of enlightening, well-documented exhibits
Drawbacks Parts of site a little dilapidated; café/restaurant areas rather bleak and dated

What's there This popular heritage attraction occupies an extensive site in lovely countryside on the western fringes of Cardiff. The generous donation of an Elizabethan manor house with 100 acres of grounds and farmland from the Earl of Plymouth enabled this ambitious project to get under way in 1946. Since then it has gradually built up into its present size. It now contains over 40 **period dwellings and workplaces** which have been dismantled and transported from all over Wales and reconstructed here in a folk-park setting. Buildings include a tannery, a Victorian school, a cockpit, a chapel and a toll-house, as well as all sorts of cottages, farmhouses and shops.

Unlike the museum exhibits, the large 1970s-style entrance block near the car park lacks period charm, but efficiently houses shops, a ticket desk, café/restaurant and galleries, along with lecture halls and exhibition space. The fascinating galleries contain well-displayed collections of **agricultural and domestic bygones** – the medical instruments, costumes and patchwork quilts are especially interesting.

Special events, festivals and exhibitions are held throughout the year, including open-air theatre performances in summer. **St Fagans Castle**, the sixteenth-century furnished manor whose grounds host the museum, is also open to visitors, along with its walled gardens, rosery and mulberry grove.

Seeing everything in detail could take the best part of a day.

Information/tours/guides There are no formal tours. Each building or point of interest is numbered in sequence and annotated by clear on-site display boards. The full-colour Visitor Guide is worth picking up at the reception desk (£1.95), not least for the plan at the back. Staff demonstrate traditional crafts like saddlery and blacksmithing, while others are on hand to explain notable aspects of the buildings. All are approachable, knowledgeable and helpful.

When to visit Fine spring or summer weekends and special events, particularly bank holidays, bring out the crowds, but the site is so large that serious hold-ups are rare. Occasionally, buildings may be closed for renovation.

Age appeal Popular with all ages. There's a fair bit of walking involved, though a useful little tractor train chugs round the site in summer to save your legs, stopping at intervals. Visitors can get on or off where they like, free of charge. An adventure playground of climbing frames and slides keeps children happy in the picnic area.

Food and drink The main café/restaurant is upstairs at the rear of the reception block. Décor is dreary and functional, but a fair range of sandwiches, salads, cakes and hot meals is served (e.g. steak and ale pie or Anglesey cake). The snack bar downstairs confines itself to commercialised ice-cream and humdrum packaged snacks. There's a picnic site if you want to eat outside.

Shops Two sizeable, well-stocked shops are located near reception (one is accessible without paying an entrance charge). Both sell similar ranges of typically Welsh souvenirs such as dragon toys (£1.95 to £10.95), preserves and lovespoons. There are also T-shirts, guidebooks, tea towels and videos of the museum, along with rather more imaginative craft products – silver jewellery in Celtic patterns (£3.40 to £12.50), animal clocks, wood or slate carvings, sheepskin slippers, woollen rugs and lace bobbins. An unusual line includes ornaments carved from the concrete rubble of the old Cardiff Arms Park (now replaced by the state-of-the-art Millennium Stadium, *qv*) from £4.99 to £120.

As part of the exhibition, the Gwalia Stores (from Ogmore Vale) contains a period museum shop selling quality Welsh 'hamper produce' such as cheeses, preserves, laverbread, confectionery, biscuits and wine.

Other facilities Toilets are scattered throughout the site, many of the 'portaloo' type; better, permanent ones with baby-changing facilities and disabled access are near the reception block.

🚗 From M4, take junction 33 or follow signs from the city's western exit roads. Museum is on A4232, four miles west of Cardiff. Large free car park near main entrance. ⊖ Bus routes 32, 32A or 32B from city centre, Tel. (01222) 396521 for times. ⏰ July to Sept, Mon to Sun 10am to 6pm; Oct to June, Mon to Sun 10am to 5pm. Closed 25 Dec, 1 Jan. *St Fagans Castle* 10am to 5pm (6pm June to Aug). 💷 Adult £5.50; child up to 18 yrs old free; senior citizen/unemployed/student/disabled visitor £3.90; family ticket (2 adults + 2 children) £14. Reductions available for school parties. *St Fagans Castle* Summer: adult £5.50, child 3.20, senior citizen/student/unemployed £3.90, family ticket £14. Winter: adult £4.50, child/senior citizen/student/unemployed £2.65. *Season tickets* adult £17.50; child £6; couple £27; senior citizen couple £20; family ticket £32.50. Holders entitled to 10% discount in museum shops. ♿ The site is extensive but mostly flattish and exhibits are linked by fairly smooth paths; wheelchair users may not be able to see all the buildings at close quarters. Disabled toilets.

National Museum and Gallery

Cathays Park, Cardiff CF10 3NP ☎ *029-2039 7951*
🖥 *www.nmgw.ac.uk*

Quality ★★★★★　　　　**Facilities 👜👜👜👜👜**　　　　**Value for money £££££**
Highlights Superb exhibits, brilliantly displayed
Drawbacks Archaeology section a little disappointing

What's there This collection, housed in the elegant classical setting of Cardiff's **Civic Centre**, is outstanding by any standards. A flagship museum for Wales, it presides over a number of associated 'national museums' scattered throughout the country. In addition to what's actually on display, this welcoming attraction attempts to show visitors what goes on behind the scenes (such as conservation, research and unseen parts of the collections), and makes special efforts for children. Excellent multimedia presentations include textboards and video shows, with exciting special effects in the lower galleries.

Even though it is on nothing like the scale of London's British Museum (*qv*) or the Victoria & Albert Museum (*qv*), there really is too much to absorb at one go. If you are short of time, concentrate on one or two galleries, or head for the unmissables (the colour guide suggests a Top Ten list, including **Jan Van Cappelle**'s seascape *A Calm*, the **Oxwich Brooch** in rubies and cameos, and the superb **Evolution of Wales** and **Natural History** galleries).

The museum is particularly strong on Impressionist paintings – look out for **Renoir**'s Blue Lady (*La Parisienne 1874*) and **Van Gogh**'s *Rain: Auvers 1890* (his last, anguished work). Monet, Cézanne, Pissaro and Sickert are also represented. There's an interesting section on the Welsh artists **Gwen and Augustus John**, including an angelic portrait of Dylan Thomas ('if provided with a bottle of beer he sat very patiently').

Allow several hours for an initial visit, and make a note to see the collection again sometime. If stamina flags, head downstairs for a rest in the museum cafés (Icons or Brangwyn's).

Information/tours/guides The main full-colour guide is £2.45. A useful free floor plan is handed out with the admission ticket. Internal sign-posting is good, and finding your way round is fairly straightforward. No formal tours are laid on except for pre-booked groups, but room attendants or Main Hall staff (including volunteer Friends of the Museum) can give any information required and are very helpful. Labelling and lighting are superb. All signs are bilingual (Welsh and English).

When to visit The museum is mainly a wet-weather attraction. Special exhibitions and events may cause queues. Lunchtime concerts are staged from time to time.

Age appeal Admirable attempts are made to interest a wide range of ages and interests without 'dumbing down' – even quite young children should get something out of it. Great emphasis on education.

Food and drink The excellent licensed café/restaurant in the basement (Icons) is spacious, clean, smart and comfortable with lots of relaxing seating areas giving a sense of privacy. The appetising range of self-service food at various counters ranges from breakfasts, snacks and sandwiches (£1.95) to more ambitious lunchtime fare (shark supreme or mushroom stroganoff, both £5.25). Children's menus are available. Cakes (from 65p) and coffee (85p) are good, and staff pleasant. There is an additional coffee bar in the Main Hall (Brangwyn's). Both Brangwyn's and Icons are open to non-museum visitors.

Shops Shop areas stretch along the rear of the main entrance foyer behind the ticket desk, selling a fairly predictable range of content-themed 'museum' merchandise like posters, postcards, calendars and art books. Other items include Eyewitness science guides as well as a tasteful selection of craft kits, potpourri, fudge, jewellery and wildflower seeds. There are some attractive ideas for children (puzzles, toys and activity kits), and museum publications and videos are on sale.

Other facilities Ancillary facilities include exemplary toilets (with baby-changing and disabled access) and luggage lockers (no charge).

🚗 From M4, take junction 32 and follow A470 towards city centre. From central Cardiff follow signs for Civic Centre. Designated museum car park at rear of building (exit tokens for barrier available from ticket desk; £1.20 unlimited time); for roadside bays outside purchase a parking voucher from local shops or the museum (80p per hour). ⊖ Local bus from Cardiff Central bus station (8, 9, 30, 34, 35, 47, 48), or train from Cardiff Central to Cathays station. ⏰ Tue to Sun and Bank Hol Mons 10am to 5pm. Closed Mons, 24–26 Dec. 🎟 Adult £4.50; child (4 to 15 yrs old) £2.65; senior citizen, student, disabled person £2.65; family ticket (2 adults + 3 children £10.25). *Season tickets* adult £17.50; couple £27; child £6; senior citizen, unemployed £14; student £10; senior citizen couple £20; family ticket (2 adults + any number of children at same address) £32.50. Free admission to Friends of the Museum and teachers (for pre-booked education tours). 10% group discount (20 or more people). ♿ Fully accessible (wheelchair entrance is to left of main front steps – orange symbol), with excellent provision of lifts to upper galleries and basement restaurant/disabled toilets. Induction loops for hard of hearing. Staff assistance on request. Parking places at main entrance.

Oakwood Coaster Country

Oakwood, Canaston Bridge, Narberth, Pembrokeshire SA67 8DE
☎ *(01834) 891376* ⏲ *www.Oakwoood-leisure.com*
⏲ *Simon.Oakwood@Virgin.net*

Quality ★★★   **Facilities** 🛈 🛈 🛈   **Value for money £££**
Highlights Queues not too bad even in peak season; varied rides suitable for all ages
Drawbacks Vertigo ride costs an extra £30 for one to three people, putting it outside
the price range of many visitors; adult entry prices start from age 10

What's there The rural setting of Oakwood amid rolling farmland makes it an unlikely spot for gut-churning excitements, but if you have the stomach for it, some thrilling rides are to be experienced. Otherwise, try the gentler family rides and the designated children's area.

Of the seven 'thrill' rides, the one you see first – and possibly the most exciting – is **Vertigo**, a sort of bungee jump and giant swing. Up to three people are harnessed together and hoisted up to a height of 50 metres, then put into free-fall for 18 metres at 110km per hour and swung out over the crowds below like a pendulum until they are brought to a stop. The extra cost for Vertigo cuts down the queues, but if this popular ride is on your hit list you should book for it when you arrive.

Megafobia was voted the 'best wooden roller coaster in the world' by the Coaster Club of Great Britain. This 900-metre ride reaches speeds of 88km per hour, and the first drop plunges 25 metres. Less alarming is the gentler Treetops Coaster through the trees, which will still give you a buzz.

On the **Bounce** riders sit side by side facing outwards and are pulled up to a height of 47 metres, before being plunged down to reach a speed of 70 kilometres in less than two seconds. The ride then bounces several more times before releasing the riders.

The Pirate Ship swings up to suspend you momentarily before plunging back down again to swing up the other side. Tamest of the thrill rides is probably Senior Go Karts. Wet thrills are to be had on **Snake River Falls** and the Waterfall water chutes (Snake River is more exciting).

Gentler rides include the Bobsleigh, the Boating Lake and Junior Go-Karts. For non-riders, **Jake's Town** is a Wild West-themed area with a gold mine, gold panning and a Music Hall Theatre with shows throughout the afternoon and evenings. Other activities include face painting and creating your own sand bottle (coloured sands cost extra in the shops).

For smaller children, **Playland** offers miniature rides on a ferris wheel, a carousel and kiddiecoaster. Playtown Farm contains a few animals and tractor rides, and an indoor soft play centre for wet-weather activities.

New attractions opening in 2000 include Voodoo Mansion and Kidzworld – two themed interactive zones for children. A free train runs around the site.

Information/tours/guides The pictorial map exaggerates the size of the rides but is reasonably clear, as is the signposting within the park.

When to visit The park is best in dry weather. Various events throughout the year include 'After Dark' festivities with shows and fireworks, Mardi Gras celebrations at Easter, and 'Christmasland' and pantomime in December.

Age appeal Something for all ages, although height restrictions on most of the thrill rides (the minimum ranges from 1.1m to 1.45m) limit access to younger children. Non-riders can go to the shows and cinema, toddlers and small children to Playland.

Food and drink The variety of venues is reasonable, though the main restaurant is relatively bland, serving main meals such as lasagne, steak and kidney pie (£3.85), filled baguettes and sandwiches. A typical children's meal is fish fingers and chips (£2.99). Coconut Creek has a tropical theme, serving cocktails and stir-fries. Elsewhere there are chicken and burger bars, snack bars, ice-creams and sweet stalls.

Shops The main shop, at the Whistlestop station where people alight from the train, has a generally uninspiring range of novelties, and lots of T-shirts and mugs. Shops in Jakestown have a greater variety of gifts and novelties.

🚗 From A40 between Carmarthen and Haverfordwest at Canaston Bridge, take A4075 south for two miles (Oakwood is on the right). ⊖ Bus 322, 381 to Canaston Bridge, 1½ miles from Oakwood. Not safe to walk because of traffic. ⏱ Mardi Gras Festival: 15 Apr to 1 May, Mon to Sun 10am until 8pm; 2 May to 21 July, Mon to Sun 10am to 5pm; 22 July to 3 Sept, Mon to Sun 10am to 10pm; rest of Sept, Mon to Sun 10am to 5pm. Dec, open for Christmas festivities – check for details. Closed Oct to Easter. 💷 Adult £11.50, child (3 to 9 yrs old) £10.50; senior citizen, disabled person £9.50; family ticket (2 adults + 2 children) £40. ♿ Park is reasonably compact, with some hills. Disabled toilets.

Powis Castle

Nr Welshpool SY21 8RF ☎ *(01938) 557018*

Quality ★★★	**Facilities** 👚👚👚👚👚	**Value for money** ££

Highlights Fascinating display of Indian loot dating back to the seventeenth century; beautiful gardens

Drawbacks Disappointing food

What's there Built as the seat of a Welsh princedom, Powis Castle took a dive in status when the last prince was forced to renounce his royal title following Edward I's conquest of Wales at the end of the twelfth century. However, it remained in the possession of the Earls of Powis for nearly another 300 years, following its sale to Sir Edward Herbert in 1587. The Herberts' espousal of the Stuart cause resulted in a chequered history for much of the eighteenth century, at the end of which the Powis estate merged its fortunes with the house of Clive when Lord Powis's daughter married Edward Clive, the eldest son of Clive of India, who had done so much to establish the British conquest of India. Edward Clive was made Earl of Powis in 1804, and his son, the 2nd Earl, changed his name to Herbert. When the 4th Earl, George Herbert, died without issue in 1952, the estate passed into the care of the National Trust.

The castle, whose romanticised skyline (added at the beginning of the eighteenth century) almost belies its martial inheritance, is now home to a magnificent collection of antiques and paintings – many of them portraits of the owners – dating back as far as the sixteenth century and owing much to the accumulated fortune brought by the Clives. Before entering the house itself, it is probably worth visiting the **Ballroom**, where a short introductory video explains who Clive of India was. The film remains carefully neutral, allowing visitors to make up their own minds as to the ethical merits of his enterprise – as well as looking at the history of the castle. The Ballroom also houses the **Clive Museum**, where Britain's finest collection of Indian treasures outside the capital is on display. Visitors can gaze in wonder at the delicate craftsmanship of ornaments and armaments and see **Benjamin West**'s imaginative rendering of *Lord Clive Receiving the Grant of Diwani from the Great Mogul* – an event that in effect made Clive the dictator of Bengal.

To the east of the house is a beautiful **baroque garden** that falls away 450 feet from the rocky outcrop on which the castle is sited, by means of a series of Italianate hanging terraces. Below the terraces a huge lawn and daffodil paddock are flanked by a mature woodland garden to the south and east, and by an elegant formal flower garden to the west. A number of interesting statues – formerly belonging to a water garden – dot the terraces, though the finest, of Fame mounted on Pegasus, is now in the main courtyard.

Information/tours/guides There are no guided tours or information boards, but room stewards are happy to discuss the history of the castle. Visitors can also purchase an excellent and extensive guidebook (£2.90) – containing a complete inventory of all the paintings – or a smaller leaflet that is sufficient for an afternoon's excursion. Another leaflet (90p) contains a map and description of the gardens.

When to visit Any time is suitable, although the gardens are probably most enjoyable in fine weather. Four of the rooms – the State Bathroom, Walcot Room, Gallery Room and Duke's Room – are open only on Wednesdays and Thursdays.

Age appeal The castle has little appeal for children beyond the extensive grounds and the host of arms and armour in the Clive Museum.

Food and drink A light and beautifully laid-out restaurant serves lunches ranging from Clive's 'Petits Pâtés' (£3.95) – small, sweet lamb pies – to Welsh cheese and leek flan (£4.25), as well as mouth-watering afternoon teas. Our home-made soup, however, tasted strongly of stock cubes.

Shops The shop is attractively laid out and offers a range of quality merchandise ranging from jewellery to hand-thrown stoneware. An aristocratic theme runs throughout. There is also a separate shop selling plants.

🚗 Off A483 1 mile south of Welshpool (follow signs). ⊖ From Welshpool railway station, take footpath away from town centre to castle (1.75 miles). Buses D71 from Oswestry and D75 from Shrewsbury to Welshpool. ⊙ *Castle and museum* Apr to Jun, Wed to Sun 1pm to 5pm; July and Aug, Tue to Sun 1pm to 5pm; Sept and Oct, Wed to Sun 1pm to 5pm. Open bank hol Mons in season. Last admission 5.30pm. *Garden* 11am to 6pm, same days/months as castle. 💷 *Castle, museum and garden* adult £7.50; child £3.75 (5 to 17 yrs old); family ticket (2 adults + 3 children) £18.75. *Garden only* adult £5; child £2.50; family ticket £12.50. Free entry for National Trust members. ♿ The map of the garden marks a route avoiding steps and steep slopes, but the house and museum contain several flights of stairs. Tea room and shop accessible. Disabled and elderly visitors can be set down in front of castle. Wheelchair available for loan.

Rhondda Heritage Park

Lewis Merthyr Colliery, Trehafod, Porth, Rhondda Cynon Taff CF37 7NP
☎ *(01443) 682036*

Quality ★★★★	Facilities 🏛🏛🏛🏛	Value for money ££££

Highlights Underground tour and simulated thrill ride; good multimedia presentations

Drawbacks Static exhibitions rather ersatz (unconvincing waxworks etc); commentary can be overblown

What's there This popular attraction is based on the story of the Rhondda collieries and the region's 'Black Gold'. It is set on the site of the disused Lewis Merthyr Colliery, which lends an authentic air, though (unlike Big Pit, *qv*) the experiences here are mock-ups rather than 'the real thing'.

The main highlight of a visit is an entertaining tour, partly underground, with ex-miner guides. This involves several elaborate audio-visual presentations, including a breathtaking white-knuckle **simulator ride** through the coal tunnels at the end of the visit. Above ground, various exhibitions re-create a picture of social and domestic life in a coal-mining community. Temporary exhibitions are displayed in the Gallery near the coffee shop.

The old winding gear and other machinery can still be seen in the pit yard, while an additional attraction with families in mind is the **Energy Zone**, an imaginative coal-themed adventure playground (supervised at weekends and during school holidays).

Allow about three hours to see everything; the tours sometimes go on for well over 1½ hours (including the shows).

Information/tours/guides The lavishly produced guide-pack is good value at 99p. The guided tour with extrovert former mine-workers is exceptionally entertaining. Background information is conveyed by lively multimedia presentations (videos and special effects).

When to visit The sight is most popular on dull days, when the Energy Zone can be enjoyed but visitors do not mind going underground. Expect school children during term-time. Lots of talks and special events are laid on. Underground tours take place between 10am and 4.30pm (usually lasting 1¼ hours).

Age appeal Good for all age groups, but particularly children, who can learn something about their regional heritage more enjoyably and comfortably than some of their predecessors, who had no choice in the matter. Designed in the manner of a theme park, the attraction puts great emphasis on entertainment, but it has a strong educative role. There are no restrictions – babes in arms and wheelchair users can go underground. The Energy Zone is for children aged 4–12 only (those under 8 must be accompanied).

Food and drink A coffee shop above the main entrance makes a comfortable place for a snack or light meal (e.g. pit pasties, salads, sandwiches, cod and chips). Furnishings are quite plain, but tables are well spaced. Children's portions are available.

Shops The gift shop is by the ticket desk at the main entrance. Besides a typical array of Welsh souvenirs (lovespoons, dolls, Celtic jewellery, mugs, etc.), there's a good range of books and guides on related aspects of social history: *Domestic Bygones* or *Victorian Schooldays in Wales*, to name but two. You can buy yourself a Davy lamp if you like (all sizes from £17).

🚗 From M4, take junction 32 on to A470 towards Merthyr Tydfil, then A4058 from Pontypridd. From central Cardiff or A465 Heads of the Valleys Road (Abergavenny-Merthyr Tydfil), follow signs. Park is 1.5 miles east of Pontypridd. Ample free parking next to main entrance. **By public transport:** from Cardiff Central, sprinter train to Trehafod every half hour takes 29 mins. Stagecoach Rhondda bus 132 leaves Cardiff Central bus station (stand A2) at 10 past and 20 to the hour, Mon to Sat 8.40am to 5.40pm (1 hour journey). ⏲ Easter to Sept, Mon to Sun 10am to 6pm; Oct to Easter, Tue to Sun 10am to 6pm. *Energy Zone* Easter to Sept, Mon to Sun 10am to 5pm. Closed 25, 26 Dec. 💷 Adult £5.60; child (5 to 15 yrs old) £4.30; senior citizen, unemployed, disabled person £4.95; family ticket (2 adults + 2 children) £16.50; college groups £4.05; school parties £3.15; group discount 10% (10 or more people), group leaders/drivers/couriers free. ♿ All parts of the site are suitable for wheelchair users, and purpose-built paths, lifts and ramps are in place. Disabled toilets and car parking places.

Swansea Maritime and Industrial Museum

Museum Square, Maritime Quarter, Swansea SA1 1SN ☎ *(01792) 650351*

Quality ★★★	Facilities 🏛 🏛	Value for money £££££

Highlights Interesting sections on local industrial heritage; floating historic ships (if you can find them)

Drawbacks Shabby, dilapidated facilities and dated displays

What's there The Victorian premises of a brick quayside warehouse provide an authentic setting for this nostalgic but oddly jumbled assembly of exhibits relating to Swansea's long and varied industrial heritage. Themes unfurled under the building's roof include the coal- and iron-workings of the lower Swansea Valley, with the dreadful pollution and social problems they caused, and the horrors of the Blitz. Facilities at this worthy venture are somewhat jaded, and reflect its urgent need for a revamp or large injection of cash.

The transport sections contain bronchitic **automobiles and motorbikes**, accompanied by flickering film footage of old-timers doing horrendous things with petrol and cigarette lighters to get them started. The **Mumbles lifeboat** takes pride of place in a central gallery, surrounded by accounts of gallant rescues.

Upper galleries devote further space to maritime exhibits (with an interesting section on cockle-gathering, and a very dull display of model ships). A memorable section displays nineteenth-century machinery from the Abbey Woollen Mill, showing the manufacturing process from piles of coloured fluff to woven textiles.

Further along the quayside, the Tramshed, a small annexe building, presents a separate exhibition on Swansea trams and the **Mumbles Railway**, billed as the first passenger railway in the world.

The museum's pride and joy is its collection of **historic vessels** moored in the adjacent basin, a couple of which can be boarded during the summer months. Unfortunately, these are so inadequately documented within the main exhibition that it's easy to miss them altogether.

As we went to press, the museum was awaiting the results of a lottery bid to transform it into a much more modern and comprehensive National Waterfront Museum over the next three years or so.

Information/tours/guides There is no guidebook or formal tour. Exhibits are accompanied by a variety of interpretive techniques, from simple display case labelling to storyboards, timer-switch demonstrations, wobbly films and slideshows, as well as models and taped sound effects triggered by light beams. Most of these systems seem dated and many were not working or in poor order when we inspected. Display boards are sometimes located too far away to be read by anyone short-sighted. Worst of all, visitors to the main exhibition are not directed to the adjacent Tramshed or historic vessels in the nearby marina, and it is not at all clear that these form part of the museum.

When to visit Summer weekends are busiest; it is usually a wet-weather attraction, though visiting the floating exhibits means braving the elements. On average, around 250 schoolchildren visit each day.

Age appeal Most people will get something out of this museum, but it is perhaps most suited to older visitors who can relate to the rather old-fashioned methods of presentation, and who may remember Morris cars and thriving coal mines. Strong local interest.

Food and drink Rudimentary rations and drinks (sandwiches, crisps, buns, lurid ice slush) are served in a drab little snack-bar area between the shop and the exhibition space. For more enticing refreshments, head for the quayside pub by the Tramshed exhibition.

Shops Floorspace near the entrance is devoted to a range of local crafts and souvenirs, for example Laugharne glassware, local pottery and stacks of 'nostalgia' merchandise such as 'Classic Wheels' jigsaws, models of cars, bikes and ships. One section offers quality products made on the Abbey Woollen Mill machinery (rugs, blankets, etc.).

🚐 From central Swansea, museum is not clearly signed – follow signs for Swansea Museum, a separate building nearby. There is no designated parking space: park in the Leisure Centre on the A4067 (reduced charges for museum visitors). ⊖ From main railway station, museum is a 15-minute walk, also a short walk from the Quadrant Bus station. ⊙ Tue to Sun and Bank Hol Mons 10am to 5pm. Last admission 4.45pm. *Museum shop and Abbey Woollen Mill Factory Shop* close 4.45pm. *Historic vessels and Tramshed* Closed Oct to Mar. 💷 Free. ⛟ Wheelchair access is possible to main building but not on board historic vessels. One toilet is larger/wider than others but not specially equipped.

Techniquest

Stuart Street, Cardiff CF1 6BW ☎ *029-2047 5475*

Quality ★★★★　　　**Facilities** 🏛🏛🏛🏛　　　**Value for money £££**
Highlights Enthusiastic, helpful staff; hands-on, interactive approach to learning
Drawbacks Disappointing Cyber Library and written information; indifferent café

What's there Housed in a futuristic, high-tech building on Cardiff Bay's revitalised waterfront, Techniquest is a science-based educational attraction designed very much with children in mind. It is an exciting environment: airy double-decker steel-and-glass galleries linked by a huge, slow-moving lift contain about 120 **entertaining pieces of equipment** illustrating the basic principles of light, sound, pressure, heat and other mainstays of science. Ancillary attractions (not always available and incurring an extra charge) include a planetarium, a science theatre and a discovery room where shows, lectures and additional equipment are held. The **Cyber Library** is designed to provide access to on-line science databases.

Billed as a 'hands-on environment' revealing the friendly face of science, the centre's approach is entirely interactive. Excited children rush from one experiment to another, pushing or pressing anything that moves. It is obvious that some treat it simply as a game, and the equipment, though robust, already shows signs of wear. At the same time, it is heartening to see how much educational value more thoughtful children get out of it.

Allow the best part of half a day for a visit, especially if you want to see a star-show or one of the events in the **science theatre**. The foyer shop is well worth a visit, and there is a pleasant waterfront café. Both are open to non-visitors.

Information/tours/guides No formal tours are available (except for prearranged school parties). Friendly helpers in emerald T-shirts circulate constantly around the galleries, ready to demonstrate experiments such as launching a mini-hot-air balloon, making a lasting shadow or creating a vortex. Geared mainly for young audiences, the written information available is clear and simple (some may think, over-simplified). Bite-sized display panels accompany each experiment, explaining briefly what is happening. An (overpriced) souvenir guide costs £2.50. When we inspected, the Cyber Library seemed poorly equipped and less than user-friendly.

When to visit An ideal wet-weather outing for families. Expect crowds of school parties during term-time, when extensive educational programmes are held. We were lucky enough to visit Techniquest during the 1999 solar eclipse, when a reflective telescope on the roof terrace (and obligingly parted clouds) made it a memorable occasion.

Age appeal Suitable for 'inquisitive minds of all ages', as the publicity blurb has it, but mainly designed with younger children in mind. Parents get surprisingly hooked on things they have not tried for years, while their offspring delight in showing the old fuddy duddies what to do. Occasional sessions for adults only ('by popular demand').

Food and drink A light, bright self-service café with a waterfront terrace is near the foyer ticket desk. It can seem cramped and messy when crowded with children. Catering sticks to familiar child-oriented favourites and is not very imaginative or diet-conscious – typical fare includes sausages, beef curry, sandwiches and soft drinks.

Shops An attractive, well laid-out shop by the ticket desk (no entrance fee necessary to visit) majors on science-based kits, books, models and games. It is a good place to look for improving or entertaining presents for children (e.g. magnets, gyroscopes, illuminated globes, plasma balls, glowstones and moonbeam catchers). Staff try to match merchandise to topical themes like 1999's solar eclipse, so stock is constantly changing.

🚗 From M4, take junction 33, then follow A4232 to Cardiff Bay. From city centre, follow Cardiff Bay signs. Free supervised car park behind Techniquest; set-down point for disabled visitors by entrance. ⊖ By train from Cardiff Queen Street to Cardiff Bay station, alternatively bus 8 from Central Bus Station or buses 7/7A from Churchill Way. ⏰ Mon to Fri 9.30am to 4.30pm, Sat, Sun and Bank Hol Mons 10.30am to 5pm. Last admission 45 mins before closing. Closed 24–26 Dec. 💷 Adult £5.50; child (5 to 15 yrs old) £3.80; senior citizen, unemployed, disabled person £3.80; family ticket (2 adults + 3 children) £15.75; annual family season ticket £42.50; group discounts available (10 or more people). Additional charges for Planetarium (75p) and Discovery Room (50p). ♿ Fully accessible to wheelchair users, with large lifts and specially adapted WCs.

Tintern Abbey

Tintern, Chepstow, Monmouthshire NP16 6SE ☎ *(01291) 689251*

Quality ★★★★   **Facilities** 👜 👜 👜   **Value for money ££££**

Highlights Romantic Wye Valley setting; good interpretive material; attractive merchandise on sale

Drawbacks Some over-enthusiastic stonework restoration; crowded with coach tours and souvenir shops

---

What's there The skeletal remains of Wales's richest and most impressive **Cistercian monastery** stand amid emerald water meadows on the banks of the River Wye, which carves majestically through densely wooded cliffs along this scenic stretch of the Anglo-Welsh border. Even in its ruinous, post-Dissolution state, Tintern's evocative shell attracts visitors from far and wide. A source of inspiration to awestruck eighteenth-century Romantics (notably Wordsworth and Turner), its current tidy state of restoration at the hands of the Welsh conservation organisation Cadw (along with the tour coaches and souvenir shops by the West Front) perhaps makes Tintern less enthralling these days.

Founded in 1131, Tintern became an immensely wealthy and influential centre of learning for just over 400 years. In 1536 Henry VIII dissolved it literally as well as politically, by melting the lead from its roof and bells.

The great **church** was begun in about 1269, replacing an earlier and more modest Romanesque building. It was designed in the newly fashionable Decorated style, which can be seen most clearly in the pierced flowerlike tracery above the windows. The fragments of the pulpitum screen which once spanned the nave, on display near the reception block, are especially ornate. Most of the church's imposing ruins can be seen (from a distance) without paying the entrance charge.

Grand though the church is, it is the **monks' domestic quarters** that bring the abbey complex most to life and give a fuller picture of everyday monastic existence during the abbey's heyday. Wandering through a maze of lichen-blotched foundation walls linked by gravel paths and mown quadrangles, visitors can piece together the routines of work, rest and prayer which shaped the Cistercian daily round. Storyboards translate the vestigial floorplans into kitchens, dormitories and infirmary wards. The most memorable features are the refectory, the abbot's lavish chambers (which may have stretched Cistercian vows of poverty a little beyond their limits), and the oddly riveting latrine system.

A couple of hours should give ample time to see everything in detail, including the small separate exhibitions near the entrance block, as well as allowing a little spiritual contemplation. The surrounding countryside suggests many lovely walks. An easy riverside path leads from the abbey car park to the visitor centre at Tintern Old Station.

Information/tours/guides Clearly written display boards with site plans (all in Welsh as well as English) interpret the various sections of the abbey. In addition, the shop sells a good range of guidebooks, postcards and interpretive material. The main full-colour, 68-page guide (£2.75) gives details on the historical background, and an excellent ground plan shows the age of the ruins. Separate guidebooks are available on Wordsworth's and Turner's associations with Tintern. There are no audio-visual presentations or regular guided tours, but group tours can be arranged with a local historian. When we inspected, no audio tour was available but a revised version may be reinstated at some stage.

When to visit Virtually the whole of the site is open to the elements, so tog up if it looks like rain. A sudden influx of coach parties may cause temporary bottlenecks at the entrance, but the site itself is spacious enough to absorb plenty of visitors.

Age appeal Efforts are made to interest children with cheerful literature like *Gerald Meets the Monks*, but young children may find the ruins dull or hard to understand. Occasional special events are held (e.g. falconry and carol-singing) – call for details. Those with mobility problems will appreciate the fact that the site is fairly compact and generally flat with easy paths or lawns. Minimal walking is required from the car park.

Food and drink None is available on site, but the Anchor pub, opposite the car park, offers teas and bar snacks with views of the ruins from the gardens. Other options are available in Tintern village nearby – try the Abbey Mill crafts and coffee-shop.

Shops The shop, in the reception block, sells an attractive range of medieval/monastic-themed merchandise in the form of Celtic jewellery, pill-boxes, paperweights, mugs, tiles and bookmarks. Cards and books, some Welsh crafts and produce, and music recordings (plainsong and male voice choirs) are available too. Tintern Abbey specialities include prints, books, plates, videos and sweatshirts, and plenty of little mementoes for under £5.

🚗 From M4, take Junction 21 to M48, then A466 up Wye Valley. From Cardiff, take Junction 23 from M4. Free parking next to main entrance. ⊖ Train to Chepstow (6 miles from Tintern) – call Chepstow Tourist Office for details (01291) 623772. Wye Valley Bus 69 between Chepstow and Monmouth runs through Tintern Mon to Sat roughly every 2 hrs. ⊙ 29 Mar to 21 May, Mon to Sun 9.30am to 5pm; 22 May to 3 Oct, Mon to Sun 9.30am to 6pm; 4–31 Oct, Mon to Sun 9.30am to 5pm; 1 Nov to 28 Mar, Mon to Sat 9.30am to 4pm, Sun 11am to 4pm. Closed 24, 25, 26 Dec, 1 Jan. 💷 Adult £2.40; child (5 to 15 yrs old) £1.90; senior citizen, student £1.90; family ticket (2 adults + 3 children) £6.70. Free for Cadw members (entrance refunded if you join on site), and for wheelchair users and their helpers. No dogs allowed. ♿ Possible, though unassisted wheelchair users may have difficulty seeing some parts of the ruins at close quarters. Disabled toilet available.

Welsh Slate Museum

Llanberis, Gwynedd LL55 4TY ☎ *(01286) 870630* 🖱 *www.nmgw.ac.uk*
🖱 *wsmpost@btconnect.com*

Quality ★★★★ **Facilities 🏛🏛🏛🏛🏛** **Value for money ££££**
Highlights Excellent 3D audio-visual presentation; fascinating cross-section into community life in the quarrymen's houses
Drawbacks Slightly pointless sound effects in parts of the museum

What's there The Welsh Slate Museum occupies the site of the Victorian workshops of the Dinorwig quarry on the Elidr mountain. The sight has been divided into five elemental-sounding themed sections – Quarry People, Iron Road, Timber Trail, Water Way and Getting the Slate – that are intended to illustrate the culture of the slate industry. The **workshops** have been left largely intact (as though the workers had just gone home), and visitors can explore the chief engineer's house, the austere *caban* where the workers discussed everything from politics to football, the sawsheds, the iron and brass foundry, and the blacksmiths' forges. Of particular interest is the huge **water-wheel** – the largest working example on the mainland – that powered the machinery throughout the workshops by means of a complex system of cogs and cranks. Many of the rooms make use of audio recordings in an attempt to bring their activities to life, but actually convey rather a ghostly feel in the absence of the workforce.

Between the *caban* and the engineer's house is an impressive 3D multi-media presentation, 'To Steal a Mountain', which gives a highly interesting and evocative account of the slate community and the history of the site. Just beyond the workshops stands a row of four **quarrymen's houses** that were painstakingly moved to the site from another slate community at Blaenau Ffestiniog, where they had fallen into disrepair. Now they have been restored to provide glimpses into the quarrymen's lives at three significant times – the 1860s, the strike of 1910 and at the time of the closure in 1969 (the fourth house is to be used as an education centre). Outside the museum is a working incline plane where visitors can watch slate being transported down the mountainside by means of a system of counterweights.

Information/tours/guides No guided tours are conducted, and at the time of our inspection the guidebook was being rewritten (to be available Easter 2000), but there are plenty of information boards, and the knowledgeable staff are happy to discuss matters relating to the industry. A map of the site is provided with the ticket.

When to visit Any time. Demonstrations of slate-working take place during the summer.

Age appeal All ages will find something of interest here, though few of the exhibits are 'hands on'.

Food and drink A chic new cafeteria-style restaurant offers a varied menu of good-value dishes, such as minted Welsh lamb or cheese patties (both £4.50), served with generous helpings of salad.

Shops An attractively presented little shop in the reception stocks a range of slate products – from door numbers to jewellery – as well as ceramics, books on the slate industry, wrought ironwork and the ubiquitous lovespoons.

🚗 Off the A4086 in the Padarn Country Park near Llanberis. ⊖ Train to Bangor, then bus direct to Llanberis (77) or to Caernarfon (5, 5A, 5B, 5C, 5X), from where bus 88 goes to Llanberis. From bus stop in Llanberis, the museum is a short walk. ⏱ Easter to Oct, Mon to Sun 10am to 5pm; Nov to Easter, Sun to Fri 10am to 4pm. 💷 Adult £3.50; child (5 to 15 yrs old) £2; senior citizens, students, unemployed £2; disabled person free; family ticket (2 adults + 2 children) £7.90. ♿ Wheelchair access to most parts of the museum. Disabled toilet.

Directory of other tourist attractions

The tourist attractions in this directory have **not been inspected** by the Guide team and are not plotted on the maps, but, like those in the main section of the book, are some of the more popular destinations for tourists. Directory entries are listed by region, then alphabetically by name of attraction.

'*All year*' indicates that the attraction does not shut for extended periods at any time in the year, although it may close for some days each week and during the Christmas and New Year holidays. The price range covers the cheapest to the most expensive single tickets at the beginning of 2000. It is advisable to call sights in advance to determine specific opening times and prices.

Comments on these and other attractions in the main part of the Guide are welcome. Please write to Department TA, Which? Books, 2 Marylebone Road, London NW1 4DF or email *books@which.net* or *whichattractions@which.co.uk*. Our web site address is *www.which.net*

LONDON

Albert Memorial

Kensington Gore, London SW7 2AO

Queen Victoria's gothic memorial to Prince Albert, now golden again after eight years' renovation. ○ *All year.* ▣ *Free*

Barbican Art Gallery

Level 3, Barbican Centre, Silk Street, London EC2Y 8DS   ☎ *020-7382 7105*

Part of the Barbican arts centre, this gallery features art, design and photography exhibitions. ○ *All year.* ▣ *Varies according to exhibition*

Battersea Park Children's Zoo

Battersea Park, London SW11 4NJ   ☎ *020-8871 7540*

Zoo with farm animals, aviaries, deer, reptiles and otters (fed twice daily), a play area and summer pony rides. ○ *All year.* ▣ *90p–£1.80 (children under 2 free)*

British Airways London Eye

Embankment   ☎ *(0870) 5000 600*

Enormous Ferris wheel with spectacular views over London and surrounding counties. Disabled access. ○ *All year.* ▣ *£4.95—£7.50 (children under 5 free)*

Dulwich Picture Gallery

College Road, London SE21 7AD   ☎ *020-8693 5254*

England's oldest public gallery, designed by Sir John Soane, houses some fine Old Masters. ① *All year.* 🎟 *£3 (children under 17 free)*

Funland

The Trocadero, 1 Piccadilly Circus, London W1V 8DH   ☎ *020-7734 2777*

Futuristic entertainment centre featuring video games and rides over six floors. ① *All year.* 🎟 *Free (individual prices for games)*

Hall Place

Bourne Road, Bexley, Greater London DA5 1PQ   ☎ *(01322) 526574*

Tudor-cum-Jacobean mansion that houses the Bexley Museum, art galleries and Great Hall. The House is situated in rose, rock, herb and peat gardens. ① *All year.* 🎟 *Free*

Harrow Museum and Heritage Centre

Headstone Manor, Pinner View, Harrow HA2 6PX   ☎ *020-8861 2626*

Local museum in a seventeenth-century tithe barn with railway exhibits. Activities include talks and concerts. ① *All year.* 🎟 *Free*

Hayward Gallery

Belvedere Road, London SE1 8XX   ☎ *020-7960 4242*

This South Bank gallery holds four major exhibitions each year (phone for details). ① *Open when exhibitions staged.* 🎟 *Varies according to exhibition*

Horniman Museum and Gardens

100 London Road, Forest Hill, London SE23 3PQ   ☎ *020-8699 1872*

Museum in 16 acres of landscaped grounds with aquarium, natural history gallery and 'African Worlds' display. Regular events and children's activities. ① *Closed for refurbishment until late 2000.* 🎟 *Free*

Lauderdale House

Highgate Hill, Waterlow Park, London N6 5HG   ☎ *020-8348 8716*

Historic house, reputed former home of Nell Gwynn, and arts centre with views over London. ① *All year.* 🎟 *Free*

London Skyview Balloon

Spring Gardens, Vauxhall, London SE11 5HF   ☎ *(0345) 023842*

Rise above 400ft in this tethered helium balloon for city panoramas. Accommodates wheelchairs. ① *All year.* 🎟 *£7.50–£12*

London Brass Rubbing Centre

The Crypt, St Martin-in-the-Fields Church, Trafalgar Square, London WC2N 4JJ
     ☎ *020-7930 9306*

The workshop supplies instruction, materials and a choice of royal, historic and Celtic designs. ① *All year.* 🎟 *Free; brass-rubbings £2.50–£15*

The Monument

Monument Street, London EC3R 8AH ☎ *020-7626 2717*

Visitors to Sir Christopher Wren's edifice marking the Great Fire of London get certificates after climbing 311 steps to the summit (spectacular views).
🕐 *All year.* 💷 *50p–£1.50*

Photographers' Gallery

5 & 8 Great Newport Street, London WC2H 7HY ☎ *020-7831 1772*

The gallery is Britain's leading contemporary photography centre and has four exhibition areas. 🕐 *All year.* 💷 *Free*

Ragged School Museum

46-50 Copperfield Road, London E3 4RR ☎ *020-8980 6405*

Museum on the site of Barnardo's ragged school, with a reconstructed Victorian classroom and exhibits on the East End 1880–1900. 🕐 *All year.* 💷 *Free*

Royal Academy of Arts

Burlington House, Westminster, London W1V 0DS ☎ *020-7300 8000*

Britain's oldest fine-arts society stages prestigious temporary and permanent exhibitions. 🕐 *All year.* 💷 *Varies according to exhibition*

Royal Air Force Museum

Grahame Park Way, Hendon NW9 5LL ☎ *020-8205 2266*

Britain's National Aviation Museum, with over 70 full-size historic aircraft and the 'Battle of Britain Experience'. 🕐 *All year.* 💷 *£3.25–£6.50*

Royal College of Art

Kensington Gore, London SW7 2EU ☎ *020-7590 4444*

Displays of students' work in progress and visiting exhibitions. 🕐 *All year.* 💷 *Free*

Royal Mews

Buckingham Palace, London SW1A 1AA ☎ *020-7839 1377*

The home of the Queen's state carriages, including the eighteenth-century Coronation Coach, and the royal horses. 🕐 *All year.* 💷 *£2.10–£4.30 (children under 5 free)*

St Martin-in-the-Fields

Trafalgar Square, London WC2N 4JJ ☎ *020-7839 8362*

Eighteenth-century parish church and concert venue in the heart of London; its crypt contains the London Brass Rubbing Centre (see above). 🕐 *All year.* 💷 *Free*

Serpentine Gallery

Kensington Gardens, London W2 3XA ☎ *020-7402 6075*

Showcasing the work of contemporary artists, both British and international, the gallery has changing exhibitions. 🕐 *All year.* 💷 *Free*

Shakespeare's Globe Theatre and Exhibition

New Globe Walk, Bankside, London SE1 9DT ☎ *020-7902 1500*

Guided tours explain how the Renaissance-style theatre was constructed using Elizabethan techniques, while exhibits describe Shakespeare's world. ⊙ *All year.* ⊞ *£5–£7.50*

Sherlock Holmes Museum

221B Baker Street, London NW1 6XE ☎ *020-7935 8866*

Museum featuring the famous fictional detective's apartment and waxwork displays of characters from Conan Doyle's books. ⊙ *All year.* ⊞ *£4–£6*

Southwark Cathedral

Montague Close, Southwark, London SE1 9DA ☎ *020-7367 6712*

London's oldest Gothic church, with memorials to Shakespeare and the Elizabethan theatres and a chapel dedicated to John Harvard. ⊙ *All year.* ⊞ *Free*

Thames Barrier Visitors' Centre

1 Unity Way, Woolwich SE18 5NJ ☎ *020-8305 4188*

This exhibition on the world's largest movable flood barrier has a working scale model and audio-visual displays. ⊙ *All year.* ⊞ *£2–£3.40*

Thameside Park City Farm

40 Thames Road, Barking, Greater London IG11 0HH ☎ *020-8594 8449*

A farm with mixed livestock. ⊙ *All year.* ⊞ *Free*

Westminster Abbey Chapter House

East Cloisters, Westminster Abbey, London SW1P 3PE ☎ *020-7222 5897*

A meeting place for medieval monks and MPs, the Chapter House boasts some fine sculpture. See also the main entry on the Abbey. ⊙ *All year.* ⊞ *£1.30–£2.50*

Westminster Cathedral

Victoria Street, London SW1P 1QW ☎ *020-7798 9097*

England's principal Roman Catholic Church has Byzantine architecture and Stations of the Cross by Eric Gill. ⊙ *All year.* ⊞ *Free*

Whitechapel Art Gallery

Whitechapel High Street, London E1 7QX ☎ *020-7522 7888*

This gallery with an Art Nouveau façade stages temporary exhibitions, usually of modern art. ⊙ *All year.* ⊞ *Free*

Wimbledon Lawn Tennis Museum

All England Club, Church Road, London SW19 5AE ☎ *020-8946 6131*

This museum overlooking Centre Court serves up tennis memorabilia including archive film. ⊙ *All year (tournament ticket holders only during Championships).* ⊞ *£4–£5 (children under 5 free)*

ENGLAND

Alice in Wonderland Family Park, Hurn

Merritown Lane, Hurn, Dorset BH23 6BA ☎ *(01202) 483444*

Themed attractions include a maze, croquet lawn, cup-and-saucer ride and play centre. ○ *All year.* 💷 *£3.75–4.25*

American Cemetery, Coton

Coton, Cambridgeshire CB3 7PH ☎ *(01954) 210350*

Cemetery maintained by the American Battle Monuments Commission, with memorial chapel. ○ *All year.* 💷 *Free*

American Museum in Britain, Bath

Claverton Manor, Bath BA2 7BD ☎ *(01225) 460503*

The galleries contain pre-Civil War decorative arts (including Native American art), the grounds a North American arboretum. ○ *25 Mar to 29 Oct, 18 Nov to 10 Dec.* 💷 *£3–£5.50*

Amerton Working Farm, Stowe-by-Chartley

Stowe-by-Chartley, Staffordshire ST18 0LA ☎ *(01889) 270294*

Farm with animals, a craft centre, farm trail and ice cream-making demonstrations. ○ *All year.* 💷 *Free*

Animal World, Bolton

Moss Bank Park, Moss Bank Way, Bolton, Lancashire BL1 6NQ ☎ *(01204) 846157*

Animals in enclosures that reflect their natural habitats, including a 'rainforest' and Butterfly House. ○ *All year.* 💷 *Free*

ARC Arts Centre, Stockton-on-Tees

Dovecot Street, Stockton-on-Tees TS18 1LL ☎ *(01642) 666600*

A regional arts venue with two theatres, dance and recording studios and rehearsal rooms. ○ *All year.* 💷 *Free*

Art and Craft Centre, Dedham

High Street, Dedham, Essex CO7 6AD ☎ *(01206) 322666*

This craft centre in a converted church incorporates a toy museum and art gallery. ○ *All year.* 💷 *30p–50p*

Arundel Castle

Arundel, West Sussex BN18 9AB ☎ *(01903) 883136*

Stronghold with eleventh-century keep, Baron's Hall, armoury and chapel. Gainsborough and Van Dyck portraits line the gallery, and the castle has a Victorian kitchen garden. ○ *Apr to Oct.* 💷 *£4.50–£7 (children under 5 free)*

Ash End House Children's Farm, Middleton

Middleton Lane, Middleton, Staffordshire B78 2BL ☎ *0121-329 3240*

The farm comprises undercover play areas, picnic barns and a gift shop.
⏱ All year. 💷 £1.30-£3.60

Attingham Park, Shrewsbury

Shrewsbury, Shropshire SY4 4TP ☎ *(01743) 709203*

Mansion with state rooms and restored Victorian kitchen. The grounds offer several
walks. ⏱ *Late Mar to Nov.* 💷 *House and grounds £2.10–£4.20, grounds £1.05–£2.10*

Auckland Castle, Bishop Auckland

Market Place, Bishop Auckland, Co Durham DL14 7NR ☎ *(01388) 601627*

The Bishop of Durham's official residence. Public areas include the private chapel
(supposedly Europe's largest), state rooms and medieval kitchen. ⏱ *May to Sept.*
💷 *£2–3*

Baddesley Clinton Hall, Knowle

Knowle, Solihull, West Midlands B93 0DQ ☎ *(01564) 783294*

A fourteenth-century moated manor house, set in 120 acres. ⏱ *House Mar to Oct,
grounds mid-Feb to mid-Dec.* 💷 *House and grounds £2.60–£5.20, grounds
£1.10–£2.60 (children under 5 free)*

Baltic Millennium Bridge, Gateshead

South Shore Road, Gateshead, Tyne and Wear NE8 2BE ☎ *0191-477 1011*

Due for completion in May 2001, this pedestrian and cycle bridge over the Tyne will link
Gateshead and Newcastle. ⏱ *Opens May 2001.* 💷 *Free*

Banbury Museum

8 Horsefair, Banbury, Oxfordshire OX16 0AA ☎ *(01295) 259855*

A restored Edwardian building with local history exhibits and a tourist information
centre. ⏱ *All year.* 💷 *Free*

Barleylands Farm Museum and Visitor Centre, Billericay

Barleylands Road, Billericay, Essex CM11 2UD ☎ *(01268) 282090*

Visitor centre with a rural museum, working craft studios (including glass-blowing) and
miniature steam railway. ⏱ *Mar to Oct.* 💷 *£1.75–£3.25*

Bass Museum of Brewing, Burton upon Trent

Horninglow Street, Burton upon Trent, Staffordshire DE14 1YQ ☎ *(01283) 511000*

Beer museum and working micro brewery with family fun trail.
⏱ *All year.* 💷 *£2–£4.50*

Beale Park, Reading

Lower Basildon, Berkshire RG8 9NH ☎ *0118-984 5172*

A rare bird collection. Other highlights include a narrow-gauge railway, adventure playground, deer park and summer boat trips. ○ *Mar to Dec.* 🖾 *£2–£4.50 (children under 3 free)*

Bede's World, Jarrow

Church Bank, Jarrow, Tyne and Wear NE32 3DY ☎ *0191-489 2106*

The story of St Paul's monastery and the Venerable Bede, Dark Age scholar. Displays include glass, sculpture, metalwork and a recreated Anglo-Saxon farm. ○ *All year.* 🖾 *£1.50–£3 (children under 5 free)*

Beningbrough Hall and Gardens

Shipton by Beningbrough, North Yorkshire YO30 1DD ☎ *(01904) 470666*

A baroque house with pictures from the National Portrait Gallery, walled gardens and an adventure playground. ○ *Apr to Oct.* 🖾 *Gardens and exhibitions £1.70 £3.50, house, gardens and exhibitions £2.50 £5 (children under 5 free)*

Belsay Hall, Castle and Gardens

Belsay, Newcastle upon Tyne, Tyne and Wear NE20 0DX ☎ *(01661) 881636*

Castle, manor house and neo-classical hall set in 30 acres of landscaped gardens. ○ *All year.* 🖾 *£3.80–£1.90 (children under 5 free)*

Beverley Minster

Beverley, East Yorkshire HU17 0DP ☎ *(01482) 868540*

A Gothic church with a Saxon sanctuary chair and sixteenth-century misericords. ○ *All year.* 🖾 *Free*

Bewl Water, Lamberhurst

Lamberhurst, Royal Tunbridge Wells, Kent TN3 8JH ☎ *(01892) 890661*

Waterside activities at south-east England's largest lake. Amenities include picnic areas, a restaurant and visitor centre. ○ *All year.* 🖾 *Easter to Oct £3–£4 per vehicle, Nov to Easter £2.50 per vehicle (1999 prices)*

Birdland Park, Bourton-on-the-Water

Rissington Road, Bourton-on-the-Water, Gloucestershire GL54 2BN ☎ *(01451) 820480*

A landscaped home to exotic birds, with tropical/temperate houses and children's play area. ○ *All year.* 🖾 *£2.50–£4 (children under 4 free)*

Birmingham Cathedral

Colmore Row, Birmingham, West Midlands B3 2QB ☎ *0121-236 4333*

Eighteenth-century baroque church with windows by Burne-Jones. ○ *All year.* 🖾 *Free*

Birmingham International Airport Visitor Centre, Birmingham

Birmingham, West Midlands B26 3QJ ☎ *0121-767 7243*

This viewing gallery and exhibition area overlook the runway and aircraft stands.
⏱ *All year.* ▣ *30p–50p (children under 5 free)*

Birmingham Nature Centre

Pershore Road, Edgbaston, West Midlands B5 7RL ☎ *0121-472 7775*

Wild animals, birds and insects in natural enclosures. ⏱ *All year.* ▣ *£1.50 (children under 16 free)*

Blackgang Chine Fantasy Park, Chale

Chale, Nr Ventnor, Isle of Wight PO38 2HN ☎ *(01983) 730330*

Themed areas include Frontierland and Nurseryland; other attractions are dinosaurs, water gardens and a water-coaster. ⏱ *Apr to Oct.* ▣ *£4.95–£5.95 (children under 3 free)*

Blake House Craft Centre, Braintree

Blake End, Braintree, Essex CM7 8SH ☎ *(01376) 320662*

Courtyard containing listed farm buildings converted into craft shops and businesses.
⏱ *All year.* ▣ *Free*

Bluebell Railway, Uckfield

Sheffield Park, Uckfield, East Sussex TN22 3QL ☎ *(01825) 722370*

Steam-train trips through the Sussex countryside, the south's largest engine collection and a railway museum. ⏱ *All year.* ▣ *£3.90–£7.80 (children under 3 free)*

Bolton Abbey

Bolton Abbey Estate, North Yorkshire BD23 6EX ☎ *(01756) 710533*

Twelfth-century Bolton Priory lies at the heart of a country estate, surrounded by parkland and nature trails. ⏱ *All year.* ▣ *£3 per vehicle*

Bolton Castle

Castle Bolton, Leyburn, North Yorkshire DL8 4ET ☎ *(01969) 623981*

The castle, ancestral home of the Scrope family, was besieged in the Civil War.
⏱ *All year.* ▣ *£3–£4 (children under 5 free)*

Bolton Museum and Art Gallery

Le Mans Crescent, Bolton, Lancashire BL1 1SE ☎ *(01204) 522311*

Displays on geology, wildlife and archaeology, plus an aquarium. ⏱ *All year.* ▣ *Free*

Bradford Industrial Museum and Horses at Work

Moorside Mills, Moorside Road, Bradford, West Yorkshire BD2 3HP ☎ *(01274) 631756*

Nineteenth-century spinning mill complex with working shire horses and weaving demonstrations. ⏱ *All year.* ▣ *Free*

Bressingham Steam Museum and Gardens, Diss

Bressingham, Diss, Norfolk IP22 2AB ☎ *(01379) 687386*

Working steam museum with engine displays and woodland rides, plus a two-acre plant centre. ⏰ *Mar to Nov.* 💷 *Call for admission prices*

Brewhouse Yard Museum, Nottingham

Castle Boulevard, Nottingham NG7 1FB ☎ *0115-915 3600*

The Museum of Nottingham Life recreates the last 300 years with period rooms. ⏰ *All year.* 💷 *80p–£1.50 weekends/bank holidays (children under 3 free)*

Brickfields Horsecountry and Isle of Wight Shire Horse Centre, Binstead

Newnham Road, Binstead, Isle of Wight PO33 3TH ☎ *(01983) 566801*

The centre has working shire horses, miniature ponies and racing pigs; attractions include a riding stable, blacksmith's and carriage collection. ⏰ *All year.* 💷 *Mar to Nov £3.25–£4.50, Dec to Feb £2–£3 (children under 4 free)*

Brighton Museum and Art Gallery

Church Street, Brighton, East Sussex BN1 1UE ☎ *(01273) 290900*

Art nouveau, art deco, ceramics, costumes and toys housed in a Moorish-style building with local history gallery. ⏰ *All year.* 💷 *Free*

Bronte Weaving Shed, Haworth

Townend Mill, North Street, Haworth, West Yorkshire BD22 8EP ☎ *(01535) 646217*

The restored shed is home to the traditionally hand-woven Bronte Tweed and exhibitions. ⏰ *All year.* 💷 *Free*

Brownsea Island, Poole

Poole Harbour, Poole, Dorset BH15 1EE ☎ *(01202) 707744*

Views of the Dorset coast from this wooded island with a nature reserve. ⏰ *Late Mar to early Oct.* 💷 *£1.30–£2.50*

Brymor Ice Cream Parlour, Masham

High Jervaulx Farm, Masham, North Yorkshire HG4 4PG ☎ *(01677) 460377*

Ice cream parlour on a working dairy farm. Sample sorbets and other chilly delights. ⏰ *All year.* 💷 *Free*

Buckinghamshire County Museum, Aylesbury

Church Street, Aylesbury, Buckinghamshire HP20 2QP ☎ *(01296) 331441*

A garden setting for local heritage galleries and the hands-on Roald Dahl Children's Gallery. ⏰ *All year.* 💷 *Museum £1; museum and Roald Dahl Gallery (summer) £2–£3.50, (winter) £1.25–£2 (children under 3 free)*

Buckler's Hard, Brockenhurst

Beaulieu, Brockenhurst, Hampshire SO42 7XB　　　　☎　*(01590) 616203*

An eighteenth-century shipbuilding village with historical reconstructions, craft displays and maritime museum. ◷ *All year.* 💷 *£3 per car + £1–£2 per occupant, pedestrians £2–£4 (children under 4 free)*

Butlins Family Entertainment Resort, Minehead

Minehead, Somerset TA24 5SH　　　　☎　*(01643) 703331*

Amusement park with Skyline Pavilion, splash swimming pool, outdoor adventure play area and bowling alley. ◷ *All year.* 💷 *£4–£12 depending on season (children under 4 free)*

Caithness Crystal Visitor Centre, King's Lynn

9-12 Paxman Road, Hardwick Industrial Estate, King's Lynn, Norfolk PE30 4NE
　　　　☎ *(01553) 765111*

Visitors can watch glass-making demonstrations and buy Royal Doulton products in the factory shop. ◷ *All year.* 💷 *Free*

Calke Abbey, Park and Gardens, Ticknall

Ticknall, Derbyshire DE73 1LE　　　　☎　*(01332) 863822*

Eighteenth-century house in a timewarp since the 1920s, with natural history collections and gardens. ◷ *Apr to Oct, park all year.* 💷 *£2.50–£5.10*

Callestock Cider Farm, Truro

Penhallow, Truro, Cornwall TR4 9LW　　　　☎　*(01872) 573356*

Learn about cider-making and see how mead, wines and preserves are made. Tractor and trailer rides. ◷ *All year.* 💷 *Free*

Captain Cook Birthplace Museum, Middlesbrough

Stewart Park, Marton, Middlesbrough TS7 6AS　　　　☎　*(01642) 311211*

Museum celebrating Captain Cook's early life, voyages and the countries he visited. ◷ *All year.* 💷 *£1.20–£2.40 (children under 5 free)*

Carsington Water, Ashbourne

Ashbourne, Derbyshire DE6 1ST　　　　☎　*(01629) 540696*

Try watersports and activities at this lake with visitor centre and conservation areas. ◷ *All year.* 💷 *Free (charge for watersports)*

Cartwright Hall Art Gallery, Bradford

Lister Park, Bradford, West Yorkshire BD9 4NS　　　　☎　*(01274) 751212*

A baroque-style gallery with modern British art exhibits and Asian collections. ◷ *All year.* 💷 *Free*

Caudwell's Mill and Craft Centre, Matlock

Rowsley, Matlock, Derbyshire DE4 2EB ☎ *(01629) 734374*

Listed Victorian working mill with machinery and craft shop. ⏰ *All year.* 💷 *£1–£3 (children under 5 free)*

Chedworth Roman Villa, Yanworth

Yanworth, Gloucestershire GL54 3LJ ☎ *(01242) 890256*

Museum, mosaics and well-preserved remains of a 32-room villa. ⏰ *Mar to Nov.* 💷 *£1.70–£3.40 (children under 3 free)*

Chester Visitor and Craft Centre

Vicars Lane, Chester, Cheshire CH1 1QX ☎ *(01244) 402111*

Heritage demonstrations in a Victorian street scene, plus an audio-visual show on Chester and a genealogy hall. ⏰ *All year.* 💷 *Free*

Chesterholm Museum, Hexham

Vindolanda Trust, Chesterholm Museum, Bardon Mill, Hexham, Northumberland NE47 7JN ☎ *(01434) 344277*

The Roman army museum has exhibits on daily life and finds from the nearby ruined fort and settlement. ⏰ *Feb to mid-Nov.* 💷 *Site £2.80–£3.80, joint ticket £4.10–£5.60 (children under 5 free)*

Chillingham Castle

Chillingham, near Wooler, Northumberland NE66 5NJ ☎ *(01668) 215359*

Medieval castle with state rooms, dungeon, woodland walks and topiary garden. ⏰ *May to Sept.* 💷 *£4–£4.50 (children under 16 free)*

Chiltern Open Air Museum, Chalfont St Giles

Newland Park, Gorelands Lane, Chalfont St Giles, Buckinghamshire HP8 4AD ☎ *(01494) 871117*

Historic buildings reflecting Chiltern life. Nature trail. ⏰ *Apr to Oct.* 💷 *£3–£5.50*

Christchurch Mansion, Ipswich

Christchurch Park, Soane Street, Ipswich, Suffolk IP4 2BE ☎ *(01473) 433554*

This Tudor mansion contains collections of ceramics, clocks and furniture. Art exhibitions are staged in the Wolsey Art Gallery. ⏰ *All year.* 💷 *Free*

Cinque Ports Pottery, Rye

The Monastery, Conduit Hill, Rye, East Sussex TN31 7LE ☎ *(01797) 222033*

Watch pottery-making activities from a viewing gallery in this listed building. ⏰ *All year.* 💷 *Free*

Clambers Play Centre, Hastings

White Rock Gardens, Hastings, East Sussex TN34 1LD ☎ *(01424) 423778*

Activity centre for children up to 12 years old, including an outdoor paddling pool, sandpit and adventure golf course. ① *All year.* 💷 *£1.60–£3.95 (children under 18 months free)*

Clarks Shopping Village, Street

Farm Road, Street, Somerset BA16 0BB ☎ *(01458) 840064*

Development on Clarks' original manufacturing site. Attractions include a shoe museum, play areas and factory shops. ① *All year.* 💷 *Free*

Cliffe Castle Museum, Keighley

Spring Gardens Lane, Keighley, West Yorkshire BD20 6LH ☎ *(01535) 618230*

A converted Victorian mansion housing natural history, geology, archaeology and social history exhibits. ① *All year.* 💷 *Free*

Cliveden, Taplow

Taplow, Buckinghamshire SL6 0JA ☎ *(01628) 605069*

The former home of Lady Astor, now a hotel surrounded by landscaped gardens. ① *Mid-Mar to Dec.* 💷 *Grounds £2.50–£5; mansion and grounds £3–£6; car park £3*

Clovelly Village

Clovelly Estate Co Ltd, Estate Office, near Bideford, Devon EX39 5SY

☎ *(01237) 431781*

Clifftop fishing village with fourteenth-century harbour, donkey-sledge transport and audio-visual programme. ① *All year.* 💷 *£2.50–£3.50 (children under 7 free)*

Coastguard Cottages, Dunwich Heath

Dunwich Heath, Dunwich, Suffolk IP17 3DJ ☎ *(01728) 648505*

Nature conservation area with walks and access to beach. ① *All year.* 💷 *Free*

Collegiate Church of St Mary, Warwick

Old Square, Warwick CV34 4RA ☎ *(01926) 400771*

Highlights inside the church are the fourteenth-century Beauchamp Chapel and Tudor tombs. ① *All year.* 💷 *Free*

Colony Country Store, Ulverston

Lindal Business Park, Lindal-in-Furness, Ulverston, Cumbria LA12 0LL

☎ *(01229) 461102*

The store sells candles made on site and other gifts. ① *All year.* 💷 *Free*

Cotwall End Countryside and Craft Centre, Dudley

Catholic Lane, Sedgley, Dudley, West Midlands DY3 3YE ☎ *(01902) 674668*

The chance to see and feed familiar animals at close hand, or visit craft studios. ① *All year.* 💷 *Free, 50p car parking fee*

Coventry Cathedral

7 Priory Row, Coventry CV1 5ES ☎ *024-7622 7597*

Twentieth-century cathedral built on the ruins of the medieval edifice destroyed in 1940. ⏱ *All year.* 💷 *Free*

Crafter's Marketplace, Derby

Unit 4, The Coliseum Centre, Derby DE1 2NY ☎ *(01332) 267750*

Market with 250 booths selling craft and hobby items. ⏱ *All year.* 💷 *Free*

Cragside House, Gardens and Estate, Rothbury

Cragside, Rothbury, Morpeth, Northumberland NE65 7PX ☎ *(01669) 620333*

Nineteenth-century house of Tyneside industrialist Lord Armstrong, where water-generated electricity was pioneered. ⏱ *House Apr to Oct, grounds Apr to mid-Dec.* 💷 *House and grounds £3.25–£6.50, grounds £2–£4 (children under 5 free)*

Croxteth Hall and Country Park, Liverpool

Croxteth Hall Lane, Liverpool L12 0HB ☎ *0151-228 5311*

Edwardian stately home with Victorian walled garden and rare breeds. ⏱ *Hall Apr to Oct, garden Apr to Sept, farm all year round.* 💷 *Hall, farm and garden £1.80–£3.60, hall and farm each £1–£1.80, garden 55p–£1.05*

Cumberland Pencil Museum, Keswick

Southey Works, Keswick CA12 5NG ☎ *(017687) 73626*

The story of pencils, told via exhibits and audio-visuals. ⏱ *All year.* 💷 *£1.25–£2.50 (children under 5 free)*

Cusworth Hall Museum of South Yorkshire Life, Doncaster

Cusworth Lane, Doncaster, South Yorkshire DN5 7TU ☎ *(01302) 782342*

This eighteenth-century hall has displays on transport, costume and local occupations over the last 200 years. ⏱ *All year.* 💷 *Free*

Dartington Crystal, Torrington

Linden Close, Torrington, Devon EX38 7AN ☎ *(01805) 626262*

See crystal glassware being crafted, try hands-on activities and learn the history of glass-making. ⏱ *All year.* 💷 *£1–£3.50 (children under 6 free)*

David Evans World of Silk, Crayford

Bourne Industrial Park, Bourne Road, Crayford, Kent DA1 4BP ☎ *(01322) 559401*

Guided tours around a silk print workshop and museum. ⏱ *All year.* 💷 *Pre-booked tour £2.50–£3, museum £1.50–£2 (children under 5 free)*

D-Day Museum and Overlord Embroidery, Portsmouth

Clarence Esplanade, Portsmouth PO5 3NT ☎ *023-9282 7261*

Displays on D-Day and the 1944 Allied invasion of Normandy: the 83-metre tapestry depicts events. ⏱ *All year.* 💷 *£2.85–£4.75*

Derby Museum and Art Gallery

The Strand, Derby DE1 1BS ☎ *(01332) 716659*

Exhibits include Derby porcelain, antiquities and social history. ⏲ *All year.* 💷 *Free*

Dinosaur Adventure Park, Lenwade

Weston Park, Lenwade, Norfolk NR9 5JW ☎ *(01603) 870245*

Explore the dinosaur trail and woodland maze. Play area for children. ⏲ *Mar to Oct.* 💷 *£3.50–£4.50*

Drusilla's Park, Polegate

Alfriston, Polegate, East Sussex BN26 5QS ☎ *(01323) 870234*

Zoo with over 100 species in natural habitats, 'millennium bug' insects, llama paddock with train and children's activities. ⏲ *All year.* 💷 *£6–£7.60 (children under 3 free)*

Dunstanburgh Castle, Alnwick

Craster, Alnwick, Northumberland NE66 3TT ☎ *(01661) 881297*

Dramatically sited clifftop castle with ruins that include a gatehouse and curtain wall. ⏲ *All year.* 💷 *90p–£1.80*

Durham Castle

Palace Green, Durham DH1 3RW ☎ *0191-374 3863*

An eleventh-century motte-and-bailey castle with medieval great hall and kitchens. ⏲ *Mar to Sept.* 💷 *£2–£3 (children under 4 free)*

East Point Pavilion Visitor Centre, Lowestoft

Royal Plain, Lowestoft, Suffolk NR33 0AP ☎ *(01502) 523000*

Underwater-themed play area with 'Discoverig' platforms based on North Sea gas rigs. ⏲ *All year.* 💷 *£1.70–£2.20*

Exbury Gardens

Exbury Estate Office, Exbury, Nr Southampton, Hampshire SO45 1AZ
☎ *(01703) 891203*

Displays of azaleas, magnolias and camellias, a rock garden, cascades and woodland walks. ⏲ *Late Feb to Nov, Mid-Mar to June.* 💷 *Jul to Nov £4–£5, Feb to mid-Mar £2.50–£3.50 (children under 10 free)*

Farmworld, Oadby

Gartree Road, Oadby, Leicestershire LE2 2FB ☎ *0116-271 0355*

Farm park with shire horses, rare breeds, milking parlour and children's adventure playground. ⏲ *All year.* 💷 *£2–£2.50 (children under 3 free)*

Ferrers Centre for Arts and Crafts, Ashby-de-la-Zouch

Staunton Harold, Ashby-de-la-Zouch, Leicestershire LE65 1RU ☎ *(01332) 865408*

Centre offering crafts including jewellery, textiles, furniture and sculpture. ⏲ *All year.* 💷 *Free*

Filching Manor Motor Museum

Filching Manor, Jevington Road, Wannock, Polegate, East Sussex BN26 5QA
☎ *(01323) 487838*

A collection of vintage sports and racing cars at a fifteenth-century Wealden hall house containing antiques and armour. ① *Easter to Oct.* ⊞ *£2.50–£3.50 (children under 5 free)*

Fishermen's Museum, Hastings

Rock-a-Nore Road, Hastings, East Sussex TN34 3DW ☎ *(01424) 461446*

Former fishermen's church, now a museum housing memorabilia including models, nets, photos and the lugger *Enterprise*. ① *All year.* ⊞ *Free*

Fort Fun, Eastbourne

Royal Parade, Eastbourne, East Sussex BN22 7LU ☎ *(01323) 642833*

A children's fun park with runaway train, roller-coaster, crazy golf, jet ride and bouncy castle. ① *All year.* ⊞ *Children £1.75–£3.75, adults free*

Framlingham Castle, Woodbridge

Framlingham, Woodbridge, Suffolk IP8 9BT ☎ *(01728) 724189*

This castle with twelfth-century curtain walls was built by the Earls of Norfolk. ① *All year.* ⊞ *£1.60–£3.20 (children under 5 free)*

Fun Farm, Weston

High Road, Weston, Lincolnshire PE12 6JU ☎ *(01406) 373444*

Indoor and outdoor activities for children, craft sessions and a gift shop. ① *All year.* ⊞ *£2.29–£3.79 (children under 1 and adults free)*

Gatwick Airport Skyview and Spectator Gallery, Gatwick

South Terminal Building, Gatwick, West Sussex RH6 0NP ☎ *(01293) 502244*

Skyview features a historic Herald airliner, cinema, simulation ride and airfield views. ① *All year.* ⊞ *Viewing gallery 75p–£1.50, gallery, cinema, airliner and simulator £3–£4.50 (children under 5 free)*

Gibside, Burnopfield

Burnopfield, Newcastle upon Tyne, Tyne and Wear NE16 6BG ☎ *(01207) 542255*

The restored mausoleum of the Bowes family (forbears of the Bowes-Lyons and the Queen Mother), designed by James Paine. ① *Mar to Oct, grounds all year.* ⊞ *£1.50–£3*

Glastonbury Abbey

Magadelene Street, Glastonbury, Somerset BA6 9EL ☎ *(01458) 832267*

Britain's oldest Christian sanctuary, reputedly King Arthur's burial-place. Museum and abbot's kitchen. ① *All year.* ⊞ *£1–£3 (children under 5 free)*

Gloucester Cathedral

Westgate Street, Gloucester GL1 2LR ☎ *(01452) 528095*

Exhibition, chapter house and cloisters. ① *All year.* ⊞ *Free*

Godstone Farm

Tilburstow Hill Road, Godstone, Surrey RH9 8LX ☎ *(01883) 742546*

Farm in wooded scenery, home to a variety of animals (some can be petted). Extensive play areas. ◷ *All year.* ▣ *£3.80 (adults accompanying children and children under 2 free)*

Goonhilly Earth Station, Helston

Nr Helston, Cornwall TR12 6LQ ☎ *(0800) 679593*

The world's largest satellite earth station. Shuttles take visitors to an audio-visual show and interactive displays. ◷ *Closed Nov to mid-Mar.* ▣ *£2.50–£4 (children under 6 free)*

Graves Art Gallery, Sheffield

Surrey Street, Sheffield, South Yorkshire S1 1XZ ☎ *0114-273 5158*

Exhibits include British and European paintings and Islamic, Japanese and Indian art. ◷ *All year.* ▣ *Free*

Great Western Designer Outlet Village, Swindon

Kemble Drive, Swindon, Wiltshire SN2 2DY ☎ *(01793) 507605*

A listed building housing the UK's largest covered outlet for discount fashion, and the Swindon Railway Heritage Museum. ◷ *All year.* ▣ *Free*

Grosvenor Museum, Chester

27 Grosvenor Street, Chester, Cheshire CH1 2DD ☎ *(01244) 402012*

Museum containing interactive displays on Roman life, period rooms and local craftware. ◷ *All year (to reopen in July 2000 after refurbishment).* ▣ *Free*

Guisborough Priory

Church Street, Guisborough, Redcar TS14 6HG ☎ *(01287) 633801*

A ruined Augustinian priory, once one of the region's greatest monasteries, overlooking the Cleveland Hills. Open-air plays in July. ◷ *Jan to Sept.* ▣ *40p–90p*

Hall Hill Farm, Lanchester

Lanchester, Co Durham DH7 OTA ☎ *(01388) 730300*

As well as farm animals, attractions include a trailer ride, riverside walk and play area. ◷ *Apr to Nov.* ▣ *Call for admission prices*

Hall's Croft, Stratford-upon-Avon

Old Town, Stratford-upon-Avon, Warwickshire CV37 6BG ☎ *(01789) 292107*

The home of Shakespeare's daughter and her doctor husband contains Elizabethan and Jacobean artefacts and medical exhibits. ◷ *All year.* ▣ *£1.70–£3.50 (children under 5 free)*

Sir Harold Hillier Gardens and Arboretum, Ampfield

Jermyns House, Jermyns Lane, Ampfield, Hampshire SO51 0QA ☎ *(01794) 368787*

A large (180-acre) collection of cultivated and woody plants. Seasonal displays. ◷ *All year.* ▣ *Apr to Oct £1–£4.25, Nov to Mar £1–£3.25 (children under 5 free)*

Harris Museum and Art Gallery, Preston

Market Square, Preston, Lancashire PR1 2PP   ☎   *(01772) 258248*

The museum contains British paintings, ceramics and costume, and tells the story of Preston. ⊙ *All year.* 🖼 *Free*

Harvey's Wine Cellars, Bristol

12 Denmark Street, Bristol BS1 5DQ   ☎   *0117-927 5036*

Learn about wine through the ages in the thirteenth-century cellars, birthplace of Harveys Bristol Cream. ⊙ *All year.* 🖼 *Museum £4–£5; additional charge for tours and tastings*

Hatton Country World

Dark Lane, Hatton, Warwickshire CV35 8XA   ☎   *(01926) 843411*

Craft centre and farm park with adventure playground and nature trail. ⊙ *All year.* 🖼 *Farm park £3.40 (children under 3 free)*

Hawes Ropemakers

W.R. Outhwaite & Son, Town Foot, Hawes, North Yorkshire DL8 3NT
    ☎   *(01969) 667487*

Observe traditional rope-making skills and visit the shop. ⊙ *All year.* 🖼 *Free*

Herbert Art Gallery and Museum, Coventry

Jordan Well, Coventry CV1 5QP   ☎   *024-7683 2565*

Interactive exhibits on 1,000 years of Coventry's history, ceramics and paintings. ⊙ *All year.* 🖼 *Free*

Heritage Motor Centre, Gaydon

Banbury Road, Gaydon, Warwickshire CV35 0BJ   ☎   *(01926) 641188*

The world's largest collection of historic British cars. Activities include quad bikes and a children's roadway. ⊙ *All year.* 🖼 *£4–£6 (children under 5 free)*

High Lodge Forest Centre, Brandon

Brandon Downham, Brandon, Suffolk IP27 0TJ   ☎   *(01842) 810271*

Thetford Forest can be explored via waymarked walks and wildlife observed at the centre. ⊙ *All year.* 🖼 *Call for admission prices*

Hop Farm Country Park, Beltring

Beltring, Nr Tonbridge, Kent TN12 6PY   ☎   *(01622) 872068*

Oast houses contain the Hop Story museum. Shire horses, a nature trail and adventure playgrounds also keep visitors amused. ⊙ *All year.* 🖼 *£3.80–£5.80 (children under 4 free)*

Hornsea Freeport

Hornsea Freeport Ltd, Rolston Road, Hornsea, East Yorkshire HU18 1UT

☎ *(01964) 534211*

Landscaped gardens contain family leisure attractions and discount shops.
⏱ *All year.* 🎫 *Free*

Ickworth House Park and Gardens, Horringer

Horringer, Suffolk IP29 5QE ☎ *(01284) 735270*

Oval house dating from 1795, surrounded by Italian gardens and 'Capability' Brown walks. ⏱ *Mar to Oct.* 🎫 *Park and garden 80p–£2.40, house, park and garden £2.40–£5.50*

Impressions Gallery of Photography, York

29 Castlegate, York YO1 9RN ☎ *(01904) 654724*

Temporary photographic exhibitions, talks and workshops. ⏱ *All year.* 🎫 *Free*

Isle of Wight Pearl, Brighstone

Chilton Chine, Military Road, Brighstone, Isle of Wight PO30 4DD ☎ *(01983) 740352*

The workshop at this showroom for real, cultured and simulated pearls has stringing demonstrations. ⏱ *All year.* 🎫 *Free*

Jane Austen Centre, Bath

40 Gay Street, Bath BA1 2NT ☎ *(01225) 443000*

This exhibition in a Georgian town house tells the story of Jane Austen's Bath. ⏱ *All year.* 🎫 *£1.95–£3.95 (children under 6 free)*

Jorvik Glass, Castle Howard

Castle Howard, Stableyard, York YO60 7DA ☎ *(01653) 648555*

See glass-blowing demonstrations in the grounds of Castle Howard. ⏱ *Mid-Mar to Oct.* 🎫 *Free*

Jungle Jungle, Andover

3a West Way, Walworth Industrial Estate, Andover, Hampshire SP10 5AS

☎ *(01264) 336360*

Children aged up to 11 can take the Amazon Trail and use the indoor adventure play area. ⏱ *All year.* 🎫 *£2.50–£3*

Kedleston Hall

Kedleston, Derbyshire DE22 5JH ☎ *(01332) 842191*

A Palladian mansion with Adam interiors and an Indian museum. ⏱ *Apr to Oct.* 🎫 *£2.50–£5 (children under 5 free)*

Keighley and Worth Valley Railway

Haworth Station, Keighley, West Yorkshire BD22 8NJ ☎ *(01535) 645214*

This preserved branch line takes in stations including that seen in the film *The Railway Children.* ⏱ *All year.* 🎫 *£3–£8 (children under 5 free)*

Kettle's Yard, Cambridge

Castle Street, Cambridge CB3 0AQ   ☎ *(01223) 352124*

A collection of twentieth-century paintings and sculpture, and temporary exhibits.
🕐 *All year.* 🎟 *Free*

Kings College Chapel

Kings College, Cambridge CB2 1ST   ☎ *(01223) 331100*

Chapel with magnificent fan-vaulting, stained glass and Rubens' *Adoration of the Magi*.
An exhibition explains its founding by Henry IV and subsequent history.
🕐 *All year.* 🎟 *£2.50–£3.50 (children under 12 free)*

Kirkleatham Old Hall Museum, Redcar

Kirkleatham, Redcar TS10 5NW   ☎ *(01642) 479500*

Displays on local life and commerce, including the fishing industry. 🕐 *All year.* 🎟 *Free*

Lakeland Sheep and Wool Centre, Cockermouth

Egremont Road, Cockermouth, Cumbria CA13 0QX   ☎ *(01900) 822673*

Nineteen breeds of sheep, shearing and displays about Cumbria's western Lakes. 🕐 *All year.* 🎟 *Sheep show £2–£3 (children under 3 free)*

Lakes Glass Centre, Ulverston

Oubas Hill, Ulverston, Cumbria LA12 7LB   ☎ *(01229) 581385*

See craftspeople at work, view an exhibition on the local area, and purchase lead crystal
and coloured glass. 🕐 *All year.* 🎟 *Factory tour £1–£2*

Lancaster Leisure Park

G B Antiques Ltd, Wyresdale Road, Lancaster, Lancashire LA1 3LA   ☎ *(01524) 68444*

Leisure complex with children's rides in parkland, a factory shop and antiques centre.
🕐 *All year.* 🎟 *75p–£1.50*

Lands End

Sennen, Penzance, Cornwall TR19 7AA   ☎ *(01736) 871501*

The cliffs at England's most westerly point offer panoramas, interactive exhibits and a
Hall of Fame. 🕐 *All year.* 🎟 *£3 admission, attractions £1.50–£2.50*

Lichfield Cathedral

The Close, Lichfield, Staffordshire WS13 7LD   ☎ *(01543) 306240*

This medieval cathedral with three spires houses the Lichfield gospels.
🕐 *All year.* 🎟 *Free*

Lindisfarne Castle

Holy Island, Berwick-upon-Tweed, Northumberland TD15 2SH   ☎ *(01289) 389244*

Built in 1550 to defend the harbour, the castle was converted into a private house by
architect Edwin Lutyens in 1903. 🕐 *Apr to Oct.* 🎟 *£2–£4*

Linton Zoo

Hadstock Road, Linton, Cambridgeshire CB1 6NT   ☎   *(01223) 891308*

Animals. including big cats, wallabies, zebras and parrots. and attractive gardens.
🕐 *All year.* 💷 *£3–£4*

Liverpool Cathedral (C of E)

Liverpool L1 7AZ   ☎   *0151-709 6271*

This grand building is Britain's largest Anglican cathedral. 🕐 *All year.* 💷 *Free; tower and embroidery exhibition £1–£2*

Liverpool Museum

William Brown Street, Liverpool L3 8EN   ☎   *0151-478 4399*

The museum has collections from all over the world, a planetarium and aquarium.
💷 *All year.* 💷 *£1.50–£3 (children under 16 free)*

Lower Barn Farm Craft Centre and Cultural Centre, Rayleigh

London Road, Rayleigh, Essex SS6 9ET   ☎   *(01268) 780991*

A focus for cultural events and antique fairs, with over 20 craft studios, a farm, falconry centre and tea room. 🕐 *All year.* 💷 *Free*

Manchester Craft and Design Centre

17 Oak Street, Northern Quarter, Manchester M4 5JD   ☎   *0161-832 4274*

The centre has 16 studios selling contemporary craftwork and designs.
🕐 *All year.* 💷 *Free*

Manchester Museum

The University, Oxford Road, Manchester M13 9PL   ☎   *0161-275 2634*

The museum includes archaeology and ethnology exhibits; undergoing refurbishment until Dec 2001. 🕐 *All year.* 💷 *Free*

Manning's Amusement Park, Felixstowe

Sea Road, Felixstowe, Suffolk IP11 2DN   ☎   *(01394) 282370*

Traditional amusement park with rides (including a ghost train), a quasar arena and nightclub. 🕐 *End Mar to Sept.* 💷 *Free*

Manor Farm, Bursledon

Manor Farm Country Park, Pylands Lane, Bursledon, Hampshire SO30 2ER   ☎   *(01489) 787055*

A traditional working farmstead with a thirteenth-century church and Victorian schoolroom. 🕐 *All year.* 💷 *£2.50–£3.90*

Mary Arden's House, Wilmcote

Wilmcote, Warwickshire CV37 9UN   ☎   *(01789) 293455*

A Tudor farmstead, the childhood home of Shakespeare's mother. Blacksmith's and falconry displays. 🕐 *All year.* 💷 *£2.50–£5 (children under 5 free)*

Meres Visitor Centre, Ellesmere

Mereside, Ellesmere, Shropshire SY12 1PA ☎ *(01691) 622981/623461*

Nesting herons in spring and nature walks from this centre containing natural history displays. ○ *Mar to Dec.* ⊞ *Free*

Merriments Gardens, Hurst Green

Hawkhurst Road, Hurst Green, Etchingham, East Sussex TN19 7RA ☎ *(01580) 860666*

Four-acre site with herbaceous borders, water gardens, unusual plants and a 'Monet'-style garden. ○ *Garden Apr to Sept, nursery and café all year.* ⊞ *£1–£2.50 (children under 5 free)*

Middle Farm Countryside Centre, Firle

Middle Farm, Firle, Lewes, East Sussex BN8 6LJ ☎ *(01323) 811411*

Farm centre with animals, craft workshops and cider barn. Attractions include the British Barnyard Fowl Centre and afternoon milking demonstrations.
○ *All year.* ⊞ *Farm animals and play area £1 (children under 3 free)*

Mid-Hants Railway plc 'Watercress Line', Alresford

Alresford Station, Alresford, Hampshire SO24 9JG (01962) 733810 ☎ *(01962) 733820*

Steam locomotives travel ten miles of track, visiting four restored stations. ○ *Feb to Oct.* ⊞ *£5–8 (children under 5 free)*

Minack Theatre, Porthcurno

Porthcurno, Penzance, Cornwall TR19 6JU ☎ *(01736) 810694*

This open-air cliffside theatre presents a 16-week season of plays and musicals; the exhibition centre tells its story. ○ *All year.* ⊞ *£1–£2.50 (children under 12 free)*

Minsmere Nature Reserve, Westleton

Westleton, Suffolk IP17 3BY ☎ *(01728) 648281*

Reserve on Suffolk heritage coast with visitor centre, nature trails and bird-watching hides. ○ *All year.* ⊞ *£1–£4*

Model Village, Bourton-on-the-Water

The Old New Inn, High Street, Bourton-on-the-Water, Gloucestershire GL54 2AF
☎ *(01451) 820467*

A model of Bourton-on-the-Water, built in Cotswold stone to a scale of one-ninth.
○ *All year.* ⊞ *£1.50–£2 (children under 3 free)*

Moors Centre, Danby

Lodge Lane, Danby, North Yorkshire YO21 2NB ☎ *(01287) 660654*

Former shooting lodge in 13 acres, with 'living landscape' exhibition and amenities.
○ *All year.* ⊞ *Free*

Moors Valley Railway, Ashley Heath

Moors Valley Country Park, Horton Road, Ashley Heath, Dorset BH24 2ET

☎ *(01425) 471415*

Ten steam locomotives ply this narrow gauge railway. A full-size signal box is among the highlights. ① *All year.* 💷 *80p–£2.20*

Moyse's Hall Museum, Bury St Edmunds

Cornhill, Bury St Edmunds, Suffolk IP33 1DX ☎ *(01284) 757488*

Norman domestic building housing exhibits on local history and archaeology. ① *All year.* 💷 *£1–£1.60*

Muckleburgh Collection, Weybourne

Weybourne Old Military Camp, Weybourne, Holt, Norfolk NR25 7EG

☎ *(01263) 588210*

Collection of armoured vehicles dating from World War II, some still roadworthy, against a coastal backdrop. ① *Mid-Feb to Oct.* 💷 *£2.50–£4*

Muncaster Castle, Gardens and Owl Centre, Ravenglass

Ravenglass, Cumbria CA18 1RQ ☎ *(01229) 717614*

A castle and owl centre in rhododendron gardens, redeveloped in 'Third Millennium' project. New for 2000: Vernon the vole. ① *Castle mid-Mar to early Nov, gardens and owl centre all year.* 💷 *£4–6 (children under 5 free)*

Museum of British Road Transport, Coventry

Hales Street, Coventry CV1 1PN ☎ *024-768 32425*

Over 275 vehicles tell the story of local transport. Exhibits include cycles and the story of the land speed record. ① *All year.* 💷 *Free*

Museum of Oxford

St Aldates, Oxford OX1 1DZ ☎ *(01865) 252761*

Sited in the town hall, the museum tells the story of the city and the university. ① *All year.* 💷 *50p–£2 (children under 5 free)*

Mustard Shop, Norwich

15 The Royal Arcade, Norwich, Norfolk NR2 1AQ ☎ *(01603) 627889*

Nineteenth-century-style shop telling the story of Colman's mustard. ① *All year.* 💷 *Free*

Nature's World at the Botanic Centre, Middlesbrough

Ladgate Lane, Acklam, Middlesbrough TS5 7YN ☎ *(01642) 594895*

Among environmental exhibits are gardens including a 'white' one, wildlife pond and model of river Tees. ① *All year.* 💷 *£1.25–£3.50 (children under 5 free)*

Needles Old Battery, West Highdown

West Highdown, Totland Bay, Isle of Wight PO39 0JH ☎ *(01983) 754772*

Fort with original gun barrels and restored cells. A 65m tunnel leads to coastal views.
🕓 *Mar to Oct; closed in adverse weather conditions.* 💷 *£1.20–£2.50*

Needles Park, Alum Bay

Alum Bay, Isle of Wight PO39 0JD ☎ *(01983) 752401*

Park with beach chairlift, children's rides and craft shops overlooking the Needles and
the coloured sand cliffs. 🕓 *Apr to Oct.* 💷 *Free*

New Place and Nash's House, Stratford-upon-Avon

Chapel Street, Stratford-upon-Avon, Warwickshire CV37 6EP ☎ *(01789) 292325*

The site of Shakespeare's last home. Adjacent Nash's House contains historical displays.
🕓 *All year.* 💷 *£1.70–£3.50 (children under 5 free)*

New Walk Museum and Art Gallery, Leicester

53 New Walk, Leicester LE1 7EA ☎ *0116-255 4100*

Galleries have displays on dinosaurs, ancient Egypt, geology and decorative arts.
🕓 *All year.* 💷 *Free*

Norfolk Lavender, King's Lynn

Caley Mill, Heacham, King's Lynn, Norfolk PE31 7JE ☎ *(01485) 570384*

Lavender, herb and cottage garden collections, distillery processes on view, and a gift
shop. 🕓 *All year.* 💷 *Free*

North of England Lead Mining Museum, Killhope

Cowshill, Weardale, Co Durham DL13 1AR ☎ *(01388) 537505*

Britain's most complete lead mine, with water wheel, crushing mill, reconstructed
machinery and views of miners' accommodation. 🕓 *Apr to Oct.* 💷 *£1.70–£3.40,
including mine tour £2.50–£5*

North Yorkshire Moors Railway, Pickering

Pickering Station, Park Street, Pickering, North Yorkshire YO18 7AJ ☎ *(01751) 472508*

This historic railway's route takes in Goathland (seen in TV's *Heartbeat*) and several
countryside walks. 🕓 *All year.* 💷 *£1.50–£9.50 (children under 3 free)*

Nottingham Castle Museum and Art Gallery

Nottingham NG1 6EL ☎ *0115-915 3700*

Mansion converted into a toy museum and art gallery. Explore passages beneath the
castle. 🕓 *Closed Nov to Feb.* 💷 *£1–£2 weekends/bank holidays (children under 3 free)*

Oakwell Hall & Country Park, Birstall

Nutter Lane, Birstall, Batley, West Yorkshire WF14 9LG ☎ *(01924) 326240*

Elizabethan manor house conveying the flavour of late seventeenth-century life, with
period gardens. 🕓 *All year.* 💷 *Mar to Oct 50p–£1.20, Nov to Feb free*

Oceanarium, Bournemouth

Pier Approach, West Beach, Bournemouth, Dorset BH2 5AA ☎ *(01202) 311993*

All·kinds of underwater creatures, including reef life in the tropical lagoon tunnel.
🕐 *All year.* 💷 *£3.95–£5.25 (children under 3 free)*

Old MacDonald's Educational Farm Park, South Weald

Weald Road, South Weald, Essex CM14 5AY ☎ *(01277) 375177*

The story of British livestock farming. Animal pens and wildlife hospital.
🕐 *All year.* 💷 *£1.75–£2.75*

Ormesby Hall

Church Lane, Ormesby, Middlesbrough TS7 9AS ☎ *(01642) 324188*

Georgian mansion with grand stables and model railway exhibit. Entrance is on Ladgate Lane. 🕐 *Apr to Oct.* 💷 *£1–£3.50 (children under 5 free)*

Otter Trust's North Pennines Reserve, Bowes

Vale House Farm, Bowes, Barnard Castle, Co Durham DL12 9RH ☎ *(01833) 628339*

This wildlife reserve over 230 acres is home to otters, deer and rare farm breeds.
🕐 *Apr to Oct.* 💷 *Call for admission details*

Paignton and Dartmouth Steam Railway

Queen's Park Station, Torbay Road, Paignton, Devon TQ4 6AF ☎ *(01803) 553760*

Steam train trips through coastal and country scenery. Services combine with river trips on the Dart. 🕐 *Closed end Oct to early Apr.* 💷 *£3.40–£5.50 (children under 5 free)*

Parish Church of St Peter and St Paul, Lavenham

Lavenham Rectory, Lavenham, Sudbury, Suffolk CO10 9SA ☎ *(01787) 248207*

Perpendicular building which commemorates the Battle of Bosworth.
🕐 *All year.* 💷 *Free*

Park Farm, Snettisham

Snettisham, Norfolk PE31 7NQ ☎ *(01485) 542425*

Safari tours, indoor and outdoor animal attractions plus a craft centre and play area.
🕐 *All year.* 💷 *£2.75–£7*

Park Rose East Coast Leisure and Retail Park, Bridlington

Carnaby Covert Lane, Bridlington, East Yorkshire YO15 3QF ☎ *(01262) 602823*

Make your own pottery or visit the bird of prey centre, bee exhibition or factory shop.
🕐 *All year.* 💷 *Free*

Pavilion Gardens, Buxton

St John's Road, Buxton, Derbyshire SK17 6XN ☎ *(01298) 23114*

Twenty-three acres of wooded gardens surround a complex including the Octagon Hall and swimming pool. 💷 *All year.* 💷 *Free*

Penshurst Place

Penshurst, Tonbridge, Kent TN11 8DG   ☎ *(01892) 870307*

Medieval manor with ornate state rooms, once home to poet Sir Philip Sidney. The grounds contain a lake, adventure playground and plant centre. ⏰ *House Mar to Oct, grounds Mar to Oct.* 💷 *House and grounds £4–£6, grounds £3–£4.50 (children under 5 free)*

Peterborough Cathedral

12a Minster Precincts, Peterborough, Cambridgeshire PE1 1XX   ☎ *(01733) 343342*

The cathedral is noted for its thirteenth-century painted ceiling and Catherine of Aragon's tomb. ⏰ *All year.* 💷 *Free*

Peto Gardens at Iford Manor, Bradford on Avon

Bradford on Avon, Wiltshire BA15 2BA   ☎ *(01225) 863146*

Terraced Italianate garden surrounding Tudor house with eighteenth-century façade (closed to public). ⏰ *Closed Nov to Easter.* 💷 *£2.50–£3 (children under 10 free; not admitted weekends)*

Pettitt's Animal Adventure Park, Reedham

Camphill, Reedham, Norfolk NR13 3UA   ☎ *(01493) 700094*

Theme park with animals, craft demonstrations and Black Mamba roller-coaster. ⏰ *Late Mar to Oct.* 💷 *£5.50–£5.95*

Pilchard Works, Penzance

Tolcarne, Newlyn, Penzance, Cornwall TR18 5QH   ☎ *(01736) 332112*

Displays on fishing heritage (pilchard salting), the Newlyn Arts and Crafts movement and stencilling activities. ⏰ *Closed Nov to Mar.* 💷 *£2.20–£2.95 (children under 4 free)*

Playbarn, Poringland

West Green Farm, Shotesham Road, Poringland, Norfolk NR14 7LP   ☎ *(01508) 495526*

Themed adventure centre for the under-7s with children's farm and nature trails. ⏰ *All year.* 💷 *Children £3*

Playzone, Portsmouth

Oak Park Industrial Estate, North Harbour Road, Portsmouth PO6 3TJ

     ☎ *(01705) 379999*

Children's indoor adventure playground with a Toddler Zone for the under-4s. ⏰ *All year.* 💷 *£2.70–3.70*

Pleasure Beach, Great Yarmouth

South Beach Parade, Great Yarmouth, Norfolk NR30 3EH   ☎ *(01493) 844585*

Rides and attractions on this nine-acre site include a wooden roller-coaster, crazy golf and pleasure gardens. ⏰ *Late Mar to mid-Sept.* 💷 *Individual rides vary, wristbands £8*

Piece Hall, Halifax

Halifax, West Yorkshire HX1 1RE ☎ *(01422) 358087*

A restored eighteenth-century building containing a shopping courtyard, tourist information centre and art gallery. ◷ *All year.* 🖭 *Free*

Pitt Rivers Museum, Oxford

Parks Road, Oxford OX1 3PP ☎ *(01865) 270927*

This important anthropology collection in a Victorian setting houses artefacts from all over the world. ◷ *All year.* 🖭 *Free*

Poole Pottery

The Quay, Poole, Dorset BH15 1RF ☎ *(01202) 666200*

Factory tours take in a museum, cinema and craft area. Throwing and painting demonstrations. ◷ *All year.* 🖭 *£1.50–£2.50*

Prinknash Abbey Visitors Centre, Cranham

Cranham, Gloucestershire GL4 8EX ☎ *(01452) 812066*

Benedictine abbey with pottery, play area and shop. ◷ *All year.* 🖭 *Free*

Quay Arts Centre, Newport

Sea Street, Newport Harbour, Newport, Isle of Wight PO30 5BD ☎ *(01983) 528825*

A renovated eighteenth-century warehouse containing art galleries, craft shops and a theatre. ◷ *All year.* 🖭 *Free*

Raby Castle, Staindrop

PO Box 50, Staindrop, Darlington, Co Durham DL2 3AH ☎ *(01833) 660202*

Medieval castle featuring a carriage collection, deer park and walled gardens. ◷ *Easter to Sept.* 🖭 *Castle and grounds £2–£5, grounds £2–£3 (children under 5 free)*

Ragley Hall, Alcester

Alcester, Warwickshire B49 5NJ ☎ *(01789) 762090*

Palladian home with fine décor and 'Capability' Brown park. ◷ *Apr to Oct.* 🖭 *£3.50–£5*

Ravenglass and Eskdale Railway

Ravenglass, Cumbria CA18 1SW ☎ *(01229) 717171*

Steam locomotives traverse the scenic Scafell mountain range. ◷ *All year (trains run Easter to Oct).* 🖭 *£3.40–£6.80*

Rheged – The Upland Kingdom Discovery Centre, Penrith

Redhills, Penrith, Cumbria CA11 0DQ ☎ *(01768) 868000*

Grass-covered building with giant screen showing film about 2,000 years of Cumbria, a sound-and-light show and exhibitions. ◷ *All year.* 🖭 *£4.25–£4.95*

Rievaulx Abbey

Rievaulx, York YO62 5LB ☎ *(01439) 798228*

A ruined twelfth-century Cistercian monastery in peaceful surroundings.
🕐 *All year.* 🎫 *£1.50–£3 (children under 5 free)*

Rochester Cathedral

The Precinct, Rochester, Kent ME1 1SX ☎ *(01634) 401301*

A Norman and Gothic building consecrated in 604, boasting a fine crypt and medieval wall paintings. 🕐 *All year.* 🎫 *Free*

Rode Bird Gardens

Rode, Bath BA3 6QW ☎ *(01373) 830326*

Exotic birds located in parkland with lakes, a play area, pets' corner and miniature steam railway. 🕐 *All year.* 🎫 *£2.90–£5.50*

Romsey Abbey

Romsey, Hampshire SO51 8EN ☎ *(01794) 513125*

A medieval church with fine Saxon crucifixes, the burial-place of Earl Mountbatten.
🕐 *All year.* 🎫 *Free*

Royal Air Force Museum, Cosford

Cosford, Shifnal, Shropshire TF11 8UP ☎ *(01902) 376200*

A collection of British, American and Japanese aircraft, plus rockets and missiles.
🕐 *All year.* 🎫 *£3–£5 (children under 5 free)*

Russell-Cotes Art Gallery and Museum, Bournemouth

Russell-Cotes Road, East Cliff, Bournemouth BH1 3AA ☎ *(01202) 451800*

Galleries on mythology/storytelling, contemporary art and Japan, in an elaborate Victorian building. 🕐 *Limited opening from Feb 2000.* 🎫 *Free*

St Nicholas' Cathedral, Newcastle

Newcastle upon Tyne, Tyne and Wear NE1 1PF ☎ *0191-232 1939*

Created a cathedral in 1882, the Cathedral Church of St Nicholas has fifteenth-century bells and Britain's oldest lantern tower. 🕐 *All year.* 🎫 *Free*

Sea Life Aquarium, Tynemouth

Grand Parade, Long Sands, Tynemouth, Tyne and Wear NE30 4JF ☎ *0191-257 6100*

Journey beneath the North Sea and come face-to-face with all kinds of aquatic creatures. 🕐 *All year.* 🎫 *£2.99–£4.50 (children under 4 free)*

Shanklin Chine

Old Village, Shanklin, Isle of Wight PO37 6PF ☎ *(01983) 866432*

A gorge with rare flora, waterfalls and a nature trail. The heritage centre displays include 'A Century of Solent Sea and Sail'. 🕐 *Early Apr to Oct.* 🎫 *£1–£2.50*

Sherborne Abbey

The Close, Sherborne, Dorset DT9 3LQ ☎ *(01935) 812452*

Church dating from Saxon times with fan vaulting and modern Great West Window.
🕐 *All year.* 💷 *Free*

Shire Hall Gallery, Stafford

Market Square, Stafford ST16 2LD ☎ *(01785) 278345*

Arts venue in an eighteenth-century hall with an exhibition and craft programme.
🕐 *All year.* 💷 *Free*

Shrewsbury Abbey

Abbey Foregate, Shrewsbury, Shropshire SY2 6BS ☎ *(01743) 232723*

Founded in 1083, the church is the fictional home of TV's *Brother Cadfael.*
🕐 *All year.* 💷 *Free*

Snowshill Manor

Snowshill, Worcestershire WR12 7JU ☎ *(01386) 852410*

A Tudor house with collections of musical instruments, clocks, toys and bicycles.
🕐 *Apr to Oct.* 💷 *House and grounds £3–£6, grounds £1.50–£3 (children under 5 free)*

South Shields Museum and Art Gallery

Ocean Road, South Shields, Tyne and Wear NE33 2JA ☎ *0191-456 8740*

The museum features a reconstructed street, Catherine Cookson exhibit and regular
events. 🕐 *All year.* 💷 *Free*

Southwell Minster

Bishop's Drive, Southwell, Nottinghamshire NG25 0JP ☎ *(01636) 814189*

Fine carvings in the chapter house of this medieval church. 🕐 *All year.* 💷 *Free*

Spalding Butterfly and Wildlife Park

Long Sutton, Spalding, Lincolnshire PE12 9LE ☎ *(01406) 363833*

Butterfly house, insectarium and reptile land. Attractions include falcon displays, pets'
corner and 9-hole golf. 🕐 *Mid-Mar to late Oct.* 💷 *Call for admission prices*

Stapehill Abbey, Crafts and Gardens

276 Wimborne Road West, Stapehill, Wimborne Minster, Dorset BH21 2EB
☎ *(01202) 861686*

A Cistercian chapel, craft centre and Victorian kitchens, surrounded by gardens with
artisan workshops and a tractor collection. 🕐 *Closed Jan.* 💷 *£4.50–£7 (summer),
reduced winter rate (children under 4 free)*

Stonham Barns Leisure Complex, Stowmarket

Pettaugh Road, Stonham Aspal, Stowmarket, Suffolk IP14 6AT ☎ *(01449) 711755*

This rural pursuits centre features craft and antique shops, a golf academy and exhibits
on birds of prey, fish and reptiles. 🕐 *All year.* 💷 *Free*

Story of Rye

Tourist Office, Strand Quay, Rye, East Sussex TN31 7AY   ☎   *(01797) 226696*

A sound-and-light show brings bygone Rye and its smuggling history to life.
🕓 *All year.* 💷 *£1–£2 (children under 5 free)*

Stowe Landscape Gardens, Buckingham

Buckingham MK18 5EH   ☎   *(01280) 822850*

Landscape gardens with 32 temples and monuments, including works by Vanbrugh and Gibbs. 🕓 *All year.* 💷 *Garden £2.25–£4.50, house £2 (children under 5 free)*

Stratford-upon-Avon Butterfly Farm

Tramway Walk, Swans Nest Lane, Stratford-upon-Avon, Warwickshire CV37 7LS
   ☎   *(01789) 299288*

Tropical butterflies in a jungle setting, plus 'Insect City'. 🕓 *All year.* 💷 *£2.75–£3.75 (children under 3 free)*

Sudbury Hall

Sudbury, Derbyshire DE6 5HT   ☎   *(01283) 585305*

A seventeenth-century house with a fine interior; a museum details children's life from late Victorian times. 🕓 *Apr to Oct.* 💷 *£1.80–£3.70*

Swanage Railway

Station House, Swanage, Dorset BH19 1HB   ☎   *(01929) 425800*

Steam-train rides on the scenic Purbeck line offer views of Corfe Castle.
🕓 *All year.* 💷 *£3–£6 (children under 5 free)*

Tank Museum, Bovington

Bovington, Dorset BH20 6JG   ☎   *(01929) 405096*

Collections of armoured fighting vehicles from World War I to the Gulf War, and interactive displays. 🕓 *All year.* 💷 *£4.50–£6.90 (children under 5 free)*

Taurus Crafts, Lydney

The Old Park, Lydney Park Estate, Lydney, Gloucestershire GL15 6BU
   ☎   *(01594) 844841*

Potters at work and a gift shop. 🕓 *All year.* 💷 *Free*

Tewkesbury Abbey

Church Street, Tewkesbury, Gloucestershire GL20 5RZ   ☎   *(01684) 850959*

The abbey, once a Benedictine monastery, has much surviving Norman architecture.
🕓 *All year.* 💷 *Free*

Thomas Bewick Birthplace Museum, Stocksfield

Cherryburn, Station Bank, Mickley, Stocksfield, Northumberland NE43 7DB
   ☎   *(01661) 843276*

Birthplace cottage of the illustrator and engraver, with farmyard and exhibits on printing and the countryside. 🕓 *Apr to Oct.* 💷 *£1.50–£3 (children under 5 free)*

Thrigby Hall Wildlife Gardens, Filby

Thrigby Hall, Filby, Norfolk NR29 3DR ☎ *(01493) 369477*

Asian mammals, crocodiles and storks in landscaped surroundings which include willow pattern gardens. ◐ *All year.* 🖃 *£3–£5.50*

Tilgate Park and Nature Centre, Crawley

Crawley, West Sussex RH10 5PQ ☎ *(01293) 521168*

Centre surrounded by parkland featuring rare wild and domestic breeds, craft units, themed gardens and shire horse stables. ◐ *All year.* 🖃 *Free, £1 car park fee*

Tiptree Tea Room

Wilkin & Sons Ltd, Tiptree, Essex CO5 0RF ☎ *(01621) 815407*

Tea room and shop with a museum on past times and the art of jam-making. ◐ *All year.* 🖃 *Free*

Tropical Butterfly Gardens and Bird Park, Great Ellingham

Long Street Nursery, Great Ellingham, Norfolk NR17 1AW ☎ *(01953) 453175*

Heated butterfly gardens with tropical vegetation. Falconry displays daily. ◐ *End Mar to early Nov.* 🖃 *£1.70–£3.45*

University of Cambridge Botanic Garden, Cambridge

Cory Lodge, Bateman Street, Cambridge CB2 1JF ☎ *(01223) 336265*

Garden covering 40 acres in central Cambridge with glasshouses, lake and scented garden. ◐ *All year.* 🖃 *£1.50–£2*

Vale and Downland Museum and Visitor Centre, Wantage

The Old Surgery, Church Street, Wantage, Oxfordshire OX12 8BL ☎ *(01235) 771447*

Displays on local history, crafts and archaeology, including a barn exhibit on agricultural life. ◐ *All year.* 🖃 *Free*

Ventnor Botanic Garden

The Undercliff Drive, Ventnor, Isle of Wight PO38 1UL ☎ *(01983) 855397*

Gardens containing rare trees and shrubs, a temperate house and a children's playground. ◐ *All year.* 🖃 *Temperate house 20p–50p*

The Vyne, Sherbourne St John

Sherbourne St John, Hampshire RG24 9HL ☎ *(01256) 881337*

Country house dating from Tudor times, renovated in classical style. ◐ *House Apr to Oct, grounds all year.* 🖃 *House £1.50–£3, house and grounds £2.50–£5 (children under 5 free)*

Warwickshire Museum

Market Place, Warwick, Warwickshire CV34 4SA ☎ *(01926) 412501*

The local exhibits include geology, wildlife and the Sheldon tapestry map. ◐ *All year.* 🖃 *Free*

Washington Old Hall

The Avenue, District 4, Washington, Tyne and Wear NE38 7LE　　☎　*0191-416 6879*

The ancestral home of US President George Washington's family, this manor house was restored in 1936. ○ *Apr to Oct.* 🖾 *£1.40–£2.80 (children under 5 free)*

Wedgwood Visitor Centre, Barlaston

Barlaston, Staffordshire ST12 9ES　　☎　*(01782) 204141*

Craftsmen at work in the factory. and the chance to put your own skills to the test. ○ *All year.* 🖾 *£3.95–£4.95 (children under 5 free)*

West Midlands Safari and Leisure Park, Bewdley

Spring Grove, Bewdley, Worcestershire DY12 1LF　　☎　*(01299) 402114*

Drive-through safari park with animal encounters, amusement rides and shops. ○ *Late Mar to Oct.* 🖾 *£5.75 (children under 4 free)*

Wet'n'Wild, North Shields

Rotary Way, Royal Quays, North Shields, Tyne and Wear NE29 6DA　☎　*0191-296 1333*

Indoor tropical water playground with rapids, slides and whirlpools. ○ *All year.* 🖾 *Under 3ft 11in £2.75–£3.65, over 3ft 11in £4.50–£6.75*

Whitby Lifeboat Museum

Pier Road, Whitby, North Yorkshire YO21 3PU　　☎　*(01947) 602001*

The museum houses the last pulling lifeboat, model vessels and Whitby RNLI memorabilia. ○ *End Mar to Oct.* 🖾 *Free*

White Scar Caves, Ingleton

Ingleton, North Yorkshire LA6 3AW　　`　　☎　*(01524) 241244*

Britain's longest show cave boasts underground waterfalls and an ice-age cavern. ○ *All year.* 🖾 *£3.45–£6.25 (children under 4 free)*

Wildfowl and Wetlands Trust, Washington

District 15, Washington, Tyne and Wear NE38 8LE　　☎　*0191-416 5454*

Observe and feed over 1,000 wildfowl including ducks, geese, swans, flamingos and herons. ○ *All year.* 🖾 *£2.75–£4.75 (children under 4 free)*

Willis Museum of Basingstoke Town and Country Life

Old Town Hall, Market Place, Basingstoke, Hampshire RG21 7QD ☎　*(01256) 465902*

Displays on natural history, clocks, watches and 'Basingstoke, the last 200 years'. ○ *All year.* 🖾 *Free*

Wollaton Hall Natural History Museum, Nottingham

The Yard Gallery, Wollaton Park, Nottingham NG8 2AE　　☎　*0115-915 3900*

Botany, zoology and geology collections occupy this Elizabethan house with deer park, lake and gardens. ○ *All year.* 🖾 *80p–£1.50 weekends/bank holidays (children under 3 free)*

Wolverhampton Art Gallery

Litchfield Street, Wolverhampton WV1 1DU ☎ *(01902) 552055*

Eighteenth- and nineteenth-century and contemporary art, and a hands-on 'Ways of Seeing' room. ○ *All year.* ⊞ *Free*

Worcester Cathedral

10a College Green, Worcester WR1 2LH ☎ *(01905) 611002*

The cathedral is famous for its Norman crypt and medieval cloisters. ○ *All year.* ⊞ *Free*

The World of Beatrix Potter™ Attraction, Bowness-on-Windermere

The Old Laundry, Crag Brow, Bowness-on-Windermere, Windermere, Cumbria LA23 3BX ☎ *(015394) 88444*

Models of famous characters from the books, and exhibits on the author's life. ○ *All year.* ⊞ *£2–£3.50 (children under 4 free)*

Wroxham Barns Craft Centre, Hoveton

Tunstead Road, Hoveton, Norwich NR12 8QU ☎ *(01603) 783762*

Rural craft centre with 13 workshops in restored barns, plus a junior farm and fairground rides. ○ *All year (fair seasonal).* ⊞ *Free, farm £2.25*

Wyld Court Rainforest Conservation Centre, Newbury

Hampstead Norreys, Thatcham, Newbury, Berkshire RG18 0TN ☎ *(01635) 202444*

Rare plant species and tropical creatures in three rainforest climates under 20,000 sq ft of glass. ○ *All year.* ⊞ *£2.50–£4 (children under 5 free)*

Yorkshire Museum, York

Museum Gardens, York YO1 7FR ☎ *(01904) 629745*

The collection includes Roman, Anglo-Saxon and medieval treasures including the Middleham Jewel. ○ *All year.* ⊞ *Winter £2.40–£3.75, summer varies depending on exhibition (children under 5 free)*

SCOTLAND

Abbot House Heritage Centre, Dunfermline

Maygate, Dunfermline KY12 7NE ☎ *(01383) 733266*

A medieval building containing displays on the history of Dunfermline. ○ *All year.* ⊞ *£2–£3 (children under 15 free)*

Aberdeen Art Gallery

Schoolhill, Aberdeen AB10 1FQ ☎ *(01224) 523700*

Gallery with paintings, sculpture, costumes, ceramics and touring contemporary exhibits. ○ *All year.* ⊞ *Free*

Aberdeen Maritime Museum

Shiprow, Aberdeen AB11 5BY ☎ *(01224) 337700*

Exhibits include interactive displays on the North Sea oil and gas industries, plus fishing and ship-building displays. ◷ *All year.* ⊞ *£2.50–£3.50*

Aquatec, Motherwell

1 Menteith Road, Motherwell ML1 1AZ ☎ *(01698) 276464*

Water park with tropical swimming pool, flume and adjacent ice rink. ◷ *All year.* ⊞ *Varies depending on activity*

Baxter's Visitor Centre, Fochabers

Fochabers, Moray IV32 7LD ☎ *(01343) 820666*

The museum charts the soup company's history since 1868. Cookery demonstrations, Scottish food and gifts. ◷ *All year.* ⊞ *Free*

Biblical Garden, Elgin

King Street, Elgin, Moray ☎ *(01343) 563367*

Garden next to the cathedral ruins containing sculptures and every plant mentioned in the Bible. ◷ *May to Sept.* ⊞ *Free*

Botanic Gardens, Glasgow

730 Great Western Road, Glasgow G12 0UE ☎ *0141-334 2422*

Gardens dating from 1817 containing the Kibble Palace and glasshouses with orchids, ferns and begonias. ◷ *All year.* ⊞ *Free*

Breadalbane Folklore Centre, Killin

St Fillan's Mill, Falls of Dochart, Killin, Stirling FK21 ☎ *(01567) 820254*

Centre overlooking Falls of Dochart which explains the mythology of Breadalbane. ◷ *All year.* ⊞ *£1.50–£3*

Broughty Castle Museum, Dundee

Castle Approach, Dundee DD5 2PE ☎ *(01382) 436916*

Fifteenth-century estuary fort, now a museum with exhibits on local history, arms and marine biology. ◷ *All year.* ⊞ *Free*

Cawdor Castle, Nairn

Nairn IV12 5RD ☎ *(01667) 404615*

Castle mentioned in Shakespeare's *Macbeth*; grounds include gardens, nature trails and nine-hole golf. ◷ *May to Oct.* ⊞ *£2.90–£5.60 (children under 5 free)*

Chatelherault, Hamilton

Carlisle Road, Ferniegair, Hamilton ML3 7UE ☎ *(01698) 426213*

Country park with a restored eighteenth-century hunting lodge, ruined castle and Hamilton family mausoleum. ◷ *All year.* ⊞ *Free*

Clan Donald Visitor Centre, Skye

Armadale Castle & Gardens, Sleat, Isle of Skye IV45 8RS ☎ *(01471) 844305*

Museum on island life and family history centre. Outdoor attractions include Victorian gardens and guided walks. ⏲ *Visitor Centre Apr to Oct, gardens all year.*
💷 *£2.60–£2.85 (children under 5 free)*

Collins Gallery, Glasgow

University of Strathclyde, 22 Richmond Street, Glasgow G1 1XQ ☎ *0141-548 2558*

Gallery of contemporary arts including paintings, ceramics and interior design.
⏲ *All year.* 💷 *Free*

Craigie Horticultural Centre, Ayr

Craigie Estate, Ayr KA8 0SS ☎ *(01292) 263275*

The centre has a tropical glasshouse, tea room and demonstration gardens.
⏲ *All year.* 💷 *Free*

Crossraguel Abbey, Maybole

Maybole, Ayrshire KA19 8HQ ☎ *(01655) 883113*

Thirteenth-century abbey founded by the Earl of Carrick. Religious and domestic buildings are among the remains. ⏲ *Summer.* 💷 *75p–£1.80*

Dean Castle Country Park, Kilmarnock

Dean Road, Kilmarnock KA3 1XB ☎ *(01563) 522702*

The castle contains armour, tapestries and musical instruments; exterior attractions include animals, nature trails and an adventure playground. ⏲ *All year.* 💷 *Castle £1.30–£2.60*

Dick Institute Museum, Kilmarnock

Elmbank Avenue, Kilmarnock KA1 3BU ☎ *(01563) 526401*

Collections on geology, archaeology and natural history, plus genealogy research facilities. ⏲ *All year.* 💷 *Free*

Edinburgh Crystal Visitor Centre, Penicuik

Eastfield, Penicuik, Midlothian EH26 8HB ☎ *(01968) 675128*

Observe glassblowing, cutting and engraving techniques on a factory tour.
⏲ *All year.* 💷 *£2–£3*

Falls of Shin Visitor Centre, Lairg

Achany Glen, Lairg IV27 4EE ☎ *(01549) 402231*

See wild salmon in their natural habitat at this centre, which has forest walks and an activity playground. ⏲ *All year.* 💷 *Free*

Fort George, Ardersier

Ardersier, Inverness IV1 2TD ☎ *(01667) 462777*

A 200-year-old working garrison with period reconstructions and museums.
⏲ *All year.* 💷 *£1.20–£3.50 (children under 5 free)*

Fruitmarket Gallery, Edinburgh

45 Market Street, Edinburgh EH1 1DF ☎ *0131-225 2383*

The venue stages exhibitions of contemporary art from Scotland and around the world. ⏲ *All year.* ▣ *Free*

Glasgow Cathedral

Cathedral Square, Glasgow G4 0QZ ☎ *0141-552 6891*

Pre-Reformation cathedral with a plain exterior concealing impressive vaulting and stonework. ⏲ *All year.* ▣ *Free*

Glenfiddich Distillery, Dufftown

William Grant & Sons Ltd, Dufftown, Moray AB55 4DH ☎ *(01340) 820373*

Tour the distillery and bottling hall and taste the whisky. ⏲ *All year.* ▣ *Free*

Gorgie City Farm, Edinburgh

51 Gorgie Road, Edinburgh EH11 2LA ☎ *0131-538 7263*

Community farm with animals, herb garden, children's play area and produce for sale. ⏲ *All year.* ▣ *Free*

House for an Art Lover, Glasgow

Bellahouston Park, Dumbreck Road, Glasgow G41 5BW ☎ *0141-353 4770*

Distinctive house designed by Charles Rennie Mackintosh, with contemporary exhibitions and design shop. ⏲ *All year.* ▣ *£2.50–£3.50 (children under 10 free)*

Hunterian Museum and Art Gallery, Glasgow

Museum: University of Glasgow, University Avenue, Glasgow G12 8QQ
☎ *0141-330 4221*

Gallery: 82 Hillhead Street, Glasgow G12 8QQ ☎ *0141-330 5431*

The museum features archaeology, geology and numismatics, while the Art Gallery across the road has art by Whistler and Rembrandt. ⏲ *All year.* ▣ *Free*

Huntly House Museum, Edinburgh

142 Canongate, Royal Mile, Edinburgh EH8 8DD ☎ *0131-529 4143*

The historic collections include pottery, glass and shop signs. ⏲ *All year.* ▣ *Free*

Inveraray Castle

Argyll Estate Office, Inveraray, Argyll PA32 8XE ☎ *(01499) 302203*

Eighteenth-century Gothic-revival castle, the ancestral home of the Campbell Clan. ⏲ *Apr to Oct.* ▣ *£2.50–£4.50 (children under 5 free)*

Inveraray Jail

Church Square, Inveraray, Argyll PA32 8TX ☎ *(01499) 302381*

Reconstructed prison with staff and inmates, life-sized models and 'trials' in an 1820s courtroom. ⏲ *All year.* ▣ *£2.30–£4.75*

Inverness Museum and Art Gallery

Castle Wynd, Inverness IV2 3EB ☎ *(01463) 237114*

Displays on archaeology, natural history and local history plus temporary exhibits.
◷ *All year.* ⊡ *Free*

Iona Abbey

Isle of Iona, Argyll PA76 6SN ☎ *0131-668 8800*

This restored abbey was the home of Celtic Christianity. ◷ *All year.* ⊡ *£2.50*

Italian Chapel, Holm

St Mary's, Holm, Orkney KW7 2RT ☎ *(01856) 781268*

A Nissen hut transformed into a chapel by Italian prisoners-of-war. ◷ *All year.* ⊡ *Free*

Johnston's Cashmere Visitor Centre, Elgin

Newmill, Elgin, Moray IV30 4AF ☎ *(01343) 554099*

Mill tours and an audio-visual presentation explain factory history and garment
manufacture. ◷ *All year.* ⊡ *Free*

Kilmahog, Trossachs Woollen Mill

Kilmahog, by Callander, Stirling FK17 8HD ☎ *(01877) 330178*

Weaving demonstrations, knitwear and tartans for sale. ◷ *All year.* ⊡ *Free*

Loudoun Castle Family Theme Park, Galston

Loudoun Castle, Galston, Ayrshire ☎ *(01563) 822296*

Castle, rides and animals in 500 acres of parkland. ◷ *Apr to Oct.* ⊡ *£9–£10 (visitors
under 90cm tall free)*

Melrose Abbey

Abbey Street, Melrose, Borders TD6 9LG ☎ *(01896) 822562*

This fifteenth-century church is the burial-place of the casket thought to contain Robert
the Bruce's heart. ◷ *All year.* ⊡ *£1–£3*

Mill Trail Visitor Centre, Alva

Mill Trail Visitor Centre, West Stirling Street, Alva FK12 5EN ☎ *(01259) 769696*

See displays on local mill history and visit a modern working mill and shop.
◷ *All year.* ⊡ *Free*

Museum of Childhood, Edinburgh

42 High Street, Royal Mile, Edinburgh EH1 1TG ☎ *0131-529 4142*

Museum housing childhood memorabilia, from soft toys to castor oil.
◷ *All year.* ⊡ *Free*

National Wallace Monument, Stirling

Abbeycraig, Stirling FK9 5LF ☎ *(01786) 472140*

Victorian Gothic monument containing William Wallace mementoes (including his sword), and a Hall of Heroes. ⏱ *All year.* 💷 *£2.30–£3.30*

Paisley Abbey

Abbey Close, Paisley PA1 1JG ☎ *0141-889 7654*

A medieval abbey noted for its royal tombs, stained glass and choir stalls.
⏱ *All year.* 💷 *Free*

Paisley Museum and Art Galleries

High Street, Paisley PA1 2BA ☎ *0141-889 3151*

Displays of weaving techniques, Paisley shawls, ceramics and paintings.
⏱ *All year.* 💷 *Free*

People's Story Museum, Edinburgh

163 Canongate, Tolbooth, Royal Mile, Edinburgh EH8 8BN ☎ *0131-529 4057*

Audio-visual exhibition describing eighteenth- and nineteenth-century Edinburgh life with added smells. ⏱ *All year.* 💷 *Free*

Perth Museum and Art Gallery

George Street, Perth PH1 5LB ☎ *(01738) 632488*

Museum with art displays, natural history, local history, and temporary exhibitions.
⏱ *All year.* 💷 *Free*

Regimental Museums of Edinburgh Castle

Scottish United Services Museum	☎	*0131-225 7534*
Royal Scots Museum	☎	*0131-310 5016*
Royal Scots Dragoon Guards Museum	☎	*0131-310 5100*

The Castle, Edinburgh EH1 2YT

Three museums on Scottish military history. The Royal Scots Museum is devoted to the infantry regiment, and the Museum of the Royal Scots Dragoon Guards to Scotland's only cavalry regiment. ⏱ *All year.* 💷 *Free (charge to enter castle – see main entry on Edinburgh Castle)*

Rothiemurchus Estate, Aviemore

Rothiemurchus Visitor Centre, by Aviemore, Inverness-shire PH22 1QH
☎ *(01479) 810858*

Attractive scenery for guided tours and walks, clay pigeon shooting and 4 × 4 driving.
⏱ *All year.* 💷 *Varies depending on activity*

Royal Burgh of Stirling Visitor Centre

3 Castle Wynd, Stirling SK8 1EH ☎ *(01786) 462517*

Centre relating the history of Stirling from medieval times to the present day.
⏱ *All year.* 💷 *Free*

St Abbs Head

Ranger's Cottage, Northfield, St Abbs, Eyemouth, Borders TD14 5QF
☎ *(018907) 71443*

Nature reserve and location for cliff-nesting seabirds, with headland walks and a wildlife exhibition. ① *All year, exhibition Apr to Oct.* ▣ *Free*

St Andrews Castle

St Andrews KY16 9AR ☎ *(01334) 477196*

Former bishop's palace and prison strikingly sited on the sea's edge.
① *All year.* ▣ *£1–£2.50 (children under 5 free), joint tickets with cathedral available*

St Mungo Museum of Religious Life and Art, Glasgow

2 Castle Street, Glasgow G4 0RH ☎ *0141-553 2557*

The museum explores world religions. Artefacts and paintings include Salvador Dali's *Christ of St John of the Cross.* ① *All year.* ▣ *Free*

Scotland Street School Museum, Glasgow

225 Scotland Street, Glasgow G5 8QB ☎ *0141-287 0500*

School designed by Charles Rennie Mackintosh, restored in 1990. Classrooms illustrate education practice 1906–72. ① *All year.* ▣ *Free*

Scottish Food and Crafts Centre, Kelty

The Butterchurn, Kelty, Fife KY4 0JR ☎ *(01383) 830169*

Traditional farm with a restaurant, craft centre, play park and pet animals. ① *All year.*
▣ *Free*

Scottish National Gallery of Modern Art, Edinburgh

75 Belford Road, Edinburgh EH4 3DR ☎ *0131-624 6200*

Twentieth-century works by Picasso, Matisse and Moore support the Scottish national collection. ① *All year.* ▣ *Varies depending on exhibition*

Scottish National Portrait Gallery, Edinburgh

1 Queen Street, Edinburgh EH2 1JD ☎ *0131-624 6200*

The gallery contains portraits of famous Scots who have influenced history.
① *All year.* ▣ *Free*

Selkirk Glass Visitor Centre

Dunsdale Haugh, Selkirk TD7 5EF ☎ *(01750) 20954*

Visitors can observe craftspeople at work and buy gifts from the showroom.
① *All year.* ▣ *Free*

Storybook Glen, Aberdeen

Maryculter, Aberdeen AB12 5FT ☎ *(01224) 732941*

Family theme park in landscaped gardens, featuring nursery-rhyme characters and fairy castles. ① *All year (weather permitting).* ▣ *£1.80–£3.60*

WALES

Aberglasney Gardens, Llangathen

Llangathen, Carmarthenshire SA32 8QH ☎ *(01558) 668998*

A restored sixteenth-century garden complex with kitchen garden, cloisters and pool. The house has a repaired façade with a portico. ◷ *Apr to Oct.* ▣ *£1.95–£3.95 (children under 5 free)*

Aberystwyth Arts Centre

University of Wales, Aberystwyth SY23 3DE ☎ *(01970) 622882*

The exhibitions, theatre shows and films staged at this centre showcase local and touring talent. ◷ *All year.* ▣ *Free, charge for performances*

Beaumaris Castle

Castle Street, Beaumaris, Anglesey LL58 8AP ☎ *(01248) 810361*

A well-proportioned medieval fortress, the incomplete final link in Edward I's 'ring of steel'. ◷ *All year.* ▣ *£1.70–£2.20*

Bodelwyddan Castle

Bodelwyddan Castle Trust, Bodelwyddan, Denbighshire LL18 5YA ☎ *(01745) 584060*

The castle contains portraits, sculpture and hands-on Victorian inventions; play areas in the wooded grounds. ◷ *All year.* ▣ *Castle and grounds £1.50–£4.30, grounds 50p–£1 (children under 5 free)*

Cardiff Bay Visitor Centre

Inner Harbour, Harbour Drive, Capital Waterside, Cardiff Bay ☎ 029-2046 3833

Part of the Millennium Waterfront, the centre features the regeneration of Cardiff's docklands and has a large-scale model of the area. ◷ *All year.* ▣ *Free*

Centre for Visual Arts, Cardiff

Working Street, The Hayes, Cardiff CF10 1GG ☎ 029-2039 4040

Wales' largest venue for contemporary art, with local and global craft, design and architecture plus a hands-on gallery. ◷ *All year.* ▣ *£2.50–£3.50 (children under 6 free)*

Corris Craft Centre

Corris, Machynlleth, Powys SY20 9RF ☎ *(01654) 761584*

Centre surrounded by mountain scenery presents crafts from ceramics to wood-turning, plus 'King Arthur's Labyrinth'. ◷ *All year.* ▣ *Free, labyrinth £3.10–£4.40 (children under 3 free)*

Dany-yr-Ogof Showcaves, Swansea

National Showcase Centre for Wales, Brecon Road, Pen-y-Cae, Swansea SA9 1GJ
☎ *(01639) 730284*

The extensive caverns feature impressive rock formations and underground lakes. ◷ *Apr to Oct.* ▣ *£4–£6.95*

Greenfield Valley Heritage Park, Holywell

Basingwerk House, Greenfield Road, near Holywell, Flintshire CH8 7GH

☎ *(01352) 714172*

The park contains reconstructed industrial buildings and an agricultural museum.
🕔 *Museum and farm Apr to Oct, park all year.* 💷 *£1–£2.25 (children under 5 free)*

Harlech Castle

Castle Square, Harlech, Gwynedd LL46 2YH ☎ *(01766) 780552*

This concentric castle, spectacularly sited between mountain and sea, was the backdrop
to Owain Glyndwr's uprising. 🕔 *All year.* 💷 *£2–£3 (children under 5 free)*

Mermaid Quay, Cardiff

Cardiff Bay CT10 5BZ ☎ *029-2048 0077*

A mix of retail, leisure and commercial outlets and restaurants. 🕔 *All year.* 💷 *Free*

Millennium Coastal Park, Llanelli

Project Office, North Dock, Llanelli, Carmarthenshire SA15 2LF ☎ *(01554) 777744*

Coastal park over a distance of 20km with extensive restoration of the coastline, the
location for the National Eisteddfod of Wales 2000. 🕔 *Opens summer 2000.*
💷 *Charge for wetlands*

Millennium Stadium, Cardiff

First Floor, West Wing, St David's House, Wood Street, Cardiff CF1 1ES

☎ *029-2023 2661*

A 72,500-seater stadium with retractable roof, inaugurated during the 1999 Rugby
World Cup finals. Admittance only to concerts and other events. 🕔 *All year.* 💷 *Varies
depending on event*

National Botanic Garden of Wales, Llanarthne

Middleton Hall, Llanarthne, Carmarthenshire SA32 8HG ☎ *(01558) 668768*

Garden dedicated to science, education, conservation and leisure, with water discovery
centre and glasshouse re-creation of a Mediterranean ecosystem. 🕔 *Opens May 2000.*
💷 *£3–£6.50 (children under 5 free)*

Newport Museum and Art Gallery

John Frost Square, Newport NP20 1PA ☎ *(01633) 840064*

The museum contains a notable 'four seasons' Roman mosaic and covers archaeology,
industrial history and wildlife. 🕔 *All year.* 💷 *Free*

Pembroke Castle

Pembroke, Pembrokeshire SA71 4LA ☎ *(01646) 681510*

The 24m great keep of this medieval castle, once a Norman power base, provides fine
views of the town. 🕔 *All year.* 💷 *£2–£3 (children under 5 free)*

Penrhyn Castle, Bangor

Bangor, Gwynedd LL57 4HN ☎ *(01248) 353084*

This neo-Norman, nineteenth-century stately home overlooks the Menai Straits.
🕐 *Late Mar to Oct.* 💷 *£2.50–£5*

Portmeirion Village

Portmeirion Village, Gwynedd LL48 6ET ☎ *(01766) 770228*

Sir Clough Williams-Ellis created this Italianate village full of architectural flourishes, the
location for cult TV show *The Prisoner*. 🕐 *All year.* 💷 *£2.25–£4.50 (children under 4
free)*

Ruthin Craft Centre

Park Road, Ruthin, Denbighshire LL15 1BB ☎ *(01824) 704774*

Complex of studio workshops around a courtyard, with a wide range of crafts on view.
🕐 *All year.* 💷 *Free*

Swansea Leisure Centre

Oystermouth Road, Swansea SA1 3ST ☎ *(01792) 649126*

Large leisure centre with pool, aqua-slides and wave machine plus a variety of sports
facilities. 🕐 *All year.* 💷 *Varies depending on activity*

Wales Millennium Centre, Cardiff

Site: Millennium Waterfront, Cardiff Bay ☎ *029-2040 2000*

Office: West Bute Street, PO Box 2001, Cardiff CF10 6YS ☎ *029-2034 4888*

This arts and entertainment centre, under construction, will be the permanent home of
the Welsh National Opera from late 2001. 🕐 *Opening times to be confirmed.* 💷 *Prices
will vary according to events*

List of attractions by category

If you are looking for a certain type of attraction, use these lists to find sights in London, England, Scotland and Wales by category. The best and worst examples in each are listed on pages 16–17.

Animal attractions

London
London Aquarium
London Zoo

England
Abbotsbury Swannery
Aquarium of the Lakes, Lakeside
Banham Zoo, Diss
Blue Planet Aquarium, Ellesmere Port
Bristol Zoo Gardens
Cannon Hall and Open Farm, Cawthorne
Chessington World of Adventures
Chester Zoo
Colchester Zoo
Cotswold Wildlife Park, Burford
Cricket St Thomas Wildlife Park, Chard
Drayton Manor Family Theme Park, Tamworth
Dudley Zoo and Castle
Flamingoland Theme Park and Zoo, Kirby Misperton
Hawk Conservancy, Andover
Howletts Wild Animal Park, Bekesbourne
Knowsley Safari Park, Prescot
Longleat, Warminster
Lotherton Hall and Bird Garden, Aberford
Marwell Zoological Park, Colden Common
Monkey World, East Stoke
National Marine Aquarium, Plymouth
Paignton Zoo
Paradise Wildlife Park, Broxbourne
Sea Life Centre, Brighton
Skegness Natureland Seal Sanctuary
Slimbridge Wildfowl and Wetlands Trust
South Lakes Wild Animal Park, Dalton-in-Furness

Suffolk Wildlife Park, Kessingland
Tropical World, Leeds
Twycross Zoo
Whipsnade Wild Animal Park, Dunstable
White Post Modern Farm Centre, Farnsfield
Wimpole Hall and Home Farm, Arrington
Woburn Safari Park
Woodland Leisure Park, Blackawton

Scotland
Blair Drummond Safari and Leisure Park
Edinburgh Zoo

Wales
Anglesey Sea Zoo, Brynsiencyn
Folly Farm, Begelly

Theme parks, thrills and spills

England
Alton Towers
American Adventure World, Ilkeston
Blackpool Pleasure Beach
Butlins Family Entertainment Resort, Skegness
Camelot Theme Park, Charnock Richard
Chessington World of Adventures
Drayton Manor Family Theme Park, Tamworth
Dreamland, Margate
Flambards Village Theme Park, Helston
Frontierland, Morecambe
Legoland, Windsor
Lightwater Valley Theme Park, North Stainley
Paultons Park, Ower
Pleasure Island, Cleethorpes
Pleasureland, Stockport
Pleasurewood Hills Theme Park, Corton
Sundown Adventureland, Rampton
Thorpe Park, Chertsey
Woodland Leisure Park, Blackawton

Wales
Oakwood Coaster Country, Narberth

Heritage and history

London
Apsley House
Banqueting House
British Library
Buckingham Palace
Cabinet War Rooms
Chiswick House
Eltham Palace
Ham House
Hampton Court
Kensington Palace
Kenwood House
Leighton House
Marble Hill House
Syon House and Park
Tower of London

England
Althorp House, Northampton
Anne Hathaway's Cottage, Shottery
Audley End House, Saffron Walden
Battle Abbey and Battlefield
Belton House
Blenheim Palace, Woodstock
Bletchley Park
Blickling Hall
Cannon Hall and Open Farm, Cawthorne
Castle Howard, Malton
Chartwell, Westerham
Chatsworth House, Bakewell
Chesters Roman Fort, Chollerford
Down House, Downe
Elsecar Heritage Centre
Haddon Hall, Bakewell
Hardwick Hall, Doe Lea
Harewood House
Hartlepool Historic Quay
Hatfield House
Holkham Hall, Wells-next-the-Sea
Housesteads Roman Fort and Museum, Haydon Bridge
Kentwell Hall, Long Melford
Kingston Lacy House and Garden, Wimborne Minster
Knebworth House
Lanhydrock House and Gardens, Bodmin
Lotherton Hall and Bird Garden, Aberford

Newby Hall and Gardens, Ripon
Nunnington Hall
Osborne House, East Cowes
Polesden Lacey, Great Bookham
Port Sunlight Heritage Centre and Village
Quarry Bank Mill, Styal
Roman Baths and Pump Room, Bath
Royal Pavilion, Brighton
St Michael's Mount, Marazion
Sandringham House
Shakespeare's Birthplace, Stratford-upon-Avon
Stonehenge, Amesbury
Stourhead, Stourton
Tatton Park, Knutsford
Temple Newsam, Leeds
Waddesdon Manor
Wallington House, Cambo
Warwick Castle
Whitby Abbey
Wigan Pier
Wilton House
Wimpole Hall and Home Farm, Arrington
Woburn Abbey

Scotland
Archaeolink Prehistory Park, Oyne
Bannockburn Heritage Centre, Stirling
Culloden Battlefield and Visitor Centre, Culloden Moor
Palace of Holyrood House, Edinburgh
Rob Roy and Trossachs Visitor Centre, Callander
Royal Yacht *Britannia*, Edinburgh

Wales
Erddig Hall, Wrexham
Llancaiach Fawr Manor, Nelson
Rhondda Heritage Park, Porth

Outdoor attractions

London
Kew Gardens

England
Beamish North of England Open Air Museum
Birmingham Botanical Gardens
Black Country Living Museum, Dudley
Cheddar Caves and Gorge, Somerset

Crealy Park, Clyst St Mary
Fountains Abbey and Studley Royal Water Gardens, Ripon
Harlow Carr Botanical Gardens, Harrogate
Heights of Abraham, Matlock Bath
Hidcote Manor Garden, Hidcote Bartrim
Ironbridge Gorge Museums
Legoland, Windsor
Lost Gardens of Heligan, Pentewan
Paradise Family Leisure Park, Newhaven
RHS Garden, Wisley
Sewerby Hall and Gardens
Southend Pier
Stourhead, Stourton
Stonehenge, Amesbury
Tatton Park, Knutsford
Wakehurst Place Gardens, Ardingly
Waterperry Gardens
Weald and Downland Open Air Museum, Singleton
Westonbirt Arboretum, Tetbury
Wimpole Hall and Home Farm, Arrington
Wookey Hole Caves
Yorkshire Sculpture Park, West Bretton

Scotland
Archaeolink Prehistory Park, Oyne
Bannockburn Heritage Centre, Stirling
Culloden Battlefield and Visitor Centre, Culloden Moor
Inverewe Garden, Poolewe
New Lanark Mills, Lanark
Royal Botanic Garden, Edinburgh

Wales
Bodnant Garden, Tal-y-cafn
Tintern Abbey

Castles

England
Bamburgh Castle
Carisbrooke Castle, Newport
Colchester Castle
Corfe Castle
Dover Castle and Tunnels
Hever Castle
Kenilworth Castle
Leeds Castle, Maidstone
Ludlow Castle

Skipton Castle
Sudeley Castle and Gardens, Winchcombe
Tintagel Castle
Warwick Castle
Windsor Castle

Scotland
Blair Castle, Pitlochry
Crathes Castle and Gardens, Banchory
Culzean Castle and Country Park, Maybole
Edinburgh Castle
Glamis Castle
Stirling Castle
Urquhart Castle, Drumnadrochit

Wales
Caernarfon Castle
Cardiff Castle
Conwy Castle
Powis Castle, Welshpool

Churches

London
St Paul's Cathedral
Westminster Abbey

England
Canterbury Cathedral
Carlisle Cathedral
Chester Cathedral
Durham Cathedral
Ely Cathedral
Exeter Cathedral
Hereford Cathedral
Lincoln Cathedral
Norwich Cathedral
Ripon Cathedral
Salisbury Cathedral
Winchester Cathedral
York Minster

Museums and galleries

London

Bethnal Green Museum of Childhood
British Museum
Courtauld Gallery
Design Museum
Geffrye Museum
Imperial War Museum
London Transport Museum
MCC Museum
Museum of London
National Army Museum
National Gallery
National Maritime Museum
National Portrait Gallery
Natural History Museum
Science Museum
Sir John Soane's Museum
Tate Gallery
Theatre Museum
Victoria & Albert Museum
Wallace Collection

England

Ashmolean Museum, Oxford
Birmingham Museum and Art Gallery
Bowes Museum, Barnard Castle
City Museum and Mappin Art Gallery, Sheffield
Dinosaur Museum, Dorchester
Fitzwilliam Museum, Cambridge
Imperial War Museum, Duxford
Laing Art Gallery, Newcastle upon Tyne
Leeds City Art Gallery
Manchester United FC Museum
Merseyside Maritime Museum, Liverpool
Museum of East Anglian Life, Stowmarket
Museum of Science and Industry, Manchester
National Glass Centre, Sunderland
National Horse-racing Museum, Newmarket
National Motor Museum, Beaulieu
National Museum of Photography, Film and Television, Bradford
National Railway Museum, York
National Waterways Museum, Gloucester
Newcastle Discovery Museum
Preston Hall Museum, Stockton-on-Tees
Royal Armouries, Leeds
Sewerby Hall and Gardens

Tate Gallery, Liverpool
Tate Gallery, St Ives
Tullie House Museum and Art Gallery, Carlisle
Walker Art Gallery, Liverpool
York Castle Museum
York City Art Gallery

Scotland
Burrell Collection, Glasgow
Gallery of Modern Art, Glasgow
Kelvingrove Art Gallery and Museum, Glasgow
Museum of Transport, Glasgow
National Gallery of Scotland, Edinburgh
National Museum of Scotland, Edinburgh
People's Palace, Glasgow
Royal Museum of Scotland, Edinburgh

Wales
Museum of Welsh Life, Cardiff
National Museum and Gallery, Cardiff
Swansea Maritime and Industrial Museum
Welsh Slate Museum, Llanberis

Themed attractions

London
BBC Experience
Bethnal Green Museum of Childhood
British Library
Cabinet War Rooms
Clink Prison Museum
Cutty Sark
Design Museum
The Dome
FA Premier League Hall of Fame
Geffrye Museum
HMS Belfast
House of Detention
Imperial War Museum
London Dungeon
London Transport Museum
Madame Tussaud's
MCC Museum
Museum of London
National Army Museum
National Maritime Museum
Natural History Museum

Rock Circus
Science Museum
Theatre Museum
Tower Bridge Experience
Vinopolis

England
Babbacombe Model Village, Torquay
Beatles Story, Liverpool
Bekonscot Model Village, Beaconsfield
Blackpool Tower
Brighton Palace Pier
Cadbury World, Birmingham
Dinosaur Museum, Dorchester
Earth Centre, Doncaster
Eden Camp, Malton
Eureka!, Halifax
Flagship Portsmouth
Galleries of Justice, Nottingham
Imperial War Museum, Duxford
Jodrell Bank Science Centre and Arboretum, Macclesfield
Jorvik Viking Centre, York
Legoland, Windsor
Louis Tussaud's Waxworks, Blackpool
Manchester United FC Museum
Merseyside Maritime Museum, Liverpool
National Centre for Popular Music, Sheffield
National Fishing Heritage Centre, Grimsby
National Glass Centre, Sunderland
National Horse-racing Museum, Newmarket
National Motor Museum, Beaulieu
National Museum of Photography, Film and Television, Bradford
National Railway Museum, York
National Waterways Museum, Gloucester
Oxford Story
Royal Armouries, Leeds
Sellafield, Seascale
Sizewell Visitor Centre
Snibston Discovery Park, Coalville
Thursford Collection, Thursford Green
York Dungeon

Scotland
Discovery Point, Dundee
Dynamic Earth Centre, Edinburgh
Glenturret Distillery, Crieff
Old Blacksmith's Shop, Gretna Green

Official Loch Ness Monster Exhibition Centre, Drumnadrochit
Rob Roy and Trossachs Visitor Centre, Callander
Scotch Whisky Heritage Centre, Edinburgh
Vikingar!, Largs

Wales
Big Pit Mining Museum, Blaenafon
Centre for Alternative Technology, Machynlleth
Llechwedd Slate Caverns, Blaenau Ffestiniog
Museum of Welsh Life, Cardiff
Swansea Maritime and Industrial Museum
Techniquest, Cardiff
Welsh Slate Museum, Llanberis

WHICH? BOOKS

General reference (legal, financial, practical, etc.)

Be Your Own Financial Adviser
420 Legal Problems Solved
150 Letters that Get Results
What to Do When Someone Dies
The Which? Computer Troubleshooter
The Which? Guide to an Active Retirement
The Which? Guide to Changing Careers
The Which? Guide to Choosing a Career
The Which? Guide to Computers
The Which? Guide to Computers for Small Businesses
The Which? Guide to Divorce
The Which? Guide to Doing Your Own Conveyancing
The Which? Guide to Domestic Help
The Which? Guide to Employment
The Which? Guide to Gambling
The Which? Guide to Getting Married
The Which? Guide to Giving and Inheriting
The Which? Guide to Home Safety and Security
The Which? Guide to Insurance
The Which? Guide to the Internet
The Which? Guide to Money
The Which? Guide to Pensions
The Which? Guide to Renting and Letting
The Which? Guide to Shares
The Which? Guide to Starting Your Own Business
The Which? Guide to Working from Home
Which? Way to Buy, Own and Sell a Flat
Which? Way to Buy, Sell and Move House
Which? Way to Clean It
Which? Way to Save and Invest
Which? Way to Save Tax
Wills and Probate

Action Pack (A5 wallet with forms and 28-page book inside)

Make Your Own Will

Health

Understanding HRT and the Menopause
The Which? Guide to Children's Health
The Which? Guide to Complementary Medicine
The Which? Guide to Managing Asthma
The Which? Guide to Managing Stress
The Which? Guide to Men's Health
The Which? Guide to Women's Health
Which? Medicine

Gardening

The Gardening Which? Guide to Patio and Container Plants
The Gardening Which? Guide to Small Gardens
The Gardening Which? Guide to Successful Perennials
The Gardening Which? Guide to Successful Propagation
The Gardening Which? Guide to Successful Pruning
The Gardening Which? Guide to Successful Shrubs

Do-it-yourself

The Which? Book of Do-It-Yourself
The Which? Book of Plumbing and Central Heating
The Which? Book of Wiring and Lighting
The Which? Guide to Painting and Decorating
The Which? HomePlanner
Which? Way to Fix It

Travel/leisure

The Good Bed and Breakfast Guide
The Good Food Guide
The Good Walks Guide
The Which? Guide to Country Pubs
The Which? Guide to Pub Walks
The Which? Guide to Weekend Breaks in Britain
The Which? Hotel Guide
The Which? Wine Guide

For credit-card orders phone FREE on (0800) 252100

The Which? Hotel Guide

'*The Which? Hotel Guide* . . . tops my list of [hotel guides] because it has the most information, painting word pictures for each one, with details of furniture, fittings, food, ambience, even proprietors.' *The Mail on Sunday*

Whether you are looking for a hotel for business purposes, a romantic break, a family holiday, an inexpensive night's accommodation or just sheer luxury, this guide presents you with a huge choice. Practical details and evocative descriptions of over 1,000 of the best hotels in England, Scotland and Wales are covered. The wonderful places to stay range from homely B&Bs through to converted castles, stately homes and smart city-centre hotels.

Our rigorous selection process for entry into the Guide, based on professional inspections and visitors' reports, means that all the recommended hotels offer exceptional hospitality. The Guide is proudly independent, taking no advertising or payment for inclusion. Similarly, neither our editors nor their inspection team accept free hospitality.

The Guide is rewritten every year, and includes up-to-date prices and other essential practical information. It features many places that offer accommodation from under £35 per person per night; over 50 London hotels; the best hotels for food, good value or a peaceful location; colour photographs of award-winning hotels; and directions to all hotels along with easy-to-read colour maps.

Paperback   210 x 120mm   704 pages   £14.99

Available from bookshops, and by post from
Which?, Dept TAZM, Castlemead,
Gascoyne Way, Hertford X, SG14 1LH
or phone FREE on (0800) 252100
quoting Dept TAZM and your credit card details

The Which? Guide to Weekend Breaks in Britain

What do you look for in a short holiday break? Beautiful countryside to walk in, perhaps stopping off at the occasional hostelry? Somewhere you can pursue an interest, like Britain's industrial heritage or natural history? Or simply relaxation in lovely surroundings, with some memorable meals and a spot of shopping?

This new guide to mini-breaks in Britain will provide you with plenty of inspiration, plus all the practical data you are likely to need, and includes touring routes through areas such as 'Constable Country', Snowdonia and the Yorkshire Dales; the best seaside resorts and historic cities; and special sections on subjects as diverse as gardens and vineyards, bird-watching, maritime history, Hadrian's Wall, fossil-hunting in Dorset, and the Boswell/Johnson trail on Skye.

Paperback   210 x 120mm   528 pages   £13.99

Available from bookshops, and by post from
Which?, Dept TAZM, Castlemead,
Gascoyne Way, Hertford X, SG14 1LH
or phone FREE on (0800) 252100
quoting Dept TAZM and your credit card details

The Which? Guide to Pub Walks

Whether you're planning a ramble with the family, a relaxed lunch with friends plus the chance to walk it off, or a romantic stroll in the countryside with one special person, you'll find plenty of suggestions in this guide for both interesting routes and reliable pubs.

Over 50 great walks in the south-east of England, from the South Downs to the Chilterns, are meticulously described, each with easy-to-follow directions and a specially drawn map. Each (circular) route has its own special character – fine scenery, rivers, lakes or wildlife, for example – and features an attractive and welcoming pub. Many of the pubs are noteworthy in their own right – some for their history, or their location, or for the high quality of the food and drink served. Information for each walk includes: length and duration (between 4 and 8 miles); difficulty – walks are graded 1 to 5 according to how taxing they are (from easy to energetic); how to reach the starting point (by public transport or by car, and where to park); details of the pub's address, opening hours and food provided.

Paperback   210 x 120mm   192 pages   £9.99

Available in May 2000 from bookshops, and by post from
Which?, Dept TAZM, Castlemead,
Gascoyne Way, Hertford X, SG14 1LH
or phone FREE on (0800) 252100
quoting Dept TAZM and your credit card details

The Good Bed and Breakfast Guide

Independence and breadth of choice are still the keynotes in this, the market leader among guides to B&Bs in Britain. More than 1,100 establishments have been carefully selected for their warmth of welcome, high standards of comfort and cleanliness, and excellent value for money (most charge £20-£35 per person per night, some even less). A diverse range of establishments in an equally wide range of locations is included, taking in Victorian townhouses and rambling country cottages, modern family homes and elegant former vicarages, working farmhouses and converted barns, and even a lighthouse.

Each entry describes the character of the B&B, indicating any particularly interesting or unusual features, as well as giving useful information on the locality and local attractions. Entries also include all the practical details needed to make a suitable choice of B&B for any special needs: number and types of rooms, facilities (such as en suite bathrooms, TV, tea and coffee), prices, accessibility for wheelchair users, provision of evening meals, and policy on children, smoking and dogs.

The Good Bed and Breakfast Guide:

- includes colour photos of award-winning B&Bs
- accepts no advertising, free hospitality or payment for inclusion
- features 25 pages of full-colour maps and is fully indexed
- recommends over 1,100 B&Bs, many charging under £25 per person per night.

Paperback   210 x 120mm   672 pages   £14.99

Available from bookshops, and by post from
Which?, Dept TAZM, Castlemead,
Gascoyne Way, Hertford X, SG14 1LH
or phone FREE on (0800) 252100
quoting Dept TAZM and your credit card details

The Which? Guide to Scotland

Scotland, beneath the whisky and tartan image so often peddled to visitors, is a country of dramatic variety and long-lived traditions. Its history as a fiercely proud nation that has frequently been in conflict is revealed in its legacy of castles, battlefields, abbeys and monuments.

For the holiday-maker who appreciates the great outdoors, there are few better destinations for fishing, climbing, bird-watching, golf or simply walking in the unspoilt moorland and mountain terrain. Conversely, Scotland's cities offer a wealth of cultural activities as well as insights into the country's past, so often shaken by political and religious controversy.

This popular guide from *Which?* covers the whole of Scotland, from the Borders to Shetland. Each chapter focuses on a different region, recommending the best sights and things to do, where to eat and stay, together with maps to help you get around.

Paperback   210 x 120mm   528 pages   £12.99

Available from bookshops, and by post from
Which?, Dept TAZM, Castlemead,
Gascoyne Way, Hertford X, SG14 1LH
or phone FREE on (0800) 252100
quoting Dept TAZM and your credit card details

The Which? Guide to Country Pubs

'Invaluable.' Tim Atkin, *The Observer*

Eating out in country pubs is a great British pastime, but with so many to choose from you need the advice of a trusted friend to help find the best. *The Which? Guide to Country Pubs,* produced by the *Good Food Guide* team to the same high standards, presents the cream of Britain's country inns and pubs, selected for their atmosphere, value for money, good food and drink, and, often, something else that sets them apart, such as a stunning location or colourful history.

Entries provide details of style, setting, décor and ambience, plus opening times, children's facilities, accommodation and much more. The *Guide* also gives awards to pubs with excellent real ale, a superior wine list, or outstanding home-cooked bar food, and indicates special points of interest.

The Which? Guide to Country Pubs is totally rewritten and re-researched for every edition; is rigorously independent, charges no payment for inclusion and accepts no free hospitality of any kind; includes full-colour maps, showing where recommended pubs are located and indicating which offer accommodation; and selects entries on the strength of readers' recommendations, supported by anonymous inspection.

Paperback   210 x 120mm   574 pages   £14.99

Available from bookshops, and by post from
Which?, Dept TAZM, Castlemead,
Gascoyne Way, Hertford X, SG14 1LH
or phone FREE on (0800) 252100
quoting Dept TAZM and your credit card details